Fodor's

The Netherlands, Belgium, Luxembourg

PRAISE FOR FODOR'S GUIDES

"Fodor's guides . . . are an admirable blend of the cultural and the practical."
—The Washington Post

"Researched by people chosen because they live or have lived in the country, well-written, and with good historical sections . . . Obligatory reading for millions of tourists."
—The Independent, *London*

"Usable, sophisticated restaurant coverage, with an emphasis on good value."
—*Andy Birsh,* Gourmet *restaurant columnist, quoted by Gannett News Service*

"Packed with dependable information."
—Atlanta Journal Constitution

"Fodor's always delivers high quality . . . thoughtfully presented . . . thorough."
—Houston Post

"Valuable because of their comprehensiveness."
—Minneapolis Star-Tribune

Fodor's Travel Publications, Inc.
New York • Toronto • London • Sydney • Auckland

Second Edition

ISBN 0–679–02739–4

Fodor's The Netherlands, Belgium, Luxembourg

Editor: Jillian L. Magalaner
Editorial Contributors: Robert Blake, Rodney Bolt, Linda Burnham, Nancy Coons, Fionn Davenport, Echo Garrett, Laura M. Kidder, Bevin McLaughlin, Mary Ellen Schultz, Eric Sjogren, Nancy van Itallie
Creative Director: Fabrizio La Rocca
Cartographer: David Lindroth
Illustrator: Karl Tanner
Cover Photograph: Peter Guttman

Design: Vignelli Associates

Special Sales

Fodor's Travel Publications are available at special discounts for bulk purchases for sales promotions or premiums. Special editions, including personalized covers, excerpts of existing guides, and corporate imprints, can be created in large quantities for special needs. For more information, contact your local bookseller or write to: Special Markets, Fodor's Travel Publications, 201 East 50th Street, New York, NY 10022. Inquiries from Canada should be directed to your local Canadian bookseller or sent to Random House of Canada, Ltd., Marketing Dept., 1265 Aerowood Drive, Mississauga, Ontario L4W 1B9. Inquiries from the United Kingdom should be sent to Fodor's Travel Publications, 20 Vauxhall Bridge Road, London SW1 2SA, England.

MANUFACTURED IN THE UNITED STATES OF AMERICA
10 9 8 7 6 5 4 3 2 1

Contents

Contents

Foreword

We would like to express our gratitude to Elisabeth Puttaert of the Office de Tourisme et d' Information de Bruxelles, Annette Beautrix of the Office de Promotion du Tourisme de la Communauté Française, Ingrid Van Hoorebeke of the Vlaams Commissariatt-Gerneraal voor Toerisme, Barbara Veldkamp and Eline van Bon of the Netherlands Board of Tourism, Frédérique Raeymaekers and Marleen Bervoets of the Belgian Tourist Office, and Anne Bastian and Jean-Claude Conter of the Luxembourg National Tourist Office for their generous cooperation during the preparation of *Fodor's The Netherlands, Belgium, Luxembourg*.

While every care has been taken to ensure the accuracy of the information in this guide, the passage of time will always bring change, and consequently, the publisher cannot accept responsibility for errors that may occur.

All prices and opening times quoted here are based on information supplied to us at press time. Hours and admission fees may change, however, and the prudent traveler will avoid inconvenience by calling ahead.

Fodor's wants to hear about your travel experiences, both pleasant and unpleasant. When a hotel or restaurant fails to live up to its billing, let us know and we will investigate the complaint and revise our entries where the facts warrant it.

Send your letters to the editors of Fodor's Travel Publications, 201 E. 50th Street, New York, NY 10022.

Highlights and Fodor's Choice

Highlights

The Netherlands   **Amsterdam celebrates its canals** in 1995 with a series of waterway-related exhibits and events. In August, the Cutty Sark Tall Ships Race will finish in Amsterdam Harbor with **Sail Amsterdam 1995,** a festival complete with fireworks and jazz.

In the northern provinces, two major museums will have opened in new locations by April 1995. November 1994 saw the opening of the **Groningen Museum** of modern art in a zanily designed new building opposite Groningen's railway station, and the **Fries Museum,** with exhibits on the history and culture of Friesland, will move from other locations in town to the restored 16th-century Chancellery in time for an April 1995 opening. More museum news: The art and archaeology collections of the **Bonnefanten Museum** have found a more spacious new home in Maastricht's newly developed Céramique District. At press time, the museum was scheduled to reopen in its new quarters in early 1995.

In May 1993, **Amsterdam Schiphol Airport,** the national airport of the Netherlands, opened Terminal West and further expands its passenger capacity from 18 million to 27 million passengers per year. The new terminal, reserved for non-European arrivals and departures, is connected to the existing facility, which handles only flights from European Union member nations. Terminal West incorporates state-of-the-art technical systems, an expanded laser-managed baggage handling operation, and a full-service business travelers' meeting and communications center. Work continues on a 3,500-car parking garage and an expanded rail station.

Belgium   On June 17 and 18, 1995, 3,000 local citizens will don the uniforms of French, English, and Prussian soldiers in a reenactment of the 1815 **Battle of Waterloo.** The realistic mock battle will include the firing of muskets and field guns. Unlike the real battle, which resulted in more than 40,000 deaths in a single day, this one ends with a grand parade. This event will be the last reenactment of the Battle of Waterloo until the year 2000.

In medieval Brugge, the **Procession of the Holy Blood** on Ascension Day (May 25 in 1995) is a magnificent pageant and one of Belgium's oldest traditions, dating back to 1291. After performances of scenes from the Old and New Testaments, the relic that was allegedly brought from Jerusalem to Brugge in 1150 is carried through the streets of the city enclosed in a golden reliquary whose embellishments include a crown given by Mary of Burgundy and the "black diamond" donated by Mary Queen of Scots.

In neighboring Ghent, the **Floralies** international flower show is held only every fifth year at the Flanders Expo Hall—the next one takes place April 22–May 1, 1995. For many years, this has been one of the world's most important flower events, with more than 300 exhibitors. Azaleas and begonias, grown in profusion in the Ghent area, have pride of place.

Luxembourg Although designated Cultural Capital of Europe for 1995, Luxembourg, with characteristic modesty, has chosen to call itself simply **Cultural City.** Events will be held throughout the country, including a major retrospective of works by Luxembourg's underrated expressionist master Joseph Kutter; the world premiere of Mikos Theodorakis's new opera, "Elektra"; a summer concert series of popular music in a giant marquee holding 2,000 people; and Berlioz' "Requiem," performed outdoors by three symphony orchestras and three choirs, in honor of the Grand Duchy's National Day on June 22.

Summer 1995 will see the opening of the new **Musée d'Histoire de la Ville de Luxembourg (Luxembourg Historical Museum)** in Luxembourg City. The museum, which traces the city's thousand-year history, is partially underground, with the lowest five levels showing the town's preserved ancient stonework. A glass-walled elevator gives a wonderful view of the ravine from the upper floors.

Fodor's Choice

No two people will agree on what makes a perfect vacation, but it's fun and helpful to know what others think. We hope you'll have a chance to experience some of Fodor's Choices yourself while visiting the Benelux countries. For detailed information about each entry, refer to the appropriate chapters within this guidebook.

Hotels

Netherlands The Grand Amsterdam *($$$$)*

Hotel de l'Europe, Amsterdam *($$$$)*

Hotel Derlon, Maastricht *($$$$)*

Auberge Corps de Garde, Groningen *($$)*

Canal House, Amsterdam *($$)*

Kasteel Elsloo, Elsloo *($$)*

City Hotel, Scheviningen *($)*

Belgium De Rosier, Antwerp *($$$$)*

De Tuilerieën, Brugge *($$$$)*

SAS Royal Hotel, Brussels *($$$$)*

Amigo, Brussels *($$$)*

Firean, Antwerp *($$$)*

Oud Huis Amsterdam, Brugge *($$$)*

Egmond, Brugge *($$)*

Erasmus, Ghent *($$)*

Manos Stephanie, Brussels *($$)*

Welcome/Truite d'Argent, Brussels *($)*

Luxembourg Auberge du Coin, Luxembourg City *($$)*

Hiertz, Vianden, Luxembourg *($$)*

Hostellerie du Grunewald, Luxembourg City *($$)*

Restaurants

Netherlands Excelsior, Amsterdam *($$$$)*

Prinses Juliana, Valkenburg aan de Geul *($$$$)*

Nolet's Restaurant Het Reymerswale *($$–$$$$)*

Café Americain, Amsterdam *($$$)*

De Silveren Spiegel, Amsterdam *($$$)*

Kastel Doorwerth, Arnhem (*$$$*)

Bodega Keyzer, Amsterdam (*$$*)

Polman's Huis, Utrecht (*$$*)

Haesje Claes, Amsterdam (*$*)

Belgium De Karmeliet, Brugge (*$$$$*)

La Truffe Noire, Brussels (*$$$$*)

Les Brigittines, Brussels (*$$$*)

Neuze Neuze, Antwerp (*$$$*)

La Quincaillerie, Brussels (*$$*)

Siphon, Damme (*$–$$*)

Chez Leon, Brussels (*$*)

Du Midi, La Roche (*$*)

Luxembourg Le Bergerie, Echternach, (*$$$$*)

Clairefontaine, Luxembourg City (*$$$$*)

Bamberg's Ehnen (*$$*)

Mousel's Cantine, Luxembourg City (*$$*)

Lëtzebuerger Kaschthaus, Frisange (*$–$$*)

Aal Vienen, Vianden (*$*)

Ancre d'Or, Luxembourg City (*$*)

Landmarks and Monuments

Netherlands Begijnhof, Amsterdam

Caves of St. Peter, Maastricht

Dom Tower, Utrecht

"Long John" Abbey Tower, Middelburg

Nieuwe Kerk, Delft

Portuguese Synagogue, Amsterdam

Prinsenhof, Delft

Sint Servaas Basilik, Maastricht

St. John's Cathedral, Hertogenbosch

Belgium Abbaye d'Orval, Orval

Bouillon Castle, Bouillon

Burg and canals, Brugge

Butte de Lion, Waterloo

Cathédrale Notre-Dame, Tournai

Cloister, Onze Lieve Vrouw-basiliek, Tongeren

Eglise St-Jacques, Liège

Graslei and Spires, Ghent

Grand'Place, Brussels

Onze-Lieve-Vrouwekathedraal, Antwerp

Luxembourg Eglise St-Laurent, Diekirch

Vianden Castle, Vianden

Museums

Netherlands Anne Frank House, Amsterdam

Kröller-Müller Museum, Otterloo

Paleis Het Loo, Apeldoorn

Rijksmuseum, Amsterdam

Vincent Van Gogh Museum, Amsterdam

Belgium Centre Belge de la Bande Dessinée (Belgian Comic Strip Center), Brussels

David and Alice Van Buuren Museum, Brussels

Groeninge Museum, Brugge

Horta Museum, Brussels

Museum Mayer van den Bergh, Antwerp

Musée d'Art Moderne, Brussels

Plantin-Moretus Museum, Antwerp

Royal Museum of Fine Arts, Antwerp

Luxembourg Battle of the Bulge Museum, Diekirch

Art Treasures

Netherlands *Destroyed City* by Zadkine, Rotterdam

The Night Watch by Rembrandt, Rijksmuseum, Amsterdam

Rietveld-Schroeder House by Rietveld, Utrecht

Sunflowers by Van Gogh, Vincent Van Gogh Museum, Amsterdam

Belgium *Adoration of the Mystic Lamb* by van Eyck, Sint Baafskathedraal, Ghent

Dulle Griet (Mad Meg) by Bruegel, Mayer van den Bergh Museum, Antwerp

Descent from the Cross by Rubens, Onze-Lieve-Vrouwekathedraal, Antwerp

Works of Magritte, Ensor, and Delvaux, Modern Art Museum, Brussels

Madonna with Canon van der Paele by van Eyck, Groeninge, Brugge

Altarpiece of St. John the Baptist and St. John the Evangelist by Memling, Memling Museum, Brugge

Baptismal font by Renier de Huy, St-Barthelemy, Liège

Perfect Moments

Netherlands Eating oysters fresh from the Oosterschelde in Zeeland.

Joining the merriment of Carnival in Maastricht.

Riding a bike along a dike road anywhere in the country.

Walking along the canals of Amsterdam after dark.

Watching fireworks over the beach in Scheveningen.

Belgium Antiquing around Grand Sablon, Brussels

Wandering at dusk through the churchyard of l'Eglise de Notre Dame, Damme

Walking the windmill-lined canal between Damme and Brugge

Following a winter walk along a North Sea beach with a plate of steaming mussels in a café with a view of the sea

Horseback riding in the beech woods of the Forêt de Soignes near Brussels

Listening to the Last Post being blown for the soldiers of World War I at the Menin Gate in Ieper

Finding a quiet side street where time has stood still in Brugge

Munching french fries out of a twist of paper at a roadside stand

Walking the misty moorland of the Hautes Fagnes near Malmedy

Singing along with amateur performers in a *café chantant* in Liège

Luxembourg Looking out over the Alzette Valley from Sigefroid's Bock.

Wandering through the beech-and-fir woods of the Müllerthal, with its limestone bluffs and twisting brooks.

The Netherlands, Belgium, and Luxembourg

Europe

World Time Zones

Numbers below vertical bands relate each zone to Greenwich Mean Time (0 hrs.).
Local times frequently differ from these general indications,
as indicated by light-face numbers on map.

Algiers, **29**	Berlin, **34**	Delhi, **48**	Istanbul, **40**
Anchorage, **3**	Bogotá, **19**	Denver, **8**	Jerusalem, **42**
Athens, **41**	Budapest, **37**	Djakarta, **53**	Johannesburg, **44**
Auckland, **1**	Buenos Aires, **24**	Dublin, **26**	Lima, **20**
Baghdad, **46**	Caracas, **22**	Edmonton, **7**	Lisbon, **28**
Bangkok, **50**	Chicago, **9**	Hong Kong, **56**	London (Greenwich), **27**
Beijing, **54**	Copenhagen, **33**	Honolulu, **2**	Los Angeles, **6**
	Dallas, **10**		Madrid, **38**
			Manila, **57**

Introduction

By Nancy Coons

Slate-colored skies curve like a pewter bowl over an undulating landscape, the long, low horizon punctuated by blunt steeples and a scattering of deep-roofed farmhouses that seem to enfold the land like a mother goose spreading wings over her brood. Inky crows wheel over spindle-fingered pollards, jackdaws pepper the ocher grainfields, and a magpie, flashing black and white, drags a long, iridescent tail through the damp air. These are the 16th-century landscapes of Bruegel the Elder—stained-glass planes in sepia tones, leaded by black branches, crooked spires, dark-frozen streams.

And these, too, are the 20th-century landscapes of Belgium, the Netherlands, and Luxembourg—a wedge of northern Europe squeezed between the massive and ancient kingdoms of France and Germany, bounded by the harsh North Sea to the northwest, defined by the rough, high forests of the Ardennes to the southeast. No wonder so much of their appeal, past and present, is interior—bountiful, sensual still lifes, the glowing chambers of Vermeer, the inner radiance in the portraits of Rembrandt: Their weather-beaten cultures have turned inward over the centuries, toward the hearth. Indoors, Bruegel's otherwise sepia scenes warm subtly with color—earthy browns, berry reds, loden greens, muted indigos, coral cheeks. So it is today: The Netherlanders gather in gold-lit, smoke-burnished "brown cafés," old bentwood chairs scraping across weathered stone floors; the Flemish nurse goblets of mahogany beer by candlelight in dark-beamed halls, a scarlet splash of paisley runner thrown over the pine tabletop; red-vested Walloons—French-speaking Belgians—read the newspaper in high-backed oak banquettes polished blue–black by generations of rough tweed. In Luxembourg, the glass of light beer and *drüp* of eau-de-vie go down behind the candy-colored leaded glass of spare, bright-lit *stuff* or pubs, where village life finds its social focus, day in, day out. In each of these small northern lands, so often lashed by rain, soaked by drizzle, wrapped in fog, with winter dark closing in at 4 PM and winter daylight dawdling until 9 AM, the people live out the rich-hued interior scenes of the Old Masters.

Yet the skies do clear, come spring, and at last the light lingers until well after 10 at night. Then the real pleasure begins—an intense appreciation that residents of moderate climates would be hard-put to understand. As if the people's gratitude took physical form, it manifests itself in flowers, a frenzy of color spilling from every windowsill, spreading like ocean waves across tulip fields, over rose trellises, through wisteria-woven archways. Fruit trees explode like fireworks, and whole orchards shimmer pink. Chestnut branches sag under the weight of their leaves and the heavy, grapelike clusters of blossom that thrust upward, defying gravity. In the midst of this orgy of scent and color, Dutch university students bicycle along canals in loose batik-print cotton; blueoveralled Flemish farmers open their half-doors and bask; the international bankers of Luxembourg swing their Versace suit coats over their shoulders and head for the benches in the green Petrusse Valley.

Then café society, and home life with it, moves lock, stock, and barrel outdoors, to bask lizardlike in the rare warmth. Terrace cafés on the Grote Markts and Grand'Places rival any piazza in Italy. And when there's no café around, the family simply sets out a cluster of folding chairs, perhaps a checkered-cloth-covered card table, whether smack on the sidewalk or behind the barn door, to make the most of fine weather. A suntan remains (as it does in sun-starved North Germany) the most sought-after of status symbols—doubly prestigious if flaunted in midwinter, as northerners, once pale and prune-skinned, return from the ski slopes of the Alps or the beaches of the Canary Islands.

The extremes of their climate, from inexorable gray to luxurious sun, may form a common bond, but the three countries of the Netherlands, Belgium, and Luxembourg sustain sharply different cultures, languages, and terrain. The Netherlands itself is a tangle of inner conflicts—Catholic versus Protestant (they lean 60–40 toward the latter, that 60 percent still functioning as one of Europe's Reformation strongholds); puritanical versus prurient (though you can't buy liquor on Sunday in some areas, in others prostitutes sit, gartered and whalebone-stayed, in display windows like so much grade-A beef). In fact, in narrow, low row houses up and down town streets, whole blocks-full of ordinary people live without curtains, their evening lives and possessions open to viewing by passersby. Open to the North Sea for hundreds of miles, each summer the Netherlanders turn their backs on the beach, load up their trailers, and migrate south; though they're leaving behind the most heavily populated land on the Continent, they flock together in crowded trailer parks wherever they go, rank on cozy rank decked with lace curtains and black-and-yellow Dutch license plates.

The Belgian situation goes beyond mere contradiction: It is a country torn in two, split by two tongues and two distinct cultures. The division between Wallonie and Flanders traces back to Merovingian times, and the Walloon patois and Belgian French represent the last northward wave of the Roman empire and its lingual residue. Twice in this century Flemish citizens (and possibly a king) were known to collaborate with German invaders, allying themselves against what they saw as French-speaking domination. And today the bickering over bilingual rights leaves Brussels a no-man's-land, with extra-wide enamel signs naming every street and alley in two tongues. The cultures are as different as their languages: The Flemish are proud and tidy, their homes filled with the exterior light that pours in tall, multipaned windows; a spare, avant-garde current in fashion, film, and literature shows their Dutch leanings. The Walloons, on the other hand, remain more laissez-faire, their homes often dark, cozy, and cluttered with knickknacks and lace. A women's clothing shop in Ghent is likely to include progressive, trendy, severe clothing, while the equivalent in Liège will show cardigans, A-line skirts, and fussy florals. These two separate worlds share a Catholic culture which, beyond the spiritual realm, finds expression in a shared appreciation of the good things in life, such as the pleasures of the table.

If Belgium and the Netherlands show inner conflict, the natives of little Luxembourg present a solid front to the outside, interacting in French, German, or English, but maintaining their private world in their own native *Lëtzebuergesch* (Luxembourgish). Thus, having survived centuries of conquest and occupation, they can open their country to European Union "Eurocrats" and more than a hundred international banks, and still keep to themselves. Luxembourg sustains two, parallel cultures, with some cafés catering to trendy, international, or tourist crowds and others reserved for the loden-coated locals, who may greet an aberrant visitor with stunned silence as thick as the cigarette smoke that fills the air.

The Netherlands, Belgium, and Luxembourg—as diverse within themselves as they are to one another. And yet all this diversity has been thrown together by the dominant cultures pressing in at the borders—France and Germany. Having been conquered, war-torn, and economically dwarfed for generations, the three little countries felt compelled, in 1958, to form an alliance, an early and seminal economic union that served as a foundation for the European Union. Since then, "Benelux" has become a convenient abbreviation for a small, independent wedge of northern Europe where even fruit juice is labeled in French and in Dutch; only a few, local products have yet been labeled in Luxembourgish.

But, of course, Benelux is considerably more than an arbitrary economic unit. It is a rich and varied region, laced with canals, sprinkled with orchards, its cities burnished with age, where museum visitors can browse through the landscapes of Bruegel and Van Ruisdael and the interiors of Van Eyck, Vermeer, and Rembrandt—then experience their inspiration firsthand, in the magnificent, brooding countryside and time-polished interiors that remain much unchanged since they first inspired the Old Masters.

1 Essential Information

Before You Go

Government Information Offices

In the United States Belgian Tourist Office, 780 3rd Ave., Suite 1501, New York, NY 10017, tel. 212/758–8130, fax 212/355–7675. **Luxembourg National Tourist Office,** 17 Beekman Pl., New York, NY 10022, tel. 212/935–8888, fax 212/935–5896. **Netherlands Board of Tourism,** 355 Lexington Ave., New York, NY 10017, tel. 212/370–7360; 225 N. Michigan Ave., Suite 326, Chicago, IL 60601, tel. 312/819–0300, fax 312/819–1740; 9841 Airport Blvd., 10th Floor, Los Angeles, CA 90045, tel. 310/348–9333, fax 310/348–9344.

In Canada **Netherlands Board of Tourism,** 25 Adelaide St. E, Suite 710, Toronto, Ont. M5C 1Y2, tel. 416/363–1577, fax 416/363–1470.

In the United Kingdom **Belgian Tourist Office,** 29 Princes St., London W1R 7RG, tel. 0171/629–0230. **Luxembourg National Tourist Office,** 122 Regent St., London W1R 5FE, tel. 0171/434–2800. **Netherlands Board of Tourism,** 25–28 Buckingham Gate, London SW1E 6LD, tel. 0171/828–7900.

U.S. Government Travel Briefings The U.S. Department of State's **Overseas Citizens Emergency Center** (Room 4811, Washington, DC 20520; enclose S.A.S.E.) issues Consular Information Sheets, which cover crime, security, political climate, and health risks as well as embassy locations, entry requirements, currency regulations, and other routine matters. For the latest information, stop in at any U.S. passport office, consulate, or embassy; call the interactive hot line (tel. 202/647–5225; fax 202/647–3000); or, with your PC's modem, tap into the Bureau of Consular Affairs' computer bulletin board (tel. 202/647–9225).

Tours and Packages

With their wealth of artistic treasures, medieval castles, storybook villages, and picturesque landscapes, Belgium, Luxembourg, and the Netherlands (Holland) offer nearly limitless options to the visitor. How to enjoy them is up to you. If you're heading to the region for the first time, consider an escorted tour. Just sit back and enjoy yourself; all the details will have been taken care of. Group tours also tend to save you money on airfare and hotels. If you prefer more independence, there are still plenty of creative alternatives available. You can enjoy a fly/drive package, follow a prearranged itinerary independently, or plan a visit from an à la carte menu of package options.

Before selecting a tour, be sure to find out exactly what expenses are included (particularly tips, taxes, service charges, side trips, additional meals, and entertainment) and expect only what is specified. In addition, check the ratings of all hotels on the itinerary and their facilities, cancellation policies for you and the tour operator and, if you are traveling alone, the cost of a single supplement.

Listed below is a sample of the tours and packages available. Most tour operators request that bookings be made through a travel agent—there is no additional charge for doing so. For additional resources, contact your travel agent or the tourist offices of the Netherlands, Belgium, and Luxembourg.

Fully Escorted Tours From the United States

Abercrombie & Kent (1520 Kensington Rd., Oak Brook, IL 60521, tel. 708/954–2944 or 800/323–7308) takes a six-night cruise through the waterways of Holland and Belgium, including stops in Amsterdam, Rotterdam, Ghent, and Brugge. **Brendan Tours** (15137 Califa St., Van Nuys, CA 91411, tel. 818/785–9696 or 800/421–8446) offers tours that range from one or two cities to one, two, or all three countries, usually in combination with visits to other cities on the Continent. **Caravan Tours** (401 N. Michigan Ave., Chicago, IL 60611, tel. 312/321–9800 or 800/227–2826) offers a "Four-Country Highlight" of Holland, Belgium, Luxembourg, and Germany in 12 days. **Central Holiday** (206 Central Ave., Jersey City, NJ 07307, tel. 201/798–5777 or 800/935–5000) specializes in both escorted and independent fly/drive packages. **Collette Tours** (162 Middle St., Pawtucket, RI 02860, tel. 401/728–3805 or 800/832–4656) spends nine days touring Paris, the beaches of Normandy, Brugge, and Amsterdam. **DER Tours** (11933 Wilshire Blvd., Los Angeles, CA 90025, tel. 800/937–1234) specializes in deluxe escorted tours. **Globus** (5301 S. Federal Cir., Littleton, CO 80123, tel. 303/797–2800 or 800/221–0090) also includes Holland and Belgium in many of its tours of continental Europe. **Maupintour** (Box 807, Lawrence, KS 66044, tel. 913/843–1211 or 800/255–4266) offers the highlights of Belgium and Germany in 10 days, including Brussels, Ghent, and a Rhine cruise. A 10-day tour of Luxembourg and Paris includes side trips to Belgium and Germany. Another tour offers Holland and Brussels for 10 days. **Olson Travelworld** (Box 10066, Manhattan Beach, CA 90226, tel. 310/546–8400 or 800/421–2255) begins its two-week excursion with highlights of Holland, heads into Belgium and Luxembourg, then winds up in Paris. **Trafalgar Tours** (11 E. 26th St., Suite 1300, New York, NY 10010, tel. 212/689–8977 or 800/854–0103) includes Holland and Belgium on a number of its trips through continental Europe. **Travcoa** (Box 2630, Newport Beach, CA 92658, tel. 714/476–2800 or 800/992–2004) offers "Medieval Holland and Flanders," an 18-day tour including Antwerp, Ghent, Brugge, Brussels, The Hague, Amsterdam, and the cities of Northern Holland.

From the United Kingdom

Amsterdam Travel Services Ltd. (Bridge House, Ware, Herts SG12 9DF, tel. 01920/467444) has short breaks and package holidays to Amsterdam. Cycling holidays, excursions, and packages to Delft, The Hague, and Scheveningen are available. **Cresta Holidays** (Cresta House, 32 Victoria St., Altringham, Cheshire WA14 1ET, tel. 01345/056511) offers package holidays to Amsterdam with optional bulb-field excursions, day trips, and canal cruises. Three-center holidays, which include Brussels and Paris, are also available. **Holland Travel Service** (Holland House, 24–28 The Broadway, Old Amersham, Buckinghamshire HP7 0HP, tel. 01494/729333) offers weekend breaks to Amsterdam and packages based in seven Dutch cities; Valkenburg is ideally placed for visiting Belgium, Luxembourg, and Germany. Castle and country house holidays are also available. **Shearing Holidays** (Miry La., Wigan, Lancashire WN3 4AG, tel. 01942/824824) features five-day city breaks centered in Brugge or Amsterdam, with excursions to Brussels and other places of interest; seven-day tours covering Belgium, Luxembourg, and Holland, and holidays based in various Dutch cities. **Time Off Ltd.** (Chester Close, Chester St., London SW1X 7BQ, tel. 0171/235–8070) has two- to seven-night packages to Brussels, Brugge, and Luxembourg. A Rhine cruise and excursions to Ghent, Antwerp, and Waterloo are available. Holidays to Amsterdam and The Hague feature optional tours to see the windmills, tulip fields, a cheese market, and a Delft pottery factory. **Travelscene Ltd.** (Travelscene House, 11–15 St. Ann's Rd., Harrow, Middlesex HA1 1AS, tel.

0181/427–4445) offers short breaks to Amsterdam in all price ranges, with optional sightseeing excursions and canal cruises. **Wallace Arnold Tours Ltd.** (8 Park La., Croyden CR0 1JA, tel. 0181/686–2378) has several coach tours featuring sights in Belgium and Holland.

Special-Interest Tours Among the operators of special-interest tours that include two or more countries of the Benelux area:

Art and Culture **Art Express** (4500 Campus Dr., Suite 410, Newport Beach, CA 92660, tel. 800/325–7103), **Art Horizons International** (1430 Broadway, 6th Floor, New York, NY 10018, tel. 212/921–5583), **Eduard Maurer & Co.** (24169 Alicia Pkwy., Suite E, Mission Viejo, CA 92691, tel. 714/859–7919 or 800/888–6262), **Swan Hellenic/Esplanade Tours** (581 Boylston St., Boston MA 02116, tel. 617/266–7465 or 800/426–5492), **Travel Time** (203 N. Wabash Ave., Chicago, IL 60601, tel. 312/726–7197 or 800/621–4725), and **Unitours** (8 S. Michigan Ave., Chicago IL 60603, tel. 312/782–1590 or 800/621–0557) offer various explorations of the artistic and historical riches of the region.

Castles and Flowers **Endless Beginnings** (9825 Dowdy Dr., Suite 105, San Diego, CA 92126, tel. 619/566–4166 or 800/822–7855), **First Dutch Tour Operators** (Box 608439, 5401 Kirkman Rd., Suite 715, Orlando, FL 32819, tel. 305/866–5555), **Passages Unlimited** (10 Liberty Sq., Boston, MA 02109, tel. 617/482–6760 or 800/232–2939), **Swan Hellenic/Esplanade** (*see* Art and Culture, *above*), and **Tauck Tours** (11 Wilton Rd., Westport, CT 06880, tel. 203/226–6911 or 800/468–2825) chart courses through gardens, countryside, museums, and castles in Flanders, the kingdom of Orange, and other regions.

Cruising If the idea of exploration on wheels does not appeal, consider sailing the Rhine and Moselle Rivers through Belgium, Holland, and Germany. Contact **Abercrombie & Kent** (*see* General Interest Tours, above), **EuroCruises** (303 W. 13th St., New York, NY 10014, tel. 212/691–2099 or 800/688–3876), **KD River Cruises of Europe** (2500 Westchester Ave., Purchase, NY 10577, tel. 914/696–3600 or 800/346–6525 in the eastern U.S.; or 323 Geary St., San Francisco, CA 94102, tel. 415/392–8817 or 800/858–8587 in the west), **Le Boat, Inc.** (Box E, Maywood, NJ 07507, tel. 201/342–1838 or 800/922–0291), **Sea Air Holidays** (733 Summer St., Stamford, CT 06901, tel. 800/732–6247), **Swan Hellenic/Esplanade Tours** (*see* Art and Culture, above), or **The BargeLady** (225 N. Michigan Ave., Chicago, IL 60601, tel. 312/540–5500 or 800/880–0071).

Cycling Contact **Classic Adventures** (Box 153, Hamlin, NY 14464, tel. 716/964–8488 or 800/777–8090), **College Bicycle Tours** (Sept.–Apr.: 415 W. Fullerton Pkwy., Chicago, IL 60614, tel. 312/404–1710; May–Aug.: 2188 Harvard, Southfield, MI 48076, tel. 800/736–2453), **Euro-Bike Tours** (Box 990, DeKalb, IL 60115, tel. 800/321–6060), **Van Gogh Bicycle Touring** (Box 57, Winchester, MA 01890, tel. 617/721–0850 or 800/435–6192), and **Vermont Bicycle Touring** (Box 711, Bristol, VT 05443, tel. 802/453–4811).

Food & Wine **Annemarie Victory Tours** (136 E. 64th St., New York, NY 10021, tel. 212/486–0353) combines historical and edible feasts for the eye and stomach on a nine-day exploration of some of the best of Belgium, Luxembourg, and France's castles, museums, châteaux, restaurants, and wine cellars. **Endless Beginnings** (*see* Castles and Flowers, *above*) also arranges deluxe food and wine tours.

Music The cooler climes of the Low Countries complement the rhythms of *le jazz hot*, and **Ciao! Travel** (810 Emerald St., Suite 107, San Diego,

CA 92109, tel. 619/272–1543 or 800/942–2426) has tours featuring visits to local clubs. **Adventures and the Arts Opera Tours** (357 Tehama St., San Francisco, CA 94103, tel. 415/433–1306) specializes in opera and art tours. **Dailey Thorp** (330 W. 58th St., New York, NY 10019, tel. 212/307–1555) offers packages including classical music, opera, and ballet performances.

Independent Packages

American Airlines Fly Away Vacations (tel. 800/832–8383) offers independent packages for as long as you like for visits to Brussels, Brugge, and Antwerp. **Extra Value Travel** (683 S. Collier Blvd., Marco Island, FL 33937, tel. 813/398–4848 or 800/255–2847) offers self-drive tours of Belgium, Luxembourg, and Holland, including hotel choices and car rental. **Jet Vacations** (1775 Broadway, New York, NY 10019, tel. 212/474–8700 or 800/538–0999) offers Flexiplan Europe, a choice of hotels, car rentals, airport transfers, and sight-seeing options for Brussels, Antwerp, Brugge, Liège, Luxembourg, and a number of cities in Holland. **Northwest WorldVacations** (tel. 800/692–8687) provides visitors to Amsterdam or Brussels with preferred hotel and car-rental rates and tour options for a minimum of two nights. **Travel Bound** (599 Broadway, Penthouse, New York, NY 10012, tel. 212/334–1350 or 800/456–8656) offers a week-long "Brussels Grand" package for independent travelers, as well as packages to Holland, Belgium, and/or Luxembourg for a minimum of three to six nights. **TWA Getaway Vacations** (tel. 800/438–2929) and **United Vacations** (tel. 800/328–6877) will customize your itinerary to this region.

When to Go

Late spring, when the northern European days are long, but the summer crowds have not yet filled the beaches, the highways, or the museums, and fall are the best times to visit these three countries.

Climate *See* individual country chapters, below, for temperature charts.

Information Sources For current weather conditions and forecasts for cities in the United States and abroad, plus the local time and helpful travel tips, call the **Weather Channel Connection** (tel. 900/932–8437; 95¢ per minute) from a Touch-Tone phone.

What to Pack

Clothing In the Netherlands, Belgium, and Luxembourg a sweater and a raincoat are indispensable. More expensive restaurants tend toward formality, making a jacket and tie useful items for men.

Miscellaneous Bring an extra pair of eyeglasses or contact lenses in your carry-on luggage. If you have a health problem that requires a prescription drug, pack enough to last the duration of the trip or have your doctor write a prescription using the drug's generic name, because brand names vary from country to country (you'll need a prescription from a doctor in the country you're visiting to get the medication from a pharmacy there). Always carry prescription drugs in their original packaging to avoid problems with customs officials. Don't pack them in luggage that you plan to check in case your bags go astray. Pack a list of the offices that supply refunds for lost or stolen traveler's checks.

Electricity The electrical current in the Netherlands, Belgium, and Luxembourg is 220 volts, 50 cycles alternating current (AC); the United

States runs on 110-volt, 60-cycle AC current. Unlike wall outlets in the United States, which accept plugs with two flat prongs, outlets in the Netherlands, Belgium, and Luxembourg take Continental-type plugs, with two round prongs.

Adapters, Converters, Transformers
To use U.S.-made electric appliances abroad, you'll need an adapter plug. Unless the appliance is dual-voltage and made for travel, you'll also need a converter. Hotels sometimes have 110-volt outlets for low-wattage appliances marked "For Shavers Only" near the sink; don't use them for a high-wattage appliance like a blow-dryer. If you're traveling with an older laptop computer, carry a transformer. New laptop computers are auto-sensing, operating equally well on 110 and 220 volts, so you need only the appropriate adapter plug. For a copy of the free brochure "Foreign Electricity is No Deep Dark Secret," send a S.A.S.E. to adapter-converter manufacturer Franzus Company (Customer Service, Dept. B50, Murtha Industrial Park, Box 142, Beacon Falls, CT 06403, tel. 203/723–6664).

Luggage *Regulations*
Free airline baggage allowances depend on the airline, the route, and the class of your ticket; ask in advance. In general, on domestic flights and on international flights between the United States and foreign destinations, you are entitled to check two bags—neither exceeding 62 inches, or 158 centimeters (length + width + height), or weighing more than 70 pounds (32 kilograms). A third piece may be brought aboard; its total dimensions are generally limited to less than 45 inches (114 centimeters), so it will fit easily under the seat in front of you or in the overhead compartment. In the United States, the Federal Aviation Administration (FAA) gives airlines broad latitude to limit carry-on allowances and tailor them to different aircraft and operational conditions. Charges for excess, oversize, or overweight pieces vary.

If you are flying between two foreign destinations, note that baggage allowances may be determined not by piece but by weight—generally 88 pounds (40 kilograms) of luggage in first class, 66 pounds (30 kilograms) in business class, and 44 pounds (20 kilograms) in economy. If your flight between two cities abroad *connects* with your transatlantic or transpacific flight, the piece method still applies.

Safeguarding Your Luggage
Before leaving home, itemize your bags' contents and their worth in case they go astray. To minimize that risk, tag them inside and out with your name, address, and phone number. (If you use your home address, cover it so that potential thieves can't see it.) Put a copy of your itinerary inside each bag, so that you can easily be tracked. At check-in, make sure that the tag attached by baggage handlers bears the correct three-letter code for your destination. If your bags do not arrive with you, or if you detect damage, immediately file a written report with the airline before you leave the airport.

Taking Money Abroad

Traveler's Checks
Traveler's checks are preferable in metropolitan centers, although you'll need cash in rural areas and small towns. The most widely recognized are **American Express, Citicorp, Diners Club, Thomas Cook,** and **Visa,** which are sold by major commercial banks. Both American Express and Thomas Cook issue checks that can be countersigned and used by you or your traveling companion. Typically the issuing company or the bank at which you make your purchase charges 1% to 3% of the checks' face value as a fee. Some foreign banks charge as much as 20% of the face value as the fee for cashing travelers' checks in a foreign currency. Buy a few checks in small denominations to

cash toward the end of your trip, so you won't be left with excess foreign currency. Record the numbers of checks as you spend them, and keep this list separate from the checks.

Buy some checks in the currency of the country you are visiting; banks will cash them with no fee, and you can use them as readily as cash in many hotels, restaurants, and shops.

Currency Banks offer the most favorable exchange rates. If you use currency
Exchange exchange booths at airports, rail and bus stations, hotels, stores, and privately run exchange firms, you'll typically get less favorable rates, but you may find the hours more convenient.

You can get good rates and avoid long lines at airport currency exchange booths by getting a small amount of currency at **Thomas Cook Currency Services** (630 5th Ave., New York, NY 10111, tel. 212/757–6915 or 800/223-7373 for locations in major metropolitan areas throughout the U.S.) or **Ruesch International** (tel. 800/424–2923 for locations) before you depart. Check with your travel agent to be sure that the currency of the country you will be visiting can be imported.

Getting Money from Home

Cash Many automated-teller machines (ATMs) are tied to international
Machines networks such as **Cirrus** and **Plus.** You can use your bank card at ATMs to withdraw money from an account and get cash advances on a credit-card account if your card has been programmed with a personal identification number, or PIN. Check in advance on limits on withdrawals and cash advances within specified periods. Ask whether your bank-card or credit-card PIN will need to be reprogrammed for use in the area you'll be visiting. Four digits are commonly used overseas. Note that Discover is accepted only in the United States. On cash advances you are charged interest from the day you receive the money from ATMs as well as from tellers. Although transaction fees for ATM withdrawals abroad may be higher than those for withdrawals at home, Cirrus and Plus exchange rates are excellent, because they are based on wholesale rates only offered by major banks. They also may be referred to abroad as "a withdrawal from a credit account."

Plan ahead: Obtain ATM locations and the names of affiliated cash-machine networks before departure. For specific foreign Cirrus locations, call 800/424–7787; for foreign Plus locations, consult the Plus directory at your local bank.

Wiring Money You don't have to be a cardholder to send or receive a **MoneyGram from American Express** for up to $10,000. Go to a MoneyGram agent in retail and convenience stores and American Express travel offices, pay up to $1,000 with a credit card and anything over that in cash. You are allowed a free long-distance call to give the transaction code to your intended recipient, who needs only present identification and the reference number to the nearest MoneyGram agent to pick up the cash. MoneyGram agents are in more than 70 countries (tel. 800/926–9400 for locations). Fees range from 3% to 10%, depending on the amount and how you pay.

You can also use **Western Union.** To wire money, take either cash or a cashier's check to the nearest agent or call and use MasterCard or Visa. Money sent from the United States or Canada will be available for pick up at agent locations in 100 countries within minutes. Once the money is in the system it can be picked up at *any* one of 25,000 locations (call 800/325–6000 for the one nearest you; 800/321–2923 in

Canada). Fees range from 4% to 10%, depending on the amount you send.

Currencies

The monetary unit in Belgium is the Belgian franc (BF); in Luxembourg, the Luxembourg franc (Flux); and in the Netherlands, the guilder (Fl). The currency exchange rates quoted in the following chapters fluctuate daily, so check them at the time of your departure.

Long-Distance Calling

AT&T, MCI, and Sprint have several services that make calling home or the office more affordable and convenient when you're on the road. Use one of them to avoid pricey hotel surcharges. **AT&T** Calling Card (tel. 800/225–5288) and the AT&T Universal Card (tel. 800/662–7759) give you access to the service. With AT&T's USA Direct (tel. 800/874–4000 for codes in the countries you'll be visiting) you can reach an AT&T operator with a local or toll-free call. **MCI's** Call USA (MCI Customer Service, tel. 800/444–4444) allows that service from 85 countries or from country to country via MCI WorldReach. From MCI ExpressInfo in the United States you can get 24-hour weather, news and stock quotes. MCI PhoneCash (tel. 800/925–0029) is available through American Express and through several convenience stores and retailers nationwide. **Sprint** Express (tel. 800/793–1153) has a toll-free number travelers abroad can dial using the WorldTraveler Foncard to reach a Sprint operator in the United States. The Sprint operator can offer international directory assistance to 224 countries. All three companies offer message delivery services to international travelers and have added debit cards so that you don't have to fiddle with change.

Passports and Visas

If your passport is lost or stolen abroad, report the loss immediately to the nearest embassy or consulate and to the local police. If you can provide the consular officer with the information contained in the passport, he or she will usually be able to issue you a new passport promptly. For this reason, keep a photocopy of the data page of your passport separate from your money and traveler's checks. Also leave a photocopy with a relative or friend at home.

U.S. Citizens All U.S. citizens, even infants, need a valid passport to enter the Netherlands or Belgium for stays of up to 90 days. U.S. citizens need a valid passport to enter Luxembourg, but their length of stay is not restricted. You can pick up new and renewal application forms at any of the 13 U.S. Passport Agency offices and at some post offices and courthouses. Although passports are usually mailed within four weeks of your application's receipt, allow five weeks or more from April through summer. Call the Department of State Office of Passport Services' information line (tel. 202/647–0518) for fees, documentation requirements, and other details.

Canadian Citizens Canadian citizens need a valid passport to enter the Netherlands, Belgium, or Luxembourg for stays of up to 90 days. Application forms are available at 23 regional passport offices as well as post offices and travel agencies. Whether for a first or a subsequent passport, you must apply in person. Children under 16 may be included on a parent's passport but must have their own to travel alone. Passports are valid for five years and are usually mailed within two weeks of an application's receipt. For fees, documentation requirements, and other information in English or French, call the passport office (tel. 514/283–2152 or 800/567–6868).

U.K. Citizens Citizens of the United Kingdom need a valid passport to enter the Netherlands, Belgium, or Luxembourg for stays of up to 90 days. Applications for new and renewal passports are available from main post offices as well as at the six passport offices, in Belfast, Glasgow, Liverpool, London, Newport, and Peterborough. You may apply in person at all passport offices, or by mail to all except the London office. Children under 16 may travel on an accompanying parent's passport. All passports are valid for 10 years. Allow a month for processing.

A British Visitor's Passport is valid for holidays and some business trips of up to three months to the Netherlands, Belgium, or Luxembourg. It can include both partners of a married couple. Valid for one year, it will be issued on the same day that you apply. You must apply in person at a main post office.

Customs and Duties

On Arrival *See* the chapters below for regulations applying to visitors entering individual countries.

Returning Home
U.S. Customs If you've been out of the country for at least 48 hours and haven't already used the exemption, or any part of it, in the past 30 days, you may bring home $400 worth of foreign goods duty-free. So can each member of your family, regardless of age; and your exemptions may be pooled, so one of you can bring in more if another brings in less. A flat 10% duty applies to the next $1,000 worth of goods; above $1,400, the rates vary with the merchandise. (If the 48-hour or 30-day limits apply, your duty-free allowance drops to $25, which may not be pooled.) Please note that these are the *general* rules, applicable to most countries, including the Netherlands, Belgium, and Luxembourg.

Travelers 21 or older may bring back 1 liter of alcohol duty-free, provided the beverage laws of the state through which they re-enter the United States allow it. In addition, 100 non-Cuban cigars and 200 cigarettes are allowed, regardless of your age. Antiques and works of art more than 100 years old are duty-free.

Gifts valued at less than $50 may be mailed to the United States duty-free, with a limit of one package per day per addressee, and do not count as part of your exemption (do not send alcohol or tobacco products or perfume valued at more than $5); mark the package "Unsolicited Gift" and write the nature of the gift and its retail value on the outside. Most reputable stores will handle the mailing for you.

For a copy of "Know Before You Go," a free brochure detailing what you may and may not bring back to the United States, rates of duty, and other pointers, contact the **U.S. Customs Service** (Box 7407, Washington, DC 20044, tel. 202/927–6724).

Canadian Customs Once per calendar year, when you've been out of Canada for at least seven days, you may bring in C$300 worth of goods duty-free. If you've been away less than seven days but more than 48 hours, the duty-free exemption drops to C$100 but can be claimed any number of times (as can a C$20 duty-free exemption for absences of 24 hours or more). You cannot combine the yearly and 48-hour exemptions, use the C$300 exemption only partially (to save the balance for a later trip), or pool exemptions with family members. Goods claimed under the C$300 exemption may follow you by mail; those claimed under the lesser exemptions must accompany you.

Alcohol and tobacco products may be included in the yearly and 48-hour exemptions but not in the 24-hour exemption. If you meet the age requirements of the province through which you re-enter Canada, you may bring in, duty-free, 1.14 liters (40 imperial ounces) of wine or liquor *or* two dozen 12-ounce cans or bottles of beer or ale. If you are 16 or older, you may bring in, duty-free, 200 cigarettes, 50 cigars or cigarillos, and 400 tobacco sticks or 400 grams of manufactured tobacco. Alcohol and tobacco must accompany you on your return.

An unlimited number of gifts valued up to C$60 each may be mailed to Canada duty-free. These do not count as part of your exemption. Label the package "Unsolicited Gift—Value under $60." Alcohol and tobacco are excluded.

For more information, including details of duties on items that exceed your duty-free limit, ask the Revenue Canada Customs and Excise and Taxation Department (2265 St. Laurent Blvd. S, Ottawa, Ont., K1G 4K3, tel. 613/957–0275) for a copy of the free brochure "I Declare/Je Déclare."

U.K. Customs If your journey was wholly within European Union (EU) countries, you no longer need to pass through customs when you return to the United Kingdom. According to EU guidelines, you may bring in 800 cigarettes, 400 cigarillos, 200 cigars, and 1 kilogram of smoking tobacco, plus 10 liters of spirits, 20 liters of fortified wine, 90 liters of wine, and 110 liters of beer. If you exceed these limits, you may be required to prove that the goods are for your personal use or are gifts.

For further information or a copy of "A Guide for Travellers," which details standard customs procedures as well as what you may bring into the United Kingdom from abroad, contact HM Customs and Excise (Dorset House, Stamford St., London SE1 9PY, tel. 0171/928–3344).

Traveling with Cameras, Camcorders, and Laptops

Film and Cameras If your camera is new or if you haven't used it for a while, shoot and develop a few test rolls of film before you leave. Store film in a cool, dry place—never in the car's glove compartment or on the shelf under the rear window.

Airport security X-rays generally aren't harmful to film with an ISO of below 400. To protect your film, carry it with you in a clear plastic bag and ask for a hand inspection. Such requests are honored at U.S. airports, usually not abroad. Don't depend on a lead-lined bag to protect film in checked luggage—the airline may increase the radiation to see what's inside. Call the Kodak Information Center (tel. 800/242–2424) for details.

Camcorders and Videotape Before your trip, put camcorders through their paces, invest in a skylight filter to protect the lens, and check all the batteries. Most newer camcorders are equipped with batteries that can be recharged with a universal or worldwide AC adapter charger (or multivoltage converter) usable whether the voltage is 110 or 220. All that's needed is the appropriate plug.

Videotape is not damaged by X-rays, but it may be harmed by the magnetic field of a walk-through metal detector, so ask for a hand-check. Airport security personnel may ask you to turn on the camcorder to prove that it's what it appears to be, so make sure the battery is charged. Note that rather than the National Television System Committee video standard (NTSC) used in the United States and Canada, the Netherlands, Belgium, and Luxembourg use PAL/SECAM technology. You will not be able to view your tapes through the local TV set or view movies bought there in your home VCR. Blank tapes bought in the Netherlands, Belgium, and Luxembourg can be used for NTSC camcorder taping, but they are pricey.

Laptops   Security X-rays do not harm hard-disk or floppy-disk storage, but you may request a hand-check, at which point you may be asked to turn on the computer to prove that it is what it appears to be. (Check your battery before departure.) Most airlines allow you to use your laptop aloft except during takeoff and landing (so as not to interfere with navigation equipment). For international travel, register your foreign-made laptop with U.S. Customs as you leave the country. If your laptop is U.S.-made, call the consulate of the country you'll be visiting to find out whether it should be registered with customs upon arrival. Before departure, find out about repair facilities at your destination, and don't forget any transformer or adapter plug you may need (*see* Electricity, *above*).

Languages

Belgium has three official languages: Flemish, French, and German. In Flemish-speaking parts of the country you are likely to get a better reaction if you speak English rather than French. Luxembourg's languages are mixed throughout the population rather than divided geographically; they include Luxembourgish (a language descended from an ancient dialect of the Franks), French, and German—as well as a fair amount of English. In the Netherlands, Dutch is the official language, but most people know some English as well.

Staying Healthy

If you have a health problem that may require the purchase of prescription drugs, have your doctor write a prescription using the drug's generic name, as brand names vary from country to country.

Finding a   The **International Association for Medical Assistance to Travellers**
Doctor   (IAMAT, 417 Center St., Lewiston, NY 14092, tel. 716/754–4883; 40 Regal Rd., Guelph, Ontario N1K 1B5; 57 Voirets, 1212 Grand-Lancy, Geneva, Switzerland) publishes a worldwide directory of English-speaking physicians whose qualifications meet IAMAT standards and who have agreed to treat members for a set fee. Membership is free.

Assistance   Pretrip medical referrals, emergency evacuation or repatriation,
Companies   24-hour telephone hot lines for medical consultation, dispatch of medical personnel, relay of medical records, cash for emergencies, and other personal and legal assistance are among the services provided by several organizations specializing in medical assistance to travelers. Among them are **International SOS Assistance** (Box 11568, Philadelphia, PA 19116, tel. 215/244–1500 or 800/523–8930; Box 466, Pl. Bonaventure, Montréal, Que. H5A 1C1, tel. 514/874–7674 or 800/363–0263), **Medex Assistance Corporation** (Box 10623, Baltimore, MD 21285, tel. 410/296–2530 or 800/874–9125), **Near Services** (450 Prairie Ave., Suite 101, Calumet City, IL 60409, tel. 708/868–6700 or 800/654–6700), and **Travel Assistance International**

(1133 15th St. NW, Suite 400, Washington, DC 20005, tel. 202/331–1609 or 800/821–2828). Because these companies will also sell you death-and-dismemberment, trip-cancellation, and other insurance coverage, there is some overlap with the travel-insurance policies discussed under Insurance, *below.*

Publications *The Safe Travel Book* by Peter Savage (Lexington Books, 866 3rd Ave., New York, NY 10022, tel. 212/702–4771 or 800/257–5755, fax 800/562–1272; $12.95) is packed with handy lists and phone numbers to make your trip smooth. *Traveler's Medical Resource* by William W. Forgey (ICS Books, Inc., 1 Tower Plaza, 107 E. 89th Ave., Merrillville, IN 45410, tel. 800/541–7323; $19.95) is also a good, authoritative guide to care overseas.

Insurance

For U.S. Residents Most tour operators, travel agents, and insurance agents sell specialized health-and-accident, flight, trip-cancellation, and luggage insurance as well as comprehensive policies with some or all of these features. Before you make any purchase, review your existing health and homeowner policies to find out whether they cover expenses incurred while traveling.

Health-and-Accident Insurance Specific policy provisions of supplemental health-and-accident insurance for travelers include reimbursement for from $1,000 to $150,000 worth of medical and/or dental expenses caused by an accident or illness during a trip. The personal-accident, or death-and-dismemberment, provision pays a lump sum to your beneficiaries if you die or to you if you lose one or both limbs or your eyesight; the lump sum awarded can range from $15,000 to $500,000. The medical-assistance provision may reimburse you for the cost of referrals, evacuation, or repatriation and other services, or it may automatically enroll you as a member of a particular medical-assistance company (*see* Assistance Companies, *above*).

Flight Insurance Often bought as a last-minute impulse at the airport, flight insurance pays a lump sum when a plane crashes either to a beneficiary if the insured dies or sometimes to a surviving passenger who loses eyesight or a limb. Like most impulse buys, flight insurance is expensive and basically unnecessary. It supplements the airlines' coverage described in the limits-of-liability paragraphs on your ticket. Charging an airline ticket to a major credit card often automatically entitles you to coverage and may also embrace travel by bus, train, and ship.

Baggage Insurance In the event of loss, damage, or theft on international flights, airlines' liability is $20 per kilogram for checked baggage (roughly about $640 per 70-pound bag) and $400 per passenger for unchecked baggage. On domestic flights, the ceiling is $2,000 per passenger. Excess-valuation insurance can be bought directly from the airline at check-in for about $10 per $1,000 worth of coverage. However, you cannot buy it at any price for the rather extensive list of excluded items shown on your airline ticket.

Trip Insurance **Trip-cancellation-and-interruption insurance** protects you in the event you are unable to undertake or finish your trip, especially if your airline ticket, cruise, or package tour does not allow changes or cancellations. The amount of coverage you purchase should equal the cost of your trip should you, a traveling companion, or a family member fall ill, forcing you to stay home, plus the nondiscounted one-way airline ticket you would need to buy if you had to return home early. Read the fine print carefully, especially sections defining "family member" and "preexisting medical conditions." **Default or bankruptcy insurance** protects you against a supplier's failure to deliver. Such policies often do not cover default by a travel agency, tour operator, airline, or cruise line if you bought your tour and the coverage directly from the firm in question. Tours packaged by one of the 33 members of the United States Tour Operators Association (USTOA, 211 E. 51 St., Suite 12B, New York, NY 10022; tel. 212/750–7371), which requires members to maintain $1 million each in an account to reimburse clients in case of default, are likely to present the fewest difficulties.

Comprehensive Policies Companies supplying comprehensive policies with some or all of the above features include **Access America, Inc.** (Box 90315, Richmond, VA 23230, tel. 800/284–8300); **Carefree Travel Insurance** (Box 310, 120 Mineola Blvd., Mineola, NY 11501, tel. 516/294–0220 or 800/323–3149); **Near** (450 Prairie Ave., Suite 101, Calumet City, IL 60409, tel. 708/868–6700 or 800/654–6700); **Tele-Trip** (Mutual of Omaha Plaza, Box 31762, Omaha, NE 68131, tel. 800/228–9792); **The Travelers Companies** (1 Tower Sq., Hartford, CT 06183, tel. 203/277–0111 or 800/243–3174); **Travel Guard International** (1145 Clark St., Stevens Point, WI 54481, tel. 715/345–0505 or 800/826–1300); and **Wallach and Company, Inc.** (107 W. Federal St., Box 480, Middleburg, VA 22117, tel. 703/687–3166 or 800/237–6615).

For U.K. Residents Most tour operators, travel agents, and insurance agents sell policies covering accident, medical expenses, personal liability, trip cancellation, and loss or theft of personal property. You can also buy an annual travel-insurance policy valid for every trip (usually of less than 90 days) you make during the year in which it's purchased. Make sure you will be covered if you have a preexisting medical condition or are pregnant.

For advice by phone or a free booklet, "Holiday Insurance," that sets out what to expect from a holiday-insurance policy and gives price guidelines, contact the Association of British Insurers (51 Gresham St., London EC2V 7HQ, tel. 0171/600–3333; 30 Gordon St., Glasgow G1 3PU, tel. 0141/226–3905; Scottish Providence Bldg., Donegall Sq. W, Belfast BT1 6JE, tel. 01232/249176; call for other locations).

Car Rentals

All major car-rental companies are represented in the Netherlands, Belgium, and Luxembourg, including **Alamo** (tel. 800/522–9696); **Avis** (tel. 800/331–1084, 800/879–2847 in Canada); **Budget** (tel. 800/527–0700); **Hertz** (tel. 800/654–3001, 800/263-0600 in Canada); and **National** (tel. 800/227–3876), known internationally as InterRent and Europcar. In cities, unlimited-mileage rates range from $34 per day for an economy car to $112 for a large car; weekly unlimited-mileage rates range from $156 to $395. This does not include tax, which in the Netherlands is 17.5% on car rentals, in Belgium 20.5%, and in Luxembourg, 15%.

Requirements Your driver's license is acceptable. An International Driver's Permit, available from the American or Canadian Automobile Association, is a good idea.

Extra Charges Picking up the car in one city and leaving it in another may entail substantial drop-off charges or one-way service fees. The cost of a collision or loss-damage waiver (*see below*) can be high, also. Some rental agencies will charge you extra if you return the car *before* the time specified on your contract. Ask before making unscheduled drop-offs. Be sure the rental agent agrees *in writing* to any changes in drop-off location or other items of your rental contract. Fill the tank before you turn in the vehicle to avoid being charged for refueling at what you'll swear is the most expensive pump in town. In Europe manual transmissions are standard and air-conditioning is a rarity and often unnecessary. Asking for an automatic transmission or air-conditioning can significantly increase the cost of your rental. Find out what the standard rentals are in the country you'll be visiting and weigh that factor when making your reservation.

Cutting Costs Major international companies have programs that discount their standard rates by 15% to 30% if you make the reservation before departure (anywhere from 24 hours to 14 days), rent for a minimum number of days (typically three or four), and prepay the rental.

Several companies operate as wholesalers. They do not own their own fleets but rent in bulk from those that do and offer advantageous rates to their customers. Rentals through such companies must be arranged and paid for before you leave the United States. Among them are **Auto Europe** (Box 7006, Portland, ME 04112, tel. 207/828–2525 or 800/223–5555, 800/458–9503 in Canada); **Europe by Car** (mailing address, 1 Rockefeller Plaza, New York, NY 10020; walk-in address, 14 W. 49th St., New York, NY 10020, tel. 212/581–3040, 212/245–1713, or 800/223–1516; 9000 Sunset Blvd., Los Angeles, CA 90069, tel. 800/252–9401 or 213/272–0424 in CA); **Foremost Euro-Car** (5658 Sepulvada Blvd., Suite 201, Van Nuys, CA 91411, tel. 818/786–1960 or 800/272–3299); and **The Kemwel Group** (106 Calvert St., Harrison, NY 10528, tel. 914/835–5555 or 800/678–0678). You won't see these wholesalers' deals advertised; they're even better in summer, when business travel is down. Always ask whether the prices are guaranteed in U.S. dollars or foreign currency and if unlimited mileage is available. Find out about any required deposits, cancellation penalties, and drop-off charges, and confirm the cost of any required insurance coverage.

Insurance and Collision Damage Waiver Until recently standard rental contracts included liability coverage (for damage to public property, injury to pedestrians, and so on) and coverage for the car against fire, theft, and collision damage with a deductible. Due to law changes in some states and rising liability costs, several car rental agencies have reduced the type of coverage they offer. Before you rent a car, find out exactly what coverage, if any, is provided by your personal auto insurer. Don't assume that you are covered. If you do want insurance from the rental company, secondary coverage may be the only type offered. You may already have secondary coverage if you charge the rental to a credit card. Only Diners Club (tel. 800/234–6377) provides primary coverage in the United States and worldwide.

In general if you have an accident, you are responsible for the automobile. Car rental companies may offer a collision damage waiver (CDW), which ranges in cost from $4 to $14 a day. You should decline the CDW only if you are certain you are covered through your personal insurer or credit card company.

Rail Passes

The **EurailPass,** valid for unlimited first-class train travel through 20 countries, including the Netherlands, Belgium, and Luxembourg, is an excellent value if you plan to travel around the Continent.

Standard passes are available for 15 days ($498), 21 days ($648), one month ($728), two months ($1,098), and three months ($1,398). **Eurail Saverpasses** valid for 15 days cost $430 per person, for 21 days $550, for one month $678 per person; you must do all your traveling with at least one companion (two companions from April through September). **Eurail Youthpasses,** which cover second-class travel, cost $578 for one month, $768 for two; you must be under 26 on the first day you travel. **Eurail Flexipasses** allow you to travel first class for five ($348), 10 ($560), or 15 ($740) days within any two-month period. **Eurail Youth Flexipasses,** available to those under 26 on their first travel day, allow you to travel second class for five ($255), 10 ($398), or 15 ($540) days within any two-month period. Apply through your travel agent or **Rail Europe** (226–230 Westchester Ave., White Plains, NY 10604, tel. 914/682–5172 or 800/848–7245; or 2087 Dundas E., Suite 105, Mississauga, Ont. L4X 1M2, tel. 416/602–4195), **DER Tours** (Box 1606, Des Plaines, IL 60017, tel. 800/782–2424, fax 800/282–7474), or **CIT Tours Corp.** (342 Madison Ave., Suite 207, New York, NY 10173, tel. 212/697–2100 or 800/248–8687; 310/670–4269 or 800/248–7245 in western U.S.).

Rail Europe also offers the **Benelux Tourrail Pass,** a special unlimited mileage ticket for travel in the Netherlands, Belgium, and Luxembourg, good for any five days in a one-month period, for $205 first class and $137 second class. The **Benelux Junior Pass** costs $102 second class for travelers under 26 years old and is free for children under 4.

Student and Youth Travel

Travel Agencies **Council Travel Services (CTS),** a subsidiary of the nonprofit Council on International Educational Exchange (CIEE), specializes in low-cost travel arrangements abroad for students and is the exclusive U.S. agent for several discount cards. Also newly available from CTS are domestic air passes for bargain travel within the United States. CIEE's twice-yearly *Student Travels* magazine is available at the CTS office at CIEE headquarters (205 E. 42nd St., 16th Floor, New York, NY 10017, tel. 212/661–1450) and in Boston (tel. 617/266–1926), Miami (tel. 305/670–9261), Los Angeles (tel. 310/208–3551), and at 43 branches in college towns nationwide (free in person, $1 by mail). **Campus Connections** (1100 E. Marlton Pike, Cherry Hill, NJ 08034, tel. 800/428–3235) specializes in discounted accommodations and airfares for students. The **Educational Travel Centre** (438 N. Frances St., Madison, WI 53703, tel. 608/256–5551) offers low-cost domestic and international airline tickets, mostly for flights departing from Chicago, and rail passes. Other travel agencies catering to students include **TMI Student Travel** (1146 Pleasant St., Watertown, MA 02172, tel. 617/661–8187 or 800/245–3672), and **Travel Cuts** (187 College St., Toronto, Ont. M5T 1P7, tel. 416/979–2406).

Discount Cards For discounts on transportation and on museum and attractions admissions, buy the **International Student Identity Card** (ISIC) if you're a bona fide student or the **International Youth Card** (IYC) if you're under 26. In the United States the ISIC and IYC cards cost $16 each and include basic travel accident and illness coverage and a toll-free travel assistance hot line. Apply to **CIEE** (*see* Travel Agencies, *above*, tel. 212/661–1414; the application is in *Student Travels*). In Canada the cards are available for C$15 each from **Travel Cuts** (*see* Travel Agencies, *above*). In the United Kingdom they cost £5 and £4 respectively at student unions and student travel companies, including Council Travel's London office (28A Poland St., London W1V 3DB, tel. 0171/437–7767).

Hostelling A **Hostelling International** (HI) membership card is the key to more than 5,000 hostels in 70 countries; the sex-segregated, dormitory-style sleeping quarters, including some for families, go for $7 to $20 a night per person. Membership is available in the United States through **Hostelling International-American Youth Hostels** (HI-AYH, 733 15th St. NW, Suite 840, Washington, DC 20005, tel. 202/783–6161), the U.S. link in the worldwide chain, and costs $25 for adults 18 to 54, $10 for those under 18, $15 for those 55 and over, and $35 for families. Volume 1 of the *AYH Guide to Budget Accommodation* lists hostels in Europe and the Mediterranean ($13.95, including postage). HI membership is available in Canada through **Hostelling International-Canada** (205 Catherine St., Suite 400, Ottawa, Ont. K2P 1C3, tel. 613/748–5638) for $26.75, and in the United Kingdom through the **Youth Hostel Association of England and Wales** (Trevelyan House, 8 St. Stephen's Hill, St. Albans, Herts. AL1 2DY, tel. 01727/855215) for £10.

Tour Operators **AESU Travel** (2 Hamill Rd., Suite 248, Baltimore, MD 21210, tel. 410/323–4416 or 800/638-7640) and **Contiki** (300 Plaza Alicante #900, Garden Grove, CA 92640, tel. 714/740–0808 or 800/266–8454) specialize in package tours for travelers 18 to 35.

Traveling with Children

Publications *Newsletters* *Family Travel Times,* published 10 times a year by **Travel With Your Children** (TWYCH, 45 W. 18th St., New York, NY 10011, tel. 212/206–0688; annual subscription $55), covers destinations, types of vacations, and modes of travel. TWYCH also publishes *Cruising with Children* ($22) and *Skiing with Children* ($29).

Books *Traveling with Children—And Enjoying It,* by Arlene K. Butler (Globe Pequot Press, Box 833, 6 Business Park Rd., Old Saybrook, CT 06475, tel. 800/243–0495, or 800/962–0973 in CT; $11.95 plus $3 shipping per book) helps plan your trip with children, from toddlers to teens. *Innocents Abroad: Traveling with Kids in Europe,* by Valerie Wolf Deutsch and Laura Sutherland (Penguin USA, 120 Woodbine St., Bergenfield, NJ 07621, tel. 800/253–6476; $15.95 or $4.95 paperback), covers child- and teen-friendly activities, food, and transportation.

Tour Operator **Grandtravel** (6900 Wisconsin Ave., Suite 706, Chevy Chase, MD 20815, tel. 301/986–0790 or 800/247–7651) offers tours for people traveling with their grandchildren. The catalogue, as charmingly written and illustrated as a children's book, positively invites armchair traveling with lap-sitters aboard.

Getting There *Airfares* On international flights, the fare for infants under age 2 not occupying a seat is generally either free or 10% of the accompanying adult's fare; children ages 2 to 11 usually pay half to two-thirds of the adult fare. On domestic flights, children under 2 not occupying a seat travel free, and older children currently travel on the "lowest applicable" adult fare.

Baggage In general, infants paying 10% of the adult fare are allowed one carry-on bag, not to exceed 70 pounds or 45 inches (length + width + height) and a collapsible stroller; check with the airline before departure, because you may be allowed less if the flight is full. The adult baggage allowance applies for children paying half or more of the adult fare.

Safety Seats The FAA recommends the use of safety seats aloft and details approved models in the free leaflet **"Child/Infant Safety Seats Recommended for Use in Aircraft"** (available from the FAA, APA–200, 800 Independence Ave. SW, Washington, DC 20591, tel. 202/267–3479; Information Hot Line, tel. 800/322–7873). Airline policy varies. U.S. carriers allow FAA-approved models bearing a sticker declaring their FAA approval. Because these seats are strapped into regular passenger seats, airlines may require that a ticket be bought for an infant who would otherwise ride free. Foreign carriers may not allow infant seats, may charge the child's rather than the infant's fare for their use, or may require you to hold your baby during take-off and landing, thus defeating the seat's purpose.

Facilities Aloft Some airlines provide other services for children, such as children's meals and freestanding bassinets (only to those with seats at the bulkhead, where there's enough legroom). Make your request when reserving. Biannually the February issue of *Family Travel Times* details children's services on three dozen airlines (*see* Publications, *above*; $12). "Kids and Teens in Flight" (free from the U.S. Department of Transportation's Office of Consumer Affairs (R-25, Washington, DC 20590, tel. 202/366–2220) offers tips for children flying alone.

Lodging At the **Best Western** hotels (reservations tel. 800/528–1234) in Brussels, Oostende, and Brugge in Belgium; the city of Luxembourg; and more than 40 cities in the Netherlands, children under 12 may stay free when sharing a room with two paying adults. A maximum of five persons is allowed per room. The **Intercontinental** hotels (reservations tel. 800/327–0200) in Amsterdam, The Hague, and Luxembourg allow one child of any age to stay free in his or her parents' room. **Hilton** hotels (reservations tel. 800/445–8667) in Amsterdam, Rotterdam, Antwerp, and Brussels also allow one child of any age to stay free in his or her parents' room. Many hotels throughout the region have family rooms.

Baby-Sitting Services Check with your hotel concierge or the tourist office for information about local child-care services.

Hints for Travelers with Disabilities

Hotels The **Ramada Inns** (reservations tel. 800/228–2828) in Liège and Amsterdam have rooms for guests with disabilities. The **Intercontinental Hotel** (reservations tel. 800/327–0200) in Luxembourg has two accessible rooms. Wheelchair-accessible rooms are also available at the **Hilton** hotels (reservations tel. 800/531–5900) in Brussels, Amsterdam, and Rotterdam.

Organizations Several organizations provide travel information for people with disabilities—usually for a membership fee—and some publish newsletters and bulletins. Among them are the **Information Center for Individuals with Disabilities** (Fort Point Pl., 27–43 Wormwood St., Boston, MA 02210, tel. 617/727–5540 or 800/462–5015 in MA between 11 AM and 4 PM, or leave message; TTY 617/345–9743); **Mobility International USA** (Box 10767, Eugene, OR 97440, tel. and TTY 503/343–1284, fax 503/343–6812), the U.S. branch of an international organization based in Britain (*see below*) that has affiliates in 30 countries; **MossRehab Hospital Travel Information Service** (tel. 215/456–9603, TTY 215/456–9602); the **Travel Industry and Disabled Exchange** (TIDE, 5435 Donna Ave., Tarzana, CA 91356, tel. 818/344–3640, fax 818/344–0078); and **Travelin' Talk** (Box 3534, Clarksville, TN 37043, tel. 615/552–6670, fax 615/552–1182).

In the United Kingdom	Important information sources include the **Royal Association for Disability and Rehabilitation** (RADAR, 12 City Forum, 250 City Rd., London EC1V 8AF, tel. 0171/250–3222), which publishes travel information for people with disabilities in Britain, and **Mobility International** (228 Borough High St., London SE1 1JX, tel. 0171/403–5688), an international clearinghouse of travel information for people with disabilities.
Travel Agency and Tour Operator	**Flying Wheels Travel** (143 W. Bridge St., Box 382, Owatonna, MN 55060, tel. 507/451–5005 or 800/535–6790) is a travel agency specializing in domestic and worldwide cruises, tours, and independent travel itineraries for people with mobility problems.
Publications	Several free publications are available from the U.S. Consumer Information Center (Pueblo, CO 81009): "New Horizons for the Air Traveler with a Disability" (include Dept. 608Y in the address), a U.S. Department of Transportation booklet describing changes resulting from the 1986 Air Carrier Access Act and from the 1990 Americans with Disabilities Act, and the Airport Operators Council's *Access Travel: Airports* (Dept. 5804), which describes facilities and services for people with disabilities at more than 500 airports worldwide.

The 500-page *Travelin' Talk Directory* (*see* Organizations, *above;* $35 check or money order with a money-back guarantee) lists names and addresses of people and organizations who offer help for travelers with disabilities. Twin Peaks Press (Box 129, Vancouver, WA 98666, tel. 206/694–2462 or 800/637–2256) publishes the *Directory of Travel Agencies for the Disabled* ($19.95, plus $2 for shipping), listing more than 370 agencies worldwide.

Hints for Older Travelers

Organizations	The **American Association of Retired Persons** (AARP, 601 E St. NW, Washington, DC 20049, tel. 202/434–2277) provides independent travelers who are members of the AARP (open to those age 50 or older; $8 per person or couple annually) with the Purchase Privilege Program, which offers discounts on lodging, car rentals, and sightseeing, and arranges group tours, cruises, and apartment living through AARP Travel Experience from American Express (400 Pinnacle Way, Suite 450, Norcross, GA 30071, tel. 800/927–0111 or 800/745–4567).

Two other organizations offer discounts on lodgings, car rentals, and other travel products, along with such nontravel perks as magazines and newsletters: the **National Council of Senior Citizens** (1331 F St. NW, Washington, DC 20004, tel. 202/347–8800; $12 annually) and **Mature Outlook** (6001 N. Clark St., Chicago, IL 60660, tel. 800/336–6330; $9.95 annually).

Note: For reduced rates, mention your senior-citizen identification card when booking hotel reservations, not when checking out. At restaurants, show your card before you're seated; discounts may be limited to certain menus, days, or hours. If you are renting a car, ask about promotional rates that might improve on your senior-citizen discount.

Educational Travel	The nonprofit **Elderhostel** (75 Federal St., 3rd Floor, Boston, MA 02110, tel. 617/426–7788) has offered inexpensive study programs for people 60 and older since 1975. Held at more than 1,800 educational institutions, courses cover everything from marine science to Greek myths and cowboy poetry. Participants usually attend lectures in the morning and spend the afternoon sightseeing or on field

trips; they live in dorms on the host campuses. Fees for two- to three-week international trips—including room, board, and transportation from the United States—range from $1,800 to $4,500.

Interhostel (University of New Hampshire, 6 Garrison Ave., Durham, NH 03824, tel. 800/733–9753 or 603/862–1147) caters to a slightly younger clientele—50 and over—and runs programs in some 25 countries. The idea is similar: Lectures and field trips are mixed with sightseeing, and participants stay in dormitories at cooperating educational institutions or in modest hotels. Programs usually last two weeks and cost $1,500–$2,100, excluding airfare.

Tour   If you want to take your grandchildren, look into **Grandtravel** (*see*
Operators Traveling with Children, *above*). **Saga International Holidays** (222 Berkeley St., Boston, MA 02116, tel. 800/343–0273), caters to those over age 50 who like to travel in groups.

Publications *The 50+ Traveler's Guidebook: Where to Go, Where to Stay, What to Do* by Anita Williams and Merrimac Dillon (St. Martin's Press, 175 5th Ave., New York, NY 10010; $12.95) is available in bookstores and offers many useful tips. "The Mature Traveler" (Box 50820, Reno, NV 89513, tel. 702/786–7419; $29.95), a monthly newsletter, contains many travel deals.

Hotels SAS Royal hotels in Brussels and Amsterdam offer weekend reductions for senior citizens and traveling companions based on age. If you're 65 years old, you qualify for a 65% reduction, those aged 75 are eligible for a 75% reduction, and so on. Travelers aged 100 stay for free.

Hints for Gay and Lesbian Travelers

Organizations The **International Gay Travel Association** (Box 4974, Key West, FL 33041, tel. 305-292-0217 or 800/999–7925 or 800-448-8550), which has 700 members, will provide you with names of travel agents and tour operators who specialize in gay travel. The **Gay & Lesbian Visitors Center of New York Inc.** (135 W. 20th St., 3rd Floor, New York, NY 10011, tel. 212/463–9030 or 800/395–2315 in NY; $100 annually) mails a monthly newsletter, valuable coupons, and more to its members.

Travel   Tour operator **Olympus Vacations** (8424 Santa Monica Blvd., #721,
Agencies and West Hollywood, CA 90069; tel. 310/657–2220) offers all-gay-and-
Tour   lesbian resort holidays. **Skylink Women's Travel** (746 Ashland Ave.,
Operators   Santa Monica, CA 90405, tel. 310/452–0506 or 800/225-5759) handles individual travel for lesbians all over the world and conducts international and domestic group trips annually.

Publications The premier international travel magazine for gays and lesbians is *Our World* (1104 N. Nova Rd., Suite 251, Daytona Beach, FL 32117, tel. 904/441–5367; $35 for 10 issues). **"Out & About"** (tel. 203/789-8518 or 800/929–2268; $49 for 10 issues, full refund if you aren't satisfied) is a 16-page monthly newsletter with extensive information on resorts, hotels, and airlines that are gay-friendly.

Arriving and Departing

From North America by Plane

Flights are either nonstop, direct, or connecting. A **nonstop** flight requires no change of plane and makes no stops. A **direct** flight stops at least once and can involve a change of plane, although the flight number remains the same; if the first leg is late, the second waits. This is not the case with a **connecting** flight, which involves a different plane and a different flight number.

Airlines Major airlines that fly nonstop or direct from the United States, Canada, or Great Britain to the Benelux countries include **KLM Royal Dutch** (tel. 800/777–5553), **Sabena** (tel. 800/955–2000), **Martinair** (tel. 800/366–4655), **Air Canada** (tel. 800/776–3000), **Icelandair** (tel. 800/223–5500), **American** (tel. 800/433–7300), **Delta** (tel. 800/221–1212), **TWA** (800/892–4141), **United** (tel. 800/241–6522), and **British Airways** (tel. 800/247–9297).

Flying Time Flights from New York to Amsterdam take just over seven hours; to Brussels, just under seven; to Luxembourg, eight. There are no scheduled nonstop flights to Luxembourg. Flights from Los Angeles to Amsterdam take 10½ hours, from London to Brussels, one hour.

Cutting Costs The Sunday travel section of most newspapers is a good source of deals. When booking, particularly through an unfamiliar company, call the Better Business Bureau and your local or state Consumer Protection Bureau to find out whether any complaints have been registered against the company, pay with a credit card if you can, and consider trip-cancellation and default insurance (*see* Insurance, *above*). A helpful resource is *Airfare Secrets Exposed*, by Sharon Tyler and Matthew Wonder (Universal Information Publishing, $16.95), available in bookstores.

Promotional Less expensive fares, called promotional or discount fares, are
Airfares round-trip and involve restrictions, which vary according to the route and season. You must usually buy the ticket—commonly called an APEX (advance purchase excursion) when it's for international travel—in advance (seven, 14, or 21 days are usual), although some of the major airlines have added no-frills, cheap flights to compete with new bargain airlines on certain routes.

With the major airlines the cheaper fares generally require minimum and maximum stays (for instance, over a Saturday night or at least seven and no more than 30 days). Airlines usually allow some return date changes for a $25 to $50 fee, but most low-fare tickets are nonrefundable. Only a death in the family would prompt the airline to return any of your money if you cancel a nonrefundable ticket. However, you can apply an unused nonrefundable ticket toward a new ticket, again with a small fee. The lowest fare is subject to availability, and only a small percentage of the plane's total seats will be sold at that price. Contact the U.S. Department of Transportation's Office of Consumer Affairs (I–25, Washington, DC 20590, tel. 202/366–2220) for a copy of "Fly-Rights: A Guide to Air Travel in the U.S." *The Official Frequent Flyer Guidebook* by Randy Petersen (4715-C Town Center Dr., Colorado Springs, CO 80916, tel. 719/597–8899 or 800/487–8893; $14.99, plus $3 shipping and handling) yields valuable hints on getting the most for your air travel dollars. Also new and helpful is *202 Tips Even the Best Business Travelers May Not Know* by Christopher McGinnis, president of the Travel Skills Group (Box 52927, Atlanta, GA 30355, tel. 404/659–2855; $10 in bookstores).

Consolidators Consolidators or bulk-fare operators—"bucket shops"—buy blocks of seats on scheduled flights that airlines anticipate they won't be able to sell. They pay wholesale prices, add a markup, and resell the seats to travel agents or directly to the public at prices that still undercut the airline's promotional or discount fares (higher than a charter ticket but lower than an APEX ticket, and usually without the advance-purchase restriction). Moreover, some consolidators sometimes give you your money back. Carefully read the fine print detailing penalties for changes and cancellations. If you doubt the reliability of a company, call the airline once you've made your booking and confirm that you do, indeed, have a reservation on the flight.

The biggest U.S. consolidator, C. L. Thomson Express, sells only to travel agents. Well-established consolidators selling to the public include: **UniTravel** (Box 12485, St. Louis, MO 63132, tel. 314/569–0900 or 800/325–2222); **Council Charter** (205 E. 42nd St., New York, NY 10017, tel. 212/661–0311 or 800/800–8222); and **Travac** (989 6th Ave., New York, NY 10018, tel. 212/563–3303 or 800/872–8800).

Discount Travel clubs offer members unsold space on airplanes, cruise ships,
Travel Clubs and package tours at as much as 50% below regular prices. Membership may include a regular bulletin or access to a toll-free hot line giving details of available trips departing from three or four days to several months in the future. Most also offer 50% discounts off hotel rack rates, but double check with the hotel to make sure it isn't offering a better promotional rate independent of the club. Clubs include **Discount Travel International** (114 Forrest Ave., Suite 203, Narberth, PA 19072, tel. 215/668–7184; $45 annually, single or family), **Entertainment Travel Editions** (Box 1014 Trumbull, CT 06611, tel. 800/445–4137; price, depending on destination, $25–$48), **Great American Traveler** (Box 27965, Salt Lake City, UT 84127, tel. 800/ 548–2812; $49.95 annually), **Moment's Notice Discount Travel Club** (425 Madison Ave., New York, NY 10017, tel. 212/486–0503; $45 annually, single or family), **Privilege Card** (3391 Peachtree Rd. NE, Suite 110, Atlanta GA 30326, tel. 404/262–0222 or 800/236-9732; domestic annual membership $49.95, international, $74.95), **Travelers Advantage** (CUC Travel Service, 49 Music Sq. W, Nashville, TN 37203, tel. 800/548–1116; $49 annually, single or family), and **Worldwide Discount Travel Club** (1674 Meridian Ave., Miami Beach, FL 33139, tel. 305/534–2082; $50 annually for family, $40 single).

Publications Both "Consumer Reports Travel Letter" (Consumers Union, 101 Truman Ave., Yonkers, NY 10703, tel. 914/378–2562 or 800/234– 1970; $39 a year) and the newsletter "Travel Smart" (40 Beechdale Rd., Dobbs Ferry, NY 10522, tel. 800/327–3633; $37 a year) have a wealth of travel deals and tips in each monthly issue. *The Official Frequent Flyer Guidebook* by Randy Petersen (*see* Promotional Airfares, *above*) yields valuable hints on getting the most for your air travel dollars, as does *Airfare Secrets Exposed*, by Sharon Tyler and Matthew Wonder (*see* Cutting Costs, *above*). Also new and helpful is *202 Tips Even the Best Business Travelers May Not Know* by Christopher McGinnis (*see* Promotional Airfares, *above*).

Enjoying the Fly at night if you're able to sleep on a plane. Because the air aloft is
Flight dry, drink plenty of fluids while on board. Drinking alcohol contributes to jet lag, as do heavy meals. Bulkhead seats, in the front row of each cabin—usually reserved for people who have disabilities, are elderly, or are traveling with babies—offer more legroom, but trays attach awkwardly to seat armrests, and all possessions must be stowed overhead.

Smoking Since February 1990, smoking has been banned on all domestic flights of less than six hours' duration; the ban also applies to domestic segments of international flights aboard U.S. and foreign carriers. On U.S. carriers flying to the Netherlands, Belgium, and other destinations abroad, a seat in a no-smoking section must be provided for every passenger who requests one, and the section must be enlarged to accommodate such passengers if necessary as long as they have complied with the airline's deadline for check-in and seat assignment. If smoking bothers you, request a seat far from the smoking section.

Foreign airlines are exempt from these rules but do provide no-smoking sections, and some nations, including Canada as of July 1, 1993, have gone as far as to ban smoking on all domestic flights; other countries may ban smoking on flights of less than a specified duration. The International Civil Aviation Organization has set July 1, 1996, as the date to ban smoking aboard airlines worldwide, but the body has no power to enforce its decisions.

From North America by Ship

Cunard Line (555 5th Ave., New York, NY 10017, tel. 212/880–7500 or 800/528–6273) operates the *Queen Elizabeth 2 (QE2)* on the only regular transatlantic crossings, sailing between New York City and Southampton, England, from April through December. Ferries connect with Belgium and the Netherlands from ports on the English Channel.

Other cruise lines whose ships are in Europe for the summer and the Caribbean for the winter make repositioning crossings: eastbound in spring and westbound in fall. Check the travel pages of your Sunday newspaper or contact a travel agent for lines and sailing dates.

If time is not a problem and the idea of taking a slow boat across the ocean sounds tempting, contact **Freighter World Cruises** (180 South Lake, Suite 335, Pasadena, CA 91101, tel. 818/449–3106 or 800/531–7774) for a listing of current cargo ships en route to Belgium, the Netherlands, the United Kingdom, or other nearby ports.

From the United Kingdom by Plane, Train, Bus, and Car

See individual country chapters.

Staying in the Benelux Countries

Getting Around

Travel in the Netherlands, Belgium, and Luxembourg is convenient by almost any mode of transportation.

By Plane Both KLM and Sabena airlines have flights between Amsterdam and Brussels, KLM has flights from Amsterdam to Luxembourg, and Sabena has flights from Brussels to Luxembourg. There are no domestic air services.

By Car A network of well-maintained superhighways and other roads covers the three countries, making car travel convenient. Traffic can be heavy around the major cities; on the roads to southern Europe in late June and late July, when many Belgians begin their vacations; and on those approaching the North Sea beaches on summer weekends.

By Train Several express trains daily connect the main cities of the Benelux region; regularly scheduled frequent service links smaller cities as well. *See* individual country chapters for specific information.

By Bus Bus service among the Benelux countries is minimal.

Shopping

These three countries, in the center of the EU and participating in the sophisticated, modern, high-tech culture of 1990s Europe, offer a full spectrum of goods, but they are especially known for diamonds, lace, porcelain, antiques, women's fashions, tulip bulbs, chocolate, and cheese.

Sports and the Outdoors

Bicycling, boating, camping, and hiking rate high among the outdoor activities available in the Benelux countries. *See* individual country chapters for specific information.

Beaches

The long North Sea coast of Belgium and southern Holland attracts droves of sun lovers during the long northern days of summer, despite the bracing temperature of the water.

Dining

In these cosmopolitan countries food from around the world is readily available. Currently the single strongest influence, even on Dutch cooking, seems to be the cuisine of France—at least in restaurants. All three countries revel in the bounty of the sea: mussels and shrimp, as well as fish, are major delicacies. Vegetables and fruit are freshest here where they are grown. Paralleling these are the local, old-fashioned specialties of each country: *waterzooi* (a rich chicken or fish stew) or *carbonnade* (beef stew with beer) in Belgium; *judd mat gardebounen* (smoked pork shoulder with fava beans) or *gromperekichelcher* (fried potato patties) in Luxembourg; and soup, sausage, and potatoes in the Netherlands.

Belgium supports a significant number of the foremost restaurants in Europe; the Netherlands offers Indonesian *rijstafel* (rice served with many small meat, poultry, and vegetable dishes and sauces) rivaling the original halfway around the world; and tiny Luxembourg has more *gastronomique* restaurants per capita than any other country in Europe.

Lodging

All three countries offer a range of choices, from the major international hotel chains and small, modern local hotels to family-run restored inns and historic houses to elegant country châteaux and resorts. Prices in metropolitan areas are significantly higher than those in outlying towns and the countryside.

Home Exchange You can find a house, apartment, or other vacation property to exchange for your own by becoming a member of a home-exchange organization, which then sends you its annual directories listing available exchanges and includes your own listing in at least one of them. Arrangements for the actual exchange are made by the two parties to it, not by the organization. For more information contact the **International Home Exchange Association** (IHEA, 41 Sutter St., Suite 1090, San Francisco, CA 94104, tel. 415/673–0347 or 800/788–2489). Principal clearinghouses include: **HomeLink International** (Box 650, Key West, FL 33041, tel. 305/294–3720 or 800/638–3841), with thousands of foreign and domestic listings, publishes four annual directories plus updates; the $50 membership includes your listing in one book. **Intervac International** (Box 590504, San Francisco, CA 94159, tel. 415/435–3497) has three annual directories; membership is $62, or $72 if you want to receive the directories but remain unlisted. **Loan-a-Home** (2 Park La., Apt. 6E, Mount Vernon, NY 10552, tel. 914/664–7640) specializes in long-term exchanges; there is no charge to list your home, but the directories cost $35 or $45 depending on the number you receive.

Apartment and Villa Rentals If you want a home base that's roomy enough for a family and comes with cooking facilities, a furnished rental may be the solution. It's generally cost-wise, too, although not always—some rentals are luxury properties (economical only when your party is large). Home-exchange directories do list rentals—often second homes owned by prospective house swappers—and some services search for a house or apartment for you (even a castle if that's your fancy) and handle the paperwork. Some send an illustrated catalogue and others send photographs of specific properties, sometimes at a charge; up-front registration fees may apply.

Among the companies are: **Europa-Let** (92 N. Main St., Ashland, OR 97520, tel. 503/482–5806 or 800/462–4486); **Property Rentals International** (1 Park West Cir., Suite 108, Midlothian, VA 23113, tel. 804/378–6054 or 800/220–3332); **Rent-a-Home International** (7200 34th Ave. NW, Seattle, WA 98117, tel. 206/789–9377 or 800/488–7368); and **The Invented City** (*see* IHEA, *above*).

Credit Cards

The following credit card abbreviations are used throughout this guide: AE, American Express; D, Discover; DC, Diners Club; MC, MasterCard; and V, Visa. It's a good idea to call ahead to check current credit card policies.

Great Itineraries

Haute Cuisine and Country Air

The peripatetic gourmet first chooses overnight stops to ensure that each evening meal is a feast. It is a bonus that many of the finest small hotels with outstanding restaurants are in out-of-the-way places that you might not otherwise visit. This kind of travel obviously does not come cheap.

Length 14 days

Getting Around *By Car* In the Netherlands the drive from Amsterdam to Kerkrade by way of Oisterwijk is 380 kilometers (228 miles). In Belgium, highways link Antwerp and Noirefontaine by way of the coast for an arc of some 600 kilometers (370 miles). To travel from meal to meal in Luxembourg, you'll cover a lot of ground, much of it inaccessible except by car.

By Train In the Netherlands there are good train and taxi connections from Amsterdam by way of Middelburg and Den Bos. Trains in Belgium connect through Brussels with the main towns on the route; a car is necessary in the Ardennes. In Luxembourg, only Luxembourg City is easily reached by direct rail lines.

The Main Route **Three Nights: Netherlands.** From Amsterdam, travel south toward Middelburg; take the Yerseke-Kruiningen exit on the highway toward **Kruiningen**. Restaurant Inter Scaldes sits alone in the countryside, offering fine French cuisine and luxury accommodations.

The following day can be a leisurely drive to **Oisterwijk** between Tilburg and 's-Hertogenbosch, for an overnight stay at Hotel-Restaurant De Swaen, in the town square. The following day travel south through Limburg province to **Kerkrade** for dinner in the castle at Hotel Kasteel Erenstein and overnight in the luxury accommodations of the half-timbered former Limburg farmstead. A word of advice: Book your overnight stays well in advance.

Nine nights: Belgium. Start the Belgian portion of your trip in **Antwerp,** where De Matelote is the top restaurant. The 10 exquisite rooms of De Rosier are only minutes away. Make your next stop **Brugge,** to eat at the revered De Karmeliet or the young, imaginative Den Gouden Harynk, both within easy walking distance of the aristocratic rooms of De Tuilerieen. As an eating alternative, Waterput in nearby **Oostkerke** is highly recommended. From Brugge, head for the coast and **Oostende,** where you can stay and dine at the sumptuous Oostendse Compagnie, overlooking the sea. At the west end of the coast, dine and stay in **De Panne** at the exquisite Le Fox.

As you head inland, stop first at Eddy Vandekerckhove's Gastronomic Village just outside **Kortrijk,** where the rooms have views of a tropical garden or the Flemish countryside, and the cuisine will delight you. Your next stop should be **Geneval,** near Brussels, where the Château du Lac's restaurant, Le Trefle à Quatre, offers lake views and superb food. Farther east, just west of **Hasselt,** the world-class Scholteshof restaurant provides extraordinary dining and superb accommodations. The Clos Saint-Denis in nearby **Tongeren** runs a close second, but offers no lodging. Head south to **Noirefontaine** in Belgian Luxembourg, and treat yourself to an overnight stay at the luxurious Moulin Hideux, where you can savor fine, leisurely meals and work off the calories by taking enchanting walks in the woods.

Three nights: Luxembourg. In **Luxembourg City,** settle for the night in either the traditional Hotel Cravat or the modern luxury of Le Royal. You'll dine in the medieval intimacy of St-Michel, in the oldest quarter of town. The next day, head south toward the French border for **Frisange,** where Lea Linster will serve a world-class lunch. Drive through the vineyards of the Moselle Valley, and spend the night in atmospheric little **Ehnen,** where you can dine and sleep at either waterfront landmark: Bamberg's or Simmer. The next day, visit **Echternach,** and book for the night in La Bergerie. You can drive or be shuttled from there into the country for an extraordinary meal at the restaurant of the same name.

The North Sea Coast

From De Panne to Knokke on the Dutch border the pattern does not change: beach, largely covered by the sea at high tide, then a sea wall that is often lined with shops, restaurants, and hotels, and dunes partially covered by marram grass. While sea dikes block your view of the water from the road throughout much of the Netherlands, you can approach the water and, in places where you see boardwalks and staircases, walk over the dikes to the beaches and the dunes. As if to make up for blocking your view while you are on land, there are roads over the two major enclosing dikes, one in the south and one in the north, that more than compensate with sweeping water views.

Length   6 days (or more)

Getting Around By Car The trip from De Panne to Breskens in Holland is about 90 kilometers (56 miles), so theoretically driving time should not be much more than an hour. In fact it is likely to take two, three, or even more during the holiday season. From Vlissingen to Harlingen by way of the Benelux tunnel is 370 kilometers (222 miles).

By Train There is train service from Brussels to several points on the coast. Along the coast you have to rely on the tram service, which operates all the way from De Panne to Knokke-Heist. Train service in the Netherlands runs between major cities and coastal towns but not along the coast.

The Main Route **Three nights: Belgium. De Panne,** where the beach is at its widest, and neighboring resorts are your best choice for a stay if you are traveling with children. Sports lovers tend to make the yacht harbor of **Nieuwpoort** their base, while **Oostende,** the largest city on the coast, offers more sophisticated pleasures in the form of a casino, a race track, and museums. The most fashionable resort is **Knokke-Heist,** where the stylish shops are open on Sunday and the casino attracts not only gamblers but also world-class entertainers. Right on the border you'll find the peaceful and fascinating bird sanctuary of **Het Zwin.**

Two nights: The Netherlands. On the Dutch side of the border, the beach continues, and **Cadzand Bad** is one of the attractive resorts. Farther on, in **Breskens,** you can take the car ferry to **Vlissingen** on the island of Walcheren. Follow the Zeeland coastal route across the Oosterscheldekering sea dike, with its massive storm surge barriers towering over the road and the Delta Expo museum. Stay overnight in **Scheveningen** to enjoy the busy beach and the nightlife. You can get to the beach next at towns such as **Katwijk** or **Egmond aan Zee.** Beyond there, the drive across the 35-kilometer (22-mile) Afsluitdijk enclosing dike offers you kilometer after kilometer of sweeping views over the water on two sides. **Harlingen** is the port for ferries to the Wadden Islands, where you can enjoy the natural beauty of the seaside.

Information *See* Chapters 3 and 4.

Ancient Crafts of the Low Countries

The extraordinary flourishing of decorative crafts in the Low Countries in the Middle Ages was the result of the insatiable appetite for ornamentation of their rulers and shared by local gentry and wealthy burghers. The clothing and jewelry lovingly depicted in 15th-century Flemish paintings indicate the very high standards of the artisans of the era, and those artisanal traditions have been continued to the present.

Length 11 days

Getting Around By Car Luxembourg City is easy to reach by car, though difficult to negotiate once you're inside. The Villeroy & Boch complex lies just outside the center, on the northwest edge, toward Wiltz. The Belgian section of the itinerary (Luxembourg City to Rotterdam) is about 780 kilometers (485 miles), driving time some 10 hours. The Dutch section (Antwerp to Delft to Amsterdam to Hindeloopen) is about 290 kilometers (175 miles).

By Train If you're visiting Luxembourg by train, city buses pass the Villeroy & Boch outlet. All Belgian cities on this itinerary are accessible by train, but you'll have to double back from Brugge to Brussels to get to Antwerp. Train travel in the Netherlands is efficient.

The Main Route

One night: Luxembourg. A weekday stop in **Luxembourg** will give you a chance to visit the on-site factory outlet store of Villeroy & Boch, whose popular vitro-porcelain sells here at discount prices. Watch for specials on patterns being phased out, and be sure to dig through the bargain bin. The factory does not ship, so be prepared to schlep. If you can round up a group of 20, you can take a guided tour of the factory.

Two nights: Liège and Sint-Truiden. Arriving from Luxembourg, start your Belgian crafts tour in **Liège.** The Val Saint-Lambert glassworks in Seraing, on the outskirts of the city, is one of the finest in the world; you can visit the showroom and watch glassblowers in action. Lace-making is an age-old Belgian specialty. You'll have an opportunity to see traditional lace-making elsewhere, but in **Sint-Truiden** one can inspect the results of a modern revival of this craft at the Kanttentoonstelling (Lace Exhibition) in the school of the Ursuline Sisters.

Three nights: Brussels. Mechelen, halfway between Brussels and Antwerp, boasts the only workshops in Belgium where traditional tapestry weaving is still practiced; Gaspard De Wit's Royal Tapestry Manufacture (open for visits Saturday mornings only) is at the Refuge van Tongerlo. In **Brussels,** some of the finest examples of Belgian tapestry from the 14th to 16th century are on view in the Musées Royaux d'Art et d'Histoire (Royal Museums of Art and History), and lace and needlework are on view in the Musée du Costume et de la Dentelle (Costume and Lace Museum). Tapestry weaving has been revived in **Tournai** (southwest of Brussels), one of the old centers of this craft, where the new Museum of Tapestry (and Textile Arts) shows how it is done.

One night: Brugge. Brugge is intimately associated with lace-making, and there are a large number of shops selling everything from lace souvenirs to works of art. The best place to get a real understanding of the craft is the Kantcentrum (Lace Center), incorporating a museum and a lace-making school.

One night: Antwerp. Diamonds are big business in **Antwerp,** where the origins and history of diamond cutting are shown at the Provincial Diamond Museum, while Diamondland, where you can also see diamond cutting demonstrations, is probably the most spectacular diamond showroom in the world.

Three nights: Netherlands. Begin in **Delft** with a visit to the factory De Porcelyn Fles to see painting of the famous blue and white ceramic ware known as Delft. Continue to **Amsterdam** for a visit to a diamond factory. Continue north to the village of **Makkum** in Friesland, where the prized Dutch multicolor ceramic ware is produced at the factory of Tichelaars Koninklijk Makkumer Aardewerk en Tegelfabriek (Tichelaars Royal Makkum Pottery and Tile Factory). In nearby **Hindeloopen** you can see the traditional painted furniture of Friesland in Museum Hidde Nieland Stichting.

Information *See* Chapters 3, 4, and 5.

The Ardennes

To experience the Ardennes fully, you owe it to yourself to take your time. Explore the hamlets and river valleys off the highway. Stop in the small towns along the way for a meal of hearty Ardennaise fare—smoked ham, cheese and farm bread, crayfish and trout from the rushing streams—enjoy the inns, visit the churches and castles. You will be amply rewarded!

Length 8 days

Getting The Belgian portions of the trip add up to about 430 kilometers (270
Around miles). Much of this is on secondary routes, so reckon on a driving
By Car time of some eight hours. To see the best of the Luxembourg Ardennes, you'll need a car for the *routes nationales* and secondary
roads that snake through the forests.

By Train The cities on the itinerary are accessible by train, but they are not
necessarily interconnected in the same sequence. Rail connections
in Luxembourg are minimal, though a train does run from Luxembourg City to Clervaux, in the north.

The Main **Two nights: Belgium.** From Liège, go by way of Eupen toward Mal-
Route médy, stopping to explore the high moorland known as the Hautes
Fagnes.

One night: La-Roche-en-Ardenne. Passing Stavelot, continue to La-
Roche-en-Ardenne in the heart of the Belgian mountain range. Here
in the valley of the River Ourthe, you will see the finest scenery the
Ardennes has to offer.

Two nights: Luxembourg. Enter the Grand Duchy of Luxembourg
from the north, stopping to visit **Clervaux's** castle museums before
winding through rolling countryside toward **Vianden,** where the
spectacular castle dominates the hill village. Head south to **Diekirch**
to visit the Romanesque church with its Merovingian sarcophagi
and the evocative Battle of the Bulge museum. Then, though it falls
just below the Ardennes plateau, drive on into **Luxembourg City,** for
the medieval fortifications, cathedral, and old-town streets.

Three nights: Belgium. Driving west from Luxembourg City you follow the Semois River, with a stop to see the romantic ruins of Orval
Abbey, to **Bouillon** with its mountaintop fort. Through dense woods
you reach **Saint-Hubert,** going on to **Han-sur-Lesse** with its remarkable caves and nature reserve. Follow the Lesse to **Dinant**—part of
the way by kayak, if you wish—spectacularly situated on the River
Meuse. As you drive along the Meuse, sheer cliffs line the riverbank
on the opposite side. Continuing along the river, with stops in **Huy**
and **Modave,** you arrive back in Liège.

2 Portraits of the Netherlands, Belgium, and Luxembourg

The Netherlands, Belgium, and Luxembourg: A Chronology

55 BC Julius Caesar's legions extend Roman control to the Meuse and Waal rivers.

ca AD 300 Inundation of the Frisian plain causes Rome to abandon it.

ca 400 Roman rule retreats before invading Frisians in the north and Franks in the south.

481–511 Under their king, Clovis, the Frankish Merovingians extend their rule north.

ca 700 Christianity is extended to the Netherlands by Saints Willibrord and Boniface.

800 Charlemagne, king of the Franks, is crowned emperor of the Romans by the pope. His domains extend from the marches of Denmark to Spain.

843 The Treaty of Verdun divides Charlemagne's empire into three. Luxembourg and the Netherlands are included in the middle kingdom of Lotharingia; Belgium is divided at the Scheldt River between France and Lotharingia. Viking attacks begin along the coast.

862 Baldwin Iron-Arm establishes himself as first count of Flanders, but rule of the Lotharingian lands is constantly disputed.

963 Siegfried, count of Ardennes, purchases an old Roman castle named Lucilinburhuc along the Alzette river. His descendants are named counts of Luxembourg.

1196–1247 Reign of Countess Ermesinde of Luxembourg, who enlarges and unifies the county, grants privileges to its cities, and founds the ruling house of Luxembourg-Limburg.

ca 1200 With the rise of towns, the collection of duchies and counties that constitutes the Low Countries gains economic power.

1302 The men of Flanders revolt against French attempts at annexation and defeat Philip the Fair's army at the Battle of the Golden Spurs, near Kortrijk. Flanders remains a desirable prize.

1308 Henry VII of Luxembourg is elected Holy Roman emperor; he grants the rule of the county of Luxembourg to his son, John the Blind (d. 1346).

1354 John's son, Charles, also Holy Roman emperor, raises the status of Luxembourg to a duchy.

1361 Philip the Bold, son of John II of France, establishes the great duchy of Burgundy, which, by Philip's marriage in 1369 to Marguerite, heiress of the count of Flanders, grows to include Flanders, Artois, Limburg, and Brabant.

1419–1467 Philip's grandson Philip the Good extends Burgundian rule over Holland, Zeeland, and Hainaut and presides over the golden age of the Flemish Renaissance. Painters include the van Eycks, Hans Memling, and Rogier van der Weyden.

1443 Philip gains Luxembourg.

1464 Philip calls the deputies of the states—nobles, merchants, and churchmen—to meet together, thus beginning the States-General, the Dutch representative assembly.

1477 The death of Philip's son Charles leaves his granddaughter Mary of Burgundy as heiress. Mary marries the Hapsburg heir, Maximilian of Austria; their son Philip marries Juana, heiress to the throne of Spain.

1500 Birth in Ghent of Charles, son of Philip and Juana, who inherits the collective titles and holdings of Burgundy, Spain, and Austria as Charles V, Holy Roman emperor.

ca 1520–1540 Protestantism spreads through the Netherlands.

1549 By the Pragmatic Sanction, Charles declares that the 17 provinces constituting the Netherlands will be inherited intact by his son Philip.

1555 Charles V abdicates, dividing his empire between his brother Ferdinand and his son Philip, who inherits Spain and the Netherlands. A devout Catholic, Philip moves to suppress Protestantism in the Netherlands.

1566 Revolt in Antwerp against Spanish rule provokes ruthless suppression by the Spanish governor, the duke of Alva.

1568 Beginning of 80 years of warfare between the 17 provinces and Spain.

1572 The "Sea Beggars" under William of Orange take to the natural Dutch element, water, and harass the Spanish.

1579 The Spanish succeed in dividing the Catholic south from the Protestant north with the Treaty of Arras. The seven Protestant provinces in the north—Holland, Friesland, Gelderland, Groningen, Overijssel, Utrecht, and Zeeland—declare themselves the United Provinces, under the hereditary *stadtholder* (city elder), William the Silent of Orange.

1585 Antwerp falls to the Spanish, and the division of the Netherlands between north and south is effectively completed; the Dutch close the Scheldt to navigation, depriving Antwerp of its egress to the sea and leading to its rapid decline.

1602 With the founding of the Dutch East India Company, the United Provinces emerges as a major trading nation and a cultural force. Rembrandt, Vermeer, and Hals chronicle an era of wealth, while in Belgium, Rubens and Van Dyck epitomize Flemish Baroque.

1609 The Twelve-Years' Truce temporarily ends fighting between the United Provinces and Spain.

1624 The Dutch land on Manhattan and found New Amsterdam.

1648 By the Treaty of Westphalia, the Spanish finally recognize the independence of the United Provinces. What will become Belgium remains under Spanish control, but is a battleground between the ambitions of France and a declining Spain.

1652–1654 First Anglo-Dutch War, over trading rivalries.

1653–1672 The Dutch fail to elect a new stadtholder and are ruled as a republic under the grand pensionary Johan de Witt.

1667 By the terms of the Peace of Breda, which ends the second Anglo-Dutch War, the Netherlands exchanges New Netherland, renamed New York, for England's Suriname.

1672 William III of Orange, great-grandson of William the Silent, is named stadtholder; de Witt is murdered.

1678 By the Treaty of Nijmegen William ends yet another war with France.

1689 William III is named joint ruler of England with his wife, Mary Stuart.

1697 The Treaty of Ryswick ends the War of the League of Augsburg against France, instigated by William.

1701–17 The War of the Spanish Succession ends with the Treaty of Utrecht, which transfers the Spanish Netherlands (including Luxembourg) to Austria. Depleted of men and money, the Netherlands declines in the 18th century.

1785–1787 Revolt of the Patriot Party in the Netherlands, which temporarily drives out the stadtholder William V; he is restored with the help of his brother-in-law, Frederick William of Prussia.

1789–1790 Inspired by events in France, the Brabançonne revolution succeeds in overthrowing Austrian rule in Belgium, but divisions between conservatives and liberals allow the Austrians to regain their territory.

1795 In the Netherlands, the Patriots eject the stadtholder and establish the Batavian Republic; the French defeat the Austrians and annex the Belgian provinces and Luxembourg.

1806–1810 Napoleon establishes the Kingdom of Holland, ruled by his brother Louis Bonaparte, but finally annexes the Netherlands to France.

18 Upon Napoleon's defeat at Leipzig, the prince of Orange is called back to the Netherlands, not as stadtholder but as King William I.

1815 Napoleon defeated at Waterloo, near Brussels. By the terms of the congress of Vienna, the Netherlands and Belgium are reunited under William I, but the union proves an unhappy one. Luxembourg is divided between William and Prussia.

1830 Again inspired by a revolution in France, the Belgians rise against William I and declare their independence.

1831 With the guarantees of the great powers, the Belgians draw up a constitution and elect as king Leopold of Saxe-Coburg (an uncle to soon-to-be-Queen Victoria of England).

1839 The Netherlands finally recognizes Belgium as an independent, neutral state. Luxembourg is again divided, with 60% going to Belgium while the rest remains a duchy, with William I of the Netherlands as grand duke.

1840 Faced by mounting popular opposition, William I abdicates in favor of his more liberal son, William II, who enacts reforms.

1865 Leopold II succeeds his father as king of the Belgians; begins reign as empire builder in Africa and rebuilder of Brussels at home. By the terms of an international agreement, the Prussian garrisons withdraw and Luxembourg's independence and neutrality are guaranteed.

1885 The establishment of the Congo Free State brings Belgium into the ranks of colonial powers.

1890   King William III of the Netherlands is succeeded by his daughter Wilhelmina; because Luxembourg bars female succession, the grand duchy passes to the house of Nassau-Weilburg.

1903   Birth of Georges Simenon (d. 1989), creator of Inspector Maigret and Belgium's most widely read author.

1908   Congo Free State annexed to Belgium.

1909   Albert succeeds Leopold II of Belgium; leads Belgian resistance from exile during World War I.

1914   In violation of the terms of the 1839 treaty, Germany invades and conquers Belgium at the outset of World War I. Luxembourg is also occupied; the Netherlands remains neutral.

1919   The Franco-Belgian alliance ends Belgian neutrality and signals the dominance of the French-speaking Walloons. Universal male suffrage is granted; in the Netherlands, where this had been enacted in 1917, women are now given the right to vote. In Luxembourg, a plebiscite confirms the continuation of the grand duchy under Grand Duchess Charlotte.

1934   Leopold III succeeds Albert on Belgian throne.

1940   May 10: Nazi Germany launches blitzkrieg attacks on Belgium, the Netherlands, and Luxembourg. The Dutch army surrenders May 14, the Belgians May 28. Grand Duchess Charlotte and Queen Wilhelmina flee; King Leopold III remains in Belgium, where he is eventually imprisoned. The Nazi occupation leaves lasting imprints on all three countries.

1942   Dutch Indonesia falls to the Japanese.

1944   Luxembourg City is liberated.

1947   The Marshall Plan helps rebuild devastated areas. Belgium, Netherlands, and Luxembourg form customs union.

1948   Queen Wilhelmina abdicates in favor of her daughter Juliana; the first of a series of Socialist governments initiates a Dutch welfare state. Women gain the vote in Belgium.

1949   The Netherlands and Luxembourg join NATO; the Dutch recognize Indonesian independence after much fighting.

1951   Amid controversy over his wartime role and continued ethnic dissension, King Leopold III of Belgium abdicates in favor of his son, Baudouin.

1957   Belgium, Netherlands, Luxembourg are charter members of the European Economic Community (EEC).

1960   A 50-year treaty establishes the Benelux Economic Union. The Belgian Congo gains independence.

1964   Grand Duchess Charlotte of Luxembourg abdicates in favor of her son, Jean.

1967   Already the center of the EC, Brussels becomes host to NATO.

1975   Suriname wins its independence from the Netherlands.

1981   Queen Juliana of the Netherlands abdicates in favor of her daughter, Beatrix.

1989   The latest of many Belgian attempts to establish greater linguistic and regional autonomy is enacted.

Moules à Volonté

By Nancy
Coons

Damp and cold mist the leaded-glass windows, but inside the café glows a scene worthy of a Flemish Master. The burnished wooden banquettes are Rembrandt's; the lace curtain, Vermeer's. Hals would have painted the diner, a lone bearded man in rumpled black leather and heavy, worn wool, his thick fingers clasping a broad-stemmed bowl of mahogany-brown beer. Before him lies a spread of crockery and mollusks, a still-life in themselves: The two-quart pot is heaped high with blue-black mussels, their shells flecked with bits of onion and celery, the broth beneath them steaming; beside them a bowl piled high with yellow *frites* (french fries), crisp and glistening; in the corner, a saucer of slabs of floury-gold cracked-wheat bread. The man works studiously, absorbed in a timeless ritual: Fish out the shell from the broth with fingers inured to the heat by years of practice. Pluck out the plump flesh with a fork and, while chewing the morsel, chuck the shell aside on a crockery plate. Sometimes he sets down the fork and uses the empty shell as pincers to draw out the meat of the next shell. As the meal progresses, the pile in the pot shrinks and the heap of empty shells grows. As the beer follows the mussels, its strong tonic paints the man's cheeks until two ruby patches radiate above his beard. The painting's caption: "Man eating moules."

It is the central image of the Flemish lowlands—the Netherlands, Flanders, even leaking into landlocked Wallonie and Luxembourg.

But this warmly lit interior scene wouldn't be as striking without its harsh exterior foil: Mussels, like the Dutch and the Flemish, are creatures of the sea; they flourish in cold, inky waters along rock-crusted shores, clustered and stacked like blue-black crystals in muddy tidal pools. They're a product of caustic sea winds and briny, chilly damp, and their bite tastes like salt air itself.

Most of the mussels consumed in the Benelux region come from the North Sea, above all in the Waddenzee, off the northern coast of the Netherlands. Captured by the billions in great nets along the bottom of specially protected, fenced-off nursery beds, they are sorted by weight and auctioned to wholesalers in Zeeland, who return them to shallow tidal waters to recover from the trip, to mature, and to purge themselves of sandy mud. From there, they are harvested en masse and shipped live across Europe.

The cultivation of mussels dates from Roman times, though legend credits an Irish shipwreck victim who settled in La Rochelle, on the west coast of France; he is said to have noticed great colonies of the mollusks clinging to posts he planted to hold fishing nets. By placing posts closer together and arranging branches between them, he was able to create an ideal breeding ground and, in essence, mass-produce the delicacy. (The French, predictably enough, prefer their own, smaller mussels from the coasts of Brittany and Normandy, insisting that North Sea mussels are fleshy, dull, and vulgarly oversized.)

Scrubbed with stiff brushes under running water, soaked with salt to draw out the sand, and often fed flour to plump and purge them, mussels are served throughout the region in dozens of ways. The building block for French or Walloon recipes: simmering them *à la marinière*, in a savory stock of white wine, shallots, parsley, and butter. It's difficult to improve on this classic method, which brings out the best in mussels' musky sea essence—but chefs have been trying for centuries. Another common version is *à la crème*, the marinière stock thickened with flour-based white sauce and a generous portion of heavy cream. Flemish mussels, on the other hand, are nearly always served in a simple, savory vegetable stock, with bits of celery, leek, and onions creeping into the shells. The Dutch have been known to pickle them, or even to fry them in batter. Those who don't want to get their fingers messy may order their mussels *meunière*, removed from the shells in the kitchen and baked in a pool of garlicky butter. Regardless of the preparation, the Belgians and the Dutch wash their mussels down with beer, the Luxembourgers with an icy bottle of one of the coarser Moselle wines—an Elbling or a Rivaner.

Mussels rations are anything but stingy here, and on your first venture you may be appalled by the size of the lidded pot put before you. It's the shells that create the volume, and once you've plucked out the tender flesh, thrown away the shells, and sipped the broth and succulent strays from a colossal soup spoon, you'll soon find yourself at the bottom of the pot. Don't worry: Many restaurants will whisk it away and come back with Round Two—another mountain of the steamy blue creatures, another pool of savory broth. It's called *moules à volonté* (all you can eat), so gird yourself for a feast: The locals have been doing it for 2,000 years.

Battle Scars from the Bulge

By Nancy Coons

The first thing the sleepy American soldiers noticed was light—pinpoints of light blinking to the east, distinct in the pitch-black of an early midwinter morning. A second, or seconds, later (depending on their distance from the German frontier), there followed the roar of a thousand exploding shells, the pounding percussion of heavy artillery. Rockets and mortars screamed overhead while at five well-spaced points German foot soldiers poured through gaps in the sparsely protected front line, their way lit by searchlights that bounced off the clouds, flooding the land with eerie, artificial "moonlight."

It was 5:30 AM on December 16, 1944, along the eastern border of Belgium and Luxembourg. The Allied armed forces—having landed at Normandy in June and southern France in August and pressed steadily inland; having pushed the German armies back to the old Siegfried line and liberated France, Belgium, and Luxembourg by September; and having fought viciously, died in droves, and been hungry, filthy, and sleepless for weeks at a time—were reveling in the role of heroes in the relatively calm days before Christmas. That morning they were caught with their pants down in one of the most massive and successful surprise attacks in World War II. It was Hitler's last, desperate effort to regain western Europe, and it was one of the greatest failures of Allied intelligence in the war.

In September 1944, when Hitler first announced secret plans for an all-out attack on the western front, his army could scarcely have been in more desperate straits. More than 3½ million German men had died over the preceding five years, and massive Allied bombing raids were leveling German cities day by day. Not only had the enemy driven the Wehrmacht out of France, Belgium, and Luxembourg, but Italy was being lost in bitter fighting as well, and Russia had penetrated west to Warsaw and Bucharest. The Third Reich was in danger of being choked off from all sides, and Hitler— though not his more prudent commanders—saw no option but to strike out offensively. His goal: to take the all-important port at Antwerp, from where the River Schelde flowed from Belgium through the Netherlands and into the North Sea. By closing in on Antwerp, they would not only cut off the most likely source of new supplies, but also surround and capture some 1 million remaining Allied forces. His strategy: to surprise the Allies by attacking through the improbably rough, virtually impassable forest terrain of the Ardennes in southeastern Belgium and northern Luxembourg. He intended to overwhelm them with massive artillery fire, press on to take the strategic bridges of the River Meuse, reinforce with a second wave, and close out defenders with strong flanks at the north and south. Antwerp could be reached in a week, he insisted, and the Allies would be crippled by winter fog, snow, and mud.

For the task of inspiring a bitter, war-weary army to what seemed even then to be a suicidal mission, Hitler named the aristocratic Gerd von Rundstedt commander in chief in the West. And, in a decision that was to set the tone for one of the most vicious and bloody conflicts in the war, in charge of the Sixth Panzer Army he placed Joseph "Sepp" Dietrich, an early Nazi loyalist and SS commander, chief executioner in the 1934 Nazi Party purge (the Night of the Long Knives), notorious for ordering the execution of more than 4,000 prisoners taken over three days at the Russian front. His kindred spirit: SS Lt. Col. Joachim Peiper, in charge of the SS Panzer Division called Leibstandarte Adolf Hitler and also notorious for brutal executions in Russia. It was Dietrich who passed on Hitler's inspirational message that this was "the decisive hour of the German people," that the attacking army was to create a "wave of terror and fright" without "humane inhibitions."

While the Germans were building up staggering quantities of materiel along the Siegfried line—tanks, artillery, rafts, and pontoons—and moving in men from all corners of the shrinking Reich, the Allied command remained remarkably unperceptive. Reconnaissance pilots flew over unwonted activity near Bitburg, Trier, and Koblenz— trains, truck convoys, heaps of equipment along the roads. Messages were intercepted and deciphered, some asking for increased forces, some for more detailed information on Ardennes and Meuse terrain. Yet Generals Bradley, Eisenhower, Middleton, and Patton continued to misinterpret, anticipating instead a predictable counterattack around Aachen and Cologne, well north of the Ardennes. (Hitler, in fact, counted on this interpretation, strutting a visible buildup of forces in the north while secretly preparing to attack elsewhere.) On December 12, an optimistic Allied intelligence summary described the vulnerability and "deathly weakness" of German forces in the area.

On the evening of December 15, the German soldiers—until then as unaware of the plan as the Allies—were finally told what morning would bring. The message from von Rundstedt: "We gamble everything . . . to achieve things beyond human possibilities for our Fatherland and our Führer!" Some, convinced the cause was lost, faced the news of further carnage with dismay; others saw a final opportunity to avenge the civilian death toll in German cities. Members of the SS, the greatest believers in the Nazi effort and thus the least restrained by the niceties of the Geneva Convention, welcomed the "holy task" with a blood lust that was to be more than sated in the weeks to come.

That night, across the border in Luxembourg, German-born film star Marlene Dietrich performed for American soldiers and went to bed early.

They attacked at 5:30 AM with a thoroughness and a ruthlessness that impressed soldiers even through their bewilderment. The assault crippled communications, and word moved as slowly as in the era before telegraph. Twenty miles from one prong of the attack, Gen. Omar Bradley had breakfast at the Hotel Alfa in Luxembourg City and, blithely unaware of the change in situation, headed toward Paris for a meeting with Eisenhower, who had just that day been promoted to five-star General of the Army. Neither heard of the conflict until late afternoon; neither believed, at first sketchy report, that it was anything more than a flash in the pan.

It was. From the first wave of "artillery-prepared" assaults—meaning systems stunned by a barrage of shells, followed by a surge of infantry attacks—to the sharp, startled, and for the most part instinctive defense of the Allies, the offensive was to escalate quickly into a battle of staggering scale, the Americans surprising the Germans in their tenacity, the Germans surprising the Americans with their almost maniacal dedication.

Over a month and a half, the two sides bludgeoned each other, struggling through harsh terrain and winter muck, reducing medieval castles to smoking rubble, and razing villages that had been liberated only months before. The ferocious tone of the fight was set early on: On December 17, SS officers of Lieutenant Colonel Peiper ordered the execution of 130 American prisoners outside Malmédy. The victims were left where they fell, periodically kicked for signs of life, and shot again. A few who survived, hiding the steam of their breath, crawled away when night fell and told their story, and the massacre at Malmédy became a rallying point for the bitter Allies. Prisoners of war were murdered on both sides, and at times the gunfights took on a guerrilla aspect, with those in danger of capture, fearing execution, dissolving into the dense forest to go it alone.

And not only soldiers were killed. On December 18, in and near Stavelot, Peiper's SS troops ordered whole families of civilians from their cellars—women, children, elderly men—and shot them methodically; the toll reached 138. On December 24, SS security men assembled all the men of Bande, screened out those over 32, stripped them of watches and rosaries, and executed them one by one. The sole survivor, before he slugged his way free and dashed for the forest, noticed that his would-be executioner was weeping.

And on December 23, Americans wrought their own kind of horror in Malmédy when Army Air Corps Marauders, headed for the German railroad center of Zulpich, mistakenly emptied 86 bombs on the village center, killing as many of its own troops as innocent citizens. As the people dug out from the rubble on December 24, another misguided swarm of American bombers dropped an even more lethal load, leveling what was left of the center. On December 25, four more planes mistook Malmédy for St. Vith and dropped 64 more bombs. Civilian victims—refugees and residents alike—were laid in rows in the school playground.

It wasn't a very merry Christmas anywhere in the Ardennes that year. Sleepless, shell-shocked, often out of touch, soldiers from both sides huddled in icy pillboxes and snowy foxholes. Propaganda flyers fluttered down, carefully phrased in the recipients' mother tongue. For the Americans, the not-so-inspirational message admonished them: "Why are you here? What are you doing, fighting somebody else's war? You will die and your wife, your mother, your daughters will be left alone. Merry Christmas!" For the Germans, the American pamphlets simply assured them they were losing the war, and that they'd long since lost the battle.

That wasn't altogether clear until well into January. By the time the carnage slowed and the tide turned, the Germans had pressed deep into Belgium, the central thrust "bulging" west to within miles of the Meuse and Dinant. Though Hitler grudgingly ordered retreat from the farthest point of the Bulge on January 8, the Germans fought through January 28, as they were driven all the way back to the Siegfried line.

Some 19,000 American soldiers died, and at least as many Germans. Hundreds of Belgian and Luxembourg citizens died as well, and survivors came back to find their villages flattened, their churches gaping shells, their castles—having survived assault for centuries—reduced to heaps of ancient stone. In Luxembourg, the towns of Diekirch, Clervaux, Vianden, and Echternach were prime battle zones, charred and crumbled. In Belgium, St. Vith, Houffalize, and myriad Ardennes resort towns like La Roche were wasted by artillery "preparation" and the gun-and-grenade battles that ensued. And Bastogne, surrounded, besieged, and pounded by artillery for days, lost what was left of its town center in the concentrated bombing Hitler ordered for Christmas Eve.

Today, throughout the Ardennes region, the faces of monuments and main streets are incongruously new and shiny, their resourceful owners having taken charred, roofless, windowless shells and made the best of the worst by installing new plumbing, modern wiring, efficient windows, central heat. Yet there are scars, visible and invisible. Behind the caulked shrapnel holes, which pock foundations and farmhouse walls here and there, lurk bitter memories that weren't altogether appeased at Nuremburg. And the ugliness of the conflict, distorted by a new generation, occasionally rears its head: On the stone memorial at the crossroads outside Malmédy, where the names of the victims of the massacre have been carved, someone has spraypainted a swastika.

The cultural chasm between the two sides of the battle seems embodied in the two military cemeteries outside Luxembourg City. The American plot at Hamm is a blaze of white-marble glory, its 5,000 graves radiating in graceful arcs under open sun, its well-tended grass worn by the shoes of visitors. The German plot, just down the road at Sandweiler, lies apart, heavily shaded and concealed from view, with a few hundred low, darkstone crosses marking the graves of some 5,000 men. Yet another 5,000, gathered in battle by the U.S. Army Burial Service and dumped unceremoniously in mass graves, were transferred here and buried under one heavy cross, as many as possible identified in fine print crowded on a broad bronze plaque. Those graves are tended today by busloads of German schoolchildren, who visit in the name of a concept long overdue: *Versöhnung über den Gräbern—Arbeit für den Frieden* (Reconcilation over the graves—work for peace).

Through the Dutch Waterways

By William Golding

The Nobel Prize–winning English novelist here describes a boat trip in the Netherlands that he took with his family. The piece first appeared in Holiday magazine in January 1962.

My old boat, the *Wild Rose,* is technically a converted Whitstable oyster smack. She has a sort of eccentric inelegance and ought to be in a maritime museum, for she was built in 1896. My wife and I, with our children David and Judith, planned a trip in her through the canals of Holland and across the old Zuider Zee. We took my friend Viv with us, partly because we like him, partly because he knew a little about Holland and partly because he is the only man I know who can keep the *Wild Rose*'s ancient auxiliary engine running.

We started at Flushing—an ancient port, clinging to, rambling along, and at one point piercing the ancient sea-wall, the dike that surrounds the island of Walcheren. We moved in through two locks, and then into a yacht basin, and at once some Dutch characteristics commended themselves to our notice. Except in show places like Cowes, a yachtsman expects the smell of decaying wood, slime, weed, mud, rusted and insecure ladders, and stanchions which once had a use but now are nothing but paint-threatening hazards. But the basin at Flushing was an oblong of still water with a neat, cemented edge, and a wooden gangway leading round it. At each berth there were piles driven into the bottom, enamelled white, their iron caps picked out in vivid orange. There was no notice forbidding the dumping of rubbish in the water; and there was no rubbish either. There was no rubbish anywhere, unless you count my ancient boat; for the basin was crowded with Dutch craft, eccentric in build, but charming—and all more glossily enamelled than the piles.

We were to find that this is a Dutch habit, and sometimes a mania. When you cannot think what else to do with something in Holland, you give it a coat of paint. Out of any ten Dutchmen you see, as they go about their business, at least one will be covering an object with bright paint—a fence, or a post, or a gate, or a stone, or a hole in the road—anything that has a paint-holding surface.

We had barely realized our status as a slumship in these spotless surroundings when we saw a number of tradesmen waiting for us on the gangway. They took our orders politely, with neither truculence nor subservience. Then they rode off on bicycles. Out of our ten typical Dutchmen, at least three will be riding bicycles. They came back quickly, with goods of moderate price and high standard; and I have always found this to be the case in Holland, whether it be car rental at the Hook, boat rental at Rotterdam, theater tickets in Amsterdam, a haircut in Groningen, lunch in Enkhuizen or a bunch of flowers in Utrecht. A Dutchman trades fairly, asking a fair price and giving a fair service, and the same cannot be said of Europe as a whole. In Holland a sucker is safe, though frowned on with a sort of tut-tutting compassion.

We stocked up, spent a quiet night and then moved out into the canal that divides Walcheren in two. In the center of Flushing we came to a bridge and had to wait while it was opened for us. Perhaps because we were in the mood to enjoy anything, the bridge, flooded with traffic and neat and powerful in construction, seemed to us wholly charming. As we approached, the red-and-white bars descended to cut off the traffic, and the middle span lifted. It was a stripped mechanism, functional, with long arms that seemed to need no effort to raise a weight of many tons. Yet the whole was so exactly balanced that there was a dream quality of ease in the movement. Nothing of the whole mechanism but had a use and was confined to it; and yet the occasion, the smooth water, the silent bridge, the calmly controlled traffic, combined to make what I can only call the poetry of order. As we moved through, we exclaimed and nodded to one another. The bridge was so modern, we said, it had the delicate elegance you see in a high-speed plane or racing car. It was the Dutch equivalent of achievements in that engineering world which produced jet aircraft and atomic submarines, the world of streamlining and calculations to the nth. This is not mere tourist country, we said—even their bridges are the newest in the world!

Viv put his head out of the hatch.

'This dam' engine won't run much longer.'

'Never mind,' said Ann. 'Enjoy yourself. Look at that bridge. Whatever will they think of next?'

Viv wiped his forehead with a wad of waste, and peered aft.

'*That* bridge?'

He gave a short, cynical engineer's laugh and disappeared again.

The bridge sank into place behind us and we turned to look forward at the most typical sight in Holland. The canal that would take us across the island lay like a sword-blade, shining and drawn to a point. There were trees looking at us over the bank, clouds and blue sky mirrored, a towpath, and miles away, a huddle of buildings that looked quaint even at that distance.

There was something shining in the air over the houses. At first we thought it might be an airliner catching the sun. But since when have airliners been made of gold and hung motionless? My wife said it was a captive balloon, and the children decided it was a flying saucer. Yet this single gleaming point of light in the soft, blue sky seemed to be causing no distraction. Dutchmen passed along the towpath on their inevitable bicycles, and they were as phlegmatic as ever. Whatever was gleaming there, in a local suspension of the law of gravity, was causing no panic. But could anything in Holland cause a panic? Would not the day of judgement find them doing no more than insuring that the dikes were holding and all accounts in order? With one of those flashes of common sense which come late in such situations, I got out the binoculars and focused them on the gleam.

The huddle of quaint houses was a town—Middelburg, in the center of the island. The gleam suspended over it was a golden crown; and with the binoculars I could see that this topped a fantastic, not to say frivolous, tower. This, then, is the scene which repeats itself all over Holland—a canal leading to a huddle of houses, with a golden crown hanging over them. Sometimes you see the gleam first, then gradually make out the tower or spire hardening into sight below it. All spires in Holland, apart from the crowns, have an air of modest fantasy. This one at Middelburg rose up first as a tower with tall, lancet windows. The tower supported a bulbous structure, topped at last by the golden crown. The whole thing looked like a graceful piece from some antique chess set.

Viv appeared once more in the hatch.

'You'd better cut the motor.'

'Can't we even go slow ahead?'

'Not unless you want to blow up. What d'you think these blue fumes are?'

There was indeed a faint haze of gasoline round the afterend of the boat. David dropped his book, ran for'ard and hoisted our tattered brown staysail as I switched off. There was the faintest breath of wind to give us way, but so little that the ripples from our bow were moving up and down against the bank before our stern had passed them. Viv sat down on the deck. Ann turned over on the catwalk in the sun, said 'Mmmm!' and went to sleep again.

Holland is a huge country. I say this in the full knowledge that I am stating an apparent paradox. I have flown across Holland in a few minutes. I have driven a car from one end to the other in a single day. But for all that, I declare Holland to be a huge, ample country, full of silences and vast airs. Moving stealthily towards the gold crown over Middelburg, we knew that the right speed for a visitor to Holland is the speed of a slow boat. That way you get the feel of the country into your blood. How else to appreciate the most remarkable quality of geographical Holland, its wide, wide light? The sky seems always not moist, but soft, as though water were hung in it like scent in a girl's hair. The softness conditions the light. We saw no hard shadows, only defined luminosities.

How strange that the Dutch, these foursquare, practical people, these sailors, farmers and engineers, should live in a pastel country that seems woven of light itself! The water-heart of Holland is a scatter of islands—mudpats, if you like—lying at the mouths of the great rivers of northern Europe. They are part of a plain that stretches from the Pennines of England to the Urals in Russia. To be out-of-doors in the water-heart of Holland is like being at sea. Uninterrupted sky comes right down to a horizon that is close at hand at every point of the compass. Whenever we went below, dazzled by this abundance of light, we descended into a darkness that drove us on deck again, into the bland, enormous air, where the fluffy white clouds rode high, and the gold crown sparked nearer. This happened wherever we went. The pastel earth seems to swing like a basket from a balloon of sky.

Halfway to Middelburg we met what must have been almost our only example of Dutch rubbish. We drew alongside a pair of wooden objects floating in the water and found they were castoff clogs. What unusual Dutchman had been so carefree as to fling them into the sparkling water? We felt this was so unlikely that there must have been an accident; and indeed the clogs, floating soles upward, looked for all the world as though a drowned Dutchman were hanging from them, his feet on the surface and his head brushing the bottom. But there was no Dutchman, of course. If there had been, he would have been rescued, neatly and methodically, and fined for causing a disturbance. So the ownerless clogs drifted astern, turning their toes apart slowly.

The Dutch call these wooden boots *klompen*, which is exactly what they are. For presently we passed another Dutchman busy being typical. He was repairing an inch or two of canal bank that had got out of place. He wore bright yellow *klompen* and whenever he moved they went 'Klomp! klomp!' over the stones.

Out of our ten Dutchmen we have not many left. One, we said, would be painting something, three riding bicycles—and now we found that another two would be repairing an earthwork. All over Holland all the time, armies are at work repairing earthworks to keep the sea out, or to keep a canal in. In Friesland I have seen them busy in a field in high summer, cutting back the long grass to insure that a mere runnel of water went where is was wanted, and more important still, did not go where it was not wanted.

We docked with surprising neatness in Middelburg, under sail only. David and Judith got the dinghy into the water and sailed it. Viv emerged from the engine room.

'I think she may last a few hours longer now. Next time may I bring my own engine? Ah—Middelburg! Come with me.'

He led us away through the cobbled streets with an expression of deep purpose and stopped at last in front of an antiques shop.

'Yes. It's still there. See?'

There was the usual display in the window—every sort of disused article from copper warming-pans, through nineteenth-century jewelry, to some not very inspiring prints.

'See what?'

'Your bridge.'

It was our lovely bridge at Flushing, accurate in every detail, even to the red and white bars that regulated traffic. But *this* bridge was made of wood, and the picture had been made in the seventeenth century.

'They were building that sort of bridge when Newton was writing his *Principia*. It's a design even older than your engine.'

I can hardly describe the revolutionary effect of this discovery on our ideas about Holland. What we had taken, in our innocence, as a triumph of technology, we now saw to be an old Dutch custom. In this country, men have always worked sensibly with things, always made a bank as wide as it need be, and no more, given the span of a bridge the exact thickness it required. That print saved us from making the common tourist's mistake. We were not to be deceived by the fairy-tale charm of the houses, their quaint gables and profuse ornamentation, into thinking that this was a doll's country. The houses were the homes of commercial giants of the seventeenth century, and those imposing buildings backing on to the inner canal, decorated as if for some eternal party, were warehouses that had held the riches of the world.

Yet this love of decoration is a strange quirk in the Dutchman's character. Wherever you go you find even the cottages are not thought properly dressed until they have been set with patterns of different-colored brick, or plaster molding. More important buildings—town halls, guildhalls and churches—sometimes break out into sheer fantasy. The result is usually pleasant to see; and perhaps this is reason enough for a practical people. . . .

We sailed across to Staveren in Friesland and entered canals again. Friesland, famous for cattle, impressed us most by its barns. These are vast structures with the farmhouses built into one end. They ride in the lush countryside like ships and the foliage of trees breaks against their tall sides like spray. We dawdled in winding canals not much wider than our boat, through an Arcadian country, a land of woods and shallow lakes, and sunshine and flowers. Each little town is a knot of canals filled with small boats of every description. It is a place in which to waste time, to refuse to move, to be indifferent to everything but the birds perched in the rigging, the waterlilies in the side canals, the sun sleeping in a green glade.

And then it was time to think about home.

We returned to the Ijsselmeer and came to our last, perhaps most impressive, vision of Holland. We stood north from Staveren and presently there appeared a stain on the horizon, a stain that hardened, lifted. It looked like a cliff but it was man-made: the Afsluitdyk, the Enclosing Dam. It cuts off the whole of the Ijsselmeer from the open sea, a bank in the sea that is eighteen miles long. There are small harbours of refuge inside it, probably built for the ships that worked on the original construction, but now very convenient for small boats. So we were able to moor, and climb on the bank.

It is stupendous. There is a motorway across it and sheep crop the short turf where so many Germans died in the retreating army. There is an observation tower too, built at the point where the breach was finally closed. There are sluices at either end a hundred yards wide. As the tide falls, the captive waters of the Ijsselmeer run through them and as the tide rises, the sluices close. The rivers of Holland bring in new water all the time. Nature is harnessed to defeat herself. Hoorn was once a saltwater port; but now the waters of the Ijsselmeer are fresh.

There is a lock at the west end of the Afsluitdyk, but the day was a Sunday; and by a mixture of business and piety only too familiar to an Englishman, the lock was closed on Sundays. So we waited there for the morrow, the Texel and the long haul home.

There was an old Dutchman beside us in his small yacht, who taught us more about the truth of the country than anyone else. He was a very distinguished old man, the equivalent of a judge of the supreme court. When he discovered how much we liked Holland, he expanded. He told us of the awful fix the Dutch were in, with the Ijsselmeer and the project for Port Europe. Both schemes were running out of money.

'But,' said he thoughtfully, 'it is more sensible than making H-bombs, don't you think?'

I looked at the fresh waters of the Ijsselmeer.

'Haven't you done enough,' I said, 'Can't you stop for a moment?'

'While there is still land to be reclaimed? My dear sir! We have a proverb. "God made the world, but the Dutch made Holland."'

And you feel that this is true. You feel it in the opening of a bridge or a lock, in the rich, cultivated earth of a polder, in the sight of a factory, looming like a ship over the level land. Is not this how men should live, making their country and keeping it? On the map of the world Holland is a very small country: but in every way save mere extent of miles it is a very great country indeed.

3 The Netherlands

By Linda Burnham

Updated by Rodney Bolt

If you come to the Netherlands expecting to find its residents shod in wooden shoes, you're years too late; if you're looking for windmills at every turn, you're looking in the wrong place. The bucolic images that brought tourism here in the decades after World War II have little to do with the Netherlands of the '90s. Sure, tulips grow in abundance in the bulb district of Noord and Zuid Holland provinces, but today's Netherlands is no backwater operation: This tiny nation has an economic strength and cultural wealth that far surpass its size and population. Sophisticated, modern Netherlands has more art treasures per square mile than any other country on earth, as well as a large number of ingenious, energetic people with a remarkable commitment to quality, style, and innovation.

The 41,040 square kilometers (15,785 square miles) of the Netherlands are just about half the number in the state of Maine, and its population of 15 million is slightly less than that of the state of Texas. Size is no measure of international clout, however. Only Great Britain and Japan invest more than the Netherlands in the American economy. The Netherlands encourages internal accomplishments as well, particularly of a cultural nature. Within a 120-kilometer (75-mile) radius are 10 major museums of art and several smaller ones that together contain the world's richest and most comprehensive collection of art masterpieces from the 15th to the 20th centuries, including the majority of paintings by Rembrandt and nearly every painting produced by Vincent van Gogh. In the same small area are a half dozen performance halls offering music, dance, and internationally known performing arts festivals.

The marriage of economic power and cultural wealth is nothing new to the Dutch; in the 17th century, for example, money raised through their colonial outposts overseas was used to buy or commission portraits and paintings by young artists such as Rembrandt, Hals, Vermeer, and van Ruisdael. But it was not only the arts that were encouraged: the Netherlands was home to the philosophers Descartes, Spinoza, and Comenius; the jurist Grotius; the naturalist van Leeuwenhoek, inventor of the microscope; and others like them who flourished in the country's enlightened tolerance. The Netherlands continues to subsidize its artists and performers, and it supports an educational system in which creativity in every field is respected, revered, and given room to express itself.

The Netherlands is the delta of Europe, where the great Rhine and Maas rivers and their tributaries empty into the North Sea. Near the coast, it is a land of flat fields and interconnecting canals; the center of the country is surprisingly wooded, and the far south has rolling hills. The country is too small for there to be vast natural areas, and it's too precariously close to sea level, even at its highest points, for there to be dramatic landscapes. Instead, the Netherlands is what the Dutch jokingly call a big green city. Amsterdam is the focal point of the nation; it also is the beginning and end point of a 50-kilometer (31-mile) circle of cities that includes The Hague (the Dutch seat of government and the world center of international justice), Rotterdam (the industrial center of the Netherlands and the world's largest port), and the historic cites of Haarlem, Leiden, Delft, and Utrecht. The northern and eastern provinces are rural and quiet; the southern provinces that hug the Belgian border are lightly industrialized and sophisticated. The great rivers that cut through the heart of the country provide both geographical and sociological borders. The area "above the great rivers," as the Dutch phrase it, is peopled by tough-minded and practical Calvinists; to the south are more ebullient Catholics. A tradition of tolerance pervades this densely populated land; aware that they cannot survive alone, the Dutch are bound by common traits of ingenuity, personal honesty, and a bold sense of humor.

Before You Go

Government Tourist Offices

In the United States Netherlands Board of Tourism (355 Lexington Ave., 21st Floor, New York, NY 10017, tel. 212/370–7367, fax 212/370–9507; 90 New Montgomery St., Suite 305, San Francisco, CA 94105, tel. 415/543–6772, fax 415/495–4925; 225 N. Michigan Ave., Suite 326, Chicago, IL 60601, tel. 312/819–0300, fax 312/819–1740; 9841 Airport Blvd., 10th Floor, Los Angeles, CA 90045, tel. 310/348–9333).

In Canada Netherlands Board of Tourism (25 Adelaide St., Suite 710, Toronto, Ont. M5C 1Y2, tel. 416/363–1577, fax 416/363–1470).

In the United Kingdom Netherlands Board of Tourism (25–28 Buckingham Gate, London SW 1E 6LD, tel. 0171/828–7900).

Tour Groups

General-Interest Tours **Abercrombie & Kent** (1520 Kensington Rd., Oak Brook, IL 60521, tel. 708/954–2944 or 800/323–7308) runs six-night barge cruises through the waterways of Holland in the early spring. **Holland Approach, Inc.** (550 Mountain Ave., Gillette, NJ 07933, tel. 908/580–9200 or 800/225–1699 outside NJ) offers nine-day tours, and **Maupintour** (Box 807, Lawrence, KS 66044, tel. 913/843–1211 or 800/255–4266) offers eight-day tulip-time excursions through Holland while the flowers are blooming. **Olson Travelworld** (Box 10066, Manhattan Beach, CA 90226, tel. 310/546–8400 or 800/421–2255) tailors tours for individuals and groups.

Special-Interest Tours The **Netherlands Board of Tourism** (NBT) offices in North America maintain a data bank for special-interest travel that includes specialized tours for senior citizens, gays, and travelers with disabilities; information is continually updated, and printouts of requested material are available.

Architecture **Art Express** (4500 Campus Dr., Suite 410, Newport Beach, CA 92660, tel. 800/325–7103, fax 714/852–1234); **Art Horizon International** (14 E. 63rd St., New York, NY 10021, tel. 212/888–2299, fax 212/888–2148); and **Horizon Holidays** (160 John St., Toronto, Ont. M5V 2X8, tel. 416/585–9911 or 800/387–2977, fax 416/585–9614) all offer tours.

Arts, Culture, and Music **Unitours** (8 S. Michigan Ave., Chicago IL 60603, tel. 312/782–1590 or 800/621–0557, fax 312/726–0339); **International Education** (301 Alhambra Pl., Madison, WI 53713, tel. 608/274–8574 or 800/558–0215, fax 608/274–8421); **Travel Time** (203 N. Wabash Ave., Chicago IL 60601, tel. 312/726–7197 or 800/621–4725, fax 312/726–0718); **Witte Travel** (3250 28th St. SE, Grand Rapids, MI 49512-1640, tel. 616/957–8113 or 800/253–0210, fax 616/957–9716); and **Ciao! Travel** (810 Emerald St., Suite 107, San Diego, CA 92109, tel. 619/272–5116 or 800/942–2426, fax 619/272–1543) offer a variety of arts and music tours.

Bicycling **Country Cycling Tours** (140 W. 83rd St., New York, NY 10024, tel. 212/874–5151 or 800/284–8954, fax 212/874–5286); **International Bicycle Tours** (Box 754, 7 Champling Sq., Essex, CT 06426, tel. 203/767–7005, fax 203/767–3090); **Four Seasons Cycling** (Box 203,

The Netherlands

North Sea

Wadden Islands

Schiermonnikoog

Ameland

Terschelling

Vlieland

Texel

Den Helder

Dokkum

Leeuwarden

Harlingen

Bolsward

Sneek

Waddenzee

IJsselmeer

Enkhuizen

Alkmaar

Hoorn

Purmerend

Zaanstad

Haarlem

Amsterdam

Bussum

Hilversum

Leiden

Utrecht

Den Haag
(The Hague)

Delft

Rotterdam

Dordrecht

Haringvliet

Overflakkee

Grevelingen

Schouwen/
Duiveland

Tholen

Oosterschelde

Walcheren

Beveland

Goes

Middelburg

Westerschelde

Breskens

Terneuzen

Steenbergen

Bergen op Zoom

Antwerp

Delfzijl

Groningen

Winschoten

Drachten

Assen

Emmen

N1

A7/E22

N34

N371

N28/E232

Hoogeveen

Meppel

N34

N48

Zwolle

Almelo

N36

Hengelo

N35

Deventer

Enschede

Lelystad

A6

A50

A32

Apeldoorn

A28/E232

Amersfoort

Arnhem

Winterswijk

Doetinchem

Rijn

A2

A9

A4/E19

E30

A12

Rijn

Lek

A12/E35

Tiel

E25

Nijmegen

Rhine

GERMANY

A50

Oss

Waal

'sHertogenbosch

A15/E31

Maas

A59

Veghel

A27

A16/E22

Breda

Tilburg

A67/E34

Eindhoven

Weert

A2/E25

Roermond

A58

Maastricht

Sittard

Aachen

Vaals

Liège

BELGIUM

Brussels

KEY

- - - - Ferry

0 _____ 40 miles

0 _____ 60 km

N

Williamsburg, VA 23187, tel. 804/253–2985); and **Revatours** (1256 Philips Sq., Suite 906, Montréal, Qué. H3B 3G1, tel. 514/392–9016 or 800/363–6339, fax 514/392–9015) arrange cycling vacations.

Barge Cruising **The Barge Lady** (230 E. Ohio St., Suite 210, Chicago IL 60611, tel. 312/944–2779); **European Waterways** (230 S. Beverly Dr., Suite 203, Beverly Hills, CA 90212, tel. 310/247–8612 or 800/438–4748, fax 310/247–9460); **Waterways & Byways** (1027 S. Palm Canyon Dr., Palm Springs, CA 92264, tel. 619/320–5754, 800/925–0444); **SeaAir Holidays Ltd.** (733 Summer St., Stamford, CT 06901, tel. 203/356–9033, 800/732–6247); and **Inclusive Tours** (2 Carleton St., Suite 910, Toronto, Ont. M5B 1J3, tel. 416/977–5074, fax 416/977–7759) offer cruising on Holland's waterways.

Horticulture **Quinn's International Holidays** (333 Vaughn St., Suite 2, Winnipeg, Man. R3B 3J9, tel. 204/942–5380 or 800/665–2626, fax 204/957–0322) and **Silverline Tours** (112 Athol St. 204, Whitby, Ont. H3B 3G1, tel. 416/666–1404 or 416/436–2253, fax 416/430–2911) specialize in Holland's flora.

Package Deals for Independent Travelers

Jet Vacations (1775 Broadway, New York, NY 10019, tel. 212/474–8700 or 800/538–0999) offers a Flexiplan Europe package, which includes a choice of hotels, car rentals, airport transfers, and sightseeing options for a number of cities in Holland. **Northwest WorldVacations** (call your travel agent or 800/692–8687) provides visitors to Amsterdam with hotel, car rental, and tour options for a minimum of two nights. **Travel Bound** (599 Broadway, Penthouse, New York, NY 10012, tel. 212/334–1350 or 800/456–8656) offers packages for a minimum of three to six nights. **United Vacations** (106 Calvert St., Harrison, NY 10528, tel. 800/678–0949) will plan customized itineraries.

When to Go

The Netherlands' high season begins in late March to late April, when the tulips come up, and runs through October, when the Dutch celebrate their Autumn Holiday. June, July, and August are the most popular traveling months with both international visitors and the Dutch themselves—it can be difficult to obtain reservations, particularly in beach towns on the North Sea coast and at campgrounds, during midsummer. The cultural season lasts from September to June, but there are special cultural festivals and events scheduled in summer months.

Climate The Netherlands has a mild maritime climate, with bright, clear summers and damp, overcast winters. The driest months are from February through May; the sunniest, May through August. In the eastern and southeastern provinces, winters are colder and summers warmer than along the North Sea coast. The following are average daily maximum and minimum temperatures for Amsterdam.

Jan.	40F	4C	May	61F	16C	Sept.	65F	18C
	34	1		50	10		56	13
Feb.	41F	5C	June	65F	18C	Oct.	56	13C
	34	1		56	13		49	9
Mar.	47F	8C	July	70F	21C	Nov.	47F	8C
	38	3		59	15		41	5
Apr.	52F	11C	Aug.	68F	20C	Dec.	41F	5C
	43	6		59	15		36	2

Festivals and Seasonal Events

Jan.–Feb.: The international **Filmfestival Rotterdam** celebrates avant-garde cinema.

Mar./Apr. (end of Lent): Carnival dances through the cities of Brabant and Limburg provinces.

Mar.: European Fine Arts Fair gathers artists and works in Maastricht, and international crews compete in Amsterdam's **Head of the River Race.**

Apr.: Rotterdam Marathon draws runners from around the globe, and the **Flower Parade** passes through Lisse to open the **National Floral Exhibition** at Keukenhof gardens.

May: National Bicycle Day races through the Netherlands; an international modern dance festival, **Spring Dance,** bounces into Utrecht; and the **International Traditional Jazz Festival** makes Breda jump.

May/June: The **Eleven Cities by Bicycle Race** and the five-day **Eleven Cities Walking Tour** circle Friesland.

June: Holland Festival of the Performing Arts captures Amsterdam, spilling over to The Hague, Rotterdam, and Utrecht; **Parkpop,** a pop music festival, livens up The Hague; and **Pinkpop** bursts into Landgraf.

July: The Hague hosts the **North Sea Jazz Festival;** the **International Organ Competition** brings musicians to Haarlem in even-numbered years; and the **International Four Days Walking Event** strides through Nijmegen.

July/Aug.: *Skutsjesilen* **Sailing Regattas** skim the lakes in Friesland.

Aug.: Utrecht enjoys the **Festival of Ancient Music.**

Sept.: The **Floral Parade** makes a day-long procession of floats from Aalsmeer to Amsterdam; **Gaudeamus Muziekweek** honors music in Amsterdam; and the **Opening of Parliament** takes place in The Hague on the third Tuesday—the queen arrives in her golden coach.

Oct.: Delft Art and Antiques Fair fills the Prinsenhof with treasure.

Nov.: With the **St. Nicolas Parade** in Amsterdam and in cities throughout the country, the arrival of Sinterklaas launches the Christmas season.

What to Pack

The best advice for a trip to the Netherlands in any season is to pack light, be flexible, bring an umbrella (and trench coat with a liner in winter), and always have a sweater or jacket available. For daytime wear and casual evenings, turtlenecks and flannel shirts are ideal for winter, alone or under a sweater, and cotton shirts with sleeves are perfect in summer. Blue jeans are popular and are even sometimes worn to the office; sweat suits, however, are never seen outside of fitness centers. For women, high heels are nothing but trouble on the cobblestone streets of Amsterdam and other old cities, and sneakers or running shoes are a dead giveaway that you are an American tourist; a better choice is a pair of dark-colored walking shoes and for women, with skirts, low-heeled pumps.

Dutch Currency

The official monetary unit of the Netherlands is the **guilder,** which may be abbreviated as Dfl, Fl, F, Hfl, and occasionally as NLG. There are 100 cents in a guilder; coins are minted in denominations of 5, 10, and 25 cents, and 1, 2½, and 5 guilders. Bank notes are printed in amounts of 10, 25, 50, 100, 250, and 1,000 guilders, with the denominations embossed in Braille in the corner of each bill. Bank notes in denominations of more than Fl 100 are seldom seen, and some shops refuse to accept Fl 1000 notes. In August 1994 the exchange rate was 1.77 guilders to the dollar, 1.23 to the Canadian dollar, and 2.73 to the pound sterling.

What It Will Cost

Prices in the Netherlands include a 17.5% **BTW/VAT** (value added tax). Residents of countries outside the European Union (EU) are entitled to a refund of the BTW on purchases over Fl 300 that are personally carried out of the country within 30 days of purchase. Shops have different systems for granting refunds: Some shops will credit your credit card account, but most require you to present some form of proof of purchase at the customs desk at Schiphol Airport on your way home. Some stores will give you a special "cheque" that may be cashed at the airport; otherwise, you'll receive your refund in the mail. The amount of the refund varies (some organizations deduct a commission), but a refund of 10% to 15% is standard.

Sample Costs Cup of coffee, Fl 2.75; glass of beer, Fl 3.50; glass of wine, Fl 4; soda or juice, Fl 2.50 to Fl 4; a sandwich Fl 4 to Fl 10; a pastry or dessert, Fl 4 to Fl 8.

Customs and Duties

On Arrival Customs barriers within the EU began to be removed in 1993. Today there are no limits on goods (such as perfume, cigarettes, or alcohol) brought into the Netherlands from another EU country, provided that they are bought duty-paid (i.e., not in a duty-free shop) and are for personal use. If you enter from a non-EU country, or have purchased goods duty-free, you may bring in 200 cigarettes or 50 cigars or 100 small cigars or 250 grams of tobacco; 1 liter of alcohol (more than 22%) or 2 liters (less than 22%), 50 grams of perfume and .25 liter cologne, 500 grams of coffee, 100 grams of tea, and other goods with a total value of up to Fl 125.

There are no restrictions regarding the import or export of currency.

On Departure To export Dutch flower bulbs, a health certificate issued by the **Nederlandse Planteziektenkundige Dienst** (Dutch Phytopathological Service) is required; these are provided with packages you buy from specialized flower bulb companies.

Language

Dutch is the official language of the Netherlands, though local dialects are used in Friesland and Limburg provinces. Almost everyone speaks good English, but in rural areas you may need a phrase book, at least until the residents overcome their shyness about using the English they know.

Staying Healthy

Travelers covered by medical insurance are entitled, by law, to medical care in Holland. All inquiries about medical care should be addressed to **Afdeling Buitenland van het Ziekenfond** (ANOZ, Health Service Foreign Affairs Department) Box 85315, 3508 AH Utrecht, tel. 030/565300.

Car Rentals

Major international car rental companies, including **Alamo, Avis, Hertz, Europcar/National,** and **Eurodollar/Dollar** operate desks at Amsterdam Schiphol Airport and have rental offices in Amsterdam and other key cities throughout the Netherlands. In addition, the Dutch firm **Van Wijk Amsterdam** (Amsterdam Schiphol Airport, tel. 020/601–5277) operates at the airport and other locations.

Rail Passes

If you plan to travel a lot by train, consider buying one of the following passes before you leave. The **Benelux Tourrail** gives you unlimited travel throughout Holland, Belgium, and Luxembourg on any five days within one month ($205 first class, $137 second class). A **Euro Domino Holland** ticket allows unlimited travel throughout Holland for three, five, or 10 days within any 30-day period (first class: three-day $81, five-day $135, 10-day $243; second class: three-day $63, five-day $88, 10-day $159). A **Railrover** entitles you to unlimited travel within Holland for seven consecutive days (first class $127, second class $85). For an additional $14, the Linkrover offers free travel on public transportation as well. The NBT offices have information on train services, as do overseas offices of Netherlands railways. You may need your passport to purchase these passes.

Student and Youth Travel

In addition to the YHA hostels, young visitors to Holland may want to consider staying at a **youth hotel,** or "sleep-in," which provides basic, inexpensive accommodations for young people. A list of these is available from the NBT (tel. 212/370–7367 in New York). In summer (and in some cases all year round), the Institute for Nature Protection Education (IVN, Postbus 20123, 1000 HC Amsterdam, tel. 020/622–8115) organizes **work camps** in scenic locations, popular among English-speaking visitors aged 15–30. Another organization to consider for **voluntary work experiences** in Holland is S/W, International Volunteer Projects (Willemstraat 7, 3511 RJ Utrecht, tel. 030/317721).

Hints for Travelers with Disabilities

The Netherlands leads the world in providing facilities for people with disabilities. Train and bus stations are equipped with special telephones, elevators, and toilets. Visitors can obtain special identity cards to ensure free escort service on all public transportation (tel. 030/316416 or 030/368340). Modern intercity train carriages have wheelchair-accessible compartments, and many have a free Red Cross wheelchair available. Train timetables are available in Braille, and some restaurants have menus in Braille. There are also special gardens for visitors who are blind at some tourist sites. For information on accessibility in the Netherlands, contact the national organization, **De Gehandicaptenraad** (Postbus 169, 3500 AD Utrecht, tel. 030/313–454). **Stichting Dienstverleners voor Gehandicapten** (Jacobistraat 14, 3500 AE Utrecht, tel. 030/331121) publishes a guide to the Netherlands for travelers with disabilities.

Each year the **NBT** publishes a booklet listing hotels, restaurants, hostels and campsites, museums and tourist attractions, as well as gas/petrol stations with 24-hour services and boat firms with adapted facilities. For assistance at railway stations, contact the NS/

Nederlandse Spoorwagen (Netherlands Railways) before noon at least one day in advance or by 2 PM Friday for travel Saturday, Sunday, Monday, or on public holidays (weekdays 8–4, tel. 030/355–5555). For travelers who are blind, all Dutch paper currency is embossed in Braille with the applicable denomination. For information on tours and exchanges for travelers with disabilities, contact **Mobility International Nederland** (Postbus 165, 6560 AD Groesbeek, tel. 08891–97138).

Hints for Older Travelers

There are special discount museum admissions available to senior citizens in the Netherlands. **Saga International Holidays** (120 Boylston St., Boston, MA 02116, tel. 617/434–0273 or 617/451–6808 or 800/343–0273, fax 617/451–6474) operates special-interest tours and cruises for travelers aged 60 and up.

Further Reading

A visit to the Netherlands is greatly enhanced by a knowledge of the nation's history and a familiarity with its rich art heritage. Books of particular value and interest include *Amsterdam: The Life of a City*, by Geoffrey Cotterell (Little, Brown; 1972), a comprehensive history of the city; *Diary of Anne Frank*, by Anne Frank, the diary of young Jewish girl that details the experience of living in hiding in Amsterdam during World War II; and *Images of a Golden Past*, by Christopher Brown (Abbeville, 1984), a guide to Dutch genre painting of the 17th century.

Some worthwhile histories include *The Dutch Revolt*, by Geoffrey Parker (Peregrine/Penguin, 1977), a history of the development of the Dutch nation; *The Dutch Seaborne Empire 1600–1800*, by C.R. Boxer (Penguin, 1965), which traces the development of the great Dutch trading companies in the 17th and 18th centuries; and *The Embarrassment of Riches*, by Simon Schama (Alfred A. Knopf, 1987/University of California Press, 1988), which interprets the Dutch culture in its Golden Age. *Evolution of the Dutch Nation*, by Bernard H.M. Vlekke (Roy, 1945), is a comprehensive history of the Netherlands.

In addition, Janwillem Van de Wetering's mystery novels (Ballantine), set in Amsterdam, can make for good light reading on the plane.

Arriving and Departing

From North America by Plane

Airports and Airlines   **Amsterdam Schiphol Airport** (tel. 06/35034050) is 25 kilometers (15 miles) southeast of Amsterdam and is linked by rail to every part of the country.

KLM Royal Dutch Airlines (tel. 800/374–7747) is the national carrier of the Netherlands. Other airlines serving the country include **Delta** (tel. 800/241–4141), **Northwest** (tel. 800/225–2525), **TWA** (tel. 800/221–2000), and **United** (tel. 800/241–6522).

Flying Time   Flying time to Amsterdam from New York is just over seven hours; from Chicago, closer to eight hours; and from Los Angeles, 10½ hours.

Discount Flights   **Martinair** (tel. 800/366–4655) offers reduced-fare flights to Amsterdam from Detroit, Fort Lauderdale, Los Angeles, Miami, New York, Oakland, San Francisco, Seattle, Tampa, and Toronto.

From the United Kingdom by Plane, Car, Train, Bus, and Ferry

By Plane   *Airlines*   Airlines that serve the Netherlands from the United Kingdom include **KLM City Hopper** (tel. 0181/750–9000), **British Airways** (tel. 0181/897–4000), and **Aer Lingus** (tel. 0181/899–4747).

Flying Time   Flying time to Amsterdam from London is one hour; from Belfast, 1½ hours.

By Car   *The Channel Tunnel*   The Channel Tunnel opened officially in May 1994, providing the fastest route across the Channel—35 minutes from Folkestone to Calais, or 60 minutes from motorway to motorway. It consists of two large 50-kilometer (31-mile)-long tunnels for trains, one in each direction, linked by a smaller service tunnel running between them. **Le Shuttle** (tel. 0345/353535 in the U.K., 800/388–3876 in the U.S.), a special car, bus, and truck train, which was scheduled to begin service in June 1994, operates a continuous loop, with trains departing every 15 minutes at peak times and at least once an hour through the night. No reservations are necessary, although tickets may be purchased in advance from travel agents. Most passengers stay in their own car throughout the "crossing"; progress updates are provided on display screens and radio. Motorcyclists park their bikes in a separate section with its own passenger compartment, while foot passengers must book passage by coach (*see* By Train, *below*).

The Tunnel is reached from exit 11a of the M20/A20. Drivers purchase tickets from toll booths, then pass through frontier control before loading onto the next available service. Unloading at Calais takes eight minutes. Ticket prices start at £130 for a low-season five-day round trip in a small car and are based on season, time of day, length of stay, and car size regardless of the number of passengers. Peak season fares are not always competitive with ferry prices.

By Train   **British Rail International** (tel. 0171/834–2345 or 0171/828–0892) runs three trains a day from London to Amsterdam.

The Channel Tunnel   **Eurostar** (for information, tel. 0171/922–4486 in the U.K., 800/942–4866 in the U.S.) high-speed train service was scheduled to begin in July 1994, with passenger-only trains whisking riders between new stations in Paris (Gare du Nord) and London (Waterloo) in three hours and between London and Brussels (Midi) in 3¼ hours. The service of one train daily each way was scheduled to increase in January 1995 to 15 trains daily in each direction. At press time, ticket prices had not been set. Tickets are available in the United Kingdom through **British Rail International** (London/Victoria Station, tel. 0171/834–2345 or 0171/828–0892 for credit-card bookings), and in the United States through **Rail Europe** (tel. 800/942–4866) and **BritRail Travel** (1500 Broadway, New York, NY 10036, tel. 800/677–8585).

By Bus   Bus/ferry combination service between the United Kingdom and the Netherlands is operated from London to Amsterdam by **Euro-City Tours** (tel. 0171/828–8361).

By Ferry   Ferries are run between Harwich and Hook of Holland twice daily by **Sealink/Stena** (tel. 01233/646801), and overnight between Hull and Rotterdam by **North Sea Ferries** (tel. 01482/795141). The trip can last between six and 14 hours, depending on the route taken.

Staying in the Netherlands

Getting Around

By Plane **KLM City Hopper** (tel. 020/474–7747) provides regular service between Amsterdam Schiphol Airport and Rotterdam, Eindhoven, and Maastricht, though air travel in a country this small is really unnecessary.

By Train **NS/Nederlandse Spoorwagen** (Netherlands Railways) (tel. 06/9292 in the Netherlands, 020/620–2266 outside the Netherlands) operates a minimum of one train per hour throughout its system, and major cities are connected by three or more trains each hour. Nearly every corner of the country is covered, supplemented by local and regional bus services. The modern, clean trains have first- and second-class coaches and no-smoking and smoking cars. Rail fares are based upon distance; there are one-way fares and day-return fares for same-day round-trip travel; and bicycles may be carried aboard for a nominal fee. Children under 3 travel free and children under 11 are charged just Fl 1 if they are accompanied by an adult. (*See* Chapter 1, Essential Information, for details on special multiday train fares.)

If you produce your rail ticket at a station ticket office, you can buy a traintaxi ticket for Fl 6 per person. Taxis from a special stand outside the station will take you anywhere within a certain area (usually defined by the town boundaries). Taxis are shared, but waiting time is guaranteed to be no longer than 10 minutes. The scheme also operates for journeys back to the station. Although not available in the large cities, traintaxis are ideal for getting to sights on the outskirts of smaller towns, such as Paleis Het Loo outside Appeldoorn.

By Ferry An extensive ferry system serves the Netherlands. Ferries in **Zeeland** province operate from Breskens (tel. 01172/1663 or 01172/3350), Vlissingen (tel. 01184/65905 or 01184/78899), and Perkpolder (tel. 01148/1234 or 01148/2692). In **Friesland** province they run from Lauwersoog (tel. 05193/49050 or 05193/49079), Harlingen (tel. 05620/2969 or 05620/2770), and Holwerd (tel. 05191/42001) to the Frisian Islands, and from Den Helder (tel. 02220/69600) in **Noord Holland** province. Ferries across the IJsselmeer run from Enkhuisen to Stavoren (tel. 02290/17341; no cars) or Urk (tel. 05277/3407).

By Car The Dutch superhighway system is extensive and very well maintained; there are European, national, provincial, and local roads designated as E, A, N, and S, respectively. The **ANWB (Royal Dutch Touring Club)** operates telephone road information services (tel. 06/9622) and has a 24-hour fleet of bright yellow cars and trucks equipped to handle routine repairs free of charge for members of AAA, CAA, or any affiliate of Alliance International du Tourisme. The speed limit in the Netherlands is 120 kilometers (75 miles) per hour, and driving is on the right. A valid driver's license from your home country is all that is required to operate a vehicle in the Netherlands.

Telephones

The country code for the Netherlands is 31.

The area code for Amsterdam is 020 (or simply 20 if you are calling from outside the Netherlands), and it is used only when you call from other parts of the Netherlands to Amsterdam. Within the immediate environs of any municipality you do not need to use an area code.

Local Calls Coin-operated telephones are becoming a rarity in the Netherlands; most public phones take PTT (Dutch telephone company) credit cards. The public telephones take Fl .25 and FL 1 coins, and most modern ones also accept Fl 2.5 and Fl 5 coins. Short local calls may only require one *kwartje* (25-cent coin), but for longer calls or calls to other parts of the country insert several coins before dialing, and they will drop automatically as needed during your conversation. Calls will be cut off abruptly when all the coins are used, so keep an eye on how many are left and add more accordingly.

International Calls To call outside the Netherlands, dial 09 followed by the country code (1 for the United States and Canada, 44 for the United Kingdom), area code, and number. In Amsterdam, **Telehouse** (Raadhuisstraat 28-50, tel. 020/674-3654) is open daily 8 AM–2 AM; it also has a fax service.

Operators and Information Dial 06/8008 for **directory assistance** within the Netherlands, 06/0418 for numbers elsewhere. Operators speak English. Dial 06/022–9111 to reach an **AT&T USA Direct** operator in the United States, or 06/022–9122 to reach an **MCI Call USA** operator, or 06/0410 for an international operator.

Mail

Postal Rates Airmail letters up to 20 grams (⅔ ounce) cost Fl 1.60 to the United States or Canada, 90¢ to the United Kingdom; postcards to the United States or Canada cost 90¢, to the United Kingdom 70¢. Aerograms cost Fl 1.10.

Tipping

Service is included in the prices you pay in the Netherlands, though it is customary to round up to the nearest guilder or two on small bills, and up to the nearest 5, 10, or even 25 guilders for good service on large bills.

Opening and Closing Times

Banks are open weekdays from 8 or 9 to 4 or 5; post offices are open weekdays from 8:30 to 5 and often on Saturday from 8:30 to noon. Shopping hours, regulated by the government, are Monday 1–6, Tuesday–Friday 9–6, and Saturday 9–5; each city may designate one night a week as a late shopping night, when stores are open until 9. Drugstores are open weekdays from 8 or 9 to 5:30, with a rotating schedule in each city to cover nights and weekends. Most national museums are closed on Mondays.

Shopping

The Netherlands is a good place to shop for diamonds, Delft and Makkumware, art, antiques, tulip bulbs, and cheese. Amsterdam has numerous department stores, shops, and boutiques that range in character from conservative to funky; Utrecht is the site of the largest enclosed shopping malls in the Netherlands for general shopping; and Maastricht is known for its elegant shops and boutiques. Diamonds are found exclusively in Amsterdam, as is the best selection of antiques. Amsterdam, The Hague, 's-Hertogenbosch, and Eindhoven are art centers. Delft and Makkumware are available throughout the country. And though tulip bulbs are available in the bulb district and cheese can be bought directly from farmers in Noord Holland province, it is easier to buy these items at the airport where bulbs are packaged with the required health certificates attached. Amsterdam's floating flower market will also sell bulbs packaged with a health certificate on request.

Sports and the Outdoors

Biking   To the Dutch, biking is not a sport, it's a primary means of transportation. Wherever you go in the Netherlands, even in a city as bustling as Amsterdam, there are separate bike lanes on major thoroughfares and special road signs and traffic signals for cyclists on smaller streets. In Amsterdam and other major cities, be sure to lock your bike to something immovable, or it may not be there when you return.

Boating and Sailing   Pleasure sailing was invented by the Dutch, who are among the world's best designers of small sailing craft, and in the Netherlands you'll find a variety of boating opportunities ranging from the rough North Sea to the wide river deltas of Zeeland province and the gentler Frisian lakes. **ANWB** (Royal Dutch Touring Club) stores in Amsterdam (Museumplein 5, tel. 020/673–0844) sell very good nautical maps.

Camping   Prices at the country's numerous camping locations range from Fl 25 to Fl 35 per site per night. Reservations can be made through the **Netherlands Reservation Centre** (Postbus 404, 2260 AK Leidschendam, tel. 070/320–3611, fax 070/320–2611).

Canoeing   Canoeing and kayaking are popular on the small rivers and canals in the eastern regions of the country. The **Netherlands Board of Tourism** booklet "Canoeing in Holland" provides a good overview of canoeing sites throughout the country and annual canoeing events. For more detailed information on canoeing in the Netherlands, contact the **Dutch Canoe Union** (Postbus 1160, 3800 BD Amersfoort, tel. 033/622341).

Fishing   Visitors need a national fishing document, or *sportvisakte*, which is valid for one year and is available at any post office. Additional licenses to fish certain areas are also necessary and are available from local fishing clubs. No license is required for saltwater fishing on the North Sea or the Wadden Sea. Ports throughout the Netherlands offer deep-sea trips; tackle and bait can be rented or bought.

Golf   There are a number of public courses throughout the Netherlands that are open to players of all levels; most are open year-round, except during tournaments. **De Nederlandse Golf Federatie** (Postbus 221, 3454 ZL De Meern, tel. 03406/21888) can provide information on golfing around the country.

Beaches

The North Sea is visited by the Dutch and their German neighbors in droves during the summer months. The principal beach areas of the Netherlands are in Zeeland at **Zoutelande, Westkapelle,** and **Domburg;** along the coast of Zuid Holland province at **Oostvoorne, Brielle, Hook of Holland, Kijkduin, Scheveningen, Katwijk,** and **Nordwijk;** and in Noord Holland at **Zandvoort, Ijmuiden, Egmond aan Zee, Bergen,** and **Den Helder.** There also are beaches on the

Frisian islands of **Texel, Vlieland, Terschelling, Ameland,** and **Schiermonnikoog.**

Dining

The Dutch have a dining advantage over other Europeans in the quantity and quality of the fresh ingredients available to them. Their national green thumb produces the Continent's best and greatest variety of vegetables and fruits, and their dairy farms supply a rich store of creams, cheeses, and butter for sauces; the forests yield a wide range of game meats in the winter wild season, and the sea dikes are covered with rare herbs and other vegetation that offer a rich diet to their lambs and calves to produce exceptionally tasty, tender meats year-round; plus, the waters of the Netherlands, both salt and fresh, are well known for the extraordinary quality and variety of the fish and shellfish they yield. Remarkably, for centuries Dutch cuisine failed to take advantage of this national bounty. But the days of home-style, stick-to-the-ribs cooking are nearly gone in the Netherlands, even in many smaller cities and rural areas. In its place are imaginative dishes prepared with the high-quality fresh ingredients so readily available. Many Dutch chefs also have spent time in the kitchens of France and Belgium to learn the techniques of both traditional and nouvelle cuisine. The rest of the population travels as well, and that fact has influenced dining in the Netherlands. You find Chinese, Italian, Mexican, and Indian restaurants even in small cities, and Indonesian restaurants are found everywhere because the Dutch, having colonized the country, developed a taste for the multidish Indonesian meal *rijsttafel* (rice served with several small meat, poultry, and vegetable dishes). Potatoes, cabbage, sausage, and other ingredients of traditional cooking remain important to the cuisine; soup continues to be the appropriate, and delicious, beginning of a meal on a daily basis. Also unchanging in the Netherlands is fresh flowers on the tables.

The Dutch prefer small, formal restaurants that emphasize service and leisurely dining; quick, casual meals can be had in French-style *grandes cafés* and café-pubs, also called *eetcafes* (eat cafés).

In Amsterdam and major cities dinner is served until 10 PM or later in most restaurants, though most diners eat between 7 and 9; elsewhere, dining hours vary by local custom. In the northern and eastern provinces, people dine from as early as 6, while in the southern provinces, dinner is later, 8 to 9.

Fixed-price and pretheater menus are found at restaurants throughout the country; vegetarian menus also are available, particularly in university cities.

The price ranges below are for an average three- or four-course meal and include taxes and tip, but not wine or drinks. The most highly recommended restaurants in each price category are indicated with a star ★.

Category	Amsterdam, The Hague, & Rotterdam	Metro Cities & Maastricht	Other Cities
$$$$	over Fl 85	over Fl 75	over Fl 65
$$$	Fl 60–Fl 85	Fl 55–Fl 75	Fl 45–Fl 65

$$	Fl 35–Fl 60	Fl 35–Fl 55	Fl 30–Fl 45
$	under Fl 35	under Fl 35	under Fl 30

Lodging

Accommodations in the Netherlands of the 1990s have changed from Old Dutch "cozy" to European cosmopolitan: Even small hotels and family-owned inns have redecorated in trendy colors and added televisions to guest rooms. International chains have opened hotels throughout the country, and golf and fitness resorts are being widely developed. In the southern province of Limburg, castles and manor houses have been converted to luxury hotels, and in many ancient city centers, a new generation of hoteliers has created attractive family-run hotels in canal houses and historic buildings.

The **Netherlands Reservation Center** (NRC, Postbus 404, 2260 AK Leidschendam, tel. 070/320–3611, fax 070/320–2611) handles bookings for most lodgings in the Netherlands.

Rates are for two people sharing a double room, including taxes and service; breakfast is generally included in the lower price categories only. Highly recommended hotels are indicated with a star ★.

Category	Amsterdam, The Hague, & Rotterdam	Metro Cities & Maastricht	Other Cities
$$$$	over Fl 450	over Fl 400	over Fl 300
$$$	Fl 300–Fl 450	Fl 300–400	Fl 200–Fl 300
$$	Fl 300–Fl 400	Fl 200–Fl 300	Fl 150–Fl 200
$	under Fl 300	under Fl 200	under Fl 150

Amsterdam

Amsterdam is a city with a split personality: It's a gracious, formal cultural center built on canals, and it's the most offbeat metropolis in the world. There is an incomparable romance about the canals at night, and a depth of cultural heritage in its great art museums; but there is also a houseboat crawling with stray cats permanently parked in front of an elegant gabled canal house, and prostitutes display their wares in the windows facing the city's oldest church. Only in Amsterdam can you marvel at the acoustics of the Concertgebouw one evening and be greeted by a hurdy-gurdy barrel organ pumping out happy tunes on the shopping street the next morning. When you know what to expect, Amsterdam is a delight to visit; when you don't, it can be disconcerting.

The city is laid out in concentric rings of canals around the old center, crosscut by a network of access roads and alleylike connecting streets; visitors easily can see the city on foot, though there are also trams and water taxis for the weary. Most of the art museums are clustered conveniently at the edge of the canal district.

Important Addresses and Numbers

Tourist Information The **VVV Amsterdam Tourist Office** is in front of Amsterdam's neo-baroque Centraal Station. *Stationsplein 10, tel. 06/340–34066 (costs*

50¢ per minute), fax 020/625–2869. Open daily 9–5. A second information office at Leidsestraat 106 operates daily 9–7 in summer.

Consulates **U.S. Consulate** (Museumplein 19, Amsterdam, tel. 020/664–5661). **British Consulate** (Koningslaan 44, Amsterdam, tel. 020/676–4343).

Emergencies The **National Emergency Alarm Number** is 06/11 for police, ambulance, and fire.

Police Call 555–5555 to report **accidents**. The **police** can be reached at 622–2222. City police stations are at Elandsgracht 117, Lijnbaansgracht 219, Warmoesstraat 44–46, and at the entrance to IJtunnel.

Hospital **Academisch Medisch Centrum** (Meibergdreef 9, tel. 020/566–9111),
Emergency **Boven 't IJ Ziekenhuis** (Statenjachtstraat 1, tel. 020/634–6346), **VU**
Rooms **Ziekenhuis** (de Boelelaan 1117, tel. 020/548–9111), **Lucas Ziekenhuis** (Jan Tooropstraat 164, tel. 020/510–8911), **Onze Lieve Vrouwe Gasthuis** (le Oosterparkstraat 197, tel. 020/599–9111), and **Slotervaartziekenhuis** (Louwesweg 6, tel. 020/512–9333).

Doctors, Call 020/612–3766 for a 24-hour referral service for all medical ser-
Dentists, vices. For dental emergencies, contact **Dentist Surgery AOC** (W.G.
Pharmacy Plein 167, tel. 020/616–1234).

Where to **GWK/Grenswisselkantoren** (Centraal Station, tel. 020/3206–0566,
Change Mon.–Sat. 8–8, Sun. 10–4) is a nationwide financial organization
Money specializing in foreign currencies, where travelers can exchange cash and traveler's checks, receive cash against major credit cards, and receive Western Union money transfers. Many of the same services are available at banks, and cash can be exchanged at any post office.

Books in The Dutch read English as well as they read their own language, so
English you will find English-language book sections in most bookstores in Amsterdam. The city's best selection of English-language reading material, including magazines, is at the **American Discount Book Center** (Kalverstraat 185, tel. 020/625–5537).

Travel Major travel agencies in Amsterdam include **American Express In-**
Agencies **ternational** (Damrak 66, 020/520–7777), **Thomas Cook** (Van Baerlestraat 40, tel. 020/676–6101 and Leidseplein 31A, tel. 020/ 626–7000), **Holland International Travel Group** (Rokin 54, tel. 020/ 551–2812), **Key Tours** (Dam 19, tel. 020/624–7310 or 623–5051), **Lindbergh Excursions** (Damrak 26, tel. 020/622–2766), and, for student travel, **NBBS** (Rokin 38, tel. 020/624–0989).

Arriving and Departing by Plane

Airports and **Amsterdam Schiphol Airport** (tel. 020/601–0966) is 25 kilometers (15
Airlines miles) southeast of the city, to which it is directly linked by rail.

Between the **KLM Road Transport** (tel. 020/649–5651 or 020/649–1393) operates a
Airport and regular morning shuttle bus service between Amsterdam Schiphol
Center City Airport and major city hotels. The trip takes about half an hour and
By Bus costs Fl 17.50.

By Train The **Schiphol Rail Line** (tel. 06/9292) operates between the airport and the city 24 hours a day, with service to the central railway station or to stations in the south part of the city. The trip takes about 15 minutes and costs Fl 5.50.

By Taxi There is a taxi stand directly in front of the arrival hall at Amsterdam Schiphol Airport. All taxis are metered, and the fare is approximately Fl 50 to various points within central Amsterdam. Service is included, but small additional tips are not unwelcome.

Arriving and Departing by Car or Train

By Car Major European highways leading into the city from the borders are E22 from western Belgium, E25 from eastern Belgium, and E22, E30, and E35 from Germany. Follow the signs for *Centrum* to reach center city. Traffic is heavy but not stationary at rush hour.

By Train The city has several substations, but all major Dutch national as well as European international trains arrive at and depart from **Centraal Station** (tel. 06/9292 for national services information, tel. 020/620–2266 for international service). The station also houses the travel information office of **NS/Nederlandse Spoorwagen** (Netherlands Railways).

Getting Around Amsterdam

Amsterdam is a small city, and most major sites are within its central district. The canal-laced central core is surrounded by concentric rings of 15th- to 17th-century canals, built following the pattern of earlier city walls and drainage ditches. Six roads link the city center with the more modern outer neighborhoods. Once you understand the fanlike pattern of Amsterdam's geography, you will have an easier time getting around. All trams and most buses begin and end their journeys at Centraal Station, sightseeing and shopping are focused at Dam Square, and the arts and nightlife are centered in the areas of Leidseplein, Rembrandtsplein, and Waterlooplein.

By Tram, Bus, and Metro The transit map published by **GVB** (main information office at Prins Hendrikkade 108–114, tel. 020/551–4911) and available at the GVB ticket office across from the central railway station is very useful. You also can get a copy at the VVV tourist information offices next door. It is also reprinted as the center spread in *What's On in Amsterdam*, the weekly guide to activities and shopping published by the tourist office. The map shows the locations of all major museums, monuments, theaters, and markets, and it tells which trams to take to reach each of them. Single-ride tickets valid for one hour can be purchased from the tram and bus drivers for Fl 3, but it is far more practical to buy a *strippenkaart* (strip ticket) that includes from two to 45 "strips," or ticket units. The best buy for most visitors is the 15-strip ticket for Fl 11. By tradition, Dutch trams and buses work on the honor system: Upon boarding the vehicle, punch your ticket at one of the machines situated in the rear or center section of the tram or bus. The city is divided into zones, which are indicated on the transit map, and it is important to punch the correct number of zones on your ticket (one for the basic tariff and one for each additional zone traveled). Occasional ticket inspections can be expected: A fine of Fl 60 is the price for "forgetting" to stamp your ticket.

By Taxi Taxi stands are at the major squares and in front of the large hotels. Or you can call **Taxicentrale** (tel. 020/677–7777), the central taxi dispatching office. Fares are Fl 5.80, plus Fl 2.75 per kilometer.

By Water Taxi A **Water Taxi** (tel. 020/622–2181) can be hailed anytime you see one cruising the canals of the city. The boats are miniature versions of the large sightseeing canal boats, and each carries up to seven passengers. The cost is Fl 60 for the first 30 minutes plus an Fl 30 pickup charge, then Fl 2 per minute. The rate is per ride, no matter how many passengers are traveling.

By Bicycle There are bike lanes on all major streets, bike racks in key locations in the city, and special bike parking indentations in the pavement. For information on renting a bicycle, *see* Sports and Fitness, *below*.

Opening and Closing Times

Opening and closing times are uniform throughout the Netherlands (*see* Staying in the Netherlands, *above*). Most state museums are closed on Mondays.

Guided Tours

Orientation The quickest, easiest way to get your bearings in Amsterdam is to take a canal-boat cruise. Trips last from one to 1½ hours and cover the harbor as well as the main canal district; a taped commentary is available in four languages. Excursion boats leave from piers in various locations in the city every 15 minutes from March to October, and every 30 minutes in winter. Most launches are moored in the inner harbor in front of Centraal Station. Fares are around Fl 11. Operators of canal cruises include **Rederij D'Amstel** (Nicolaas Witsenkade, opposite Heineken Brewery, tel. 020/626–5636), **Holland International** (Prins Hendrikkade, opposite Centraal Station, tel. 020/662–7788), **Rederij P. Kooy B.V.** (Rokin, near Spui, tel. 020/623–3810 or 020/623–4186), **Rederij Lovers B.V.** (Prins Hendrikkade 26, opposite Centraal Station, tel. 020/622–2181), **Meyers Rondvaarten** (Damrak, quays 4–5, tel. 020/623–4208), **Rederij Noord/Zuid** (Stadhouderskade 25, opposite Parkhotel, tel. 020/679–1370), and **Rederij Plas C.V.** (Damrak, quays 1–3, tel. 020/624–5406 or 020/622–6096).

Bus Tours Afternoon bus tours of the city operate daily. Itineraries vary, and prices range from Fl 25 to Fl 35. A three-hour city tour that includes a drive through the suburbs is offered by **Key Tours** (Dam 19, tel. 020/624–7304 or 020/624–7310). A three-hour tour focusing on the central city and including a canal-boat cruise is offered by **Lindbergh Excursions** (Damrak 26, tel. 020/622–2766).

Special- Several boat trips to museums are available: **Canalbus** (Nieuwe
Interest Tours Keizersgracht 8, tel. 020/623–9886), which makes three stops along
By Boat a route between the Centraal Station and the Rijksmuseum, costs Fl 12.50. Following a longer route is **Museumboot Rederij Lovers** (Stationsplein 8, tel. 020/622–2181), which makes seven stops near 20 different museums. The cost is Fl 19 for a day ticket that entitles you to a 50% discount on admission to the museums, or Fl 35 for a combination ticket that includes admission to three museums of your choice.

By Bike During the extended summer season, March through October, guided 3½-hour bike trips through the central area of the city are available through the **VVV Amsterdam Tourist Office** (Stationsplein 10, tel. 06/340–34066).

On Foot Walking tours focusing on art and architecture are run by **Stichting Arttra** (Staalstraat 28, 1011 JM, tel. 020/625–9303) and **Archivisie** (Postbus 14603, 1001 LC, tel. 020/625–8908). For walking tours of the Jewish Quarter, contact **Joods Historisch Museum** (Jonas Daniel Meyerplein 2–4, Postbus 16737, 1001 RE, tel. 020/626–9945, fax 020/624–1721), and for a guided walk through the red-light district, contact **Stichting FIS** (Postbus 1566, 1001 ND, tel. 020/624–5720).

Personal The **VVV Amsterdam Tourist Office** (Stationsplein 10, tel.06/340–
Guides 34066, fax 020/625–2869) maintains lists of guides and can advise

you on making arrangements. The costs range from Fl 80 to Fl 350 for a half day and from Fl 120 to Fl 650 for a full day.

Self-Guided The **VVV Amsterdam Tourist Office** (Stationsplein 10, tel. 06/340–
Tours 34066, fax 020/625–2869) sells brochures outlining easy-to-follow theme tours through the central part of the city. Among them are "A Journey of Discovery Through Maritime Amsterdam," "A Walk Through the Jordaan," "Jewish Amsterdam," and "Rembrandt and Amsterdam."

Highlights for First-Time Visitors

Amsterdam Historisch Museum (*see* Tour 1: City of the Arts)
Anne Frankhuis (*see* Tour 3: The Canals)
Museum het Rembrandthuis (*see* Tour 2: The Jewish Quarter and the Old Town)
Museum van Loon (*see* Tour 1: City of the Arts)
Rijksmuseum (*see* Tour 1: City of the Arts)
Rijksmuseum Vincent Van Gogh (*see* Tour 1: City of the Arts)

Exploring Amsterdam Tour 1: City of the Arts

Numbers in the margin correspond to points of interest on the Amsterdam map.

1 Your tour begins where Amsterdam began. In the 12th century **Dam (Dam Square)** was the site of a dam across the Amstel River and the location of the local weigh house. The monument in the center was erected in 1956 to commemorate the liberation of the Netherlands at the end of World War II.

Follow the shopping street Kalverstraat south to the entrance to the
2 **Amsterdam Historisch Museum** (Amsterdam Historical Museum). In the halls of this former orphanage you will learn all you need to know about the history of Amsterdam, from its beginnings in the 13th century as a marketplace for farmers and fishermen through the glorious period in the 17th century when Amsterdam was the richest, most powerful trading city in the world. A towering, skylighted gallery is filled with the guild paintings that document that period of power. *Kalverstraat 92, tel. 020/523–1822. Admission: Fl 6.50 adults, Fl 3 children. Open weekdays 10–5 and weekends 11–5.*

Passing through the painting gallery of the historical museum
3 brings you to the entrance of the **Begijnhof** (Beguine Court). Walk inside and you are in the courtyard of a peaceful residential hideaway. Built in the 14th century as a conventlike residence for unmarried lay women, it is typical of many found throughout the Netherlands. No. 34 is the oldest house in Amsterdam. The small church is the Church of Scotland. *Begijnhof 29, tel. 020/623–3565. Admission free. Open weekdays 11–4.*

Time Out At the end of the alley that passes the Beguine Court you come to Spui, an open square that is the focal point of the University of Amsterdam and the site of its library. Several of the pubs and eateries here are good places to take a break, including **Caffe Esprit** (Spui 10, tel. 020/622–1967), attached to the store of the same name. Try **Broodje van Kootje** (Spui 28, tel. 020/623–7451) for a classic Amsterdam *broodje* (sandwich).

Cut through the canals by way of the Heisteeg and its continuation, the Wijde Heisteeg. The corner of Herengracht and Leidsegracht,

❹ the **Gouden Bocht** (Golden Bend), was the most prestigious section of the city in the 17th century, and still is. The houses are wide, the doors centrally placed, and the architecture imposing. Follow Herengracht to the left to Vijzelstraat and turn right. Cross the Keizersgracht and turn left to find the **Museum van Loon.** This is the city's best look at life in those magnificent canal houses. Still a private residence for a descendant of one of Amsterdam's powerful families, the house is filled with portraits, many of them traditional paired marriage portraits and paintings of children. *Keizersgracht 672, tel. 020/624–5255. Admission: Fl 5 adults, Fl 4 children. Open Mon. 10–5, Sun. 1–5.*

Turn left and follow Keizersgracht to Nieuwe Spiegelstraat, where you take another right and walk toward Museumplein. Amsterdam's wealth of art is largely concentrated around this grassy plain, which also serves as a transition point between the central canal area and the modern residential sections of the city.

❺ The **Rijksmuseum** (State Museum), which occupies a turreted, turn-of-the-century building designed by Petrus J. Cuypers, has more than 150 rooms displaying paintings, sculpture, and objects from both the West and Asia, dating from the 9th through the 19th centuries. The primary collection is of 15th- to 17th-century paintings, mostly Dutch (the Rijksmuseum has the largest concentration of these masters in the world); there are also extensive holdings of Dutch drawings and prints from the 15th to the 20th centuries. The main attraction of the Rijksmuseum is the work of Rembrandt, including *The Night Watch. Stadhouderskade 42, tel. 020/673–2121. Admission: Fl 10 adults, Fl 5 children. Open Tues.–Sat. 10–5, Sun. and holidays 1–5.*

When you leave the Rijksmuseum, walk through the covered gallery that divides the building. Directly ahead is Museumplein; to your right is Paulus Potterstraat (look for the diamond factory on the far ❻ corner), where you'll find the **Rijksmuseum Vincent Van Gogh** (Vincent van Gogh Museum). As the Rijksmuseum honors Rembrandt, so this light-filled building designed by Gerrit Rietveld and opened in 1973 honors the short, but prolific, career of the 19th-century Dutch painter with a collection that includes *nearly all* of his paintings, drawings, and letters. The galleries present, step by step, van Gogh's development as an artist, from the early dark and rough-hewn drawings of potato farmers he did in the Dutch province of Drenthe to his brooding final painting of crows circling above a wheat field. *Paulus Potterstraat 7, tel. 020/570–5200. Admission: Fl 10 adults, Fl 5 children. Open Tues.–Sat. 10–5, Sun. 1–5, Mon. 10–5 Easter–Sept.*

Continuing along Paulus Potterstraat, at the corner of Van Baerle-❼ straat, you reach the **Stedelijk Museum** (Municipal Museum), where you'll find a collection of paintings and sculptures by Cézanne, Picasso, Monet, and other artists dating from 1850 to the present. Major movements that are well documented here are COBRA (Appel, Corneille), American pop art (Johns, Oldenburg, Liechtenstein), American action painting (de Kooning, Pollock), and neorealism (de Saint-Phalle, Tinguely). *Paulus Potterstraat 13, tel. 020/573–2911. Admission: Fl 7.50 adults, Fl 3.50 children. Open daily 11–5.*

Facing the back of the Rijksmuseum across Museumplein is the ❽ **Concertgebouw** (Concert Building), filled since the turn of the century with the music of the Concertgebouw Orchestra as well as visiting international artists. There are two concert halls in the building,

Grote (large), and Kleine (small): It is the larger hall that is well known to music lovers and musicians around the world as one of the most acoustically perfect anywhere. You will recognize the building at once (it is topped with a lyre); enter through the glass extension along the side. There are no tours of the building, so you will need to buy a ticket to a concert to see beyond the broad lobby, or, if you visit on a Wednesday before 12:30 September–June, you can attend a free lunchtime concert. *Concertgebouwplein 2–6, tel. 020/675– 4411 (24-hr concert schedule and information hot line) or 020/671– 8345 (box office). AE, DC, MC, V.*

Time Out On the corner of Van Baerlestraat and Brouwersstraat, facing the side of the Concertgebouw, is **Restaurant Bodega Keyzer** (Van Baerlestraat 96, tel. 020/671–1441), something of an institution in the neighborhood as the spot for a meal before or after a performance.

Tour 2: The Jewish Quarter and the Old Town

Start on Waterlooplein, where the large and modern **Muziektheater/Stadhuis** (Music Theater/Town Hall) complex is the cornerstone of a revival of this part of the city. Built as a home for everything from opera performances to welfare applications, it is a multifunctional complex that includes theaters, offices, shops, and even the city's wedding chamber (Dutch marriages all must be performed in the Town Hall, with church weddings optional). Feel free to wander through the lobbies; there is interesting sculpture as well as a display that dramatically illustrates Amsterdam's position below sea level. Tours of the backstage areas are run twice weekly. *Tel. 020/551–8054. Admission: Fl 8.50. Tours: Wed. and Sat. 4 PM.*

Wrapped around two sides of the Music Theater/Town Hall complex is the **Waterlooplein** flea market. The wooden pushcarts that were used when the market began (before World War II) are gone, but a stroll past the stalls provides a colorful glimpse of Amsterdam entrepreneurship in action, day in and day out, in every sort of weather. *Waterlooplein. Admission free. Open weekdays 9–5, Sat. 8:30– 5:30.*

From the time in the 15th century when the diamond cutters of Antwerp first arrived to find refuge from the Spanish Inquisition, the area east of the Zwanenburgwal has traditionally been Amsterdam's Jewish Quarter.

East of Waterlooplein, across Mr. Visserplein, is a statue erected after World War II to honor a solidarity strike by Amsterdam's dockworkers in protest of the deportation of Amsterdam's Jews during the war. Facing it is the entrance to the **Joods Historisch Museum** (Jewish Historical Museum) complex, which incorporates four synagogues and contains documents, paintings, and objects related to the history of the Jewish people in Amsterdam and the Netherlands. *Jonas Daniel Meyerplein 2–4, tel. 020/626–9945. Admission: Fl 7 adults, Fl 3.50 children. Open daily 11–5.*

Just to the east, on the corner of Mr. Visserplein and Jonas Daniel Meyerplein, is a square brick building behind brick courtyard walls. This is the **Portugees Israelitische Synagogue** (Portuguese Israeli Synagogue), built between 1671 and 1675 by the Sephardic Jewish community that had emigrated from Portugal during the preceding two centuries. Its spare, elegantly proportioned, wood interior has remained virtually unchanged since it was built and still is lighted

Amsterdam

Het IJ

de Ruyterkade

Oosterdokskade

Oosterdok

CENTRAAL STATION Front

Centraal Station

CENTRAL STATION

Hendrikkade

Prins Hendrikkade

Ofen

Haven

Nieuwendijk

Spuistr.

Singel

Damrak

Nieuwendijk

Oudebrugsteeg

Beursstraat

Warmoesstraat

Zijds Voorburgwal

burgwal

Achter

Oude

Zijds

Oude Hoogstr.

Nieuwe Hoogstr.

Raamgr.

Kloveniersburgwal

Groen burgwal

Zwan nenburg

Nes

Nieuwe Doelenstr.

Staalstraat

Kalverstraat

Rokin

Spui

Singel

nieuwezijdsvoorburgwal

Dam

Rokin

Damstraat

St. Antoniesbreestr.

NIEUW-MARKT

Oude

Schans

Oude

Nieuwe Uilenburgerstraat

Uilenburgergracht

Valkenburgerstraat

Rapenburgerstraat

Rapenburg

Anne Frank str.

Jodenbreestraat

Mr. Visser plein

Muiderstraat

gracht

Wertheim Park

Plantage Parklaan

Plantage Middenlaan

Zeedijk

Oudezijds Kolk

Geldersekade

Prins

Binnen kant

Waals

Bantam Oude waal

Recht Boomsloot

Binnen eilandsgracht

Konings str.

Kramer Koningslt

Amstel

Amstel

Amstelstr.

Blauwbrug

Nieuwe Amstel

WATERLOOPLEIN

Nieuwe

Nieuwe

Nieuwe

Nieuwe

Amstel

Heren

Keizersgracht

Kerkstraat

Prinsengracht

Nieuwe Achter

Valckenierstraat

Weesperstraat

WEESPERPLEIN

Sarphatistraat

Mauritskade

Reguliersdwarsstraat

Rembrandt plein

Heren gracht

Keizersgracht

Prinsengracht

Noorderstr.

Nieuwe Looiersstr.

Reguliers gracht

Utrechtsestraat

Kerkstraat Magere Brug

Utrechte dwarsstraat

Amstel

Frederiks plein

Sarphatistraat

Vijzelgracht

Vijzelstraat

Weteringschans

Wetering Schans

Wetering Pl.

Den Texstraat

Nicolaas Witsen Kade

Stadhouderskade

F. Bol Straat

dwarstr.

N

KEY

🛈 Tourist Information

Ⓜ Metro Stops

Metro Lines

Tram Lines

Railroad

0   220 yards

0   200 meters

by candles in two immense candelabras during services. *Mr. Visserplein 3, tel. 020/624–5351. Admission: Fl 5. Open May–Oct., Sun.–Fri. 10–4; Nov.–Apr., Mon.–Thurs. 10–4, Fri. 10–3.*

Up Jodenbreestraat (once the main street of the Jewish Quarter) from Mr. Visserplein, the second house from the corner by the Zwanenburgwal is **Museum het Rembrandthuis** (Rembrandt's House). This was the house that Rembrandt, flush with success, bought for his family. He later lost it to bankruptcy when he fell from popularity following his wife's death. He came under attack by the Amsterdam burghers, who refused to accept his liaison with his housekeeper. The house today is a museum of Rembrandt prints and etchings and includes one of his presses. *Jodenbreestraat 4–6, tel. 020/624–9486. Admission: Fl 5 adults, Fl 3 children. Open Mon.– Sat. 10–5, Sun. and holidays 1–5.*

Time Out Grab a bite in the Waterlooplein flea market or in the café of the Muziektheater.

Cross the bridge into St. Antonies Brestraat and follow it to the **Zuiderkerk** (South Church), built between 1603 and 1611. The city planning office maintains a display here that offers a look at the future of Amsterdam. *Zandstraat. Admission free. Tower open June– Oct., Wed. 2–5, Thurs.–Fri. 11–2, Sat. 11–4.*

Cut through on Zandstraat to Kloveniersburgwal and follow it north to **Nieuwmarkt** (New Market) square. The **Waag** (Weigh House) in the center of the square was built between 1488 and 1614 as a town gate, and it was part of the city walls in 1500. After 1617 this was the weighing house; one of its towers became a teaching hospital for the academy of surgeons of the Surgeons' Guild. It was here that Rembrandt came to watch Professor Tulp in action prior to painting *The Anatomy Lesson*.

Take Koningsstraat to the Kroomboomsloot canal and turn left; turn right at Rechtboomsloot canal and follow it through its homey neighborhood to Montelbaans Straat, turn left, and cut through to **Oudewaal** canal. Follow it right to **Montelbaanstoren** (Montelbaans Tower), which dates from 1512 and now houses the City Water Office. Since 1878, this department has maintained the water levels in the canals and engineered the nightly flushings of the entire city waterway system, closing and opening the sluices to change the direction of the flow and cleanse the waters. (The canals remain murky green despite the process, due to algae.) The elegant clock tower was added early in the 17th century. Up Kalk Markt from the tower, at Prins Hendrikkade, is the **Oosterdok** (Eastern Dock) of Amsterdam Harbor. Continue west along Prins Hendrikkade to Gelderskade and **Schreierstoren** (Weeper's Tower). There's a shop for nautical instruments, maps, and books in the building now, but in the 16th century it was a lookout tower for the women whose men were fishing at sea. A plaque on the side of the building tells you that it was from this location that Henry Hudson set sail on behalf of the Dutch East India Company to find a shorter route to the East Indies, discovering instead Hudson's Bay in Canada and, later, New York harbor and the Hudson River.

Follow Oudezijds Kolk south to the small alley of **Zeedijk,** once known throughout the country as the black hole of Amsterdam for its concentration of drug traffickers and users. In one night in the late 1980s, the city fathers cleared the area with an onslaught of horse patrols and fire hoses. These attackers were immediately followed by a brigade of carpenters, who reclaimed the area's dilapidated buildings; many of these buildings now house shops, restaurants, and galleries. No. 1 Zeedijk, now a café, is one of only two timbered houses left in the city.

⑲ From Zeedijk, take Oudezijds Voorburgwal south to **Museum Amstelkring** ("Our Lord in the Attic" Museum). It looks to be just another canal house, and on the lower floors, it is. The attic of the building is unique, however; it is a small chapel that dates from the Reformation in Amsterdam, when open worship by Catholics was outlawed. *Oudezijds Voorburgwal 40, tel. 020/624–6604. Admission: Fl 5 adults, Fl 3 children. Open Mon.–Sat. 10–5, Sun. 1–5.*

Continue south on Oudezijds Voorburgwal through part of the red-light district (where semi-nude women display their wares in canal-
⑳ side windows) to the **Oude Kerk** (Old Church), built between 1366 and 1566 and restored from 1955 to 1979. Rembrandt's wife, Saskia, is buried here. *Oudekerksplein 23, tel. 020/624–9183. Admission: Fl. 3.50. Open Apr.–Oct., Mon.–Sat. 11–5, Sun. 1:30–5; Nov.–Mar., Fri.–Sun. 1–5.*

From here you can continue south on Oudezijds Voorburgwal through more of the red-light district to Damstraat and the Dam.

Tour 3: The Canals

This tour, too, begins at Dam Square. On its western side are two of
㉑ Amsterdam's most imposing structures. **Het Koninklijk Paleis te Amsterdam** (Royal Palace at Amsterdam), built in the mid-17th century as the city's town hall, is Dutch classical in design and stands solidly on 13,659 pilings sunk deep into the marshy soil of the former riverbed. Restored as a royal residence during the Napoleonic period and filled with furnishings of that time, it has been the official residence of the House of Orange since 1808. Queen Beatrix, like her mother and grandmother before her, uses it only on the highest of state occasions, however. If you are in Amsterdam while it is open, be sure to visit; this is the Dutch equivalent of touring the White House. *Dam, tel. 020/624–8698. Admission: Fl 5 adults, Fl 1.50 children. Open Easter, summer, and autumn holidays, Mon.–Sun. 12:30–4; most Wed. afternoons rest of the year.*

㉒ To the right of the palace is the **Nieuwe Kerk** (New Church). Built in the 16th and early 17th centuries, this is the royal church of the Netherlands, in which every monarch has been crowned since 1815. It is often the site of special exhibitions. *Dam, tel. 020/626–8168. Admission free (except to special exhibitions). Open daily 11–5.*

Circle around behind the Royal Palace, follow the tram tracks into the wide and busy Raadhuisstraat, and continue along it to the
㉓ Westermarkt. The **Westerkerk** (Western Church) is on the right, facing the next canal. Built between 1602 and 1631, it has a tower topped by a copy of the crown of the Habsburg emperor Maximilian I. Its carillon is the comforting "clock" of the canal area of Amsterdam whose chiming was mentioned often in the famous diary of Anne Frank, who lived around the corner. Rembrandt and his son Titus are buried here; the philosopher René Descartes lived on the square facing the church. *Prinsengracht (corner of Westermarkt), tel. 020/624–7766. Tower open June–Sept., Tues.–Wed. and Fri.–Sat. 2–5.*

㉔ Make a right past the church and follow the Prinsengracht canal to the **Anne Frankhuis** (Anne Frank House), one of the most frequently visited places in the world. It was in this unimposing canal house that two Jewish families hid from the Nazis for more than two years during World War II. They were eventually discovered and sent to concentration camps, but young Anne's diary survived as a detailed record of their life in hiding. If you have time to see nothing else in Amsterdam, don't miss a visit to this house. *Prinsengracht 263, tel. 020/556–7100. Admission: Fl 8 adults, Fl 4 children. Open Sept.–Apr., Mon.–Sat. 9–5, Sun. and public holidays 10–5; May–Aug., Mon.–Sat. 9–7, Sun. and public holidays 10–7.*

Time Out Sugared or fruit-filled crepe-style pancakes are a Dutch specialty, and the **Pancake Bakery** (Prinsengracht 191, tel. 020/625–1333) is one of the best places in Amsterdam to try them; the menu offers a choice of more than 30 combinations.

Continue north along the Prinsengracht canal. The neighborhood to your left, across the canal, is known as the **Jordaan,** the traditional working-class area of the city. Developed during the Napoleonic era and filled with streets and former canals named for flowers and trees, it was originally referred to as the *jardin,* French for "garden."

At the intersection of the Prinsengracht and Brouwersgracht canals, turn right. A leisurely stroll along the **Brouwersgracht** (Brewers Canal) is one of the prettiest in the city; the canal is lined with homes and former warehouses of the brewers who traded here in earlier centuries and is blessed with long views down the canals and plenty of sunlight. Cross the canal at Willemsstraat and follow it back to the Singel canal. On the other side, follow the tram tracks to the left toward the harbor. Ahead is **Centraal Station** (Central Station), an imposing example of Dutch Renaissance style. It opened in 1885 and has been the hub of transportation for the Netherlands ever since.

The inner harbor along the broad avenue leading to the station is the **Damrak** (Dam Port), once completely filled with piers bringing fish and other cargo to the weigh house at the Dam and now lined with a curious assortment of shops, attractions, hotels, and eating places. On the far side, the **Beurs** (Stock Exchange), built at the turn of the century, overlooks the Dam.

Amsterdam for Free

Free demonstrations are given at a number of Amsterdam's diamond-cutting factories and showrooms, including the **Amsterdam Diamond Centre** (Rokin 1–5, at Dam Square, tel. 020/624–5787), **Coster Diamonds** (Paulus Potterstraat 2–4, behind the Rijksmuseum, tel. 020/676–2222), and **Van Moppes Diamonds** (Albert Cuypstraat 2–6, in the middle of the daily green market street, tel. 020/676–1242). Free lunchtime concerts are given on Wednesdays at 12:30 between September and June at the Concert Building.

What to See and Do with Children

Keep young travelers entertained with a visit to the **Plantage quarter,** east of the city center beyond the expressway leading to the IJ Tunnel. Built in the mid-19th century as a garden city, this area includes a 37-acre park called **Artis** that is home to Amsterdam's collection of natural-history museums, a zoo with an aviary and an aquarium, and a planetarium. A special Artis Express canal boat from the central railway station provides an amusing means of transportation. *Plantage Kerklaan 40, tel. 020/523–3400. Admission: Fl 19 adults, Fl 12.50 children. Open daily 9–5. Zoological Museum closed Mon., planetarium opens Mon. at 1.*

The Netherlands' link to Indonesia and the West Indies is honored at the Tropen Museum (*see* Off the Beaten Track, *below*) beyond the Artis complex. The **Kindermuseum** (Children's Museum) was recently added here. Adults may visit, but only under the supervision of a child aged 6 to 12. *Linnaeusstraat 2, tel. 020/568–8295. Admission: Fl 7.50 adults, Fl. 4.50 children. Open weekdays 10–5, weekends and holidays noon–5.*

The nearby **Museumwerf 't Kromhout** (Museum Wharf The Kromhout), a small 19th-century shipyard in which old ships are being restored, is sure to hold the attention of nautically minded youngsters. *Hoogte Kadijk 147, tel. 020/627–6777. Admission: Fl 3.50 adults, Fl 1.50 children. Open weekdays 9–4.*

A replica of the VOC (Dutch East India Company) ship *Amsterdam* (*see* Off the Beaten Track, *below*) is permanently moored at the end of the harbor.

A branch of the world-famous wax museum, **Madame Tussaud's,** is at Dam Square above the P&C department store. *P&C Bldg., Dam 20, tel. 020/622–9949. Admission: Fl 17 adults, Fl 12 children. Open daily 10–5:30.*

Off the Beaten Track

The early development of Western civilization, from the Egyptians to the Romans, and of the Near Eastern cultures (Anatolia, Persia, Palestine) are documented in the displays of the **Allard Pierson Museum,** the archaeological collection of the University of Amsterdam. *Oude Turkmarkt 127, tel. 020/525–2556. Admission: Fl 10 adults, Fl 4 children 12–14. Open Tues.–Fri. 10–5, weekends and holidays 1–5.*

Well beyond the bustle of the city center, housed in a magnificent tiered, galleried, and skylighted building decorated in gilt and marble, is the **Tropen Museum** (Tropical Museum), where displays and dioramas portray everyday life in the world's tropical environments. *Linnaeusstraat 2, tel. 020/568–8295. Admission: Fl 7.50 adults, Fl 4.50 children. Open weekdays 10–5, weekends and holidays noon–5.*

If you have always wanted to sort out your knowledge of the Dutch role in the development of world trade, the **Rijksmuseum Nederlands Scheepvaart/VOC Schip** *Amsterdam* (State Museum of Netherlands Shipping/East India Ship *Amsterdam*) is the place to do it. Once the warehouse from which trading vessels were outfitted for their journeys with everything from cannons to hardtack, the building now incorporates room after room of displays related to the development and power of the Dutch East and West Indies companies as well as the Dutch fishing industry. Moored alongside the building at the east end of Amsterdam Harbor is the replica trading ship *Amsterdam. Kattenburgerplein 1, tel. 020/523–2222. Admission: Fl 7.50 adults, Fl 8 children. Open Tues.–Sat. 10–5, Sun. and holidays 1–5.*

In the Plantage section of the city is the remarkable **Hortus Botanicus,** a botanical garden that was first laid out as an herb garden for doctors and pharmacists in 1638. It has since been expanded to incorporate an ornamental garden, where 6,000 species are represented. *Plantage Middenlaan 2, tel. 020/625–8411. Admission: Fl 7 adults, Fl 3.50 children. Open Apr.–Sept., weekdays 9–5, weekends and holidays 11–5; Oct.–Mar., weekdays 9–4, weekends and holidays 11–4.*

Shopping

The variety of goods available here and the convenience of a shopping district that snakes through the city in a continuous parade of boutiques and department stores are the major joys of shopping in Amsterdam. Be sure to visit the year-round outdoor flea market at Waterlooplein, a holdover from the pushcart days in the Jewish Quarter. Shopping hours in the Netherlands are regulated by law: One night a week is reserved for late shopping. In Amsterdam, department stores and many other shops are closed Monday morning but open Thursday evening.

Shopping Districts and Streets **Dam Square** is home to two of Amsterdam's main department stores, and several popular shopping streets lead away from the square in different directions: **Nieuwendijk** is good for bargain buys, **Rokin** for high-priced fashion and jewelry items. **Kalverstraat** is the city's main pedestrian-only shopping street. **Leidsestraat** offers a range and variety of shopping similar to Kalverstraat's. **Max Euweplein** is a small plaza-style shopping mall surrounding a summer café and adjacent to the Amsterdam Casino. The posh and prestigious **P.C. Hooftstraat,** generally known as the P.C. (pronounced "pay-say"), and its companion shopping avenue, **Van Baerlestraat,** leading to the Concertgebouw, are both good choices. For a variety of trendy shopping opportunities, try **Utrechtsestraat.**

Department Stores The city's best-known department store is **De Bijenkorf,** on one of the main corners of Dam Square. Directly across the square is **P&C,** specializing in clothing. In the middle of the Kalverstraat are the gracious and conservative **Maison de Bonneterie en Pander,** for clothing and household items, and the Amsterdam branch of England's **Marks & Spencer,** a good bet for low-priced clothing. Other lower-priced department stores include **C&A,** spanning the block between Nieuwendijk and Damrak, and **Vroom & Dreesman,** at the end of the Kalverstraat near Muntplein. One other department store to mention is **Metz & Company,** at the corner of Leidsestraat and Keizersgracht.

Street Markets Few markets compare with Amsterdam's **Waterlooplein** flea market, which partially surrounds the city's Music Theater/Town Hall complex at the convergence of the Oude Schans canal and the Amstel River. It is a descendant of the haphazard pushcart trade that gave this part of the city its distinct and lively character in the early part of the century. You're unlikely to find anything of value here, but it's a good spot to look for the secondhand clothing young Amsterdammers favor, and it is a gadget lover's paradise. The **Bloemenmarkt** on the Singel between Koningsplein and Muntplein is another of Amsterdam's must-see markets, where flowers and plants are sold from permanently moored barges. Both the Waterlooplein flea market and the Bloemenmarkt are open Monday–Saturday 9:30–5 (some flower stalls in the Bloemenmarkt stay open until 6). Sunday art markets are held in good weather from April to October on **Thorbeckeplein** and from April through November at **Spui.** The **Postzegelmarkt** stamp market is held twice a week (Wed. and Sat. 1–4) on Nieuwezijds Voorburgwal.

Specialty Stores *Antiques* Antiques always have been a staple item of shopping in Amsterdam, and the array of goods available at any time is broad. There are more than 150 antiques shops scattered throughout the central canal area of the city. The greatest concentration of those offering fine antiques and specialty items is in the **Spiegel Quarter.** Nieuwe Spiegelstraat and its continuation, **Spiegelgracht,** constitute the main thoroughfare of the quarter, with shops on both sides of the street and canal for five blocks, from the Golden Bend of the Herengracht nearly to the Rijksmuseum, including several dealers under one roof in the **Amsterdams Antiques Gallery** (Nieuwe Spiegelstraat 34, tel. 020/625–3371). **Rokin,** which runs between Dam and Muntplein, is the location of the Amsterdam branch of **Sotheby's** (Rokin, tel. 020/627–5656). Shops on **Rozengracht** and along **Prinsengracht** near the Westerkerk tend to offer country Dutch furniture and household items; you'll also find antiques and curio shops along the side streets in that part of the city. For a broad range of vintage and antique furniture, curios, jewelry, clothing, and household items, try **Antique Market de Looier** (Elandsgracht 109, tel. 020/624–9038; open Sat.–Wed. 11–5, Thurs. 11–9), which houses more than 50 dealers. Nearby is an indoor flea market, **De Rommelmarkt** (Looiersgracht 38, tel. 020/627–4762; open Sat.–Thurs. 11–5).

There are sure to be old maps and prints (including botanicals) in antiques shops all over Amsterdam, but for a broad selection of high quality, visit **A. van der Meer** (P.C. Hooftstraat 112, tel. 020/662–1936), a gallery that has specialized in 17th-, 18th-, and 19th-century works for more than 30 years. Daumier etchings, hunt prints, and cityscape engravings can be found here.

There is considerable interest in Art Deco and Jugendstil items in the Netherlands, particularly in Amsterdam. **Tangram** (Herenstraat, tel. 020/624–4286), **De Haas** (Kerkstraat 155, tel. 020/626–5952), and **Galerie Frans Leidelmeyer** (Nieuwe Spiegelstraat 58, tel. 020/625–4627) are good sources.

Art   *What's On in Amsterdam,* published by the tourist office, is a good source of information on current exhibitions; another is the Dutch-language publication *Uit Krant/Going Out News,* which has the most comprehensive listings available. Among the dealers specializing in 20th-century art in Keizersgracht are **Collection D'Art 1970** (Keizersgracht 516, tel. 020/622–1511), **Kunsthandel M.L. De Boer** (Keizersgracht 542, tel. 020/623–4060), **Galerie Espace** (Keizersgracht 548, tel. 020/624–0802); and in the Spiegel Quarter, **E. Den Biemen de Haas** (Nieuwe Spiegelstraat 44, tel. 020/626–1012), **Marie-Louise Woltering** (Nieuwe Spiegelstraat 53, tel. 020/622–2240), **C.M. Kooring Verwindt** (Spiegelgracht 14–16, tel. 020/623–6538), **Galerie Asselijn** (Lange Leidsedwarsstraat 200, tel. 020/624–9030), **Galerie Oppo** (Spiegelgracht 30, tel. 020/624–1192), **Wetering Galerie** (Lijnbaansgracht 288, tel. 020/623–6189), and **Galerie Guido de Spa** (2e Weteringdwarsstraat 34, tel. 020/622–1528). Also dealing in art, including old paintings, engravings, and Asian art, are **Waterman** (Rokin 116, tel. 020/623–2958), **E.H. Ariens Kappers** (Nieuwe Spiegelstraat 32, tel. 020/623–5356), **Eurasia Antiques** (Nieuwe Spiegelstraat 40, tel. 020/626–1594), **Cserno Antiek** (Spiegelgracht 28, tel. 020/626–3697), **Art Galerie Bruns** (Lijnbaansgracht 290, tel. 020/626–6777), **Couzijn Simon** (Prinsengracht 578, tel. 020/624–7691), **Kunsthandel J. Polak** (Spiegelgracht 3, tel. 020/627–9009), **Aalderink** (Spiegelgracht 15, tel. 020/623–0211). In the Spiegel Quarter, **Galerie Animation Art** (Berenstraat 19, tel. 020/627–7600) offers original Disney and other cartoon sketches.

Books   The Dutch love books, and most read in at least two or three languages. You'll have no trouble finding reading material in English. **Allert de Lange** (Damrak 60–62, tel. 020/624–6744) has a good selection of travel books, history, and fiction, as does **W.H. Smith** (Kalverstraat 152, tel. 020/638–3821). Near the art museums and the Concertgebouw, **Premsela** (Van Baerlestraat 78, tel. 662–4266) specializes in art books. The very best, and best located, place to shop for English-language books in Amsterdam is **American Discount Book Centers** (Kalverstraat 185, tel. 020/625–5537). True to its name, American Discount Book Centers' selection is strongly oriented to American tastes and expectations.

Ceramics, Crystal **Focke & Meltzer** (P.C. Hooftstraat 65–67, tel. 020/664–2311; Hotel Okura Shopping Arcade, tel. 675–2774) is the primary source in Amsterdam of authenticated Delft and Makkumware as well as fine crystal.

Cigars and Smokers' Materials Dutch cigars are famous for their unique taste and character; a cigar is also a customary after-dinner offering among men in the Netherlands. One of the best places in the world to buy cigars and other smoking materials is **Hajenius** (Rokin 92, tel. 020/623–7494), in business since 1826. Another option near the Concert Building is **Davidoff** (Van Baerlestraat 84, tel. 020/671–1042).

Coffee, Tea, Spices While other nations sent ships to plunder the world's stores of gold and jewels, the 17th-century Dutch got rich carrying shiploads of coffee, tea, and cinnamon. **Jacob Hooy & Co.** (Kloveniersburgwal 12, tel. 020/624–3041), in the same canalside location since 1743, sells spices and herbs from goldlettered wooden drawers, barrels, and bins, and offers a daunting array of *dropjes* (hard candies and medicinal drops) as well as teas. Directly across town near the Anne Frank House is **H. Keijzer's Koffie- en Theehandel N.V.** (Prinsengracht 180, tel. 020/624–0823), which offers nearly 100 different kinds of tea and more than two dozen coffees.

Diamonds, Jewelry The Amsterdam Diamond Center (Rokin 1, tel. 020/624–5787), housing several diamond sellers, is across the street from Bonebakker (Rokin 88/90, tel. 020/623–2294), one of the city's oldest and finest jewelers. At the head of the Kalverstraat is the century-old Schaap and Citroen (Kalverstraat 1, tel. 020/626–6691), dealing in jewelry and watches.

Premsela & Hamburger (Rokin, tel. 020/624–9688; closed weekends) has sold fine antique silver and jewelry since 1823. Two other dealers are **Schilling** (Nieuwe Spiegelstraat 23, tel. 020/623–9366) and Hemke Kuilboer (Nieuwe Spiegelstraat 52, tel. 020/624–6285).

Duty-Free If you find you have no time to shop in Amsterdam, save your guilders for the airport. **Amsterdam Airport Shopping Centre** (Box 7501, 1118 ZG, Amsterdam Schiphol Airport Holland, tel. 020/601–2497) is bigger, better, and cheaper than almost any other airport duty-free shopping area in the world. The departure hall at Amsterdam Schiphol Airport looks more like a shopping mall than a transportation facility, and auxiliary shops for the most popular items (liquor, perfume, chocolates) are found in every wing of the terminal.

Men's Clothes In addition to the main department stores, which have good men's departments, the best places to shop for menswear in Amsterdam are on the Kalverstraat or in the P.C. Hoofstraat/Van Baerlestraat shopping district. Two of the best shops are **Meddens** (Heiligeweg 11–17, tel. 020/624–0461) and **The English Hatter** (Heiligeweg 40, tel. 020/623–4781). There are nearly a dozen shops on the P.C. For conservative clothes, try **Richfield** (P.C. Hooftstraat 58, tel. 020/675–6203), **McGregor** (P.C. Hooftstraat 113, tel. 020/662–7425), **Mulberry Company** from England (P.C. Hooftstraat 46, tel. 020/673–8080), and **Society Shop** (Van Baerlestraat 20, tel. 020/664–9281). For more highly styled apparel, head to **Players** (P.C. Hooftstraat 31, tel. 664–5243), **Dik** (P.C. Hooftstraat 35, tel. 020/662–4328), **Inpetto** (P.C. Hooftstraat 53, tel. 020/675–1676), **Oger**

(P.C. Hooftstraat 81, tel. 020/676–8695), and **Gaudi** (P.C. Hooftstraat 116, tel. 020/679–9319).

Shoes and Hats For men, try **Smit Bally** (Leidsestraat 41, tel. 020/624–8862). For women's shoes, three of the best shops are **Bally Shoes** (Leidsestraat 8–10, tel. 020/622–2888), **Charles Adams** (P.C. Hooftstraat 90, tel. 020/662–3835), and **Shoe Ba Loo** (Koningsplein 7, tel. 020/626–7993). The well-stocked **Houden M/V** (422 Herengracht, tel. 020/626–3038), in a canal house, carries Borsalino hats for men and women as well as Dutch and international designer hats.

Women's Clothes Dutch women are conscious of their clothes, although they tend to be conservative in both style and colors. The department stores carry mainstream styles, but boutiques along the side streets between the canals and in the Jordaan neighborhood are where generation after generation of experimental designers have set up shop to show their imaginative creations. Antique- and used-clothing shops also can be found in these parts of town. Two Dutch minichains stand out among the crowd for the quality of both design and craftsmanship: **Claudia Strater** (Beethovenstraat 9, tel. 020/673–6605) and **Boetiek Pauw** (van Baerlestrasse 66 and 72, tel. 020/662–6253), which also operates men's and children's shops. At Spui, you will find **Esprit** (tel. 020/626–3624), but some of the best shopping for women's clothes in a variety of styles is in the P.C. Hooftstraat/Van Baerlestraat shopping area, including **Reflections** (P.C. Hooftstraat 66, tel. 020/664–0040), **Champs Élysées** (Strawinskylaan 63, tel. 020/671–6499), **Benetton** (P.C. Hooftstraat 72, tel. 020/679–5706), **Alain Manoukian** (P.C. Hooftstraat 95, tel. 020/673–3822), **Max Mara** (P.C. Hooftstraat 110, tel. 020/671–7742), **Leeser** (P.C. Hooftstraat 117, tel. 020/679–5020), **Azzurro** (Van Baerlestraat 17, tel. 020/671–6804), and designer **Edgar Vos** (P.C. Hooftstraat 134, tel. 020/662–6336).

Sports and Fitness

Biking The most convenient places to rent a bicycle are **Centraal Station** (Stationsplein 12, 1012 AB, tel. 020/624–8391) and **McBike** (Marnixstraat 220, 1016 TL, tel. 020/626–6964). Expect to pay from Fl 10 per day, plus a deposit from Fl 50 to Fl 200 per bicycle.

Golf The new and luxurious **Golf Resort Purmerend** (NHM Hotels, Westerweg 60, 1445 AD Purmerend, tel. 02990/81666) is now open outside Amsterdam in Noord Holland province.

Health Clubs Several hotels in Amsterdam have fitness facilities for guests; these facilities generally include exercise machines, weights, sauna, and whirlpool. The **Holiday Inn Crowne Plaza** (N.Z. Voorburgwal 5, 1012 RC, tel. 020/620–0500) has a large indoor swimming pool. Two of the more comprehensive hotel-based fitness facilities are **Splash Sonesta** (Kattengat 1, tel. 020/621–2223) and **Splash Palace Executive Fitness Club** (Prins Hendrikkade 59–72, tel. 020/556–4899), both of which offer personal training, aerobics, weight training, massage, solarium, Turkish bath, sauna, and whirlpool. **Sporting Club Leidseplein** (18 Korte Leidsedwarsstraat, tel. 020/620–6631) offers fitness facilities, sauna, and superfast tanners. Day rates at all of the above are Fl 25, with extra charges for special services.

Jogging Sunday morning is about the only time when Amsterdam's city center gets enough of a break from foot, bike, and car traffic to allow for a comfortable jog. **Vondelpark** (Vondel Park), near the art museums, and **Oosterpark** (Eastern Park), behind the Tropenmuseum, are the only parks within the city proper. Beyond the city near the suburb of

Amstelveen, **Amsterdamse Bos** (Amsterdam Woods) is a large, spacious place to run.

Squash   The **Sporting Club Leidseplein** (18 Korte Leidsedwarsstraat, tel. 020/620–6631) is a squash and fitness club. There are eight courts; the use of a sauna is included, and you can rent equipment and take lessons. Day cards for all facilities are Fl 25, weekdays until 4 PM; services are priced separately evenings and weekends.

Spectator Sports

Rowing   There are monthly rowing events organized by Stedelijk Beheer Sport en Recreatie (tel. 020/643–1414) in **Amsterdamse Bos** (Amsterdam Woods), a large park south of the city. There are also canoeing events four times a year in the Bos. In the city the **Dutch Marine Academy** stages a rowing event (tel. 020/624–7699) on the canals in September.

Soccer   Soccer is a near obsession with the Dutch, and if you want to impress an Amsterdam host, you would best be advised to know the current standing of the local team, Ajax (pronounced "eye-axe"), relative to that of its archrivals, Rotterdam's Feyenoord (pronounced "fienord") and PSV (Philips Sports Vereninging). The Dutch soccer season runs from August to June, with a short break in midwinter; matches are played at the **Ajaxstadion** (Ajax Stadium; Middenweg 401, tel. 020/665–4440).

Beaches

After their long, dreary winter, Amsterdammers count the days until they can hit the beaches at **Zandvoort,** a beach community directly west of the city, beyond Haarlem, where clean beachfront stretches for miles and many of the dunes are open for walking. The train station is close by, and there are lifeguards on duty. Separate areas of the beach are reserved for nudists, though topless bathing is common practice everywhere in the Netherlands.

Dining

Amsterdammers enjoy good food, particularly when shared with good company. In couples or small groups, they seek out the quieter, cozier places or go in search of the new culinary stars of the city; to celebrate or entertain, they return to the institutions that never disappoint them with the quality of their cuisine or service; and in large groups, you invariably find the Dutch trooping into their favorite Indonesian restaurant to share a rijsttafel. The city's more than 700 restaurants span a wide variety of ethnic cuisines; you'll find everything from international fast-food joints to chandeliered waterfront dining rooms frequented by the royal family. In between are small, chef-owned establishments on the canals and their side streets, restaurants that have stood the test of time on the basis of service, ambience, and consistency.

$$$$ **Beddington's.** The decor is eye-catching, and the location is good: Near the Concertgebouw and the art museums, Beddington's sits at the junction between the business district and the city's most prestigious modern residential neighborhoods. The chef, an Englishwoman, takes a multicultural approach in the kitchen, mixing Japanese and other East Asian flavors and concepts with others from England, Spain, and the West Indies. A sample of the sort of imaginative meal you might put together for yourself here would be

zeeduivel (monkfish) tandoori followed by—why not?—trifle. *Roelof Hartstraat 6–8, tel. 020/676–5201. Reservations advised. Jacket required. AE, DC, MC, V. Closed Sun.*

$$$$ Dikker en Thijs. This gracious restaurant, which opened in 1915, overlooks the busy corner of the Leidestraat and the Prinsengracht from the second floor of a French-style, late-19th-century building. It is a quiet place, with large well-spaced tables and patient service that encourages you to linger over coffee. Chefs Wim Bastiaanse and Jan Borst have brought an imaginative touch to the establishment's traditional cuisine. Try the turbot salad on artichoke hearts with olive paste, lamb cutlet with salami, or zeeduivel with sauerkraut. *Prinsengracht 444, tel. 020/626–7721. Reservations advised. Jacket and tie required. AE, DC, MC, V. Closed Sun. and Aug. 3–16.*

$$$$ Excelsior. The Excelsior's view over the Amstel River, to the
★ Muntplein on one side and to the Music Theater on the other, is the best there is in Amsterdam. The dining room is a gracious, chandeliered hall with plenty of room for diners, waiters, dessert trolleys, preparation carts, towering palms, tall candelabras, and the grand piano. The approach is traditional French with a twist: You might choose a lobster bisque or an adventurous dish such as smoked veal over a mound of marinated tuna, or cod with truffle galettes. For dessert, try the orange pie with frozen yogurt. There are five fixed-price menus. *Hotel de L'Europe, Nieuwe Doelenstraat 2–8, tel. 020/623–4836. Reservations advised. Jacket and tie required. AE, DC, MC, V.*

$$$$ De Kersentuin. The name of this cheerful, high-ceilinged restaurant, which means "cherry orchard," signals the overwhelming color scheme that extends from the dinnerware to the decor. It is a good place for a leisurely meal, although service occasionally leaves something to be desired. Although there are large windows overlooking a residential street, the star of the show is chef Rudolf Bos: The kitchen is open behind glass panels, and you are welcome to watch the chef and his staff prepare French dishes with a Far Eastern twist, such as perch flavored with coconut and spicy Thai sauce, or calf's sweetbreads marinated in soya sauce and ginger. *Dijsselhofplantsoen 7, tel. 020/664–2121. Reservations required. Jacket and tie required. AE, DC, MC, V. Closed Sun. No lunch.*

$$$$ 't Swarte Schaep. This cozy upstairs restaurant overlooking the
★ noisy Leidseplein, named after a legendary black sheep that roamed the area in the 17th century, is a study in traditional Dutch decor, with copper pots hanging from the wooden beams and heavily framed paintings on the walls. Together with this Old Holland atmosphere, the excellent French cuisine—which includes chateaubriand with béarnaise sauce and lobster mousse with asparagus salad—sometimes attracts members of the Dutch Royal Family during their incognito visits to the capital. Dinner orders are accepted until 11 PM—late even for Amsterdam. *Korte Leidsdwarsstraat 24, tel. 020/622–3021. Reservations required. Jacket and tie advised. AE, DC, MC, V.*

$$$$ De Trechter. This very small restaurant beside a canal in the residential part of the city has a very big reputation, so reservations are absolutely necessary—if you can get them. Chef Jan de Wit offers such specialties as carpaccio of Angus beef and Scotch salmon, fillet of lamb in potato crust with ratatouille and rosemary sauce, or smoked oxtails with cubes of goose liver, garlic mayonnaise, and croutons. *Hobbemakade 62–63, tel. 020/671–1263, fax 020/685–2571. Reservations required.Jacket and tie required. AE, DC, MC, V. Closed Sun.–Mon. No lunch.*

$$$ Café Americain. Though thousands of buildings in Amsterdam are
★ designated as historic monuments, the one that houses this restau-

rant is the only structure whose interior, an Art Deco treasure, is also protected. Opened in 1882 and said to have been the site of Mata Hari's wedding reception, the Americain is a hybird restaurant-café serving everything from light snacks to full dinners. To one side are formal tables draped with white linens, where traditional entrées such as medallions of beef with béarnaise sauce are served; to the other side are tiny bare-topped tables, perfect for a quick coffee and pastry. There is a well-stocked buffet complete with hot dishes, salads, and desserts. *American Hotel, Leidsekade 97, tel. 020/624–5322. No reservations. Dress: casual but neat. AE, DC, MC, V.*

$$$ **Christophe.** After Christophe Royer opened his *eet tempel* (eating temple) on a small cross canal between the Keizersgracht and Prinsengracht, not far from the Anne Frank House, he and his all-French kitchen staff quickly became recognized for their fine French cuisine. Specialties include Indian corn soup with oysters, *crevettes à l'orange* (shrimp with orange sauce), and *pigeon à la marocaine* (pigeon cooked with coriander and other tangy spices); there is also a selection of vegetarian dishes. The menu may be special, but at Christophe's, the welcoming atmosphere and personalized service are worth noting as well. *Leliegracht 46, tel. 020/625–0807. Reservations required. Jacket and tie required. AE, DC, MC, V. Closed Sun.–Mon., New Year's week, and 2 weeks in July–Aug.*

$$$ **Dynasty.** At this trendy, interesting spot, the decor is a fanciful mating of Oriental and art deco. A mural in red, white, and black encircles the room, and dozens of amber and dove-gray Chinese paper umbrellas hang upended from the ceiling. Chef K. Y. Lee's menu is as fascinating as the decor: The medley of Asian cuisines includes authentically prepared, classic Chinese dishes, such as Three Meats in Harmony, and selections from the cuisines of Thailand, Malaysia, and Vietnam. There are two fixed-price menus. *Reguliersdwarsstraat 30, tel. 020/626–8400. Reservations advised. Jacket required. AE, DC, MC, V. Closed Tues.*

$$$ **De Silveren Spieghel.** Owner Ben van den Nieuwboer gives you his
★ personal attention, including offering wines from his own French vineyard, as you sit at one of the scattered tables of this restaurant in a delightfully crooked 17th-century house. The cuisine is French-influenced but uses the best of such local ingredients as the lamb from the island of Texel and the honey of Amsterdam's Vondelpark. The seasonally changing game dishes are always worth trying and the fixed-price menus represent excellent value for the money. *Kattengat 4–6, tel. 020/624–6589. Reservations required. Jacket and tie advised. AE, MC, V.*

$$$ **Tout Court.** Chef John Fagel, who hails from a well-known Dutch
★ family of chefs, has stuck by his intention to serve "good food without a fuss." This comfortable, casual restaurant is tucked away on a side street between the canals: You'll know it by the napkins that hang in the window, as if strung on a laundry line. The menu is direct and uncomplicated, with selections such as roast rib of lamb with basil, guinea fowl stuffed with mushrooms, roast brill with leeks, and watercress soup. At dinner there are three menus, including a seven-course feast. *Runstraat 13, tel. 020/625–8637. Reservations advised for dinner. Dress: casual but neat. AE, DC, MC, V. Closed Sun.–Mon.*

$$$ **D'Vijff Vlieghen.** Dining in a traditional canal-house environment is part of the Amsterdam experience, though you are more likely to find yourself seated among closely packed tables of Swedes and Japanese than among Dutch diners. But don't let that stop you; the "Five Flies" is a charming spot. Housed in five adjoining houses that date from 1627, the restaurant incorporates a series of small, timbered dining rooms, each well adorned with mementoes and bric-a-brac ranging from music boxes, liqueur kegs, and violin cases to two etchings by Rembrandt. The kitchen, long a bastion of traditional Dutch meat-and-potatoes cooking, is now drawing on fresh local ingredients in such dishes as smoked calves' tongue on spinach, baby turbot with bay, and pheasant with endive. Judge for yourself whether it's overpriced, as some diners attest. *Spuistraat 294–302, tel. 020/624–8369. Reservations advised. Jacket and tie required. AE, DC, MC, V.*

$$$ **Yamazoto.** The chef at this restaurant, lauded by Japanese residents as the best in town, tempers his fidelity to the traditions in which he has been trained with a few concessions to local taste—there are more beef dishes than usual on a traditional Japanese menu. A full seasonal set menu costs Fl 100, but there are scores of less pricey options. There is a separate sushi bar and a teppanyaki restaurant, which specializes in table-side grilling. *Hotel Okura, Ferdinand Bolstraat 333, tel. 020/678–7111. Reservations required. Jacket and tie advised. AE, DC, MC, V.*

$$–$$$ **Lucius.** The plain setting and the simple service belie the fact that this is one of the best fish restaurants in town. On the marine menu, your choices range from fishburgers with gorgonzola cheese to grilled lobster. The wine list includes a good selection from California and even a Dutch wine from Apostlehoeve in Limburg province, the country's only vineyard. *Spuistraat 247, tel. 020/624–1831. Reservations required. Dress: casual but neat. AE, DC, MC, V. Closed Sun.*

$$–$$$ **Pier 10.** This intimate restaurant, perched on the end of a pier be-
★ hind the Centraal Station, was built in the 1930s as a shipping office. Ask for a table in the tiny glass-enclosed room at the far end of the restaurant, where you can see the water lap gently beneath the windows and the harbor lights twinkle in the distance. Owner-chef Steve Muzerie sometimes comes up with odd combinations such as licorice mousse with a sauce made from *advocaat* (a liqueur made with beaten egg yolks, sugar, and spirit), but his culinary inventions are usually delicious. Try the eel with herb sauce or goose with smoked mushrooms. *De Ruyterkade Steiger 10, tel. 020/624–8276. Reservations required. Dress: casual but neat. AE, MC, V.*

$$ **Bodega Keyzer.** After 85 years spent serving musicians, concert
★ goers, and residents of the neighborhoods surrounding the art museums and Concertgebouw, this half restaurant, half café-bodega has evolved into something as familiar and comfortable as an old shoe. You can come in almost any attire, at almost any hour, for a simple drink or a full meal. The interior is paneled with dark woods, the lights are dim, and Oriental carpets cover the tables. The menu is equally traditional—among the meat and fish selections are tournedos, schnitzel, and sole meunière—though you may also come across a more adventurous *ris de veau* (veal sweetbreads) with orange and green pepper sauce or fricassee of veal with nut-basil sauce. *Van Baerlestraat 96, tel. 020/671–1441. Reservations advised. Dress: casual but neat. AE, DC, MC, V. Closed Sun.*

$$ **Brasserie Lido.** The Brasserie is the heart of the new Lido dining and casino complex at Leidseplein; it is a relaxing place, with tall windows overlooking the boardwalk and terrace to the canal. It's open all day and into the night for everything from breakfast and light snacks to complete suppers. Choices include quiche and French or Dutch breakfasts, and for dinner, leg of rabbit with leeks and prunes. *Leidsekade 105, tel. 020/626–2106. No reservations. Dress: casual. AE, DC, MC, V.*

$$ **Brasserie van Baerle.** Begun as a neighborhood lunch and Sunday brunch restaurant, this bright, appealing spot with an uncompli- cated European modern decor now even draws late diners who come

Dining

Beddington's, **35**
Bodega Keyzer, **33**
Brasserie Lido, **26**
Brasserie
van Baerle, **34**
Cafe Americain, **19**
Caffe Esprit, **16**
Christophe, **7**
De Kersentuin, **36**
De Keuken van 1870, **3**
De Kooning
van Siam, **9**
De Oesterbar, **21**
De Silveren
Spieghel, **2**
De Trechter, **38**
Dikker en Thijs, **16**
D'Vijff Vlieghen, **14**
Dynasty, **22**
Excelsior, **25**
Haesje Claes, **15**
Lucius, **11**
Meghna, **30**
Padi Mas, **27**
Pier 10, **5**
Rose's Cantina, **23**
Sama Sebo, **29**
Sluizer, **31**
't Swarte Schaep, **20**
Tony's Pasta and Pizza
Company, **24**
Toscanini, **1**
Tout Court, **12**
Yamazoto, **37**

Lodging

Ambassade, **13**
American, **19**
Amstel Hotel, **39**
Botel, **6**
Canal House, **8**
Hotel de l'Europe, **25**
Golden Tulip Barbizon
Palace, **4**
Grand Amsterdam, **17**
Hotel de Filosoof, **32**
Jan Luyken, **28**
Pulitzer, **10**
Quentin Hotel, **18**

Amsterdam Dining and Lodging

Het IJ

5

ⓘ M CENTRAAL STATION Front

Centraal Station

M

de Ruyterkade

2
3

Ofen
Prins Hendrikkade
Haven
Nieuwendijk
Spuistr.
Singel

4

Zeedijk
Oudezijdskolk

Oosterdokskade
6

Damrak
Oudebrugsteeg
9
Zeedijk
Geldersekade
Prins
Waals
Binnen
Hendrikkade

Oosterdok

N

Damrak
Beursstraat
Warmoesstraat

Bantam Oude waal
kant eilandsgracht
Recht Boomssloot

Dam ⓘ
Damstraat
Oude Zijds Voorburgwal
Achter
burgwal
St. Antoniebreestr.
Koningsstr.
M NIEUW- MARKT

Schans
Rapenburg

Kalverstraat
Rokin
Nes

Oude
Zijds
Oude Hoogstr.
Nieuwe Hoogstr.
Raamgr.
Krombogntstoat
Oude

Nieuwe Uilenburgerstraat
Anr. rankstr.
Valkenburgerstraat
Rapenburgerstraat

17
Oude
Klovenniersburgwal
nenburwal
Jodenbreestraat
Uilenburggracht

6
UI

Nieuwe Doelenstr.
Staalstraat
Groen
Zwd burgwal
25

Mr. Visser- plein
Muiderstraat
gracht
Heren
Wertheim Park
Plantage Parklaan
Plantage Middenlaan

Rokin
Singel
Amstel
Amstel
Nieuwe Amstel
M WATERLOOPLEIN
Heren

24
Reguliersdwarsstraat
Rembrandt plein
Amstelstr.
Blauwbrug
Nieuwe

3
Vijzelstraat
Heren
gracht
Utrechtsestraat
Amstel
Nieuwe
Keizersgracht
Weesperstraat
Kerkstraat

Keizersgracht
Reguliers
Kerkstraat Magere Brug
Nieuwe
Prinsengracht

Prinsengracht
gracht
30 31
Nieuwe
Nieuwe Achter
gr.

arstr.
Vijzelgracht
Noorderstr.
Nieuwe Looiersstr.
Utrechtse dwarsstraat
Amstel
Valckenierstraat
M Sarphatistraat
WEESPERPLEIN

F. Bol Straat
etering Pl.
Wetering Scharis
Frederiks plein
Sarphatistraat
39
Mauritskade

Den Texstraat
Nicolaas Witsen Kade
Stadhouderskade

KEY

ⓘ Tourist Information
M Metro Stops
Metro Lines
Tram Lines
Railroad

0   220 yards
0   200 meters

following performances at the nearby Concertgebouw. The chef's creativity is the main attraction. Imaginative dishes from the kitchen include spicy Oriental salads and heavier fare such as duck in truffle sauce. There is outdoor dining in good weather. *Van Baerlestraat 158, tel. 020/679–1532. Reservations accepted. Dress: casual but neat. AE, DC, MC, V. Closed Sat., Dec. 25–Jan. 2.*

$$ Haesje Claes. This is as Old Dutch cozy as you can get. The beams are dark and heavy, the walls are chockablock with copper pots and farmstead curios, and the lamp shades that hang low over the tabletops are draped with kerchiefs in the traditional way to shadow the light. The food, too, is Old Dutch. Come here for calves' liver with bacon and onions, or tournedos with pepper sauce. A nightly tourist menu is served; there also is a children's menu. The prices are as basic as the food. *Spuistraat 273–275, tel. 020/624–9998. Reservations advised. Dress: casual. AE, DC, MC, V. Closed Sun.*

$$ De Kooning van Siam. This Thai restaurant, which is favored by the city's Thai residents, sits smack in the middle of the red-light district, but don't let that keep you away. Although the beams and wall panels are still visible in this old canal house, there is nothing Old Dutch about the furniture or the wall decorations. Choices are somewhat limited: Selections might include very hot stir-fried beef with onion and chili peppers, or a milder chicken and Chinese vegetables with coconut, curry, and basil. *Oude Zijds Voorburgwal 42, tel. 020/623–7293. Reservations accepted. Jacket advised. AE, DC, MC, V. Closed Feb.*

$$ Meghna. This comfortable, friendly Indian eatery is part of a small restaurant row among the neighborhood shops of the Utrechtsestraat. Small and darkly decorated, it is the pride and joy of owner–chef Roy Sankar. Prices are quite reasonable, and there are two fixed-price menus: Choices include *rogan josh* (lamb cooked with tomatoes and spices), a mild and creamy East Indian fish curry, or chicken tandoori badami with cashew nuts. *Utrechtsestraat 28, tel. 020/625–1392. Reservations accepted. Dress: casual but neat. AE, DC, MC, V.*

$$ De Oesterbar. "The Oyster Bar," like its namesake in New York, is an Amsterdam institution and the first place to think of when you hanker for a half-dozen oysters fresh from the Oosterschelde or the simply prepared catch of the day. The choices are straightforward: grilled, baked, or fried fish served with tartar sauce, potatoes, and salad. Live lobster is also available in season. The no-nonsense main-floor room, which has a small bar at the back, has white tile walls incorporating nautical murals and a long row of eerily lighted fish tanks along one side. In the upstairs dining room, the mood is oddly bordellolike, with the elaborately patterned wallpaper and the assortment of innocuous paintings punctuating the walls. *Leidseplein 10, tel. 020/623–2988. Reservations advised. Dress: casual but neat. AE, DC, MC.*

$$ Padi Mas. The new owners have high hopes that, with their fresh, lively interpretations of traditional Indonesian dishes, this restaurant will be the next star in the firmament of top Dutch restaurants. Found among the shops on the fashionable P.C. Hooftstraat shopping street, this small dining room is also convenient to the Concertgebouw and the art museums. Two rijsttafels are served (with 15 and 17 dishes), and a children's menu is available. *P.C. Hooftstraat 87, tel. 020/664–6421. Reservations advised. Dress: casual but neat. AE, DC, MC, V.*

$$ Rose's Cantina. A perennial favorite of the sparkling set, this restaurant serves up spicy Tex-Mex food and lethal cocktails. The noise level can be lethal, too. Pop in for a full meal or sundowner.

Reguliersdwarsstraat 38, tel. 020/625–9797. Dress: casual. Reservations advised. AE, DC, MC, V.

$$ Sluizer. Sluizer is really two side-by-side restaurants—one serves only meat, the other only fish. Both are simply decorated and unpretentious; both are known for good food that is honestly prepared without a lot of fanfare or creativity; both are known to be reasonably priced; and, not surprisingly, both are crowded every night. *Utrechtsestraat 43–45, tel. 020/622–6376 (meat restaurant) or 020/626–3557 (fish restaurant). Reservations advised. Dress: casual. AE, DC, MC, V.*

$$ Toscanini. This cavernous, noisy Italian restaurant is very popular
★ with local trendies. The food is superb. You'll find pasta with game sauce, subtle fresh fish dishes such as trout with fresh basil, and other delights as well as such familiar favorites as antipasti, which are scrumptious here. And there's not a pizza in sight. *Lindengracht 75, tel. 020/623–2813. Reservations required. Dress: casual. No credit cards. Closed Tues. No lunch.*

$ Caffe Esprit. Clean-cut and trendy, it has tall windows that overlook
★ the busy Spui square; the decor is simple black, white, and gray. There is just a handful of small tables, with a small counter to take care of overflow. The menu is contemporary American in character, with choices such as a Surf Burger garnished with avocado and bacon, or an Archie Bunker burger covered with melted Swiss cheese. Salads include Chinese almond chicken and spinach salad with hot tarragon mustard dressing. There also are pastas, pizzas, and sandwiches; at breakfast (served until noon) fresh-squeezed orange juice is available, as well as yogurt with muesli and scones with butter and jam. There is a children's menu. *Spui 10, tel. 020/627–8281. No reservations. Dress: casual. No credit cards. Closed Sun.*

$ De Keuken van 1870. "The Kitchen of 1870" was a soup kitchen throughout the Great Depression and two world wars and now serves up hearty Dutch food at unbeatably low prices. Tourists, punks, and pensioners sit at plain wooden tables spread about a traditional black-and-white tiled floor. The steamy kitchen maintains a constant outpouring of enormous white plates piled high with substantial meat stews, potatoes, and vegetables. Late-nighters take note: The kitchen closes at 8 PM. *Spuistraat 4, tel. 020/624–8965. No reservations. Dress: casual. No credit cards.*

$ Sama Sebo. Come to this small, busy, and relaxed neighborhood Indonesian restaurant near the State Museum for rijsttafel, a simple *bami goreng* (spicy fried rice with vegetables), or a lunch of *nasi goreng* (spicy fried noodles with vegetables). The colors are muted tans and browns with rush mats covering the walls. When things are busy, the restaurant can be somewhat cramped. *P.C. Hoofstraat 27, tel. 020/662–8146. Reservations accepted. Dress: casual. AE, DC, MC, V. Closed Sun.*

$ Tony's Pasta and Pizza Company. Not all the restaurants on the Reguliersdwarsstraat are expensive. Tony's is a bright, cheerful place decorated in Italian red, white, and green, with small white tables and stiff black chairs that don't encourage anyone to linger. Pizzas, pastas, and simple grilled meats are on the menu. *Reguliersdwarsstraat 55, tel. 020/627–3833. Reservations not necessary. Dress: casual. AE, DC, MC, V.*

Lodging

There are some 270 hotels from which to choose in Amsterdam, though most are small mom-and-pop operations, best described as pensions, found along and among the canals or in residential neighborhoods beyond the center. The larger hotels, including the expensive international chains, are clustered in the area around Central Station, at Dam Square, and near Leidseplein. Amsterdam is a busy city; reservations are advised at any time of the year and absolutely necessary in tulip season (late Mar.–June). Should you arrive without a room, the **VVV Logiesservice** (VVV Accommodation Service, Stationsplein 10 or Leidsestraat 106, open Easter–Sept., daily 9–5; Oct.–Easter, Mon.–Sat. 9–5), a same-day hotel booking service, can help you find a room for a modest service charge of Fl 3.50.

$$$$ ★ **Amstel Hotel.** This grand 125-year-old hotel reopened in 1992 with a completely new interior designed by Pierre Yves Rochon of Paris, who has created a Dutch atmosphere with a European touch. Rooms are still the most spacious in the city; the new decor is like that of a gracious home, with Oriental rugs, brocade upholstery, Delft lamps, and a color scheme that borrows from the warm tones of Makkum pottery. Everything about this hotel has been reconsidered and redesigned, including the format of its well-known restaurant, La Rive, where there's now a special table from which you can watch your meal being prepared. *Professor Tulpplein 1, tel. 020/ 622–6060, fax 020/622–5808. 79 rooms.Facilities: 2 restaurants, sauna, fitness center, swimming pool. AE, DC, MC, V.*

$$$$ **Golden Tulip Barbizon Palace.** One of the newest hotels in Amsterdam also has one of the most convenient locations, directly across from the Centraal Station. The exterior was designed to blend with the neighboring row of old houses, which overlook the inner harbor. Inside, the historic mood disappears in the face of the towering, skylighted, Roman-atrium-style lobby, which stretches across the length of the hotel, with cafés, shops, restaurants, and club rooms opening to the sides. Guest rooms are small, but they are decorated nicely and support the Old Dutch theme with dark beams across the ceilings. *Prins Hendrikkade 59–72, tel. 020/556–4564, fax 020/624– 3353. 268 rooms. Facilities: 2 restaurants, fitness center. AE, DC, MC, V.*

$$$$ **The Grand Amsterdam.** This hotel is on a historically important site: it was built into a group of buildings dating from the 14th century that served for more than 185 years as the Town Hall of Amsterdam. Maria de Medici once stayed here, as did William of Orange, and it was the site of Queen Beatrix's wedding. Today's hotel is deluxe, with Gobelin tapestries, Jugendstil stained-glass windows, and, in the café, a wall mural by Karl Appel created early in his career to repay a debt to the city of Amsterdam. The rooms, which vary in size, are attractively done in deep tones of burgundy damask and bold floral prints; the best of them overlook the garden courtyard. *Oude Zijds Voorburgwal 197, tel. 020/555–3111, fax 020/555–3222. 166 rooms. Facilities: 2 restaurants, sauna, solarium, heated swimming pool. AE, DC, MC, V.*

$$$$ ★ **Hotel de l'Europe.** Quiet, gracious, and understated in both decor and service, this hotel overlooking the Amstel River, the Muntplein, and the flower market, near the Music Theater boasts one of Amsterdam's most convenient locations. The city-side rooms, recently redecorated, are full of warm, rich colors; the riverside rooms are done in pastel shades and brilliant whites, and have French windows to let in floods of light. The marble baths are large and luxurious. A junior suite might be a worthwhile choice here. *Nieuwe Doelenstraat 2–8, tel. 020/623–4836, fax 020/624–2962. 101 rooms. Facilities: restaurant, sauna, solarium, fitness room, small swimming pool. AE, DC, MC, V.*

$$$ ★ **American.** The American, one of the oldest hotels in Amsterdam, is housed in one of the city's most fancifully designed buildings. Its location directly on the Leidseplein is ideal for anyone who likes to be in the middle of everything—nightlife, dining, sightseeing, and shopping are all at hand. Rooms are comfortably sized and furnished in an art deco style. *Leidseplein 28, tel. 020/624–5322, fax 020/625–3236. 188 rooms. Facilities: restaurant, fitness room. AE, DC, MC, V.*

$$$ Pulitzer. Twenty-four 17th-century houses were combined to create this hotel, which faces both the Prinsengracht and the Keizersgracht canals and is just a short walk from Dam Square; the place retains a historic ambience. Most guest rooms have beamed ceilings; there are gardens in the middle of the block. From here you may hear the hourly chiming of the nearby Westerkerk clock. Recent renovations have added comfort and convenience. *Prinsengracht 315–331, tel. 020/523–5235, fax 020/626–2646. 236 rooms. Facilities: restaurant. AE, DC, MC, V.*

$$ ★ Ambassade. Nine 17th- and 18th-century canal-side houses have been joined to create this hotel, which is elegantly decorated with Oriental rugs, chandeliers, and antiques. The canal-side rooms are spacious, with large windows and solid, functional furniture. The rooms at the rear are quieter, but smaller and darker. Service is attentive and friendly. *Herengracht 355–353 (entrance at 341), tel. 020/626–2333, fax 020/624–5321. 44 rooms, 5 suites, 1 apartment. Facilities: lounge. AE, DC, MC, V.*

$$ ★ Canal House. This is what you imagine a canal-house hotel to be like: a beautiful old home with high plastered ceilings, antique furniture, and old paintings, and a backyard garden bursting with plants and flowers. Every room is unique in both size and decor. The elegant chandeliered breakfast room overlooks the garden, and there is a small bar in the front parlor. The American owners have put a lot of love and style into the Canal House: The result is an intimate hotel that seems more like the private home of a well-to-do family. *Keizersgracht 148, tel. 020/622–5182, fax 020/624–2962. 26 rooms with bath. Facilities: breakfast room, elevator. AE, DC, MC, V.*

$$ Hotel de Filosoof. This hotel in a quiet street near the Vondel Park attracts artists, thinkers, and people looking for something a little different; bona fide Amsterdam philosophers are regularly to be found in the salon's comfy armchairs. Each room is decorated with a different cultural motif—there's an Aristotle room furnished in Greek style, with passages from the works of Greek philosophers hung on the walls, and a Goethe room adorned with Faustian texts. *Anna van den Vondelstraat 6, tel. 020/683–3013, fax 020/685–3750. 27 rooms, 23 with bath. Facilities: lounge, bar. AE, MC, V.*

$ Botel. This floating hotel, moored near the Centraal Station, is an appropriate lodging in watery Amsterdam. The rooms are cabinlike, but the portholes have been replaced by windows that provide fine views of the city across the water. Make sure you don't get a room on the land side of the vessel, or you'll end up staring at an ugly postal sorting office. *Oosterdokskade 224, tel. 020/626–4247, fax 020/639–1952. 176 rooms. AE, DC, MC, V.*

$ ★ Jan Luyken. This small, out-of-the-way place is barely noticeable among the homes and offices of a residential Amsterdam neighborhood. The personal approach is a relaxing alternative to the large hotels, yet it also is well equipped to handle the needs of the many business travelers who stay here regularly, with office services and small meeting rooms available. *Jan Luykenstraat 58, tel. 020/573–0730, fax 020/676–3841. 63 rooms. Facilities: elevators. AE, DC, MC, V.*

$ Quentin Hotel. This small, family-run hotel is just a stone's throw from the hectic Leidseplein. It is simply decorated with plain colors and modern prints, and large windows allow for a flood of light. The best rooms are the spacious corner ones that overlook a canal. Unfortunately, no room has its own bathing facilities. *Leidsekade 89, tel.*

020/626–2187, fax 020/622–0121. 16 rooms without bath. AE, MC, V.

The Arts and Nightlife

The Arts More than 18,000 performances are staged each year in Amsterdam's theaters, churches, museums, and assorted venues. The arts overflow into the streets as well: There are barrel organs playing on the shopping streets, carillon concerts from the church towers, and impromptu street performances at locations such as Dam Square and Leidseplein.

The grand and elegant new **Muziektheater** (Music Theater, Waterlooplein) is Amsterdam's equivalent of Lincoln Center in New York. It seats 1,600 people and is home to both the Netherlands Opera and the Netherlands National Ballet; it also hosts international opera, ballet, and chamber orchestra performances throughout the year.

Amsterdam's theater and music season begins in September and runs through June, when the Holland Festival of Performing Arts is held. *What's On in Amsterdam* is a comprehensive, English-language publication distributed by the tourist office that lists art and performing-arts events around the city. Look, too, for a magazine called *Time Out Amsterdam;* it is a bimonthly English-language publication sold on newsstands that includes advertisements and listings for movies and clubs. Reserve tickets to performances at the major theaters before your arrival through the **National Reservation Center** (Postbus 404, 2260 AK Leidschendam, tel. 3170/320–2500, fax 070/320–2611). Tickets can also be purchased in person at the tourist information offices through the **VVV Theater Booking Office** (Stationsplein 10; open Mon.–Sat. 10–4), at the **AUB Ticketshop** (Leidseplein/corner Marnixstraat; open Mon.–Sat. 10–6, tel. 020/ 621–1211), or at theater box offices.

Multicultural Performances Three stages known for their eclectic mix of offerings are **Akhnaton** (Nieuwezijdskolk 25, tel. 020/624–3396), which is a multicultural stage that offers, for example, South American or African music at Friday and Saturday night performances; **Paradiso** (Weteringschans 6, tel. 020/623–7348), a former church with a calendar of various national and international offerings; and **De Melkweg** (Lijnbaansgracht 234A, tel. 020/624–1777 or 020/624–8492), internationally known as a multicultural center for music, theater, film, and dance, with live music performances at least four nights a week.

Music Amsterdam's critically acclaimed **Koninklijk Concertgebouworkest** (Royal Concert Orchestra) is often joined by other internationally known performers. There are two concert halls, large and small, under one roof at the **Concertgebouw** (Concertgebouwplein 2–6, tel. 020/671–8345). Contemporary music is on the program at **IJsbreker** (Weesperzijde 23, tel. 020/668–1805).

Opera and Ballet **De Nederlandse Opera** (The Netherlands National Opera) and **Het Nationale Ballet** (The Netherlands National Ballet) are the resident companies at Amsterdam's **Muziektheater** (Waterlooplein, tel. 020/ 625–5455). Both offer largely classical repertoires, but the dance company has, in recent years, gained a large measure of fame throughout Europe for its performances of 20th-century ballets as well.

Theater/Cabaret Performances of American and British plays as well as English-language revues and cabaret are common in multilingual Amsterdam, and touring companies from Broadway and West End musical hits come to town on a regular basis. For traditional theater, check the program of **Stadsschouwburg** (Leidseplein 26, 020/624–2311); for large-scale productions, **Koninklijk Theater Carre** (Amstel 115–125, tel. 020/622–5225); and for cabaret, **Kleine Komedie** (Amstel 56–58, tel. 020/624–0534). Amsterdam's off-Broadway-type theaters, **Frascati** (Nes 63, tel. 020/623–5723 or 020/623–5724) and **Brakke Grond** (Nes 45, central box office tel. 020/626–6866), are found on a small street off Dam Square.

Film First-run American feature films are common and are usually shown undubbed: It's like you never left home. Cinemas are concentrated near the Leidseplein; the largest is the seven-screen **City 1–7** (Kleine Garmanplantsoen 13–25, tel. 020/623–4579); directly across the street is the four-screen **Alfa 1–4** (Kleine Gartmanplantsoen 4A, tel. 020/627–8806). Also near Leidseplein are **Alhambra 1–2** (Weterinschans 134, near Frederiksplein, tel. 020/623–3192), **Bellevue Cinerama** (Marnixstraat 400, tel. 020/623–4876), and **Calypso** (Marnixstraat 402, tel. 020/626–6227). Worth visiting if only to have the pleasure of sitting in its Art Deco auditorium is the **Tuschinski** (Reguliersbreestraat 26, tel. 020/626–2633).

Puppets/ The young and the young at heart will enjoy puppet and marionette
Marionettes shows at **Amsterdam Marionette Theater** (Nieuwe Jonkerstraat 8, tel. 020/620–8027).

Nightlife Most of Amsterdam's nightlife is concentrated at Leidseplein and Rembrandtsplein, which bustle until late on weekends, and even until a relatively late hour during the week. The city has something for everyone, be it disco or jazz club, piano bar or rowdy revue, gay or straight; and if all else fails, you can always fall back on the quieter pleasure of downing a few Dutch beers in a brown café (*see* Brown Cafés *below*). Amsterdam also has a full-scale casino right in the heart of the city.

Nightclub/ One of the best additions to the nightlife scene of Amsterdam in re-
Casino cent years is the **Lido Dinner Show** (Leidsestraat 105, tel. 020/626–2106) and, under the same roof, the **Holland Casino Amsterdam** (Max Euweplein 62, tel. 020/620–1006), which is one of the largest in Europe (more than 9,500 square meters/90,000 square feet) and offers everything from your choice of French or American roulette to computerized bingo, with the obligatory slot machines to eat up your supply of loose guilders.

Brown Cafés *Bruine cafes* (brown cafés), loosely equivalent to English pubs, are an indispensable part of the city's lifestyle, and they can be found on many corners throughout Amsterdam. A few bruine cafes you may come across in your travels are **De Admiraal** (Herengracht 319, tel. 020/625–4334), **De Drie Fleschjes** (Gravenstraat 18, tel. 020/624–8443), and **In de Wildeman** (Kolksteeg 3, tel. 020/638–2348). In the Jordaan neighborhood are **Nol** (Westerstraat 109, tel. 020/6245380), **Rooie Nelis** (Laurierstraat 101, tel. 020/624–4167), and **'t Smalle** (Eglantiersgracht 12, tel. 020/623–9617). **De Reiger** (Nieuwe Leliestraat 34, tel. 020/624–7426) has a distinctive Jugendstil bar and serves food. When you want to hear the locals sing folk music on Sunday afternoons, stop by **De Twee Zwaantjes** (Prinsengracht 114, tel. 020/625–2729).

Jazz Clubs The Dutch love jazz, and a number of establishments in Amsterdam have been meccas for music lovers for years. At **Bimhuis** (Oude Schans 73–77, tel. 020/623–3373), the best-known jazz place in town, you'll find top musicians, including avant-gardists, performing on Friday and Saturday nights, and weeknight jam sessions. Other jazz clubs include **Alto** (Korte Leidsedwarsstraat 115, tel. 020/626–

3249), **Bamboo Bar** (Lange Leidsedwarsstraat 64, tel. 020/624–3993), **Bourbon Street Jazz & Blues Club** (Leidsekruisstraat 6–8, tel. 020/623–3440), **Grand Jazzcafe de Heeren van Amstel** (Thorbeckeplein 5, tel. 020/620–2173), and **Joseph Lam** (Van Diemenstraat 242, tel. 020/622–8086), which specializes in Dixieland and is open only on Saturdays. The most recent addition to the scene is **Parker's Podium Café** (Voetboogstraat 5a, tel. 020/420–1711).

Piano Bars Hotel piano bars include **Le Bar** (Hotel de l'Europe, Nieuwe Doelenstraat 2–8, tel. 020/623–4836) and **Golden Palm Bar** (Grand Hotel Krasnapolsky, Dam 9, tel. 020/554–9111). Another, near Leidseplein, is **Pianobar Maxim** (Leidsekruisstraat 35, tel. 020/624–1920).

Discos and Among the hotel discos are **Boston Club** (Kattengat 1, tel. 020/624–
Rock Clubs 5561) and **Royal Club Dance** (Oudezijds Voorburgwal 3, tel. 020/638–1461). Near Leidseplein are **Cash** (Leidseplein 12, tel. 020/627–6544), open Thurs.–Sun. 10 PM–4 AM, and **Hard Rock Cafe** (Korte Leidsedwarsstraat 28–32, tel. 020/626–6422). At Rembrandtsplein there is the huge, popular **Escape** (Rembrandtsplein 11–15, tel. 020/622–3542; open Thurs. and Sun. to 4 AM, Fri.–Sat. to 5 AM), which can handle 2,500 people dancing to a DJ or live bands. There are also laser light shows and videos here. Not far away is the theatrical **Roxy** (Singel 465, tel. 020/620–0354; open Sun., Wed., and Thurs. to 4 AM, Fri.–Sat. 11 PM–5 AM), which is considered the trendiest discotheque in the Netherlands at the moment. **(36 Op de Schaal Van) Richter** (Reguliersdwarsstraat 36, tel. 020/626–1573) is an intimate club with two small dance floors and soul and soul-derivative sounds. **It** (Amstelstraat 24, tel. 020/625–0111; open Thurs.–Sun. to 4 AM) has four bars, special acts and bands, and celebrities in the crowd. This place tends toward a gay crowd on Friday and Saturday nights, straight on Thursday and Sunday nights. Also attracting an artsy crowd, both gay and straight, is **Mazzo** (Rozengracht 114, tel. 626–7500; open weeknights to 4 AM, Fri.–Sat. to 5 AM), which features trendy dance music and specialty acts and bands.

Gay Bars Gay visitors to Amsterdam should check the major newsstands for one of the specialized publications that include ads and listings for entertainment possibilities oriented to the interests of gays and lesbians. The gay scene in Amsterdam is concentrated mostly on Warmoestraat, Reguliersdwarsstraat, Amstelstraat and along the Amstel, and Kerkstraat near Leidseplein. The **Gay & Lesbian Switchboard** can provide information (tel. 020/623–6565, open 10–10), as can **COC** action group (Rozenstraat 14, tel. 020/626–3087), which also operates a coffee shop, youth café, pub, and weekly dance.

Gay cafés include **Amstel Taveerne** (Amstel 54, tel. 020/623–4254), **Chez Manfred** (Halvemaansteeg 10, tel. 020/626–4510), **Downtown** (Reguliersdwarsstraat 31, tel. 020/622–9958), and, for lesbians, **Saarein** (Elandsstraat 119, tel. 020/623–4901). **Exit** (Reguliersdwarsstraat 42, tel. 020/625–8788) is a gay discotheque with a large bar.

Excursions from Amsterdam

Numbers in the margin correspond to points of interest in the Excursions from Amsterdam map.

Excursions from Amsterdam

The Bulb Fields and Flower Auction

Though the bulb fields are in full bloom in April and May, flowers are a year-round business in the Netherlands: Visitors in the dead of winter can still gain a sense of the magnitude and magnificence of Dutch tulips and countless other varieties of flowers.

The **Bollenstreek Route** (Bulb District Route) is a special itinerary through the heart of the flower-growing region that was designed by the Dutch auto club, ANWB. The route begins in Oegstgeest, near Leiden, and circles through Rijnsburg (site of one of Holland's three major flower auction houses), the beach communities of **①** **Katwijk** and **Noordwijk, Hillegom, Lisse** (site of Keukenhof Gardens, *see below*), and **Sassenheim.** The route is marked with small blue and white signs that read "Bollenstreek."

Keukenhof is a 70-acre park and greenhouse complex that are planted each year to be a special spring exhibition of bulb flowers. It also serves to introduce the newest hybrids developed by Dutch botanists. Keukenhof is open only in April and May. *Lisse, tel. 02521/ 19034. Admission: Fl. 15 adults, Fl. 7 children. Open late Mar.– late May, daily 8–8.*

At any time during the year, it is an easy trip from Amsterdam to **②** the small village of **Aalsmeer.** This is the site of the **Bloemenveiling Aalsmeer** (Aalsmeer Flower Auction) that is held five days a week from the predawn hours until mid-morning. It is the largest flower auction in the world, with three auction halls operating continuously in a building the size of several football fields. You walk on a catwalk above the rolling four-tier carts that wait to move on tracks past the auctioneers. The buying system is what is called a Dutch auction; the price goes down, not up, on a large "clock" on the wall. The buyers sit lecture-style with buzzers on their desks; the first to register a bid gets the bunch. *Legmeerdijk 313, tel. 02977/34567. Admission: Fl. 4 adults, children under 11 free. Open weekdays 7:30–11.*

Folkloric Holland ❸ Over the Noordzee Kanaal from Amsterdam and just beyond the city of **Zaandam** is the restored village of **Zaanse Schans,** gateway to the windmill-studded countryside of Noord Holland province. Many of the buildings here have been restored as private homes, but a small cluster along the river edge includes a clock museum, the shops of a clog maker and a cheese maker, a bakery museum, and a restaurant. *Kraaienest 2, tel. 075/152221. Admission: Fl. 3.50 adults, Fl. 1.50 children. Open daily 10–5.*

❹ ❺ Open-air **cheese markets** are held in **Alkmaar** (tel. 072/114284; Apr.– Sept., Fri. mornings) and **Purmerend** (tel. 02990/52525 Feb.–Aug., Thurs. mornings). To see how cheese is made, visit one of more than a dozen *kaasboerderij* (cheese farms) in the area: **Kaasboerderij De Witte Saander** (Braakdijk 37, Zaandam, daily 9–6), **Kaasboerderij De Domme Dirk** (Roomeinde 17, Broek in Waterland, daily 10–5), and **Kaasboerderij Zeilzicht** (Westdijk 15, Alkmaar, Tues. and Thurs. 10–4) are three of them.

Metropolitan Holland and The Hague

Like filings around the end of a magnet, the population of the Netherlands clusters in the arc of Amsterdam's attraction. More than 25% of the country's 15 million residents live in and around 10 small to medium-size cities that are within 80 kilometers (50 miles) of the capital. And that doesn't count the tulip growers, vegetable farmers, dairy farmers, and villagers who fill in what little open land remains in this area. The Dutch refer to the circle formed by the four cities of Amsterdam, Den Haag (The Hague in English), Rotterdam, and Utrecht as the Randstad (Ridge City), because the cities lie along the same ridge. The megalopolis also is called "The West" by young Randstad wanna-bes waiting for their opportunity to hit the big time in the same way young Americans and Britons dream of making it in New York, Los Angeles, or London. In addition to harboring the capital of international justice (The Hague) and the world's largest port (Rotterdam), Metropolitan Holland is the political and historic heart of the Dutch nation.

Important Addresses and Numbers

Tourist Information **VVV Delft** (Markt 85, tel. 015/126100; open Apr.–Sept., weekdays 9–6, Sat. 9–5, Sun. 11–3; Oct.–Mar., Sat. 9–5). **VVV Haarlem** (Stationsplein 1, 2011 LR, tel. 023/319059, fax 023/340537; open Apr.–Sept., Mon.–Sat. 9–5:30; Oct.–Mar., Sat. 10–4). **The Hague Information Office** (Koningin Julianaplein 30, Babylon shopping center, tel. 06/34035051; open mid-Apr.–mid-Sept., Mon.–Sat. 9–9, Sun. 10–5; mid-Sept.–mid-Apr., Mon.–Sat. 9–6, Sun. 10–5). **Scheveningen Information Office** (Gevers Deynootweg 1134, Palace shopping center Promenade, tel. 070/354–6200). **VVV Leiden** (Stationsplein 210, tel. 071/146846) open Apr.–Aug., Mon.–Sat. 9–6; Sept.–Mar., weekdays 9–5:30, Sat. 10–4). **VVV Rotterdam** (Coolsingel 67, tel. 06/34034065, fax 010/4130124; open Mon.–Thurs. 9–5:30, Fri. 9–9, Sat. 9–5, and Sun. 10–4; Oct.–Mar., Mon.–Thurs. 9–5:30, Fri. 9–9, and Sat. 9–5). **VVV Utrecht** (Vredenburg 90, tel. 06/34034085, fax 030/331417; open weekdays 9–6, Sat. 9–4).

Emergencies The **National Emergency Alarm Number** for police, fire, and ambulance is 06/11.

Hospital Emergency care is available in **Delft** (R. De Graafweg 3–11, tel. 015/
Emergency 603060), **Haarlem** (Velserstraat 19, tel. 023/141516), **The Hague**
Rooms (Bronovolaan 5, tel. 070/312–4141), **Leiden** (Rijnsburgerweg 10, tel.
071/269111), **Rotterdam** (Dr. Molewaterplein 40, tel. 010/463–9222),
and **Utrecht** (Heidelberglaan 100, tel. 030/509111).

Late-Night In **Delft** (tel. 015/121568), in **Haarlem** (tel. 023/319148), in **The Hague**
Pharmacies (tel. 070/345–1000), in **Rotterdam** (tel. 010/411–0370), and in **Utrecht**
(tel. 030/441228).

Arriving and Departing

By Car N5/A5 goes to **Haarlem** from Amsterdam (from there N208 leads through the bulb district to Leiden); to reach **Leiden, The Hague, Delft,** and **Rotterdam** directly from Amsterdam, take E19 via Amsterdam Schiphol Airport; to continue to **Utrecht** from Rotterdam, take E25, or to reach **Utrecht** directly from Amsterdam, take E35. Take E30/A12 from The Hague to Utrecht to bypass the congestion of Rotterdam.

By Train **Intercity express trains** (tel. 06/9292) run twice an hour between Amsterdam and Leiden, The Hague, and Rotterdam, and four times an hour between Amsterdam and Haarlem and Utrecht. To get to Delft from Amsterdam, change trains in The Hague. Four trains an hour also run between The Hague and Rotterdam, and three per hour between The Hague and Utrecht, and Rotterdam and Utrecht. There are two railway stations in The Hague (one in the central business district and another in the residential area); for reasons that have more to do with politics than practicality, trains from Amsterdam do *not* stop at the central station, which means you either must change trains in Leiden to disembark directly at the central station, or take a bus from the high station into the center.

Getting Around Metropolitan Holland and The Hague

By Bus or Bus service is available in all cities in this region, and trams run in
Tram The Hague, between Delft and The Hague, in Rotterdam, and in Utrecht; Rotterdam also has an excellent underground metro system with two major lines (east–west and north–south) that extend into the suburbs and cross in the city center for easy transfers from one to the other. For **information** on public transportation (trains, buses, trams, and ferries) in all major Dutch cities, call 06/9292 from anywhere in the country.

By Taxi Taxis are available at railway stations, at major hotels, and, in larger cities, at taxi stands in key locations. Call to order a taxi in Delft (tel. 015/620621), Haarlem (tel. 023/151515), The Hague (tel. 070/390–7722 or 070/364–2828), Leiden (tel. 071/212144), Rotterdam (tel. 010/462–6060 or 010/425–7000), or Utrecht (tel. 030/515151 or 030/331122).

By Bike Bicycles can be rented at railway stations or by contacting local rental facilities (*see* Sports and Fitness, *below,* for names of firms in each town).

Guided Tours

In Leiden, **Jaap Slingerland** (tel. 071/413183; fare: Fl 15 per person) runs 3½-hour boat trips every summer afternoon except Saturdays from the *haven* (harbor) across the Braassemer Lake and the Kager Lakes, including a windmill cruise. In July and August there are also day trips across the Braassemer Lake to visit the bird and recreation center **Avifauna** in Alphen aan den Rijn (tel. 01720/87575; fare: Fl 9.50 adults, Fl 7 children; includes admission to Avifauna park). In The Hague, a **Royal Tour** (tel. 070/354–6200) is run during the summer that takes in the palaces and administrative buildings associated with Queen Beatrix. The cost is Fl 19 adults, Fl 15 children. The **Rotterdam City Tour** (Coolsingel, tel. 06/3403–4065) is available daily from May through September for Fl 25. The best way to see Rotterdam's waterfront is by boat. **Spido Harbor Tours** (Willemsplein, tel. 010/413–5400), offer excursions lasting from just over an hour to a full day. In Utrecht, carriages drawn by Gelderland horses tour the city on weekends from April through October. Another option in Utrecht is the **Walkman Tour,** available from the tourist office (Vredenburg 90, tel. 06/3403–4805) for Fl 5.

Exploring Metropolitan Holland

Numbers in the margin correspond to points of interest on the Metropolitan Holland map.

Haarlem Often eclipsed by Amsterdam, **Haarlem** is an important small city in
❶ its own right. It is home to one of the finest church organs in the world, and its museums contain art that fills in gaps or expands upon the collections of Amsterdam's major museums.

The heart of any Dutch town is its market square. Surrounding Haarlem's Grote Markt are the medieval town hall, the old fish- and meat-market halls dating from the 17th century and often used by the Frans Hals Museum for special exhibitions, and the imposing late-Gothic **Grote Kerk** (St. Bavo's Church) built on the square in the 15th century and the burial place of Frans Hals. The church is the home of the world-famous Müller Organ, on which both Handel and Mozart played (Mozart at age 10). Installed in 1738 and long considered to be the finest in the world, this gilded and gleaming instrument has been meticulously maintained and restored through the years to protect the sound planned by its creators, the master organ builder Christian Müller and the sculptor Jan van Logteren. Between May and October the official town organists of Haarlem give free weekly or twice-weekly concerts. *Grote Markt. Admission: Fl 2 adults, Fl 1 children. Open Apr.–Aug., Mon.–Sat. 10–4; Sept.–Mar., Mon.–Sat. 10–3:30.*

Time Out On the Grote Markt, across the square from St. Bavo's church, the spacious **Grand Café Brinkman** (Grote Markt 9–13, tel. 023/323111) is a good place for a reasonably priced snack or light meal.

Just off the Grote Markt in a small gabled town building is the **Corrie ten Boom House,** which honors a family of World War II resistance fighters who successfully hid a number of Jewish families before being captured themselves by the Germans in 1944. Most of the ten Boom family lost their lives in the concentration camps, but Corrie survived and returned to Haarlem to tell the story in her book, *The Hiding Place.* The family clock shop is preserved on the street floor, and their living quarters now contain displays, documents, photographs, and memorabilia. Visitors can also see the hiding closet, which the Gestapo never found, although they lived six days in the house hoping to starve out anyone who might be hiding there. *Barteljorisstraat 19, tel. 023/310823. Admission free (donations ap-*

Metropolitan Holland

KEY
— Rail Lines

North Sea

's-Gravenhage/
Den Haag
(The Hague)

*preciated). Open Apr.–Oct., Mon.–Sat. 10–4:30; Nov.–Mar.,
Mon.–Sat. 11–5:30.*

Crossing back through the Grote Markt, take Warmoesstraat and its
continuations, Schagchelstraat and Groot Heilig Land, to the entrance to the **Frans Hals Museum.** What once was a series of small
houses is now galleries for paintings, period furniture, silver, and
ceramics. The 17th-century collection of paintings that is the focal
point of this museum includes the works of Frans Hals and other
masters of the Haarlem School, including Hendrick Goltzius, Judith
Leyster, Johannes Verspronck, Pieter Claesz, Willem Heda,
Adriaen van Ostade, and Jacob van Ruisdael. The museum has a
modern art collection as well, with the works of Dutch impression-
ists and expressionists, including sculpture, textiles, and ceramics,
as well as paintings and graphics; there are also an 18th-century
dollhouse and a re-created 18th-century pharmacy. *Groot Heilig
Land 62, tel. 023/319180. Admission: Fl 6.25 adults, Fl 3 children.
Open Mon.–Sat. 11–5, Sun. and public holidays 1–5.*

From the Hals Museum, follow the canals around to the left, past the
Turfmarkt to Spaarne to reach the **Teylers Museum.** This is the oldest museum in the Netherlands and possibly the most curious in the
world. The major artistic attraction is the collection of master drawings and prints by Michelangelo, Rembrandt, and others that once
belonged to Queen Christina of Sweden. Among the scientific curiosities are collections of fossils and crystals and examples of early
machines and scientific tools. There is also a collection of coins and
medals and even a rare 31-pipe Fokker organ. *Spaarne 16, tel. 023/
319010. Admission: Fl 6.50 adults, Fl 3 children. Open Tues.–Sat.
10–5; Sun. and public holidays 1–5.*

Leiden Birthplace of Rembrandt and site of the nation's oldest and most
❷ prestigious university, **Leiden** is also noted for its significant historic role. In 1574, Leiden was the object of a major siege at the hands of
the Spanish; the story of that siege, and the city's deliverance by the
uniquely Dutch tactic of breaching the dikes to flood out an invader,
is an important part of national lore. A place where windmills still
rise over the cityscape, Leiden derives its charm today from its relaxed and spirited university-town atmosphere.

Founded in 1575, **Leiden University** was a mecca for the great think-
ers and scientists of the 16th and 17th centuries, including the philosopher René Descartes. Follow the wide Rapenburg canal from
the center of town to the university's **Hortus Botanicus.** This botanical garden is the oldest in Europe and includes extensive beds filled
with flowers, rare plants, and towering trees; there is an orangery, a
Japanese garden, and several greenhouses. *Rapenburg 73, tel. 071/
275188. Admission: Fl 3.50. Open Apr.–Oct., Mon.–Sat. 9–5, Sun.
10:30–5; Nov.–Mar., weekdays 9–4:30, Sun. 10:30–3.*

After visiting the gardens, continue into Kaiserstraat to the next canal, where you will find the **Pilgrim Collection.** In a small house behind the city archives, this collection includes documents, models,
and books related to the period when a group of English Puritans
later known as the Pilgrims lived in Leiden before sailing to found
the Plymouth Colony in what is now Massachusetts. *Vliet 45, tel.
071/120191. Admission free. Open weekdays 9:30–4:30.*

Return to the gardens and cross the canal; take Kloksteeg to the
square in front of the **Pieterskerk** (St. Peter's Church), which is the
oldest church in the city, dating from 1428. Also on the church
square is the Gravensteen, which once was the home of the Counts of
Holland. *Pieterskerkhof, tel. 071/124319. Admission free. Open daily 1:30–4.*

Behind the church on Pieterskerkchoorsteeg is the former home of
William Brewster, spiritual leader of the Pilgrims. At the entrance
is a small plaque placed by the Society of Mayflower Descendants.
Return to the Rapenburg canal and stroll past the city's most gracious houses to reach the **Rijksmuseum van Oudheden** (National Museum of Antiquities), which has a particularly fine Egyptian and
classical collection, as well as Dutch archaeological artifacts. Pass
through a soaring gallery in which the Egyptian temple of Taffah
has been reconstructed, and continue through two floors of Greek
and Roman sculpture, Egyptian tombs, funerary urns, and collections of everyday items from the pre-Christian eras, including glassware, ceramics, jewelry, and weapons. *Rapenburg 28, tel. 071/
163163. Admission: Fl 5 adults, Fl 4 children. Open Tues.–Sat.
10–5, Sun. noon–5.*

Time Out Just past the end of the Rapenburg canal, in one of the most attractive spots in town, **De Waterlijn** (Prinsessekade, tel. 071/121279) is a
strikingly modern, glass-walled café on a moored boat, offering
views of old boats, gabled houses, and a windmill. The Dutch apple
tart is good here.

Continue straight ahead through the Turfmarkt to the second canal,
the Oude Singel. On the far side is the **De Lakenhal** museum, which
contains an impressive collection of paintings as well as furniture
and silver and pewter pieces. The galleries are hung with paintings
by Rembrandt, Gerrit Dou, Jan Steen, and Salomon van Ruysdael,
as well as an impressive collection of the works of Lucas van Leyden,
including his triptych, *Last Judgment.* Also of interest here are the

reconstructed guild rooms. *Oude Singel 28–32, tel. 071/165361. Admission: Fl 5 adults, Fl 2.50 children. Open Tues.–Sat. 10–5, Sun. and public holidays noon–5.*

The Hague and Scheveningen While Amsterdam is the official capital of the Netherlands, 's-Gravenhage/Den Haag (The Hague) is the seat of government and home of the reigning monarch, Queen Beatrix. An elegant city dotted with parks and open squares, it exudes a graciousness that Amsterdam lacks, and has a formal and traditional lifestyle that befits its role as a diplomatic capital and world center of international peace and justice. Almost seamlessly connected to The Hague is the fishing port and stylish beach resort community of Scheveningen, where a small and dwindling community of women still dresses in traditional costumes on a daily basis.

Numbers in the margin correspond to points of interest on The Hague map.

❸ ❹ ❺ The governmental heart of the Netherlands is the Parliament Complex, which is in the center of The Hague beside the **Hofvijver** (Court Lake), a small rectangular reflecting pool. The late-13th-century **Ridderzaal** (Knight's Hall) is where the queen comes each fall to address her government at the annual Opening of Parliament (the third Tuesday in September). Built around this is the **Binnenhof** (Inner Court) complex; it incorporates the buildings used by the First and Second Chambers of the Staten Generaal (States General, equivalent to the U.S. Senate and House of Representatives). There is a special exhibition on the origin and methods of the Dutch governmental system, and there are guided tours into the legislative chambers (when they are not in session) and the Knight's Hall, with its provincial flags and stained-glass windows displaying the coats of arms of the major Dutch cities. *Binnenhof, tel. 070/364–6144. Reservations required. Admission: tour Fl 5.50, Parliament exhibition free. Open Mon.–Sat. 10–4; last guided tour at 3:55 PM.*

❻ Tucked into a corner behind the Parliament Complex and overlooking the waters of the Court Lake is a small 17th-century palace, the **Mauritshuis,** known as the Royal Gallery of Paintings, which contains an outstanding collection of Dutch masterpieces, including three Rembrandt self-portraits and his breakthrough painting, *The Anatomy Lesson.* Also here are three highly prized paintings by Vermeer *(Girl with the Pearl, View of Delft, Diana with the Nymphs);* more than a dozen works by Jan Steen, who portrayed daily life and ordinary people in the Netherlands in the 17th century; and paintings by other Dutch and Flemish masters, including Hals, Ruysdael, Potter, Rubens, and Van Dyck. *Korte Vijverberg 8, tel. 070/346–9244. Admission: Fl 7.50 adults, Fl 3.50 children. Open Tues.–Sat. 10–5, Sun. 11–5.*

Included in the admission to the Mauritshuis is the opportunity to visit the **Painting Gallery of Prince Willem V,** which is on the far side of the Parliament Complex on the open Buitenhof (Outer Court). This small gallery in a Louis XIV–style town house contains additional works by 17th-century masters that illustrate life in the Netherlands in that time. *Buitenhof 35, tel. 070/318–2487. Admission: Fl 2.50 adults, Fl 1 children. Open Tues.–Sun. 11–4.*

❼ Facing the Parliament Complex across the Court Lake is **Museum Bredius.** Housed in an 18th-century mansion, it displays a former private collection that includes additional works by the masters as well as lesser-known works of the period. *Lange Vijverberg 14, tel. 070/362–0729. Admission: Fl 6 adults, Fl 4 children. Open Tues.–Sun. noon–5.*

The Hague

Time Out Follow Gravenstraat toward the center to a small square facing the old Town Hall. Opening onto the square is 'T Goude Hooft (De Groenmarkt 13, tel. 070/346–9713), the oldest restaurant in The Hague, with both a street café and a traditional Dutch dining room.

8 Beyond the city center and facing the world across a broad lawn is the **Vredespaleis** (Peace Palace), which houses the International Court of Justice. The court was initiated in 1899 by Czar Nicolas II of Russia, who invited 26 nations to meet in The Hague to set up a permanent world court of arbitration. The present building was constructed in 1903 with a $1.5 million gift from the Scots-American industrialist Andrew Carnegie. Gifts from each of the participating nations embellish the architecture with examples of their national craftsmanship in the form of statuary, stained-glass windows, gates, doors, clocks, and such. *Carnegieplein 2, tel. 070/346–9680. Admission: Fl 5 adults, Fl 3 children. Open May–Oct., weekdays 10–4; Nov.–Apr. weekdays 10–3; guided tours 10 AM, 11 AM, 2 PM, and 3 PM; May–Oct., additional guided tour 4 PM.*

9 Continuing by way of Groot Hertoginnelaan to Stadhouderslaan, you find the **Haags Gemeentemuseum** (Hague Municipal Museum), which is best known for housing the world's largest collection of works by Piet Mondrian, as well as 50 drawings by Karl Appel. In addition there are paintings from the Hague school and an arts-and-crafts section that displays magnificent local silverware, old glass, earthenware, ceramics, and Dutch and Chinese porcelain. *Stadhouderslaan 41, tel. 070/351–2873. Admission: Fl 8 adults, Fl 6.50 children. Open Tues.–Sun. 11–5.*

⑩ Also at the Hague Municipal Museum is the **Museon,** which incorporates science exhibits on the origins of the universe and evolution with three themes: Earth, Our Home; Between Man and the Stars; and Ecos, an environmental show. *Stadhouderslaan 41, tel. 070/ 338–1338 and 070/338–1305. Admission: Fl 5 adults, Fl 3 children. Open Tues.–Fri. 10–5, weekends and public holidays noon–5.*

⑪ Next door to Museon is the IMAX theater **Omniversum,** which shows a rotating program of spectacular presentations, including several with natural and futuristic themes, on a film screen that is six stories high. *Pres. Kennedylaan 5, tel. 070/354–5454. Reservations advised. Admission: Fl 15 adults, Fl 13 children. Shows Tues.–Thurs. hourly 11–4, Fri.–Sun. and holidays hourly 11–9.*

Numbers in the margin correspond to points of interest on the Metropolitan Holland map.

⑫ Leaving Omniversum, follow Johan De Wittlaan to Scheveningseweg, which leads to the beach resort community of **Scheveningen.** Here you can enjoy a variety of relaxing pleasures, including a walk on the beach promenade or a swim in a wave pool. The famous and grand old hotel, the **Kurhaus,** (*see* Dining and Lodging, *below*) houses a casino as well as several restaurants. There is also shopping seven days a week (it is the only Sunday shopping in the Netherlands). Scheveningen is the departure point for deep-sea fishing trips.

Delft Perhaps more than any other in the Netherlands **Delft** preserves a
⑬ historic look that is best appreciated by simply wandering along its small canals with their graceful, humpbacked bridges. It rivals Leiden in its importance to the history of the Netherlands; it was here that William of Orange (known as William the Silent), founder of the nation, was assassinated in 1584. The Dutch monarchs that followed him are all buried here in the Nieuwe Kerk (New Church), in the shadow of which the painter Jan Vermeer was born and lived. And, of course, Delft also is the crafts center known around the world for its famous blue-and-white porcelain.

Begin your tour of Delft at the market square, flanked at one end by the **Stadhuis** (Town Hall). Facing it across the square is the 14th-century **Nieuwe Kerk** (New Church), which is the royal burial church of the House of Orange; it entombs all but a few of the Dutch monarchs. The mausoleum of William the Silent, a massive and ornate structure of black marble and alabaster, dominates the chancel. Nearby in the floor is the stone that covers the entry to the royal crypt, and throughout the church are paintings, stained-glass windows, and memorabilia associated with the Dutch royal family. In summer it is possible to climb the church tower for the view that stretches as far as The Hague and Scheveningen. *Markt, tel. 015/123025. Admission: Fl 2.50 adults, Fl 1 children. Combination card (Old and New churches): Fl 3.50 adults, Fl 1.50 children. Open May–Oct., Mon.– Sat. 9–5; Nov.–Apr., Mon.–Sat. 11–4. Tower Admission: Fl 3.50 adults, Fl 2.50 children. Open May–Aug., Tues.–Sat. 10–4:30; July 15–Aug. 19, daily 10–4:30.*

Time Out On a corner at the center of the market square is a small pastry shop and tearoom, **Bankerbakkerij van Leeuwen** (Markt 57, tel. 015/ 123720), in a building also identified as *In Den Beslagen Bijbel,* honoring the fact that it was in this building that the first Dutch printed Bible was produced.

Behind the Town Hall is a row of buildings that formerly served as the butter market, the town weigh house, and the guild halls of gold- and silversmiths and pharmacists. Cut through and cross the second canal, which is the **Oude Delft.** This was the first canal dug in the city and is said to be the first city canal dug in the Netherlands. If you turn right, you walk toward the now-leaning tower of the **Oude Kerk** (Old Church). Founded in 1200, this is the oldest church in Delft and the final resting place of several important Dutch military and naval heroes and of Antonie van Leeuwenhoek, the Delft resident who invented the microscope. The tower, which now leans too precariously to be ascended, holds the largest carillon bell in the Netherlands; weighing nearly 20,000 pounds, it now is used only on state occasions. *Heilige Geestkerkhof, tel. 015/123015. Admission: Fl 2 adults, Fl 0.75 children. Combination card (Old and New churches): Fl 3.50 adults, Fl 1.50 children. Open Apr.–Nov., Mon.– Sat. 10–5.*

Directly across the canal from the Oude Kerk is **Het Prinsenhof** (Prince's Court), the most famous sight in Delft. Built as a convent in the early 15th century, the complex of buildings was taken over by the government of the new Dutch Republic in 1572 and given to William of Orange for his use as a residence. It was here that William was assassinated. The complex of buildings now houses a museum devoted to the history of the Dutch Republic; there is also a museum of ethnology and a church. *St. Agathaplein 1, tel. 015/602358. Admission: Fl 3.50 adults, Fl 1.75 children. Open Tues.–Sat. 10–5, Sun. 1–5.*

Rotterdam
14

Were it not for the devastation of World War II, when the city and its port were leveled in the cross fire between Hitler's forces and the Allies, **Rotterdam** might never have become the dynamic and influential world port it is today. A busy harbor since the 17th century, it built bigger facilities in the 19th and early 20th centuries, playing a key role in European trade. The massive 48-kilometer-long (30-mile-long) **Europoort** complex of piers, warehouses, and refineries is best seen by boat (*see* Guided Tours, *above*).

Walk along the Leuvehaven inner harbor past several old ships moored along the quay to the nautical museum at the head of the harbor. This is the **Prins Hendrik Maritime Museum,** devoted to the history of Rotterdam harbor and its historic role in world trade. The museum building contains both changing exhibitions and a permanent collection of models and memorabilia; the warship *De Buffel,* moored alongside the museum, is part of the collection. *Leuvehaven 1, tel. 010/413–2680. Admission: Fl 6 adults, children free; free Wed. Open Tues.–Sat. 10–5, Sun. and holidays 11–5.*

Take a westbound line from the Metro station outside the museum to the next stop at Eendrachtsplein; walk along Westersingel toward the park and turn right on Mathenesserlaan. The **Boymans-van Beuningen Museum** is another of the Netherlands' exceptional fine-arts museums. Its collection spans the 15th to 20th centuries and includes a number of extraordinary early primitives by painters such as Hieronymus Bosch, Sint Jans, and the van Eycks, as well as Bruegel the Elder and van Scorel. Later painters, including Rubens and Van Dyck, are also represented. Rembrandt's portrait of his son Titus is part of the collection, as are prints and drawings by Dürer, da Vinci, and later artists such as Cezanne and Picasso. Add to this a remarkable collection of impressionist, surrealist, and contemporary art, and as the final fillip, a fine collection of objects that includes glassware, silverware, and earthenware. *Mathenesserlaan*

18–20, tel. 010/441–9400. Admission: Fl 6 adults, children free; free Wed. Open Tues.–Sat. 10–5, Sun. and holidays 11–5.

Alongside the museum is the spanking new **Nederlands Architectuurinstituut**, with changing exhibits on architecture and interior design. Across the square is the 1992–93 **Kunsthal**, which hosts all manner of major temporary exhibitions—from Andy Warhol retrospectives to rows of compact cars. *Nederlands Architectuurinsituut: Museumpark 25, tel. 010/440–1200. Admission: Fl 6. Open Tues.–Sat. 10–5, Sun. 11–5. Kunsthal: Westzeedijk 341, tel. 010/440–0300. Admission: Fl 10. Open Tues.–Sat. 10–5, Sun. 11–5.*

Three stops farther west along the Metro line is **Delfshaven.** (From the Metro station, double back along Schiedamseweg, then turn right down Aelbrechtskolk.) This last remaining nook of old Rotterdam has rows of gabled houses lining the waterfront, and even a windmill. Today Delfshaven is an up-and-coming area of trendy galleries, cafés, and restaurants.

Utrecht Birthplace of the 16th-century Adrian VI, the only Dutch pope, **⓯** **Utrecht** has been a powerful bishopric since the 7th century and is still is a major religious center. It was here that the Dutch Republic was established in 1579 with the signing of the Union of Utrecht.

Although the surrounding city is among the busiest and most modern in the Netherlands, the central core of Utrecht retains a historic character, particularly along its two main canals. The best place to begin a tour is from the bridge that connects Lange Viestraat to Potterstraat just beyond Vredenburg square. There's a pleasant view over the **Oude Gracht** (Old Canal), which winds through the central shopping district. The unique feature of this lively esplanade is that there are upper and lower levels, with shops opening onto the street level, restaurants and cafés opening onto the walkway that is just above water level.

Time Out For a tasty lunch, visit **De Soepterrine** (Zakkendragerssteeg 40, tel. 030/317005), a snug restaurant that serves bowls of steaming homemade soups and hefty salads. Some 10 varieties of soup are made daily, including the traditional Dutch *erwtensoep* (thick pea soup). Soups come with crusty bread and herb butter.

Follow the canal along to the Steenweg and jog left to visit one of the most delightful museums in the Netherlands. Housed in an old church, the **Rijksmuseum van Speelklok tot Pierement** (National Museum from Musical Clock to Street Organ) is a happy place filled with ticking clocks, music boxes, player pianos, and traditional Dutch barrel organs. *Buurkerkhof 10, tel. 030/312789. Admission: Fl 7.50 adults, Fl 3.50 children. Open Tues.–Sat. 10–5, Sun. and public holidays 1–5; guided tours every hr.*

Return to the Old Canal and cross at the Zadelstraat bridge. The **Domtoren** (Dom Tower) in front of you is the highest tower in the Netherlands (112 meters/367 feet), and it is well worth the effort to climb its 465 steps for the panoramic view of the city and surrounding countryside of Utrecht province. Built in the late 14th century, the stone tower was originally the bell tower of a cathedral that was destroyed in a hurricane late in the 17th century (the outline of its nave can still be seen in the paving squares of the Domplein). Soaring lancet windows add to the impression of majestic height. *Domplein, tel. 030/310403. Admission: Fl 3.50 adults, Fl 1 children. Open Apr.–Nov., weekdays 10–5, Sat. 11–5, Sun. and public* *holidays noon–5; Dec.–Mar., Sat. 11–5, Sun. and public holidays noon–5, last tour at 4.*

Across the square is the Gothic-style **Domkerk** (Dom Church), built in the 13th and 14th centuries and designed after the pattern of the Tournai Cathedral in Belgium. It has five chapels radiating around the ambulatory of the chancel, as well as a number of funerary monuments, including that of a 14th-century bishop. *Domplein, tel. 030/ 310403. Admission free; guided tours Fl 4. Open May–Sept., Mon.–Sat. 10–5, Sun. 2–4; Oct.–Apr., Mon.–Sat. 11–4, Sun. 2–4.*

The 15th-century cloister garden adjacent to the Dom Church, the **Pandhof** (House Garden) of the Dom, is planted with herbs and offers a peaceful respite. *Between Domplein and Achter den Dom. Admission free. Open Dec.–Mar., Sat. 11–5, Sun. noon–5; Apr. and June–Nov., weekdays 10–5, Sat. 11–5, Sun. noon–5; May, Mon., Wed., and Fri. 10–5, Tues. and Thurs. 10–8:30, Sat. 11–5, Sun. noon–5.*

Turn right on Achter den Dom and walk toward the **Nieuwe Gracht** (New Canal). **Het Catharijneconvent,** a vast and comprehensive museum of religious history and sacred art housed in a former convent is just past the second bridge. There are magnificent altarpieces, ecclesiastical garments, manuscripts, sculptures, paintings, and the country's primary collection of medieval art. *Nieuwegracht 63, tel. 030/317296 or 030/313835. Admission: Fl 5 adults, Fl 2.50 children. Open Tues.–Fri. 10–5, weekends and public holidays 11–5.*

Continue to the end of the Nieuwegracht and turn right at Agnietenstraat, where you will find the **Centraal Museum,** also housed in a former convent. Primarily dedicated to painting and the decorative arts, it contains collections of costumes, coins, and medals and an archaeological section as well. The paintings here include excellent works from the 16th-century Utrecht school, reflecting the strong Italian influence on painters such as van Scorel, van Heemskerk, and Terbrugghen. There are also examples of the 20th-century Dutch de Stijl movement, though this school is best represented at the Rietveld-Schroder House (*see* Off the Beaten Track, *below*). *Agnietenstraat 1, tel. 030/362362 or 030/362359. Admission: Fl 5. Open Tues.–Sat. 10–5, Sun. and public holidays noon–5.*

What to See and Do with Children

Leiden's **Molenmuseum de Valk** (Windmill Museum de Valk) may be the best place and the best way to learn more about the windmill heritage of the Netherlands. *2e Binnenvestgracht 1, tel. 071/165355. Admission: Fl 3 adults, Fl 1.50 children. Open Tues.–Sat. 10–5, Sun. and holidays 1–5.*

Near Leiden, in the beach community of Noordwijk, is Europe's first permanent space exhibition, **Noordwijk Space Expo,** which includes real satellites, engines, and space stations, as well as models and pieces of moon rock. *Keplerlaan 3, Noordwijk, tel. 01719/46446 or 01719/46448. Admission: Fl 12.50 adults, Fl 7.50 children. Open Tues.–Sun. 10–6.*

Madurodam, in The Hague, is a collection of small reproductions of typically Dutch buildings set into a sprawling "village" with pathways, tram tracks, and railway stations. All of the most important buildings of the Netherlands have been reproduced; if you are here at sunset you will see the lights come on in the houses. In July and August, there is also an after-dark sound-and-light presentation, free to park visitors. *Haringkade 175, tel. 070/355–3900. Admis-*

sion: Fl 14 adults, Fl 11 senior citizens, Fl 8.50 children. Open Mar.–May, daily 9 AM–10:30 PM; June–Aug., daily 9 AM–11 PM; Sept., 9 AM–9:30 PM; Oct.–Mar., 9–6.

Off the Beaten Track

June is the time to visit **Westbroek Park** in The Hague, when its 20,000 rosebushes are in magnificent bloom. *Kapelweg. Admission free. Open daily 9–1 hr before sunset.*

The **Euromast** tower affords a panorama of Rotterdam Harbor. You reach it on the **Spacetower** revolving elevator. *Parkhaven 20, tel. 010/436–4811. Admission: Fl 14.50 adults, Fl 9 children. Open Apr.–Sept., daily 10–7; Oct.–Mar., daily 10–5; July–Aug., Tues.– Sat. 10 AM–10:30 PM, Sun. and Mon. 10–7.*

An imaginative program of postwar building has given Rotterdam an extraordinary concentration of adventurous modern architecture. The oddest buildings are a series of cube-shaped apartments turned to balance on one corner on the top of a tall stem. One of these precarious-looking houses, the **Kijk-Kubus,** just east of the center of town, is open to the public. *Overblaak 70, tel. 010/414–2285. Admission: Fl 2.50. Open Tues.–Fri. 10–5, weekends 11–5.*

An adjunct exhibit of Utrecht's Centraal Museum, several blocks away, the **Rietveld–Schröder House** exemplifies several key principles of the de Stijl movement—its open plan, the direct communion with nature from every room, and the use of neutral white or gray on large surfaces with primary colors to identify linear details. *Prins Hendriklaan 50A, tel. 030/326310. Reservations required. Admission (includes guided tour): Fl 9 adults, Fl 6 children. Open Wed.– Sat. 11–5.*

The charming old city of **Dordrecht,** at the busiest river junction in Europe, rewards a visit with medieval town gates, a 15th-century church with a leaning tower, and an 18th-century period house museum. It is the oldest town in Holland, given its charter in 1220.

Shopping

The late shopping nights in this region: in **Leiden,** Thursdays; in **The Hague,** Thursdays; in **Scheveningen,** Fridays and, during the summer at the Palace Promenade, Mondays through Saturdays; in **Rotterdam,** Fridays; and in **Utrecht,** Thursdays.

Shopping Districts
The best shopping in this region of the Netherlands is in the larger cities of The Hague, Rotterdam, and particularly Utrecht, which has two American-style enclosed shopping malls.

Street Markets
Street markets are an integral part of Dutch city life. **Leiden's** street market is held in the city center on the Nieuwe Rijn on Wednesday and Saturday 9–6 and at Vijf Mei plein on Tuesday 9–2. In **The Hague,** the Farmers' Market is Wednesday 10–6, and there is an antiques market on Lange Voorhout on summer Thursdays. In **Delft,** market day is Thursday 9–5, and there is a flea market on the canals in the town center on summer Saturdays. In **Rotterdam** an antiques, curiosities, and general market is held on Mariniersweg on Tuesday and Saturday 9–5, and the stamp, coin, and book market on Grotekerkplein is on Tuesday and Saturday 9:30–4; there is also a Sunday market at Schiedamsedijk April–September 11–5. In **Utrecht** the general market at Vredenburg is Wednesday 9–5 and Saturday 8–5; the antiques market at the Ossekop (Voorstraat 19) is Saturday 9–5; flowers and plants are sold at Janskerkhof on Satur-

day 7–4, and by the Old Canal on Saturday 8–5; there is a health-food market at Vredenburg on Friday noon–6; and a flea market at Waterstraat is held Saturday 8–2.

Specialty Stores Delft **De Porceleyne Fles** (The Royal Delftware Factory, Rotterdamseweg 196, tel. 015/560234) is home to that famous blue-and-white Delft pottery. The galleries here exhibit famous pieces from throughout Delft's history, and regular demonstrations of molding and painting pottery are given by the artisans. Other Delftware pottery factories are **De Delftse Pauw** (Delftweg 133, tel. 015/124920 or 015/124743), and **Atelier de Candelaer** (Kerkstraat 13, tel. 015/131848).

Sports and Fitness

Biking Bicycling is popular in this flat land, and rentals are available in virtually every city. Delft: the **railway station** (tel. 015/143033). Leiden: **Bicycle Depot** (next to the railway station, tel. 071/131304). Haarlem: **Van Bentum** (Stationsplein, tel. 023/317066) and **De Volken-fietser** (Koningstraat 36, tel. 023/325577). The Hague: **Cycle Garage** (Hollands Spoor, tel. 070/389–0830; or at Central Station, tel. 070/385–3235) and **Garage du Nord** (Keizerstraat 27, Scheveningen, tel. 070/355–4060). Rotterdam: **Stationsrijwielstalling Centraal Station** (Stationsplein 1, tel. 010/412–6220). Utrecht: **Bicycle Parking** (Central Station Utrecht, tel. 030/311159), and **Verleun and Co.** (Van Bijnkershoeklaan 413, tel. 030/936368).

Canoeing A canoe may be the very best way to get a close view of the bulb fields that fill the countryside between Haarlem and Leiden. The **VVV Leiden tourist office** (tel. 071/146846) has mapped out four different routes of varying lengths through the Dune and Bulb Area. Ask, too, about the Singel sightseeing route through Leiden's canals and moats. For information on canoe rentals contact **Jac. Veringa** (tel. 071/149790).

Sea Fishing Sea fishing is one of the main reasons many people visit Scheveningen. For information and reservations, contact **Sportviscentrum Trip** (Dr. Lelykade 3, Scheveningen, tel. 070/354–1122 or 070/354–0887).

Sports Complex In Utrecht, the sports center **De Vechtsebanen** (Mississippidreef 151, tel. 030/627878) is a multisport complex offering bowling, badminton, volleyball, squash, curling, and a number of other sports; there is a small running track as well as both indoor and outdoor tennis courts and ice-skating rinks.

Tennis/Squash In Leiden, you can play squash and tennis at the **Holiday Inn Racket Center** (Haagse Schouwweg 10, tel. 071/355100). In Delft, squash courts are available at **Squash Delft** (Sportring 3, tel. 015/146983). In Utrecht, both squash and tennis are available at the sports center **De Vechtsebanen** (Mississippidreef 151, tel. 030/627878).

Spectator Sports

Auto Racing One of Europe's best-known auto racing tracks is **Circuit Park Zandvoort** (Burgemeester van Alphenstraat, tel. 02507/16004 or 02507/18284); the racing season runs from April to October.

Horse Racing Near The Hague, **Duindigt Racecourse** (Waalsdorperlaan 29, Wassenaar, tel. 070/324–4427) is one of two racetracks in the Netherlands (the other is in Hilversum, between Utrecht and Amsterdam). The racing season runs from mid-March to mid-November and includes both flat and trotting races with betting. Race days are Wednesday and Sunday.

Marathon Run in late April each year (in close time proximity to both the Boston and London marathons), the City of Rotterdam Marathon is the major European running event of the year, where world records are routinely broken.

Soccer Rotterdam's Feyenoord team (pronounced "fie-nord") plays at **Feyenoord Stadion** (Olympiaweg 50, tel. 010/492–9499 or 010/492–9444).

Beaches

The beach community of **Scheveningen** has a boardwalk and amusement pier. Beaches near Leiden are at **Katwijk** and **Noordwijk.** Near Haarlem, **Zandvoort** is also the principal beach for Amsterdam (busy, but very large); the beaches at **Bloemdaal** are also open to the public.

Dining and Lodging

Delft　**De Prinsenkelder.** In the old storerooms of the former convent that
Dining　now is the Prinsenhof Museum, this restaurant has a sedate, elegant atmosphere. Classic French dishes, including veal and duck choices, are wonderfully prepared and beautifully presented. Entry is by way of a small alley opening onto the Oude Delft canal. *Schoolstraat 11, tel. 015/121860. Reservations advised. Jacket and tie advised. AE, DC, MC, V. Closed Sun. $$$$*
L'Orage. The owner/chef of this bright and gracious small French restaurant facing the Old Canal is Jannie Munk, who won the Netherlands' Lady Chef of the Year award in 1994. She creates delicious fish dishes, many based on recipes from her native Denmark. *Oude Delft 111b, tel. 015/123629. Reservations advised. Jacket and tie required. AE, DC, MC, V. Closed Sun.–Mon. $$$*

Lodging　**Delft Museumhotel & Residence.** This small, elegant hotel has been created within a complex of 11 historic buildings in the prime neighborhood of Delft. Among the choices are small apartments in the adjacent Residence building that opens onto the side alley. *Oude Delft 189, 2611 HD, tel. 015/140930, fax 015/140935. 51 rooms. Facilities: bar. AE, DC, MC, V. $$*
Hotel Leeuwenbrug. Facing one of Delft's canals, this traditional hotel has an Old Dutch–style canal-side lounge. The rooms are large, airy, and contemporary in decor; those in the annex are particularly appealing. *Koornmarkt 16, 2611 EE, tel. 015/147741. 30 rooms with bath or shower. Facilities: bar. AE, MC, V. $–$$*
Les Compagnons. This is a one-family hospitality package in the heart of Delft. The younger generation operates a small and comfortable hotel on the market square that offers a variety of brightly decorated rooms with a range of amenities that you wouldn't expect in so small a hotel. Dad hosts a restaurant on the next canal, and Mom operates a deli and tearoom in the adjoining store. In the early 1990s the family took over a pension farther along the market square and a four-star hotel on the other side of town. *Markt 61, 2611 GS, tel. 015/140102. 11 rooms with bath. AE, DC, MC, V. $–$$*

Haarlem　**Peter Cuyper.** This gracious restaurant is convenient to both the
Dining　Frans Hals and the Teyler museums. Its small, traditional beamed dining rooms are brightened with flowers, crisp linens, and light from an enclosed garden (open in summer) filtering through the windows. *Kleine Houtstraat 70, 2011 DR, tel. 023/320885. Reservations advised. Jacket and tie advised. AE, DC, MC, V. Closed Mon. dinner and Sun. $$$*

Lodging **Carlton Square Hotel.** This modern high-rise hotel in a residential district beyond the center has rooms that are bright and spacious with white art deco–inspired furniture. *Baan 7, 2012 DB, tel. 023/319091, fax 023/329853. 106 rooms. Facilities: restaurant bar. AE, DC, MC, V. $$$*

Golden Tulip Lion d'Or. This traditional hotel near the railway station has been here since the early 18th century. Thoroughly modernized, it has spacious rooms. A jogging path runs behind the hotel. *Kruisweg 34–36, 2011 LC, tel. 023/321750, fax 023/329543. 36 rooms with bath. Facilities: restaurant, garage, business center. AE, DC, MC, V. $$–$$$*

Hotel Faber. Within walking distance of the beaches of Zandvoort, this is a small, family-style hotel with bright, tidy rooms and a summer terrace. *Kostverlorenstraat 15, 2042 PA Zandvoort, tel. 02507/12825, fax 02507/16886. 30 rooms with bath. Facilities: lounge. AE, MC, V. $*

The Hague **Le Haricot Vert.** In a 1638 former staff house for the nearby palace,
Dining this intimate, candlelighted restaurant combines Dutch simplicity and French flair. Succulent meats swimming in sauce are served on large white plates with tangles of colorful vegetables. The menu changes seasonally. *Molenstraat 9a–11, tel. 070/365–2278. Reservations advised. Jacket and tie advised. AE, MC, V. $$–$$$*

Lodging **Hotel Des Indes.** With a grace and graciousness that make it one of the world's very special hotels, it is on one of The Hague's most prestigious squares. Once a private residence, the mansion was built principally for grand balls and entertainments. The former inner courtyard is now a towering reception area leading to the restaurant. The spacious, stylish rooms were renovated in 1993–94. One suite, which enjoys a magnificent view over the city toward the beach, is fought over by rock stars who come to perform in nearby Rotterdam. *Lange Voorhout 54–56, 2514 EG, tel. 070/363–2932, fax 070/345–1721. 76 rooms. Facilities: restaurant, bar. AE, DC, MC, V. $$$$*

Kurhaus Hotel. Holding the prime position at the center of the beach at Scheveningen, this grand hotel of the old school is nevertheless fully modern and bustling. Now engulfed by shops and apartments on the street side, it still has its famous turn-of-the-century profile from the amusement pier, and you still can dine in the magnificent Kurzaal with its fancifully painted, coffered ceiling high overhead. Rooms here are grand and grandly decorated in a variety of modern and traditional styles. *Gevers Deynootplein 30, 2586 CK, Scheveningen, tel. 070/416–2636, fax 070/416–2646. 241 rooms. Facilities: 2 restaurants, sauna, casino. AE, DC, MC, V. $$$$*

Corona Hotel. Elegant lodging seems appropriate to an elegant city of diplomacy, and this hotel fits in perfectly. It is conveniently located across from the Parliament Complex, near the Mauritshuis and Museum Bredius at the edge of the shopping district. The rooms are restfully decorated in a muted scheme of white, cream, and dove gray. *Buitenhof 39–42, 2513 AH, tel. 070/363–7930, fax 070/361–5785. 26 rooms with bath. Facilities: restaurant, bar. AE, DC, MC, V. $$$*

Novotel Hotel. Well located for both the sights and the shopping of The Hague, Novotel is a new and well-appointed full-service hotel with modestly sized rooms; the decor is a bland but restful beige and white. *Hofweg 5–7, 2511 AA, tel. 070/364–8846, fax 070/356–2889. 106 rooms. Facilities: restaurant, bar, sauna. AE, DC, MC, V. $$*

Hotel Petit. On a residential boulevard between the Peace Palace and The Hague Municipal Museum, this quiet, family-style mid-20th-century brick hotel is operated by a young couple. Bright and graciously furnished, it has a pleasant guests-only bar-lounge for relaxing after a day of sightseeing. *Groot Hertoginnelaan 42, 2517 EH, tel. 070/346–5500, fax 070/346–3257. 20 rooms with bath. Facilities: bar. AE, DC, MC, V. $–$$*

Hotel Sebel. The friendly owners of this hotel have expanded into two buildings between the city center and the Peace Palace. Tidy and comfortable, the rooms are large and have high ceilings and tall windows for lots of light and air. *Zoutmanstraat 38, 2518 GR, tel. 070/360–8010, fax 070/345–5855. 14 rooms with bath. Facilities: bar-lounge. AE, DC, MC, V. $–$$*

City Hotel. Just off the beach in Scheveningen, this spanking clean, brightly decorated, and very friendly small family hotel spreads through several houses on a main street leading to the waterfront. It has its own restaurant, rare in a hotel of this size. *Renbaanstraat 1–3 and 17–23, 2586 EW, Scheveningen, tel. 070/355–7966, fax 070/354–0503. 20 rooms with bath. Facilities: restaurant, bar. AE, DC, MC, V. $*

Leiden
Dining

Bistro La Cloche. This chic, attractive French-Dutch restaurant, just off the Rapenburg canal on the small street leading to St. Peter's Church, is done up in soft pastels, with flowers everywhere. It has a pleasant, but small, streetside café area and quieter dining upstairs. *Kloksteeg 3, tel. 071/123053. Reservations advised. Jacket and tie advised. AE, DC, MC, V. $$$*

Oudt Leyden/'t Pannekoekenhuysje. These side-by-side restaurants with a shared kitchen have totally different menus and environments. Oudt Leyden is a formal, Old Dutch–style restaurant with a traditional menu of simple grilled and sautéed meats and fishes; 't Pannekoekenhuysje is a traditional Dutch pancake house with red-checked tablecloths, a relaxed mood, and easy-on-the-budget prices. *Steenstraat 51–53, tel. 071/133144. Reservations advised. O.L.: jacket and tie advised; 't P.: casual. AE, DC, MC, V. Closed Sun. Oudt Leyden: $$$; 't Pannekoekenhuysje: $*

Mangerie de Koekop. Just a few minutes from the old De Valk Windmill, near the center of old Leiden, this restaurant is popular with students and locals. The turn-of-the-century building was gutted and has been refurbished with tasteful but no-frills decor, including cream ceramic-tile floors, apple-green tablecloths, and wicker chairs. The good-value, excellent food draws the crowds: Less than Fl 40 buys a three-course meal that includes such mouthwatering dishes as artichoke hearts wrapped in fillets of sole or sweetbreads with shiitake mushrooms simmered in sake. *Lange Mare 60, 2312 GS, tel. 071/141937. Reservations advised. Dress: casual. No credit cards. $$*

M'n Broer. Run by a pair of twins, "My Brother" is a cozy brasserie with a brown café atmosphere. The kitchen serves up such hearty meals as seafood pie and roast duck with port sauce; the portions are generous, and the food is good. *Kloksteeg 7, tel. 071/125024. No reservations. Dress: casual. No credit cards. $$*

Annie's Verjaardag. This restaurant consists of a low-ceilinged, arched cellar, often full of chatty students, and a water-level canalside terrace. During the day, there is a modest selection of salads and sandwiches on baguettes, and at least one more substantial offering. After 6 PM you can choose from a fuller menu that includes cheese fondue, grilled trout, and spareribs. *Hoogstraat 1a, tel. 071/125737. No reservations. Dress: casual. No credit cards. $–$$*

Lodging

Holiday Inn Leiden. Just off the secondary highway between Leiden and The Hague and not far from the beaches at Katwijk, this is more a resort than a hotel. There is a vast interior garden lobby, and the decor of the guest rooms carries out the garden theme with bold colors and floral-patterned curtains. *Haagse Schouwweg 10, 2332 KG, tel. 071/355555, fax 071/355553. 200 rooms. Facilities: 2 restaurants, bar, swimming pool, tennis and squash, bowling, sauna/solarium, casino. AE, DC, MC, V. $$$*

De Ceder. This is a small, friendly, and very tidy family-style hotel in a converted home out near the teaching hospital of Leiden University. The garden rooms are particularly desirable, but the breakfast room overlooks the garden, too. *Rijnsburgerweg 80, 2333 AD, tel. 071/17 59 03, fax 071/15 70 98. 16 rooms, 9 with bath/shower. Facilities: bar-lounge for guests, garden. AE, DC, MC, V. $*

Rotterdam
Dining

Raden Mas of Rotterdam. At this elegant and exotically decorated Indonesian restaurant, rijsttafel is served both traditional style (from a number of small dishes) and Oriental style (all on your plate from the kitchen). Among the traditional elements of a rijsttafel you will find *sate* (a kebob of chicken or pork in peanut sauce), *gado-gado* (Oriental vegetables), and *sambal* (a red-pepper condiment that is very, very hot). *Kruiskade 72, tel. 010/411–7244. Reservations advised. Jacket and tie advised. AE, DC, MC, V. $$$$*

La Gondola. In this Italian restaurant there is a picture wall that reads like a history of modern pop music. Directly across from the Rotterdam Hilton, where pop stars tend to stay, it is a relaxing, friendly place with a good selection of traditional Italian specialties. *Kruiskade 6, tel. 010/411–4284. Reservations advised. Jacket required. AE, DC, MC, V. $$$*

Millers. This restaurant in attractive Delfshaven is housed in a converted warehouse dating from 1620. There's a spacious bistro downstairs for drinks and light meals, and intimate nooks under the rafters upstairs for dinners by candlelight. The menu displays Japanese, Italian, and French influences. *Voorhaven 3, tel. 010/477–5181. Reservations advised. Dress: casual but neat. AE, DC, MC, V. $$–$$$*

De Wagon. This pleasant little restaurant is an old railway dining car now at Leuvehaven harbor. It is a casual place with a friendly bar and a traditional menu of grilled meats and fish. *Geldersekade 10, tel. 010/433–1728. No reservations. Dress: casual. AE, DC, MC, V. $$*

Dining and
Lodging

Rotterdam Holiday Inn. This 10-story, business-oriented hotel is next to the major theater of Rotterdam and across from the congress center. It has attractive, art deco–style rooms, renovated in 1993–94, and an appealing small restaurant overlooking the street that offers a fixed-price dinner arrangement with private limousine transportation for nonguests. *Schouwburgplein 1, 3012 CK, tel. 010/433–3800, fax 010/414–5482. 100 rooms. Facilities: restaurant, café. AE, DC, MC, V. $$$*

Hotel New York. The twin towers rising over the water of the Nieuwe Maas across from the city center for decades were known to Rotterdammers as the headquarters of the Holland-America Line. In 1993, the old building was renovated and opened as a hotel. Rooms are individually decorated and modern. The enormous restaurant (it seats 400) somehow maintains an intimate, café atmosphere, and the fine, eclectic cuisine attracts Rotterdam's fashionable set. *Koninginnenhoofd 1, tel. 010/486–2066, fax 010/484–2701. 73 rooms. Facilities: restaurant, gym, meeting rooms. AE, DC, MC, V. $–$$*

Lodging

Rotterdam Hilton. Don't be surprised if you run into Mick Jagger or Diana Ross if you stay here. This is the hotel of choice for many of the pop and rock performers who bring their tours to Holland; it provides top facilities, a number of suites, and luxury appointments and amenities. It also has one of the best downtown locations in Rotterdam. *Weena 10, 3012 CM, tel. 010/414-4044, fax 010/411-8884. 247 rooms, 7 suites. Facilities: restaurant, café, bar, discotheque, garage, casino, barber/beauty shop. AE, DC, MC, V. $$$$*

Hotel Inntel Rotterdam. All the rooms in this modern high rise, built at the opening to the Leuvehaven inner harbor in 1990, have water views, as do the dinner restaurant and the rooftop health club. *Leuvehaven 80, 3011 EA, tel. 010/413-4139, fax 010/413-3222. 150 rooms. Facilities: restaurant, café, sauna, indoor swimming pool. AE, DC, MC, V. $$$*

Hotel Van Walsum. On a residential boulevard within walking distance of the Boymans–van Beuningen Museum, Hotel van Walsum is not far from the Euromast. The gregarious owner proudly restores and reequips his rooms, floor by floor, on a continuously rotating basis, with the always-modern decor of each floor determined by that year's best buys in furniture, carpeting, and bathroom tiles. There is a bar-lounge and a small restaurant that has a summer garden extension. *Mathenesserlaan 199–201, 3014 HC, tel. 010/436-3275, fax 010/436-4410. 25 rooms. Facilities: restaurant, café. AE, DC, MC, V. $*

Utrecht
Dining

Het Grachtenhuys. There is the feeling of a gracious home at this restaurant in a canal house that overlooks the fashionable New Canal. The young owners offer a choice of four- or five-course menus of traditionally French-influenced Dutch cuisine. Tempting selections might include rabbit fillet with a puree of various nuts, or truffle and potato soup with smoked eel. *Nieuwegracht 33, tel. 030/317494. Reservations advised. Jacket and tie advised. AE, DC, MC, V. Closed Mon. and weekend lunch. $$$-$$$$*

Le Piano. One of the restaurants on the lower quay of Utrecht's main canal, it has waterside tables in the summer. The dining room is hung with amusing art; the menu offers traditional grilled dishes, including choices such as salmon with chervil, and lamb with honey and rosemary. *Oudegracht a/d Werf 101–103, tel. 030/334939. Reservations advised. Dress: casual but neat. AE, DC, MC, V. $$*

Polman's Huis. This grand café of the old school is a Utrecht institution. Its Jugendstijl/Art Deco interior is authentic. Other reasons to find your way to Polman's are its relaxing atmosphere and range of meal choices, from a simple quiche to a steamed fish dinner. *Keistraat 2, tel. 030/313368. No reservations. Dress: casual. No credit cards. Closed Dec. 25. $$*

Lodging

Holiday Inn. Primarily a business hotel (it looks like an office building), it serves the convention and exhibition hall next door and makes a convenient choice for other travelers as well. It has the only hotel swimming pool in town. *Jaarbeursplein 24, 3521 AR, tel. 030/910555, fax 030/943999. 280 rooms. Facilities: restaurant, bar, sauna, indoor swimming pool. AE, DC, MC, V. $$$*

Hotel Smits. On the main square between the station and the old city center, this medium-size hotel has all the comforts of the larger, business-oriented establishments. The rooms are bright, comfortable, and decorated in mauve and black, in an art deco–influenced manner; no-smoking rooms are available. *Vredenburg 14, 3511 BA, tel. 030/33 12 32, fax 030/328451. 85 rooms. Facilities: restaurant, bar. AE, DC, MC, V. $$*

Malie Hotel. On a quiet residential street in a 19th-century row house, this is a modern and attractive family hotel. Rooms are brightly decorated though simply furnished. The bar-lounge doubles as a small art gallery. *Maliestraat 2–4, 3581 SL, tel. 030/316424, fax 030/340661. 29 rooms with baths. Facilities: bar. AE, DC, MC, V. $$*

Hotel Ouwi. A convivial family hotel, it is just off one of the main transit routes to the city center. The rooms are tight and simple in furnishings and decor, but they're very clean and tidy. *F.C. Dondersstraat 12, 3572 JH, tel. 030/716303, fax 030/714619. 21 rooms, 18 with bath/shower. No credit cards. $*

The Arts and Nightlife

The Arts The cities of the Randstad are a cultural mecca, harboring world-class music and dance programs, master classes, major festivals, and pop/rock extravaganzas.

For information on cultural events, call the *Uit (Going Out)* **information** telephone numbers in The Hague (Uitpost Den Haag, tel. 070/363–3833) and Rotterdam (Uit Promotie Rotterdam, tel. 010/413–6540; or VVV Rotterdam, tel. 06/3403–4065), or contact the VVV tourist information office in Utrecht (Vredenburg 90, tel. 06/3403–4085) for both schedules and ticket information. In addition, in The Hague you can pick up the monthly *Info: Den Haag, Scheveningen en Kijkduin, Day to Day Tourist Information*, which lists (in Dutch) what's going on in major theaters in that area, with English copy describing major events. Similar publications are *Inside Out* in Rotterdam, and *Uit in Utrecht* in Utrecht.

Music Haarlem hosts the **International Organ Competition** in even-numbered years during the first week of July. In The Hague, the **Residentie Orkest** is the city's excellent orchestra, which performs at **Dr. Anton Philipszaal** (Houtmarkt 17, tel. 070/360–9810) and **Nederlands Congresgebouw** (Churchillplein 10, tel. 070/354–8000). In Rotterdam, the concert orchestra is the fine **Rotterdam Philharmonic Orchestra,** which performs at the large concert hall **Concert-en Congresgebouw de Doelen** (Kruisstraat 2/Schouwburgplein 50, tel. 010/217–1700). Utrecht is the site of the **Festival of Early Music** (tel. 030/340921) late in each summer. It also offers a full program of concerts in its fine churches, including the Dom Church (tel. 030/310403), St. Peter's Church (tel. 030/311485), and St. Catharine's Church (tel. 030/314030), and there are programs including both concerts and master classes in the **Conservatory** of the **K&W-gebouw/Arts and Sciences Building** (Mariaplaats 27, tel. 030/314044).

Dance **Nederlands Danstheater** is the national modern dance company of the Netherlands, which makes its home in The Hague and performs at the **AT&T Danstheater** (Schedeldoekshaven 60, tel. 070/360–4930). **Scapino Ballet** is Rotterdam's resident dance company; performances are at **Rotterdamse Schouwburg** (Schouwburgplein 25, tel. 010/411–8110), which was designed by Dutch architect Wim Quist. In Utrecht you will find dance on the programs of **Stadsschouwburg** (Lucas Bolwerk 24, tel. 030/331343), which has a major performance hall as well as the Blauwe Zaal (Blue Room) for small productions.

Theater/Opera In The Hague, the national theater company **Het Nationale Toneel** performs at **Royal Schouwburg** (Korte Voorhout 3, tel. 070/346–9450); the **De Appel** company performs at its own **Appeltheater** (Duinstraat 6–8, tel. 070/350–2200). **Musicals,** including occasional world tours from Broadway, can be seen at **Nederlands Congresgebouw** (Churchillplein 10, tel. 070/354–8000) or in the adjoining beach resort community of Scheveningen at **Circustheater** (G. Deijnootplein 50, tel. 070/351–1212). The theater company of Rotterdam is **RO-theatergroup,** which performs at the new **Rotterdamse Schouwburg** (Schouwburgplein 25, tel. 010/411–8110);

cabaret and musicals in Rotterdam are performed at **Luxor Theater** (Kruiskade 10, tel. 010/413–8326). Theater (and opera) in Utrecht is performed in the *zaals* (auditoriums—large and small) at **Stadsschouwburg** (Lucas Bolwerk 24; tel. 030/331343).

Film Films are shown in the original language, except Disney movies and other films for the very young. In addition to the annual avant-garde **Film Festival Rotterdam** (tel. 010/413–6540), Rotterdam offers mixed media and film performances at **Lantaren/Venster** (Gouvernestraat 129–133, tel. 010/436–1311) and has a special publication for film listings titled *Cargo*, available in bars, cafés, and some shops.

Pop/Rock When the big stars come to Rotterdam, they perform either at the **Sportpaleis Ahoy** (Zuiderparkweg 20–30, tel. 010/410–4204) or at the major soccer stadium, **Feyenoord Stadion** (Olympiaweg 50, tel. 010/492–9499 or 010/492–9444).

Jazz One of the festivals for which the Netherlands is well known is the annual **North Sea Jazz Festival** (tel. 070/350–2034), which is the largest of its kind in the world. It is held in The Hague and Scheveningen for four days in July and regularly attracts the greats of jazz as well as thousands of jazz lovers from around the world. In addition, the **Heineken Jazz Festival** (tel. 010/413–3972) is held in Rotterdam's streets and cafés in August.

Nightlife You'll find brown cafés in every town in the Netherlands and discos in any of the student towns, such as Leiden, but for real nightlife, with plenty of variety, look to the large cities. In The Hague, you will find discos in the streets around Centraal Station, especially on Herengracht, and in the beach resort of Scheveningen; in Rotterdam, nightlife is concentrated in Oude and Nieuwe Binnenweg, on 's Gravendijkswal, Oude Haven, Katshoek, Witte de Wittsstraat, and at Stadhuisplein; and in Utrecht, cafés are found on Oude Gracht and at 't Wed (near the canals, in the center). Among the favorite newer places to go are the Paris-style grand cafés and brasseries, which have terraces (open or covered) on busy streets and squares of the major cities.

Cafés In the beach community of Scheveningen, **Plaza Bar** (Gevers Deynootplein 118, tel. 070/355–5056) is a chic and exclusive place, open until 4 AM, that offers all sorts of music, live and recorded. In Rotterdam, **De Consul** (Westersingel 28B, tel. 010/436–3323) offers movies, New Age and pop music; **Zolcher's** (Badenpowellaan 12, tel. 010/436–4249), in the middle of Het Park, has a busy terrace, casual café, and smart restaurant. In Utrecht, **Het Oude Pothuis** (Oude Gracht 279, tel. 030/318970) has both music and meals six nights a week, plus a stage with instruments available for jam sessions; another place in Utrecht is **Polman's Huis** (*see* Dining and Lodging, *above*), which stays open until 2 AM on weekdays, 3 AM on weekends.

Discotheques In The Hague, the huge **Marathon** (Wijndaelerweg 3, tel. 070/368–0324) offers a wide variety of music, as does **Rock Inn** (Herengracht 7, tel. 070/345–7616). In Scheveningen, **Thahiti** (Strandweg 43, tel. 070/350–2068) has some live performances. In Rotterdam, **Hallo** (Stadhuisplein 43, tel. 010/414–6400), with a well-stocked bar and an intimate dance floor, has a wide range of music; **Carrera** (Karel Doormanstraat 10–12, tel. 010/213–0534, open Thurs.–Sun. to 5 AM) has a variety of music and an all-night French terrace serving snacks; **Full Moon** ('s Gravendijkswal 130, tel. 010/436–7172) has dance music until 4 AM nightly except Monday (no house music). In Utrecht, the top place is **Fellini** (Stadshuisbrug 3, tel. 030/317271), in the cellars of the old town hall.

Dancing   In Rotterdam, **Tudor** (Nieuwe Binnenweg 210212) has dance music Thursday through Sunday until 6 AM. **Le Toucan** (L. Berchmakerstraat 4, tel. 030/317107) in Utrecht is a "swing-café" with a dance floor that's open Wednesday to Saturday until 3 AM.

Jazz/Blues   After Amsterdam, Rotterdam is the place for jazz. **Dizzy** ('s Gravendijkswal 127A, tel. 010/477–3014) is a jazz café with a big terrace out back that has performances by Dutch and international musicians every Tuesday and Sunday. **Thelonious** (Witte de Withstraat 16, tel. 010/433–0421) has concerts on Friday and Saturday nights, with jam sessions on Thursdays. **De Twijfelaar** (Mauritsstraat 173, tel. 010/413–2671, open Tues.–Sat.) has jazz sessions on Wednesdays. In Utrecht, **Zeezicht** (Nobelstraat 2, tel. 030/319957) offers jazz and blues on Tuesdays.

For Gays   In Rotterdam, **Gay Palace** (Schiedamnsesingel 139, tel. 010/414–1486) is a discotheque that's open Thursday–Monday until 4 AM; and in Utrecht, **De Roze Wolk** (Oude Gracht 45, tel. 030/322066) is a canal-side gay and lesbian disco with two bars that's open Thursday–Saturday until 4:30 AM.

The Border Provinces and Maastricht

The long border between the Netherlands and Belgium runs like a drunkard's test path from the North Sea coast to the German frontier. The shared heritage of religion, architecture, food, and lifestyle makes Brussels as alluring as Amsterdam to the residents of the southern provinces of the Netherlands: These southern Dutch are more gregarious and outspoken than those of the north; they also pursue the good life of food, drink, and conviviality with more gusto, and less guilt, than their Calvinist-influenced countrymen who live "above the Great Rivers."

Three provinces hug the Belgian border: Zeeland (Sea Land) is a collection of flat, open, and windswept islands and peninsular extensions of the mainland, known for its agriculture and shellfish; Noord Brabant, also known simply as Brabant, is a wooded and water-laced industrial area bordered on both east and north by the River Maas; Limburg is a region of hills and half-timbered farmhouses that extends along the River Maas deep into the south, a peninsula of land surrounded on one side by Belgium and the other by Germany.

Important Addresses and Numbers

Tourist Information   The tourist information offices of the major cities of the border provinces are **VVV Breda** (Willemstraat 17–19, 4811AJ, tel. 076/222444), **VVV Eindhoven** (Stationsplein 17, 5611 AC, tel. 040/449231), **VVV 's-Hertogenbosch** (Markt 77, Box 1039, 5200 BA, tel. 073/123071), **VVV Maastricht** (Het Dinghuis, Kleine Staat 1, 6211 ED, tel. 043/252121, fax 043/213746), and **VVV Middelburg** (Markt 65a, Postbus 730, 4330 AS, tel. 01180/16851).

Emergencies   The **National Emergency Alarm Number** for police, fire, or ambulance is 06/11.

Medical   There are **hospitals** in Breda (tel. 076/258000), Eindhoven (tel. 040/335933), 's-Hertogenbosch (tel. 073/869111), Maastricht (tel. 043/876543), and Middelburg (tel. 01184/25000).

Arriving and Departing

By Plane There are airports in Eindhoven and Maastricht. In addition to regular flights to both cities from Amsterdam, **KLM City Hopper** (tel. 081/750–9000) also operates service direct from London Gatwick to Maastricht and from London Heathrow to Eindhoven. Additional services to Eindhoven from the United Kingdom are scheduled by **Base Business Airlines** (tel. 061/489–2988) from Birmingham and Manchester.

By Car To reach **Zeeland** take E19 from Amsterdam to Rotterdam and pick up A29 south; connect with N59 west to Zierikzee and N256 across the Zeelandbrug toll bridge to Goes, where you can pick up E312/A58 west to Middelburg, capital of Zeeland province.

To reach the provinces of Brabant and Limburg take E25/A2 from Amsterdam south through Utrecht. Pick up A27 south to Breda, or stay on E25 through Den Bosch to reach Eindhoven and other points south.

By Train There are **Intercity express trains** (tel. 06/9292) twice each hour from Amsterdam direct to 's-Hertogenbosch and Eindhoven, once each hour direct to Middelburg or Maastricht. To reach Breda by train, it is necessary to connect either in Roosendaal or 's-Hertogenbosch.

Getting Around the Border Provinces and Naastricht

By Bus The **national bus information** number is 06/9292. Operators can also give you information about local bus routes. Local and regional buses leave from and return to the Dutch railway stations.

By Train There is an Intercity train line (tel. 06/9292) that crosses the country, west to east **within the Border Provinces,** twice each hour. From Breda there also is twice-hourly service direct to Eindhoven, for connections to Maastricht.

By Taxi To summon a taxi, call in **Breda** (tel. 076–222111), **Eindhoven** (tel. 040/525252), **'s-Hertogenbosch** (tel. 073/313131), **Maastricht** (tel. 043/477777), and **Middelburg** (tel. 01180/12600).

Guided Tours

The **Maastricht Tourist Office** (Kleine Staat 1, tel. 043/252121) offers a guided tour of the city for Fl 5.25 for adults, Fl 3 for children. Tours last from one to 1½ hours. For cruises on the River Maas, contact **Stiphout Cruises** (Maaspromenade 27, 6211 HS Maastricht, tel. 043/254151). Fares start at Fl 8 adults and Fl 5 children.

The **Middelburg Tourist Office** (Markt 65a, tel. 01180/16851) occasionally offers guided walking tours during the summer for Fl 2 (1 hr) to Fl 4 (2 hrs) per person. Tours of the province also are available through **Holland International Reisbureau Van Fraassen** (Londensekaai 19, tel. 01180/27758), **Carlier Tours** (Elektraweg 9, tel. 01180/15015), and **Holland International Reisbureau** (Langeviele 7, tel. 01180/27855).

Exploring the Border Provinces and Maastricht

Numbers in the margin correspond to points of interest on the Border Provinces map.

Zeeland On the fingerlike peninsulas and islands of the province of Zeeland you are never more than a few kilometers from a major body of water. You also are never more than a meter or two above sea level, if you are above it at all: Floods have put this province almost completely under water on several occasions, most recently in 1953. Today, major dikes, dams, and bridges connect the four chief islands and peninsulas of Zeeland, guarding against the possibility of the sea's reclaiming the land already reclaimed by the Dutch.

From the north, follow A29 to N59, which leads to the small old city ❶ of **Zierikzee,** a yachting port with a canal connecting it to the open waters of the Oosterschelde. Continue on N59 to Serooskerke, where you can turn onto N57 to cross the Oosterscheldekering dam. This dramatic ride may be restricted in times of high winds; you have the North Sea to one side, the Oosterschelde bay to the other, and the looming storm surge barriers beside the road remind you that it requires massive constructions of steel and concrete to resist the forces of the sea. Your destination is Neeltje Jans Island, approximately halfway across the dam. Used as a work island during the two decades this massive enclosure was under construction, it ❷ now is the site of **Delta Expo,** which documents the 2,000-year history of Dutch hydraulic engineering. There are films and slide shows, working scale models, and displays of the materials used to construct dikes, dams, and underwater supports. The visit includes a boat trip in good weather, and there is an opportunity to walk inside a sample of one of the multistory pilings that make up the support system of the storm surge barriers. *Eiland Neeltje Jans, Burgh-Haamstede, tel. 01115/2702. Admission: Apr.–Oct., Fl 15 adults, Fl 10 children; Nov.–Mar., Fl 9 adults, Fl 6 children. Open Apr.–Oct., daily 10–5; Jan.–Feb., Thurs.–Mon. 10–5; Mar. and Nov.–Dec., Fri.–Tues. 10–5.*

Beyond the dam you briefly cross a corner of Noord Beveland Island and travel over another small dam, the Veersegatdam. Take the dike ❸ road to **Veere,** one of the prettiest small towns in the Netherlands, complete with a fairy-tale Gothic **Stadhuis** (Town Hall) begun in 1474. Now the principal sailing port of the Veerse Meer (Veerse Lake), the town was an important seaport in the 16th century, with a busy trade in items such as wool, linen, and salt. The **Museum De Schotse Huizen** (The Scots' Houses), which faces the town's small inner harbor, is actually side-by-side 16th-century buildings that once were the offices and warehouses of Scots wool merchants. Highly decorated, the buildings are named Het Lammetje (The Little Lamb) and De Struys (The Ostrich); you'll know which is which by the facade stones. Inside is a collection of local costumes, porcelain, household items, and paintings. *Kaai 25–27, Veere, tel. 01181/1744. Admission: Fl 2 adults, Fl 1.25 children. Open Apr.–Oct., Mon. 1–5, Tues.–Sat. 10–5.*

❹ From Veere take the local road to **Middelburg,** the capital of the province of Zeeland and an important trading post of the Dutch East and West India companies in the 17th century. The **Stadhuis** (Town Hall) on the market square is an elaborately decorated structure begun in the mid-15th century. The heart of this small city, however, is the 12th-century **Abdij** (Abbey Complex), which incorporates three churches, countless provincial government offices, a major research library, the provincial cultural and historical museum, and a tall tower that overlooks the city and surrounding countryside. Although it was badly damaged in World War II, the entire complex has been faithfully reconstructed. **Onze Lieve Vrouwe Abdij** (Our Beloved Lady Abbey) was founded in 1150 as a Premonstrant abbey and served as a monastery until 1574. A multimedia presentation about the design and history of the abbey includes a 20-minute video

The Border Provinces

North Sea

GERMANY

BELGIUM

Brussels

Ghent

Brugge

Antwerp

Rotterdam

Dordrecht

Breda **6**

's-Hertogenbosch **7**

Eindhoven **8**

Venlo

Tilburg

Helmond

Weert

Roermond

Maastricht **9—20**

Margraten **21**

Heerlen **22**

Hoensbroek **23**

Sittard

Zierikzee **1**

Delta Expo **2**

Veere **3**

Middelburg **4**

Yerseke **5**

Vlissingen

Goes

KEY

Rail Lines

Ferry

20 miles

30 km

TO DÜSSELDORF

TO KÖLN

in English. *Abdij 9, tel. 01180/16851. Admission: Fl 6 adults, Fl 4 children. Open Mar.–Nov., Mon.–Sat. 10–6, Sun. noon–6.*

Part of the Abdij complex, the **Zeeuwse Museum** (Zeeland Museum) is best known for its series of tapestries illustrating the major Dutch sea battles with Spain during the 16th century. The varied collection also includes an Egyptian mummy, votive stelae dating from the Roman period, a rare seashell collection of the Royal Zeeland Science Association, and a costume hall that is one of the best in the Netherlands. *Abdij, tel. 01180/26655. Admission: Fl 4.50 adults, Fl 1 children. Open Tues.–Fri. 10–5, Sat.–Mon. 1:30–5.*

Time Out   **Restaurant De Abdij** (Abdijplein 5, tel. 01180/35022 or 01180/36196) is a convenient place to stop for a bite of lunch. Within the Abbey Complex next to the Zeeuwse Museum, it offers a menu of sandwiches, salads, and light meals.

Also part of the Abbey complex, and of particular interest to American visitors to Zeeland, is the **Roosevelt Studiecentrum** (Roosevelt Study Center), a library, research center, and exhibition hall. Theodore Roosevelt and Franklin Delano Roosevelt were descendants of a Zeeland family; the purpose of this center is to make known the historical links between the United States and the Netherlands and particularly to publicize the role of the United States in Europe during the 20th century. *Abdij 9, tel. 01180/31590. Admission free. Open weekdays 10–12:30 and 1:30–4:30.*

You can climb the 207 steps to the top of the octagonal **"Lange Jan" Abdijtoren** ("Long John" Abbey Tower), which is attached to the Choral Church of the Abbey Complex. The 85-meter (280-foot) stone tower was constructed in the 14th century and is topped with an onion-shaped dome from the 18th century. *Abdij, tel. 01180/82255. Admission: Fl 2.50 adults, Fl 1.75 children. Open Apr.–Sept., Mon.–Sat. 10–5.*

❺   Leave Middelburg on E312/A58 toward Bergen Op Zoom. At the Kruiningen/Yerseke exit, follow signs to **Yerseke,** a small fishing port that is the oyster nursery of Europe. Along the waterfront here, you'll see lobster boats docked at the piers; below the seawalls in pits are the beds in which are nurtured what some say are the finest, sweetest, and most flavorful oysters and mussels in the world. Peek into the small buildings on the docks and you will see shellfish being sorted and packed for shipment.

Brabant   Follow A58 all the way to **Breda.** Dotted with parks, this small city **❻**   maintains a quiet medieval charm that is unexpected in a city also known as a major manufacturing center.

From the railway station, walk toward the center through **Stadspark Valkenburg** (Valkenburg Park), which dates from 1350 and was originally the castle garden of the counts of Breda. The former castle, **Kasteel van Breda** (Breda Castle), sits imposingly beyond the moat; it now houses the KMA (Royal Military Academy) and can be visited only on the city walks organized by the VVV during the summer.

Follow Kasteelplein to Kerkplein and the imposing 15th- and 16th-century **Grote Kerk** (Great Church). Built in the French-influenced Brabant Gothic style in brick and sandstone, it was the family church of the House of Orange-Nassau: William of Orange's first wife and child are buried here, as are several of his ancestors. The church was looted of its brass ornamentation when Napoléon's soldiers used it as a barracks. The splendor of the architecture remains, as does the magnificence of the blue-and-gold-painted 18th-century organ. *Kerkplein, tel. 076/218267. Admission: Fl 2. Open weekdays 10–5, Sat. 10–5, Sun. 1–5.*

Facing the Grote Markt just beyond the church is the **Stadhuis** (Town Hall), which counts among its treasures a copy of the Velázquez painting of the surrender of Breda in 1625. Also on this elongated square is the municipal museum, **Breda's Museum,** worth a quick visit to learn something of the city's eventful history. *Grote Markt 19, tel. 076/223110. Admission: Fl 1.50 adults, Fl 0.75 children. Open Tues.–Sun. 1–5.*

Time Out When it's time to take a break, you'll find a good selection of restaurants and cafés surrounding the Grote Markt. **Brasserie-Café Beecker & Wetselaar** (Grote Markt 45–49, tel. 076/221100), next to the Great Church, is a traditional high-ceilinged café with a brasserie upstairs.

From the head of the Grote Markt behind the church, follow Catharinastraat to the **Waalse Kerk** (Walloon Church, Catherinastraat 83a, tel. information 076/218267), which marks the entrance to the **Begijnhof** (Beguine Court). A home for unmarried or widowed lay women who dedicate their lives to prayer and charitable works, this is one of only two remaining cloisters of this type in the Netherlands (the other is in Amsterdam).

From Breda, take E311/A27 north to Raamsdonksveer and connect ❼ with A59 to **'s-Hertogenbosch.** 'S-Hertogenbosch means The Duke's Woods in Dutch, and while that is the official name of this stylish medieval city, the name you will hear more commonly is simply Den Bosch (pronounced "den-boss"), The Woods. Not much remains of the woods for which it was named, however: The forests have been replaced by marshes and residential and industrial development. The principal attraction of Den Bosch is the magnificent **St. Janskathedraal** (St. John's Cathedral), the only cathedral in the Netherlands. Built between 1380 and 1520 in the Brabant Gothic style, it is a cruciform, five-aisle basilica with numerous side chapels and a Romanesque tower. Abundantly decorated with statuary, sculptural details, and grotesques, its nave is supported by double flying buttresses that are unique in the Netherlands. *Parade, tel. 073/139740. Admission free. Open weekdays 10–5.*

Time Out There is a very special sweet treat in store for you in 's-Hertogenbosch. Called a *Bossche bol,* it is a whipped-cream-filled, ball-shaped *choux* (cream puff) pastry that is completely dipped in dark chocolate and served cool. **Patisserie Jan de Groot** (Stationsweg 24, tel. 073/133830), on the road leading to the railway station, is the only producer in town.

From the Parade, follow Lange Putstraat to Verwersstraat and turn left for the **Noordbrabants Museum** (North Brabant Museum), the foremost provincial museum in the country. Housed in the imposing former residence of the provincial governor, the museum contains historical, archaeological, and cultural exhibits related to the history of Brabant, as well as an outstanding art collection that includes many 17th- and 18th-century Dutch floral paintings and works by Brabant artists of various periods. *Verwersstraat 41, tel. 073/866877. Admission: Fl 7.50 adults, Fl 4.50 children. Open Tues.–Fri. 10–5, weekends noon–5.*

❽ From 's-Hertogenbosch, take E25/N2 to **Eindhoven.** This bustling, modern city has no traditional, historic center to explore, thanks to heavy bombing in World War II, but there are remarkable examples of contemporary architecture throughout the city (even the bus shelters are designed by well-known architects), and there is an exceptional museum of modern art. The **Stadelijk Van Abbemuseum** (Municipal van Abbe Museum) began in 1936 as the simple wish of a local cigar maker, Henri van Abbe, to visit a museum in his own town; today it has one of the world's finest collections of contemporary art and owns more works than can be displayed at one time. The galleries and exhibitions are rotated and rearranged continually. The collection includes major works by artists such as Picasso and Christo. There are examples here of every major trend of the last 100 years, including cubism, constructivism, de Stijl, German expressionism, minimalism, and American pop. *Bilderdijklaan 10, tel. 040/389730. Admission: Fl 5 adults, Fl 2.50 children. Open Tues.– Sun. 11–5.*

Leaving the Van Abbe Museum, you can take an interesting walk past shops and art galleries. Turn right on Wal and left at Grote Berg, right again at Bergstraat and take another right at Kleine Berg.

Time Out | **Grand Cafe Berlage** (Kleine Berg 16, tel. 040/457481) is a spacious, Art Deco brasserie with a streetside terrace that serves standard Dutch café fare such as spareribs, salads, and *uitsmijters* (fried eggs on toast with a variety of accompaniments, including tomatoes, ham, bacon, and cheese).

Continue left onto Keizersgracht and its continuation, Willemstraat, or return from Keizersgracht to the tourist office and railway station.

Numbers in the margin correspond to points of interest on the Maastricht map.

Maastricht From Eindhoven, take E25/A2 south through Limburg province to reach the city of Maastricht. The oldest city in the Netherlands, established by the Romans more than 2,500 years ago, Maastricht has enjoyed a long history as a crossroads between Germanic and Latin cultures. The lighthearted lifestyle, the meticulous attention to service, and the exceptionally fine French cuisine further reflect the blending of these influences. Maastricht straddles the River Maas: The old city is on the river's western bank, its newer neighborhoods and the railway station are on the eastern side. Connecting the two **❾** is **St. Servaasbrug** (St. Servatius Bridge), one of the oldest and busiest bridges in the Netherlands. Built solidly of gray Namur stone in the late 13th century, it replaced an earlier wooden bridge. It offers the best views of the old city—an expanse of jumbled rooflines and whitewashed houses facing the river. The St. Servatius Bridge leads directly into both the old city and the heart of the shopping district. Follow Maastrichter Brugstraat to its end and bear right on Kleine Staat to find the tourist office, housed in a building that dates from 1470. Take Muntstraat directly ahead to Markt, the market **❿** square, dominated by the 1662 **Stadhuis** (Town Hall). Every Wednesday and Friday are market days in Maastricht, when this square is chockablock with stalls and stands offering fruits, vegetables, meats, and household items. You'll notice that business here is conducted in three currencies (Dutch, Belgian, and German) and four languages (Dutch, French, German, and English). *Markt 78,*

Maastricht

tel. 043/292222. *Admission free. Open weekdays 8:30–12:30 and 2–5:30.*

⑪ Leave the market square by way of Spilstraat, near the jolly statue of a roly-poly woman carrying a basket of vegetables, known affectionately as **Moosewief** (Greengrocer's Wife).

⑫ Turn right onto Grote Street and continue to the large open **Vrijthof** square. Ringed with restaurants, grand cafés, discotheques, and traditional pubs, this is the major public gathering place of Maastricht and the focal point of the annual Carnival.

Time Out   A cheerful place to stop at any time of the day is the plant-filled, Jugendstil-decorated **Cafe Britannique** (Vrijthof 6, tel. 043/218691). It serves breakfast (with champagne if you like) as well as simple, light meals throughout the day and drinks, including a house beer, until midnight.

⑬ Tucked into a corner of Vrijthof are two churches. The larger of these is the magnificent and historic 7th-century **St. Servaasbasiliek** (St. Servatius Basilica) named for and built above the site of the burial place of a 4th-century saint whose choice of Maastricht for his see stimulated the development of the city following the departure of the Romans in 402. The basilica's 1993 restoration included a fresh paint job using the bright colors of the somewhat gaudy original design. The focal points of the church are the richly carved 13th-century **Berg Portal,** and the **Schatkamer van Sint Servaas** (Treasure Chamber of St. Servatius) in the 12th-century chapel. The extraordinary collection dates from 827 and contains religious relics (some of them donated by Charlemagne) and exquisitely wrought liturgical objects. The most important item in the collection is the 12th-century Noodkist, an elaborately decorated oak chest that is adorned with gold and silver figures and contains bones and relics of St. Servatius and other local bishops. *Vrijthof, tel. 043/25 21 21. Admission: Fl 3.50 adults, Fl 1 children. Open Dec.–Mar., daily 10–4, Apr.–June and Sept.–Nov. 10–5; July–Aug., daily 10–6.*

⑭ Next to St. Servatius is the 14th-century Gothic **St. Janskerk** (St. John's Church), the white interior of which is a notable contrast to the bright colors of St. Servatius Basilica. *Vrijthof (enter Henric van Veldekeplein), tel. 043/252121. Admission free. Open mid-June–mid-Sept., Tues.–Fri. 11–4; July–Aug. Tues.–Sat. 11–4.*

Cross the Vrijthof in front of the Spanish Government House and continue on the Bredestraat to reach the intimate residential square **⑮** **Onze Lieve Vrouweplein** (Our Beloved Lady Square). Dominating **⑯** the tree-shaded, quiet square is the **Onze Lieve Vrouwebasiliek** (Our Beloved Lady Basilica). Recent excavations on the square indicate that the basilica may have replaced a Roman temple. The Westwork, a massive flat facade in Romanesque style that is topped with two round turrets, is the oldest part of the structure, dating from the 11th and 12th centuries. Inside is a two-story apse with a double row of columns and a half-domed roof. *Onze Lieve Vrouweplein, tel. 043/251851. Admission to church free; admission to treasure chamber: Fl 3.50 adults, Fl 1 children. Open Easter–Oct., Mon.–Sat. 11–5, Sun. 1–5.*

From Onze Lieve Vrouweplein, take Plankstraat to the small entry **⑰** to **Op de Thermen.** This small interior square was discovered in 1840 to be the site of the Roman baths; recently laid paving stones indicate the outline of the chambers of the ancient complex. Beyond the **⑱** entry to the square, the next street is **Stokstraat,** a fashionable residential street that extends on either side of Plankstraat and was the heart of the original Roman settlement of Maastricht.

Turn right onto the Maas Boulevard, where a pedestrian bridge leads across the river to the newly developed (1994–95) Céramique **⑲** District. Here you'll find the **Bonnefantenmuseum** (Bonnefanten Museum), the provincial museum of Limburg. Among the displays are one on the archaeological history of the province, a model of the city of Maastricht, and an art collection that focuses on 13th- to 15th-century Romanesque and Gothic Mosan sculpture of the Meuse region, 14th- to 16th-century Italian painting, and 16th- to 18th-century paintings of the South Netherlands, including works by Jan Bruegel and Pieter Bruegel the Younger. There also is a collection of contemporary art by important Dutch painters of the 20th century, several of whom are from Limburg. At press time, the museum was in the process of moving from its old location at Dominikanerplein 5 (tel. 043/251655), and planned to open here in early 1995. As the treasures are packed away and there is less to see at the old address, the admission price will dwindle to zero. *Ave. Ceramique 250, tel. 043/290190. Admission: Fl 10 adults, Fl 5 children. Open Tues.–Fri. 10–5, weekends 11–5.*

South beyond Maastricht's city walls and the busy Prins **⑳** Bisshopsingel (N278) encircling highway are the **Grotten St. Pieter** (Caves of St. Peter), man-made corridors carved deep into the limestone hills since Roman times to produce building stone. There are approximately 200 kilometers (124 miles) of chambers and passageways here; in some areas the mining has been so extensive that the ceiling height now is nearly 12 meters (40 feet); this means that graffiti left by the Romans are now far above your head, while the signatures of such visitors as Napoléon can still be seen. The caves are complex and can be visited only with a guide; they are also chilly and damp, so bring a sweater. *Grotten Noord (Northern System) Luikerweg 71; Zonneberg Caves, Slavante 1 (near Enci Cement Works); tel. 043/217878 for times of tours and for an English-speaking guide. Admission: Fl 5.25 adults, Fl 3 children. Open hrs vary; call ahead.*

Numbers in the margin correspond to points of interest on the Border Provinces map.

South Limburg Take the encircling highway N278 east from the caves toward Vaals and Aachen. Approximately 10 kilometers (6 miles) beyond the city, **㉑** near the town of **Margraten,** you will find the entrance to the 65-acre **Netherlands American Cemetery and Memorial.** This is the only American military cemetery in the Netherlands and is the final resting place of more than 8,000 Americans killed in World War II. *Rijksweg 2, tel. 04458/1208. Admission free. Open summer, daily 8–6; winter, daily 8–5.*

㉒ From here, take N281 toward **Heerlen,** the second of the Roman cities in this part of the Netherlands. The discovery in 1940 of the foundations of a large and elaborate Roman bathhouse was proof of the importance of Heerlen as a meeting place for the Roman troops stationed in this northern outpost. Now enclosed in a large, open, glass-encircled building, the **Thermenmuseum** (Thermae Museum) has catwalks over the perfectly preserved complex. The *thermae* (baths) incorporated open-air sports fields, a large swimming pool, shops, restaurants, and the enclosed bathhouse complex, which included a large dressing room, the hot-air sweating room, and a series of baths (warm, lukewarm, cold, and immersion). *Coriovallumstraat 9, Heerlen, tel. 045/604581. Museum admission: Fl 3 adults, Fl 2 children. Open Tues.–Fri. 10–5, weekends and holidays 2–5.*

㉓ Follow N281 northwest to **Hoensbroek** and the largest and best preserved of the castles in South Limburg, the **Kastel Hoensbroek** (Hoensbroek Castle), which incorporates sections dating from the 13th century and represents various architectural styles, including Baroque and Maasland-Renaissance. You can visit several sparsely but appropriately furnished rooms and an unexpected small museum of Afro-Asian art. There is an art gallery in the attic and a photography gallery in the gatehouse. *Klinkertstraat 118, tel. 045/211182. Admission: Fl 5 adults, Fl 3.50 children. Open May–Sept., 10–5:30; Oct.–Apr., 10–noon and 1–5:30.*

What to See and Do with Children

Miniatuur Walcheren (Miniature Walcheren) is a miniature city in a garden not far from the Abbey Complex in Middelburg. Typical buildings and landmarks of the area have been duplicated at 1:20 scale, including houses, churches, and windmills. Even the trees and plants are miniature, and there is a reconstruction of Veerse Lake, with motorized boats. *Molenwater, Middelburg, Zeeland, tel. 01180/12525. Admission: Fl 8 adults, Fl 4 children. Open Apr. 12–Oct. 21, daily 9:30–5; July–Aug., daily 9:30–7:30.*

The **Remschip de Schorpioen** (Ramship *Scorpion*) is one of only three iron ramming ships of its kind in the world and the oldest surviving Dutch naval vessel. It is docked across from the railway station in Middelburg and can be visited in summer. *Loskade,*

Middelburg, Zeeland, tel. 01180/39649. Admission: Fl 3.50 adults, Fl 2.50 children. Open Apr.–Oct., daily 10–5.

De Efteling is a children's fairy-tale park in Brabant, approximately halfway between Breda and 's-Hertogenbosch. Rides and amusements are enhanced by the fanciful and witty depiction of classic fairy tales by the Dutch artist Anton Pieck. *Box 18, 5170 AA Kaatsheuvel, Brabant, tel. 04167/88111, fax 4167/81095. Admission: Fl 30, children under 3 free. Open mid-Apr.–late Oct., daily 10–6.*

Hundreds of animals live in an open, natural environment at **Safaripark Beekse Bergen** in Brabant, near Tilburg. There is a safari bus to take you through the park, or you can rent your own safari jeep (Fl 50 for 1½ hours). There is also a children's farm. *Beekse Bergen 1, Hilvarenbeek, Brabant, tel. 013/360035. Admission: Fl 17 adults, Fl 14 children. Open Apr.–Oct.*

Off the Beaten Track

Just east of Tilburg is **Oisterwijk,** a wooded community and resort town that's perfect for a weekend getaway or a quiet day in the country. The charming central square is planted with lime trees, and there is a bird sanctuary with a number of exotic species.

As you travel south toward Maastricht, the small town of **Thorn,** known as the "white village" because of its abundance of white-painted 18th-century houses and buildings, is also well worth a detour. Visit the 10th-century abbey church, which has an outstanding Baroque altar and three choirs (for canons, princesses, and noblewomen); there also is a small museum.

Shopping

While there is shopping in every city mentioned in this section, you are well advised to save your guilders for Maastricht. This sophisticated small city is a mecca for goods from all over Europe, drawing merchants and shoppers from as far as Amsterdam, Brussels, and Cologne.

In Maastricht, as well as Breda, 's-Hertogenbosch, and Middelburg, stores are open late (until 9 PM) on Thursday; in Eindhoven, on Friday.

Shopping Districts The concentration of shopping in **Maastricht** is in the pedestrian cross streets that connect and surround the three main squares of the old city. Maastrichter Brugstraat takes you into the network of shopping streets from the St. Servaasbrug. Maastrichter Smedenstraat and Plankstraat are lined with exclusive shops, with Wolfstraat and the exceptionally fashionable Stokstraat intersecting both of them. In the other direction, Kleine Staat and Grote Staat lead to Vrijthof, with a mixed bag of shopping opportunities. Off Grote Staat is a trio of small shopping streets—Spilstraat, Nieuwestraat, and Muntstraat—that end at the Markt. Off Helmstraat is a shopping square, W. C. Entre Deux.

Street Markets **Breda** has a general market at Grote Markt Tuesday through Friday, and a secondhand market on Wednesday; **'s-Hertogenbosch** holds a large general market every Wednesday and Saturday; **Maastricht** has its tri-country general market in front of the Town Hall on Wednesday and Friday mornings, and a flea market opposite the railway station on Saturday; **Middelburg's** market day is Thursday, and the fruit market is held there on Saturday. The summer antiques and curiosities market is held at the Vismarkt from mid-June through August on Thursdays from 9 to 4.

Art and Antiques Fair Each year Maastricht's MECC Congress and Exhibition Hall is the site of the **European Fine Art Fair** (European Fine Art Foundation, Box 1035, 5200BA, 's-Hertogenbosch, tel. 073/145165), for a week beginning in mid-March. Major dealers in antiques and fine art from all over Europe participate, showing paintings, drawings, and prints (traditional and contemporary), furniture and objects, textiles, tapestries, and rugs; there also are music programs and lectures.

Specialty Stores *Antiques/Art Galleries* Eindhoven is an art and antiques mecca. Among the dealers in modern art is **Kunsthandel Beckers B.V.** (Kleine Berg 14, tel. 040/441381). Antiques dealers include **Mimore** (Keizersgracht 22, tel. 040/444470) for 20th-century articles, including Art Deco; and **'t Harlekijntje** (Bergstraat 38, no phone) for small antique items.

Art Books The shop of the **North Brabant Museum** (Verwersstraat 41, tel. 073/877800) in 's-Hertogenbosch offers an exceptional collection of art books covering many periods and styles of Dutch and international art.

Sports and the Outdoors

Biking To rent a bicycle, contact, in Breda, **Rijwielstalling NS** (Stationsplein 16–20, tel. 076/210501); in 's-Hertogenbosch, **Stationsfietsstalling** (Stationsplein 22, 5211 AP, tel. 073/134737 or 073/134033) or **Cyclepoint** (Hoek Zuid-Willems-vaart-Hinthamereinde, tel. 073/139020); in Middelburg, **Stationsrijwielstalling** (Kanaalweg 22, tel. 01180/12178) or **L. Petiet** (Kinderdijk 92, tel. 01180/24394); in Maastricht, the **Railway Station** (Stationsplein, Maastricht, tel. 043/211100).

Canoeing/ Kayaking There are two areas of interest to canoeists in Noord Brabant province. One is the **Biesbosch** area near Breda, which combines small creeks with stretches of open water (busy with powerboats in the summer season); the other is the tiny **Dommel River,** which meanders through the countryside between 's Hertogenbosch and Eindhoven and beyond. To rent a canoe in the Biesbosch area, contact **Nion Watersport** (Oosterhoutseweg 20, Raamsdonksveer, tel. 01621/12997); along the Dommel, contact **Adventure Trips** (Sint Oedenrode, tel. 04138/77267), **De Kanovriend** (Geenhovensedreef 10, Valkenswaard, tel. 04902/14632), or **Kanobouw/kanoverhuur Rofra** (Luikerweg 74, Valkenswaard, tel. 04902/42593). To kayak on the River Maas in Maastricht, contact **Kayak Tours Limburg** (Grote Dries 8, 6223 AE Borgharen, tel. 043/632242).

Sailing To arrange a day on the water in Zeeland, contact **Jachtwerf Oostwatering** (Polredijk 13 B, Veere, tel. 01181/1665), **WSVW en RYCB,** (Wolphaartsdijk, tel. 01198/1565), **Keur Marina B.V.** (Kanaalweg wz 5, Veere, tel. 01181/1223), or **Jachtwerf Wolphaartsdijk** (Zandkreekweg 5, Wolphaartsdijk, tel. 01198/1562).

Spa One of the special treats of South Limburg is a luxurious hill spa that offers a complete range of services, including indoor and outdoor spring-fed pools, sauna, steam bath, yoga/meditation and hydrogymnastics, aerobics, sports massage, herbal and mud baths, and more. **Thermae 2000** (Cauberg 27, 6301 BT Valkenburg aan de Geul, Valkenburg, tel. 04406/19419) is open daily 9 AM–11 PM.

Tennis/Squash To play in Maastricht, visit **Squash Centre Erik van der Pluijm** (Brusselsestraat 74a, tel. 043/216387), **Tennis Centre De Dousberg**

(Dousbergweg, tel. 043/434404), or **Sportpark Mulder** (Mockstraat 36–38, tel. 043/637295). Rates are about Fl 20 per 30 minutes of court time during the day; Fl 40, after 5 PM.

Spectator Sports

Trotting Races There is Friday-night racing at the **Limburg Race** in Landgraff (Hofstraat 13–15, tel. 045/319191) starting at 7.

Soccer Eindhoven's team, **PSV** (Philips Sport Vereniging), plays from September through May at **PSV-stadion Eindhoven** (Frederiklaan 101A, tel. 040/501505).

Beaches

In the vicinity of Middelburg, you will find the best beaches at the towns of **Domburg, Kouderkerke, Oostkapelle, Vrouwenpolder/ Serooskerke, Westkapelle,** and **Zoutelande;** all have beach houses to rent, and all but Vrouwenpolder/Serooskerke have beach pavilions.

Dining and Lodging

When Amsterdammers want to spend a weekend eating well and staying in luxurious small hotels, they think first of the southern provinces of their own country. The freshness of Zeeland shellfish and the Burgundian lifestyle and French kitchens of the border provinces make for restaurants of exceptional quality, and Limburg's castles are often the site of luxurious hotels.

Breda Dining **Auberge De Arent.** The ceiling murals in this elegant white, step-gabled 15th-century house, thought to be among the oldest in western Brabant, are of pheasants, rabbits, and snails, all of which are found on the menu in wild season (the fall and winter months). The Arent has a French kitchen; there is a separate bistro and also a wine cellar with a tasting room. *Schoolstraat 2, tel. 076/144601. Reservations advised. Jacket and tie required. AE, DC, MC, V. Closed Sat. lunch and Sun. Restaurant $$$; Bistro $$*

Dining and Lodging **De Klok.** This small hotel is a busy and friendly part of the lively market square of Breda. There is a café on the street in summer, and a bar and restaurant take up the lobby. Double rooms are generously sized, and beds have *dekbedden* (comforters) to keep you warm. Baths may have shower or tub; some quads are available. *Grote Markt 26–28, 4811 XR, tel. 076/214082, fax 076/14343. 28 rooms with bath/shower. Facilities: restaurant/café, bar. AE, DC, MC, V. $$*

Lodging **Hotel Mercure.** Next to the railway station in a building that formerly housed the offices of the telephone company, this member of the French hotel chain is a straightforward business hotel with a no-nonsense approach to decorating. Still, rooms are spacious, and the staff exhibits a certain degree of Gallic charm. *Stationsplein 14, 4811 BB, Breda, tel. 076/220200, fax 076/214967. 40 rooms. Facilities: restaurant, bar. AE, DC, MC, V. $$–$$$*

Eindhoven Dining **Ravensdonck.** The Ravensdonck is in a large and elegant house with tall windows. The dining room, on the second floor, with windows all around, serves a variety of simple but tasty grilled dishes. A café with a friendly atmosphere occupies the first floor. There is an amusing touch here, in that you can buy boxes of chocolates in the shape of light bulbs. Why not? It was a light-bulb factory that transformed Eindhoven from a sleepy village at the turn of the century to an international business mecca. *Ten Hagestraat 2, tel. 040/443142. Reservations advised. Jacket and tie required. AE, DC, MC, V. Closed weekend lunch. $$*

Dining and **The Mandarin Hotel.** Prepare yourself for a pleasant surprise: The
Lodging Mandarin is unique in that it was designed to meet East Asian standards of service. Its Asian decor includes small bridges spanning water gardens as part of the traffic pattern through the lobby. The restaurants are all Asian in theme and cuisine: One serves fine Chinese specialties, another offers a range of Indonesian and Oriental dishes, and the third is a Japanese steak house; there also is a Parisian coffee shop. No-smoking rooms are available. *Geldropseweg 17, 5611 SC, tel. 040/125055, fax 040/121555. 105 rooms and suites. Facilities: 3 restaurants, café, indoor swimming pool, saunas, parking. AE, DC, MC, V. $$$*

Elsloo **Kasteel Elsloo.** This manor-house castle with its own park and bo-
Dining and tanical garden sits at the edge of the village, which owns and oper-
Lodging ates the hotel restaurant. Rooms are spacious and restfully decorated. The restaurant, too, has a manor house ambience; the kitchen is traditional French. *Maasberg 1, 6181 GV, tel. 046/37 76 66, fax 046/377570. 27 rooms with bath. Facilities: restaurant, bar, botanical garden. AE, DC, MC, V. Hotel $$; restaurant $$$*

's-Herto- **Auberge de Koets.** *Koets* means "carriage" in Dutch, and that is the
genbosch theme of the decor of this moderately formal restaurant on the Pa-
Dining rade, near the cathedral. Bridles, old saddles, and brass carriage lamps decorate the walls on all five dining levels. The interior is light and bright, with touches of brass. The menu is French influenced. *Korte Putstraat 23, tel. 073/132779. Reservations advised. Jacket advised. AE, DC, MC, V. $$$*

Dining and **Hotel Central.** This is more than just your typical full-service busi-
Lodging ness hotel: The Hotel Central is a family-run place that has grown along with the city, and the warmth of the service here reflects this. The rooms have a modern, tailored look. The restaurant, De Leeuwenborgh, with a separate entrance on the square, is graciously appointed and intimate; mirrors are etched with views of the city's important buildings; the menu is traditional and French. *Burg. Loeffplein 98, 5211 RX, tel. 073/125151, fax 073/145699. 125 rooms. Facilities: restaurant, bar. AE, DC, MC, V. $$$*

Kerkrade **Hotel Kasteel Erenstein.** A 14th-century moated château houses the
Dining and restaurant; a traditional whitewashed Limburg farmstead across
Lodging the road is the luxury hotel. Many of the rooms have beamed ceilings, and some are bi-level and skylighted; others have rooftop balconies. The menu and the wine cellar are French. *Oud Erensteinerweg 6, 6468 PC, tel. 045/461333, fax 045/460748. 44 rooms. Facilities: restaurant, bar, fitness center, sauna, massage. AE, DC, MC, V. Hotel $$$; restaurant $$$$*

Kruiningen **Restaurant Inter Scaldes.** In the past 25 years the owner/chef of this
Dining and small, gracious country restaurant has earned acclaim in the Euro-
Lodging pean culinary world for her imaginative use of the products of her region. To accommodate the diners who were traveling from all over the Netherlands and Belgium to sample her French cooking, a luxuriously appointed 12-room *manoir* was added on the far side of the small formal garden beyond the windows of the restaurant. *Zandweg 2, 4416 HA, tel. 01130/81753, fax 001130/81763. Reservations required. Jacket and tie required. AE, DC, MC, V. Closed Mon.–Tues. $$$$*

Maastricht
Dining

Chateau Neercanne. This gracious château has a wide summer terrace and a wine cellar carved into the hillside overlooking the Belgian border. Dining in the elegant and quietly decorated dining rooms is like attending a dinner party in a private home. The cuisine, regularly honored in European culinary circles, is French, with an emphasis on seasonal and country specialties. In a former chapel there is a second, less formal, lunch restaurant, L'Auberge. *Cannerweg 800, tel. 043/251359, fax 043/213406. Reservations required. Jacket and tie required. AE, DC, MC, V. Closed Mon. $$$$*

't Kläöske. This pleasant, somewhat formal restaurant facing Onze Lieve Vrouweplein is owned by an established Limburg restaurant family. Oyster-shell globe lamps hang from the beamed ceiling to light the tables of the spacious open dining room. French and Belgian country cuisine are the inspiration for the original dishes served here; a children's menu offers simpler fare. *Plankstraat 20, tel. 043/218118. Reservations advised. Jacket and tie advised. AE, DC, MC, V. Closed Sun. $$$*

't Hegske. This romantic spot is near St. Amorsplein off Vrijthof. Window boxes full of flowering plants decorate the street side, and there is a bubbling fountain in the interior courtyard. The warmth of half-timbered walls, hanging baskets, and antique collectibles here and there add to the intimacy. The kitchen is open, the cuisine classic French. *Heggenstraat 3a, tel. 043/251762. Reservations advised. Jacket and tie advised. AE, DC, MC, V. Closed Tues. $$–$$$*

De Blindgender. Not far from Onze Lieve Vrouweplein, De Blindgender is a particularly warm and cheerful eating pub with large windows looking onto the street. The tables are plain and unadorned, the service is relaxed, and the menu has a good selection of fish dishes, including salmon with a saffron sauce. *Koestraat. 3, tel. 043/250619. No reservations. Dress: casual. No credit cards. $$*

Dining and Lodging

Old Hickory. The location seems at first to be an odd one (behind the railway station), but it is in fact quite convenient to both the city of Maastricht and the surrounding Limburg countryside. You might not want to walk back to the hotel at night, though, as the area is rather deserted. The spacious restaurant, focused around a large central fireplace, emphasizes traditional French gastronomy. Fish and shellfish are the basis for many dishes, and game is served in season. The owner/chef often invites overnight guests to visit his extensive, naturally climate-controlled wine cellar. Most rooms are spacious and bright, decorated in a country-house manner, but the standards of decor may vary. Because of the hotel's proximity to the railway goods yard, the views are ugly, and rooms can get some early-morning noise. *Meerssenerweg 372/6224 AL, tel. 043/620548. 8 rooms with bath. Facilities: restaurant. AE, DC, MC, V. Hotel $$; restaurant $$$*

Lodging

Hotel Derlon. The relaxed and quiet elegance of Onze Lieve Vrouweplein is perfectly reflected in this small luxury hotel. Guest rooms are graciously sized and decorated in relaxing, muted, sand-and-sea-shell tones, and each has its own work of art, most often a contemporary painting; they face either the medieval side street or, if you are particularly fortunate, the tree-filled square. There is a personal quality to the service. *Onze Lieve Vrouweplein 6, 6211 HD, tel. 043/216770, fax 043/251933. 42 rooms. Facilities: restaurant, shops. AE, DC, MC, V. $$$$*

Hotel Du Casque. Smack-dab in the center of old Maastricht, this hotel has a tradition that dates back to a 15th-century inn, although today's building is a completely modern, post-war structure. Some rooms overlook the Vrijthof square, and there's direct access to a steak house with a terrace on the square. *Helmstrat 14, 6211 TA, tel.*

043/214343, fax 043/255155. 38 rooms with bath or shower. Facilities: garage. AE, DC, MC, V. $$

Hotel Bergere. The family-owned Bergere occupies an elegant 19th-century building not far from the railway station. There's an elevator, a *grand café* with a separate entrance, and comfortable and well-appointed rooms (some rooms have showers rather than tubs). The color scheme is light and fresh in pinks, grays, and beiges. *Stationsstraat 40, 6221 BR, tel. 043/251651, fax 043/255498. 40 rooms with bath or shower. Facilities: restaurant, parking. AE, MC, V. $–$$*

Middelburg **Het Groot Paradys.** Facing the market square in a house that dates
Dining from the mid-16th century, this intimate restaurant retains a traditional town-house decor. Dishes feature ingredients from the region, and fresh-baked breads are the pride of the kitchen. *Damplein 13, tel. 01180/26764. Reservations advised. Jacket advised. AE, DC, MC, V. Closed Sun.–Mon. $$$$*

Lodging **Le Beau Rivage.** This attractive hotel occupies a gabled, brick, turn-of-the-century canal-side building near the city center. The rooms are comfortable and decorated in pale colors with modern prints on the walls; the management is efficient and friendly. *Loskade 19, 4331 HW, tel. 01180/38060, fax 01180/29673. 9 rooms with shower. Facilities: restaurant. AE, MC, V. $–$$*

Oisterwijk **Hotel Restaurant De Swaen.** This French-Victorian streetside town
Dining and hotel faces a tree-shaded square and is more the sort of place you
Lodging expect to see in the American Southwest, not the middle of the Netherlands. The shallow front porch is equipped with rocking chairs and a café terrace in the summer; there is also a patio terrace. The crystal-chandeliered restaurant, overlooking the elegant formal garden in back of the hotel, serves excellent French cuisine. There is also a small *auberge* (inn) restaurant, De Jonge Swaen (The Young Swan), that serves simpler, less expensive, traditional Dutch choices. The Swan's hotel rooms are gracious and homey; baths are marble. *De Lind 47, 5061 HT, tel. 04242/19006, fax 04242/85860. 18 rooms with bath. Facilities: restaurant, bar, lounge, garden. AE, DC, MC, V. $$$*

Valkenburg **Prinses Juliana.** Food is everything here; the French cuisine served
Dining and here was recognized internationally more than 10 years ago and con-
Lodging tinues to be honored by even the harshest French food critics. The decor is elegant in an unadorned way so you can pay attention to the food. The suite-style rooms are bright and spacious. *Broekhem 11, Postbus 812, 6300 AV Valkenburg a/d Geul, tel. 04406/12244, fax 04406/14405. 15 rooms with bath. Facilities: lounge, restaurant. AE, DC, MC, V. $$$$*

Wittem **Kasteel Wittem.** This fairy-tale castle hotel, with its duck-filled
Dining and moat, spindle-roofed tower, and series of peekaboo dormers dotting
Lodging the roof is human in scale. The family who has owned it for more than 25 years welcomes you to a comfortable environment of vintage Dutch furnishings. The intimate dining room, where the cuisine is French, has towering windows open to the view of gardens and fields. There is even a summer terrace beside the moat. *Wittemer Allee 3, 6286 AA, tel. 04450/1208, fax 04450/1260. 12 rooms with bath. Facilities: restaurant, lounge. AE, DC, MC, V. $$$*

Yerseke **Nolet's Restaurant Het Reymerswale.** After a stroll along the harbor,
Dining stop in at the Nolet family's restaurant for a bite. The traditional, beamed second-floor dining room overlooking the water is spacious and graciously decorated with a comfortable lounge area with a fireplace and a summer porch to the back. The menu's focus is on sea-

food, traditionally and simply prepared to finest French standards. In a separate building, with shared kitchen, is an informal bistro. *Jachthaven 6, tel. 01131/1642. Reservations advised. Dress: casual. AE, DC, MC, V. Closed Feb. and Tues.–Wed. Bistro: $$; restaurant $$$–$$$$.*

The Arts and Nightlife

The Arts Maastricht is the arts capital of the border provinces. It has a resident orchestra, a well-known men's choir, and several small theater companies. For information on what is going on during your visit, check *Maandagenda*, a monthly calendar you will find around town, or *Uit in Maastricht*, published biweekly by the VVV tourist office.

Music In Maastricht, the **Limburgse Symfonie Orkest** (Limburg Symphony Orchestra), the leading regional orchestra, performs at the Theater aan Het Vrijthof (Vrijthof 47, tel. 043/210380; box office open Mon. 1–4, Tues.–Fri. 11–4, Sat. 11–2). In addition, there are regular student and amateur performances at both the Conservatoire Concert Hall (Bonnefanten 15, tel. 043/466680) and the College of Music Concert Hall (St. Maartenspoort 2, tel. 043/29 31 41). Also of interest are the free twice-weekly open rehearsals of Maastreechter Staar, the male choir of Maastricht, which are held Monday and Thursday at 8 PM (except July–Aug.).

Carillon Once a week, 's-Hertogenbosch offers back-to-back carillon recitals
Concerts from two sets of bells. The town hall bells play every Wednesday morning from 10 to 11, followed by another carillon concert from the cathedral from 11:30 to 12:30. In **Maastricht,** there is a summer series of evening concerts played by carillonneurs on various church bells of the city; and throughout the year there are midday concerts every Friday from 11:30 to 12:30 from the cheerful carillon on the town hall in the market square.

Theater The main theater of Maastricht is the **Theater aan Het Vrijthof** (Theater at Vrijthof, Vrijthof 47, tel. 043/210380); in addition, there is a small theater hall, Podium (Het Generaalshuis, Vrijthof 47, tel. 043/210380), and next door, Het Verlog Theater (Vrijthof 47a, tel. 043/255333). The student theater is Studio Toneelacademie (Drama Academy, Lenculenstraat 31–33, tel. 043/466690).

Nightlife Among the bars and cafés in the heart of the old city of **Maastricht** on
Bars or near Onze Lieve Vrouweplein are **De Boonte Kooi** (Koestraat 14–16, tel. 043/214812); **De Lanteern** (O.L. Vrouweplein 26, tel. 043/214326); and **Charlemagne** (O.L. Vrouweplein 24, tel. 043/219373). A special pub to visit is the very old **In den Ouden Vogelstruys** (Vrijthof 15, tel. 043/214888); first mentioned in town records in the 13th century, it has remained virtually unchanged since 1730 (except, of course, for the modern conveniences of electricity and beer on tap).

In 's-Hertogenbosch, try **Silva Ducis** (Parade 6–7, tel. 073/130405), **Galaxy** (Karrenstraat 29, tel. 073/143658), or the late-night **King's Cross** (Vughterstraat 99a, tel. 073/134479).

Casinos There are two casinos in this part of the Netherlands: **Holland Casino Breda** (Bijster 30, tel. 076/227600) and **Holland Casino Valkenburg** (Odapark, tel. 04406/15550), not far from Maastricht.

Discos The disco life of Maastricht is in, on, or near the main nightlife squares. On Vrijthof, **Momus** (Vrijthof 8, tel. 043/211937) is a Top 40 discotheque with a neoclassical decor of marble and statues; **Satyricon** (St. Bernardusstraat 16, tel. 043/210321) is a mellow, jazz-oriented place.

Gay Bars Two gay bar/dancing cafés in the city of Maastricht are **Cafe Rembrandt** (Markt 32, tel. 043/214218), on the market square, and on the "new" side of the city, **La Ferme** (Rechtstraat 29). Both are open until 2 AM.

Carnival The Catholic heritage of the southern provinces of the Netherlands is most dramatically felt during the days preceding Ash Wednesday each year. The public celebration of Carnival survives in its full bloom of conviviality and relative recklessness in both **Breda** and **Maastricht,** with celebrations also in 's-Hertogenbosch and Eindhoven.

The Green Heart

Like a mystery package that opens in a series of ever smaller, ever more intriguing boxes, the wooded heart of the Netherlands is an unfolding treasure. The national park is the wrappings; its ultimate and most precious gift is a museum of art that is buried deep in the forest; another of its surprises is a small palace.

Important Addresses and Numbers

Tourist Information The tourist offices in the region are: **Apeldoorn** (Stationsplein 6, tel. 055/788421), **Arnhem Region** (Stationsplein 45, tel. 085/420330), **Deventer** (De Drie Haringen aan de Brink 55, tel. 05700/16200), **Zutphen** (Groenmarkt 40, tel. 05750/19355), and **Zwolle** (Grote-Kerkplein 14, tel. 038/213900).

Emergencies The **National Emergency Alarm Number** for police, fire, and ambulance is 06/11.

Hospital Emergency Rooms Hospital numbers are: **Apeldoorn** (tel. 055/811111), **Arnhem** (tel. 0085/210000), **Deventer** (tel. 05700/46666; or ambulance, tel. 05700/56000), **Zutphen** (tel. 05750/92911; or ambulance, tel. 05750/15555), and **Zwolle** (tel. 038/299911 or 038/262222).

Arriving and Departing

By Car From Amsterdam, take A1 to Apeldoorn and Deventer or Zutphen; A2 and A12 to Arnhem; or A1 and A28 to Zwolle. Nijmegen is easily reached from Arnhem by A52.

By Train There are **express Intercity trains** (tel. 06/9292) twice each hour from Amsterdam to Apeldoorn and Deventer, Zwolle, and Arnhem; there is hourly service to Nijmegen, with an additional train each hour connecting in Arnhem. To reach Zutphen by train, change in either Arnhem or Zwolle.

Getting Around the Green Heart

By Bus For local and regional bus service, contact tourist offices (*see* Tourist Information, *above*).

By Taxi Taxis wait at city railway stations; additional stands may be available in central shopping and hotel districts. To call a taxi: **Apeldoorn** (tel. 055/413413 or 055/223223), **Arnhem** (tel. 085/450000), **Deventer** (tel. 05700/26200 or 05700/22537); **Nijmegen** (tel. 080/226000 or 080/233000); **Zutphen** (tel. 05750/25345, 05750/12935, 05750/19217, or 05750/13717); **Zwolle** (tel. 038/551133, 038/213000, or 038/660077).

By Bike Free bicycles are provided in the national park De Hoge Veluwe for visitors. In the cities of this region, you can also rent a bicycle at railway stations or from **Blakborn** (Soerenseweg 3, tel. 055/215679), **Harleman** (Arnhemseweg 28, tel. 055/334346), and **M. Janssen** (Koninginnelaan 54, tel. 055/212582) in Apeldoorn; **Mantel** (95 Lawick van Pabststraat, tel. 085/420624), **H. Matser** (784 Kemperbergweg, tel. 085/423172), or **R.W. Roelofs** (1 G.A. van Nispenstraat, tel. 085/426014) in Arnhem; and **Scholten** (Luttekestraat 7, tel. 038/217378) in Zwolle.

Guided Tours

The tourist offices *(see* Tourist Information, *above)* in most cities in the region organize walking tours in the summer months. Inquire for times, minimum group size, and whether or not English translation is offered or can be arranged.

In summer (late June–late Aug.) the VVV Apeldoorn offers a nature tour of the royal forests on weekday evenings, called **Game Quest** (tel. 055/788421). The 2½-hour drive brings visitors into sections of the woods normally closed to the public to observe the wildlife and the indigenous trees and plants. The tours are by reservation only; the cost is Fl 14.50.

Exploring The Green Heart

Numbers in the margin correspond to points of interest on the Green Heart map.

The Royal Forest The small and gracious city of **Apeldoorn** is the gateway to the royal forest. On its outskirts you will find **Palace Het Loo.** Built in 1685 on the site of a 14th- and 15th-century castle and hunting lodge as a country residence for William III and his wife Mary Stuart (daughter of James II of England), it was further expanded into a full-blown royal palace when the couple became king and queen of England, with Mary's quarters in the east wing and William's to the west. Built of brick and outfitted with what are said to be the world's first sash windows, the palace is Dutch Baroque in style and has formal French gardens. An avenue of tall beeches leads to the central courtyard, where you enter through a high, grilled fence. Exhibits fill some of the rooms, and there is a video that documents the building's history and restoration prior to its opening to the public in 1984. Many other rooms are furnished as they had been for William and Mary, but rooms are also maintained in the manner in which they were used by later Dutch monarchs, including Queen Wilhelmina, who was the grandmother of the current queen. Wilhelmina was the last regent to make this her home and died here in 1962. Queen Mary's kitchen, where she made jam, is particularly appealing for the sense of homeyness it gives to the palace. The four gardens, meticulously and formally planted, are decorated with statues and fountains, and lined with tall trees. There are separate King's and Queen's Gardens; the King's is dominated by plantings in blue and orange, the colors of the Dutch royal family. Don't miss the stable; it is full of old royal carriages, including the toy car that was used by the current crown prince of the Netherlands when he was a child. *Koninklijk Park 1, tel. 055/212244. Admission: Fl 10 adults, Fl 5.50 children. Open Tues.–Sun. 10–5.*

De Hoge Veluwe (tel. 08382/1041) is a public nature reserve that covers more than 13,000 acres. The traditional hunting land of the Dutch royal family is populated with deer, boar, and many birds; it is also filled with towering pines and hardwood trees (oak, beech, and birch), dotted with small villages (Hoge Soeren, near Apeldoorn, is

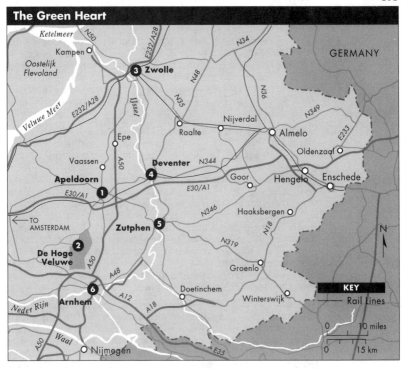

The Green Heart

particularly charming), and riddled with paths for cars, bicycles, and walkers. There is a landlocked, always shifting sand dune to marvel at, the world's first museum of all things that live (or have lived) underground, plus an old hunting lodge beside a dam that provides a nice stopping place. You'll find racks of bikes here and there in the park, available free of charge; just be sure to return the bike to any bike rack when you are finished using it. If you need an idea for a destination, there is a visitors' center that contains exhibits on the park and also an observation point for animal-watching.

In the heart of the national park is the **Kröller-Müller Museum,** the third most important museum of art in the Netherlands, after the Rijksmuseum and the Vincent van Gogh Museum in Amsterdam. Opened in 1938, it is the repository of a remarkable private collection of late-19th-century and early 20th-century paintings, including 278 works by van Gogh that, when combined with the collection in the Amsterdam museum, constitute nearly his entire *oeuvre*. Helene Kröller, née Müller, the wife of a prosperous industrialist, had a remarkable eye for talent and a sixth sense about which painters and paintings would be important. Her first purchase was van Gogh's *Sunflowers*. Among his other well-known paintings in her collection are *Potato Eaters*, *The Bridge at Arles*, and *L'Arlesienne*, copied from a drawing by Gauguin. But Helene Kröller-Müller was not myopic in her appreciation and perception. She added to her collection of van Goghs works by Seurat, Picasso, Redon, Braque, and Mondrian. The collection also contains 16th- and 17th-century Dutch paintings, ceramics, Chinese and Japanese porcelain, and contemporary sculpture. The museum building itself, which was designed by Henry van de Velde, artfully brings nature into the galleries through its broad windows, glass walkways, and patios. The gardens and woods around the museum form another gallery in the open air, with a collection of 20th-century sculptures by Aristide Maillol, Jean Dubuffet, Richard Serra, and Claes Oldenburg; works by Barbara Hepworth and Alberto Giacometti are under a special pavilion added in 1953. *National Park De Hoge Veluwe, tel. 08382/ 1041. Admission (to park and museum): Fl 7.50 adults, Fl 3.75 children, cars Fl 7.50. Open Tues.–Sun. 10–5. Sculpture Garden open Tues.–Sun. 10–4:30.*

Hanseatic Towns Seven hundred years before the European Common Market or the European Union, there was an association of northern European trading cities called the Hanseatic League. It began as a pact among itinerant merchants to travel together for mutual safety, but in time it became an alliance of more than 80 cities scattered over the Continent, including major ports such as London, Lübeck, Bremen, Hamburg, Cologne, Danzig, Stockholm, Novgorod, and Bergen, as well as 17 cities on the rivers and coastline of what is now the Netherlands. Their purpose was to consult with one another on matters of trading routes, tolls, and uniformity of regulations governing trade. Three of the cities that were important Dutch members of that league are scattered along the River IJssel, which connects the Rhine with the body of water known today as IJsselmeer, an open sea (the Zuider Zee) in the 13th century.

❸ The small city of **Zwolle** was an important depot for trade between the Netherlands and Germany during the time of the Hanseatic League, located as it is between the IJssel and another important Dutch river, the Vecht. Founded in 800, it officially became a town in the 12th century. An important Latin school was in Zwolle, and the religious philosopher Thomas à Kempis lived here in the early 1400s, when he wrote his influential work, *Imitation of Christ.* Zwolle continued in this century as an important center of cattle trading, grain processing, coffee roasting, and linen manufacture.

A pleasant short walk through the town begins at the brick- and stone-embellished **Sassenpoort,** which is the only one of the original town gates of 1406 left standing on the eastern edge of the city center. From there you can weave your way on and off Sassenstraat to the **Grote Kerkplein,** the main square of Zwolle. It is the site of the Town Hall as well as the local tourist office and a charming shop, **Zwolse Balletjes Huis** (Grote Kerkplein 13, tel. 038/218815), that sells the local sweet specialty, *Zwollse balletjes* (fruit-and-spice-flavored hard candies).

Time Out A pleasant place to stop for lunch in the middle of your wandering might be **De Librije** (Broerenkerkplein 13, tel. 038/212083). Specializing in game and fish dishes, the restaurant is housed in the former library of a 15th-century monastery.

The Romanesque **St. Michaelskerk,** which dates from 1040, dominates the square; within are a fine organ and the final resting place of the 17th-century painter of interiors Gerard Terborch, who was born in Zwolle. Farther along on the Voorstraat is the provincial **Overijssel Museum,** housed in a building that dates from the mid-16th century. Its principal display is the wainscoted living-dining Blokzil Room, which came from a house in the north part of the province and exemplifies the lifestyle of a well-to-do 17th-century family. *Melkmarkt 41 or Voorstraat 34, tel. 038/214650. Admission: Fl 3.50 adults, Fl 1 children. Open Tues.–Sat. 10–5, Sun. 2–5.*

Leaving Zwolle, follow signs for Wijhe-Olst for a scenic drive along the IJssel River, passing rich marshes filled with wildlife and lush plants. This region between the river and the German border, known as the Salland, is the Provence of Holland, a quiet farming area that has a local dialect and produces asparagus and offers food specialties such as *kruitmoes* (hot porridge with raisins).

❹ As you near **Deventer,** follow signs to *Centrum.* Founded late in the 8th century by an English cleric named Lubuinus, whose mission in life was to convert the Saxons to Christianity, by the 9th century Deventer was already a prosperous port and a powerful bishopric; the town center still reflects this medieval heritage. A center of learning as well, it had a printing industry to disseminate the thoughts of its scholars. It was home at various times to Thomas à Kempis, Pope Adrian VI, Erasmus, and, in the 17th century, French philosopher René Descartes. Still under restoration, Deventer has won prizes for the renovation of its historic houses and public buildings. In Brink, the main square, the late-Gothic **Waag** (Weigh House), begun in 1528, holds periodic exhibits on town history. Uphill is the 13th-century Romanesque-Gothic **Bergkerk** high on a square with pleasing views down medieval side streets (Bergstraat and Roggestraat are particularly appealing). *Admission free. Open Tues.–Fri. 11–5, weekends 1–5.*

Time Out Just below the Bergkerk is **Chez Antoinette** (Roggestraat 10–12, tel. 05700/16630), a restaurant-pub whose menu honors the owners' fascination with everything Portuguese. The building dates from 1303, and the pub (open for lunch and snacks) is the oldest in the city (from 1881).

The principal sight in Deventer is **Lubuinuskerk,** a huge stone cross basilica that was built in the 10th century on the site of Lubuinus's small wooden church. It is known for its mural paintings, its massive size, and its 15th-century tower, which can be climbed in the summer months for a wide view over the town; the carillon is played at least twice a week. *Grote Kerkhof. Admission free. Open weekdays 10–5, Sat. 1:30–5.*

Known as the Tower City for the many spires that rise above the city center, **Zutphen** is on a small hill at the juncture of the Rivers IJssel and Berkel. It was one of the region's wealthiest towns in the 14th and 15th centuries. The tourist office offers town tours twice a week from mid-June to mid-September (Tues. and Thurs. at 1:30). The charming, once-walled town has medieval houses and courtyards, churches and monasteries, and towers and water gates. The small **Henriette Polak Museum** contains a portrait of the Dutch queen, Wilhelmina, at age 10, by Mari Andriessen. *Zaadmarkt 88, tel. 05750/16878. Admission: Fl 3 adults, Fl 2.50 children. Open Tues.– Fri. 11–5, weekends 1:30–5.*

Time Out Not far from the Henriette Polak Museum is **De Pelikaan** (Pelikaanstraat 6, tel. 05750/12024), a coffee and tea emporium dating from the late 1880s; the adjacent tearoom is a good place to stop for refreshment.

St. Walburgskerk (St. Walburgis Church) was begun in the 12th century in Romanesque style and enlarged in the 16th century in Gothic style. It is busy with roofs and a wide variety of building materials. Within, the side walls and vaults are ornamented with 14th- and 15th-century frescoes; the richly decorated organ loft contains a Baeder organ. In the **Librije** side chapel are found the true treasures of Zutphen: This library dates from 1561, and under its white vaulted ceilings are rare and beautiful early manuscripts and incunabula, chained to rows of reading stands. *Kerkhof. Admission: Fl 3.50 adults, Fl 2 children; combined with the walking tour, Fl 5 adults, Fl 3 children. Open May–Sept., tours Mon. at 2 and 3, Tues.–Sat. at 11, 2, and 3.*

Arnhem **Arnhem** is best known as the "bridge too far." Near the end of World
❻ War II the Allies followed up the invasion of Normandy by seeking to cut off the German army entrenched in the eastern Netherlands. The battle involved the largest airborne operation of the war, and 3,000 British, American, and Canadian lives were lost in three weeks of fighting that left the Allies still short of their goal, which was finally achieved seven months later. **Airborne Museum** includes a large scale model of the region and incorporates memorabilia, weapons, and equipment to depict the battle. Tanks and guns sit on the lawn, and an audiovisual presentation describes the progress of the battle. *Utrechtseweg 232, Oosterbeek, tel. 085/337710. Admission: Fl 4 adults, Fl 2.50 children. Open Mon.–Sat. 11–5, Sun. and holidays noon–5.*

Among the other attractions of Arnhem are its parks (including the 185-acre **Sonsbeek Park**), its trolley buses, its weekly market held in the shadows of the **Grote Kerk** (Great Church), and its cozy entertainment area, the **Korenmarkt,** where old warehouses have become pubs, cafés, restaurants, and discotheques. On the River Rhine, Arnhem also is the southern gateway to the national park De Hoge Veluwe (*see above*). North of the city in a 44-acre park is the **Nederlands Openlucht Museum** (Open Air Museum), which recreates Dutch country life through farm buildings typical of their regions, transported to the site from every province of the Netherlands. Here you can see furnished farmhouses, outbuildings, windmills, and crafts shops in a setting that reflects the variety of the Dutch landscape. *Schelmseweg 89, tel. 085/576111. Admission: Fl 12.50 adults, Fl 8 children. Open Apr.–Oct., weekdays 9:30–5, weekends 10–5.*

What to See and Do with Children

More than 2,000 animals inhabit **Burgers' Zoo** in Arnhem. Established in 1913 on the principle that there should be as few barriers as possible between human beings and animals, this zoo includes a large safari park with roaming lions, zebras, giraffes, and rhinos, plus a tropical rain forest. *Schelmseweg 85, 6816 SH Arnhem, tel. 085/424534 or 085/450373. Admission: Fl 20 adults, Fl 15 children. Open summer 9–7, last safari 5 PM; winter 9–sunset, last safari 4 PM.*

In Apeldoorn's **Apenheul** park, more than 300 monkeys, apes, chimpanzees, and gorillas wander free in the woods. *J.C. Wilslaan 31, tel. 055/552556. Admission: Fl 13.50 adults, Fl 9 children. Open Apr.–June, daily 9:30–5; July–Aug., daily 9:30–6, Sept.–Oct., daily 10–5.*

The **Speelgoed- en Blikmuseum** (Toys and Tin Museum) is an enchanting collection of toys (including mechanical toys), dolls, puppets, and electric trains in a town house just off the main square and only a few doors down from the tourist office in Deventer. *Brink 47, tel. 05700/93786. Admission: Fl 5 adults, Fl 3 children. Open Tues.–Sat. 10–5, Sun. 2–5.*

Off the Beaten Track

From Zwolle it is a short drive to another Hanseatic town, **Kampen.** Once a herring port, it lies near the point where the IJssel River empties into IJsselmeer. To see the oft-painted skyline at its best, approach the city from across the river by way of the old bridge rather than the highway: Take N50 and follow signs for IJsselmuiden. The **Schepenzaal** (Magistrates' Hall) in the 14th-century Oude Raadhuis (Old Town Hall) is an excellent example of a medieval courtroom.

Near Zutphen on the road to Doetinchem is **Bronkhorst,** the tiniest town in the Netherlands; its population is 160, and the entire town is protected by the national historic preservation program. There are curious little museums and shops here, as well as a choice of gracious restaurants. The 14th-century chapel is particularly attractive and peaceful.

From Arnhem it is an easy 30-minute drive to the pre-Roman city of **Nijmegen,** situated strategically near the junction of the Maas–Waalkanal and the River Waal. The river is the main branch of the Rhine and the second of the "great rivers" of the Netherlands that lead to the North Sea. Nijmegen is a lively university town and shopping center for the region, as well as the gateway to the southern provinces. The city's **Belvedere Park** offers a splendid view over the river below and a restaurant in a tower. The nearby Waalkade riverfront esplanade, lined with restaurants, shops, and a casino, is also a pleasant place to stroll.

Shopping

The late shopping nights in the cities in this region are: in Apeldoorn, Thursday in the city center, Friday in the suburbs; in Arnhem, Thursday; in Nijmegen, Thursday; in Zutphen, Friday; and in Zwolle, Thursday.

Street Markets The market days in the region are: in Apeldoorn, Monday and Wednesday mornings and on Saturday at Marktplein in the city center; in Arnhem, Friday morning and Saturday at Kerkplein; in Deventer, Tuesday–Friday morning and Saturday (also antiques); in Nijmegen, Monday and Saturday at Agustijnenstraat, Grote Markt, and Burchstraat; in Zutphen, Thursday mornings; in Zwolle, Friday morning and Saturday.

Sports and the Outdoors

Biking There is a program of *free* bicycles (a total of 400 vehicles) for use on the 42 kilometers (26 miles) of bicycle paths in **De Hoge Veluwe National Park** (*see above*); special cycles for people with disabilities are also available.

Canoeing In summer it's possible to canoe on the canals of Zwolle. **Vadesto Kanocentrum** (Veenrand 5, 8051 DW Hattem, tel. 05206/45428) at the Potgietersingel rents canoes. The VVV Zwolle tourist information office (*see* Tourist Information, *above*) sells canoeing maps.

Fishing Fishing in the streams of Overijssel province near Zwolle is easy and pleasurable. The VVV Zwolle tourist information office (*see* Tourist Information, *above*) sells one-day fishing licenses for Fl 5. The license includes a list of the fishing places, and the tourist office also has a helpful map of the area.

Golf Among the best golf facilities in the area are **Publi Golf De Berendonck** (Panhuysweg 39, Wijchen, tel. 08894/20039) and **Golfbaan Het Rijk van Nijmegen** (Postweg 17, 6561 KJ Groesbeek, tel. 08891/76644), near Nijmegen, and **Golfclub Zwolle** (Heinoseweg 26, Zwolle, tel. 05290/1930).

Jogging There is a training circuit in Zwolle at the **Haersterveerweg**. Near the center of town are two places suitable for jogging, **Park De Weezenlanden** and **Park 't Engelse Werk**.

Tennis/Squash Facilities in the region include **Squash Matenpark** (Heemradenlaan 130, tel. 055/296222) and **De Maten Sports** (Ambachtsveld 2, tel. 055/425044) in Apeldoorn; **Tennis en Squashcentrum** (Bremenweg 29, tel. 05700/22107) in Deventer; **Jan Massinkhal** (Nieuwe Dukenburgseweg, tel. 080/564260) in Nijmegen; and in Zwolle, **Squash Zwolle** (near Winkelcentrum Aalanden, tel. 038/548485), **Sportpark Wilhelmina** (Wilhelminastraat, tel. 038/214826), **Sportpark de Marslanden** (Marsweg, tel. 038/217189), **Sportpark De Pelikaan** (Haersterveerweg, tel. 038/537177), **Tenniscentrum Zwolle** (Palestrinalaan, tel. 038/545100), and **Tenniscomplex Zwolle** (Peterskampweg, tel. 038/544204).

Spectator Sports

Walking/ Cycling Each summer during the third week of July the **Nijmegen Annual Four-Day Walking Event** is held; it draws as many as 30,000 participants from all over the world. A similar event is held for cyclists.

Dining and Lodging

The Royal Game Reserve in the north and the fruit- and vegetable-growing region to the east provide the restaurants of the Green Heart with abundant, high-quality ingredients. The area is well supplied with hotels of all sizes and types, small resorts, and country inns in the woods.

Apeldoorn **Echoput.** Not far from Palace Het Loo, Echoput is a much-honored
Dining and gracious country restaurant. The large fireplace in the lounge welcomes in winter; the terrace invites in summer. With the royal hunting grounds so nearby, the restaurant manages to offer fine game dishes nearly year-round. *Amersfoortseweg 86, tel. 05769/1248. Reservations advised. Jacket and tie advised. AE, DC, MC, V. Closed Mon. $$$*

Lodging **De Keizerskroon.** A nice cross between a business hotel and a country inn, it is within easy walking distance of Palace Het Loo. Renovations over the past 25 years have obliterated all traces of traditional architecture; in its place is a stylish hotel, with rooms decorated in pastels, with furniture that, like the hotel, is a blend of business practical and weekend comfortable. *Koningstraat 7, 7315 HR, tel. 055/217744, fax 055/214737. 101 rooms. Facilities: sauna, solarium, swimming pool. AE, DC, MC, V. $$$*
Astra. On a quiet residential side street, Astra is a small pension-style family hotel that is comfortably furnished in the manner of a Dutch home. Rooms are large for this type of accommodation. *Bas Backerlaan 12–14, 7316 DZ, tel. 055/223022, fax 055/223021. 27 rooms with bath. Facilities: recreation room. AE, DC, MC, V. $*

Arnhem **Kasteel Doorwerth.** This restaurant offers a rare experience: to dine
Dining in a moated castle near the Rhine 8 kilometers (5 miles) from Arnhem. The timbered dining room, once the castle's coach house, is furnished with antiques, and the cuisine is in the new, French-in-

spired Dutch mode; vegetables and herbs come from the castle gardens. *Fonteinalle 4, Doorwerth, tel. 085/333420. Reservations advised. Jacket and tie advised. AE, DC, MC, V. Closed Tues. $$$*

Lodging **Hotel de Bilderberg.** In a wooded setting in the suburb of Oosterbeek, de Bilderberg caters to business travelers as well as weekenders. The rooms are spacious and bright, with comfortable modern furnishings. *Utrechtseweg 261, 6862AK, Oosterbeek, tel. 085/340843, fax 085/334651. 144 rooms. Facilities: indoor swimming pool, sauna/solarium, fitness room, tennis courts. AE, DC, MC, V. $$$*

Hotel Blanc. This small hotel is not far from the railway station in central Arnhem. In a turn-of-the-century town house, the Blanc offers bright and comfortable rooms and a friendly café for guests. *Coehoornstraat 4, 6811 LA, tel. 085/428072, fax 085/434749. 22 rooms, 4 with bath, others with shower. Facilities: café, lounge. AE, DC, MC, V. $*

Hotel Molendal. In an Art Deco–era house in a residential neighborhood near Sonsbeek Park, the hotel has spacious and high-ceilinged rooms; decorative elements carry out the Art Deco heritage of the building. *Cronjestraat 15, 6814 AG, tel. 085/424858, fax 085/436614. 32 rooms with bath. Facilities: lounge. AE, DC, MC, V. $*

Bronkhorst **Herberg de Gouden Leeuw.** This peaceful country restaurant is in the
Dining and smallest town in the Netherlands. There are formal and informal
Lodging dining areas and a fireplace in the lounge, and on Saturday nights diners are entertained with piano music. The cuisine is traditional Continental, with such choices as beef bourguignonne and veal cordon bleu. The guest rooms are simple. *Bovenstraat 2, 7226LM, tel. 05755/1231. 8 rooms, 2 with shower. Facilities: restaurant. AE, DC, MC, V. Hotel $; restaurant $$$*

Hoog Soeren **Hotel Oranjeoord.** In a small woodland village that seems to be right
Lodging out of a Grimms' fairy tale, the Oranjeoord is a relaxed country hotel with garden rooms, terraces, and a sunny dining room. It is a pleasant choice for a country weekend. *Hoog Soeren 134, 7346AH, tel. 05769/1227, fax 05769/1451. 27 rooms with bath. Facilities: restaurant. MC. $*

Nijmegen **Belvedere.** Housed in a tall tower set high on a hill in the middle of a
Dining park overlooking a wide bend in the River Waal, it has possibly the best river view in the Netherlands. In the beamed dining room are only a handful of tables; the menu is new Dutch cooking, including choices such as duck breast in an envelope of goose liver. *Kelfkensbos 60, tel. 080/226861. Reservations required. Jacket and tie advised. AE, DC, MC, V. Closed Sat. lunch and Sun. $$–$$$*

Zutphen **Berkhotel.** With a stream running by outside, and rooms decorated
Dining and in English Country–style (with pastels and floral prints), it's hard
Lodging to believe that this hotel is almost in the heart of town. The restaurant has a rather grand ambience, with chandeliers, live piano music, palms, and candlelight; the cuisine is strictly vegetarian, prepared with an Oriental touch. *Marspoortstraat 19, 7201 JA, tel. 05750/11135, fax 05750/41950. 19 rooms, 10 with bath or shower. Facilities: restaurant, lounge, terrace. AE, MC, V. $*

Zwolle **Grand Hotel Wientjes.** Convenient to both the railway station and
Lodging the city center, this hotel occupies a stately old building. Most rooms are in the modern wings and are both spacious and brightly decorated. It also has theme rooms, including one styled in Old Dutch and a Chinese-style bridal suite with a two-person tub. *Stationsweg 7, tel. 038/254254, fax 038/254260. 57 rooms. Facilities: restaurant. AE, DC, MC, V. $$$*

The Arts and Nightlife

The Arts In Apeldoorn, there are concerts the last Friday of every month at **Paleis Het Loo** (Koninklijk Park 1, tel. 055/212244); in Nijmegen, performances take place at **Stadsschouwburg Nijmegen Concertgebouw De Vereeniging** (tel. 080/221100 or 080/228344).

Nightlife In Deventer, there is a concentration of brown cafés at the main square, including **Het Wapen van Overijssel** (also known as **Floors**; Brink 37, tel. 05700/13811), **La Balance** (Brink 72, tel. 05700/19277), and **De Waagschaal** (Brink 77, tel. 05700/17190); in Zutphen, there is **Oma** (Beukerstraat 52a, tel. 05750/18003); and in Zwolle, **Catastrofe** (Gasthuisplein 11, tel. 038/214234) and **La Galleria** (Oude Vismarkt 9a, tel. 038/212153).

The North

In the northern provinces of the Netherlands, life is more peaceful; there are quiet streams and a chain of sparkling lakes 64 kilometers (40 miles) long to tempt you to sample the outdoor life. For the most part, museums are small and quiet but have surprisingly rich displays, and there are luxury resorts hidden in small wooded villages that rival the attractions of the more cosmopolitan parts of the country. Particularly in Friesland, there are opportunities to watch an unusual array of sporting activities, including sailing regattas, bike races, long-distance walks, a local version of pole-vaulting, and—*if* the canals freeze in the winter—one of the world's most famous ice-skating races, which flashes through 11 cities before it is done.

Important Addresses and Numbers

Tourist Information The tourist office in **Groningen** (Gedempte Kattendiep 6, 9711 PN, tel. 06/32023050, fax 050/136358) provides information on the capital city and also the province of the same name. The tourist office in **Leeuwarden** (Stationsplein 1, 8911 AC, tel. 06/32024060, fax 058/136555) is the central source for information for both the city and the province of Friesland.

Emergencies The **National Emergency Alarm Number** for police, fire, and ambulance is 06/11.

Police **Groningen:** tel. 050/162222; for breakdown and towing service, tel. 050/565274. **Leeuwarden:** tel. 058/132423.

Hospital Emergency Rooms **Groningen:** tel. 050/619111 or 050/258888. **Leeuwarden:** tel. 058/933333.

Arriving and Departing by Car, Train, or Ferry

By Car To reach the northern provinces from Amsterdam, you can take A6 across the province of Flevoland to Emmeloord, then A50 to Joure, and from there E22 to Groningen. Turn north on N32 for Leeuwarden. You can also follow E22 through Noord Holland province and across the 35-kilometer (22-mile) Afsluitdijk (Enclosing Dike) that divides the IJsselmeer from the North Sea; from the end of the Enclosing Dike, take A31 to Leeuwarden or continue on E22 to Groningen. A third option is to drive to Enkhuizen and take the car ferry to Urk (*see* By Ferry, *below*). From Urk, take N351 to A50 and continue as above.

By Train **Intercity** express trains (tel. 06/9292) operate once an hour direct from Amsterdam to both Leeuwarden and Groningen; there is an additional hourly Intercity service to both cities that requires a connection in Amersfoort. Whatever train you take, however, be sure you are in the right car; trains split en route, so there are separate cars for each destination in both classes of service.

By Ferry Two ferry lines cross the IJsselmeer from May to September to connect the town of **Enkhuizen** with the northern provinces of Friesland and Flevoland. Both lines are operated by **Rederij Naco B.V.** (de Ruyteskade, Steiger 7, Amsterdam, tel. 020/626–2466), and both accept bicycles but not cars. One takes travelers to **Stavoren**, from where there is a direct train connection to Leeuwarden; the ferry operates three times a day and there is no need for a reservation. Adult fare is Fl 9.50 one way, Fl 15 round-trip; children pay Fl 4.75 one way, Fl 7.75 round-trip. The other goes to **Urk** in Flevoland province (Fl 12 per person, Fl 6.50 per bicycle).

Getting Around the North

By Car Roads are excellent throughout the northern provinces of Friesland and Groningen. In Friesland signs are in two languages, however, with the town names shown in Frisian as well as in Dutch. For example, the provincial capital Leeuwarden also is seen on signs by its Frisian name, Ljouwert.

By Train In addition to the national rail lines connecting Leeuwarden with the south, local trains link the Enkhuizen–Stavoren ferry service to Leeuwarden; another connects Leeuwarden with Harlingen (departure point for ferry and hydrofoil services to the Wadden Islands); and another links Leeuwarden with Groningen and continues to the German border. A small local train in Groningen province connects Groningen with Winsum (a canoeing center), Uithuizen (departure for guided walks to the Wadden Islands at low tide), and the port of Eemshaven. For **train information** in Leeuwarden or Groningen, call 06/9292.

By Taxi Taxis wait at the railway stations in both Leeuwarden and Groningen. For a taxi in Leeuwarden, call 058/122222 or 058/123333; in Groningen, call 050/128044.

Guided Tours **Canal cruise trips** are available in summer; in Leeuwarden, contact **H. Geertsma** (Tijnjedijk 31, tel. 058/887588); in Groningen, **Verbindingskanaal Groningen** (tel. 050/128379 or 050/122713). Another guided option, as much sport as sightseeing, is to join a **wadlopen** excursion to the Wadden Islands. Permissible *only* with a guide who knows well the timing of the tidal waters on the Wadden Sea, these are walks across the sand at low tide from the mainland to the islands from May to September. Don't even think about attempting this on your own; the tides are very, very tricky. If you are interested, the tourist offices can give you information and recommend qualified guides, or you can contact **De Stichting Wadloopcentrum Pieterburen** (Postbus 1, Pieterburen, tel. 05952/300).

Exploring the North

Numbers in the margin correspond to points of interest on the North map.

Leeuwarden An odd mixture of distinctions identifies the small provincial capital
❶ of **Leeuwarden.** On one hand, it was the official residence of the first hereditary *stadhouder* (king) of the Netherlands; on the other, it is believed to have been the birthplace of the notorious dancer/spy, Mata Hari. It is well known as the focal point of the Dutch dairy in-

dustry and site of one of the largest cattle markets in Europe, yet it also is home to the one of the world's finest collections of Oriental ceramics. The world-famous 200-kilometer (124-mile) Elfenstedentocht (Eleven Cities Tour) ice-skating race departs from Leeuwarden when—or if—there is ice on the canals connecting the capital with 10 other cities of the province (including Harlingen, Franeker, Workum, Hindeloopen, Stavoren, and Sloten).

From the railway station, follow the wide street just ahead, across the Nieuwestade canal, where you jog left to the next bridge before continuing along Kleine Kerkstraat. At Grote Kerkstraat is the **Museum Het Princessehof** (Netherlands Ceramic Museum), housed in the former residence of Marie-Louise of Hesse-Kassell, who was the widow of the first prince of Orange and whose gracious dining room has been preserved. The museum documents the history of fine ceramics, Oriental as well as European, and modern as well as ancient. The remarkable collection of Chinese stoneware and porcelain dates from the third millennium BC through the 20th century. Look closely at the plates and tiles commissioned in China by the Dutch East India Company; you'll notice decidedly Asian features on Dutch-costumed merchants and their ladies. *Grote Kerkstraat 9–15, tel. 058/ 127438. Admission: Fl 6.50 adults, Fl 4.50 children. Open Mon.–Sat. 10–5, Sun. 2–5.*

The 13th-century **Grotekerk** (Great Church), a Jacobin church, has been reconstructed and restored over the centuries, most recently in 1976; it is the traditional burial place of the Nassau line, ancestors of the royal family. *Jacobinerkerkhof, tel. 058/151203. Admission free. Open June–Aug., Tues.–Fri. 2–4.*

From the church, follow Bij de Put and its continuation, Sacramentsstraat, across the Voorstreek canal; follow Tuinen canal and turn right at Turfmarkt. Here is the ornate Renaissance building known as the **Kanselarij** (Chancellery), which was the residence of George of Saxony when he governed the region in the 16th century. Two museums have moved to the Chancellery from other locations in town and are scheduled to open here in April 1995. One is the provincial **Fries Museum** (Frisian Museum), which has a varied collection documenting the history and culture of Friesland. Among its treasures is a portrait by Rembrandt of his wife, Saskia; she was the daughter of the mayor of Leeuwarden. The couple married in 1634 in the nearby village of St. Annaparochie. The other is the **Verzetsmuseum Friesland** (Resistance Museum), an intriguing collection of memorabilia and exhibits honoring the strong Frisian resistance movement under the German occupation during World War II. *Turfmarkt 11, tel. 058/123001. Admission prices not set at press time; call ahead. Open Tues.–Sat. 10–4, Sun. 1–4.*

From the Kanselarij, continue along Turfmarkt to Korfmakersstraat and turn right. At the canal you will see a tiny statuette of a dancer. You guessed it; this is **Mata Hari,** a statue erected in the late 1970s to honor the town's most colorful citizen.

Time Out | If you follow the canal into the center, you will come to the Waagplein, which is dominated by the redbrick **Waag** (Weigh House), decorated with heraldic lions. Built at the end of the 16th century, it was used as a weigh house for butter and cheese until the late-19th century; it now houses a cozy restaurant called **De Waag** (Nieuwestad 148B, tel. 058/137250).

Beyond the Weigh House, take Weerd to the Raadhuisplein and its extension, the Hofplein. Facing one another here are the **Stadhuis**

The North

(Town Hall) and the **Hof,** which was the former residence of the Frisian stadhouders. In the center of the square is a statue of Willem Louis, the first stadhouder, locally known as *Us Heit* (Our Father).

Friesland The province of Friesland offers a number of fascinating small museums, particularly in the craft towns that dot the coast of the IJsselmeer. To explore the province, take N355 from Leeuwarden toward Harlingen. In the late 18th century a clergyman in the town of **Franeker** convinced the inhabitants that the end of the world was imminent due to a collision of the planets. When his dire prediction failed to materialize, a local scoffer set out to help his neighbors understand why. The **Eise Eisinga Planetarium** is one man's attempt to demonstrate why the planets do not collide. One wonders what his wife must have thought, but Eise spent years turning his living-room ceiling into a continuously moving display of interplanetary action, and his home's closets and attic into the storage place for the workings needed to carry out his unusual experiment in education and home decoration. *Eise Eisingastraat 3, Franeker, tel. 05170/ 93070. Admission: Fl 4 adults, Fl 3 children. Open Oct.–Apr., Tues.–Sat. 10–12:30, and 1:30–5; May–Sept., Mon.–Sat. 10–12:30 and 1:30–5, Sun. 1–5.*

Just a short drive farther on is the small port city of **Harlingen.** A walk along its main canal will remind you of Amsterdam in that several homes are copies of canal houses in the capital.

Time Out Facing the main canal is the pleasant, small hotel-restaurant **Anna Caspari** (Noorderhaven 69, tel. 05178/12065), where you can have a bite of lunch or dinner while overlooking the canal.

Take the scenic coastal road south along the dike toward Zurich and ④ from there toward **Makkum.** If you are a lover of fine pottery, you will know that multicolored Makkumware is as important and treasured in Dutch homes as the better-known blue-and-white Delft-ware. The small, family-owned factory, **Tichelaars Koninklijke Makkumer Aardewerk en Tegelfabriek** (Tichelaar's Royal Makkum Pottery and Tile Factory), which has made Makkumware under license from the royal family for 10 generations, invites you to watch the craftsmen at work; they also operate a shop where you can buy the products of the sole supplier of Makkumware to the world. *Turfmarkt 63, Makkum, tel. 05158/31341. Admission: Fl 4. Open weekdays 10–11:30 and 1–3:45; factory showrooms open weekdays 9–5:30, Sat. 9–4.*

Nearby, in a former weigh house, is the **Fries Aardewerkmuseum DeWaag** (Frisian Pottery Museum), a small collection of ceramic tiles and other pottery that includes many contributions by the Tichelaar family. *Waaggebouw, Pruikmakershoek 2, Makkum, tel. 05158/31422. Admission: Fl 3. Open Apr.–Sept. 15, Mon.–Sat. 10–5, Sun. 1:30–5; Nov.–Mar., weekdays 10–noon and 1–4.*

Continuing along the dike road through the villages of Piamm and Gaast, you come to **Workum,** where, in a house on the main street ⑤ near the church, you will find the **Jopie Huisman Museum.** This is an art museum devoted to one man who was born in Workum and lives here still in a house by an eel stream where he fishes every night. What is unusual about the man, and his art, is that he was a junk man all his life; sketching and painting every chance he had, without benefit of formal instruction, he produced an abundance of fine canvases and drawings, many reminiscent of the careful duplication of fabric and texture in the work of the early Dutch masters. Jopie Huisman, however, has made haunting compositions of the rags, worn shoes, and discarded dolls he collected in his travels. *Noard 6, Workum, tel. 05151/43131. Admission: Fl 4 adults, Fl 2.50 children. Open Mar.–Nov., Mon.–Sat. 10–5, Sun. 2–5.*

⑥ Just beyond Workum is the coastal town of **Hindeloopen,** which is known for its traditional painted furniture. The **Museum Hidde Nijland Stichting** is an exhibition of the local craft that is worth a quick detour. *Dijkweg, tel. 05142/1420. Admission: Fl 3.50 adults, Fl 1.75 children. Open Mar.–Nov., Mon.–Sat. 10–5, Sun. 1:30–5.*

From Hindeloopen you are within easy driving distance of the **Frisian Lakes,** which lure Dutch and international sailors and boating enthusiasts every summer. N359 just outside Hindeloopen or Workum takes you across the countryside and across the connecting land between one of the largest lakes and its outlet. The small forti-⑦ fied towns of **Sloten** and **Balk** are focal points in this area of south-western Friesland known as **Gaasterland.**

Groningen **Groningen** is a university town; it also is a major commercial center **and Environs** of the northern provinces of the Netherlands. A member of the Han-⑧ seatic League in medieval times, it enjoyed six centuries of prosperity as a grain market. The province still leads Western Europe in the production of sugar beets; another of its riches is a large supply of natural gas. Street life is busy in the city, and the region offers pleasant drives in the countryside.

To tour the town on foot, start at the Grote Markt, the market square in front of the **Stadhuis** (Town Hall). Walking by way of Sint Jansstraat, you come to the **Martinikerk**, which dates from 1230 and was begun as a Romanesque-Gothic cruciform basilica. Finished in the 15th century, it has an organ that was installed in 1470, as well as splendid murals from that period; the stained-glass windows date from the late 18th century. *Martinikerkhof, tel. 050/120798. Admission: Fl 1. Open May–Aug., Tues.–Sat. noon–5.*

Behind the church is the **Prinsenhoftuin** herb and rose garden, which has an 18th-century sundial in its gate and hedges cut in the shapes of *A* and *W*, after the first names of former governors of Friesland and Groningen provinces. *St. Walburgstraat Kattenh, no phone. Admission free. Open mid-Mar.–mid-Oct.*

Leaving the garden, follow the canal around to the left. Turn back into the city at Oude Boteringestraat, where you will pass a number of fashionable homes built by prominent 18th-century citizens and, on the corner of the Broerstraat, a medieval stone house that is one of the oldest in town.

Turn there and you will pass the main building of the **university.** Founded in 1614 and today one of the largest in the Netherlands, it was chosen by Descartes in 1645 to arbitrate his conflicts with Dutch theologians. The university building you see is neo-Renaissance in style, built in 1909. Allegorical figures of Science, History, Prudence, and Mathematics adorn the gable; across the street is the University Library opened in 1985.

Time Out   As might be expected in a university town, there are plenty of cafés clustered around the Grote Markt. When you are hungry or want to take a break, head for **Time Out** (Poelestraat 34, tel. 050/131535) or **Bunders** (Oude Boteringestraat 9, tel. 050/183535).

Ten sculptures on major city access roads are part of the **City Identification Project,** conceived by the Municipal Physical Planning Department to restore to the city the identity once derived from its medieval city gates. Two architects, three artists, a historian, a philosopher, a choreographer, a playwright, and an economist were each commissioned to design an "identification feature," each of which was given an identifying letter spelling out *Cruoningae*, an ancient name for the city; the resulting sculptures and structures circle the city clockwise from the south and carry such mystifying titles as *Earth, water and gas flames; A steel book on posts; The missing factor X.*

Walk south from the Grote Markt, following signs for the railway station. Opposite Groningen Station is the town's newest landmark, the zanily designed, brightly colored **Groningen Museum.** The complex of three buildings connected by walkways was, at press time, scheduled to open in November 1994. Conceived by Italian architect Alessandro Mendini, the adventurous design was made even zanier by additions by three "guest architects." You'll find exhibits on Groningen history, art and crafts (including a good collection of Oriental porcelain), and visual art from the 16th century to the present. *Museum Island, no phone at press time (call museum administration at 050/183-3431). Admission: FL 9 adults, FL 7.50 children. Open Tues.–Sat. 9–5, Sun. 1–5.*

What to See and Do with Children

From April through October you can follow the **Aldfaers Erf** (Our Forefathers' Heritage) route, which weaves through the Frisian countryside in a small area bounded by the towns of Makkum, Bolsward, and Workum, stopping at 12 restored buildings and workshops. In Exmorra you can visit the agricultural museum, a village grocery, and a schoolroom; in Allingawier, a farm, a church, a painter's workshop, a forge, a bakery, and two residences; in Piaam, an ornithological museum; and in Ferwoude, a carpenter's workshop. *Postbus 176, 8700 AD Bolsward, tel. 05157/5681. Open Apr.–Nov., daily 10–5.*

Near Groningen, children will enjoy a stop at **Abraham's Mostermakerij**, a museum-restaurant in the village of Eenrum/Pieterburen. The convivial manager invites diners and visitors into the mustard factory to see how mustard and vinegar are made. *Molenstraat 5, 9967SL Eenrum/Pieterburen, tel. 05959/1600. Open daily 10–9.*

Off the Beaten Track

If you happen to be in Leeuwarden on Friday morning, find your way to the Frieslandhal on the perimeter of town for the **weekly cow market**. It is one of the largest in Europe and offers a look into what this part of the Netherlands is really all about.

Of all the unexpected places in the Netherlands, perhaps the most intriguing are the offshore **Wadden Islands,** which shelter the northern coastline from the North Sea. They offer varying degrees of seclusion or socialization and plenty of opportunity for water sports, beach walking, and birding. Ferries leave from Harlingen to Terschelling (tel. 05620/2141) and Vlieland (tel. 05620/4141; no cars); ferries to Ameland leave from Holwerd (tel. 05191/42001), and to Schiermonnikoog from Lauwersoog (tel. 05193/9050). For information on accommodations on the islands, contact the VVV Friesland (Stationsplein 1, 8911 AC Leeuwarden, tel. 06/32024060, fax 058/136555).

Shopping

Shopping is not the lure of the northern provinces, though standard merchandise is available. The late shopping night in both Leeuwarden and Groningen is Thursday, until 9 PM.

Street Markets Market days in **Leeuwarden** are Friday (to 3:30) and Monday afternoon at Wilhelminaplein and Wednesday morning at Akkerstraat. In **Groningen** the market is held on the Grote Markt on Tuesday, Wednesday, Friday, and Saturday; there also is a Sunday flea market between June and mid-October in Groningen on the Grote Markt.

Antiques/ Antique Books There are a number of antique book dealers in the city center of Groningen, including **De Groninger Boekverkoper** (Oude Kijk-in-'t-Jatstraat 60, tel. 050/135858) and **Isis Antiquarian Bookshop** (Folkingestraat 20, tel. 050/184233). A number of general antiques shops are clustered on the broad shopping street **Gedempte Zuiderdiep.**

Ceramics There is a particular pleasure in buying from a factory store, even if no special savings are involved. The factory shop at the **Tichelaars**

Koninklijke Makkumer Aardewerk en Tegelfabriek sells a good selection of Makkumware (*see* Friesland, *above*).

Sports and the Outdoors

Camping   With more than 100 campgrounds in the province of Friesland alone, the North offers plenty of opportunity for camping. The national reservations service, **NRC/National Reservations Centre** (Box 404, 2260 AK Leidschendam, tel. 070/320–2500, fax 070/320–2611), takes campsite reservations. For camping in Leeuwarden, **De Kleine Wielen** (De Groene Ster 14, 8926 XE, tel. 05118/31660; may be closed mid-Oct.–mid-Mar.) has sites for 350 tents and touring caravans and has places for hikers. **Camping Stadspark** (Campinglaan 6, 9727 KH, tel. 050/251624; may be closed Nov.–Mar.) in Groningen has 200 sites; it also has accommodation for hikers.

Canoeing   In both Friesland and Groningen, canoeing routes have been laid out and special maps have been printed. Check with the respective tourist offices. Three of the largest canoe renting facilities in Friesland are **Watersportbedrijf De Drijfveer** (U. Twijnstrawei 31, 8491 CJ Akkrum, tel. 05665/2789), **Pean** (Pean 1, 8490 AB Akkrum, tel. 05663/1392), and **De Ulepanne/Balk** (Tsjamkedijkje 1, 8571 MS Balk, tel. 05140/2982). In the province of Groningen, **Horizon** (Witherenweg 26 9977 SB Kleine Huisjes, tel. 05958/1980), **De Zijlsterhoeve/HR** (Zijlsterweg 5, 9892 TE Aduarderzijl, tel. 05941/1423), and **Hinrichs Watersport** (Damsterweg 32, 9629 PD Steendam, tel. 05960/29137) rent canoes.

Sailing/   Friesland is bordered by the large and windswept IJsselmeer (Lake
Boating   IJssel). The province is also cut with a swath of lakes, canals, and small rivers that offer sailing or boating opportunities. The more than 150 boat- and sailboat-rental firms throughout Friesland include **Watersportbedrijf Anja** (Meersweg 9a, 9001 BG Grouw, tel. 05662/1373), **Botenverhuurbedrijf Grouw** (Wilhelminastraat 9001 BT Grouw, tel. 05662/3810), **A.E. Wester en Zn., 'De Blieken'** (Garde Jagersweg 4–5, Postbus 51, 9001 ZB Grouw, tel. 05662/1335, fax 05662/3840), **Watersportcamping Heeg** (De Burd 25a, 8621 JX Heeg, tel. 05154/2328), **Jachtwerf Frisia** (Oude Oppenhuizerw 79, 8606 JC Sneek, tel. 05150/12814, fax 05150/18182), and **Top En Twel Zeilcentrum** (It Ges 6, 8606 JK Sneek, tel. 05150/19192).

Although less blessed with open water, the province of Groningen offers opportunities for sailing and boating as well, particularly on the Schildmeer from the boating center at Steendam; contact **Hinrichs Watersport** (Damsterweg 32, 9629 PD Steendam, tel. 05960/29137) for information on boat rentals.

Windsurfing   Where the sailboats go, so go the Windsurfers. In Friesland the following firms rent both equipment and wet suits: **De Ulepanne/Balk** (Tsjamkedykje 1, 8571 MS Balk, tel. 05140/2982), **Jeugdherberg Oer 'T Hout** (Raadhuisstraat 18, 9001 AG Grouw, tel. 05662/1528), and **Top En Twel Zeilcentrum** (It Ges 6, 8606 JT Sneek, tel. 05150/19192).

Spectator Sports

Kaatsen   During the summer months, you will find local matches of the Frisian ball game *kaatsen* (similar to baseball) played in the villages throughout Friesland; major tournaments are held in August.

Polsstok-   Another uniquely Frisian sport is *polsstokspringen*, which involves
springen   pole-vaulting over canals. The main competition is held in Winsum in August.

Sailing Throughout the summer you will find weekend racing on the Frisian lakes. The summer's main event, however, is the two-week series of **Skûtjesilen Races** (late July) using the uniquely Dutch vessels, *skûtjes*, which are wide-bottom sailing barges.

Beaches

The need for dikes to hold back the sea makes broad beaches impossible along the long northern coastline of the Netherlands, but there are plenty of wide sandy beaches on the offshore Wadden Islands (*see* Off the Beaten Track, *above*).

Dining and Lodging

Beetsterzwaag **Hotel Lauswolt.** This golf and spa resort is in a sprawling manor-
Dining and house hotel at the back of a sweeping lawn in a quiet wooded village.
Lodging The fine restaurant is a member of the Alliance Gourmandise Néerlandaise. The rooms are large, and suites have separate living rooms. Special golf, spa, and gastronomic packages are available. *Van Harinxmaweg 10, 9244 ZN, tel. 05126/1245, fax 05126/1496. 54 rooms. Facilities: restaurant, sauna, swimming pool, tennis/ squash courts. AE, DC, MC, V. $$$*

Groningen **Ni Hao.** Across the canal from the city center, not far from the rail-
Dining way station, this antiques-filled and elaborately decorated Chinese-Indonesian restaurant is large, but thanks to an imaginative layout of open dining areas alternating with semiprivate rooms for groups, there is no feeling of the crowd that regularly fills the tables. Groups (4–6 people) can order from the extravagant 10-course menus, but if it's just two of you, the Surprise Menu mixes a variety of Chinese regional specialties; another possibility is an all-duck dinner, including whole roast Peking duck. *Hereweg 1, tel. 050/181400. Reservations advised. Jacket and tie advised. AE, DC, MC, V. $$$*
De Pauw. This chic, highly styled restaurant done in cream and black has a sophisticated and imaginative menu influenced by the cuisines of Provence and of other sunny climes. Dishes include fresh paprika soup and spring chicken with pasta and pesto. Art decorates the walls, and the bouquets are peacock feathers. *Gelkingestraat 52, tel. 050/181332. Reservations advised. Jacket and tie advised. AE, DC, MC, V. $$$*
Salle a Manger. This restaurant is not far from Grote Markt. Despite the traditional Dutch decor of the three dining rooms, the menu looks to Provençal France for its inspiration, with lots of tomato-and-herb–based sauces. The emphasis here is on meat dishes, although there are some vegetarian options. *Poelestraat 41, tel. 050/ 181114. Reservations advised. Dress: casual. AE, DC, MC, V. $$*

Dining and **Auberge Corps de Garde.** This small family-owned hotel is in a gra-
Lodging cious 17th-century barracks house facing the city center's encircling canal. Partially furnished with antiques, it is a congenial place with pleasant, spacious rooms that are brightly decorated in tones of green and rose. The restaurant serves excellent new Dutch cuisine. *Oude Boteringestraat 74, 9712 GN, tel. 050/145437, fax 050/136320. 8 rooms, 6 with bath. Facilities: restaurant, lounge. AE, DC, MC, V. Hotel $$; restaurant $$$*
Golden Tulip Familiehotel. In a comfortable suburb of Groningen on the edge of the area's largest lake, this small family hotel has grown over the years into a semiresort. There is a spaciousness and an elegantly modern but homey feeling about the rooms and suites. The lakeside café is particularly busy and entertaining in summer; boats can be rented nearby. *Groningerweg 19, 9765 GA Paterswolde, tel.*

05907/95400, fax 05907/91157. 78 rooms. Facilities: 3 restaurants, bikes, whirlpool, sauna, tennis, indoor swimming pool, pier, bus to city center. AE, DC, MC, V. $$$

Lodging **Hotel Mercure.** Essentially a business traveler's hotel that serves the local exhibition hall across the street, the Mercure is well located on one of the major roadways to the city center. The rooms have a bland but restful pastel-and-white decor. *Expositielaan 7, 9727 KA, tel. 050/258400, fax 050/217828. 157 rooms. Facilities: restaurant, bar, sauna, indoor swimming pool. AE, DC, MC, V. $$$*

Leeuwarden **Het Leven.** Just off the main shopping street of Leeuwarden, this in-
Dining formal brasserie-style restaurant on two levels serves good-value, delicious food such as cheese fondue, mussels, and stews. *Druifstreek 57–59, tel. 058/121233. Reservations advised. Dress: casual. AE, MC, V. $$*

Dining and **Oranjehotel.** Primarily a business hotel, Oranjehotel is directly
Lodging across from the railway station. The rooms are comfortable; the hotel is a local gathering place with a busy pub and a fine restaurant serving traditional Continental cuisine. *Stationsweg 4, 8911 AG, tel. 058/126241, fax 058/121441. 78 rooms. Facilities: restaurant, bar. AE, DC, MC, V. Closed Dec. 25–26. $$$*

Oudkerk **De Klinze.** In a wooded town not far from Leeuwarden, De Klinze is a
Dining and semiresort created from a 17th-century country estate. The roomy
Lodging suites in the manor house are decorated with vintage furniture and antiques; the bright and spacious guest rooms, decorated in a cheerful lemon-yellow and white, are in a separate, modern wing that also includes the spa. Dinner here is in the former parlors, with views of the woods. The cuisine is French. *Van Sminiaweg 32–36, 9064 KC Oudkerk; tel. 05103/61050; fax, 05103/61060. 22 rooms and 5 suites, all with bath. Facilities: indoor swimming pool, sauna, whirlpool, solarium, beauty salon. AE, DC, MC, V. $$$$*

Nightlife

Casino **Holland Casino** (Gedempte Kattendiep 150, tel. 050/123400), the only casino in the northern half of the Netherlands, is in Groningen.

Discos The influence of 20,000 university students in **Groningen** ensures that there is plenty of dancing to the latest music. In the Grote Markt neighborhood are **Die Unie** (Gelkingestraat 5, tel. 050/130192), with live music; **Gdansk** (Poelestraat 53, tel. 050/188200); **The Palace** (Gelkingestraat 1, tel. 050/139100); **Troubadour** (Peperstraat 19, tel. 050/132690); and **Warhol** (Peperstraat 7, tel. 050/121350).

Jazz/Rock In **Leeuwarden** the generally tame nightlife scene is enlivened by
Clubs two music cafés. **De Brouwershoeck** (Poststraat 21) offers jazz, and **Kings Inn** (Nieuwesteeg 1) has a novel combination of gospel and rock.

Gay Bars In Groningen there are two gay discotheques: **Duke** (Hoogstraatje 9, tel. 050/134609) and **MacDonald** (Hoge der A–3, tel. 050/127188).

4 Belgium

By Eric Sjogren

Belgium packs just over 5 million Dutch-speaking Flemings and almost as many French-speaking Walloons into a country only slightly larger than the state of Vermont. The presence of two language cultures inevitably creates tension, but it also enriches the cultural heritage. A diversity of geography, too, enhances the country's attractions. The Belgian landscape ranges from the beaches and dunes of the coast and the tree-lined, placid canals of the "platte land" (flat land) to the sheer cliffs of Ardennes River valleys and the dense forests of the south.

In many ways, Belgium is a country for connoisseurs: This is the land of van Eyck, Bruegel, and Rubens, and this is where their best work can be seen. The spirit of the Middle Ages and its great humanists—Erasmus, his friend Thomas More, and others—lives on in cities of great renown like Brugge and Ghent, and in others that are waiting to be discovered, like Mechelen and Lier. The art of living well has been cultivated in Belgium since the days of the great Burgundian feasts. Today, the country boasts an astonishing number of gourmet restaurants, including some of the world's finest.

In Belgium flourishes an unapologetically bourgeois culture. Dukes, counts, and lesser lords have built many a feudal castle on Belgian land, and abbots and cardinals have constructed towering religious edifices, but it was the merchants who built the cities and commissioned the works of art we admire today. The endless variations of Art Nouveau in the town houses of the Belle Epoque are another manifestation of bourgeois individualism. So are the comfortable proportions of today's private homes and public spaces.

Until quite recently the Belgians had no common history. Rather, their fate was determined by the dynastic marriages whereby princely families sought to extend their influence and perpetuate their power. It was through marriage that the possessions of the dukes of Flanders passed into the hands of the dukes of Burgundy in the 14th century, and then to the Habsburg family in 1477. A scion of that family, born in Ghent, became Emperor Charles V in 1519 when he inherited the Holy Roman Empire from his father and Spain from his mother. This was the beginning of 200 years of Spanish rule, and when eventually the Austrian branch of the Habsburg family gained the upper hand, the only real difference for Belgium was that it came to be ruled from Vienna instead of Madrid.

After the fall of Napoléon in 1815, the victorious powers aimed to settle matters by awarding the Belgian provinces to the Netherlands. But a cultural divide had opened up between the Low Countries to the north and those to the south, and it was a foregone conclusion that the staunchly Catholic southerners would not get along with the adamantly Protestant northerners. In military terms Belgium's 1830 war of independence did not amount to more than a few skirmishes, but the purpose was served. The new nation included the former principality of Liège, which under elected prince-bishops had maintained its independence for 800 years.

Colonialism, too, was thrust upon the Belgians. The Congo was the personal fiefdom of King Leopold II (son of Leopold I, first king of independent Belgium), who bequeathed it to the nation in 1908 only shortly before his death. The Belgians may have reaped the reward, but they also had to pay the consequences when colonialism came to its painful end and the independent Congo (now known as Zaire) was born 52 years later.

When Belgian forces put up unexpected resistance against the Germans in 1914, the country became known, a little patronizingly, as "brave little Belgium." In 1940 another war that Belgium basically had nothing to do with ravaged the country.

This is perhaps why Belgium is one of the staunchest supporters of the European Union (EU). Brussels is the home of the European Commission, where most decisions affecting the EU are made. Writers and politicians tend to refer to "Brussels" as a synonym for the commission, and this can be a bit of a mixed blessing. It is a heady sensation, but of secondary importance, to be the capital of Europe. What matters is the commonality of interests. The EU will survive only if it is successful in fashioning unity out of diversity. Exactly the same thing applies to the kingdom of Belgium.

Before You Go

Government Tourist Offices

In North America **Belgian Tourist Office** (780 3rd Ave., Suite 1501, New York, NY 10017, tel. 212/758–8130, fax 212/355–7675).

In the United Kingdom **Belgian Tourist Office** (29 Princes St., London W1R 7RG, tel. 0171/629–0230, fax 0171/629–0454).

Tour Groups

General-Interest Tours Listed below is a sample of the tours and packages that concentrate on Belgium. *See* Tour Groups in Chapter 1, Essential Information, for tours that cover more than one country in the region.

From the United Kingdom **Shearing Holidays** (Miry La., Wigan, Lancashire WN3 4AG, tel. 01942/824824) features a five-day city break centered in Brugge with excursions to Brussels and other places of interest, and a Belgian House Party tour. **Time Off Ltd.** (Chester Close, Chester St., London SW1X 7BQ, tel. 0171/235–8070) has packages from two to seven nights to Brussels and Brugge.

Special-Interest Tours From the United Kingdom **The Belgium Travel Service** (Bridge House, Ware, Herts. SG12 9DG, tel. 01920/467345) specializes in inclusive holidays on the Belgian coast and in the Ardennes, and it also operates tours covering all Belgium. Some include noteworthy festivals such as the Oostende Carnival. **Holts' Battlefield Tours** (15 Market St., Sandwich, Kent CT13 9DA, tel. 01304/612248) organizes tours of World War I battlefields in France and Belgium, with an emphasis on the Ypres salient. Waterloo and Battle of the Bulge tours are also available.

Package Deals for Independent Travelers

American Airlines Fly Away Vacations (tel. 800/832–8383) offers independent packages for as long as you like for visits to Brussels, Brugge, and Antwerp. **Extra Value Travel** (683 S. Collier Blvd., Marco Island, FL 33937, tel. 813/398–4848 or 800/255–2847) offers self-drive tours of Belgium, including hotel choices and car rental. **Jet Vacations** (1775 Broadway, New York, NY 10019, tel. 212/474–8700 or 800/538–0999) offers Flexiplan Europe, a choice of hotels, car rentals, airport transfers, and sightseeing options for Brussels, Antwerp, Brugge, and Liège. **Northwest WorldVacations** (tel. 800/692–8687) provides visitors to Brussels with preferred hotel and car-rental rates and tour options for a minimum of two nights. **Travel Bound** (599 Broadway, Penthouse, New York, NY 10012, tel. 212/334–1350 or 800/456–8656) offers a week-long "Brussels Grand" package for independent travelers, as well as packages to Belgium

Belgium

for three to six nights. **United Vacations** (106 Calvert St., Harrison, NY 10528, tel. 800/678–0949) will customize your itinerary in Belgium.

When to Go

Because the Belgians take vacations in July and August, these months are not ideal for visiting the coast or the Ardennes, but summer is a very good time to be in Brussels, Antwerp, or Liège. In summer you may also be able to get a break on hotel prices. On the other hand, this is also vacation time for many restaurants. For touring the country and visiting much-frequented tourist attractions like Brugge, the best times are April–June and September–October.

The following are average daily maximum and minimum temperatures for Brussels.

Brussels	Jan.	40F	4C	May	65F	18C	Sept.	70F	21C
		31	–1		47	8		52	11
	Feb.	45F	7C	June	72F	22C	Oct.	59	15C
		32	0		52	11		45	7
	Mar.	50F	10C	July	74F	23C	Nov.	49F	9C
		36	2		54	12		38	3
	Apr.	58F	14C	Aug.	72F	22C	Dec.	43F	6C
		41	5		54	12		34	1

Festivals and Seasonal Events

Jan. 18–28: Brussels's **International Film Festival,** which gains prestige each year, takes place at the Palais des Congrès (tel. 02/513–4130).

Feb. 26–28: Carnival is celebrated with great gusto, especially at Binche with its extravagantly costumed Gilles, at Malmédy, at Oostende, and at Eupen.

Mar. 4: The **Bal du Rat Mort** (tel. 059/500512, Wed. and Fri. 10–noon) in Oostende is one of Europe's most extravagant fancy-dress balls. Reservations are essential.

Mar. 19: In Stavelot, the hilarious Blancs Moussis with their long red noses swoop through town during the **mid-Lent carnival.**

Apr. 22–May 1: One of the world's leading flower shows, the **Floralies** (tel. 09/222–7336), held every fifth year in the Flanders Expo Hall in Ghent, is scheduled for 1995.

Late Apr.–early May: The **Royal Greenhouses** (tel. 02/513–0770), at Laeken Palace near Brussels, with superb flower and plant arrangements, are open to the public for a limited period.

Apr. 26–May 27: The **Queen Elisabeth International Music Competition** (tel. 02/513–0099) is one of the most demanding events of its kind. In 1995, the focus is on young pianists.

Late May: The **Brussels Jazz Rally** (tel. 02/735–8629) encompasses gigs and informal sessions in more than 60 cafés and pubs, plus outdoor concerts in the Grand'Place.

May: The **Ascension Day** Procession of the Holy Blood (tel. 050/448664) in Brugge is one of the oldest and most elaborate religious and historical processions in Europe. Early seat reservations are recommended.

May: The **Kunsten Festival des Arts** (tel. 02/223–2300) in Brussels is a month-long international celebration of contemporary drama, dance, and music.

June 11: The **Trinity Sunday** procession of the Golden Carriage and St. George's battle with Lumeçon the dragon are enacted in Mons (tel. 065/335580).

June 17–18: The **Folklore and Shrimp Festival** (tel. 058/511189) in Oostduinkerke features shrimp fishermen on horseback, brass bands, floats, and folklore ensembles.

June 17–18: A reenactment of the **Battle of Waterloo** (tel. 02/354–9910), staged every fifth year, is next scheduled for 1995.

July–Oct.: The **Festival of Wallonia** (rue du Jardin Botanique 29, 4000 Liège, tel. 041/223248) is a four-month series of concerts throughout Wallonia.

July 4 and 6: The **Ommegang** (tel. 02/512–1961) takes over Brussels's Grand'Place. It's a sumptuous and stately pageant reenacting a procession that honored Emperor Charles V in 1549.

July 15–24: The **Ghent Festivities** (tel. 091/241555) start, a 10-day sequence of music-making, entertainment, and assorted happenings in the streets of the city.

Aug.: The **Francorchamps Formula I Grand Prix** (tel. 02/287–0911) is one of the key events in the annual cycle of international motor racing.

Aug. 15: The **Outremeuse Festival** in Liège combines religious and folkloric elements in a joyous tide that sweeps through this section of the *cité ardente* (the Fiery City).

Aug. 17–26: In the **Canal Festival** (tel. 050/448686) in Brugge, events from the city's past are re-created alongside the romantic canals.

Sept.–mid-Oct.: The **Festival of Flanders** (Eugeen Flageyplein 18, 1050 Brussels, tel. 02/640–1525) brings concerts to all the old Flemish cities.

Sept.–Dec.: Every other year, the **Europalia Festival** honors a different country with exhibitions, concerts, and other events amounting to a thorough inventory of its cultural heritage. In 1996, the country thus honored in Brussels and other cities will be Turkey (tel. 02/507–8550).

Sept. 10: On **National Heritage Day** (tel. 02/511–1840) buildings of architectural or historical interest throughout Belgium that are not normally accessible to the public open their doors to all who come.

Nov. 3–12: The **European Union Championship** (tel. 03/326–1010) in Antwerp is a major event on the international tennis circuit.

Dec. 8–10: The **European Christmas Market** in the Grand Sablon in Brussels features the traditions and products of many different European countries.

What to Pack

Clothing No season is totally devoid of rainfall in Belgium, even though the rain is usually rather light. For visits from April/May to October, you would be well advised to bring a raincoat, and you will need an overcoat at other times. Bring a sweater at all times. The more expensive restaurants expect patrons to wear jacket and tie.

Miscellaneous If you're bringing electrical appliances from the United States, you'll need a converter and adapter plug. More expensive hotels often have blow-dryers and 100V shaver outlets.

Taking Money Abroad

Cash Machines The two major ATM networks in Belgium are Mister Cash and Bancontact. Provided you have a PIN code and have arranged direct debit to your bank at home, you can withdraw cash from these machines using major credit cards. There's a minimum charge of BF125 per transaction and interest is charged.

There is an American Express cash machine in the arrival hall at the National Airport in Brussels, and Diners Club, Visa, and MasterCard cash advances can be obtained at SCS Weckers, also in the arrival hall.

Belgian Currency

The monetary unit in Belgium is the Belgian franc. There are bills of 100, 500, 1,000, 2,000, and 10,000 francs, and coins of 1, 5, 20, and 50 francs. At press time (August 1994), one dollar was worth about BF32; one pound sterling, BF49; and one Canadian dollar, BF23.

What It Will Cost

The Belgian economy is stable and inflation is low to moderate, currently at less than 3%. Brussels, with its vast influx of business travelers and officials on EU business, can be very expensive. This applies especially to hotels, which can be twice as expensive as elsewhere in the country, but perfectly acceptable accommodations are available at more reasonable prices as well.

Taxes Sales tax (TVA) is always included in the price quoted for accommodations and meals. It ranges from 6% on basic items to 33% on luxury goods. *See* Shopping in Staying in Belgium, *below.*

Sample Costs A cup of coffee in a café will cost you BF45–BF60; a glass of beer, BF50–85; a glass of wine, about BF120. Train travel averages BF6 per mile, the average bus/metro/tram ride costs BF50, theater tickets are about BF600, and movie tickets cost about BF220.

Languages

Belgium is bisected by a linguistic border, with Flemish spoken to the north and French to the south of it. Written Flemish is indistinguishable from Dutch, but spoken Flemish may include dialect variations. Some French speakers have Walloon, a separate German-influenced tongue, as a second language. German, spoken by a couple of hundred thousand people at the eastern end of the country, is Belgium's third official language. Brussels is officially bilingual (Flemish/French).

Language is a sensitive subject in Belgium, loaded with political implications. A foreigner is well advised to use English rather than French in Flanders, even though both are widely understood. You will have no problem finding English-speakers in Brussels. In Wallonia you may have to muster whatever French you possess, but in tourist centers you will always be able to find people who speak at least basic English.

Staying Healthy

Medical services are highly developed in Belgium, and should the need for hospitalization arise, it's almost always possible to be admitted immediately. English is more widely spoken by doctors and paramedics of Flemish mother tongue than among French-language colleagues. This is worth bearing in mind when, as in Brussels, you have a choice among hospitals where Flemish or French predominates.

It used to be the rule that seafood should not be consumed during months without an "r" in the name. Nowadays you can safely eat mussels and the like the year-round in restaurants with good hygienic standards, but avoid those where the produce is displayed all day long (as in some places in Brussels's Ilôt Sacré area).

Car Rentals

There are 20 pages of ads for car-rental firms in the Brussels Yellow Pages, so a wide choice is available. Half a dozen firms have desks in the baggage claim area at the Brussels airport, in addition to several locations around town. Some also have offices at hotels—Avis at the Hilton, Hertz at the SAS Royal. The major firms also have offices in the larger provincial cities, supplemented by local enterprises.

Rail Passes

Belgian **rail passes** can be bought in the United Kingdom from Belgian National Railways (10 Premier House, Greycoat Pl., London SW1P 1SB, tel. 01891/516444). Passes are not available in the United States or Canada, but you can buy them once you arrive in Belgium.

Student and Youth Travel

The youth information service in Brussels is **Infor-Jeunes** (blvd. de Smet de Nayer 145, tel. 02/426–3333), and there's also an English-language **Help Line** (tel. 02/648–4014), which provides both practical information and crisis intervention. **Acotra** (rue de la Madeleine 53, tel. 02/512–8607) will help in finding inexpensive accommodations.

Youth hostels are inexpensive and numerous. For information on facilities in Wallonia, write to **Fédération Belge des Auberges de la Jeunesse** (Belgian Youth Hostel Federation, rue Van Oost 52, 1030 Brussels, tel. 02/215–3100); for Flanders, contact **Vlaamse Jeugdherbergcentrale** (Flemish Youth Hostel Center, Van Stralenstraat 40, Antwerp, tel. 03/232–7218).

Traveling with Children

Hotels Children under 12 stay free in their parents' room at Best Western hotels. The Brussels Best Western is the Bedford Hotel (rue du Midi 135); there are also Best Westerns in Brugge, Knokke, Blankenberg, and Oostende. Children under 19 stay free at Holiday Inn. Children of whatever age stay free at the Hilton.

Apartment/ Villa Rentals A large choice of properties in Wallonia is available through **Belsud Reservation** (rue Marché-aux-Herbes 61, 1000 Brussels, tel. 02/504–0280, fax 02/514–5335). This organization is part of the government tourist authority. They publish a catalogue with illustrations of all accommodations.

Hints for Travelers with Disabilities

For information on facilities for travelers with disabilities in Belgium, contact **Fonds National de Reclassement Social des Handicapés** (rue du Meiboom 14, 1000 Brussels, tel. 02/218–3080) or **Vlaamse Federatie voor Gehandicapten (VFG)** (rue St. Jean 32–38, 1000 Brussels, tel. 02/515–0260).

Two holiday complexes have facilities built especially for people with disabilities: **De Ceder** (Parijsestraat 34, 9800 Astene-Deinze, tel. 09/386–3028) in Flanders, and **Les Riezes et les Sarts** (rue Grande 84, 6404 Cul-des-Sarts, Couvin, tel. 060/377664) in the Ardennes.

Visitors with disabilities should be aware that many Belgian streets are cobblestone.

Hotels The following hotels in Brussels (listed from most expensive to least) have rooms for guests who have disabilities: Hilton, SAS Royal, Carrefour de l'Europe, Sodehotel Brussels, Conrad, Mayfair, Royal Crown, Copthorne Stephanie, Sheraton Brussels and Sheraton Brussels Airport, Cadettt Mövenpick, Le Dome, Métropole, Holiday Inn Brussels Airport, Eurovillage, Jolly Atlanta, Mercure, Jolly Grand Sablon, Novotel Brussels off Grand'Place, Palace, Albert Premier, Leopold, Fimotel Brussels Airport, Fimotel Expo, Ibis Brussels Center and Ibis Brussels Airport, Orion,Capital, Campanile, Gerfaut, Van Belle, and Sun.

The same applies for Best Western, Holiday Inn, Novotel, Mercure, and Ibis hotels throughout Belgium, for the Grand Hotel in Waterloo, Ramada Hotel in Liège, the Switel and Hilton in Antwerp, Hotel Pullman in Brugge, and Hotel Ardennes in Spa-Balmoral.

Further Reading

Barbara Tuchman's *A Distant Mirror*, describing 14th-century European affairs, gives valuable insights, illuminated by memorable vignettes, into the conflicts between Flemish towns and the crown of France. *The Guns of August* applies Tuchman's narrative technique to the events, largely in Belgium, of the first month of World War I. John Keegan's *The Face of Battle* includes a brilliant analysis of the Battle of Waterloo. Leon Wolff's *In Flanders Fields* is a classic account of the catastrophic campaign of 1917, while John Toland's *No Man's Land* covers the events on the Western Front in 1918.

Toland has also written *Battle: The Story of the Bulge*. William Wharton's *A Midnight Clear* is a fictional account of the Ardennes battle as seen by American GIs. *Outrageous Fortune* by Roger Keyes is a sympathetic account of the role played by Leopold III up to 1940. Hugo Claus's *The Sorrow of Belgium*, an outstanding novel of life during the occupation, has been translated into many languages from the original Dutch.

Two 19th-century novels well worth dipping into are Georges Rodenbach's *Bruges-la-Morte*, which was contemporaneous with the rediscovery of Brugge, and Charles de Coster's picaresque *La legende d'Ulenspiegel*, which captures the spirit of Belgian defiance of outside authority. Both have been translated into English.

Maurice Maeterlinck, Marguerite Yourcenar, and Georges Simenon were all Belgian writers working in French. So was Jacques Brel, many of whose songs also contain outstanding poetry. Hergé, finally, set many of the *Tintin* cartoon adventures in foreign lands, but Tintin himself remained always the quintessential "bon petit Belge."

Arriving and Departing

From North America by Plane

Airports and Airlines
All intercontinental and the vast majority of other international flights arrive at the Brussels National Airport at Zaventem. The airport is linked with Antwerp by coach service and with all other Belgian cities by rail.

Sabena (tel. 02/511–9030), the Belgian national carrier, flies to Brussels from New York, Boston, and Chicago; **American Airlines** (tel. 02/508–7700), from New York and Chicago; **United** (tel. 078/114376), from Washington; **Delta** (tel. 730–8200) from New York and Atlanta; and **TWA** (tel. 02/513–7916) from New York.

Sample eastbound flying times are: six hours, 50 minutes from New York to Brussels; and seven hours from Boston to Brussels. Westbound flights are about an hour longer.

From the United Kingdom by Plane, Car, Ferry/Ship, Train, and Bus

By Plane
Sabena (tel. 02/511–9030) and **British Midland** (tel. 02/772–9400) fly to Brussels from London (Heathrow); **British Airways** (tel. 02/725–3000) from London (Heathrow and Gatwick); and **Air UK** (tel. 02/507–7052), from London (Stansted). Other U.K. cities with direct or nonstop flights to Brussels include Birmingham, Manchester, Newcastle, Leeds, Bristol, Edinburgh, and Glasgow. Flying time from London to Brussels is one hour; Brussels to London is one hour, 10 minutes.

By Car
The ferry routes to Belgium are from Ramgate, Hull, or Felixstoxe to Zeebrugge. Unless you're traveling in the dead of winter, and sometimes even then, it's essential to book well in advance (*see* By Ferry/Ship, *below*, for addresses). Rates vary according to the length of your vehicle, the time of your crossing, and whether you travel in peak, shoulder, or low season.

Both the **Automobile Association** (Fanum House, Basingstoke, Hants. RG21 2EA, tel. 01345/500600) and the **Royal Automobile Club** (RAC House, Box 100, South Croydon CR2 6XW, tel. 0181/686–2525) operate on-the-spot breakdown and repair services across Belgium. Both companies will also transport cars and passengers back to Britain in case of serious breakdowns. AA has five-day, 12-day, and 31-day coverage; RAC offers 10-day and 31-day coverage.

The Channel Tunnel
The Channel Tunnel opened officially in May 1994, providing the fastest route across the Channel—35 minutes from Folkestone to Calais, or 60 minutes from motorway to motorway. It consists of two large 50-kilometer- (31-mile-) long tunnels for trains, one in each direction, linked by a smaller service tunnel running between them. **Le Shuttle** (tel. 0345/353535 in the U.K., 800/388–3876 in the U.S.), a special car, bus, and truck train, which was scheduled to begin service in June 1994, operates a continuous loop, with trains departing every 15 minutes at peak times and at least once an hour through the night. No reservations are necessary, although tickets may be purchased in advance from travel agents. Most passengers stay in their own car throughout the "crossing"; progress updates are provided on display screens and radio. Motorcyclists park their bikes in a separate section with its own passenger compartment,

while foot passengers must book passage by coach (*see* By Train, *below*).

The Tunnel is reached from exit 11a of the M20/A20. Drivers purchase tickets from toll booths, then pass through frontier control before loading onto the next available service. Unloading at Calais takes eight minutes. Ticket prices start at £130 for a low-season five-day round-trip in a small car and are based on season, time of day, length of stay, and car size regardless of the number of passengers. Peak season fares are not always competitive with ferry prices.

By Ferry/Ship There are two principal routes across the English Channel to Belgium: Ramsgate–Oostende, operated by **Oostende Lines** (try to book on their new ship, *Prins Filip*) and marketed by **Sally Line** (Argyle Centre, York St., Ramsgate, Kent CT11 9DS, tel. 01843/595522), and Felixstowe–Zeebrugge, operated by **P&O European Ferries** (tel. 01304/203388). The Ramsgate–Oostende crossing takes four hours, depending on sea states; the Felixstowe–Zeebrugge trip takes about six hours, eight hours for overnight crossings. The passengers-only Ramsgate–Oostende Jetfoil (book through Sally Line) is a good bet if you're traveling by train. It makes the crossing in only 100 minutes, but it is more expensive than the regular ferries and much more liable to be canceled in bad weather.

By Train Boat trains timed to meet ferries at Ramsgate leave London and connect with onward trains at Oostende. The Ramsgate–Oostende Jetfoil service is the fastest conventional rail connection to Brussels (about 5½ hrs, station to station). Contact **Intercity Europe,** the international wing of BritRail, at London/Victoria station (tel. 0171/834–2345, information; tel. 0171/828–8092, bookings).

The Channel **Eurostar** (for information, tel. 0171/922–4486 in the U.K., 800/942–
Tunnel 4866 in the U.S.) high-speed train service was scheduled to begin in July 1994, with passenger-only trains whisking riders between new stations in Paris (Gare du Nord) and London (Waterloo) in three hours and between London and Brussels (Midi) in 3¼ hours. The service of one train daily each way was scheduled to increase in January 1995 to 15 trains daily in each direction. At press time, ticket prices had not been set. Tickets are available in the United Kingdom through **Intercity Europe,** the international wing of BritRail (London/Victoria Station, tel. 0171/834–2345 or 0171/828–8092 for credit-card bookings), and in the United States through **Rail Europe** (tel. 800/942–4866) and **BritRail Travel** (1500 Broadway, New York, NY 10036, tel. 800/677–8585).

By Bus **City Sprint,** operated by **Hoverspeed** (tel. 01304/240241), offers bus service to Dover, Hovercraft service to Calais, and another bus connection to Brussels or Antwerp. Both trips take about seven hours.

Staying in Belgium

Getting Around

By Plane There are no domestic air services.

By Train The Société Nationale des Chemins de Fer Belge (SNCB/Belgian National Railways, rue de France 89, B-1070 Brussels, tel. 02/219–2640) provides frequent train service—first and second class—from Brussels to all major cities in the country. Very few are more than an hour away. This means that you can, if you wish, see most of the country on day trips while remaining based in Brussels and traveling on reduced-price same-day return tickets. Tickets are sold only at railway stations.

Rail Passes **Tourrail Tickets** allow unlimited travel on the Belgian network for any five days during a one-month period. For those over 26 the price is BF2,970 first class and BF1,980 second class. For those under 26, the pass costs BF2,030 first class and BF1,350 second class. A **Go-Pass,** available at BF990 for those between 12 and 26, is good for eight one-way trips in a six-month period; it is not individual and can thus be used by a group traveling together.

By Bus Intercity bus travel is not well developed in Belgium. You can, however, reach a number of localities surrounding each city by the local bus company. Generally speaking, this would correspond to getting to those places that are mentioned under Off the Beaten Track in each chapter.

By Car Belgium has a magnificent network of well-marked motorways and, in contrast with the railroads, they are not all spokes from the Brussels hub. Thus you can, for instance, drive along fast, four-lane highways from Antwerp to Ghent, or Liège to Tournai or Brugge to Kortrijk without passing through the capital. There are no tolls, and most highways are illuminated at night.

You must carry a warning triangle, to be placed well behind the car in case of a breakdown. There are emergency telephones at intervals along the motorways. The speed limit is 120 kph (74 mph) on motorways, 90 kph (56 mph) on secondary roads and 50 kph (31 mph) in built-up areas. Driving with the flow may mean higher speeds than most U.S. drivers are accustomed to. At intersections, always check traffic from the right even if you're on a thoroughfare; Belgian drivers can be reckless in insisting on "priority on the right." Gas costs about the same as in other European countries, which means quite a bit more than in the United States (almost a dollar a liter).

Telephones

Local Calls Pay phones work with 5- and 20-franc coins or (increasingly) with Telecards, available in a number of denominations starting at BF200. These cards can be purchased at any post office and at many newsstands. Most phone booths that accept Telecards have a list indicating where cards can be bought. A local call costs BF10 or BF20.

International Calls The least expensive way is to buy a high-denomination Telecard and make a direct call from a phone booth. A five-minute call to the United States at peak time will cost about BF750 by this method. Most hotel rooms are equipped with direct-call telephones, but nearly all add a service charge that can be quite substantial. It's better to ask beforehand what service charges are applied.

To call collect, or by credit card, dial 078/110010 (AT&T), 078/110012 (MCI), or 078/110014 (US Sprint) for the United States; 078/110044 for the United Kingdom.

Mail

Postal Rates A 10-gram airmail letter to the United States costs BF38; add BF4 for each additional 10 grams. Postcards cost BF38. Letters (up to 20 grams) and postcards to the United Kingdom cost BF16.

Receiving Mail If you do not know where you will be staying, you can have mail sent care of American Express (Pl. Louise 1, 1000 Brussels). The service is free for cardholders, otherwise $2 per letter.

Tipping

A service charge is included in restaurant and hotel bills, and tips are also included in the amount shown on the meter in taxis. Additional tipping is unnecessary unless you wish to say thank you for really superior service. Hotel porters generally get a gratuity of BF100 for carrying bags to your room. Tip doormen BF50 for getting you a cab. Porters in railway stations ask a fixed per-suitcase price of BF30–BF35. In movie theaters, ushers expect a BF20 tip when you present the ticket. Washroom attendants get a BF10 tip. Hairdressers usually receive 10%–20%.

Shopping

Good quality **lace** is available in several shops in Brussels (but not in cheap souvenir shops); even so, you may wish to wait until you've seen what is available in Brugge before making your choice. Similarly, if you're interested in **fashion,** wait until you've checked out the avant-garde boutiques in Antwerp. If your visit includes Liège, go first to the Val St.-Lambert factory shop before buying **crystal** elsewhere.

Chocolate is best bought as close to departure as possible. In fact, some of the best brands (Godiva, Neuhaus, Daskalides) are available in the tax-free shop at the airport. The Godiva shop in place Stephanie will mail boxes anywhere in the world.

Many shops advertise that goods are available tax-free. The procedure for overseas visitors buying merchandise tax-free has been greatly simplified. At the time of purchase by credit card, you pay the price without TVA and you also sign, with your card, a guarantee in the amount of the sales tax. You are given two invoices: One is your record and the other must be stamped by customs when you leave Belgium (or the last EU country on your itinerary). You must return the stamped invoice to the store within three months, or you forfeit the guarantee.

Keep in mind that shop clerks are often aloof in a manner that may seem rude.

Sports and the Outdoors

Two organizations provide information on all sports facilities in the country: **BLOSO** (rue des Colonies 31, tel. 02/510–3411), for Flemish speakers, and **ADEPS** (blvd. Léopold II 44, tel. 02/413–2311), for French speakers.

Cycling The flat land of Flanders is made for this sport, but it can get windy at times. The steep hills of the Ardennes separate the men from the boys. You can rent bikes cheaply at many railway stations, but they aren't your state-of-the-art models. Specialized rental shops exist in most tourist centers. The **Fédération Belge de Cyclotourisme** (Belgian Cycling Federation) is at Av. H. Limbourg 34, Brussels (tel. 02/521–8640).

Golf Until recently strictly a rich man's sport in Belgium, golfing is becoming more popular, and there are now courses near all major cities. The **Fédération Royale Belge de Golf** (Royal Belgian Golf Federation) is at Chaussée de La Hulpe 110, Brussels (tel. 02/672–2389).

Mountain-
eering The Ardennes may not be the Alps, but the many cliffs, especially along the Meuse River valley, provide excellent opportunities for

rock-face climbing. The **Club Alpin Belge** (Belgian Alpine Club) is at rue de l'Aurore 19, Brussels (tel. 02/648–8611).

Tennis There are tennis courts aplenty, but so popular is this sport that you are well advised to book one as early as you can. Your hotel concierge will generally help. For more information, contact the **Fédération Royale Belge de Tennis** (Royal Belgian Tennis Federation), Passage International 6, Centre Rogier, Brussels (tel. 02/217–2200).

Water Sports All along the coast, but also on lakes and man-made bodies of water, you'll see large numbers of people windsurfing. For information on this and other sports, contact the **Vlaamse Watersportvereiningen** (Flemish Water Sport Association), Beatrijslaan 25, Antwerp (tel. 03/219–6967).

Beaches

Belgium's entire North Sea Coast is one long beach, and some resorts are so close to each other that you can wander from one to the next without really noticing. Generally speaking, Knokke-Heist draws a youngish, well-heeled clientele, De Haan is more middle-aged, Oostende caters to a mixed crowd, and De Panne attracts families with young children. If you crave a secluded beach, cross the border into the Dutch province of Zeeuwsch-Vlaanderen.

Dining

The Belgians, by and large, take dining seriously and are discerning about fresh produce and innovative recipes. Because they put a high value on the pleasures of the table, they are also prepared to pay a price that in the best restaurants can be quite steep. You will almost always find families or groups of friends sharing a celebratory meal even in the most expensive restaurants.

As in France, nouvelle cuisine has meant a liberation of creative spirits, and the standards have improved greatly over the past few decades. More recently, the trend has been back to regional and traditional dishes, and now you can enjoy old-fashioned recipes with a modern twist in many restaurants. These may include such hearty dishes as *waterzooi* (a rich chicken or fish hot pot), *faisan à la brabançonne* (pheasant with braised chicory), *lapin à la bière* (rabbit cooked in beer), or *carbonnade* (chunky beef stew with beer).

The quintessential Belgian vegetable is not the brussels sprout but the *witloof* (*chicon* to French-speakers, and endive or chicory to the rest of the world). We owe it to an act of pure serendipity. During one of the many wars in Belgium, a farmer near Mechelen had to abandon the chicory roots (used to produce a coffee substitute) that he had just harvested. When he returned, he found they had sprouted leaves; he tried them and found them good. The witloof was born, and you'll find it in many guises—braised, au gratin, or in salads, always with a slightly bitter edge. Many other good things come from Belgium: superb asparagus, smoked ham and sausages from the Ardennes, crayfish, and trout. But the mussels the Belgians eat with such gusto and proclaim as their own actually come from Holland.

Belgians also swear by the humble *frites*—chips or french fries. They are served in every restaurant and home. You can also get them on street corners and at roadside stands known as *fritures* (Dutchified *frituur*), served with mayonnaise, catsup, or, catering to more advanced tastes, béarnaise or curry sauce. You're not likely to encounter a cheaper or more Belgian dish.

Mealtimes Most hotels serve breakfast until 10. Belgians usually eat lunch between 1 and 3, but restaurants are open from noon. The two-hour lunch is generally expense-account related. The main meal of the day is dinner, generally eaten between 8 and 10. Peak dining time used to be about 8 but seems to be getting later, and reservations are readily accepted for 9 or 9:30.

Dress Belgians are becoming less formal, and conservative dress is now de rigueur only in the most expensive restaurants. The younger generation in particular favors stylish but casual dress when dining out.

Ratings Prices are per person and include appetizer, entrée, and dessert, but no beverages. *See also* separate ratings for Brussels, *below*. Highly recommended restaurants are indicated by a star ★.

Category	Cost: Belgium except Brussels
$$$$	over BF3,000
$$$	BF1,750–BF3,000
$$	BF750–BF1,750
$	under BF750

Lodging

You can trust Belgian hotels, almost without exception, to be clean and of a high standard. Modern hotels catering to business travelers, especially in Brussels, can be very expensive, but there is also a wide choice of perfectly acceptable and reasonably priced hotels, where the only difference is the size of the room and number of amenities. Hotel prices in the rest of the country are considerably lower than in the capital. Taxes and service charges are always included in the quoted price. Hotel lists are available from local tourist offices.

Apartment Hotels If you are staying for a week or longer, this may be an interesting option. There are 20-odd such hotels in Brussels, with prices ranging from BF15,000 to BF40,000 per week for a furnished flat with kitchenette.

Pensions Pensions offer a double room with bath or shower and full board from BF2,500 to BF3,500 in Brussels, about BF500 less elsewhere. There's often a minimum stay requirement of two to three days. For information, check the local tourist office.

Youth Hostels *See* Student and Youth Travel in Before You Go, *above*.

Camping Belgium is well supplied with camping and caravaning sites. For details, contact the **Royal Camping and Caravaning Club of Belgium** (Avenue Albert 30, Brussels, tel. 02/344–9446).

Ratings Hotel prices are exclusive and are posted in each room. All prices in this book are for two people sharing a double room. *See also* separate ratings for Brussels, *below*. Highly recommended hotels are indicated by a star ★.

Category	Cost: Belgium except Brussels
$$$$	over BF6,000
$$$	BF3,500–BF6,000
$$	BF2,500–BF3,500
$	under BF2,500

Brussels

Brussels (Bruxelles in French, Brussel in Flemish) is a provincial city at heart, even though it has assumed a new identity as capital of the EU. Within the Belgian framework, Brussels has equal status with Flanders and Wallonie as an autonomous region. It is a bilingual enclave just north of the border that divides the country into Flemish- and French-speaking parts.

The battle for dominance of the city began long ago. A village on the site of present-day Brussels had begun to emerge during the latter half of the 10th century. A population of craftsmen and traders settled gradually around the castle of the counts of Leuven, who were later succeeded by the dukes of Brabant.

Philip the Good, duke of Burgundy, took possession of Brabant in 1430, and Brussels became a center for the production of tapestry, lace, and other luxury goods. When Charles V abdicated in 1555, his son, Philip II of Spain, dealt ruthlessly with advocates of the Reformation, which had taken hold in the Low Countries. His governor, the duke of Alva, had the leaders of the revolt, the counts of Egmont and Hoorn, executed in the Grand'Place. A monument to them stands in the square of the Petit Sablon.

In 1695, the French Marshal Villeroy had the city bombarded with red-hot cannonballs. Four thousand houses and 16 churches were destroyed by the ensuing fires, including all of the Grand'Place with the exception of the Town Hall. The Austrian Habsburgs, nominal masters of the Low Countries from 1713 on, recovered the lands in 1744. A new era of prosperity began, and the Upper Town around place Royale, the Sablon, and the Parc de Bruxelles was restyled in something like its present form.

The next large-scale rebuilding of Brussels was initiated by Leopold II in the second half of the 19th century. He applied the profits from what was the Congo Free State to grand urban projects. Present-day Brussels is indebted to him for the generous proportions of the city's avenues and thoroughfares.

At the end of the 19th century, Brussels was one of the liveliest cities in Europe, known for its splendid cafés and graceful Art Nouveau architecture. The Germans stamped out that gaiety when they occupied the city during World War I, and again from 1940 to 1945. The comeback of Brussels on the international scene was heralded by the World's Fair and Universal Exposition of 1958.

International business has invaded the city in a big way, but a few steps from the steel-and-glass office blocks there are cobbled streets and forgotten spots where the city's eventful past is plainly visible, and all over the city fanciful Art Nouveau town houses testify to the individualistic tastes of their builders.

Over the centuries, Brussels has been shaped by the different cultures of the foreign powers that have been its rulers. It has learned the art of accommodating them and in the process prepared itself for the role of capital of Europe.

Important Addresses and Numbers

Tourist Information The **Tourist Information Brussels** (TIB) office is in the Hotel de Ville (Town Hall) on the Grand'Place (tel. 02/513–8940), open Monday–Saturday 9–6; Sunday, same hours in summer, 10–2 in winter, closed December–February. There's a separate tourist office in Waterloo at Chaussée de Bruxelles 149 (tel. 02/354–9910), open April–November 15, daily 9:30–6:30; November 16–March, daily 10:30–5.

Embassies **U.S.:** blvd. du Regent 27, tel. 02/513–3830. **Canadian:** av. de Tervuren 2, tel. 02/735–6040. **U.K.:** rue d'Arlon 85, tel. 02/287–6211.

Emergencies **Police,** tel. 101. **Ambulance,** tel. 100. **Hospital emergency rooms:** Hôpital St. Pierre (rue Haute 322, tel. 02/535–4051) and Institut Edith Cavell (rue Edith Cavell 32, tel. 02/348–4001). **Doctors,** tel. 02/648–8000. **Dentists** (nights and weekends only), tel. 02/426–1026.

Late-Night Pharmacies One pharmacy in each district stays open 24 hours; the roster is posted in all pharmacy windows. In an emergency, call 02/479–1818.

Where to Change Money Major banks have offices at the airport and all over the city. Many *bureaux de change* stay open outside banking hours but may charge a higher rate. Your safest bet is to go to **American Express** (Pl. Louise 2, tel. 02/512–1740) or **Thomas Cook** (Grand'Place 4, tel. 02/513–2845).

English-Language Bookstores **W.H. Smith** (blvd. Adolphe Max 71, tel. 02/219–2708) carries a large selection of paperbacks, specialized hardbacks, and periodicals. The **Librairie de Rome** (av. Louise 50, tel. 02/511–7937) sells paperbacks, guidebooks, and newspapers from all over Europe.

Travel Agencies **American Express** is at place Louise 2 (tel. 02/512–1740); **Wagons-Lits** is at boulevard Anspach 1 (tel. 02/211–9990) and other locations. For travel to the United Kingdom, most requirements can be handled by the **British Reservation Centre** (av. Louise 306, tel. 02/646–4210). For others, ask at your hotel.

Arriving and Departing by Plane

Airport and Airlines All flights arrive at and depart from Brussels's national airport, **Zaventem** (tel. 02/732–3111). **Sabena, American, Delta, TWA,** and **United** fly into Brussels from the United States. **Sabena, British Midland,** and **British Airways** fly to Brussels from London's Heathrow Airport; **Air UK,** from Stansted; and **British Airways,** from Gatwick. Zaventem has been undergoing changes (both renovations and new construction); at press time, a new air terminal and half of a new embarkation wing were expected to open in December 1994, the rest of the wing in June 1995.

Between the Airport and Downtown *By Train* Express trains leave the airport for the Gare du Nord and Gare Centrale every 20 minutes (one train an hour continues to the Gare du Midi). The trip takes 20 minutes and costs BF110 one way in first class, BF70 second class. You can buy tickets at a booth in the baggage area or on the train (BF30 surcharge). The trains operate 6 AM–midnight.

By Taxi Airport taxis are plentiful. A taxi to the city center takes about half an hour and costs about BF1,000. You can save 25% on the fare by buying a voucher for the return trip if you use the Autolux taxi company.

By Bus Free courtesy buses serve airport hotels and a few downtown hotels. Inquire when making reservations.

Arriving and Departing by Car, Train, and Bus

By Car Belgium is covered by an extensive network of four-lane motorways. Brussels is 204 kilometers (127 miles) from Amsterdam on E19, 222 kilometers (138 miles) from Düsseldorf on E40, 219 kilometers (136 miles) from Luxembourg City on E411, 308 kilometers (191 miles) from Paris, and 115 kilometers (71 miles) from Oostende on E40.

Brussels is surrounded by a beltway, marked RING. Exits to the city are marked CENTER. Among several large underground parking facilities, the one close to the Grand'Place is particularly convenient for users of downtown hotels.

By Train Conventional train services from London connect with the Ramsgate–Oostende ferry or Jetfoil, and from Oostende the train takes you to Brussels. The whole journey using Jetfoil takes some six hours, but by ferry it's three hours longer. For more information, contact **British Rail** (tel. 0171/834–2345) or **Sally Line** (tel. 01843/595522).

Brussels is linked with Paris, Amsterdam, and the German rail network by fast intercity trains, and there are direct services to Switzerland, Italy, and Austria. **Belgian National Railways** (SNCB, tel. 02/219–2640) is the national rail line.

The Channel Tunnel *See* The Channel Tunnel in Arriving and Departing from the United Kingdom by Train, *above.*

Stations The main station is the **Gare du Midi** (South Station, off Boulevard du Midi). Trains also stop at the **Gare du Nord** (rue du Progrès); this is the one to use if your hotel is in the place Rogier area. In between is the **Gare Centrale** (blvd. de l'Impératrice), the most convenient for the downtown area, but served (apart from the Airport Express) mostly by commuter trains. For train information, call 02/219–2640.

By Bus From London, the **Hoverspeed City Sprint** bus connects with the Dover–Calais Hovercraft, and the bus then takes you to Brussels, where it stops at rue Antoine Dansaert 101, near the Bourse. The journey takes seven hours. For reservations and times, call **Hoverspeed** (tel. 01304/240241).

Getting Around Brussels

By Metro, Tram, and Bus The **Metro** system consists of one line running east–west and another north–south. Tram and bus routes are less predictable and subject to change. Maps of the total system are available in many Metro stations and from the TIB in the Grand'Place.

Multifare cards can be purchased in Metro stations and at newsstands. Single tickets, good for one transfer, cost BF50 and can be bought on buses and trams. The best buy is a 10-trip ticket at BF290, or a 24-hour card at BF220. You need to stamp your card in the appropriate machine on buses and trams; in the Metro your card is stamped as you pass through the turnstiles.

By Taxi Taxis are expensive, but tips are included in the fare. Even a short trip will cost you about BF250, and longer in-town trips are up to BF500. To call a cab, phone (or have the restaurant or hotel call) **Tax-**

is Verts (tel. 02/349–4949), or catch one at a cabstand. Don't expect to hail a cab—taxis don't cruise.

Opening and Closing Times

Businesses are open weekdays 9–5 or 9–5:30. Banks are open weekdays 9–4, with some open Saturday 9–noon. Administrative offices are a law unto themselves; call ahead. Shops are generally open Monday–Saturday 10–7; smaller shops often close for lunch. Nearly all museums are closed on Monday. Restaurants usually stay open until the last guest leaves; dinner orders will be accepted until about 10 PM. Theaters and concerts normally start at 8:30. In discos and nightclubs, the action begins around midnight.

Guided Tours

De Boeck Sightseeing (tel. 02/513–7744) operates city tours (BF700) with multilingual cassette commentary and guides. Passengers are picked up at major hotels and at the TIB in the Town Hall. De Boeck also operates tours of Waterloo. **Chatterbus** (tel. 02/673–1835 evenings only) organizes walking tours from June to September (BF275).

Special Interest ARAU (rue Henri Maus 37, tel. 02/513–4761) organizes a variety of city architectural tours (BF500 for a half-day tour, Sat. only) in English.

Personal Guides Qualified guides, collectively speaking a total of 14 languages, are available for individual tours from TIB in the Town Hall (tel. 02/513–8940). The cost for three hours is BF2,600, and up to 20 people can share the same guide.

Highlights for First-Time Visitors

Cathédrale St-Michel (Tour 1: The Grand'Place and Surroundings)
Grand'Place (Tour 1: The Grand'Place and Surroundings)
Grand Sablon (Tour 2: The Upper Town and the Marolles)
Manneken Pis (Tour 1: The Grand'Place and Surroundings)
Musée d'Art Ancien (Tour 2: The Upper Town and the Marolles)
Musée d'Art Moderne (Tour 2: The Upper Town and the Marolles)
Petit Sablon (Tour 2: The Upper Town and the Marolles)
Place Royale (Tour 2: The Upper Town and the Marolles)

Exploring Brussels

Start in the historic heart of Brussels, the Lower Town, centered on the Grand'Place with its 17th-century guild houses. You can devote a second day to the Upper Town of the 18th and 19th centuries.

Tour 1: The Grand'Place and Surroundings

Numbers in the margin correspond to points of interest on the Brussels map.

① The most famous citizen of Brussels is the insouciant **Manneken Pis**. The small bronze statue of a chubby boy peeing into a fountain stands at the corner of the rue de l'Etuve and the rue du Chêne, southwest of the Grand'Place. A similar stone figure, of unknown origin, is first mentioned in a document from 1377. To replace it, the city ordered the present bronze statue in 1619 from the sculptor Jerome Duquesnoy. It was hidden during the 1695 bombardment but was later briefly kidnapped by British soldiers in 1745 and French soldiers in 1747. King Louis XV of France presented Manneken Pis with a gold-embroidered suit in 1747, and the statue has many other costumes for ceremonial occasions.

❷ Rue de l'Etuve leads to the **Grand'Place,** one of Europe's most ornate market squares and a true jewel box, close to the hearts of all the people of the city. At night, you experience the full theatrical effect of the burnished facades of the guild houses and their gilded statuary. From April to September, the square is floodlighted after sundown with changing colored lights. There is a daily flower market in the Grand'Place, and a bird market on Sunday mornings.

The **Hôtel de Ville** (Town Hall), in Brabant Gothic style, is some 300 years older than the guild houses. The left wing was begun in 1402 but was soon found to be too small. Charles the Bold laid the first stone for the extension in 1444, and it was completed in just four years. The change in plans left the slender belfry, designed by Jan van Ruysbroeck, off center. It is topped by a bronze statue of St. Michael crushing a figure of the devil beneath his feet. Over the gateway are statues of the prophets, female figures representing lofty virtues, and effigies of long-gone dukes and duchesses. The Town Hall contains some excellent Brussels and Mechelen tapestries, some of them in the Gothic Hall, where there are frequent recitals and chamber-music concerts. *Grand'Place. Admission: BF75. Open for tours only; English-speaking tours given Tues. at 11:30 and 3:45, Wed. at 3:45.*

The guild houses of the Grand'Place were built soon after the 1695 bombardment in ornate Italo-Flemish Baroque style. Among the buildings on the north side of the square, No. 1–2, **La Maison du Roi d'Espagne,** belonged to the bakers' guild. It is decorated with a relief honoring Charles II of Spain, and is surmounted by a cupola on which the figure of Fame is perched. **La Maison du Sac,** No. 4, commissioned by the guild of joiners and coopers, and No. 6, **La Maison du Cornet,** built for the boatmen, were both designed by Antoon Pastorana, a gifted furniture maker. **La Maison du Renard,** No. 7, was designed for the guild of haberdashers and peddlers. A sculpture of St. Christopher, their patron, stands on top of the gable.

Time Out On the ground floor of No. 1 there's a vast and popular cafe, **Au Roy d'Espagne,** with an open fire and solid wooden furniture.

On the same side as the Town Hall, **La Maison des Brasseurs** (No. 10), the brewers's guild, appropriately houses a Brewery Museum, making it the only guild hall in the world still serving its original purpose. *Grand'Place 10, tel. 02/511–4987. Admission: BF50. Open weekdays 10–noon and 2–5, Apr.–Sept. also Sat. 10–noon.*

Next to it stands No. 9, **La Maison du Cygne,** formerly owned by the guild of butchers, now one of the city's most elegant restaurants. Before going posh, it housed a tavern frequented by Karl Marx, who lived in Brussels for three years before being expelled.

On the side opposite the Hotel de Ville stands the **Maison du Roi,** in which no king ever lived, although legend has it that it was the scene of Emperor Charles V's abdication in 1555 in favor of his son, Philip II. Now it houses the **Musée Communal,** with some fine tapestries, altarpieces, and paintings, notably Pieter Bruegel the Elder's *Marriage Procession.* On the top floor you can see the extensive wardrobe of costumes donated to Manneken Pis. *Grand'Place, tel. 02/*

9 pl. du Beguinage

pl. de Brouckère

bd. Anspach

7 pl. et Th. de la Monnaie

r. Neuve

6

r. du Pont

bd. Emile Jacqmain

r. Neuf

r. St. Pierre

bd. Adolphe Max

r. de

r. du Damier

la Blanchisserie

r. aux Choux

av. Victoria Regina

St. Lazare

bd.

av. du Boulevard

bd. du Jardin Botanique

Jardin Botanique

Botanique

ch. de Haecht

r. Traversière

r. du Méridien

r. de l'Union

porte de Schaerbeek

pl. des Barricades

r. Potagère

r. Berlolsfr.

r. Scailquin

ch. de Louvain

r. de la Charité

r. Persil

r. du Marais

bd. Pacheco

13

r. Grétry

r. des Bouchers

3

pte. de Flandre

4

r. d'Arenberg

r. d'Assaut

r. Mont. aux Herbes Potagères

bd. de Berlaimont

r. de la Banque

r. de Ligne

Koningsstraat

r. de l'Association

r. du Congrès

r. du Nord

bd. du Régent

av. des Arts

pl. Madou

2

i

r. du Marché

aux Herbes

ⓘ

bd. de l'Impératrice

5

r. de laCroix de Fer

r. de la Presse

r. de Louvain

Gare Centrale

r. des Colonies

Cantersteen

pl. de l'Albertine

r. des Sols

r. de la Loi

r. Joseph II

pl. St. Jean

mpereur

r. J. Lebeau

19

Coudenberg

20

r. Royale

21

Parc de Bruxelles

17

18

16

pl. Royale

22

r. Ducale

r. Guimard

bd. du Régent

av. des Arts

r. de la Loi

r. du Commerce

r. de l'Industrie

r. de la Science

4

r. de la Régence

15

r. des Petits Carmes

r. de Namur

r. du Pépin

r. Bréderode

r. de la Pepinière

pl. du Trône

23

r. Belliard

r. Montoyer

aux Laines

porte de Namur

av. Marnix

r. du Luxembourg

r. du Trône

Gare du Quartier Léopold

aterloo

oison d'Or

r. des Chevaliers

r. de Stassart

ch. d'Ixelles

chaussée de Wavre

r. E. Solvay

KEY

— Rail Lines

═ Metro

┄ Tram

TO WATERLOO

r. des Drapiers

r. Keyenveld

25

N

0 — 400 yards

0 — 400 meters

511–2742. Admission: BF80. Open weekdays 10–12:30 and 1:30–4 (Apr.–Sept. 10–12:30 and 1:30–5), weekends 10–1.

The alley next to the Maison du Roi leads out of the Grand'Place to rue du Marché-aux-Herbes and, across the way, the narrow Petite Rue des Bouchers. We're now in the **Quartier de l'Ilôt Sacré**, the liveliest area in Brussels, where restaurants and cafés are cheek by jowl, with tables spilling out on the sidewalk. In the evening it grows very crowded; be careful not to provide temptation for pickpockets. The restaurants make strenuous efforts to pull you in with huge displays of seafood and game. As a general rule, the more extravagant the display, the more dubious the quality (*see* Dining, *below*). Down an even narrower alley off Petite Rue des Bouchers, called Schuddeveld, lies the **Théâtre Toone** (Impasse Schuddeveld, tel. 02/511–7137), a famous old puppet theater where satirical plays are performed in broad Bruxellois dialect. You won't understand a word, but it's fun anyway.

To the right at the top of Petite Rue des Bouchers, past several more restaurants, the **Galeries St-Hubert** (also known as the Galeries Royales) branch off right and left. They were built in 1847 as the world's first covered shopping galleries, using the new engineering techniques that allowed architects to design soaring constructions of glass with iron girders. Neoclassical gods and heroes in their sculpted niches look down on the crowded scene below, and even the buskers play classical music, while from high above, diffused daylight penetrates the gallery from the glassed arches.

At the northern exit of the galleries, to the right on rue d'Arenberg and up the slight incline, is the **Cathédrale St-Michel et Ste-Gudule** (Parvis Ste-Gudule 20, tel. 02/217–3845), begun in 1226, whose twin Gothic towers gleam white after the removal of centuries of grime. Stay to the right side of the street in front of the church before crossing to the side entrance, for there are no marked crossings, and pedestrians are fair game. The restoration of the interior is underway, but the remains of an 11th-century Romanesque church can be glimpsed through glass apertures set into the floor. Among the windows, designed by various artists, those by Bernard van Orley, a 16th-century court painter, are outstanding. The window of the Last Judgment, at the bottom of the nave, is illuminated from within in the evening.

Cross the boulevard into the rue d'Assaut. Making a right on rue Montagne aux Herbes Potagères, turn into rue du Fossé-aux-Loups or proceed straight ahead and turn left through the narrow rue du Persil into the **place des Martyrs**, at long last being restored. This nobly proportioned square, in the cool style favored by the Austrian Habsburgs of the 18th century, contains an underground shrine to the 445 patriots who died in the brief war of independence against the Dutch.

If you return to rue du Fossé-aux-Loups on rue Neuve (a busy pedestrian shopping street) you arrive in place de la Monnaie, where the revolt began. It was here, during a performance of Auber's *La Muette de Portici* in the **Théâtre de la Monnaie** (pl. de la Monnaie, tel. 02/218–1202) on August 25, 1830, that some members of the audience became so inflamed by the duet "Amour sacré de la patrie" that they stormed out and started a riot that led to independence. The opera house is very pleasing, and among Europe's leading opera stages. Concerts and recitals are also given here, as are lunchtime chamber music performances.

So, you're getting away from it all.

Just make sure you can get back.

AT&T Access Numbers
Dial the number of the country you're in to reach AT&T.

*AUSTRIA†††	022-903-011	*GREECE	00-800-1311	NORWAY	800-190-11
*BELGIUM	078-11-0010	*HUNGARY	00◇-800-01111	POLAND†♦²	0◇010-480-0111
BULGARIA	00-1800-0010	*ICELAND	999-001	PORTUGAL†	05017-1-288
CANADA	1-800-575-2222	IRELAND	1-800-550-000	ROMANIA	01-800-4288
CROATIA†♦	99-38-0011	ISRAEL	177-100-2727	*RUSSIA† (MOSCOW)	155-5042
*CYPRUS	080-90010	*ITALY	172-1011	SLOVAKIA	00-420-00101
CZECH REPUBLIC	00-420-00101	KENYA†	0800-10	S. AFRICA	0-800-99-0123
*DENMARK	8001-0010	*LIECHTENSTEIN	155-00-11	SPAIN•	900-99-00-11
*EGYPT¹ (CAIRO)	510-0200	LITHUANIA♦	8◇196	*SWEDEN	020-795-611
*FINLAND	9800-100-10	LUXEMBOURG	0-800-0111	*SWITZERLAND	155-00-11
FRANCE	19◇-0011	F.Y.R. MACEDONIA	99-800-4288	*TURKEY	00-800-12277
*GAMBIA	00111	*MALTA	0800-890-110	UKRAINE†	8◇100-11
GERMANY	0130-0010	*NETHERLANDS	06-022-9111	UK	0500-89-0011

Countries in bold face permit country-to-country calling in addition to calls to the U.S. **World Connect℠** prices consist of **USADirect®** rates plus an additional charge based on the country you are calling. Collect calling available to the U.S. only. *Public phones require deposit of coin or phone card. ◇Await second dial tone. †May not be available from every phone. †††Public phones require local coin payment through the call duration. ♦Not available from public phones. • Calling available to most European countries. ¹Dial "02" first, outside Cairo. ²Dial 010-480-0111 from major Warsaw hotels. ©1994 AT&T.

Here's a travel tip that will make it easy to call back to the States. Dial the access number for the country you're visiting and connect right to AT&T. It's the quick way to get English-speaking AT&T operators and can minimize hotel telephone surcharges.

If all the countries you're visiting aren't listed above, call **1 800 241-5555** for a free wallet card with all AT&T access numbers. Easy international calling from AT&T. **TrueWorld Connections.**

AT&T

American Express offers Travelers Cheques built for two.

Cheques *for Two*^{SM} from American Express are the Travelers Cheques that allow either of you to use them because both of you have signed them. And only one of you needs to be present to purchase them.

Cheques *for Two* are accepted anywhere regular American Express Travelers Cheques are, which is just about everywhere. So stop by your bank, AAA* or any American Express Travel Service Office and ask for Cheques *for Two*.

Cross the modern Centre Monnaie and the broad and busy boulevard Anspach. On the right is the place de Brouckère, which is recovering from a past as a sort of Times Square of Brussels. Straight ahead toward the place Ste-Catherine are the rather forlorn remnants of the **Tour Noire**, which dates from the 12th century and was part of the city's oldest fortifications. Archaeological excavations have started under the tower.

The short rue des Cyprès is one of several streets that converge on the place du Beguinage and the **Eglise de St-Jean Baptiste.** Beguinages are enclosures once inhabited by an order of lay sisters. The one in Brussels exists no more, except for the beautiful Flemish Baroque–style church. The facade is divided into three bays, each with a curlicued scroll gable.

Down the block-long rue du Peuplier is the **quai aux Bois à Bruler,** formerly a quay along the harbor of the River Senne. The other side of the street is called the quai aux Briques. The river, long since gone underground, is represented only by a symbolic pool, but the legacy of the harbor is present in a collection of good fish restaurants. The Bruxellois come here for alfresco dining in summer.

To the left past the **Eglise Ste-Catherine,** which looks centuries old but is in fact barely 150, is the square of the same name, which was the old fish market. There is still generally a stall where you can taste some oysters or mussels and wash them down with a glass of chilled muscadet.

The second left on the square, **rue Antoine Dansaert,** has in recent years become a center for chic boutiques featuring young Belgian designers, home furnishings shops, galleries, and bars.

Time Out **Le Pain Quotidien** (rue Antoine Dansaert 16) is a bakery that produces superior bread, and you can enjoy it, in sandwiches or with salad, seated at a big old refectory table.

Rue du Pont de la Carpe affords a brief detour to the **place St-Géry,** the oldest part of Brussels. Some of its old brick houses have been restored, and a short stretch of the river has been uncovered.

Rue Jules Van Praet leads to boulevard Anspach opposite the rather magnificent **Bourse** (Palais de la Bourse, tel. 02/512–5110), built in 1871 on a scale that Brussels's modest stock-exchange trading has never quite justified.

Tucked away behind the Bourse and hemmed in by tiny houses is the small **Eglise de St-Nicolas** (Bourse—Grand'Place, tel. 02/511–8178). Once the parish church of Brussels's merchants, it is also the traditional church of aspiring dancers. Here Mass is said in English on Sundays at 10. One short block on rue au Beurre leads back to the Maison du Roi and the Grand'Place.

Tour 2: The Upper Town and the Marolles

There are few more pleasant places in Brussels than the **Grand Sablon,** once, as the name implies, nothing more than a sandy hill. Today it is an elegant square, surrounded by numerous restaurants, cafés, and exclusive antiques shops, some in intriguing alleys and arcades, as well as Wittamer, a pastry shop of such renown that its products are flown to Belgian embassies around the world. On Saturdays and Sunday mornings there's a lively antiques market at the upper end of the square.

At the eastern end stands the **Eglise Notre-Dame du Sablon,** a Flamboyant-Gothic church founded in 1304 by the guild of crossbowmen and rebuilt in the 15th century. Its chief glory is the stained-glass windows. After nightfall they are illuminated from within, suffusing the Grand Sablon with kindly light.

⑮ Across rue de la Régence lies the **place du Petit-Sablon.** The square is surrounded by columns topped by small bronze statues representing the city's 48 guilds. Inside the garden are statues of the Flemish patriots, Counts Egmont and Hoorn, on their way to the scaffold in 1568. On the square, the **Musée Instrumental** (Musical Instruments Museum), with more than 4,000 instruments, is one of the largest museums of its kind in the world. The saxophone family is well represented here, as befits the country of its inventor, Adolphe Sax. The collection is scheduled to be transferred to a house on the place Royale that is now undergoing restoration. *Pl. du Petit Sablon 17. Admission free. Open Tues., Thurs., Sat. 2:30–4:30, Wed. 4–6, Sun. 10:30–12:30.*

Immediately beyond the square is the **Palais d'Egmont,** where Queen Christina of Sweden, France's Louis XV, and Voltaire resided at various times. The garden is open to the public and can be entered from a gate on rue du Grand Cerf.

To the left from Petit Sablon at rue de la Régence 30 is the Conservatoire Royale (the Royal Conservatory, tel. 02/511–0427), site of numerous concerts, and Synagogue de Bruxelles (No. 32, tel. 02/512–4334), the city's main synagogue. Down rue de la Régence to **⑯** the right lies the **Musée d'Art Ancien** (Museum of Classical Art), which holds paintings by Flemish primitives of the 15th century such as Memling, Petrus Christus, and Gerard David. The collection of works by Pieter Bruegel the Elder is outstanding; it includes *The Fall of Icarus*, in which the figure of the mythological hero disappearing in the sea is but one detail while people continue going about their business. An excellent Rubens collection is on the floor above. The 19th-century collection on the ground floor includes the *Assassination of Marat* by Jacques-Louis David, who like many other French artists and writers spent years of exile in Belgium. *Rue de la Régence 3. Admission free. Open Tues.–Sun. 10–noon and 1–5.*

⑰ The new **Musée d'Art Moderne** can be reached by an underground passage, or you can enter it from the house on place Royale where Alexandre Dumas (père) once lived and wrote. This original subterranean gallery circles downward eight floors, rather like the Guggenheim Museum in reverse. Here you can see how the art movements of the past hundred years have been interpreted in works by Belgian painters. The handful of Belgians who have acquired international prominence—the expressionist James Ensor and the surrealists Paul Delvaux and René Magritte—are well represented. *Pl. Royale 1. Admission free. Open Tues.–Sun. 10–noon and 1–5.*

⑱ The white, elegantly proportioned **place Royale** is the centerpiece of the Upper Town as conceived in Louis XVI style in the 18th century. Its buildings are being restored one by one, leaving the facades intact. From the center you have a splendid view of the Lower Town and its spires. In the other direction is the attractive church of St-Jacques-sur-Coudenberg, and down the rue Montagne de la Cour **⑲** and the flight of steps on the left you reach the neoclassical **Ancien Cour** on the right, all that remains of the palace built for Charles of Lorraine in 1760.

Back on rue Montagne de la Cour, the blackened walls of the **Hotel Ravenstein** loom across the street. Built in the 15th century, it is the only aristocratic house from that period to have survived. A bit far-
⑳ ther on is the main entrance of the **Palais des Beaux-Arts,** designed in the 1920s in Art Deco style by Victor Horta, better known for the Art Nouveau architecture of his earlier years. Here stood the pension where the Brontë sisters, Charlotte and Emily, stayed in 1842.

From rue Baron Horta a flight of curving steps leads up to **rue Royale.** The white and quietly elegant buildings lining this street contain the headquarters of the Société Générale, which formerly had enormous holdings in Africa and remains powerful in Belgian
㉑ banking and industry. In front of you is the **Parc de Bruxelles,** once a wild and woodsy hunting ground but tamed into rigid symmetry in the late 18th century.

㉒ The huge **Palais Royal** occupies the entire south side of the park. It was built by Leopold II at the beginning of this century on a scale corresponding to his own megalomaniacal ambitions. The present monarch, King Albert, lives at the Laeken Palace on the outskirts of Brussels but comes here for state occasions. *Pl. des Palais. Admission free. Open July 22–early Sept., Tues.–Sun. 10–4.*

㉓ Up rue Ducale in the **place du Trône** stands Leopold II himself in the form of an equestrian statue. Here, too, is the Luxembourg Metro station; two stops on the subway take you to place Louise. Here, boulevard du Régent forms part of *la ceinture* (the belt) that surrounds the heart of the city. It changes names every few blocks and, to make the confusion complete, the two sides of the street also have different names. To the south past the intersection Porte de Namur lies the real shopping section. On the **boulevard de Waterloo** side you'll encounter the same luxury brand names as on Rodeo Drive or Fifth Avenue. The other side is appropriately named the **avenue de la Toison d'Or** (Golden Fleece Avenue). Two shopping arcades branch off from here, the warrenlike Galerie de la Toison d'Or and
㉔ the more prestigious **Galerie Louise** with its recent upmarket addition, Espace Louise. Fashion boutiques predominate in the arcades, interspersed with cafés and perfumeries. At the other end Galerie
㉕ Louise has its exit on **place Stephanie.** To the right is **avenue Louise,** the city's top shopping street, built in the mid-19th century to link the city with the Bois de la Cambre to the south.

Time Out | **Nemrod** (blvd. de Waterloo 61, near place Louise) is a popular place for a shopping break or a drink after a movie.

㉖ Past place Louise to the northwest stands the gigantic **Palais de Justice,** another of Leopold II's brainchildren, on the site of the old Gallows Hill. The terrace in front of it offers great views of the Lower Town and, to the northwest, another huge and eccentric building, the Basilique, begun in 1905 but not completed until 1970. On its right, straight north, you can see the Atomium, a 122-meter (400-foot) -high structure representing the nine atoms of an iron crystal, designed for the World's Fair in 1958.

The contrast of the grand scale of the works of Leopold II with the past is immediately apparent as you descend the ramps and proceed down rue de l'Épée into **Les Marolles,** an area once deemed dangerous and still with a slightly raffish reputation. If the Grand'Place has an ambience of old money, Les Marolles has one of old poverty. Settled by weavers in the Middle Ages, it has survived many occupations and welcomed many waves of immigrants. Here you might still hear the Brussels dialect, mixing Flemish with French and bits of Spanish.

On your right at rue Haute is the **Maison de Bruegel** (No. 132), a step-gabled building where the painter probably lived. To the left on

㉗ rue Haute and right on rue des Renards is **place du Jeu de Balle,** scene of a huge daily flea market. Early morning is the best time for spotting value. Leave your handbag at the hotel. Rue Blaes, lined with curio shops, parallels rue Haute.

㉘ At the end of rue Blaes stands the unusual **Eglise Notre-Dame de la Chapelle,** where Pieter Bruegel the Elder was married in 1563 and, just six years later, buried. The transept is Romanesque, while the nave and aisles are in Brabant Gothic style, and the church tower is Baroque. Across the place de la Chapelle is rue de Rollebeek, lined with a multitude of restaurants; it leads back to the place du Grand-Sablon.

Excursion to Waterloo

The decisive Battle of Waterloo, where Napoléon was finally stopped by the British and Prussian armies under Wellington and Blücher, was fought on June 18, 1815. Once every five years (next in 1995) the Battle of Waterloo is reenacted by thousands of volunteers in period uniforms. The town of **Waterloo** is 19 kilometers (12 miles) south of Brussels on N5. The **Waterloo Tourist Office** (Chaussée de Bruxelles 149, tel. 02/354–9910) is in the center of town. Next door is the well-laid-out **Wellington Museum,** in the building where Wellington had his headquarters. It presents maps and models of the battle along with military memorabilia. *Chaussée de Bruxelles 147, tel. 02/ 345–7806. Admission: BF60. Open Apr.-mid Nov., daily 9:30–6:30; mid-Nov.–Mar., daily 10:30–5.*

South of the city is the actual **battlefield,** where 40,000 men were killed. The **Visitors' Center** offers an introductory audiovisual presentation of the progress of the battle, followed by a mood-setting film of the battle as seen through the eyes of children. You can buy souvenirs here, too—from tin soldiers to T-shirts—as well as tokens for other attractions. *Rte. du Lion 252-254, tel. 02/385–1912. Admission (including the Butte du Lion and Panorama, see below): BF300, children BF190. Open Apr.–Oct., daily 9:30–6:30; Nov.–Mar., daily 10:30–4.*

Expert guides, **Les Guides 1815** (rte. du Lion 250, tel. 02/385–0625), can be hired to take you around the battlefield (cost: BF1,400 for a 1-hr tour and BF2,200 for a 3-hour visit; group visits in English, BF100 per person, weekends 4 PM July–Aug.).

The victorious combatants were quick to erect battle monuments. The most famous, the **Butte du Lion,** a pyramid 226 steps high and crowned by a 28-ton lion, was erected by the Dutch on a spot of no military significance, but it provides a great view of the battlefield. The adjacent **Battle Panorama Museum** contains a vast, circular painting of the battle, executed with amazing perspective and realism. It was first unveiled in 1912 and has recently been restored.

Napoléon's headquarters were at what is now the small **Musée du Caillou** in **Genappe,** south of the battlefield. It contains the room where he spent the night before the battle and some personal effects. *Chaussée de Bruxelles 66, tel. 02/384–2424. Admission: BF60. Open Apr.–Sept., Tues.–Sun. 10:30–6:30; Nov.–Mar., Tues.–Sun. 1:30–5.*

Dining **L'Auberge d'Ohain.** This country inn northeast of Waterloo has an elegant dining room decorated in shades of peach and champagne and a kitchen capable of great things: carpaccio of scallops with basil and olive oil, fillet of sole with asparagus in a parsley coulis, and lightly curried lobster fricassee. The four-course *menu découverte* (tasting menu) is an excellent value. *Chaussée de Louvain 709, tel. 02/653–6497. Reservations advised. Jacket and tie advised. AE, DC, MC, V. $$*

L'Amusoir. Popular with resident Americans, this steak house in an old wooden building in the center of town serves excellent filet mignon, prepared with a variety of sauces. *Chaussée de Bruxelles 121, tel. 02/353–0336. Reservations advised. Dress: casual. AE. $*

Dining and **Le 1815.** This new small hotel is actually on the battlefield. Each **Lodging** room is named for one of the participating generals, and decorated with his portrait. The style is art deco, but with details evocative of the period of the battle. The restaurant is much better than those clustered at the foot of the Butte du Lion. *Rte. du Lion 367, tel. 02/ 387–0060, fax 02/387–1292. 14 rooms with bath. Facilities: restaurant, bar, garden, minigolf. AE, DC, MC, V. $$*

What to See and Do with Children

There are few kids who don't fall in love with the **Musée des Enfants** (Children's Museum) even though its purpose is educational for 2- to 12-year-olds: learning to handle both objects and emotions. Kids get to plunge their arms into sticky goo, dress up in eccentric costumes, crawl through tunnels, or take photographs with an oversize camera. *Rue du Bourgmestre 15, tel. 02/640–0107. Admission: BF150. Open Sept.–July, Wed. and weekends 2:30–5.*

Under the high glass roof of the south hall in the Parc du Cinquantenaire, you'll find **Autoworld,** one of the handsomest collections of vintage cars—over 450 of them—in the world. *Palais Mondial/Cinquantenaire, tel. 02/736–4165. Admission: BF150. Open daily 10–5, Apr.–Sept. until 6.*

Mini-Europe consists of a collection of 1:25 scale models of 300 famous European buildings and high-tech achievements in a 5-acre park near the Atomium. *Blvd. du Centenaire 20, tel. 02/478–0550. Admission: adults BF350, children BF290, under 6 free. Open Apr.–Dec. weekdays 9–6 (July–Aug. until 8), weekends 9–9.*

The adjoining **Oceade** offers water slides, a wave pool, and other watery attractions. *Tel. 02/478–4320. Admission: adults BF389, children BF240. Open Tues.–Thurs. 2–10, Fri. 2–midnight, Sat. 11 AM–midnight, Sun. 10–8.*

Out of town, **Walibi** draws Brussels kids and teenagers with its advanced rides and shows, while attractions at the adjoining **Aqualibi** include a tropical river adventure. *Exit 6 (N238) at Wavre from E411, tel. 010/414446. Walibi admission: BF530. Open Apr.–Sept., daily 10–6. Aqualibi admission: BF360. Open Apr.–Sept., Tues.– Sun. 10–10; Oct.–March, Tues.–Sun. 2–10.*

From mid-July until the end of August, all of Belgium's carnival barkers and showmen and their carousels, ghost trains, Ferris wheels, shooting galleries, rides, swings, and roundabouts congregate along the boulevard du Midi for the giant and hugely popular **Foire du Midi.**

Off the Beaten Track

West of the city center, in Anderlecht, the **Maison d'Erasme/ Erasmushuis** (House of Erasmus) has been restored to its condition in 1521. In addition to Erasmus's study, the house contains portraits of Erasmus by Hans Holbein and first editions of *In Praise of Folly* and other books by Erasmus. *Rue du Chapitre 31, tel. 02/521–1383. Metro to St–Guidon; Tram 103; Buses 47 and 49. Admission: BF20. Open Wed–Thurs., Sat.–Mon. 10–12 and 2–5.*

In the boroughs just south of the center, St-Gilles and Ixelles, are Brussels's best examples of the pre–World War I Art Nouveau architecture of Victor Horta and his colleagues and followers, architects who transformed the face of Brussels in little more than 10 years, turning entire areas into unified Art Nouveau neighborhoods. Although many of their houses were demolished by developers before their true value was recognized, a good number remain. The **Horta Museum,** the house where the architect lived and worked until 1919, is the best place to see his joyful interiors and furniture. Horta's genius lay in his ability to create a sense of opulence and spaciousness where little space existed. Lamps hang from the ceilings like tendrils, and mirrored skylights evoke giant butterflies with multicolored wings of glass and steel. *Rue Américaine 25, tel. 02/ 537–1692. Trams 81 and 92; Buses 81 and 92. Admission: BF100. Open Tues.–Sun. 2–5:30.*

The **David and Alice Van Buuren Museum,** in the borough of Uccle, preserves a perfect Art Deco interior. The made-to-order carpets and furnishings are of an exceptional standard, and the art treasures include paintings by the Van Buurens' contemporaries as well as Old Masters, including one of the three versions of Bruegel's *The Fall of Icarus. Av. Leo Errera 41, tel. 02/343–4851 or 02/733–7152. Trams 23 and 90. Admission: BF100. Open Mon. 2–4 and by appointment (groups only).*

The late Hergé, creator of Tintin, elevated the comic strip to an art form. The new **Centre Belge de la Bande Dessinée** (Belgian Comic Strip Center) contains over 400 original plates by Hergé and his many successors and 25,000 cartoon works. *Rue des Sables 20, tel. 02/219–1980. Metro Rogier/Botanique: Trams 90, 92, and 93; Bus 38. Admission: BF120. Open Tues.–Sun. 10–6.*

Toward the southern end of avenue Louise is the **Bois de la Cambre,** a natural park that is a favorite among joggers and families with children. The park merges on the south into the beech woods of the 11,000-acre **Forêt de Soignes,** extending as far south as Genval with its lake and restaurants.

From Square Montgomery, Tram 44 passes the rolling Parc de Woluwe and through the forest all the way to **Tervuren.** Nearby is the **Musée Royal d'Afrique Centrale,** the final vestige of Belgium's colonial adventure. It contains a fine collection of masks, sculpture, and memorabilia of the journeys of the explorers of Africa. *Leuvensesteenweg 13, tel. 02/767–5401. Admission: BF50. Open mid-Mar.–mid-Oct., Tues.–Sun. 9–5:30; mid-Oct.–mid-Mar., Tues.–Sun. 10–4:30.*

North of the center of Brussels stands the **Atomium,** a model of a molecule enlarged 165 billion times, constructed for the 1958 World's Fair. There's an express elevator to the highest point, where you have a panoramic view of Brussels. *Blvd. du Centenaire, tel. 02/477–0977. Metro Heysel. Admission: BF150. Open mid-Mar.–mid-Oct., daily 9:45–6:30 mid-Oct.–mid-Mar., daily 9:30–5.*

Shopping

The Belgians started producing high-quality luxury goods in the Middle Ages, and this is what they are skilled at. This is not a country where you pick up amazing bargains. Value added tax (TVA) further inflates prices, but visitors from outside the European Union can obtain refunds.

Shopping Districts The chic shopping area comprises the upper end of **avenue Louise** plus the avenue branching off at a right angle from it at place Louise, **avenue de la Toison d'Or** and **boulevard de Waterloo** (the other side of the street), plus **Galerie Louise**, which links the two avenues and, a couple of blocks away, another arcade, the **Galerie de la Toison d'Or**. The **Place du Grand-Sablon** is equally expensive but more attractive. Here and in the adjoining streets and alleys you will find exclusive antiques dealers and smart art galleries. The **Galeries St-Hubert** is a rather stately shopping arcade lined with high-class shops selling men's and women's clothing, books, and interior design products. The **City 2** mall on place Rogier and the pedestrian **rue Neuve** are fun and inexpensive shopping areas (but not recommended for women alone after dark). **Rue Antoine Dansaert** and **place du Nouveau Marché aux Grains,** near the Bourse, form the newest chic shopping area, specializing in clothes by young designers, interior design, and art.

Department Stores The best department stores in town are **Inno** (rue Neuve 111, tel. 02/211–2111; Chaussée d'Ixelles 41, tel. 02/512–7800; and Chaussée de Waterloo 699, tel. 02/345–3890) and **Sarmalux** (rue Neuve 15, tel. 02/212–8714; and av. Louise 12, tel. 02/513–8494).

Street Markets Bruxellois with an eye for fresh farm produce and low prices do most of their food shopping at the animated open-air markets in almost every borough. Among the best are those in **Boitsfort** in front of the Maison Communal (Sun. morning), on **place du Chatelain** (Wed. afternoons), and on **place Ste-Catherine** (all day Mon.–Sat.). In addition to fruits, vegetables, meat, and fish, most markets include traders with specialized products, such as wide selections of cheese and wild mushrooms. The most exotic market is the **Marché du Midi** (Sun. morning), which transforms the area next to the railway station into a vast bazaar as the city's large North African community gathers to buy and sell foods, spices, and plants.

In the Grand'Place there's a **Flower Market** (every day but Mon.) and a **Bird Market** (Sun. morning). You need to get to the flea market, **Vieux Marché** (pl. du Jeu de Balle; open daily 7–2) early. The **Antiques and Book Market** (pl. du Grand-Sablon; Sat. 9–6 and Sun. 9–2) is considerably more upscale and is frequented by established dealers. The TIB (tel. 02/513–8940) has the details on other specialized markets.

Specialty Stores

Antiques **Costermans** (pl. du Grand-Sablon 5, tel. 02/512–2133) and **Jean Tollemans** (rue de la Régence 21, tel. 02/511–3405) are among the leading dealers in the Sablon area. **Afrique Congo** (av. Louise 138, tel. 02/640–6948) specializes in African art.

Books **Tropismes** (Galerie des Princes 11, tel. 02/512–8852) carries more than 40,000 titles and will help you find out-of-print books. **Libris** (Espace Louise, tel. 02/511–6400) is very well stocked with current French-language titles. The **Galerie Bortier** is devoted entirely to rare and secondhand books. Designed by the architect responsible for the Galeries St. Hubert, this small, attractive arcade runs from rue de la Madeleine to rue St. Jean. Shops specializing in comic strip albums include those at Chausséede Wavre Nos. 167, 179, and 198, and the **Tintin Shop** (rue de la Colline 13).

Chocolates **Godiva** (Grand'Place 22 and other locations) is the best known. **Neuhaus** (Galerie de la Reine 25–27 and other locations) is the runner-up and is preferred by many. **Leonidas** (Chaussée d'Ixelles 5 and other locations) is the budget alternative, still high quality. The best handmade pralines, which are the crème de la crème of Belgian chocolates, are made and sold at **Nihoul** (av. Louise 298–302, tel. 02/648–3796), **Mary** (rue Royale 73, tel. 02/217–4500), and **Wittamer** (pl. du Grand Sablon 12, tel. 02/512–3742).

Crystal **Art et Sélection** (rue du Marché-aux-Herbes 83, tel. 02/511–8448) and **Buss** (across the street at No. 86, tel. 02/511–6652) both carry Val St-Lambert handblown crystal tableware.

Home **Ligne** (galerie de la Reine 12–16, tel. 02/511–6030), **Projection**
Furnishings (blvd. Anspach 85, tel. 02/511–5452), and **Théorèmes** (pl. du Nouveau Marché-aux-Grains 22–23, tel. 02/512–5258) carry avant-garde furniture.

Lace **Manufacture Belge de Dentelle** (Galerie de la Reine 6–8, tel. 02/511–4477) and **Maison F. Rubbrecht** (Grand'Place 23, tel. 02/512–0218) sell local handmade lace. At the many souvenir shops in the area it is likely to come from the Far East. An introductory visit to the **Musée du Costume et de la Dentelle** (rue de la Violette 6, tel. 02/512–7709; admission: BF80; open weekdays 10–12:30 and 1:30–5, weekends 2–4:30) is a good idea.

Leather Goods **Delvaux** (av. de la Galerie 31, tel. 02/512–7198 and blvd. de Waterloo 27, tel. 02/513–0502) makes outstanding, classic, and long-lasting handbags, wallets, belts, and attaché cases. Be prepared to part with a hefty sum.

Men's Clothing **Dean** (av. Louise 50A, tel. 02/511–2718), **Deman** (blvd. de Waterloo 45, tel. 02/512–2367), and **De Vlaminck** (blvd. de Waterloo 32, tel. 02/512–4203) carry classic Italian and English ready-to-wear and accessories. **Stijl Men** (rue Antoine Dansaert 26, tel. 02/512–0313) caters to younger tastes.

Women's **Bouvy** (av. de la Toison d'Or 52, tel. 02/513–0748) carries a good se-
Clothing lection of upscale ready-to-wear. **Olivier Strelli** (av. Louise 72, tel. 02/511–2134) is the best-known Belgian fashion designer. Most French and Italian big-name designers are represented by boutiques in the avenue Louise and boulevard de Waterloo district.

Sports and Fitness

Golf The top clubs in the area are **Royal Golf Club de Belgique** (Château de Ravenstein, Tervuren, tel. 02/767–5801), **Royal Waterloo Golf Club** (Vieux Chemin de Wavre 50, Ohain, tel. 02/633–1850), and **Keerbergen Golf Club** (Vlieghavenlaan 50, Keerbergen, tel. 015/234961). For more information, call the Royal Belgian Golf Federation (tel. 02/672–2389).

Health and Several hotels have well-equipped fitness centers open to the public.
Fitness The best are at the **Europa Brussels** (rue de la Loi 107, tel. 02/230–1333), **Holiday Inn** (Holidaystraat 7, Diegem, tel. 02/720–5865), **SAS Royal** (rue du Fosse-aux-Loups 47, tel. 02/219–2828), and **Sheraton** (pl. Rogier 3, tel. 02/224–3111). Fees range from BF750 to BF1,000 a session. Prices are considerably lower at independent health clubs such as **European Athletic City** (av. Winston Churchill 25A, tel. 02/345–3077) and **California Club** (Chaussée d'Ixelles 298–300, tel. 02/640–9344).

Horseback Riding Stables/schools near the Forêt de Soignes include **Centre Equestre de la Cambre** (Chaussée de Waterloo 872, tel. 02/375–3408), **L'Etrier** (Champ du Vert Chasseur 19, tel. 02/374–2860), and **Le Relais Equestre de Groenendael** (Groenendalsesteenweg 139, Hoeilaart, tel. 02/657–2177). For more information, call the Fédération Royale Belge des Sports Equestres (Royal Belgian Riding Federation) (tel. 02/374–4734).

Jogging For in-town jogging, use the **Parc de Bruxelles** (rue de la Loi to the Palace); for more extensive workouts, head for the **Bois de la Cambre** (southern end of av. Louise).

Swimming Hotel swimming pools are few and far between. Among covered public pools, the best are **Calypso** (av. Wiener 60, tel. 02/673–7619), **Longchamp** (sq. de Fré 1, tel. 02/374–9005), and **Poseidon** (av. des Vaillants 4, tel. 02/762–1633).

Tennis Popular clubs include the **Racing Club** (av. des Chênes 125, tel. 02/374–4181), **Royal Leopold** (av. Dupuich 42, tel. 02/344–3666), and **Wimbledon** (Chaussée de Waterloo 220, Rhode-St-Genèse, tel. 358–3523). For more information contact the Fédération Royale Belge de Tennis (Royal Belgian Tennis Federation, tel. 02/217–2365).

Spectator Sports

Horse Racing Going to the races comes second in popularity only to soccer, and there are three major racecourses: **Boitsfort** (Chaussée de la Hulpe 51, tel. 02/660–2839), which has an all-weather flat track; **Groenendael** (Sint-Jansberglaan 4, Hoeilaart, tel. 02/673–6792), for steeplechasing; and **Sterrebeek** (Du Roy de Blicquylaan 43, Sterrebeek, tel. 02/767–5475), for trotting and flat racing. For information, contact the **Jockey Club de Belgique** (tel. 02/672–7248).

Soccer Soccer is the most popular spectator sport, and the leading club, **Anderlecht,** has many fiercely loyal fans. Their home pitch is Parc Astrid (av. Theo Verbeeck 2, tel. 02/522–1539). Major international games are played at Heysel Stadium (av. du Marathon 135, tel. 02/479–3654). For information and tickets, contact the **Maison du Football** (av. Houba de Strooper 145, tel. 02/477–1211), which is open weekdays, 9–4:15.

Dining

When the history of the European Commission is written, the real reason for the choice of Brussels as capital of Europe will be revealed: the excellence of its restaurants. There are more than 1,600 of them, and 25 are internationally acclaimed. They are not cheap; a meal with wine in a medium-class restaurant with some gastronomic distinction is likely to cost about BF2,000 per person. In this country, cooking has the status of a fine art. The Belgians take the pleasures of the table seriously and are happy to save up to give themselves, their families, and friends a treat. Formal wear is de rigueur only in very expensive ($$$$) restaurants.

You can reduce the check almost by half by choosing a set menu. Menus and prices are always posted outside restaurants. You should never feel that you're under an obligation to eat a three-course meal; many people order just a salad and a main course.

If you don't want two full restaurant meals a day, there are plenty of snack bars for a light midday meal, and most cafés serve sandwiches and light hot meals both noon and night. Vegetarian restaurants are another inexpensive alternative. The city is also richly endowed with good Oriental restaurants.

The TIB booklet "Gourmet Restaurants," which contains food journalists' evaluations of some 250 restaurants, is available for BF80 at the Tourist Office in Grand'Place. Listings include the cost of set menus and of *plats du jour* (daily specials).

Ratings Prices are per person and include a first course, main course, and dessert, but no beverages. The check always includes 6% value added tax (TVA) and 16% service charge. There is no need for any additional tipping. Highly recommended restaurants are indicated by a star ★.

Category	Cost
$$$$	over BF3,500
$$$	BF2,500–BF3,500
$$	BF1,500–BF2,500
$	under BF1,500

$$$$ **Comme Chez Soi.** Pierre Wynants, the third-generation owner/chef,
★ has redecorated the tiny restaurant in Art Nouveau style. Every detail at this temple of gastronomy is authentic, from the stained-glass panels to the stylish menus. The kitchen is larger than the dining room (there is one much-sought-after table in the kitchen), and the wine cellar bigger than the kitchen. Wynants cooked with only minimal amounts of butter and cream before nouvelle cuisine was heard of, and among his creations are *emincé* (slices) of crayfish with green asparagus and basil in a vinaigrette with ground nuts, and sautéed duck's liver with blackberry vinaigrette and angelica leaves. Tables for two are tiny and cramped. Dinner reservations need to be made well in advance. *Pl. Rouppe 23, tel. 02/512–2921, fax 02/511–8052. Reservations required. Jacket and tie required. AE, DC, MC, V. Closed Sun.–Mon., July, and Christmas week.*

$$$$ **Les Délices de la Mer.** When you make reservations, check that Michel Beyls is still commanding the brigade—this great chef gets the traveling bug more often than most. This villa in Uccle has been splendidly transformed into a restaurant, with plenty of space between tables. Seafood has pride of place on the menu, but there's also lamb, poultry, and game. Try the quickly sautéed sea scallops in a light curry sauce, or the turbot baked in a salt crust. Beyls can turn a poached egg on a bed of chopped wild mushrooms into a memorable experience, and the fixed-price menu is great value for money. *1020 Chaussé de Waterloo, tel. 02/375–5467. Reservations required. Jacket and tie required. AE, DC, MC, V. Closed Sat. lunch.*

$$$$ **La Maison du Cygne.** Dining at the Cygne is a sensuous experience. The setting, in one of the old guild houses on the Grand'Place, is incomparable. The paneled dining room upstairs is hung with old masters, while the ground floor is less formal. Tailcoated waiters glide rather than rush to attend your every wish. The cuisine is classic French: saddle of lamb, braised turbot, duckling with onions. *Rue Charles Buls 2, tel. 02/511–8244. Reservations advised. Jacket and tie required. AE, DC, MC, V. Closed Sat. lunch, Sun., Aug., Christmas week.*

$$$$ **La Truffe Noire.** Luigi Ciciriello's "Black Truffle" attracts a so-
★ phisticated clientele with its discreet modern design, well-spaced tables, and a cuisine that draws on classic Italian and modern French cooking. Carpaccio is prepared at the table and served with

long strips of truffle and Parmesan. Entrées include ravioli filled with minced truffles and wild mushrooms, John Dory stuffed with truffles and leeks, and leg of Pauillac lamb in pie crust. *Blvd. de la Cambre 12, tel. 02/640–4422. Reservations required. Jacket and tie required. AE, DC, MC, V. Closed Sat. lunch, Sun., Easter week, second half of Aug., Christmas week.*

$$$$ **Villa Lorraine.** Generations of American business travelers have been introduced to the three-hour Belgian lunch at the opulent Villa, on the edge of the Bois de la Cambre. The green terrace room is light and airy, and there's alfresco eating under the spreading chestnut tree. You can dine supremely on such standbys as red mullet in artichoke vinaigrette, crayfish cooked in chicken stock with white wine and a dash of Armagnac, and duckling with peaches and green pepper. *Av. du Vivier-d'Oie 75, tel. 02/374–3163. Reservations advised. Jacket and tie required. AE, DC, MC, V. Closed Sun. and July.*

$$$ **Les Brigittines.** Facing the church where Bruegel is buried, a couple
★ of blocks west of the Grand Sablon, this restaurant has a Belle Epoque interior that is remarkably attractive, with paintings and floral displays; one room is dominated by a splendid old bar, the other by an enormous open fireplace. Try the escalope of goose liver with caramelized apple, sea scallops with bacon and braised chicory, or grilled John Dory with lobster béarnaise. Tables are well spaced. *Pl. de la Chapelle 5, tel. 02/512–6891. Reservations advised. Jacket and tie advised. AE, DC, MC, V. Closed Sat. lunch, Sun., and Aug.*

$$$ **Les Capucines.** This pleasant restaurant stands out amid the mediocrity of most rue Jourdan eateries. The dining room is invitingly green, with huge flower arrangements. Chef Pierre Burtonboy prepares dishes such as grilled fillet of sea bream on a bed of shredded leek dressed with nut oil; lamb interleaved with goose liver, rolled and encased in pastry, with rosemary and thinly sliced potatoes; bitter chocolate mousse with *crème anglaise;* and iced peach soup with mint. *Rue Jourdan 22, tel. 02/538–6924. Reservations advised. Dress: casual but neat. AE, DC, MC, V. Closed Sun., Mon. dinner, 2 weeks in Sept.*

$$$ **Castello Banfi.** On the Grand Sablon in beige-and-brown
★ postmodern surroundings, you can enjoy classic dishes with little added refinements such as toasted pine kernels with the pesto. There's excellent carpaccio with Parmesan and celery, red mullet with ratatouille, and unbelievable mascarpone. The quality of the ingredients (sublime olive oil, milk-fed veal imported from France) is very high. The wine list is strong on fine Chianti aged in wood. *Rue Bodenbroek 12, tel. 02/512–8794. Reservations advised. Jacket and tie required. AE, DC, MC, V. Closed Sun. dinner, Mon., and second half of Aug.*

$$$ **L'Ecailler du Palais Royal.** This fish restaurant off the Grand Sablon (and at the upper end of the $$$ category) has the feel of a comfortable club, and many of the clients seem to have known each other and the staff for years. It's a favorite spot among top Belgian businessmen. Risotto of *langoustines* (spiny lobsters) au Champagne, back of salmon in a parsley crust, and suprême of sea bass with French mustard are among the offerings. *Rue Bodenbroek 18, tel. 02/512–8751. Reservations required. Jacket and tie required. AE, DC, MC, V. Closed Mon., Easter week, Aug.*

$$$ **Michel Meyers.** Only seafood is served in this tiny restaurant just off the Fish Market, which has been enlarged to serve all of 18 diners. The eponymous owner/chef is alone in the kitchen and goes to the nearby market twice daily for the freshest products of the sea. Don't hesitate to take the menu he proposes. It might consist of smoked salmon pâté, lobster with five spices, medallion of monkfish with

Central Brussels Dining and Lodging

Dining

Adrienne, **39**
Au Vieux Saint Martin, **29**
Aux Armes de Bruxelles, **13**
Boccaccio, **21**
Brasserie Georges, **51**
Café Camille, **48**
Castello Banfi, **30**
Chez Jean, **19**
Chez Leon, **16**
Comme Chez Soi, **26**

Falstaff, **15**
Gallery, **34**
In 't Spinnekopke, **5**
La Fine Fleur, **44**
La Maison du Cygne, **18**
La Manufacture, **4**
La Porte des Indes, **47**
La Quincaillerie, **46**
La Roue d'Or, **23**
La Truffe Noire, **50**

L'Armagnac, **49**
L'Ecailler du Palais Royal, **31**
Le Faste Fou, **35**
Les Brigittines, **27**
Les Capucines, **38**
Les Délices de la Mer, **53**
Les Petits Oignons, **28**
Michel Meyers, **6**
Ogenblik, **9**
Villa Lorraine, **52**
Vincent, **8**

Lodging

Albert Premier, **1**
Amigo, **17**
Beau-Site, **43**
Cadettt, **45**
Château du Lac, **54**
Clubhouse, **42**
Le Dixseptième, **22**
Conrad, **40**
Gerfaut, **12**
Hilton, **32**

Metropolitan Brussels Dining and Lodging

Manos Stephanie, **41**
Matignon, **14**
Metropole, **7**
Montgomery, **25**
Mozart, **20**
Novotel, **11**
Orion, **2**
Royal Windsor
Hotel, **12**
SAS Royal Hotel, **10**
Sofitel, **36**

Stanhope, **33**
Sun, **37**
Welcome La Truite
d'Argent, **3**

fresh garlic, and a dessert prepared by Madame la Patronne. *Pl. du Samedi 18, tel. 02/219–2616. Reservations advised. Dress: casual. AE, V. Closed Sun. and mid-July–mid Aug.*

$$$ Ogenblik. This small, split-level restaurant in a side gallery off the Galeries St-Hubert has all the appurtenances of an old-time bistro: green-shaded lamps over marble-topped tables, sawdust on the floor, and laid-back waiters. There's nothing casual about the cuisine, however: boned chicken with sweetbreads and goose liver, *mille-feuille* (thin layers of puff pastry separated by filling) of lobster and salmon, saddle of lamb with spring vegetables. The selection of Beaujolais is particularly good. The restaurant is open till midnight. *Galerie des Princes 1, tel. 02/511–6151. No reservations after 8 PM. Dress: casual. AE, DC, MC, V. Closed Sun.*

$$$ La Porte des Indes. The last days of the Raj are re-created in the city's foremost Indian restaurant—the creation of Karl Steppe, a Belgian antiques dealer turned restaurateur. The gracious staff wear traditional Indian attire. The plant-filled lobby, wood carvings, and soothing blue-and-white decor provide a restful backdrop. The cuisine ranges from a mild pilaf to a spicy *vindaloo* (very hot curry). The "brass tray" offers an assortment of specialties. A vegetarian menu is also available. *Av. Louise 455, tel. 02/647–8651. Reservations advised. Dress: casual but neat. AE, DC, MC, V. Closed Sun.*

$$ Aux Armes de Bruxelles. Hidden among the tourist traps in the Ilôt Sacré, this restaurant attracts a largely local clientele with its slightly tarnished middle-class elegance and its Belgian classics: turbot *waterzooi* (a creamy stew of potatoes, vegetable, and fish), a variety of steaks, mussels prepared every which way, and french fries, which the Belgians, with some justification, believe they prepare better than anyone else. The place is cheerful and light, and service is friendly if frequently overstretched. *Rue des Bouchers 13, tel. 02/511–2118. Reservations advised. AE, DC, MC, V. Closed Mon. and June.*

$$ Brasserie Georges.
★ This hugely successful brasserie, open every day until past midnight, was the first brasserie in Brussels and is still the best. You'll find a splendid display of shellfish at the entrance, an Art Deco interior with tile floor and potted palms, fast and friendly service by waitresses in black and white, and such traditional fare as sauerkraut, poached cod, and potted duck, as well as more adventurous dishes like salmon tartare and swordfish chop with a light chicory curry. Twenty-five different wines are sold by the glass. *Av. Winston Churchill 259, tel. 02/347–2100. Reservations advised. Dress: casual. AE, DC, MC, V.*

$$ La Fine Fleur. This neighborhood restaurant, a stone's throw from avenue Louise, attracts a young, artistic clientele. Leafy plants proliferate, and French chansons from the stereo set the mood. The owner, an artist, designed the minimalist decor and serves a sort of minimalist cuisine which includes such felicitous surprises as carpaccio with cèpes, and scallops with horseradish—but portions are not large. Arrive after nine to experience the place at its busiest. *Rue de la Longe Haie 51, tel. 02/647–6803. Reservations advised. Dress: casual. AE, DC, MC, V. Closed Sat. lunch, Sun., 2 weeks at Easter, 2 weeks in Aug.*

$$ In 't Spinnekopke. This is where true Brussels cooking has survived and continues to flourish. It was a coaching inn in the 18th century, and low ceilings and benches around the walls have remained. You can choose among a hundred artisanal beers, and many of the dishes are made with beer, including carbonnade. *Pl. du Jardin aux Fleurs 1, tel. 02/511–8695. Reservations advised. Dress: casual. AE, DC, MC, V. Closed Sat. lunch and Sun.*

$$ La Manufacture. In a former workshop where expensive Delvaux handbags were made, La Manufacture has been cleverly transformed into a contemporary-looking restaurant, with tables of polished stone, brick walls, and friendly servers wearing long leather aprons. The cooking is stylish and modern as well: lobster ravioli with pineapple conserve, ostrich fillet with green mustard mousseline. The crusty bread is great; so is the crème brulée. *Rue Notre-Dame du Someil 12, tel. 02/502–2715. Reservations advised. Dress: neat but casual. AE, DC, MC, V. Closed Sat. lunch and Sun.*

$$ Les Petits Oignons. This airy 17th-century restaurant in the heart of the Marolles has been furnished with plants and bright modern paintings. It places no demands on your palate, but the ambience makes you feel good and well looked after. Pâté of goose liver with champagne *ratafia* (liqueur) and leg of lamb with potatoes au gratin are among the choices. *Rue Notre-Seigneur 13, tel. 02/512–4738. Reservations advised. Dress: neat but casual. AE, DC, MC, V. Closed Sun. and Aug.*

$$ La Quincaillerie. The name means "The Hardware Store," and
★ that's precisely what this place used to be. It still looks the part, except now there are tables perched on the narrow balcony and a zinc oyster bar downstairs. The youngish clientele is served by even younger waitresses who run up and down the stairs with heavy trays. The menu consists mostly of brasserie grub like baked ham knuckle, but it's enlivened by dishes such as salmon fillet au gros sel, honey-baked Peking duck, and excellent game. The upwardly mobile have a soft spot for this place, and its doors stay open till midnight. *Rue du Page 45, tel. 02/538–2553. Reservations advised. Dress: neat but casual. AE, DC, MC, V.*

$$ La Roue d'Or. The murals in the Roue d'Or pay extravagant homage to Magritte, the great surrealist. Bowler-hatted gentlemen ascend serenely to the ceiling, a blue sky inhabited by tropical birds. The good cuisine includes traditional Belgian fare as well as such staples of the French brasserie repertoire as lamb's tongue vinaigrette with shallots, pig's feet salad, or veal kidneys with watercress cream. The *escargots à la bourguignonne* (snails in their shells with a garlic-butter sauce) is outstanding. Go elsewhere if you're seeking a quiet meal; the noise level here can be quite high. *Rue des Chapeliers 26, tel. 02/514–2554. Reservations advised. Dress: casual. AE, DC, MC, V. Closed weekends and mid-July–mid-Aug.*

$$ Vincent. In a town where most of the more fashionable places now concentrate on seafood, Vincent remains unapologetically a red-meat stronghold. Sides of beef and big slabs of butter in the window announce what awaits you. You pass through the kitchen on your way to the dining room, which is decorated with naive hand-painted tiles. *Rue des Dominicains 8, tel. 08/511–2303. Reservations advised. Dress: casual. AE, DC, MC, V. Closed Aug.*

$ Adrienne. It's the huge cold buffet that packs them in year after year at this upstairs restaurant just around the corner from avenue Toison d'Or. The look is rustic, with red-and-white-check tablecloths, and you can eat on the terrace in summer. The location is great for uptown shopping and movies, and it's also fun for kids. A second Adrienne (tel. 02/478–3000) is near the Atomium and Bruparck; the formula is the same. *Rue Capitaine Crespel 1A, tel. 02/511–9339. Reservations advised for lunch. Dress: casual. AE, DC, MC, V. Closed Sun.*

$ L'Armagnac. As the name implies, this restaurant specializes in dishes of southwestern France. The place may be a wee bit run-down, but the faithful, mostly middle-aged clientele appreciates the reliability of the $25-fixed-price menu, which offers a choice between half a dozen dishes for each of the three courses. Scampi in lobster sauce, lambs' tongues, fillet steak with wild mushrooms, and braised pheasant are among the favorites. *Chaussée de Waterloo 591, tel. 02/345–9279. Reservations advised. Jacket and tie required. AE, DC, MC, V. Closed Mon. dinner, Sun., and July 20–Aug. 20.*

$ **Boccaccio.** The Moroccan husband and Swedish wife who own the restaurant serve generous portions of Italian-inspired food in this super-friendly hole-in-the-wall shaped like a diner with a tiny kitchen at one end. It's popular with airline crews—not a bad recommendation. *Rue du Marché-aux-Fromages 14, tel. 02/512–2929. Reservations advised. Dress: casual. AE, DC, MC, V. Closed Sun.*

$ **Café Camille.** Named for the sculptor Camille Claudel, who has become somewhat of a cult figure in these parts, this restaurant has a large mural with a sculpture motif and a huge floral centerpiece; otherwise, it's bare floorboards and plain tables. Many of the customers, most of whom are young, seem to know one another, and as the evening progresses the noise level can become high. Service is casual and friendly, and the food (lamb noisettes with braised chicory and celery au gratin, scampi ramekin, fillet steak with shallots) is quite good. The restaurant is open till midnight. *Chaussée de Waterloo 559, tel. 02/345–9643. Reservations advised. Dress: casual. AE, DC, MC, V. No lunch on weekends.*

$ **Chez Jean.** Jean Cambien runs a reliable restaurant, unchanged since 1931, with oak benches against the walls backed by mirrors on which the dishes of the day are written up in whitewash. Waitresses in black and white serve poached cod, mussels cooked in white wine, chicken waterzooi, and other Belgian dishes. *Rue des Chapeliers 6, tel. 02/511–9815. Reservations advised. Dress: neat but casual. No credit cards. Closed Sun.–Mon.*

$ ★ **Chez Leon.** This started as a tiny restaurant 100 years ago and has expanded to occupy eight old houses in the middle of the Îlot Sacré, and it now serves a ton of mussels a day. It does serve other Belgian specialties, such as eels in green sauce, or what Belgians are pleased to call a filet Américain (in fact a large steak tartare), but potfuls of steaming mussels, served with frites and beer, are the trademark. *Rue des Bouchers 18, tel. 02/511–1415. No reservations. Dress: casual. No credit cards.*

$ **Falstaff.** This huge tavern with a pure Art Nouveau interior fills up for lunch and keeps going until 5 AM with an ever-changing crowd. The only contemporary touch to the traditional Belgian food is provided by the cordless electronic order pads wielded by the cheerful waitresses. Make sure you go to the original Falstaff at No. 19, not its next-door neighbor. *Rue Henri Maus 19, tel. 02/511–8789. No reservations. Dress: casual. AE, DC, MC, V.*

$ **Le Faste Fou.** Well situated in the place Louise area Faste Fou is crowded with office workers at lunch. There is counter service downstairs and table service upstairs in a bare and noisy dining room devoid of decor; friendly servers and good food make up for it. The menu offers substantial salads and complete meals. *Rue du Grand-Cerf 21, tel. 02/511–3832. No reservations. Dress: casual. AE, DC, MC, V. Closed Sun.*

$ **Gallery.** This popular new Vietnamese restaurant is furnished with contemporary black chairs and tables, artfully suspended spotlights, and an exhibit of black-and-white photographs. The kitchen holds no surprises, but the food is well prepared, and the helpings generous. Many come here for the large and well-stocked bar. *Rue du Grand Cerf 7, tel. 02/511–8035. Reservations advised. Dress: casual. AE, DC, MC, V. Closed Sun. lunch, first half of Aug.*

$ ★ **Au Vieux Saint Martin.** Even when neighboring restaurants on Grand Sablon are empty, this one is full. A rack of glossy magazines is a thoughtful touch for lone diners, and you're equally welcome whether you order a cup of coffee or a full meal. The short menu emphasizes Brussels specialties; portions are generous. A wine importer, the owner serves unusually good wine for the price by the glass or by the bottle. The red walls are hung with large, contemporary paintings, and picture windows overlook the pleasant square. A brass plaque marks the table where Bill Clinton took his ease during a Brussels walkabout. The kitchen is open daily from noon until midnight. *Grand Sablon 38, tel. 02/512–6476. No reservations. Dress: casual. No credit cards.*

Lodging

Brussels has seen a boom in hotel-building over the past few years in response to the increase in business and diplomatic travel; three out of four visitors come here on business. Most business travel takes place in winter, so a number of hotels offer as much as 50% off on weekends and in July and August. In the past few years, new hotels in the $$ and $ categories have opened, providing a wider choice of attractive accommodations.

Tourist Information Brussels (TIB) publishes an annual hotel guide listing prices and facilities. You can obtain a copy by writing to TIB (Hôtel de Ville, 1000 Brussels). It contains a reservation form, to be sent to Belgian Tourist Reservations (blvd. Anspach 111, 1000 Brussels, tel. 02/513–7484, fax 02/513–9277). If you arrive in Brussels without reservations, check the **Tourist Information Office** (tel. 02/722–3000) at the airport. The **TIB** at Grand'Place (tel. 02/513–8940) will also arrange reservations locally. The youth organization **Acotra** (rue de la Madeleine 53, tel. 02/512–8607) has a room-finding service for youth hostels. These services are free, but you will be asked for a deposit, which is then deducted from your hotel bill.

Quoted hotel rates always include 6% value added tax, 9% city tax and 16% service charge, so there are no surprises when you get your bill. All rooms have bath or shower, color TV, and direct-dial telephone unless otherwise indicated. The prices below are for two people in a double room and include Continental breakfast unless otherwise stated. Highly recommended hotels are indicated by a star ★.

Category	Brussels
$$$$	BF9,000–BF12,000
$$$	BF6,500–BF9,000
$$	BF3,500–BF6,500
$	under BF3,500

$$$$ **Conrad.** Opened in 1993 on the elegant avenue Louise, the Conrad has the classic facade of an 1865 mansion and a sleek, deluxe, American interior. Rooms come in many different shapes but are all spacious and have three telephones, a desk, bathrobes, and in-room checkout. The intimate, gourmet Maison de Maître restaurant wins good reviews, and Cafe Wiltcher's offers all-day dining. The large piano bar is pleasantly clubby, and there are state-of-the-art conference and banquet facilities. Bill Clinton slept here. *Av. Louise 71, 1050, tel. 02/542–4242, fax 02/542–4300. 254 rooms, 15 suites. Facilities: 2 restaurants, 2 bars, conference rooms, garage; breakfast not included. AE, DC, MC, V.*

$$$$ Hilton. One of the first high rises in Brussels back in the 1960s, it outclasses most other Hiltons in Europe and is continuously being refurbished floor by floor. The corner rooms are the most desirable. There are four floors of Executive rooms, with a separate check-in area. The location near the Porte Louise is great for high-class shopping. There is a fine panoramic view from the 27th-floor restaurant, the En Plein Ciel (buffet lunch only). The second-floor restaurant, the Maison du Boeuf, is one of the best in town, and the ground-floor Café d'Egmont stays open around the clock. *Blvd. de Waterloo 38, tel. 02/504–1111, fax 02/504–2111. 420 rooms, 30 suites. Facilities: 3 restaurants, 2 bars, sauna, garage, conference center; breakfast not included. AE, DC, MC, V.*

$$$$ Montgomery. The owners of this 1993 hotel set out to create new standards of service for the business traveler, and for the most part, they have succeeded. Fax machines, three telephones (with a private line for incoming calls), good working desks, safes, triple-glazed windows, and bathrobes are standard. Rooms are decorated in Chinese, English (for those who like frills and furbelows), or cool, clean colonial style. There's a library bar/restaurant with a wood-burning fireplace, and the small meeting rooms are well-appointed boardrooms. The inner ring road location on Square Montgomery is convenient to the European Commission. *Av. de Tervueren 134, tel. 02/741–8511, fax 02/741–8500. 61 rooms, 2 penthouses, 1 suite. Facilities: restaurant, bar, library, health club, meeting facilities, garage. AE, DC, MC, V.*

Royal Windsor Hotel. The Royal Windsor, opened in 1974 close to the Grand'Place, has been refurbished, and all rooms have blond-wood paneling and marble bathrooms. They are, however, on the small side. The lobby is businesslike, with leafy plants, comfortable sofas and chairs placed around marble-topped tables, and music wafting in from the adjacent piano bar. The elegant dining room, Les Quatre Saisons, serves light, imaginative, and expensive French cuisine. *Rue Duquesnoy 5, tel. 02/511–4215, fax 02/511–6004. 280 rooms. Facilities: restaurant, health club, piano bar, disco, garage, conference rooms. AE, DC, MC, V. $$$$*

$$$$ ★ SAS Royal Hotel. Next to the Opera, near the northern end of the Galeries St-Hubert, this hotel opened in 1990 and was an instant success. The floors are decorated in a variety of styles—Oriental (wicker furniture and Asian art), Italian (art deco fixtures and furnishings), and Scandinavian (light-wood furniture and parquet flooring). The greenery-filled atrium incorporates a 10-foot-high section of the 12th-century city wall. The Sea Grill is a first-rate seafood restaurant, and Scandinavian specialties are served in the Atrium. Children under 15 stay free; senior citizens get at least 65% off. *Rue du Fosse-aux-Loups 47, tel. 02/219–2828, fax 02/219–6262. 281 rooms. Facilities: 3 restaurants, 2 bars, garage, health club, sauna, airline check-in, business center, conference rooms. AE, DC, MC, V.*

$$$$ Stanhope. This small hotel is the most expensive in Brussels and operates on the principle that if you have to ask the price, you can't afford it. It was created out of three adjoining town houses; all the high-ceilinged, luxuriously furnished rooms and suites are different and have marble bathrooms. Each room has its own name. The Linley features furniture handmade by Viscount Linley, nephew of the queen of England. You can have English afternoon tea in the ground-floor salon, and the downstairs bar serves caviar. *Rue du Commerce 9, tel. 02/506–9111, fax 02/512–1708. 25 rooms and 25 suites. Facilities: restaurant, tearoom, bar, health club, sauna, boardrooms, garden, garage. AE, MC, V.*

$$$ **Amigo.** Just a block from the Grand'Place and decorated in Spanish
★ Renaissance with touches of Louis XV, the Amigo looks more turn-
of-the-century than its actual age of almost 40 years. Public spaces
and guest rooms were refurbished in 1993. Rooms vary in furnish-
ings, size, and price; bathrooms are on the small side. The higher
floors have views over the surrounding rooftops. Amigo is popular
with those who like understated luxury, and the service is excellent.
*Rue d'Amigo 1–3, tel. 02/547–4747, fax 02/513–5277. 183 rooms. Fa-
cilities: restaurant, bar, garage, conference rooms. AE, DC, MC,
V.*

$$$ **Château du Lac.** Half an hour from the city center and a good choice
★ for those who want a peaceful home base from which to visit the capi-
tal and the provinces, this mock-Florentine castle is a former
Schweppes bottling plant. The large rooms are light beige and well
furnished, and the decor in the public rooms is contemporary, mostly white with details picked out in red. The splendid restaurant, Le
Trèfle à Quatre, where Michel Haquin is chef, is itself worth the
journey for his superb cuisine focusing on fish and game and for the
views over the lake. *Av. du Lac 87, Genval, tel. 02/654–1122, fax 02/
653–6200. 38 rooms. Facilities: restaurant, bar, sauna, outdoor
swimming pool, conference center. AE, DC, MC, V.*

$$$ **Clubhouse.** On a quiet side street off the chic avenue Louise, the for-
mer Alfa Louise has had a major face-lift that, alas, has also lifted it
to a higher price category. The rooms have been redone with pastel
walls, salmon-pink carpeting, flower-patterned Laura Ashley–style
bedspreads and curtains, and sofa, easy chair, and desk. The large,
blue-carpeted lobby, opening on a small garden, has a fire in the
open hearth on chilly days. *Rue Blanche 4, tel. 02/537–9210, fax 02/
537–0018. 81 rooms. Facilities: bar, conference room, garage. AE,
DC, MC, V.*

$$$ **Metropole.** Stepping into the Metropole, you would think you were
on the Orient Express. The hotel has been restored to the palace it
was during the Belle Epoque. The lobby, with its enormously high
coffered ceiling, chandeliers, marble, and Oriental carpets sets the
tone. It is carried through in the bar with potted palms, deep leather sofas, and Corinthian columns; in the café, which opens onto the
sidewalk of place Brouckère; and in the Alban Chambon restaurant
(named for the architect). The rooms are discreetly modern in varying shades of pastel (some with trompe l'oeil murals), with furniture
upholstered with the same material as the bedspreads. *Pl. de
Brouckere 31, tel. 02/217–2300, fax 02/218–0220. 410 rooms. Facilities: restaurant, bar, café, conference rooms, airport courtesy bus.
AE, DC, MC, V.*

$$$ **Sofitel.** Opened in 1989, the six-floor Sofitel has a great location op-
posite the Hilton. There's a chic shopping arcade on the ground
floor, and you reach the lobby on an escalator. Public rooms and bed-
rooms are decorated in warm brown and beige tones. The restau-
rant, at the back of the lobby, is good and getting better. *Av. de la
Toison d'Or 40, tel. 02/514–2200, fax 02/514–5744. 171 rooms. Facili-
ties: restaurant, bar, conference rooms; breakfast not included.
AE, DC, MC, V.*

$$ **Beau-Site.** Gleaming white and with flower boxes suspended from
the windowsills, this former office building, opened as a hotel in
1993, makes a smart impression. The location (a block from the upper end of avenue Louise) and the attentive staff are big pluses. The
good-sized rooms come in shapes other than the standard cube, and
bathrooms have blow-dryers and bidets. The complimentary buffet
breakfast includes bacon and eggs. *Rue de la Longue Haie 76, tel.
02/640–8889, fax 02/640–1611. 38 rooms with bath. Facilities: breakfast room. AE, DC, MC, V.*

$$ Cadettt. The concept of the Cadettt (part of the Swiss Mövenpick Group) is to offer superior rooms with limited services at a moderate price. The Brussels Cadettt, completed in 1991, has large rooms, each with blond-wood furniture, a Lay-Z-Boy chair, and good work space. The beige-and-green atrium bar and restaurant serves copious Swiss breakfasts and a limited selection of specialties for lunch and dinner. *Rue Paul Spaak 15, tel. 02/645-6111, fax 02/646-6311. 128 rooms. Facilities: restaurant, 2 bars, garage, health club, sauna, seminar facilities; breakfast not included. AE, DC, MC, V.*

$$ Le Dixseptième. Opened in 1993, Le Dixseptième occupies the stylishly restored 18th-century residence of the Spanish Ambassador. Rooms surround a pleasant interior courtyard, and suites are up a splendid Louis XVI staircase. Named for Belgian artists, all units have whitewashed walls, plain floorboards, exposed beams, suede sofas, and colorful draperies. Rooms have bathrobes; some rooms have kitchenettes; and suites have working fireplaces and fax machines. One suite even has a separate office. *Rue de la Madeleine 25, tel. 02/502-5744, fax 02/502-6424. 12 rooms, 13 suites. Facilities: breakfast room, some rooms have kitchenettes. AE, DC, MC, V.*

$$ Manos Stephanie. The Louis XV furniture, marble lobby, and an-
★ tiques set a standard of elegance seldom encountered in a hotel in this price category. The rooms have rust-colored carpets, green bedspreads, and good-sized sitting areas. The hotel, opened in 1992, occupies a grand old town house, so the rooms are not rigidly standardized; the split-level Room 103 is especially appealing. The atrium restaurant is enlivened by gaily striped chair coverings. *Chaussée de Charleroi 28, tel. 02/539-0250, fax 02/537-5729. 55 rooms. Facilities: restaurant, bar, conference room, garage. AE, DC, MC, V.*

$$ Novotel. One of the newly built old-look gabled hotels on the place d'Espagne, a stone's throw from the Grand'Place, the mock-Renaissance brick Novotel was built in 1989. Some big French hotel chains mass-produce hotels that are functional but motel-like, and this Novotel is no exception. The rooms have white walls and russet carpets; all come with a sofa that can sleep an extra person, some with an additional roll-away bed. There's no extra charge for children under 16. One floor is reserved for nonsmokers. The Grill serves French hotel-chain cuisine; it's acceptable but far from exciting. *Rue du Marché-aux-Herbes 120, tel. 02/514-3333, fax 02/511-7723. 136 rooms. Facilities: restaurant, bar, conference rooms, garage. AE, DC, MC, V.*

$ Albert Premier. This hotel has been around since the 1920s, but it was totally renovated in 1988 and done up in blue and gunmetal art-deco style. Among the somewhat somber rooms, the quietest are those facing the courtyard. Quite a few tour groups use the hotel. *Pl. Rogier 20, tel. 02/217-2125, fax 02/217-9331. 285 rooms. Facilities: bar, conference rooms. AE, DC, MC, V.*

$ Gerfaut. In this cheerful hotel opened in 1991, the rooms—in light beige with colorful bedspreads—are of reasonable size. Three- and four-bed rooms are available at modest supplements. Breakfast is served in the bright and friendly Winter Garden room. The location near the Gare du Midi (South Station), though not choice, is convenient. *Chaussée de Mons 115-117, tel. 02/522-1922, fax 02/523-8991. 48 rooms. Facilities: bar. AE, DC, MC, V.*

$ Matignon. Only the facade was preserved in the conversion of this Belle-Epoque building to a hotel in 1993. The lobby is no more than a corridor, making room for the large café/brasserie that is part of the family-owned operation. Rooms are small but have generous beds, blow-dryers, and large-screen TVs, a welcome change from the dinky TVs you find in most budget hotels. Windows are double-glazed, and that's important in this busy spot across the street from the Bourse and a couple of blocks from the Grand'Place. The five duplex suites are an especially good value. Advance payment is requested. *Rue de la Bourse 10, tel. 02/511–0888, fax 02/513–6927. 22 rooms. Facilities: bar and restaurant (both closed Mon.). AE, DC, MC, V.*

$ **Mozart.** Opened in 1993, the Mozart is between two Greek pita joints, and the lobby is up a flight of stairs. For some, the attractive, spacious, oak-beamed rooms, done in shades of salmon and furnished with refrigerators and showers, may make up for the lack of an elevator. Complimentary breakfast is served in a cozy nook. The multilingual Moroccan owner, Ben, and his Swedish wife also own the remarkably inexpensive Boccaccio restaurant across the street. *Rue Marché aux Fromages 15A, tel. 02/502–6661, fax 02/502–7758. 23 rooms. Facilities: breakfast room. AE, DC, MC, V.*

$ **Orion.** Here's a really neat idea: a residential hotel where rooms and apartments can be rented by the night. Walls are whitewashed, and there are bright red accent pieces throughout. All rooms have well-equipped kitchenettes. The reception desk is always manned, but you do your own bed and tidying. Linen is changed weekly. The rates go up 15% in peak seasons, but there are special weekly and monthly rates. Rooms on the courtyard are the quietest. *Quai au Bois-à-Bruler 51, tel. 02/221–1411, fax 02/221–1599. 169 rooms. Breakfast not included. AE, DC, MC, V.*

$ **Sun.** Rooms are on the small side, in cool pastel green, with safes and beds with firm mattresses; the bathrooms are cramped. The attractive breakfast room has a striking glass mural; snacks are served there during the day. The hotel is on a quiet but slightly dilapidated side street off the busy Chaussée d'Ixelles. *Rue du Berger 38, tel. 02/511–2119, fax 02/512–3271. 22 rooms with bath or shower. Facilities: parking. AE, DC, MC, V.*

$ **Welcome/Truite d'Argent.** The smallest hotel in Brussels is much in
★ demand, in large part due to its charming young owners, Michel and Sophie Smeesters. The six rooms, which have king- or queen-size beds, are as comfortable as those in much more expensive establishments. The dining room downstairs serves three meals a day to guests of the hotel, and the rather expensive Truite d'Argent (closed Sat. lunch, Sun., first half of Aug.) around the corner on the Fish Market offers excellent seafood. *Rue du Peuplier 5, tel. 02/219–9546, fax 02/217–1887. 6 rooms. Facilities: 2 restaurants, seminar rooms, garage. AE, DC, MC, V.*

The Arts and Nightlife

The Arts A glance at the "What's On" supplement of the indispensable weekly English-language newsmagazine *The Bulletin* reveals the breadth of the offerings in all categories of cultural life. Tickets for most events can be purchased by calling **Free Time Line** (tel. 02/538–3131) or **Ticketel** (tel. 02/675–5414).

Theater Nearly all the city's 30-odd theaters stage French-language plays; only a few present plays in Dutch. Avant-garde performances are the most rewarding. Check what's on at **Théâtre Varia** (rue du Sceptre 78, tel. 02/640–8258), **Théâtre du Residence Palace** (rue de la Loi 155, tel. 02/231–0740), and **Théâtre de Poche** (Bois de la Cambre, tel. 02/649–1727).

Music The principal venue for classical music concerts is the **Palais des Beaux-Arts** (rue Ravenstein 23, tel. 02/507–8200). A smaller and more attractive hall is the **Conservatoire Royale** (rue de la Régence 30, tel. 02/511–0427). There are also many concerts in various churches, especially the **Eglise des Minimes** (rue des Minimes 62).

If you're going to be in Brussels in the spring, try to take in some of the concerts that are part of the **Queen Elisabeth Music Competition** (the penultimate round is at the Conservatoire Royale, the final week at the Palais des Beaux-Arts), for pianists, violinists, singers, and composers in successive years.

The principal venue for rock concerts is the **Forest National** (av. du Globe 36, tel. 02/347–0355). For more rock/pop as well as French *chanson*, check also the **Cirque Royal** (rue de l'Enseignement 81, tel. 02/218–2015) and **Centre Culturel le Botanique** (rue Royale 236, tel. 02/218–3732).

Opera and Dance The national opera house is **Théâtre Royal de la Monnaie** (pl. de la Monnaie, tel. 02/218–1211). Visiting opera and dance companies often perform at the **Cirque Royal** (rue de l'Enseignement 81, tel. 02/218–2015).

Art Galleries Many of the two dozen galleries in Brussels are in the avenue Louise and Grand Sablon areas. See *The Bulletin* for listings.

Film First-run English-language and French movies predominate. The most convenient movie theater complexes are **Acropole** (Galeries and av. de la Toison d'Or, tel. 02/511–4238) and **UGC de Brouckère** (pl. de Brouckère, tel. 02/218–0607). The biggest—26 theaters—is the futuristic **Kinepolis** (av. du Centenaire 1, Heysel, tel. 02/478–0450). The **Musée du Cinéma** (Cinema Museum, rue Baron Horta 9, tel. 02/507–8370) shows classic and silent movies; reserve the day of the performance.

Nightlife By 11 PM most Bruxellois have packed up and gone home. But around midnight, bars and cafés fill up again as the night people take over. Nightclubs and cabarets are by and large pale imitations of those in Paris. Locals provide their own entertainment.

Bars and Lounges There's a cafe on virtually every street corner, and they are all taprooms in disguise. The Belgians consume vast quantities of beer, some of it with a 10% alcohol content. **La Mort Subite** (rue de Montagne-aux-Herbes Potagères 7, near the northern end of the Galeries St-Hubert) is renowned as a genuine and unchanged beer hall. **Chez Moeder Lambic** (rue de Savoie 68 in St-Gilles) claims to stock 600 Belgian beers and a few hundred more foreign ones; **Fleur en Papier Doré** (rue des Alexiens 53) is quietly surrealistic; **Ultieme Hallucinatie** (rue Royale 316) is Art Nouveau. People meet for a drink at all hours in the **Falstaff** (rue Henri Maus 19), **Le Perroquet** (rue Watteeu 31), or **'t Kelderke** (Grand'Place 15). If you like Gypsy music, try **Le Huchier** (Grand Sablon 42) or the **Ateliers de la Grande Ile** (rue de la Grande Ile 33).

Brussels's sizable black population, hailing mostly from Zaire, has its own hangouts. One such is **Kwassa Quoisa** (rue de Boetendael 113, tel. 02/344–9836); another is the disco **L'Ecume des Nuits** (Galerie Louise 122A, pl. Stephanie entrance; tel. 02/512–9147; from 11 PM Thurs.–Sun.). Chaussée de Wavre is the principal street for African shops, bars, and restaurants.

Anglo-Saxons flock to **Rick's Café Américain** (av. Louise344, tel. 02/648–1451). The **James Joyce** (rue Archimède 34, tel. 02/230–9894) and the **Kitty O'Shea** (blvd. de Charlemagne 42, tel. 02/230–7875) are as Irish as they come. Among the best hotel bars are those in the **Hilton,** the **Amigo,** and the **Métropole** (*see* Lodging, *above*).

Gay bars include **Tels Quels** (rue du Marché au Charbon 81, tel. 02/512–4587), **Why Not** (rue des Riches Claires 7, tel. 02/512–7587), and **Le Féminin** (rue Bourgal 9, tel. 02/511–1719).

Cabarets **Show Point** (pl. Stephanie 14, tel. 02/511–5364) offers striptease, **Chez Flo** (rue au Beurre 25, tel. 02/512–9496) has transvestite shows, and **Do Brasil** (rue de la Caserne 88, tel. 02/513–5028) features Latin American entertainment.

Discos The disco scene warms up around midnight. Most are only open weekends and cater to the under-30 crowd. The most snobbish, where they let you in if they like the look of you, are **Jeux d'Hiver** (Chemin du Croquet 1A, Bois de la Cambre, tel. 02/647–2205) and **Mirano** (Chaussée de Louvain 38, tel. 02/218–5772). Others include **Take Off** (rue Vilain XIII 55, tel. 640–3870), **Le Vaudeville** (rue de la Montagne 14, tel. 02/514–1260), and **Griffin's** in the Hotel Royal Windsor (rue Duquesnoy 7, tel. 02/511–4215).

Jazz There are two contemporary Belgian jazz greats: Toots Thielemans (on harmonica) and the guitarist Philip Catherine. You stand a good chance of catching Catherine at **Travers** (rue Traversière 11, tel. 02/218–4086). Other places to check out are **Kaai** (quai aux Pierre de Taille 39, for info, fax 02/502–1275), **Preservation Hall** (pl. de Londres 4, tel. 02/502–1597), and **Sounds** (rue de la Tulipe 28, tel. 02/512–9250).

Excursions from Brussels

Mechelen

Tourist **City tourist office: Dienst voor Toerisme** (Stadhuis, Grote Markt, tel.
Information 015/29–76–55). **Provincial tourist office: Toeristische Federatie Provincie Antwerpen** (Karel Oomsstraat 11, Antwerp, tel. 03/216–2810).

Getting There Mechelen is 28 kilometers (17 miles) north of Brussels on the A1/E19 expressway, and just about the same distance from Antwerp (avoid the exit for the almost identically named Machelen, a Brussels suburb). The train trip takes 15 minutes.

Guided Tours The **tourist office** organizes walks to explore historic Mechelen at 2 PM on weekends from Easter to September, and daily in July and August.

Exploring **Mechelen** (known to French speakers as Malines) is the traditional
Mechelen residence of the Roman Catholic primate of Belgium and has preserved the traditional Belgian specialty of tapestry weaving. There are also furniture factories producing the heavy oak pieces favored by many Flemish families. Mechelen, finally, is also the center of vegetable production, especially asparagus and witloof, the Belgian delicacy known elsewhere as chicory or endive.

Mechelen's brief period of grandeur coincided with the reign (1507–1530) of Margaret of Austria, who established her de0vout and cultured court in this city while she served as regent for her nephew, later to become Charles V. The philosophers Erasmus and Thomas More visited her court, as did the painters Albrecht Dürer and Van Orley (whose portrait of Margaret hangs in the Musée d'Art Ancien in Brussels), and Josquin des Prés, the master of polyphony.

For the modern visitor, Mechelen's chief glory is the **St. Romboutskathedraal** on the Grote Markt and more especially the admirably proportioned tower, with its powerful but light vertical lines. It had been planned to reach a height of 167 meters (547 feet), which would have made it the tallest spire in the world, but construction came to an end in the 1520s when it was only 97 meters (318 feet) high. Even so, the tower represents a magnificent achievement by three generations of the Keldermans family of architects. Inside are two remarkable 40-ton carillons of 49 bells each; carillon-playing was virtually invented in Mechelen, and student carillonneurs still come here from all over the world. The interior of the cathedral is spacious and lofty, particularly the white sandstone nave dating from the 13th century. There are numerous paintings, notably Van Dyck's *Crucifixion* in the south transept. *Grote Markt. Open Mon.– Sat. 9:30–4 (until 7 in summer), Sun. 1–5. Check tourist office for tower tours. Carillon concerts Sat. 11:30 AM, Sun. 3 PM, Mon. 8:30 PM.*

Time Out Relax in the 't Voske on the Grote Markt with a local specialty such as *witloofsoep* (cream of endive soup), or *boerenbrood hesp* (open sandwich with ham and salad).

The **Stadhuis** (Town Hall), opposite the cathedral, consists of two contrasting parts. On the left is the palace commissioned by Charles V to accommodate the Grote Raad, the supreme court of the Burgundian Netherlands established by Charles the Bold. Work was abandoned after 20 years, in 1547, but completed in the 20th century in accordance with Rombout Keldermans's original plans. On the right is the somber, turreted, 14th-century Lakenhalle (Cloth Hall). *Grote Markt. Guided tours of the Stadhuis start at 2 at the Tourist Office, weekends Easter–June, daily July–Aug., weekends in Sept.*

Frederik de Merodestraat leads from the square to **Hof van Busleyden,** which houses the Municipal Museum. It, too, was built by the Keldermanses, for Hieronymus van Busleyden, the lawyer and humanist to whom Thomas More dedicated his *Utopia.* The dining room has survived almost intact, and the collection of paintings provides insights into the city's history. *Frederik de Merodestraat 65, tel. 015/202004. Admission: BF75. Open Wed.–Mon. 10–noon and 2–5.*

Back toward the town center is **Sint-Janskerk,** which contains a Rubens triptych, the *Adoration of the Magi.* The painter's wife posed as the Virgin. To the right off Klapgat is Schoutetstraat, with the Refuge van Tongerlo and the tapestry workshops of **Gaspard De Wit—Koninklyke Manufactuur/Manufacture Royale** (Royal Tapestery Manufacturer), the only place where the ancient and glorious Belgian art of tapestry weaving is still practiced. *Schoutetstraat 7, tel. 015/202905. Guided tours of workshops and collection of antique and contemporary tapestries mid-Aug.–July Sat. 10:30; admission BF150.*

East of the center, near the railway station, you'll find **Speelgoedmuseum Mechelen** (Mechelen's Toy Museum), which houses a vast collection of toys and games, including more than 8,000 tin soldiers ready to do battle on a model of Waterloo. There's also a play area for young and old. *Nekkerspoel 21, tel. 015/557075. Admission: BF120. Open Tues.–Sun. 10–5.*

Dining Mechelen offers a rewarding variety of restaurants where good eating takes center stage.

★ **D'Hoogh.** In a grand graystone mansion on the Grote Markt, its first-floor (second to Americans) dining room looking over the square, this glamorous landmark presents top-quality *cuisine du marché* (menus based on whatever is freshest in the local market): smoked eel terrine with pistachios, poached goose liver in port jelly with caramelized apples, turbot and zucchini spaghetti in vinaigrette and olive oil, and the most wonderful asparagus imaginable in April and May. *Grote Markt 19, tel. 015/217553. Reservations required. Jacket and tie advised. AE, DC, MC, V. Closed Sat. lunch, Sun. dinner, Mon., first 3 weeks of Aug. $$$*

Folliez. In 1990, this simple bistro was transformed into a restaurant with a futuristic but welcoming decor. The young chef turns out creative dishes such as a mille-feuille of sweetbreads and langoustines, and farm chicken with morels and leek conserve. *Korenmarkt 19, tel. 015/420302. Reservations advised. Jacket and tie advised. AE, DC, MC, V. Closed 3 weeks in Feb.–Mar. and 4 weeks in July–Aug. $$$*

't Korenveld. This tiny, old-fashioned bistro has been primly restored and decked with pretty floral wallpaper and tiled tabletops. Its cuisine is equally unpretentious, featuring simple fish and steaks at low prices. It adjoins the Alfa Hotel, and has some tables in their bar. *Korenmarkt 20 tel. 015/421469. Reservations advised. Dress: casual. AE, DC, MC, V. Closed Mon. $*

Leuven

Tourist Information
City tourist office: Town Hall (Naamsestraat 1a, tel. 016/21–15–39). **Provincial tourist office: Toeristisch Federatie Brabant** (rue du Marché-aux-Herbes 61, Brussels, tel. 02/504–0455).

Getting There
Leuven is 26 kilometers (16 miles) east of Brussels via A3/E40 (toward Liége) and A2, or 20 minutes by train.

Guided Tours
There are no regularly organized guided tours of Leuven, but you can arrange with the tourist office for an English-speaking personal guide (BF1,200 for 2 hrs).

Exploring Leuven
Leuven (Louvain to French speakers) is best known for its Catholic university, founded in 1425. One of its rectors was elected Pope Hadrian VI; Erasmus taught here in the 16th century, as did the cartographer Mercator and, in the following century, Cornelius Jansen, whose teachings inspired the anti-Jesuit Jansenist movement. The city was pillaged and burned by the Germans in 1914, when 1,800 buildings, including the university library, were destroyed. In the 1970s, after severe intercultural tensions, the old bilingual university split into a French-language university, which moved south of the linguistic border to Louvain-la-Neuve, and a Dutch-speaking one, which remained in Leuven. Present-day **Katholieke Universiteit Leuven** has a student body of more than 25,000.

The **Stadhuis** (Town Hall) escaped the 1914 fire due to its occupation by German staff. It is the work of Leuven's own architectural master of Flamboyant Gothic, Mathieu de Layens, who finished it in 1469 after 21 years' work. In photographs it looks more like a finely chiseled reliquary than a building; it is necessary to stand back from it to fully appreciate the vertical lines in the mass of turrets, pinnacles, pendants, and niches, each with its statue. The interior contains some fine 16th-century sculpted ceilings. *Grote Markt. Guided tours start from the tourist office weekdays at 11 and 3, weekends (Mar.–Oct.) at 3.*

Time Out
Under the Town Hall, and adjoining a small beer museum, is the **Raadskelder** café, strategically located for the revival of tired city officials and tourists.

Across the square stands the collegiate church, **St. Pieterskerk.**
Mathieu de Layens had a hand in this, too, as did Mechelen's Jan
Keldermans and Diest's Sulpice van der Vorst. A shifting foundation
led to the shortening of the tower in the 17th century and to the re-
placement of the spire with a cupola in the 18th. The interior is remarkable for the purity of the Gothic nave; the ambulatory and choir
are closed for restoration, but some treasures usually found here,
including Dirk Bouts's masterpiece, *The Last Supper*, are on display
elsewhere in the church. *Admission free. Open mid-Oct.–mid-
Mar., Tues.–Sat. 10–noon and 2–5, Sun. 2–5; mid-Mar.–mid-Oct.,
Mon.–Sat. 10–noon and 2–5, Sun. 2–5.*

Additional art treasures fill the **Stedelijk Museum** (Municipal Museum), just off the Grote Markt. They include works by Albrecht
Bouts (died 1549), son of Dirk, and Quentin Metsys (1466–1530), a
remarkable portraitist, as well as Brabantine sculptures from the
15th and 16th centuries. *Savoyestraat 6. Admission: BF50 (includes access to other museums). Open Tues.–Sat. 10–noon and
2–5, Sun. 2–5.*

A kilometer (½ mile) south down Naamsestraat, past several university colleges (Holy Spirit at #40, Premonstratensian College at #61,
Arras at #63, Van Dale at #80, and American College at #100) lies the
Groot Begijnhof, a city within the city where the *Beguines* (lay wom-
en members of an old religious order) once resided in their tiny individual houses. There are more than 70 of them, carefully restored
and now used by the university, as well as an attractive church.

A number of university institutes are in less congested surroundings in the splendid park of **Arenberg Castle** (tel. 016/284010) in
Heverlee, 6 kilometers (4 miles) south of the city. At Heverlee, too, is
the **Norbertine Abbey of Park** (visits Sun. 4 PM; for information call
the tourist office), founded in 1128, with its 18th-century water mill,
granary, abbey farm, and church.

Dining   **Belle Epoque.** This grand urban town house by the station offers the
most lavish dining in Leuven, served with considerable pomp. Try
the smoked salmon filled with eel mousse, and hope for wild hare, in
season. *Bondgenotenlaan 94, tel. 016/223389. Reservations required. Jacket and tie advised. AE, DC, MC, V. Closed Sun.–Mon.*
$$$

Domus. Tucked into a back street off the Grote Markt, this café ad-
joins the tiny Domus brewery, famous for its honey beer. The ambi-
ence is young and casual, the decor authentically rustic: craggy old
beams, a brick fireplace, a labyrinth of separate rooms, bric-a-brac,
and paisley table throws. The menu offers well prepared omeletes,
chicken à la king, and a cream gratin of endive, ham, and cheese, as
well as several salads and cold plates. *Tiensestraat 8, tel. 016/
201449. Dress: casual. No credit cards. $*

Hainaut

All the highways leading south from Brussels end up in France,
which may serve to remind you that you are in a proud old country
that was the nursery of French kings, the rich dowry of dynastic
marriages, and for many years the buffer between expansionist
France and quarrelsome Flanders. You go through landscape
scarred by the industrial revolution and past ancient, fortified farms
turned into centers of highly productive agriculture. You'll see the
ravages of war and some cathedrals that were spared, and wander

through parks and châteaus that are a reminder of the feudal world that was.

Important Addresses and Numbers

Tourist Information
Wallonie: tourist office (rue du Marché-aux-Herbes 61, Brussels, tel. 02/504–0390). **Province of Hainaut:** tourist office (rue des Clercs 31, Mons, tel. 065/360464). **City tourist offices: Tournai** (Vieux Marché-aux-Poteries 14, tel. 069/222045); **Mons** (Grand'Place 22, tel. 065/335580); and **Binche** (rue St-Paul 14, tel. 064/333721).

Emergencies
Police: tel. 101. **Ambulance:** tel. 100. The name of the nearest on-duty **pharmacy** is posted in all pharmacy windows.

Getting There

By Train
There is frequent train service from Brussels to Tournai (on the route to Lille) and to Mons (on the route to Paris). Each trip takes about an hour.

By Car
Roads leading south from Brussels pass through Flemish-speaking Brabant; thus roads are signposted to Bergen (Mons), Doornik (Tournai), and Rijsel (Lille).

Guided Tours

City tours are organized on request by the **tourist offices** in Tournai, Mons, and Binche. For tours of the southern part of the province, contact the tourist office in **Beaumont** (tel. 071/588191).

Exploring Hainaut

Numbers in the margin correspond to points of interest on the Hainaut map.

❶ Driving south on E19, you're in **Beersel** almost before leaving Brussels. It is the site of a stark 13th-century fort, the **Kastel van Beersel,** surrounded by a moat. One of the rooms is a well-equipped torture chamber. *Lotsestraat, tel. 02/331–0024. Admission: BF60. Open Mar.–mid-Nov., Tues.–Sun. 10–noon and 2–6; mid-Nov.–Dec. and Feb., weekends 10:30–5.*

From Beersel you can proceed west past St-Pieters-Leeuw and follow the signs to **Gaasbeek.** The area is called Pajottenland, and you may be familiar with the landscape from Bruegel's works, many of which were painted here. **Gaasbeek Château** was restored in the 19th century; it contains outstanding 15th- and 16th-century tapestries. Rubens's will is among the documents in the castle archives. The surrounding park is popular with picnickers. *Kasteelstraat 40, tel. 02/532–4372. Admission: BF120. Open Apr.–June and Sept.–Oct., Tues.–Thurs. and weekends 10–5; July–Aug., Sat.–Thurs. 10–5.*

❸ South of Gaasbeek, **Halle** is worth a stop for its ***basiliek*** (basilica), which dates from the 14th century. The south portal is decorated with a sculpture of the Virgin and Child surrounded by angels playing musical instruments. Inside, the main religious treasure is the allegedly miraculous Black Virgin; artistically, the focus is on 15th-century sculptures of the apostles from the school of Claus Sluter, the celebrated sculptor at the court of the Duke of Bourgogne in Dijon. *Open for visits daily 9–5 except during services.*

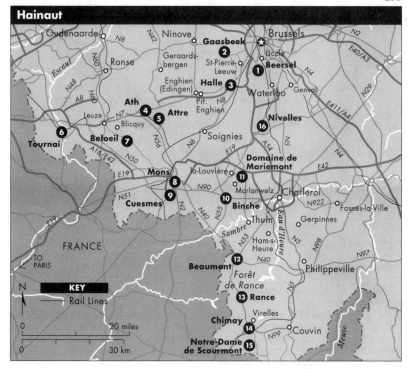

Hainaut

South of Halle on the A8 motorway, at the linguistic frontier at Enghien/Edingen, signs begin to refer to Tournai rather than **4** Doornik. From here N7 leads to **Ath,** where amid great jubilation, giants run wild on the fourth Sunday of August during the celebration of the **ducasse,** an event of unknown origin that goes back at least to the 15th century. The principal figures, 4½ meters (15 feet) high, represent Monsieur and Madame Gouyasse (Goliath), the four sons of Aymon on their steed Bayard, Samson, Ambiorix (who fought against the Romans), and Mam'zelle Victoire, representing the town of Ath.

5 In nearby **Attre** stands the splendid **Château d'Attre,** built in 1752 and preserved intact. Among its treasures are paintings by Franz Snyders and Bartolomé Murillo. *Admission: BF120. Open Apr.– Oct., weekends 10–noon and 2–6; July–Aug., Thurs.–Tues. 10– noon and 2–6.*

6 **Tournai** shares with Tongeren the distinction of being one of the oldest cities in Belgium. It was important in the time of the Romans, and later it was the home of France's Merovingian kings; Clovis was born here in 465. At various times, Tournai has been English, French, and Austrian. Through these vicissitudes the city remained a flourishing center of art. The German bombardment in May 1940 destroyed virtually all the priceless old buildings, with the exception of a few Romanesque structures from the early 13th century and some Gothic buildings, built some 200 years earlier. The **Cathédrale Notre-Dame,** with its five towers, all different, dominates the city today. Begun in 1110 and completed in 60 years, it is the most original work of religious architecture in Belgium and the progenitor of a distinctive style that spread from Tournai down the River Escaut (Scheldt).

You get the best general view of the cathedral from place Paul-Emile Janson, and you need to walk around it to get the full effect of its vast proportions and the massive silhouettes of the five towers. Inside is an overpowering Renaissance screen in polychrome marble. The transept, almost a cathedral within the cathedral, contains the remains of 12th-century frescoes and well-restored 14th-century windows. In the chapels are paintings by Rubens, Pourbus the Elder, and Martin de Vos. Foremost among the objects in the treasury are reliquaries in gilded copper and silver by two of the great 13th-century silversmiths, Nicholas de Verdun and Hugo d'Oignies. *Pl. Paul-Émile Janson. Open Easter–Sept., daily 8:30–6; Oct.–Easter, daily 8:30–4:30. Treasury open Easter–Sept., daily 10–noon and 1–6; Oct.–Easter, daily 10–noon and 1–4:30.*

Time Out **A l'Bancloque** (rue des Chapeliers 46, tel. 069/222149) is a classic Belgian drinking room with high, coffered ceilings and an old stone fireplace.

To see Tournai from the river, take a one-hour trip by sightseeing boat from the landing stage below the Pont des Trous, a 13th-century fortified bridge built to control river access. *Fare: BF80. Hrs: May–Aug., Tues.–Sun. at 11, 2:30, and 4:15.*

Tapestry-making has a long tradition in Tournai, and you can see an outstanding selection of tapestries from the Middle Ages to the present day in the new **Musée de la Tapisserie.** You can also see tapestry weaving and restoration in studios in the museum. *Pl. Reine Astrid, tel. 069/234285. Admission: BF50. Open Wed.–Mon. 10–noon and 2–5:30.*

The star-shaped **Musée des Beaux Arts** was designed by architect Victor Horta, of Art Nouveau fame. Its exceptional collection of early Flemish art includes works by native son Roger de la Pasture, better known as Roger Van der Weyden, as well as some Impressionist masterpieces by Manet, and modern Belgian art. *Enclos St. Martin, tel. 069/222045. Admission: BF50. Open Wed.–Mon. 10–noon and 2–5:30.*

From Tournai, head east on A16 in the direction of Mons, keeping an
❼ eye peeled for signs to **Beloeil,** home of the princes de Ligne since the 14th century. The 17th-century château is partially a reconstruction from the original plans, following a fire in 1900. It contains fine furniture and tapestries, and the heirlooms include gifts from Marie Antoinette and Catherine the Great, friends of the Maréchal de Ligne; his grandson was offered, but refused, the Belgian crown. The elegant park is patterned on Versailles. *Tel. 069/689426. Admission: BF280. Open Apr.–Oct., daily 10–6.*

❽ A16 takes you quickly on to **Mons,** in the heart of the Borinage mining district, administrative center of the province of Hainaut. Its hilly streets, lined with elegant if grimy 17th- and 18th-century brick houses, have considerable charm. It was at Mons that the British Expeditionary Force first joined battle with the Germans in August 1914. In September 1944, further destruction was wrought by a running battle between advancing American troops and the retreating Germans.

At the highest point stands a remarkable **belfry,** known locally as *le château,* for it is next to the site of the castle of the counts of Hainaut. The 87-meter-high (285-foot-high) Baroque tower, crowned by an onion dome, was built in the 17th century. Restoration is in progress, and the tower cannot be visited.

Rue des Clercs takes you to the **Collégiale Ste-Waudru** (Collegiate Church of St. Waudru), named for the wife of a Merovingian dignitary who, legend has it, founded a monastery in the 7th century around which the city developed. The church was begun in 1450 by the ladies of St. Waudru's noble chapter of secular canonesses. The Car d'Or (Golden Coach) carries the reliquary of St. Waudru on Trinity Sunday (first Sun. after Pentecost). *Treasury admission: BF30. Open June–Sept., Tues.–Sun. 2–5.*

Time Out   You can grab a bite or eat more ambitiously at **Le St-Germain-Saey** (Grand'Place 12), which is also a patisserie.

The area around Mons is dotted with conical slag heaps, reminders of a coal mining past that came to an end in the 1950s. **Grand-Hornu,** 13 kilometers (8 miles) west of the city, provides a striking example of an effort to humanize working conditions. The vast complex of workshops, offices, and housing, including a library, dance hall, and bathhouse, was built by Henri De Gorge in the early 19th century in a neoclassical style, with arcades, pediments, and half-moon windows. It served its purpose for well over a century. This fascinating exercise in industrial archaeology was rescued from demolition and is now a multipurpose cultural site. *Hornu, tel. 065/770712. Admission free. Open Mar.–Sept., Tues.–Sun. 10–noon and 2–6; Oct.–Feb., Tues.–Sun. 10–noon and 2–4.*

Vincent van Gogh came to the Borinage, the area south of Mons, as a preacher in 1878, and stayed with a family of miners, the Decrucqs, in **Cuesmes,** just south of the city. It was here that he began drawing the landscape and scenes of the miners' lives. The **house,** in which his room has been reconstituted, still stands. *Rue du Pavillon 3, tel. 065/355611. Open Tues.–Sun. 10–6.*

From Mons the Charleroi road, N90, leads to **Binche,** whose center is still intact behind its 25 towers and 2.4 kilometers (1½ miles) of ramparts. Binche is the only remaining walled city in Belgium, but it is for its **carnival** that the city is famed. The carnival begins the Sunday before Ash Wednesday, when, first, hundreds of transvestite Mam'zelles dance in the streets to the music of fiddles, barrel organs, and drums, and, later, 1,500 Binche dancers make a procession. Shrove Tuesday is the big day. The Gilles (dancers whose role originated in the 16th century when lords dressed as Incas or Indians, representing recently discovered America, performed to entertain Charles V; the role evolved into an incarnation of the rites of nature) start assembling at dawn, wearing their fantastic costumes of red and yellow. Their magnificent hats are crowned with huge plumes of ostrich feathers, and their white masks are painted with green spectacles and mustaches. To the rhythm of drums, the Gilles move through the streets in a slow, shuffling dance. The day ends with fireworks, but the Gilles continue dancing through the night. Traditionally, they drink nothing but champagne.

The **Musée International du Carnaval et du Masque** contains an extraordinary collection of masks and costumes from all over the world, and there's an audiovisual presentation of the local carnival, in case you're in Binche at the wrong time for the real thing. *Rue du St-Moustier 14, tel. 064/335741. Admission free. Open mid-Jan.–mid-Nov., Mon.–Thurs. 9–noon and 2–5, Sat. 2–6, Sun. 10–noon and 2–6.*

From Binche, N563 goes north to the expressway to Brussels. On
⑪ the left at the turn at Morlanwelz is the **Domaine de Mariemont.**
There's nothing left of the châteaus that have successively stood
here, but the 110-acre English park is one of the most attractive in
Belgium, decorated with sculptures by a number of artists, including Auguste Rodin and Constantin Meunier. The well-laid-out museum contains excellent collections of Chinese art, archaeological
finds, and Tournai porcelain. *Chaussée de Mariemont, tel. 064/
212193. Admission free. Open Tues.–Sun. 10–6.*

N55 south from Binche leads to the country *Entre Sambre-et-Meuse*
(between the area's two principal rivers). Turn left on N40 and
⑫ you're soon in **Beaumont** with its **Tour Salamandre,** all that remains
of a major fortified castle built in the 11th century. The tower has
been restored and houses a museum of local and regional history.
*Tel. 071/588191. Admission: BF50. Open May–Sept., daily 9–noon
and 2–7; Oct., Sun. 10–noon and 2–5.*

⑬ To the south on N53 is **Rance,** known for its quarries, which furnished the red marble for St. Peter's in Rome. The excellent **Musée
National du Marbre** (National Marble Museum), is here. *Tel. 060/
412048. Admission: BF100. Open Apr.–Oct., Tues.–Sat. 9:30–6,
Sun. 2–6.*

Continuing through the Forêt de Rance, one eventually reaches
⑭ **Chimay,** the home of Froissart, the great 14th-century historian
whose chronicles furnished the background information for some of
Shakespeare's plays.

The town has more vivid memories of Madame Tallien, a great beauty who was known to revolutionary France as Notre Dame de Ther-
midor. She narrowly escaped the guillotine, married her protector,
Citizen Tallien, and persuaded him to instigate the overthrow of
Robespierre. Eventually she was again married, to Francois-Jo-
seph Caraman, prince de Chimay, and ended her days in peace and
dignity as mistress of the **Château de Chimay.** The warrant for her
arrest, signed by Robespierre, is preserved at the château along
with other memorabilia, such as the baptismal robe worn by
Napoléon's son, the king of Rome. *Grand'Place, tel. 060/211846. Admission: BF150. Guided tours Mar.–Nov., daily 10–noon and 2–6.*

⑮ South of Chimay is the Trappist monastery of **Notre-Dame de
Scourmont.** The abbey cannot be visited (except on retreats), but
you can buy the excellent cheese and stout beer produced by the
brothers.

⑯ **Nivelles** is one more old town that suffered terribly from bombardment in May 1940, when more than 500 buildings were destroyed.
Again, it is the church that survived. The **Collégiale Ste-Gertrude**
(St. Gertrude's Collegiate Church) bears the name of the daughter
of Pepin the Old, who founded a convent here about AD 650. It is the
country's finest Romanesque building, with two transepts and
choirs at opposite ends. The size and simplicity of the interior are
impressive. The crypt contains the burial vaults of St. Gertrude and
her parents, and vestiges of the five churches that preceded the
present one on the same spot. *1-hr tours of the church at 10, 11, 2, 3
and 4. Admission: BF50. Closed Sun. AM.*

Time Out   Locals swear by **Pâtisserie Courtain** (blvd. Fleur de Lys 14) for the
local Nivelles specialty, *tarte al djote,* a succulent cheese and vegetable pie, served hot.

On N237, 13 kilometers (8 miles) east of Nivelles, is **Villers-la-Ville,** and at the crossroads north of the village lie the remarkable **Abbey Ruins.** St. Bernard himself laid the foundation stone in 1147, and the cloister, dormitories, refectory, and chapter hall, all in true Cistercian style, are impressive. *Tel. 071/879898. Admission: BF50. Open mid-Mar.–Oct., daily 10–6.*

What to See and Do with Children

There's a full-scale **old steam train** providing service between Charleroi and Mariembourg to the south. *Round-trip fare: BF200. Easter–June and Sept., weekends; July–Aug., Sat.–Tues. and Thurs.*

The **Eau-d'Heure Lakes,** on the N40 between Beaumont and Philippeville, is a wild, wooded 4,500-acre park with lakes and grassy valleys. There are aquariums, a panoramic tower, water sports, and marked trails. *Tel. 071/633534. Admission: BF180. Open Easter–Sept., daily 9–6.*

For the **Centre de Loisirs de l'Orient,** take E42 toward Tournai to Exit 32. The large center has boats, games, barbecues, and a café. *Chemin de Mons 8. Open Apr.–Sept., daily 10–10.*

At Blicquy-Aubechies, near Beloeil, the **Archeosite** is a collection of prehistoric and Gallo-Roman houses, with mud walls, thatched roofs, and authentic interiors, that have been reconstructed according to plans found during their excavation. *Tel. 069/662938. Admission: BF70. Open Nov.–Easter, weekdays 9–5; Easter–Oct., weekdays 9–5, weekends 2–6.*

Shopping

Mons The smart shops are found in the pedestrian rue de la Chaussée and around the city's Grand'Place. On Sunday mornings there is a flea market on the place Simonet.

Tournai There's a lively pedestrian area, known simply as **Le Pietonnier,** near the post office. Other shopping streets are rue Royale and the streets branching off from the Grand'Place. Lively Saturday morning **markets** take place on the Grand'Place, place St-Pierre, and place Paul-Emile Janson, as well as along the quai du Marché aux Poissons. Sunday-morning flea markets are held on place St-Pierre and in the shopping gallery off rue du Cygne. There are many **antiques** dealers in the area around the Eglise St-Jacques (St. James's Church).

Sports and the Outdoors

Archery You can practice crossbow shooting at the **Arbaletriers Beaumontois** (Parc de Paridaens, Beaumont, tel. 071/588609), or archery at the **Club Saint-Sebastien** (rue de Mons 3, Beaumont, tel. 060/512307).

Golf There's a public, 18-hole golf course west of **Mons, Golf Public** (rue du Mont Garni 3, Baudour, tel. 065/622719).

Horseback Riding Horseback riding is popular in many parts of the province, particularly in the less densely populated south. You can arrange treks with the **Centre Equestre des Fagnes** (rue de la Fagne 20, **Chimay,** tel. 060/411169).

Tennis Try the **Waux-Hall** (av. Reine Astrid 22, **Mons,** tel. 065/339089); **Se-quoia Tennis Club** (rue du Sequoia 33, **Ath,** tel. 068/285264); or **Plaine de Jeux Bozière** (av. Bozière 1B, **Tournai,** tel. 069/223586).

Dining and Lodging

From the ancient Frankish capital of Tournai to the greenery sur-rounding Chimay, there's no shortage here of memorable old inns and atmospheric restaurants.

Chimay **Hostellerie du Gahy.** Overlooking a large garden, this small inn has
Dining and six rooms decorated in traditional style. The cuisine is ambitious:
Lodging Try the lobster with vanilla flavoring in puff pastry or quails stuffed with foie gras. Half board (a good buy) is obligatory in summer. *Rue Gahy 2, tel. 060/511093, fax 060/512879. 6 rooms with bath. Facili-ties: restaurant (closed Sun. dinner, Mon., Wed. dinner). AE, MC, V. $$*

★ **Le Virelles.** Just north of Chimay, in the open greenery around the Etang de Virelles, this charming old country inn offers simple, mid-dle-class regional cooking in a pretty, well-weathered beam-and-copper setting. You can have trout or *escavèche* (a spicy, cold mari-nade of cooked fish), or a more ambitious, multicourse menu based on regional plenty (freshwater fish and game). Rooms, named after field flowers, are simple and cozy, some with four-poster beds. The adjacent nature reserve is great for long walks. *Rue du Lac 28, B-6431 Virelles-Chimay, tel. 060/212803. 8 rooms with bath or shower. Facilities: restaurant (closed Tues. dinner and Wed., except in July/Aug.), café. AE, DC, MC, V. $*

Mons **Alter Ego.** This handsome, stylish brasserie offers regionally in-
Dining spired cuisine: head cheese with sweet garlic, saddle of rabbit with rosemary, and outstanding mousse au chocolat. You get excellent value for your money here. *Rue Nimy 6, tel. 065/351730. Reserva-tions advised. Jacket and tie advised. AE, DC, MC, V. Closed Sun. dinner, Mon., mid-July–mid-Aug. $$*

Tournai **Le Pressoir.** Tucked down at the end of the Marché aux Poteries, be-
Dining tween the cathedral and the Beffroi, this chic, unpretentious restau-
★ rant combines historical atmosphere (exposed brick, illuminated oil paintings) with surprising urbanity: The bar draws BCBG (*bon chic–bon genre*) clientele, and the restaurant hosts visiting VIPs. Try the saffron-perfumed bouillabaise of *rouget* (red mullet) or confit of farm pigeon with young turnips. *Marché aux Poteries 2, tel. 069/223513. Reservations advised. Jacket and tie advised. AE, DC, MC, V. Closed Mon. dinner, Tues., Wed.–Thurs. dinner, Carnival week, last 3 weeks of Aug. $$–$$$*

Bistro de la Cathédrale. This modernized, brightly lighted store-front restaurant offers a few very reasonable menus and large por-tions of good, simple, well-prepared food: sparkling-fresh oysters, salads of *crevettes grise* (gray shrimp), sole meunière, rabbit with prunes. The ambience is casual, the staff friendly. *Vieux Marché aux Poteries 15, tel. 069/210379. Dress: casual. AE, DC, MC, V. $*

Lodging **Cathédrale** (formerly Condor). This is a fully modernized chain-style business hotel at the foot of the cathedral in the center. The rooms are laminate-spare, and some look onto the small square. *Pl. St-Pierre, B-7500, tel. 069/215077. 45 rooms. Facilities: restaurant, café. AE, DC, MC, V. $$*

L'Europe. Well placed on the Grand'Place, with rooms looking out toward the Beffroi and historic architecture, this is a comfortable hotel in an old step-gabled house. The rooms have been cheaply re-decorated with a lavish touch; most have toilets down the hall. The restaurant/tavern downstairs draws crowds of locals for stone-grilled meats. *Grand'Place 36, B-7500, tel. 069/224067. 8 rooms. Facilities: restaurant, tavern. AE, DC, MC, V. $*

The Arts and Nightlife

The Arts There are several noteworthy museums in the region: In Tournai the **Musée des Beaux-Arts** (Enclos St. Martin, tel. 069/222045; open Wed.–Mon. 10–noon and 2–5:30) has good collections of Flemish primitives and Impressionists; in Charleroi the **Musée de la Photographie** (av. Paul Pastur 11, tel. 071/435810; admission: BF100; open Tues.–Sun. 10–6) features historical photographic exhibits as well as contemporary work; and in Mons the **Musée des Beaux-Arts** (rue Neuve, tel. 065/349555; open Tues.–Sun. 10–12:30 and 2–6) has interesting temporary exhibitions. In Charleroi the **Palais des Beaux-Arts** (pl. du Manege 7, tel. 071/311212) is a multicultural center for opera, theater, dance, and popular music.

Nightlife There's hardly a village anymore that doesn't have its own disco. In **Charleroi** try **La Reserve** at the Palais des Beaux-Arts. **Parisiana** (rue du Commerce 3) has a floor show, and **Le Carré Blanc** (rue Leopold 18) is for the younger set. In **Mons**, the **Voum-Voum** (rue de la Coupe 44) is for dancing and the **New Blue Note** (av. Roi Albert 667) is for devotees of jazz.

Ghent, Brugge, and the Coast

Brugge and Ghent are the art cities of Flanders that represent the flowering of the late Middle Ages. The North Sea Coast provided irresistible sandy shores on which the Vikings beached their longboats, and it was to fend off these marauders that Baldwin of the Iron Arm, first count of Flanders, built the original fortifications at both Brugge and Ghent. The cities came to prominence as centers of the cloth trade. Flemish weavers had been renowned since the days of the Romans, but it was in the Middle Ages that they began to use the finest wool from England, Scotland, and Ireland, and their products became truly superior. Thus the English acquired an interest in keeping Flanders from the French. This early form of industrialization also prepared the ground for communal strife, pitting common weavers against patrician merchants.

The destinies of the two cities diverged in the 19th century; Brugge settled into a graceful decline from which it has only roused itself in the last few decades. Ghent, however, embraced the industrial revolution, becoming an important textile center once more. The cities of Kortrijk and Ieper to the south recall the long history of battles fought in the region since the time of Julius Caesar. The North Sea Coast continues to be irresistible to invaders, but now they are sunseekers and beach lovers.

Important Addresses and Numbers

Tourist Information The **Tourist Office for Flanders** in Brussels is at rue du Marché-aux-Herbes 61 (tel. 02/504–0390). Information on the area as a whole can be obtained from **Westtoerisme** (Kasteel Tillegem, Brugge, tel. 050/380296). Local tourist offices are as follows: **Blankenberge:** Leopold III plein (tel. 050/412227); **Brugge** (Toerisme Brugge): Burg 11 (tel. 050/448686); **Ghent** (Dienst voor Toerisme): Predikherenlei 2 (tel.

09/225–3641) and Town Hall (Botermarkt, tel. 09/224–1555); **De Haan:** Leopoldlaan 24 (tel. 059/235723); **Ieper:** Stadhuis, Grote Markt (tel. 057/200724); **Knokke-Heist:** Zeedijk 660 (tel. 050/601616); **Kortrijk:** Schouwburgplein (tel. 056/239371); **Nieuwpoort:** Marktplein 7 (tel. 058/235594); **Oostende:** Wapenplein 3 (tel. 059/701199); **De Panne:** Zeelaan 21 (tel. 058/421818).

Emergencies **Police:** tel. 101. **Ambulance:** tel. 100. **Hospital emergency room, Ghent:** tel. 09/240–2742. The name of the on-duty **late-night pharmacy** is posted in all pharmacy windows.

Arriving and Departing

By Car The six-lane A10/E40 from Brussels passes both Ghent and Brugge en route to Oostende. Traffic is sometimes bumper-to-bumper on summer weekends, making it a better alternative to take N9 from Ghent via Brugge; for Knokke, you branch off on N49. A back road to the resorts southwest of Oostende is N43 from Ghent to Deinze and then N35 to the coast. E17 links Kortrijk with Ghent. A19 links Kortrijk with Ieper and will eventually continue to the coast.

By Train **Brugge** is a major stop on the important London–Brussels–Cologne railway line. There is half-hourly service from Brussels (50 min) and Oostende (15 min). All Brussels–Oostende trains (1 hr and 10 min) also stop at **Ghent.** For train information in Ghent, call 09/221–4444; in Brugge, call 050/382382; and in Oostende, call 059/701517. There's also train service to Blankenberge, Knokke-Heist, and Zeebrugge.

By Ship **Sally Line** (in the U.K., tel. 01843/595522) car ferry has up to six sailings a day from Ramsgate to Oostende (4 hrs) and **P&O Ferries** (tel. 01304/203388) two sailings a day from Felixstowe to Zeebrugge (6 hrs). **North Sea Ferries** (in the U.K., tel. 01482/77177) offers overnight sailings from Hull to Zeebrugge (14 hrs). Foot passengers only are carried by Jetfoil from Ramsgate to Oostende (1 hr and 40 min, up to 4 daily crossings).

Getting Around Ghent, Brugge, and the Coast

Brugge The center of Brugge is best seen on foot. The winding streets may confuse your sense of direction, but if you look up, there's always the Belfry to guide you back to the Markt. Sturdy footwear is recommended.

Access for cars and coaches into the old city is restricted. There are only five routes into the city. Most of the cobbled streets have been turned into one-way routes, and the Markt is closed to through traffic. A new computer-controlled traffic light system is being installed on the ring road around Brugge.

By Bus The **De Lijn** bus company (tel. 078/113663; fare BF40, 10-trip tickets BF230) runs most buses every 20 minutes, including Sundays. New minibuses, designed to penetrate the narrow streets, are now in service.

By Taxi There are big taxi stands at the station (tel. 050/384660) and at the Markt (tel. 050/334444).

By Bicycle As traffic is of necessity slow-moving, this is a good way to get around Brugge and environs. Bikes can be rented at the **railway station** (BF150 per day with a valid train ticket), at **Eric Popelier** (Hallestraat 14, around the corner from the Belfry, tel. 050/343262; BF150 for 4 hrs, BF250 for the day), at **Koffiebontje** (Hallestraat 4, tel. 050/338027; same rates), or at **De Ketting** (Gentpoortstraat 23, tel. 050/344196; same rates).

Ghent Most of the sights in the center of town are within a radius of a kilometer (½ mile) of the Stadhuis (Town Hall), and the preferred way to see them is on foot.

By Tram If you arrive by train, take Tram 1, 11, or 12 (fare: BF40) for the city center.

By Taxi There are taxi stands at the railway station and at major squares.

By Bicycle You can rent a bike at the **train station** (BF150 a day with valid rail ticket). Note: Traffic is quite a bit heavier than in Brugge.

The Coast There's tram service—a happily preserved relic of another era—all
By Tram the way from Knokke to De Panne. The trams are modern, and it's a pleasant ride, but don't expect uninterrupted views of the sea; the tram tracks are on the leeward side of the dike. Tickets cost about BF50 depending on distance. A one-day ticket comes to BF290; a five-day ticket is BF840. For information, call 078/113663.

By Car The coastal road, N34, is very busy in summer. Allow ample time for driving between resorts.

Guided Tours

Brugge **Bruges with Bart,** (tel. 050/333709, 8–9 AM or 9–10 PM; cost: BF350)
By Bicycle offers bicycle tours of the city beginning at 10 AM every day on the Markt. They last just under two hours.

The **Back Road Bike Co.** (tel. 050/343045) organizes **bicycle** tours covering six villages near Brugge. Mountain bikes are supplied, and the guided four-hour rides take only back roads.

By Boat Independent motor launches depart from five jetties along the Dijver and Katelijnestraat as soon as they are reasonably full (every 15 minutes or so). The trips take just over half an hour. *Fare: BF150 adults, BF75 children. Operated daily 10–6 Mar.–Nov.; Dec. and Feb., weekends only.*

By You may have to wait for more than an hour for a short ride with
Horse-Drawn inadequate commentary and then be asked for "something for the
Carriage horse." Kids love it, however. Carriages wait in the Burg (cost: BF800; Wed. AM at the Belfry).

By Minibus The 50-minute **Sightseeing Line** tour gives a good if impersonal overview of Brugge's attractions. No visits are included, and the commentary is taped. *The Markt, tel. 050/311315. Fare: BF330 adults, BF200 children. Hourly July–Aug., 10–7; tapering off to Jan.–Feb., 11–1.*

Quasimodo Tours (tel. 050/370470; fare: BF840) operates a "Fields of Flanders" full-day bus tour on Monday and Saturday, April 1 through October 31.

Personal You can book an English-speaking guide through the **tourist office**
Guides (tel. 050/448686). Guides charge a minimum of BF1,200 for two hours, BF500 per extra hour. In July and August, groups are consolidated at the tourist office every day at 3 PM; cost per person is BF100 (children free).

Ghent **Benelux-Gent Watertoerist** sightseeing boats depart from the old
By Boat landing stages at Graslei and Korenlei for 35-minute trips on the Ghent waterways. *Tel. 09/282–9418. Fare: BF120 adults, BF70 children. Operated Easter–Oct.*

A full-day **Museum Line** excursion on the River Leie, leaving Ghent at 9 AM and returning at 8 PM, is operated on Thursdays from May to September. *Benelux Co., Recollettenlei 10, Ghent, tel. 09/225–1505. Bookings required.*

By Horse-Drawn Carriage Carriages wait in the Sint-Baafsplein to take you on a half-hour trip that gives a general idea of the city center. *Cost: BF700 for up to 4 persons. Operated Easter–Oct.*

Personal Guides In addition to a standard tour, you can ask for accompanied visits to other sights and museums. Guides charge BF1,200 for the first two hours and BF500 per additional hour. For bookings, call **Gidsenbond van Gent** (Association of Ghent Guides, tel. 09/233–0772, fax 09/233–0865).

The Coast **Quasimodo** (tel. 050/370470; price: BF850) has all-day minibus tours from Brugge on Wednesday and Friday in season. The English-language tour includes a drive along the coast.

Exploring Ghent, Brugge, and the Coast

The wealth of the Flemish cities was created by the weaving trade. The sumptuous clothing so lovingly depicted in numerous paintings was all locally produced. The merchants built their magnificent houses in Flemish style, and they engaged Flemish artists to paint their portraits. Flemish architects designed the churches and town halls. All of this combined to create a remarkable homogeneity, and in that sense Brugge and Ghent are indeed twin towns, and Kortrijk, Ieper, and the others are the closest of kin. It also helped shape the Flemish identity, and even today many a Fleming would, if left to his own devices, build himself a home that would not look out of place in medieval Brugge or Ghent.

Tour 1: Ghent

Numbers in the margin correspond to points of interest on the Ghent, Brugge, and the Coast map.

❶ The Flemish call it Gent; the French, Gand. The English variant, **Ghent,** exists only to prevent a mispronunciation. Long ago, however, the English called it Gaunt, as in John of Gaunt; English links with the city go back to the 14th century.

The city grew up around two 7th-century abbeys, Sint-Pieter (St. Peter) and Sint-Baafs (St. Bavo), and the 9th-century castle of 's-Gravensteen, which dominates the River Leie. The canal joining Ghent and Brugge's port at Damme was dug in the 13th century, and a hundred years later more than 5,000 men were working at the weaver's trade in Ghent.

In the early Middle Ages, the wealthy burghers were loyal to the counts of Flanders, who owed allegiance to the kings of France. But the weavers were dependent for their livelihood on wool shipments from England. Patrician families built fortified houses to make themselves secure in their own town; a few of them still stand.

In 1448, the people of Ghent refused to pay a salt tax imposed by Philip the Good, duke of Burgundy. For five years their militia stood firm against Philip's troops, and when they were finally overwhelmed, 16,000 townspeople perished. Ghent continued to rebel, again and again, against perceived injustices. The emperor himself, Charles V, who was born in Ghent, was not immune to their wrath. He responded by razing the St. Bavo Abbey and suppressing city

Ghent, Brugge, and the Coast

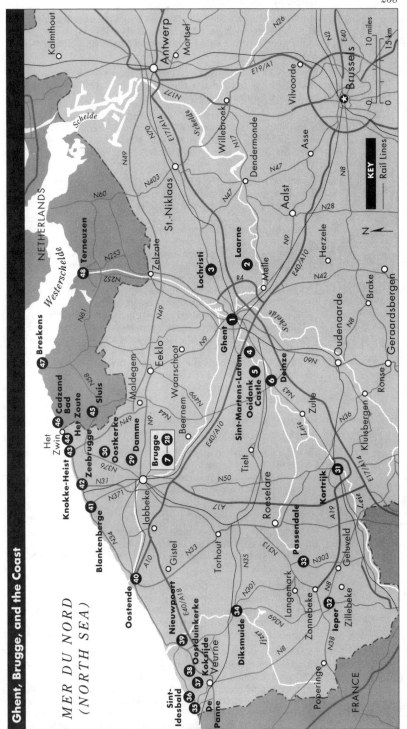

*MER DU NORD
(NORTH SEA)*

NETHERLANDS

FRANCE

Kalmhout

Antwerp
Mortsel

Brussels

Vilvoorde

Willebroek

Dendermonde

Asse

Aalst

Herzele

Brake

Geraardsbergen

Ronse

Oudenaarde

Kluisbergen

Geluweld

Zillebeke

Zonnebeke

Poperinge

Langemark

Torhout

Gistel

Ieper **32**

Diksmuide **34**

Passendale **33**

Langemark

Roeselare

Tielt

Deinze **6**

Zulte

Kortrijk **31**

Sint-Martens-Latem

Ooidonk Castle **5**

Deinze **4**

Ghent **1**

Lochristi **3**

Laarne **2**

Melle

St.-Niklaas

Zelzate

Terneuzen **48**

Breskens **47**

Cadzand Bad **46**

Sluis **45**

Het Zoute **44**

Knokke-Heist **43**

Zeebrugge **42**

Blankenberge **41**

Oostende **40**

Nieuwpoort **39**

Oostduinkerke **38**

Koksijde **37**

De Panne

Sint-Idesbald **36 35**

Veurne

Oostkerke **30**

Damme **29**

Brugge **7 — 28**

Jabbeke

Eeklo

Maldegem

Beernem

Waarschoot

Het Zwin

KEY
— Rail Lines

N
10 miles
15 km

rights. Religious fervor was added to this volatile mixture when the Calvinist iconoclasts proclaimed a republic in 1577, only to be overthrown by Spanish forces seven years later.

In the 18th century French armies marched on Ghent on four different occasions. This did little to dampen the conflict between French and Flemish speakers in the city.

Ghent was rescued from economic oblivion by a daring young man named Lieven Bauwens, who in 1800 smuggled a spinning jenny out of Britain in a neat reversal of what had happened hundreds of years earlier, when Flemish weavers emigrated to England. Bauwens's exploit provided the foundation for a textile industry that employed 160,000 workers a century later.

To facilitate textile exports, a new canal was built to link Ghent's inland port with the North Sea. It remains the foundation for modern industrial development, drawing a Volvo assembly plant and huge car carriers filled with Hondas.

The best spot to start a walk around Ghent is on **Sint-Michielsbrug** (St. Michael's Bridge), with its view of the glory of Ghent, the three great medieval steeples. Closest by is the tower of the **Sint-Niklaaskerk** (St. Nicholas's Church), the parish church of Ghent's merchants. Its sober, early Gothic style is sometimes called Scheldt Gothic, for it traveled down the River Scheldt from Tournai, where it originated. Next comes the **Belfort** (Belfry), begun in 1314 and not really completed until 1913, when the spire with its gilded details was added, based on the original 14th-century elevation. In the background stands the honey-colored sandstone tower of the **Sint-Baafskathedraal** (St. Bavo's Cathedral), begun in the 13th century but finished in the 16th in the ornate Brabant Gothic style.

Across the bridge, turn right and walk down the steps to Korenlei. Here is another magnificent view: the **Graslei** on the other side of the River Leie. The row of buildings along this old quay was restored for the World's Fair of 1913. The guild house of the **Vrije Schippers** (Free Boatmen) at No. 14 is a late-Gothic building from 1531; the guild dominated inland shipping. No. 11 is the **Korenmetershuis** (Grain Measurers' House), a late-Baroque building from 1698. Next to it is the narrow Renaissance **Tolhuis** (Toll House), where taxes were levied on grain shipments. It stands side by side with the brooding Romanesque **Koornstapelhuis** (Granary), nicknamed the *Spijker* (Spike), which was built in the 12th century and served its original purpose for 600 years; this was where the grain that the tax men had claimed was stored. The guild house of the **Metselaars** (Stone Masons), finally, is a copy of a house from 1527 constructed on this site in 1913. The original, which stands near the transept of St. Nicholas's Church, has also recently been restored. Every night in season (Fri.–Sat. nights Nov.–Apr.), the Graslei and all other historic monuments are illuminated from sunset to midnight.

From the Grasbrug at the end of Korenlei you have a fine view of the old **Groot Vleeshuis** (Great Meat Hall), an early 15th-century sandstone building on the bank of the Leie, almost at its confluence with the Lieve Canal. Turning back from the bridge and continuing north on Jan Breydelstraat you come to the **Museum voor Sierkunst** (Museum of Decorative Arts), with splendid 18th-century salons and a new contemporary design section. *Jan Breydelstraat 5. Admission: BF80. Open Tues.–Sun. 9–12:30 and 1:30–5:30.*

Time Out If you're wandering around after 7 PM, stop in at **Tap en Tepel** (Gewad 7, tel. 09/223–9000; closed Mon.–Wed. and Aug.), a wine and cheese house filled with flickering candles and lined with shelves of wine bottles.

Turn toward the canal on Burgstraat, and as you cross the Hoofdbrug, **'s-Gravensteen,** the castle of the counts of Flanders, looks rather like an enormous old battleship, improbably steaming down the Lieve Canal. Even today, there's a splendid view over the rooftops of old Ghent from its windswept battlements. Rebuilt a number of times—most recently in the 19th century to reflect what the Victorians thought a medieval castle should look like—it has little in common with the original fortress conceived by Count Baldwin (of the Iron Arm) to discourage marauding Norsemen. *Sint-Veerleplein, tel. 09/225–9306. Admission: BF80. Open Apr.–Sept., daily 9–6, 9–5 Oct.–Mar. Guided tours in English Apr.–Oct., weekends at 11 AM.*

Its purpose, too, changed from protection to oppression as the conflict deepened between feudal lords and unruly townspeople. One of the rooms contains an exhibition of instruments of torture, and there is an *oubliette* (secret dungeon), deep below the floor of another room. It was here that Lieven Bauwens's purloined spinning mule was installed, the first on the Continent; soon the castle's chambers were invaded by clattering looms and flying shuttles, and Ghent became a textile center to rival Manchester.

Many of the workers lived in the **Patershol** area. You reach it by crossing Sint-Veerleplein, taking the Kraanlei, and turning left into one of the narrow lanes. Once a badly neglected slum, this has lately become a desirable address for young and well-to-do families who have converted many of the small houses for their use, interspersed with smart cafés and restaurants.

Back on Kraanlei is the **Museum voor Volkskunde** (Folk Museum), in a 16th-century almshouse. The many small rooms have been reconstructed to convey an idea of life in Ghent a hundred years ago: One room is a grocer's shop, another a tavern, a third a weaver's workshop, and there are several bourgeois rooms. *Kraanlei 65, tel. 09/ 223–1336. Admission: BF50. Open Apr.–Oct., daily 9–12:30 and 1:30–5:30; Nov.–Mar., Tues.–Sun.10–noon and 1:30–5.*

Time Out The popular **Caffe Wolff,** in a Renaissance building at Kraanlei 27 (tel. 09/233–0157), is an excellent stop for coffee and cake, a beer, or an aperitif.

Two Baroque houses along Kraanlei have elaborately decorated facades. The panels of No. 79 represent the five senses, crowned by a figure of a flute player, while those of No. 77 illustrate six acts of mercy. The house used to be an inn, and taking in travelers was considered the seventh act.

Across the river stands a small 15th-century cannon on the right, known as Dulle Griet. Up Meersenierstraat is the **Vrijdagmarkt,** a square that becomes particularly lively during the weekly Friday market. It was here that Jacob Van Artevelde urged the people to take up arms against the French in the Hundred Years' War and here that mass meetings of socialists were held to rouse the workers earlier in this century.

Straight ahead, the second street on the right, Belfortstraat, takes you down toward the Town Hall. At the junction of Hoogport is **Sint-Jorishof** (Botermarkt 2), one of the oldest hotels in the world, in business since 1228. The present step-gabled building was constructed in the 1470s.

In the 13th century, when Ghent's population topped 60,000, there were more than a hundred private homes equipped with towers, from which merchant princes could survey the traffic on the Rivers Leie and Scheldt, and the Lieve Canal. One such family was the Van der Sickelens, and their name lives on in the 14th-century **Kliene Sikkel**, a Romanesque town house of unhewn stone on the corner of Biezekepelstraat; in the **Grote Sikkel** across the street, a less austere building from the 15th century; and in the **Achtersikkel** behind it, the most attractive of the three, with Gothic buildings grouped around a white Renaissance tower. Nowadays, this is the home of the Ghent Conservatory. None of these three buildings is open to visitors.

The **Town Hall** is built in two very different architectural styles. Antwerp's Domien de Waghemakere and Mechelen's Rombout Keldermans were called in to build it in 1516, and they designed a town hall that would put all others to shame. Among its features are the tower on the corner of Hoogpoort and Botermarkt, the balcony expressly built for the announcement of proclamations, the projecting choir of the Magistrates' Chapel, and, above all, the lacelike tracery that embellishes its facade. Before the building could be completed, the taxes imposed by Charles V had drained the city's resources. When work resumed in 1580, during the short-lived Protestant Republic, the Gothic style had fallen from favor and been replaced by that of the Renaissance. *Botermarkt, tel. 09/224–1555. Admission: BF60. Guided visits only. Weekdays 4 PM.*

Just across the Gouden Leeuwplein, named for the Golden Lion of Flanders, stands the proud **Belfort** (Belfry), 91 meters (300 feet) high, which symbolizes the power of the guilds in the 14th century. The Belfry contained the documents listing the privileges of the city, protected behind double doors with triple locks, and bells that were rung in moments of danger until Charles V ordered them removed. Now a 52-bell carillon hangs on the fifth floor, and one of the damaged old bells rests at the foot of the tower. *Sint-Baafsplein, tel. 09/223–9977. Admission: BF100. Open daily 10–12:30, with guided visits 10 min after each hr.*

The Belfry is adjoined by the **Lakenhalle** (Cloth Hall). Its vaulted basement was used as a prison for 150 years and is now a restaurant.

Across the square on the other side of the Belfry is the **Sint Baafskathedraal** (St. Bavo's Cathedral), which contains one of the greatest treasures in Christendom. Originally dedicated to St. John, it became the site for the veneration of Ghent's own saint after Charles V had the old Abbey of St. Bavo razed. The Order of the Golden Fleece—instituted in Brugge by Philip the Good in 1430 and presided over today by King Juan Carlos of Spain as grand master—was convened here in 1559 by Philip II of Spain, and the coats of arms of the 51 knights who attended still hang in the south transept. The remarkably ornate pulpit is carved in white Italian marble and black Danish oak. In one of the radiating chapels hangs a Rubens masterpiece, *Saint Bavo's Entrance into the Monastery.*

It is, however, for *The Adoration of the Mystic Lamb*, now in the De Villa chapel to the left of the entrance, that crowds throng the cathedral. This stupendous polyptych by Hubert and Jan van Eyck was completed in 1432, and it has had a history as tumultuous as that of Ghent itself. When the iconoclasts smashed St. Bavo's stained-glass windows and other treasures, the painting was hidden in the tower.

Napoléon had it carried off to Paris. The panels of Adam and Eve (which Joseph II, a Holy Roman emperor, had found prurient) disappeared and remained lost for a hundred years. The other side panels were sold and hung in a Berlin museum. In 1920 the masterpiece was again complete, but 14 years later a thief removed the panels on the lower left side. He returned St. John the Baptist but apparently died while waiting for a ransom for the panel of the Just Judges. Most people believe the panel is still hidden somewhere in Ghent, possibly even in the cathedral. The whole altarpiece was removed to France for safekeeping during World War II, but the Germans found it and had it taken away. American troops eventually found it in an abandoned salt mine in Austria.

The central panel is based on the Book of Revelations: "And I looked, and, lo, a Lamb stood on the mount Sion, and with him an hundred forty and four thousand, having his Father's name written in their foreheads." There are not quite that many people in the painting, but it does depict 248 figures and 42 different types of flowers, each botanically correct. But statistics do not even suggest its grandeur. It uses a miniaturist technique to express the universal; realism, to portray spirituality. To the medieval viewer it was an artistic *Summa Theologica,* a summation of all things revealed about the relationship between God and the world.

An old tradition identifies the horseman in the foreground of the panel to the immediate left as Hubert van Eyck, while the fourth figure from the left is believed to be his brother Jan. No other work by Hubert van Eyck has survived, and it is thought that he died in about 1426 after working on the altarpiece for four years. Jan was brought from Brugge to continue the work, using brushes so delicate that the finest consisted of a single boar's bristle. It was completed on May 6, 1432. *Sint-Baafsplein. Admission: BF50. Open Apr.–Sept., Mon.–Sat. 9:30–noon and 2–6, Sun. 1–6; Oct.–Mar., Mon.–Sat. 10–noon and 2:30–4, Sun. 2–5. Closed during services.*

In the Vicinity **Laarne Castle** lies 13 kilometers (8 miles) east of Ghent, and you reach it on R4, in the direction of Melle, and then on secondary roads ② to **Laarne.** Built in the 14th century to protect the city's eastern approaches, it was converted to peaceful use in the 17th; it is one of the best-preserved medieval strongholds in Belgium. Inside are fine examples of Brussels tapestry weaving and an outstanding collection of silver from the 15th to the 18th century. *Rte. R4, Exit 5, Heusden–Laarne, tel. 09/230–9155. Admission: BF120. Open July–Aug., daily 10–noon and 2–6; Sept.–Dec. and Feb.–June, Tues.–Sun. 10–noon and 2–6.*

③ Return to Ghent on N449 north, turning west on N70 to **Lochristi.** It is the center of the Ghent flower-growing region, and in season the city and its gardens are a riot of begonias and azaleas.

The shores of the River Leie have attracted many painters. Take ④ N43 in the direction of Deinze, and turn off to **Sint-Martens-Latem** with its 15th-century wooden windmill. Gustave van de Woestyne and his friends worked here in the early years of this century and were followed by Constant Permeke and the Expressionists after World War I. In the neighboring village of **Deurle,** the house and studio of the Ghent painter Gust De Smet has been turned into the **Museum Dhondt-Dhaenens.** It contains a major collection of expressionist paintings, including works by Permeke, Van den Berghe, and Albert Servaes. *Admission: house and studio, each BF20. Both open Mar.–Nov., Wed.–Sat. 2–5, Sun. 10–noon and 2–5.*

❺ On a bend of the river stands **Ooidonk Castle,** a magnificent and largely untouched palatial abode in Hispano-Flemish style, still inhabited. It was the property of Count Hoorn, the Flemish patriot executed in 1568 by the Spanish. *Tel. 09/282–6123. Admission: BF120. Open Easter–mid-Sept., Sun. 2–5:30; July–Aug., also Sat. same hrs. Park open daily.*

❻ In **Deinze,** finally, is an attractive Gothic church next to the river, and beside it the **Museum van Deinze en Leiestreek,** with works by the impressionist Emile Claus as well as by the Latem group of painters. *Lucien Matthyslaan 3, tel. 09/386–0011. Admission: BF40. Open Mon and Wed.–Fri. 2–5, weekends 10–noon and 2–5.*

Tour 2: Brugge

The city may be better known by its French name, Bruges, but you'll score points with the locals by using the correct Flemish form. After all, you wouldn't call Liège by the Flemish Luik.

Linked with the estuary of the Zwin on the North Sea by a navigable waterway, the city became one of the most active members of the Hanseatic League in the 13th century, exporting Flemish cloth and importing fish from Scandinavia, furs from Russia, wine from Gascony, and silk from Venice. Italian merchants from Lombardy, Tuscany, and Venice set themselves up in Brugge, and the town established Europe's first stock exchange.

In 1301, the French Queen Jeanne of Navarre was annoyed by the finery flaunted by the women of Brugge. "I thought I alone was queen," she said, "and here I am surrounded by hundreds more." The men of Brugge, in return, were annoyed at being requested to pay for the French royal couple's lavish reception. One fine morning in May 1302, they fell upon and massacred the French garrison and then went on with the men of Ghent and Ieper to defeat the French cavaliers in the Battle of the Golden Spurs—commemorated to this day as the epitome of Flemish nationalism.

Brugge is where Flemish painting began. In fact, painting with oil was invented by Hubert and Jan van Eyck in the 1420s and spread to Italy at a later date. The art of the so-called Flemish primitives represented a revolution in realism, portraiture, and perspective; it brings their era alive in astonishing detail. Jan van Eyck was named court painter to Philip the Good, duke of Burgundy, who married Isabella of Portugal in a ceremony of ostentatious luxury in Brugge's Prinsenhof in 1429.

The last Burgundian feast in Brugge was the wedding of Duke Charles the Bold to Margaret of York, sister of England's Edward IV, in 1468. In August every five years (next in 1996) it is reenacted in a splendid pageant called the Feast of the Golden Tree, with tableaux of Flemish legend and history as magistrates and guilds welcome the sovereign couple to the city.

At the end of the century adversity struck. Flemish weavers had emigrated across the Channel and taught their trade to the English, who became formidable competitors. Even worse, the Zwin had begun to silt up, and the people of Brugge did not have the nerve or the funds to build the canal that might have saved them. Instead, trade and fortune switched to Antwerp.

In the 19th century, it was British travelers on their way to view the battlefield of Waterloo who rediscovered Brugge and spread its fame as a perfectly preserved medieval town. A novel by Georges

Rodenbach, *Bruges-la-Morte* (Bruges, the Dead), brought more visitors but created an image that has been difficult to throw off. The principal industry in Brugge today is, inevitably, tourism. It is also the administrative center of West Flanders and incorporates within its city limits the new port of Zeebrugge as well as some sophisticated industries and two fiercely competitive soccer teams.

The Historic *Numbers in the margin correspond to points of interest on the*
Heart *Brugge map.*

❼ A good place to start exploring Brugge is the **Markt,** through the centuries the center of the city's commercial life. In the middle stands the statue of the city's medieval heroes, Jan Breydel and Pieter De Coninck, who led the commoners of Flanders to their short-lived victory over the aristocrats of France. On the south side of the Markt stands the 13th-century **Halle** (Cloth Hall). In its heyday it was occupied by stalls where lengths of brightly colored cloth were piled high. The **Belfort** (Belfry) towers above it, rising to a height of 82 meters (270 feet). It commands the city and the surrounding countryside with more puissance than grace. The octagonal lantern that crowns the tower, added in the 15th century, contains the 47 bells of the remarkable Brugge carillon. *Admission: BF100. Open Apr.–Sept., daily 9:30–5; Oct.–Mar., daily 9:30–12:30 and 1:30–5. Carillon concerts Sept.–June, noon Wed. and Sat.–Sun. noon; July–Aug., Mon., Wed. and Sat.–Sun. noon.*

The west and north sides of the market square are lined with old guild houses. Most of them shelter restaurants of unremarkable quality that spill out over the sidewalk. On the east stand the provincial government house and the post office, an excellent pastiche of Burgundian Gothic.

❽ Breidelstraat, on the left of the Belfry, leads directly to the **Burg.** It is an enchanted square, never more so than when discreetly floodlighted after dark. The Burg derives its name from the fortress built by Baldwin of the Iron Arm, which is long since gone. So is, alas, the Carolingian cathedral of St. Donaas, built around 900 and wantonly destroyed by French Republicans in 1799; the cathedral's site is now a small park.

In the corner of the square stands the small **Heilig Bloed Basiliek** (Basilica of the Holy Blood). The Lower Chapel has kept its austere 12th-century Romanesque character, with massive pillars supporting a low, vaulted roof. The baptismal scene carved on the tympanum is original.

A beautiful Gothic stairway leads to the Upper Chapel, which was twice destroyed—by Protestant iconoclasts in the 16th century and by French Republicans in the 18th—but both times rebuilt. There is a small museum next to the basilica containing the reliquary used to carry a phial thought to contain some drops of the blood of Christ during the annual procession and two outstanding *volets* (shutters) painted by Pieter Pourbus. *Admission: BF40. Open Apr.–Sept., Thurs.–Tues. 9:30–noon and 2–6, Wed. 9:30–noon; Oct.–Mar., daily 10–noon and 2–4 (closed Wed. PM).*

Next to the basilica, the gleaming white sandstone **Stadhuis** (Town Hall), built at the end of the 14th century in Flamboyant Gothic, served with its strong vertical lines as the model for town halls in other Flemish cities such as Brussels and Leuven. The figures that originally adorned the facade were smashed by the French Republicans and have been replaced by modern replicas. Inside, a staircase mounts to the Gothic Hall, which has a marvelous double-vaulted

Brugge

Begijnhof, **17**
Brangwyn Museum, **12**
Burg, **8**
Godshuis Onze-Lieve-Vrouw der Zeven Weeen, **19**

Godshuizen De Pelikaan, **9**
Gouden Handrei, **24**
Groeninge Museum, **11**
Gruuthuse Museum, **13**
Hof van Bladelin, **23**
Huidenvettersplein, **10**

Huize ter Buerze, **27**
Markt, **7**
Memling Museum, **15**
Minnewater, **16**
Onze-Lieve-Vrouwekerk, **14**
Saaihalle, **28**
Sint-Jakobskerk, **22**

Sint-Salvators-kathedraal, **20**
Speelmanskapel, **21**
Tolhuis, **26**
Vlissinghe, **25**
Walplein, **18**

timber roof ornamented with 19th-century romantic frescoes. *Admission: BF60. Open Apr.–Sept., daily 9:30–5; Oct.–Mar., 9:30–12:30 and 2–5.*

The Town Hall is linked with the graceful **Oude Griffie** (Office of Records) by a bridge arching over the narrow Blinde Ezelstraat. Two centuries younger than its neighbor, it is a mixture of Gothic and Flemish Renaissance elements. The building is topped by an effigy of Justice, flanked by Moses and Aaron. It is now occupied by departments of the city administration.

Squeezed into the corner beside the Office of Records is the tiny **Museum van het Brugse Vrije** (Museum of the Brugge County Council), a remnant of the 15th-century county hall. Its principal treasure is the courtroom with its huge oak and black-marble chimneypiece. A large bas-relief, carved in dark oak by Guyot de Beaugrant, depicts a robust, nearly life-size Charles V. *Admission: BF20. Open Feb.–Dec., Tues.–Sun. 10–noon and 1:30–5.*

Where the rest of the county hall once stood is the **Gerechtshof** (Court of Justice), a Baroque palace that now houses the tourist office and other city offices.

Time Out | **Opus 4** is reached through the shopping gallery Ten Steeghere, which starts next to the basilica. It's a good place for a quiet beer, snack, or cake overlooking a pleasant stretch of canal.

Blinde Ezelstraat leads from the Burg across the canal. To the left is Steenhouwersdijk, which overlooks the brick rear gables that were part of the original county hall. The Meebrug (Mee Bridge) offers an especially good view. Farther along the Groenerei stand the ⑨ **Godshuizen De Pelikaan.** These almshouses were built in the early 18th century, but others in Brugge were built as long ago as the 14th century and as recently as the beginning of the 20th.

Return to the Blinde Ezelstraat bridge and the **Vismarkt** (Fish Market), where fresh seafood from Zeebrugge is sold every day except ⑩ Sunday and Monday. Just beyond is **Huidenvettersplein** (Tanners' Square), with its 17th-century guild house.

Follow Rozenhoedkaai and its continuation, the Dijver, to the ⑪ **Groeninge Museum,** set back from the street behind a medieval gate. Although it is small, this is one of the world's essential museums and merits a half-day visit. In the very first room hangs Jan van Eyck's wonderfully realistic *Madonna with Canon Van der Paele.* Van Eyck achieved texture and depth through multiple layers of oil and varnish, and his technique has withstood the ravages of more than five centuries. All the Flemish primitives and their successors—Petrus Christus, Hugo Van der Goes, Hans Memling, Gerard David, Pieter Bruegel (both Elder and Younger), Pieter Pourbus—are represented at this feast. The survey of Belgian art continues through the romantics and realists to surrealists and contemporary art. *Dijver 12, tel. 050/339911. Admission: BF130. For BF350 you can buy a combination ticket also including the Gruuthuse, Memling, and Brangwyn museums. Open Apr.–Sept., daily 9:30–5; Oct.–Mar., Wed–Mon. 9:30–12:30 and 2–5.*

Time Out | The attractive **Taverne Groeninge** (Dijver 13) is decorated with works by Frank Brangwyn.

⑫ The **Brangwyn Museum** is in fact next door. The 18th-century house contains hundreds of drawings and paintings by Frank Brangwyn

(1867–1956). His father, an architect, had, like a number of other British romantics, settled in Brugge, and the son stayed on to paint many an homage to his adopted city. *Dijver 16, tel. 050/339911. Admission: BF80. Open Apr.–Sept., daily 9:30–5; Oct.–Dec. and Feb.–Mar., Wed.–Mon. 9:30–12:30 and 2–5.*

⑬ Next on museum row is the **Gruuthuse Museum,** once the home of Lodewijk Van Gruuthuse, a prominent and powerful nobleman of the Netherlands in Burgundian times who financed Edward IV's campaign to regain the throne of England. Room 6 is an attractive Gothic interior with a 15th-century mantelpiece and stained-glass windows. *Dijver 17, tel. 050/339911. Admission: BF130. Open Apr.–Sept., daily 9:30–5; Oct.–Mar., Wed.–Mon. 9:30–12:30 and 2–5.*

⑭ **Onze-Lieve-Vrouwekerk** (Church of Our Lady), a block away, was begun in the 13th century, and the west front with its two round towers is typical of the early Gothic style. The church's most precious treasure is the small *Virgin and Child* by Michelangelo, carved in white marble, which sits in a black marble niche in an altar at the end of the south aisle. The choir contains two mausoleums: that of Mary of Burgundy, who died in 1482 at the age of 25 after a fall from her horse; and that of her father, Charles the Bold, killed in 1477 while laying siege to Nancy in France. *Gruuthusestraat. Open Apr.–Sept., daily 10–11:30 and 2:30–5; Oct.–Mar., 10–11:30 and 2:30–4:30. Closed Sun. AM except to worshipers.*

⑮ The **Memling Museum** is right across Mariastraat, inside the medieval **Sint-Janshospitaal** (St. John's Hospice). It contains just six works, but they are paintings of breathtaking quality. Hans Memling was born in Germany about 1435 but spent the greater part of his life in Brugge, possibly attracted to the Burgundian court. In the *Altarpiece of St. John the Baptist and St. John the Evangelist,* two leading personages of the court are believed to be portrayed, Mary of Burgundy (buried in the church across the street) as St. Catherine and Margaret of York as St. Barbara. The miniature paintings that adorn the St. Ursula Shrine are marvels of fine detail and poignancy; Memling may well have been the most spiritual of early Flemish painters.

The Sint-Janshospitaal was founded in the 12th century and remained in use until the early 20th. The middle ward, the oldest of three, was built in the 13th century in Romanesque style. There is a fascinating painting from the 18th century that shows patients arriving by sedan chair and being fed and ministered to by sisters and clerics. *Mariastraat 38, tel. 050/332562. Admission: BF130. Open Apr.–Sept., daily 9:30–5; Oct.–Mar., Thurs.–Tues. 9:30–noon and 2–5.*

To return to the Markt, turn left on Mariastraat, walk up to Simon Stevinplein, and then turn right on Steenstraat.

City of The **Minnewater** (inner harbor), at the south end of the city center,
Merchants was created in the 13th century to expand the city's capacity as a
⑯ trading center. The swans of Minnewater evoke an etymological legend or perhaps a historical truth: In 1488 the people of Brugge imprisoned Maximilian of Austria and decapitated his adviser, Pieter Lanchals. Now, *Lanchals* is very close to the Dutch for "long neck," so when Maximilian was liberated, he ordered Brugge to expiate its crime by keeping swans in the canals of the city in perpetuity.

⑰ The **Begijnhof** is just off Wijngaardplein at the northern end of the Minnewater. This serene close of small whitewashed houses surrounding a pleasant green is at its best in spring when daffodils bloom. If you hear the convent bell, don't hesitate to enter the Renaissance church. The Begijnhof (Beguinage in French) was founded in 1245 by Margaret of Constantinople, primarily as a refuge for widows of Crusaders who had fallen in foreign lands, and the congregation flourished for 600 years. The Beguines have been replaced by Benedictine sisters. Most of the present-day houses are from the 16th or 17th century but have maintained the architectural style of the houses that preceded them. Silence is requested. *Monasterium de Wijngaard, Oud Begijnhof, tel. 050/330011. Admission free; BF50 for a house visit. Open Apr.–June, daily 11–noon and 1:45–5:30; July–Aug., daily 10–noon and 1:45–6; Sept.–Mar., daily 10:30–noon and 1:45–5*

18 To the left from the Begijnhof on Wijngaardstraat and almost immediately left again is **Walplein,** one of Brugge's many delightful squares.

Time Out Here you can choose between **Nieuw 't Walnutje,** for a snack or a meal, and **Straffe Hendrik,** part of the Henri Maes brewery.

19 From Walstraat, you can walk around Oude Gentweg to look at the attractive **Godshuis Onze-Lieve-Vrouw der Zeven Weeen** (Almshouse of Our Lady of the Seven Sorrows) in Drie Kroezenstraat, and additional almshouses of the 17th century in Nieuwe Gentweg.

20 Turn right up Mariastraat and branch left into Heilige-Geeststraat, which leads to **Sint-Salvatorskathedraal** (St. Savior's Cathedral), an impressive Gothic brick building with a cluster of chapels radiating from the choir. The upper part of the tower was damaged by fire in 1853 and rebuilt. Inside, the coats of arms of knights of the Order of the Golden Fleece hang above the choir stalls; a chapter was held here in 1478. The adjoining cathedral museum contains works by Dirk Bouts, Lancelot Blondeel, and Pieter Pourbus. *Steenstraat, tel. 050/330044. Admission: BF40. Open Apr.–Sept., Thurs.–Sat. and Mon.–Tues. 10–noon and 2–5, Sun. 3–5; Oct.–Mar., Thurs.–Sat. and Mon.–Tues. 2–5.*

21 Across Zuidzandstraat and through Zilverpand, a modern shopping mall, Noordzandstraat leads left to the large 't Zand square, where, on the right at the end of Speelmansrei, along the canal, stands a charming chapel. The **Speelmanskapel** was founded in 1421 by the guild of minstrels, who enjoyed exclusive rights to provide the music **22** for public functions. Farther along, on Moerstraat, is **Sint-Jakobskerk** (St. Jacob's Church). As the parish church of the mercantile community, it accumulated so much wealth that it is now almost overencumbered with works of art. Chief among them is the *Legend of St. Lucy* triptych, painted by an unknown master of the 15th century.

23 To the right on Sint-Jakobsstraat and left on Boterhuis, to Naaldenstraat, is the **Hof van Bladelin,** built in 1451 for Pieter Bladelin, counselor to Philip the Good and one of the richest men in the Burgundian Netherlands. In the courtyard is an arcade with carved stone consoles from Bladelin's time. Under the arcade on the street side, one of the consoles is decorated with three feathers passing through a ring. This was the emblem of Lorenzo the Magnificent; the Medicis bought the Bladelin house in 1466 to serve as both bank and residence. *Naaldenstraat 19. Admission free. Open Apr.–Sept., Mon.–Sat. 9–noon and 2–6, Sun. 10–noon and 2–6; Oct.–Mar., Mon.–Sat. 9–noon and 2–4, Sun. 10–noon and 2–4.*

Across Grauwwerkerstraat and through Pieter Pourbusstraat, Vlamingstraat leads left over the bridge to Augustijnenrei, one of the loveliest of quays. Directly ahead are the three arches of the Augustijnenbrug. Dating from 1391, it's the oldest bridge in Brugge. Crossing it and turning left on the cobbled **Gouden Handrei,** you arrive at the broad main canal, which once flowed all the way to the Markt.

㉕ Aross the main canal is the **Vlissinghe** (Blekersstraat 2A). This is the oldest pub in Brugge; people have been enjoying their beer here since 1552.

Follow the branch of the canal that curves right toward Jan van Eyckplein. Ahead is the **Poortersloge,** a late-Gothic building with a slender spire, once a meeting place for the burghers of Brugge. The rampant bear that occupies one niche here shares Brugge's coat of arms with the lion of Flanders.

㉖ The present-day canal ends at **Jan van Eyckplein,** which features a statue of the painter. On the right is the old **Tolhuis** (Toll House), built in 1477. Next door is a very narrow 15th-century building that was owned by the guild of porters. **Spanjaardstraat,** on the right, leads up to the quay where goods from Spain were unloaded. The house at No. 9 was owned by one Gonzalez d'Aguilera; this is where St. Ignatius of Loyola stayed when he came to Flanders on holidays from his studies at the Sorbonne in Paris.

㉗ From Jan van Eyckplein, Academiestraat leads to Vlamingstraat. This intersection was the original Beursplein (not to be confused with the present Beursplein, behind 't Zand). On it is the **Huize ter Buerze** (House of Purses), built in 1453 and recently carefully restored.

㉘ The houses of the Venetian and Florentine merchants have disappeared, but the **Saaihalle** (Serge Hall), formerly the Genoese trading house, still stands, just across the narrow Grauwwerkerstraat from the House of Purses. Originally the top floor had a similar crenelated curtain wall, but it has been replaced by a bell-shaped gable. On the other side of Vlamingstraat lies **Kraanplaats** (Crane Place). Vlamingstraat leads back to the Markt, then as now at the center of Brugge.

In the Vicinity *Numbers in the margin correspond to points of interest on the Ghent, Brugge, and the Coast map.*

㉙ The road to the small town of **Damme,** just 7 kilometers (4½ miles) north of Brugge, follows a canal lined with tall and slender poplars, all slightly bent by the prevailing breeze. You can ride a bike along the top of the levee, and if the return trip seems too daunting, you can take the bike aboard a miniature paddle steamer, the *Lamme Goedzak.*

In 1134 a tidal wave opened up an inlet of the sea from the Zwin to the neighborhood of Brugge, whose people were quick to build a canal to link up with it. Damme started life as a fishing village at the junction. It became an important port that held exclusive rights to import such varied commodities as wine from Bordeaux and herring from Sweden, and the "Maritime Law of Damme" became the standard for Hanseatic merchants.

It was in Damme's **Onze-Lieve-Vrouwekerk** (Church of Our Lady) that Charles the Bold and Margaret of York were married, and on the facade of the **Stadhuis** (Town Hall) you can see their effigies, the noble duke presenting the wedding ring to his fiancée. Damme was (erroneously) believed to be the home of the legendary Tijl Uilenspiegel, whose merry pranks, detailed in Charles de Coster's novel, *La Légende et les aventures héroïques . . . d'Ulenspiegel . . .* (1866), were often directed at the Spanish occupying force.

Another mile along the tree-planted canal is its confluence with the Leopold Canal; just past here is the village of **Oostkerke.** Less visited by tourists, it is more in keeping with the peaceful polder landscape.

Tour 3: Battlefields

The highways south from Brugge and Ghent point in the direction of Flanders Fields, where decisive battles have been waged since the time of Julius Caesar. Here longbowmen fought cavalry in heraldic colors, and here the horrors of World War I were played out.

Kortrijk (Courtrai to unreconstructed French speakers) is about 50 kilometers (31 miles) south of Brugge and Ghent. The Battle of the Golden Spurs (which the French prefer to call the Battle of Courtrai) was fought immediately outside the city walls, close to the present Groeningelaan. On that fateful July 11, 1302, the poorly armed weavers and other craftsmen from Brugge, Ghent, and Ieper took on the flower of French nobility. The battle had actually been going well for the French infantrymen, but they were brushed aside by the mounted knights, who were spoiling for a fight. A hidden canal, the Groeninge, was the Flemings' greatest ally; many of the knights plunged into it, to be speared by the Flemish pikemen. After the battle, 700 pairs of golden spurs were removed from the bodies and triumphantly hung in the Church of Our Lady in Kortrijk as a votive offering.

A 14-meter-high (45-foot-high) neo-Gothic monument has been erected on the spot where the battle was fought, and it is commemorated on the weekend closest to July 11 with a parade or a tournament (for information, tel. 056/239371). At the **Stedelijk Museum** you can inspect a large-scale model of the city as it was in the Middle Ages, showing the battle site. There is also a copy of the Oxford Chest (of unknown provenance), which is decorated with a series of scenes of the battle. *Broelkaai 6, tel. 056/211992. Open Tues.–Sun. 10–noon and 2–5.*

Like almost every self-respecting Flemish town, Kortrijk has a stadhuis, a begijnhof, and an Onze-Lieve-Vrouwekerk. In this case, the Beguinage, with its cobbled streets and whitewashed houses, is an oasis of calm in the busy city, and the church contains a beautiful alabaster figure of St. Catherine from 1380, standing in the Chapel of the Counts of Flanders.

The River Leie passes through Kortrijk on its way to Ghent. In the Middle Ages it was known as the Golden River because of the fields of flax on its banks. The story of this industry is told in a series of lifelike tableaux in the **Nationaal Vlasmuseum** (National Flax Museum), installed in an old farmhouse. *Etienne Sabbelaan 4, tel. 056/210138. Admission: BF80. Open Mar.–Nov., Tues.–Fri. 9:30–12:30 and 1:30–6, Mon. 1:30–6.*

Time Out The elegant **Tea Room D'haene** (Sint Maartenskerkstraat 4–1) serves very good pancakes, waffles, and pastries throughout the day, and pleasant light lunches.

㉜ Ieper—better known outside Flanders as Ypres, the "Wipers" of World War I—lies 32 kilometers (20 miles) due west of Kortrijk. This city was literally wiped off the face of the earth during the war of 1914–1918. Today's city is a painstaking reconstruction, which was not completed until after World War II. One tradition lives on, the **Kattenwoensdag** (Cat Wednesday) on the second Sunday of May, when cats (stuffed animals these days) are flung from the belfry by the town jester. The tradition goes back to the 10th century, and was part of a renunciation of the devil and his works. Now it is linked to a great parade of cats and floats.

The magnificent **Lakenhalle** (Cloth Hall) is a copy of a building that had stood here since 1304. It houses on the first floor the **Herinnerungsmuseum** (Museum of Remembrance). The bayonets and guns, uniforms and helmets, and medals and shells are all here, as well as useful maps of the battlefields and cemeteries, and moving photographs of soldiers. *Grote Markt, tel. 057/200724. Admission: BF30. Open Easter–mid-Nov., daily 9:30–noon and 1:30–5:30.*

From the Cloth Hall, walking around the cathedral, you can reach **St. George's,** a small British church with an abundance of war memories and the adjoining **Pilgrims' Hall,** built for those who visit Ieper looking for a relative's grave. *Elverdingsestraat 1, tel. 057/216212.*

One of the most moving of war memorials is the **Menin Gate,** five minutes' walk from the Grote Markt on Meensestraat. After World War I, the British built a vast arch in memory of the 300,000 soldiers who had perished nearby. Every night at 8, traffic is stopped at the gate as buglers sound the Last Post. The practice was interrupted during World War II and resumed the night the Germans left, September 6, 1944.

Some 44 million shells were fired over this stretch of the Western Front in the two wars, and a fair number failed to explode. Flemish farmers still turn up about 200 every month, and the bomb disposal experts have to be called in. The poison-gas canisters cause special concern.

There are more than 170 military cemeteries in the area. From Ieper, on N332 toward Zonnebeke, you can stop at **Potijze** to pay homage to the 3,748 whose resting place is the French cemetery. Just beyond **Geluveld,** halfway to Menen, on the site of the Kasteelhof 't Hooghe is one of the few places where bomb craters can still be seen. Follow the signs via Canadalaan and Sanctuary Wood to the **Museum of the Trenches,** which is highly interesting but in a state of some neglect. In addition to photographs, weapons, and assorted objects salvaged from the field of battle, the owner has preserved some of the original trenches and tunnels on his land. You'll need to wear boots to inspect them. *Canadalaan, Zillebeke, tel. 057/466373. Admission: BF100. Open daily 10–6.*

㉝ North of Geluveld is **Passendale,** which gave its name to one of the most murderous battles in history. It is perhaps a hopeful irony that today the name is better known in Belgium as that of the buttery cheese this area produces. Near here is **Tyne Cot,** a British cemetery with 12,000 graves. A few miles to the west is the German cemetery of **Langemark,** with 44,000 dead.

㉞ From Langemark, you can take N301 to **Diksmuide,** about 16 kilometers (10 miles) to the northwest. Like Ieper, this town has been completely rebuilt in its original style. A network of trenches west of the town, the Dodengang, can be visited; here Belgian troops faced their German adversaries for four years. In town, an 84-meter

(275-foot) tower, the **IJzertoren,** has been erected in honor of the defenders.

Veurne, 14 kilometers (9 miles) west on N35, was the Belgian Army headquarters during World War I. For a town of just over 10,000, Veurne has an amazingly large and sumptuous **Grote Markt,** surrounded by buildings from the 16th and 17th centuries. On the last Sunday of July, a Procession of Penitents is organized in Veurne. On the Saturday preceding August 15, there's a festive late-night market in the Grote Markt.

Tour 4: The North Sea Coast

From De Panne in the southwest to Knokke in the northeast is only 65 kilometers (40 miles), but it's a considerable distance in terms of taste, from middle class to snob appeal. There's a total of 20 resorts, but sometimes it's difficult to know where one ends and the next begins. You can walk for miles along the dike, flanked by modern apartment houses where flats are let by the week or month; for many Belgians, an apartment by the sea is the equivalent of a summer house. All along the coast, parents help their kids fly kites, youngsters ride pedal cars, horseback riders thunder by next to the water's edge, lovers walk arm in arm, dogs chase sticks, children dig in the sand, and sun worshipers laze in deck chairs protected from the North Sea breezes by canvas windbreaks.

Belgians flock to the shore over the weekend all year round. Quite a few profess to like it best in the real off-season, when you can walk along the beach in the pale winter sun, filling your lungs with bracing sea air, and then warm up in a cozy tavern with a plate of steaming mussels.

35 It was at **De Panne,** almost at the French border, that Queen Elisabeth took up residence while King Albert I directed his country's forces from Veurne during World War I. Now it is primarily a family resort, with more than 50 hotels and pensions and an amusement park. The dunes west of the resort are a nature reserve, **Westhoek** (Dynastielaan, tel. 058/421818), where guided walks are organized in season.

36 **Sint-Idesbald** is also family oriented. For art lovers, the **Paul Delvaux Museum** is dedicated to the nonagenarian painter, famous for his surrealist mix of nudes, skeletons, and trains. A pleasant outdoor restaurant is attached to the museum. *Kabouterweg 42, tel. 058/521229. Admission: BF150. Open July–Aug., daily 10:30–6:30; Apr.–June and Sept., Tues.–Sun. 10:30–6:30; Oct.–Dec., weekends and bank holidays 10:30–5:30.*

37 **Koksijde** offers more than beach life. The Hoge Blekker is at 33 meters (108 feet) the highest dune on the coast. Nearby are the ruins of the Cistercian **Duinenabdij** (Abbey of the Dunes) with an archaeological museum. *Koninklijke Prinslaan 8, tel. 058/511933. Admission: BF75. Open July–Sept., daily 10–6; Oct.–Dec. and Feb.–June, daily 9–noon and 1:30–5.*

To the north of the abbey stands a new church, **Onze-Lieve-Vrouw ter Duinenkerk** (Our Lady of Sorrows of the Dunes Church), of striking modern design that suggests both the dunes and the sea.

Time Out **Verdonck,** next to the traffic lights on the Koninklijke baan (where the coastal tram runs), has outstanding ice cream and chocolates.

㊳ At **Oostduinkerke** there are still some horseback shrimp fishers. At low tide, the sturdy horses, half immersed, trawl heavy nets along the shoreline.

㊴ **Nieuwpoort,** at the estuary of the River IJzer, is where the sluices were opened in October 1914, inundating the polder and permanently halting the German advance. The estuary makes an excellent yachting port, and some 3,000 leisure craft are moored here. Nieuwpoort is also the home of a sizable fishing fleet and a lively fish market.

㊵ **Oostende** (Ostende in French; Ostend in English) is the largest town and the oldest settlement on the coast, with a history going back to the 10th century. It was a pirate hideout for centuries, and from here Crusaders set sail for the Holy Land. In the early 17th century, Oostende withstood a Spanish siege for three years. One of continental Europe's first railways was built between Oostende and Mechelen in 1838, and regular mail packet services to Dover began in 1846. Modern Oostende leads a double life, as a communications center and fishing port on the one hand, and as a fashionable resort on the other.

The painter James Ensor, who was born and spent most of his life in Oostende, has only lately been recognized as one of the great artists of the late 19th century. Using violent colors to express his frequently macabre or satirical themes, he depicted a fantastic carnival world peopled by masks and skeletons. His home, converted into a museum, **James Ensorhuis,** includes his studio. *Vlaanderenstraat 27. Admission: BF50. Open June–Sept., Wed.–Mon. 10–noon and 2–5.*

Paintings by Ensor and his contemporaries can be seen in the **Museum voor Schone Kunsten** (Fine Arts Museum). *Wapenplein, tel. 059/805335. Admission: BF50. Open Wed.–Mon. 10–noon and 2–5.*

Oostende also has a good modern art museum, the **Museum voor Moderne Kunst** (MMK), where contemporary artists are well represented with works by Pierre Alechinsky, Roger Raveel, Pol Mara, and others. *Romestraat 11, tel. 059/508118. Admission: BF100. Open Wed.–Mon. 10–6.*

Time Out Among the pleasant brasseries and cafés around the Wapenplein in the center of the old town, **Falstaff** has a permanent exhibition of photographs of Oostende in the 1920s.

Along the **Visserskaai** (Fishermen's Wharf), next to the ferry port, fishwives hawk seafood in all its forms from stalls opposite an almost uninterrupted row of fish restaurants.

㊶ **Blankenberge,** once a small fishing port, has grown into a large resort with more than a hundred hotels and boarding houses. It has the only British-style amusement pier on the Belgian coast, with a modern aquarium and model ships. Blankenberge also has a Casino and an attractive yachting harbor.

㊷ **Zeebrugge,** or Brugge-on-the-Sea, is the same size as the parent city, which is 14 kilometers (8 miles) inland. In addition to a sandy beach and a busy fishing port, Zeebrugge's chief distinction is its commercial port. You can tour the harbor and its installations by Euro Line sightseeing boat. *Cost: BF220. 1½-hr sailings June 15–Sept. daily at 11 and 2:30.*

㊸ **Knokke-Heist,** finally, is where Belgium's BCBG come to play. It is, in fact, one resort made up of five areas, growing progressively more fashionable as you go north from Heist and Duinbergen on Albert-Strand to Knokke and the splendid villas of **Het Zoute.** Along the Kustlaan, on the leeward side of the dike, you'll find virtually every fashionable shop in Brussels represented by a boutique, and all are open on Sunday. The people strolling along the Zeedijk tend to be bronzed and well dressed. The Casino boasts an enormous chandelier of Venetian crystal, and some of the world's top entertainers come there to perform.

Time Out The Albertplein is widely known as the place M'as-tu-vu (Did-you-see-me Square); it's a gathering place for the chic. The **Belle Epoque** is a good spot to have a drink and people-watch.

The coast has one more treat in store for you, **Het Zwin** on the Dutch border, where Brugge once had its outlet to the sea. Now it's a 375-acre nature reserve where at certain times saltwater washes into the soil, and the flora and fauna are unusual. The best times to visit are in spring for the bird migrations and from mid-July to mid-August for the flowers. Next to the aviary, a former royal villa, the Pavillon du Zoute, serves as an attractive restaurant, and from the top of the dike there's a splendid view of the dunes and inlets. *Ooievaarslaan 8, tel. 050/607086. Admission: BF140 adults, BF80 children. Open daily 9–7.*

Het Zwin continues on the Dutch side of the border. **Zeeuwsch-Vlaanderen,** part of the Dutch province of Zeeland, stretches 60-odd kilometers (about 40 miles) to the mouth of the Scheldt, north of Antwerp. When Belgium declared its independence in 1830, this province stayed Dutch, mostly for religious reasons.

The best-known town is **Sluis,** reached from Knokke on N376 (N58 in the Netherlands). This small town shared the wealth of Brugge, for it was on the waterway that linked Brugge with the sea. Many Belgians come here to shop and bank.

The beach proper begins with **Cadzand Bad,** which has several good hotels, and continues to **Breskens** (where you can take a car ferry to Vlissingen on Walcheren). Zeeuwsch-Vlaanderen is well suited for a holiday with children precisely because the resorts are uncrowded, with wide and quiet beaches.

N252 south from the port city of **Terneuzen** links up with R4 to Ghent. There's a second car-ferry service east of Terneuzen, from Kloosterzande on N60 to Kruiningen on Walcheren. Going south on N60 you link up with N49 in Belgium, 26 kilometers (16 miles) from Antwerp.

What to See and Do with Children

Brugge The **Boudewijn Park and Dolphinarium** is near the motorway about 2 kilometers (just over a mile) south of the city. There are several daily shows, an educational exhibition, and other attractions. *A. De Baeckestraat 12, St-Michiels, tel. 050/383838. Admission: BF480 adults, BF430 children for all attractions; BF180 adults, BF160 children for Dolphinarium only. Park open Easter–May, daily noon–6; May–Sept., daily 10–6; Sept., Wed. and weekends noon–6. Dolphinarium open daily, shows at 11AM and 4PM, more during peak season.*

The Coast The **Meli Park** at Adinkerke (close to De Panne) has all kinds of fun rides, animals, activities, and even a magic show. *De Pannelaan 68,* *tel. 058/420202. Admission: BF575 adults, BF420 children. Open Apr.–mid-Sept., daily 10–6.*

In Oostende, youngsters like to visit the windjammer **Mercator,** which is moored in the yacht harbor. *Vindictivelaan, tel. 059/ 705654. Admission: adults BF75, children BF40. Open May, June, Sept. daily 9–noon and 1–6; July, Aug. daily 9–7; Oct., Mar., Apr. weekends 10–noon and 1–5; Nov.–Feb. Sun. 10–noon and 1–4; closed Christmas and New Year.*

Ghent The unusual **School Museum Michel Thiery** highlights geography, fossils, shells, and so on, but the biggest attraction is a sound-and-light show featuring a large scale model of Ghent as it was 400 years ago. *Sint-Pietersplein 14, tel. 09/222–8050. Admission: BF80 adults, children free. Open Mon.–Thurs. and Sat. 9–12:15 and 1:30–5:15, Fri. 9–12:15.*

Off the Beaten Track

Brugge The **Museum voor Volkskunde** (Folklore Museum) is housed in a row of whitewashed almshouses originally built for retired shoemakers and contains various reconstructed interiors: grocery shop, living room, tavern. *Rolweg 40, tel. 050/330044. Admission: BF80. Open Apr.–Sept., daily 9:30–5; Oct.–Dec. and Feb.–Mar., Wed.–Mon. 9:30–12:30 and 2–5.*

Don't miss the **Jeruzalemkerk** (Jerusalem Church), built by the Adornes brothers in 1428 and still the property of their descendants. Among several family tombs, the black marble mausoleum of Anselm Adornes and his wife is the most striking. *Jeruzalemstraat 3. Admission free. Open weekdays 10–noon and 2–6, Sat. 10–noon and 2–5.*

The **Kantcentrum** (Lace Center) is next door. It is a foundation that aims to maintain the quality and authenticity of this ancient craft. The center includes a lace museum in the Jerusalem almshouses in Balstraat, and a lace school where youngsters are taught the intricate art of the bobbins. *Peperstraat 3, tel. 050/330072. Admission: BF40 for all 3. Open weekdays 10–noon and 2–6, Sat. 10–noon and 2–5.*

Ghent The **Sint-Baafsabdij** (St. Bavo's Abbey) east of the center goes back to the 7th century. England's Edward II stayed here with his Queen Philippa, and here it was that she gave birth to John of Gaunt (or Ghent), the future regent. The abbey was already very old when Charles V, another native son, ordered it demolished in 1540. The remnants of the abbey buildings have been left as they were, mostly romantic ruins. The oldest surviving part is an octagonal building from 1171. *Gandastraat 7, tel. 09/225–1585. Admission: BF80 adults, BF20 children. Open Tues.–Sun. 9:30–5.*

The **Klein Begijnhof** (Lange Violettenstraat 71) southeast of the center is the best preserved of Ghent's three beguinages. Founded in 1234 by Countess Joanna of Constantinople, it is protected by its wall and portal. The small houses, each identified by a statue of a saint, surround a spacious green and are still occupied by a small number of Beguines, leading the life stipulated by their founder 750 years ago. You may walk through the Klein Begijnhof (quietly, please), but the houses cannot be visited.

South of the city center, in Citadel Park, stands the **Museum voor Schone Kunsten** (Museum of Fine Arts), whose collections include two outstanding paintings by Hieronymus Bosch, *Saint Jerome* and

The Bearing of the Cross; in the latter Christ is shown surrounded by grotesque faces of unmitigated cruelty. *Nicolaas de Liemaeckereplein 3, tel. 09/222–1703. Admission: BF80. Open Tues.–Sun. 9–5.*

The lively **Museum van Hedendaagse Kunst** (Museum of Contemporary Art), also in Citadel Park, includes, in addition to hyperrealism, pop art, and the rest, works of great vitality by artists of the COBRA Group from Copenhagen, Brussels, and Amsterdam. *Hofbouwlaan 28, tel. 09/221–1703. Admission: BF80. Open Tues.–Sun. 9:30–5.*

Shopping

Brugge Brugge has many trendy boutiques and shops, especially along **Steenstraat** and **Vlamingstraat,** both of which branch off from the Markt. **Ter Steeghere** mall, which links the Burg with Wollestraat, deftly integrates a modern development into the historic center. The largest and most pleasant mall is the **Zilverpand** off Zilverstraat, where 50-odd shops cluster in Flemish gable houses around a courtyard with sidewalk cafés.

Street Markets The Burg is the setting for the **Wednesday Market** (weekly except July–Aug.) with flowers, vegetables, and fruit. The biggest is the **Saturday Market** on 't Zand. The **Fish Market** is held, appropriately, on the Vismarkt, daily except Sunday and Monday. All three are morning events, from 8 to approximately 12:30. On Saturday and Sunday afternoons (Mar.–Oct.) there's a **Flea Market** along the Dijver.

Specialty Stores Some of the best known of Brugge's many **art and antiques** dealers are 't **Leerhuis** (Groeninge 35, tel. 050/330302), which specializes in contemporary art; **Guyart** (Fort Lapin 37, tel. 050/332159), which is both an art gallery and a tavern (open Thurs.–Tues. 3–10 PM); **Papyrus** (Walplein 41, tel. 050/336687), specializing in silverware; and **Classics Kunstatelier** (Oude Burgstraat 32–24), which has the best selection of Flemish hangings.

Brugge has been a center for **lace making** since the 15th century, and such intricate variations on the art as the rose pattern and the fairy stitch, which requires more than 300 bobbins, were developed here. Most tourists buy lace as a souvenir costing a few hundred francs, and you can find it in a great many souvenir shops. Handmade lace in intricate patterns, however, takes a very long time to produce, and this is reflected in the price; for work of this type you should be prepared to part with BF10,000 or more. The best shop for the serious lace lover is 't **Apostelientje** (Balstraat 11, tel. 050/337860), across the street from the Lace Museum (*see* Off the Beaten Track, Brugge, *above*).

Ghent **Veldstraat** and the **Lange Munt** are major shopping streets. There are also several exclusive shopping galleries where boutiques are interspersed with cafés and restaurants, such as the **Bourdon Arcade** (Gouden Leeuwplein) and **Braempoort** (between Brabantdam and Vlaanderenstraat).

Kortrijk Kortrijk was a pioneer in establishing pedestrian shopping streets. Two of the best known are **Steenstraat** and **Wijngaardstraat,** both lined with fashionable and expensive boutiques.

Sports and Fitness

Spectator Sports Brugge In Brugge, the main sport is **soccer**. Home games are played at the Olympia Stadium (Koning Leopold III-Laan 50, St-Andries, tel. 050/389462).

The Coast The Wellington Hippodrome in Oostende is a top track for **flat racing** (tel. 059/806055; open July–Aug., Mon., Thurs., weekends, and bank holidays), and it also holds **trotting races** (tel. 059/803636; open May–Sept., Fri. 6:45 PM).

Participant Sports Brugge Information is available from the city's **Sports Service** (Walweinstraat 20, tel. 050/448322). The green city wall is ideal for **jogging**. For a more extensive workout, try the Tillegembos provincial domain in St-Michiels.

For **swimming** try the Olympic-size pool at the new Provinciaal Olympisch Zwembad (Olympia Park, Doornstraat, St-Andries, tel. 050/390200). There's also a sauna and solarium.

For **tennis** check out the Bryghia Tennis Club (Boogschutterslaan 37, St-Kruis, tel. 050/353406). Indoor courts cost BF350 for one hour, outdoor courts BF400 per hour.

The Coast For information about sports facilities in the area, contact **BLOSO** (Flemish Sports Association, rue des Colonies 31, 1000 Brussels, tel. 02/510–3411). More detailed local information can be obtained for Knokke (tel. 050/604317); for Oostende (tel. 059/500529); and for De Panne (tel. 058/412971). For information on water sports, contact Vlaamse Vereniging voor Watersport (Beatrijslaan 25, 2050 Antwerp, tel. 03/219–6967).

There are 18-hole **golf** courses at De Haan (tel. 059/235723) and Het Zoute (tel. 050/601616) and practice courses at other locations.

The coast, with its prevailing breeze, offers splendid **sailing** opportunities. Good yacht harbors include Blankenberge, Nieuwpoort, Oostende (tel. 059/706294), and Zeebrugge (tel. 050/544197).

At De Panne and Oostduinkerke, where the beach is up to 250 meters (820 feet) wide, the facilities for **sand yachting** are excellent.

Currents can be tricky, and you should **swim** only at beaches supervised by lifeguards. A green flag means bathing is safe; yellow, bathing is risky but guards are on duty; red, bathing is prohibited. Do not ignore warnings. Many resorts also offer good public open-air pools.

Tennis tournaments are held during the season at Oostende and Het Zoute. There are hundreds of courts along the coast; check with your concierge or the local tourist office.

Windsurfing is extremely popular and special areas have been set aside for it along many beaches. In Oostende, the Flemish Sports Association has set up a water-sports center on the Spuikom waterway (also used for oyster beds).

Ghent Ghent possesses an extensive sports and recreation center only minutes away from the city, the 250-acre **Blaarmeersen** (Zuiderlaan 5, tel. 09/221–8266). It is equipped with outdoor and indoor tennis courts, squash courts, a roller-skating track, jogging and cycling tracks, and facilities for windsurfing, sailing, canoeing, and camping.

Dining and Lodging

Between historic Ghent, romantic Brugge, and the highly developed coastline, Belgium concentrates its greatest variety of hotels and restaurants in this, its most tourist-accommodating region.

Dining Naturally, this is seafood country: Brugge ships in fresh fish daily from Zeebrugge, its waterfront counterpart, and the coast towns serve North Sea delicacies from the source at terrace restaurants whipped by sand and salt air. Even in landlocked Ghent, some 50 kilometers (31 miles) from the coast, locals snack on whelks and winkles (sea snails) as if they were popcorn. You'll inevitably find sole and turbot poached, *barbue* (brill) grilled or broiled, and a limited choice of classic sauces: grilled fish with rich béarnaise or *dijonnaise* sauces and poached fish with only slightly lighter sauce mousseline.

When the Flemish aren't eating their fish straight or in a blanket of golden sauce, they consume it in the region's most famous dish, fish waterzooi. Only the citizens of Ghent, deprived of a coastline, prepare their version with chicken.

If fish is the staple of bourgeois Flemish cuisine, the workingman's essentials are *mosselen* (mussels) and *paling* (eels), the latter as common a source of protein here as chicken or beef is elsewhere in the West. Their flesh is firm, fatty, and sweet, served in long crosssections that contain an easy-to-remove backbone. The most prevalent preparation by far is "in green," stewed in a heady mix of sorrel, tarragon, sage, mint, and parsley. The side dish? Frites, of course.

For two vegetable delicacies of Flanders, it's worth arranging your visit in springtime: Asparagus, white and tender, is served either in sauce mousseline or with the traditional Flemish garnish of chopped hard-boiled egg and melted butter; and the rarer hops sprouts, sweet, delicate shoots of the hops plant, abundant in March and April in beer-making country.

Lodging Unlike Antwerp and Brussels, Brugge is not a conference town but its opposite: This is where city folk get away for a romantic weekend, and they expect atmosphere in their second-honeymoon suite. Brugge is happy to provide it. Many hotels work hard to supply appropriately Old Flemish decor in the public areas and, when possible, in the rooms. Recent changes in fire codes left Brugge struggling between the obligation to install fire escapes and the desire to preserve its historic landmarks intact: The results are discreet but comforting in this city that often glows with a thousand wood-burning hearths. Ghent, like Brugge, aims at weekend visitors but hasn't developed an industry of romantic hotels; lodgings, with few exceptions, are modern. **Note:** Check with the tourist offices of Brugge and Ghent for package arrangements, in which rooms are reserved and some restaurant meals included, all for a reasonable fixed price. Coast hotels aim for longer visits and often offer half-board plans; in summer, be sure to book well in advance.

Brugge **De Karmeliet.** In a lovely 18th-century house with a graceful En-
Dining glish garden, this culinary landmark offers Bresse pigeon in truffle
★ juice, ravioli of *foie d'oie* (goose liver), and crisp potato nests with langoustine. The wine cave lives up to the kitchen's standard, which is stratospheric; the ambience is genteel, the service flexible and pleasant. *Langestraat 19, tel. 050/338259. Reservations required. Jacket and tie advised. AE, DC, MC, V. Closed Sun. dinner, Mon.* $$$$

★ **Den Gouden Harynk.** Few of his colleagues can claim the natural flair of chef Philippe Serruys. Holding forth in a small, unpretentious, antiques-filled dining room just south of the Dijver, he serves international cuisine with an artist's gift, not only for presentation but also for planning, pacing, and inspired combination. The menu dégustation offers langoustines brushed with a light curry blend or foie d'oie on a bed of rhubarb with pink peppercorns. *Groeninge 25, tel. 050/337637. Reservations advised. Jacket and tie advised. AE, DC, MC, V. Closed Sun.–Mon. $$$$*

De Witte Poorte. Under low brick vaults and stone arches, with rear windows looking onto a lush little garden, this formal restaurant offers rich, contemporary French cooking, with an emphasis on seafood. Specialties include sweetbreads in tarragon cream sauce, sole with Zeeland oysters, and a superb dessert cart. *Jan Van Eyckplein 6, tel. 050/330883. Reservations advised. Jacket and tie advised. AE, DC, MC, V. Closed Sun.–Mon. $$$$*

't Bourgoensche Cruyce. In one of the most medieval-*looking* buildings in Brugge (though its weathered timbers and sharp-raked roofs were heavily rebuilt at the turn of the century), this restaurant claims one of the most romantic canal-side settings as well: Dining-room windows shed warm light over the water, the reflections tinted by the salmon-and-copper decor. The cuisine is equally romantic, including delicate smoked halibut, tender scallops, wild mushrooms, or saddle of hare. *Wollestraat 41, tel. 050/337926. Reservations advised. Jacket and tie advised. AE, MC, V. $$$*

Breydel–De Coninck. Directly en route between the Markt and Burg, this no-frills luncheonette looks more like a tourist trap than a place for locals to flock for their winter mosselen—but they do. Austere pink plastic tablecloths and vinyl banquettes leave the focus on the basics, and while there are token offerings of eel and steak, nothing could be more basic than a crock the size of a chamber pot heaped high with shiny blue-black shells. *Breidelstraat 24, tel. 050/339746. Dress: casual. AE, MC, V. Closed Tues. lunch, Wed. $$*

't Paardje. Off the beaten tourist track, this familial little restaurant concentrates all efforts on a few specialties: Mussels are prepared in six variations, eel in eight, and steak in 11 versions. Its terra-cotta and lace decor is cozy, clean, and unpretentious, and its cooking dependably good. *Langestraat 20, tel. 050/334009. Dress: casual. MC, V. Closed Mon.–Tues. nights. $$*

Sint Joris. Among the dozen or so competitive brasseries crowded along the Markt, this low-key spot maintains a more civilized profile than its neighbors do. Flowers, linens, candles, a roaring fire, and a comfortable clutter of ceramics and copper warm the dining room, and you'll find a choice of either sheltered or open terrace. The cooking is a cut above average as well, and regional dishes are exceptionally well prepared: fish-based waterzooi, eel in green sauce, and mussels. *Markt 29, tel. 050/333062. Dress: casual. AE, DC, MC, V. $–$$*

Steakhouse De Tassche. Though you may feel far removed from the romance of old Brugge, you'll be compensated by the attention, commitment to detail, and overall sincerity of this husband-and-wife-run restaurant. A wide range of simple dishes, from cheap steak and frites to grilled sole, are served in a setting of pink damask and copper, and the cooking comes from the heart: Even the frites are hand-cut, and the chef cruises the dining room like a true gastronome. *Oude Burg 11, tel. 050/331282. Dress: casual. DC, MC, V. $–$$*

★ **Staminee De Garre.** Tucked in an alley off the well-worn Breidelstraat, this tiny two-tiered coffeehouse is a brick-and-beam oasis, offering Mozart and magazines along with plunger coffee and 136 beers—four of them variations on the house brew. There are simple cold platters and grilled sandwiches, attractively served, and traditional nibbles of cheese with the heartier beers. *Off Breidelstraat, tel. 050/341029. Dress: casual. No credit cards. $*

Taverna Curiosa. Don't be put off by the aggressive posters, menus, and broadcast music that spill onto the street: Downstairs, this cross-vaulted crypt makes a comfortable, atmospheric hideaway from tourist traffic and an ideal place for conversation, a light meal, and one of myriad beers, many of them local. Snacks include omelettes, sandwiches, and *visschotel* (smoked fish plates), as well as pancakes and ice cream. *Vlamingstraat 22, tel. 050/342334. Dress: casual. AE, MC, V. Closed Mon. $*

Tom Pouce. Despite its somewhat geriatric air—heavy velour drapes, splashy carpet, cracked crockery, noisy open service bar— this stuffy old urban tearoom dominates the Burg every afternoon as tourists, shoppers, and loyal retirees dig into warm apple strudel, airy waffles, and their tour de force: hot *pannekoeken*, pancakes that are light, eggy, and vanilla-perfumed, with a pat of butter and a sprinkle of dark brown sugar. There are lunch plates as well. *Burg 16–17, tel. 050/330336. Dress: casual. AE, DC, MC, V. Closed Mon. $*

Dining and Lodging **Die Swaene.** Lavishly decorated in every period excess, this hotel tries harder. Its situation—facing one of the prettier canals in the heart of the tourist center—makes it particularly appropriate for splurging honeymooners, who will be rewarded with swagged tulle, crystal, and any number of marble nymphs. (Its most popular room is a relatively subdued converted Flemish kitchen with stone fireplace and carved four-poster.) The romantic, candlelit French restaurant serves such specialties as goose liver with caramelized apples, and lobster-and-spinach lasagna. *Steenhouwersdijk, B-8000, tel. 50/342798. 24 rooms with bath. Facilities: restaurant, (closed Wed., Thurs. lunch, 2 weeks in Jan., 2 weeks in Aug.), bar. AE, DC, MC, V. $$$–$$$$*

De Castillion. This hotel is named for Jean-Baptiste de Castillion, who lived here in the 18th century. Some of the guest rooms have cherry wood period furniture; others are furnished in a modern style. Filet mignon of venison in a Pomerol stock, duck's liver, and a fricassée of monkfish and wild salmon are among the restaurant's offerings; the fixed-price menus are great value for the money. Pre-dinner drinks and post-prandial coffee are served in the handsome Art Deco salon, which is decorated in shades of blue and green. *Heilige Geeststraat 1, tel. 050/343001, fax 050/339475. 18 rooms, 2 suites, all with bath. Facilities: restaurant (closed Tues., first half of Jan.), sauna, solarium, conference room. AE, DC, MC, V. $$–$$$*

Lodging **Holiday Inn Crowne Plaza.** There was inevitable skepticism when Holiday Inn got permission to build a hotel right on the Burg in the heart of the city, but the critics have been confounded: The new redbrick hotel with a red-tile roof and modern steel gables fits in remarkably well with its surroundings. Rooms are large, modern, and decorated in muted colors; the best ones have steps leading up to them, and dark-wood ceiling beams, giving you the feeling of being in the eaves. On display in the basement are remnants of the old ramparts and artifacts found during construction. *Burg 10, tel. 050/345834, fax 050/345615. 96 rooms. Facilities: restaurant, bar, museum, garage, conference room, health club with sauna and pool. AE, DC, MC, V. $$$$*

★ **De Tuileriëen.** This stately 15th-century mansion was converted to a sumptuous hotel in 1988 and furnished with genuinely patrician taste: discreet antique reproductions, weathered marble, and warm mixed-print fabrics in shades of celadon, slate, and cream. The firelighted bar is filled with cozy tartan wingbacks, and the breakfast room has a massive mantel and a coffered ceiling. Despite its aristocratic air, this is a welcoming stop. Caveat: Canal views entail traffic noise; courtyard rooms are quieter. *Dyver 7, B-8000, tel. 50/343691. 26 rooms. Facilities: breakfast rooms, bar, indoor pool, whirlpool, sauna, solarium, parking. AE, DC, MC, V. $$$$*

Bryghia. Restored in 1965 and renovated in 1989, this 15th-century landmark (once a German/Austrian trade center) now sports seamless modern room decor with beechwood cabinetry and soft pastel florals. The management works hard on details of comfort, offering in-room teakettles, flowers, valet parking, and mosquito repellent when the canal waters run slow. *Oosterlingenplein 4, B-8000, tel. 50/338059. 18 rooms with bath. Facilities: breakfast room. AE, DC, MC, V. $$$*

★ **Oud Huis Amsterdam.** Packaged like a fine gift, this snug, central retreat combines the grace of the two noble 17th-century houses it occupies with the polish and luxury of a new first-class property. Antique details—tooled Cordoba wallpaper here, rough-hewn rafters and Delft tiles there—have been preserved, and slick services—international newspapers, umbrellas—superimposed. Owner Philip Traen has even mounted ancestral art in an old master vein. Rooms with canal views also overlook a busy street; rooms with roofline views in back are calmer. *Spiegelrei 3, B-8000, tel. 50/341810. 18 rooms with bath. Facilities: garden, bar. AE, DC, MC, V. $$$*

Pandhotel. Its faded gentility dating not only from the 1830s, when it was built as a private mansion, but also from 1979, when it was renovated as a hotel, this member of the Romantik chain mixes a jewel-box neoclassical decor with modern touches—dark ceramic baths, a skylighted breakfast room. Services are business-oriented, and the location is central to tourism. *Pandreitje 16, B-8000, tel. 50/340666. 24 rooms with bath. Facilities: breakfast room, bar. AE, DC, MC, V. $$$*

★ **Egmond.** Gracefully placed along the lush Minnewater park, this manorlike inn offers garden views from every room, as well as the odd skylight, parquet floor, fireplace, or dormer-sloped ceiling. Breakfast is served in an oak-beamed hall with a Delft-tiled fireplace. With the park in front and the quiet Beguinage behind, you may feel pleasantly isolated from the touristic bustle of the center, though it's only 10 minutes' walk. *Minnewater 15, B-8000, tel. 50/341445. 9 rooms with bath. Facilities: breakfast room. AE, DC, MC, V. $$*

Europ. Run by an enthusiastic young management, this mid-price hotel focuses less on historic atmosphere than on basic comforts: Good big beds with Swiss-flex construction are placed in every room, and the breakfast buffet is generous. The hotel was first built in a 1789 house, with a modern wing added in 1970—but the current decor is spare and contemporary in both parts. *Augustijnenrei 18, B-8000, tel. 50/337975. 31 rooms, 28 with bath. Facilities: bar. AE, DC, MC, V. $$*

Ter Brughe. A 1989 renovation of this 15th-century step-gabled house created a slick, modern, efficient hotel in which the decor might seem generic (beige and bamboo) but for those heavy beams, tempera murals, and leaded-glass windows. There are exposed brick barrel vaults in the bar, and you can throw bread to the ducks from the breakfast room, which opens directly onto the canal. *Oost-Gistelhof 2, B-8000, tel. 50/340324. 24 rooms with bath. Facilities: bar. AE, DC, MC, V. $$*

★ **De Pauw.** Homey, familial, and warmly furnished, from the fresh flowers and doilies to the bronzed baby booties in the breakfast parlor, this is a welcoming little inn passed on from mother to daughter. Every room has a name instead of a number, needlepoint cushions, and old framed prints. (Two rooms with shower down the hall are super values.) Breakfast, which includes six kinds of bread plus cold cuts and cheese, is served on pretty china. *Sint-Gilliskerkhof 8, B-8000, tel. 50/337118. 8 rooms, 6 with bath. Facilities: breakfast room. AE, DC, MC, V. $*

Fevery. The living quarters of the family seem to spill over into the lounge area of this friendly, comfortable hotel; the magazines and knickknacks make you feel like personal guests. There's even a baby monitor so parents can curl up with a drink downstairs after putting a child to bed. The room decor was upgraded (new carpet, fresh chenille) in 1993, and all rooms have bathrooms. *Collaert Mansionstraat 3, B-8000, tel. 50/331269. 11 rooms with bath. Facilities: bar. AE, DC, MC, V. $*

Jacobs. With all its plush and crystal in the public rooms, this spot may look posh, but the staff are young and friendly, and the breakfast tables are garnished with plastic waste buckets. There are cheap no-bath rooms as well as full-facility doubles, with homey, plain decors. *Baliestraat 1, B-8000, tel. 50/339831. 26 rooms, 24 with bath. Facilities: bar. AE, MC, V. $*

Damme/ Oostkerke
Dining
★

De Waterput. This small whitewashed farmhouse in the middle of the polder-land contains a superb restaurant presided over by a most original chef, Willy Bataillie. There's no menu, because he uses only those products that are freshest and the best on any given day. A meal might include home-smoked wild salmon, John Dory with chives, wild duck with small onions, or crêpes suzette. *Rondsaartstraat 1, Oostkerke, tel. 050/599256. Reservations required. Jacket and tie required. AE, DC, MC, V. Closed Thurs. off-season, Tues., Wed., mid-Nov.–mid-Dec. $$$*

★ **Siphon.** This sprawling white-brick landmark, along two tree-lined canals, has great casement windows taking in green farmlands. It is often mobbed by fur-coated urbanites on outings in the country. Yet the restaurant is anything but upscale: It's delightfully down-to-earth, with brusque white-uniformed waiters busing eel and wood-grilled lamb chops at checkered-cloth tables, and as many people drink beer as delve into the stellar wine list. *Damse Vaart Oost 1, Damme, tel. 050/620202. Reservations advised. Dress: casual. No credit cards. Closed Thurs., first half of Feb., first half of Oct. $–$$*

Lodging **Wilgenhof.** Halfway between Brugge and Damme and a stone's throw from the canal, this bucolic mansion-on-the-polder is a good base for excursions in either direction and to the coast, 12 kilometers (7½ miles) away. Rooms are pleasant but fairly basic. *Polderstraat 151, Brugge, tel. 050/362744, fax 050/362821. 6 rooms with bath. Facilities: breakfast room, garden. AE, DC, MC, V. $$–$$$*

Ghent
Dining

Guido Meersschaut. With a direct connection to the nearby fish market, where Meersschaut has shipped in the freshest catch from the Channel and the North Sea, this small, stylish restaurant offers an extensive menu of seafood. Fresh cold shrimp and snails, their shells still damp with brine, are offered with the aperitif, and the menu includes a courteous four-tongue translation of the encyclopedic list of available fish. Aim for the lightly broiled or poached: The flavors are too fresh to be drowned in that ubiquitous Belgian butter. *Kleine Vismarkt 3, tel. 09/223–5349. Reservations advised. Jacket advised. AE, DC, MC, V. Closed Sun. dinner, Mon. $$$*

★ **Het Cooremetershuys.** In a small room one flight up from the waterfront on the Graslei, this venturesome little restaurant offers contemporary spins on Belgian classics (wild rabbit with ginger, smoked entrecote) as well as simple standards (lamb shoulder with lentils, fish of the day). The setting combines the best of gallery-chic simplicity and old Flemish atmosphere: wood, brick, sculpture, and a massive hearth. *Graslei 12, tel. 09/223–4971. Reservations advised. Jacket advised. AE, DC, MC, V. Closed Wed. and Sun. $$$*

Jan Breydel. This cozy corner restaurant, warmed with exposed brick, oak, and a stone fireplace, offers sophisticated, nouvelle-inspired cooking: beef sautéed with goose liver in acacia honey and raspberry vinegar; turbot stuffed with oysters; strawberry gratin with lime and almonds. Cunning presentation occasionally overshadows substance, but the genial ambience and low-key intimacy compensate for any culinary pretensions. *Jan Breydelstraat 10, tel. 09/225–6287. Reservations advised. Jacket and tie advised. AE, DC, MC, V. Closed Mon. lunch and Sun. $$$*

★ **Pakhuis.** A gesture toward see-and-be-seen urban chic, this cavernous bi-level brasserie in a former warehouse has been built in a theatrical, retro high-tech style, with copper patina, terrazzo, and Statue of Liberty *torchières*. Daily *plats à l'ancienne* include *choucroute* (sauerkraut), waterzooi, and cassoulet, but the menu's real focus is on trendy upgrades: The house salad combines carpaccio of beef, *saumon mariné minute* (marinated raw salmon), smoked salmon, and foie gras. *Schuurkenstraat 4, B-9000, tel. 09/223–5555. Reservations optional. Dress: casual. AE, MC, V. Closed Sun. lunch. $$*

't Hietekoekske. Its name is Ghent dialect for "pancakes," but the menu offers a few chic, simple daily plates as well as its warm, tender namesakes. The setting is upscale and up-to-date—hanging halogen, framed contemporary art—but the ambience is casual and comfortable, ideal for a break from shopping in this neighborhood of trendy boutiques and department stores. It's open for lunch and afternoon snacks only. *Bennesteeg 1, tel. 09/223–7566. Dress: casual. No credit cards. Closed Sun. and dinner. $*

Taverne Keizershof. Considerably slicker than its peers and offering large portions of good, solid food, this restaurant is popular with locals. Besides all-day snacks (toasted sandwiches, spaghetti), there are cheap *dagschotel* (daily plates), cold meat or fish plates, mountainous steaks, and *gentse stoverij*, the local beer-marinated stew. The dining room in back has a low vaulted ceiling, crypt-style. *Vrijdagmarkt 47, tel. 09/223–4446. Dress: casual. MC, V. Closed Sun. $*

Lodging **Gravensteen.** If you prefer historic atmosphere over modern convenience, you'll overlook the creaks and austerity within this once-glamorous 1865 structure, its exterior and public spaces restored to the heights of neoclassical excess. Rooms, in contrast, are almost painfully spare (though squeaky-clean) and surprisingly small. The location—by the s-Gravensteen castle—is very good, in the midst of the picturesque waterfront. *Jan Breydelstraat 35, B-9000, tel. 09/225–1150, fax 09/225–1850. 17 rooms with bath. Facilities: lounge, bar, breakfast room, garden, parking. AE, DC, MC, V. $$$*

Novotel. Though part of a cookie-cutter, look-alike hotel chain, this modern lodging merits mention not only because of its location, in the center of the tourist and shopping area, but also because it manages to compress a sprawl of business-class luxuries—lounges, garden, swimming pool—into what seems to be a small urban space. Some windows open onto the inner courtyard, with its pool and greenery, and some take in the city monuments; decor is slick and standardized. In a city lacking in luxury accommodation, this is the closest thing. *Goudenleeuwplein 5, B-9000, tel. 09/224–2230, fax 09/*

224–3295. 117 rooms. Facilities: restaurant, bar, swimming pool. AE, DC, MC, V. $$$

Sint Jorishof/Cour St-Georges. Billing itself as the oldest hotel in Europe, this noble old step-gabled inn has housed and feted guests since 1228, from Mary of Burgundy (1477) to Napoléon (1805). Despite generations of renovation, much of its Gothic spirit has been preserved, from the burnished-wood restaurant to the stone fireplace in the reception. Rooms, both upstairs and in the annex across the street, are considerably less atmospheric, though new and attractive, with peach-tinted wood and fabrics in Florentine prints. The restaurant serves rich French classics and a few regional specialties. *Botermarkt 2, B-9000, tel. 09/224-2424, fax 09/224-2640. 28 rooms with bath. Facilities: restaurant ($$–$$$), conference rooms, garage. AE, DC, MC, V. $$$*

★ **Erasmus.** From the flagstoned and wood-beamed library/lounge in the basement to the stone mantels in the bedrooms upstairs, every cubic centimeter of this noble 15th-century home has been scrubbed, polished, and decked with a period knickknack, an antique clock, a circle of local lace; Even the tiny garden out back has been manicured like a miniature Versailles. The delightful couple in charge answer the bell pull at night and serve guests their soft-cooked eggs in the parlor in the morning. *Poel 25, B-9000, tel. 09/224-2195, fax 09/233-4241. 11 rooms with bath. Facilities: lounge, breakfast room. AE, DC, MC, V. Closed mid-Dec.–mid-Jan. $$*

Ieper
Lodging
Regina. Directly on the Grote Markt in a sturdy neo-Gothic brick building, this is a fresh, comfortable hotel, its generous spaces full of light, its rooms up-to-date. Everything has been upgraded except the windows; traffic noise is the only drawback. *Grote Markt 45, B-8900, tel. 057/219006. 17 rooms with bath. Facilities: restaurant, bar. AE, DC, MC, V. $$*

Knokke-Heist/
Het Zoute
Dining
Aquilon. Looking like it's the subject of a society house tour in a 1953 *Holiday* magazine, this glamorous little Empire-style mansion from Knokke's nouveau-riche golden age has been converted into a sumptuous restaurant, where diners sit at lace-covered tables and look onto a miniature landscaped garden and pond. The food, prepared by chef Marguerite De Spae, is just as opulent: oysters gratin with almond butter; whole bass, its juices captured in a solid crust of rock salt; and several lobster dishes. *Bayauxlaan 70, tel. 050/601274. Reservations required. Jacket and tie advised. AE, DC, MC, V. Closed high season, Tues. dinner, and Wed.; off-season, Mon.–Wed., mid-Dec.–Jan. $$$$*

New Alpina. Despite token efforts at pink linens and multiple stemware, this is a seafood diner at heart, where a friendly, house-proud husband and wife team have served North Sea classics since 1970. Fresh *raie* (skate), turbot, sole, and shrimp are served with simple sauces; the multicourse *"menu gourmet"* is a seafood feast. It's just off the beach, by the tourist office. *Lichttorenplein 12, tel. 050/608985. Reservations advised. Dress: casual. V. Closed Mon. dinner, Tues. $$*

Lodging
La Réserve. This vast country club of a hotel, complete with a saltwater treatment center and a man-made lake, was built as a private mansion in 1964 and expanded, under various managements, into the enormous complex it is today. Flowers and antique-look details do little to warm the airport-style public spaces, but rooms are bright and lovely, in soothing sponge-painted pastels. You can buy in as far as you like, from a simple bed-and-breakfast arrangement to a full-out Thalassa-treatment package. It's across from the Casino, three minutes from the beach. The restaurant is good and get-

ting better. *Elizabetlaan 158–160, B-8300 Albertstrand, tel. 050/ 610606. 110 rooms. Facilities: restaurant, bar, treatment center, seawater pool, hair salon, sauna, 4 tennis courts, windsurfing school. AE, DC, MC, V. $$$$*

Katelijne. A bit out of place in the bustle of high-style boutiques and traffic snaking along the beachfront, this charming old whitewashed brick auberge, built in the 1930s in traditional Flemish style, offers an atmospheric retreat, with fireplace, Oriental runners, fringed plush, and darkened timbers. The rooms are equally cozy and dated, though the marble/travertine baths are deluxe. There's a garden and terrace, and a welcoming copper-decked restaurant featuring fish. *Kustlaan 166, B-8300 Knokke-Zout, tel. 050/601216. 15 rooms with bath. Facilities: restaurant, bar, garden. AE, MC, V. $$$*

Kortrijk
Dining and Lodging

Gastronomisch Dorp Eddy Vandekerckhove. Just south of Kortrijk, Eddy's "gastronomic village" is a gourmet's heaven. On the menu are such delicacies as new potatoes with langoustines and caviar, lobster and sea scallops with braised chicory and onion marmalade, and thinly sliced venison with *trompettes de la mort* (a kind of black mushroom) and celeriac mousse. The large, luxurious rooms overlook fields on one side and an exotic botanical garden and pond on the other. *Sint-Anna 9, tel. 056/224756, fax 056/227170. 7 rooms with bath. Facilities: restaurant (reservations required), garden. AE, DC, MC, V. Closed Sun. dinner, Mon., Carnival week, 2 weeks in Sept. $$$$*

Lodging
★

Damier. This is a grand little hotel, impeccably renovated and superbly appointed, right on the Grote Markt. From its lavish café, with florid plasterwork and chandeliers, to its Laura Ashley rooms, to its beeswaxed oak wainscoting and Persian carpets, it exudes grace and seamless style; there are no musty corners or creaky halls hiding behind the decor. Despite its rococo facade, the hotel dates from the French Revolution, but comforts are thoroughly modern. *Grote Markt 41, B-8500, tel. 056/221547. 49 rooms. Facilities: restaurant, café, terrace café, sauna. AE, DC, MC, V. $$$*

Oostende
Dining and Lodging

Oostendse Compagnie/Le Vigneron. This palatial villa, once a royal residence, is right on the sea, and there are views of the beach and ocean from the dining room with its splendid terrace and from the large bedrooms. The restaurant has had its ups and downs in recent years, but it's now firmly on an upward trajectory. Among new dishes are tempura of langoustines with new onions and ginger, roast turbot with spices, and pullet *à la vapeur* with truffles. *Koningstraat 79, tel. 059/704816, fax 059/805316. 13 rooms with bath. Facilities: restaurant ($$$$), beach. AE, DC, MC, V. Closed Sun. dinner, Mon., first 2 weeks of Mar., Oct. $$$*

De Panne
Dining

De Braise. Run by the parents of Le Fox's chef, who ran Le Fox (*see below*) when it was a simple tavern, this is the Buyens family's return to their roots: an old-fashioned regional restaurant, offering updated, upgraded local cooking in a homey, bourgeois setting. Though the menu reads like a thousand others in the region—eels in green, turbot poached or grilled, sauce hollandaise/dijonnaise, sole meunière—the portions are generous and the preparation is soigné, and the service is equally sophisticated. *Bortierplein 1, tel. 058/ 415999. Reservations advised. Dress: casual/jacket advised. AE, DC, MC, V. Closed Mon., Tues., second half of Jan., Oct. $$–$$$*

Dining and Lodging
★

Le Fox. Chef Stéphane Buyens, like a proper son, has made good, taking over his parents' tavern and creating a prestigious, welcoming gastronomic retreat. Developing dishes such as roast langoustine tails in sea urchin butter, and turbot in an aromatic mix of 10 oils, herbs, and beet juice, he has drawn a loyal following. They stay in graciously furnished rooms (some rooms have windows angled toward the waterfront), and work as many meals into the weekend as they can. The dining room is auberge-cozy and the ambience unstuffy. *Walckiersstraat 2, B-8660, tel. 058/412855. 14 rooms with bath. Facilities: restaurant ($$$$), bar. AE, DC, MC, V. Closed all year, Tues.; off-season, Mon., second half Jan., first 3 weeks of Oct. $$*

Lodging **Sparrenhof.** This is a self-contained oasis, cut off from the beachfront scene but only 150 meters (500 feet) from the water. Its pretty pool is cloistered in a garden haven, with many rooms facing the greenery. The original building dates from the '50s, and there are still seven comfortable rooms within; the new wing sports flashy bird's-eye veneer and modern furnishings. The restaurant is welcoming year-round, with a wood-burning fireplace and poolside tables. *Koninginnelaan 26, B-8660, tel. 058/411328. 25 rooms with bath. Facilities: restaurant, bar, poolside terrace, pool. AE, DC, MC, V. $$*

The Arts and Nightlife

The Arts The monthly *Agenda Brugge* (at the tourist office) gives details of all
Brugge events in the city. Check also listings in *The Bulletin*.

The **Festival of Flanders** is the umbrella organization for music festivals in all major Flemish cities. For program information, contact Festival van Vlaanderen (Pl. Flagey 18, Brussels 1050, tel. 02/648–1484).

There are dramatic and musical performances at the **Stadsshouwburg** (City Theater) in Vlamingstraat (tel. 050/338167).

Ghent Cultural life in Ghent is lively and varied, and it's worthwhile checking *The Bulletin*'s "What's On" section under the heading "Other Towns." Many events take place in the **Kunstencentrum Vooruit** (Vooruit Arts Center, Sint-Pietersnieuwstraat 123, tel. 09/225–5643), which includes two concert halls, a ballroom, a theater, 10 smaller halls, and an art gallery.

De Vlaamse Opera (Flemish Opera House) (Schouwburgstraat 3, tel. 09/225–2425) has been restored, with a splendid ceiling and chandelier, and its eight annual productions are of international standard.

Nightlife Among the nicest hotel bars are **The Meeting** at the Oud Huis Am-
Brugge sterdam (Spiegelrei 3, tel. 050/341810), **De Medici** (Potterierei 15, tel. 050/339833), and **Academie** (Wijngaardstraat 7–9, tel. 050/332266).

Discos, mostly catering to a clientele not much older than 20, are clustered around Eiermarkt, back of the Markt: **Coolcat** (Eiermarkt 11, tel. 050/340527), **Ambiorix** (Eiermarkt 11 bis, tel. 050/337400), **The Pick** (Eiermarkt 12, tel. 050/337638); and at 't Zand: **Ma Rica Rokk** ('t Zand 8, tel. 050/338358) and **Graffiti** ('t Zand 9, tel. 050/336909). **Villa Romana** (Kraanplein 1, tel. 050/343453) attracts an older crowd.

Ghent As in most Belgian towns, nightlife in Ghent is a laid-back affair. A few cabarets exist, but the Gentenaars much prefer their pubs and cafés. **Backstage** (Sint-Pietersnieuwstraat 128, tel. 09/233–3535), a café-restaurant across from the Vooruit center, presents occasional classical and jazz concerts. **Cirque Central** (Hoogpoort 32, tel. 09/225–1416) is both a café and a disco with an under-25 crowd. The

Brasserie Aba-jour (Oudburg 20, tel. 09/223–4208), more relaxed with its cool jazz and art deco ambience, overlooks the Leie.

The Coast The closure rate among seasonal night spots is high; make sure the place you've chosen is still in business. The best bet for quality and consistency in any town is the Casino, where gambling takings help underwrite the nightclub.

Knokke-Heist is the leader on the coast for nocturnal entertainment. The **Casino** (Zeedijk 507, tel. 050/606010) offers dinner-dancing with two orchestras, gala nights with international stars, theater, movies, ballet, exhibitions, and two discos, **Number 1** (entrance on Zeedijk) and **Dubbel's** (entrance on Canada Square). Another favorite is the **Gallery Club** (Canada Square 22, tel. 050/608133). In **Blankenberge** the popular discos are **The Beatles** (Casinoplein 6, tel. 050/411653), **Old Corner** (Casinoplein 10, tel. 050/414419), **Pebbles** (Zeedijk 104, tel. 050/416536), and **Wit Paard** (Langestraat 40, tel. 050/411100). In **Oostende**, your best bet is the **Sporting Club** (Oosthelling, tel. 059/705111), which is run by the casino. There's a wide choice of night clubs, girlie shows, and discos along Van Iseghemlaan and Langestraat.

Antwerp

The true Flemish name of Belgium's second city is Antwerpen. English speakers use an abbreviated form, and French speakers call it Anvers. Some think the name refers to the way that merchant brigantines sailed up to the central town, which was *aan het werp* (on the wharf). A more fanciful but much-favored legend tells the story of a Roman soldier, Silvius Brabo, and a giant, Druon Antigon. The giant exacted a toll from boatmen on the river and cut off the hands of those who refused, until Silvius confronted him, cut off the giant's own hand, and flung it—*handwerpen* (hand throwing)—into the River Scheldt. Believe it if you will, but it explains the presence of severed hands on Antwerp's coat of arms.

Great prosperity came to Antwerp during the reign of Emperor Charles V. Born in Ghent and raised in Mechelen, he made Antwerp the principal port of his vast domains, and it became the most important commercial center in the 16th-century world, as well as a center of the new craft of printing. The golden age came to an end with the abdication of Charles V in 1555. He was succeeded by Philip II, whose ardent Catholicism brought him into immediate conflict with the Protestants of the Netherlands. In 1566, when Calvinist iconoclasts destroyed paintings and sculptures in churches and monasteries, Philip responded by sending in Spanish troops. In what became known as the Spanish Fury, they sacked the town and killed thousands of citizens.

The decline of Antwerp had already begun when its most illustrious painters, Rubens, Jordaens, and Van Dyck, reached the peak of their fame. The Treaty of Munster in 1648, which concluded the Thirty Years' War, also sealed Antwerp's fate, for the River Scheldt was closed to shipping—not to be opened again until 1863, when a treaty obliged the Dutch, who controlled the estuary, to reopen it.

The huge and splendid railway station, built at the turn of the century, remains a fitting monument to Antwerp's second age of prosperity; the city hosted universal expositions in both 1885 and 1894. In World War I, Antwerp held off the German invaders long enough for the Belgian army to regroup south of the IJzer. In World War II, the

Germans trained many V-1 flying bombs and V-2 rockets on the city, where Allied troops were debarking for the final push.

Antwerp today is Europe's second-largest port. Although ships go in and out in a single day, and sailors on leave are a rare sight on the city streets, Antwerp has retained much of the zest often associated with a port. Some of the old ambiguity also remains. Antwerp has traditionally taken pride in being open to influences from abroad and in welcoming newcomers to the city. Yet in recent elections, a startling number of votes have been cast for the more extreme right-wing Flemish parties.

Important Addresses and Numbers

Tourist Information The **Toerisme Stad Antwerpen** (Antwerp City Tourist Office) (Grote Markt 15, tel. 03/232–0103, fax 03/231–1937; open Mon.–Sat. 9–6, Sun. 9–5) is in the heart of the old city. It will assist with hotel reservations. The **Toeristische Federatie Provincie Antwerpen** (Antwerp Provincial Tourist Office) (Karel Oomsstraat 11, tel. 03/216–2810) will help plan trips to see the rest of the province.

Emergencies **Police,** tel. 101. **Ambulance,** tel. 100. **Emergency Rooms:** Middelheim (Lindendreef 1, tel. 03/280–3111); Stuivenberg (Lange Beeldekensstraat 267, tel. 03/217–7111).

Late-Night Pharmacies The name of the pharmacy on duty is displayed in all pharmacy windows.

Where to Change Money As well as at banks, money can be changed at **American Express** (Frankrijklei 21), and at **Thomas Cook** (Koningin Astridplein 33). The Exchange Office in the Central Station and **Inter-Change** (Suikerrui 36) stay open late and on weekends.

Travel Agencies **American Express** (Frankrijklei 21, tel. 03/232–5920); **VTB** (Sint-Jacobsmarkt 45, tel. 03/220–3232); **Huybrechts** (Carnotstraat 41, tel. 03/231–9900).

Arriving and Departing by Plane

Deurne Airport (tel. 03/218–1211), 5½ kilometers (3½ miles) from the city center, is served by several flights a day to London. **Brussels National Airport** (Zaventem) is linked with Antwerp by frequent bus service (hourly 7 AM–11 PM). The trip takes 50 minutes and a round-trip ticket costs BF220.

Arriving and Departing by Car, Train, and Bus

By Car Antwerp is 48 kilometers (30 miles) north of Brussels. The city is surrounded by a ring road from which expressways shoot off like spokes in a wheel: A1/E19 south to Brussels and Paris, north to Rotterdam and Amsterdam; A14/E17 southwest to Ghent and Lille; A13 southeast to Hasselt and Liège; A21/E34 northeast to Eindhoven and the Ruhr. For car rentals there are **Avis** (Plantin en Moretuslei 62, tel. 03/218–9496), **Budget** (Frankrijklei 70, tel. 03/232–3500), and **Hertz** (Mechelsesteenweg 43, tel. 03/233–2992).

By Train There are four to five trains an hour from Brussels, and the trip takes about 45 minutes. The train ride north to Rotterdam takes an hour. International Intercity trains between Paris and Amsterdam stop at Berchem Station south of the city center rather than entering the downtown Central Station (Koningin Astridplein, tel. 03/233–3915).

Getting Around Antwerp

By Tram and Subway You can travel by tram all over central Antwerp. Some operate underground as the pre-Metro system. The most useful subway line for visitors links the Central Station (Metro stop *Diamant*) with the left bank via the Groenplaats (for the cathedral and Grote Markt). Your BF40 ticket is good for one hour on all forms of public transport; BF190 will buy you unlimited travel for one day. Tickets are available at **De Lijn** offices (tel. 03/218–1411) at the Diamant, Opera/Frankrijklei, and Groenplaats Metro stops, and at the tourist office.

By Bus Municipal bus lines (tel. 03/218–1411) mostly begin outside the Central Station in the Koningin Astridplein. Longer distance buses start from the Franklin Rooseveltplaats.

By Taxi There are taxi stands in front of the Central Station and at other principal points. It is often easier to call for one: **Antwerp Taxi** (tel. 03/238–3838), **ATM** (tel. 03/216–0160), or **Metropole Taxi** (tel. 03/231–3131).

Guided Tours

By Minibus **Sightseeing Line** (based in Brugge, tel. 050/311355) operates 50-minute orientation tours with cassette commentary. Tickets (BF330 adults, BF200 children) are sold on the bus, which departs Grote Markt daily at 2, 3, and 4 from mid-March to mid-November. It runs weekends, mid-November to mid-March.

By Boat **Flandria** (tel. 03/231–3100) operates 50-minute boat trips on the River Scheldt, departing from the Steenplein pontoon (next to the Steen) daily every hour on the hour from 10 to 4 from Easter to September (BF220 adults, BF120 children), as well as boat tours of the port (2½ hrs), which leave from Quay 13 near Londonstraat (May–Aug., daily 10:30 and 2:30; Easter–Apr. and Sept., Sun. and bank holidays only; BF350 adults, BF200 children).

Personal Guides Qualified guides can be engaged through the City Tourist Office, which requires a couple of days' notice. The price for two hours is BF1,200, and BF600 for each additional hour.

Highlights for First-Time Visitors

Bourla Theater (Tour 2: Rubens and Diamonds)
Grote Markt (Tour 1: The Old City)
Museum Mayer van den Bergh (Tour 2: Rubens and Diamonds)
Onze-Lieve-Vrouwekathedraal (Tour 1: The Old City)
Plantin-Moretus Museum (Tour 1: The Old City)
Rubenshuis (Tour 2: Rubens and Diamonds)
St. Carolus Borromeuskerk (Tour 1: The Old City)
Provinciaal Diamantmuseum (Tour 2: Rubens and Diamonds)
Steen (Tour 1: The Old City)
Zoo (Tour 2: Rubens and Diamonds)

Exploring Antwerp

Numbers in the margin correspond to points of interest on the Antwerp map.

Tour 1: The Old City The triangular **Grote Markt,** the heart of the Old City, is lined on two sides by guild houses and on the third by the Renaissance **Stadhuis** ❶ (Town Hall). Antwerp's Town Hall was built in the 1560s during the city's golden age, when Paris and Antwerp were the only European cities with more than 100,000 inhabitants. In the facade, the fanciful fretwork of the late-Gothic style has given way to the discipline and order of the Renaissance; the public rooms are suitably impressive, though the heavy hand of 19th-century restoration work is much in evidence. *Admission: BF30, Open Mon. 9–noon, Tues.–Fri. 9–3, and Sat. noon–4. No access during official receptions.*

The huge fountain splashing water over much of the square is crowned by the figure of the legendary Silvius Brabo. He has been about to fling the hand of the giant into the River Scheldt for the past hundred years. Cafés line the square, most with terraces where it is especially pleasant to linger on a Monday night in summer, listening to the cathedral carillon.

Another famous monster slayer, St. George, is perched on top of the 16th-century guild house at Grote Markt 5, while the dragon appears to be falling off the pediment. Walk around the Stadhuis and along Gildekamersstraat; as you emerge on the north side of the square, take the second street left, Wisselstraat.

Time Out Among the many Italian restaurants around the Grote Markt, **La Terrazza** (Wisselstraat 2), run by brothers Saverio and Arturo, features reasonable prices and authentic cuisine.

Turn left again on Oude Beurs and you come immediately upon little Spanjepandsteeg and the house called **De Spieghel** (The Mirror). Originally built for the archers' guild, it was bought in 1506 by Pieter Gillis, a leading humanist. At the beginning of his most famous work, Sir Thomas More describes how, on a visit to Antwerp, he is walking back from Mass in the cathedral with Gillis when they encounter a traveler who tells them of his adventures on an island named Utopia. Erasmus, another friend of Gillis's, had the first edition of *Utopia* printed in Leuven.

② You can't miss the step-gabled **Vleeshuis** (Butchers' Hall), just a block away, for it remains one of the tallest buildings in the Old City, although it was completed for the Butchers' Guild in 1503. The designer was Herman de Waghemakere, member of a family of architects who did much to embellish their native city. The walls were built of alternating bands of brick and sandstone, creating an oddly pleasing layered effect. In the old days, the ground floor was used as a meat market, while the upper floors were occupied by a banquet hall and council chambers. Most of the space is crammed with miscellaneous antiquities of local origin. *Vleeshouwersstraat 38–40, tel. 03/233–6404. Admission: BF75. Open Tues.–Sun. 10–5.*

③ The block-long Repenstraat leads to the quay and the **Steen**. The 9th-century fortress was built to protect the western frontier of the Holy Roman Empire against the counts of Flanders. Charles V had the Steen partially rebuilt, and one can distinguish the darker, medieval masonry extending midway up the walls from the lighter, 16th-century upper level. The Steen was used as a prison for centuries. It now houses the **National Scheepvaartmuseum** (National Maritime Museum), where a large collection of models, figureheads, instruments, and charts is on display. *Steenplein, tel. 03/232–0850. Admission: BF75. Open Tues.–Sun. 10–5.*

The Steen is the only survivor of the original waterfront. Many houses were torn down in the 19th century to make room for the wide, straight quays that nowadays are practically deserted, the port having moved north of the city proper. The promenade starting at the Steen, **Noorderterras,** remains a very popular place for a Sun-

Antwerp

Antwerp Zoo, **18**

Bourla Theater, **13**

Centraalstation, **17**

Diamondland, **16**

Etnografisch
Museum, **10**

Groenplaats, **11**

Grote Markt, **1**

Museum Mayer
van den Bergh, **12**

Onze-Lieve-
Vrouwekathedraal, **7**

Plantin-Moretus
Museum, **9**

Provinciaal
Diamantmuseum, **15**

Rockoxhuis, **5**

Rubenshuis, **14**

St. Carolus
Borromeus, **6**

Sint-Pauluskerk, **4**

Steen, **3**

Vlaeykensgang, **8**

Vleeshuis, **2**

day stroll along the Scheldt, 500 meters (550 yards) wide here. "God gave us the river," say the Antwerpers, "and the river gave us all the rest."

At the end of the promenade, descend the steps, veer right across the quay, and head for the newly renovated **Sint-Pauluskerk** (St. Paul's Church), whose Baroque steeple can be seen over the rooftops. The church itself is late Gothic, built for the Dominicans by Domien de Waghemakere, but the interior was subsequently embellished—crammed, some would say—with a wealth of Baroque statuary, furnishings, and paintings, including the *Scourging of Christ* by Rubens. You have to walk around the church to find the entrance. *Veemarkt, tel. 03/232-3267. Admission: BF30. Open daily May–Sept. 2–5; Oct.–Apr. 9–noon.*

From the Veemarkt in front of St. Paul's, you can zigzag through the old streets and alleys—first along Zwartzustersstraat, then right on Stoelstraat (at No. 11 stands the last remaining, but restored, wooden house in Gothic style), left on Zirkstraat, and right on Lange Koepoortstraat to the second street on the left, **Wolstraat.** This is the street where many English wool merchants settled in the 16th century, and the houses are distinguished by their Baroque portals, especially those at Nos. 7 and 30. You can enter through the gate of No. 37 to discover a well-preserved inner courtyard surrounded by 15th-century almshouses.

Turning left on Minderbroedersrui and right almost immediately on Keizerstraat, you arrive at the **Rockoxhuis,** the splendid Renaissance home of Nicolaas Rockox, first burgomaster (mayor) of Antwerp, who moved here in 1603. Rockox, a humanist and art collector, was a friend and patron of Rubens, and two of the painter's works hang here. One is *Madonna and Child,* in fact a delicate portrait of his first wife, Isabella, and their son Nicolaas; the other is a sketch for the *Crucifixion.* The collection also includes works by Van Dyck, Frans Snijders, Joachim Patinier, Jordaens, and David Teniers the Younger. The setting is important; rather than being displayed on museum walls, the paintings are shown in the context of a patrician Baroque home, furnished in the style of the period. *Keizerstraat 10, tel. 03/231-4710. Admission free. Open Tues.–Sun. 10–5.*

The Jesuit church of **St. Carolus Borromeus** is just off Wolstraat. The front and tower are generally attributed to Rubens, and his hand can certainly be seen in the clustered cherubim above the entrance. The facade suggests a richly decorated high altar, inviting the spectator to enter the church. The interior also bears the imprint of Rubens and his group. *Hendrik Conscienceplein 12, tel. 03/233-8433. Admission: BF20. Open Mon. and Wed.–Fri. 7:30–1, Sat. 7:30–noon and 3–6:15.*

The square is one of the most attractive in Antwerp, flanked by the harmonious Renaissance buildings of the Jesuit convent, now occupied by the City Library. Wijngaardstraat, with its restaurants and art galleries, leads toward the Grote Markt.

Time Out   **Het Elfde Gebod** (The Eleventh Commandment, Torfbrug 10) nestles under the cathedral. One of the most original of Antwerp's many cafés, it is crammed with plaster saints and angels salvaged from old churches. The beer is good, and you can have a pleasant meal of bread and cheese.

Continue to the cathedral entrance on Handschoenmarkt (Glove Market). **Onze-Lieve-Vrouwekathedraal** (Our Lady's Cathedral) is the city's Gothic masterpiece, recently restored. It is the largest church in the Low Countries. Work started in 1352 and continued in fits and starts until 1584, but even so the whole is a totally homogeneous monument of stone and light thanks to a succession of remarkable architects, including Peter Appelmans, Herman and Domien de Waghemakere, and Rombout Keldermans the Younger. The 123-meter (404-foot) -high north spire is a miracle of lightness. The tower contains a 47-bell carillon (played Fri. 11:30–12:30 and Mon. in summer 8 PM–9 PM).

The cathedral's art treasures were twice vandalized, first by Protestant iconoclasts in 1566, and again by the French at the end of the 18th century. The latter carried off masterpieces of art as though they were their rightful booty; some but by no means all have subsequently been returned. Other works have been donated or purchased to make up an outstanding collection of 17th-century religious art, including three Rubens altarpieces. The panels of the Descent from the Cross triptych—Mary's visit to Elizabeth and the presentation of Jesus in the temple—are among the most delicate and tender biblical scenes ever painted. The *Assumption of the Virgin Mary*, painted for the high altar, is a characteristic swirling apotheosis in which the Virgin is carried upward by massed ranks of *putti* (cherubs) and *amoretti* (cupids) toward the angel waiting to crown her. The Assumption has been cunningly hung so that the rays of the sun illuminate it exactly at noon. *Groenplaats 21, tel. 03/231–3033. Admission: BF60. Open weekdays 10–5, Sat. 10–3, and Sun. 1–4.*

A few steps to the left from the front of the cathedral is Oude Koornmarkt, with many old step-gable houses. At No. 16 begins the **Vlaeykensgang,** a quiet cobblestone lane that preserves the mood and style of the 16th century. The alley ends in Pelgrimsstraat, where there is a great view of the cathedral spire. Turning your back to the spire and walking down Pelgrimsstraat, you quickly reach Reyndersstraat, where the **house of** the painter **Jacob Jordaens** stands at No. 6. This gem of Baroque art, with its very attractive courtyard, rivals the Rubenshuis (*see* Tour 2, *below*). *Reyndersstraat 6, tel. 03/233–3033. Admission free. Open Tues.–Fri. 10–5.*

Time Out There's another secret courtyard near the Jordaens house. It's at Leeuwenstraat 18 and features a good café, **De Groote Witte Arend,** an old convent where the music tends to be by Vivaldi or Telemann. The menu lists 34 different types of beer.

Just to the left is Leeuwenstraat, which leads to Vrijdagmarkt. On the south side of this square stands the **Plantin-Moretus Museum,** named for Christophe Plantin, who established the Plantin Press here in 1576. Philip II of Spain appointed Plantin exclusive printer of liturgical books, and thousands were exported every year to Spain and its possessions. His greatest achievement was the *Biblia Regia* (in Room 16): eight large volumes containing the Bible in Latin, Greek, Hebrew, Syriac, and Aramaic, complete with notes, glossaries, and grammars.

The first three rooms were the family quarters; they contain several portraits by Rubens. Others remain as they were when occupied by accountants, editors, and proofreaders. The printing workshop, finally, contains Plantin's 16 printing presses. Two typefaces designed here, Plantin and Garamond, are still in use. The presses are still in working order, and one can, in fact, purchase a copy of Plantin's sonnet "Le bonheur de ce monde," an ode to contentment, in any of seven European languages and printed on an original press. *Vrijdagmarkt 22, tel. 03/233–0294. Admission: BF75. Open Tues.–Sun. 10–5.*

On the way back to the Grote Markt, you can cross the Suikerrui to
⑩ the **Etnografisch Museum** (Ethnographic Museum). This new museum—opened in 1988—contains excellently displayed collections illustrating art, religion, and daily life in Africa, the Americas, Asia, and the South Seas. *Suikerrui 19, tel. 03/232–0882. Admission: BF75. Open Tues.–Sun. 10–5.*

Tour 2: The bustling **Groenplaats,** just south of the cathedral, is adorned
Rubens and with a statue of Pieter Paul Rubens himself. He wears a sword as a
Diamonds badge of his rank, for he was truly a Renaissance man who in addi-
⑪ tion to his prodigious artistic output found time to undertake a number of diplomatic missions, culminating in the negotiation of a peace treaty between Spain and England and knighthoods from both Charles II and Philip IV.

From the southeast corner of the square, Schoenmarkt leads up toward Meir, Antwerp's most elegant shopping street, punctuated at this end by the **Torengebouw,** built around 1930, which Antwerpers proudly proclaim as Europe's first skyscraper.

Huidevettersstraat, to the right, leads to Lange Gasthuisstraat and
⑫ the outstanding **Museum Mayer van den Bergh,** a private art collection amassed in the 19th century by a passionate connoisseur, Fritz Mayer van den Bergh. The collection includes treasures such as a life-size polychrome statue from about 1300 of St. John resting his head on Christ's bosom. It is, however, the two Bruegel paintings that make this small museum a must. One is his witty, miniature illustrations of *Twelve Proverbs* based on popular Flemish sayings. The other is *Dulle Griet*, often referred to in English as Mad Meg. It shows an irate woman wearing helmet and breastplate—a sword in one hand, and food and cooking utensils in the other—striding across a field strewn with the ravages and insanity of war. Nothing could be further from the Bruegelian villages than this nightmare world, whose hallucinations are akin to those of Hieronymus Bosch's fevered imagination. On an emotional level, it is among the most powerful antiwar statements ever made. A footnote: Mayer van den Bergh bought *Dulle Griet* for BF488 in 1894; today it is priceless. *Lange Gasthuisstraat 19, tel. 03/232–4237. Admission: BF75. Open Tues.–Sun. 10–5.*

In Komedieplaats (by way of Huidevettersstraat), on the right, is
⑬ the restored neoclassical **Bourla Theater,** a magnificent playhouse from the 1830s, with an ornate ceiling and an enormous chandelier.

Time Out Even if you do not attend a theater performance, stop in at the **Bourla Café** in the theater's rotunda. This trendy place is open noon–midnight for coffee, drinks, and light meals.

⑭ On Wapper, one block away, stands **Rubenshuis,** the carefully reconstructed home of the painter as patrician. Only the elaborate portico and temple, designed by Rubens in Italian Baroque style, were still standing earlier in this century. They figure in several of his own paintings as well as in works by Van Dyck and Jordaens. Drawings by Rubens and his pupils and old prints were used to re-create the brick and sandstone house—kitchen, dining room, bedrooms—and the huge studio. Some Rubens paintings hang in the house (an early *Adam and Eve*, an *Annunciation*, a self-portrait), but nothing like the 300-odd pieces that his widow promptly sold off after his death in

1640. *Wapper 9, tel. 03/232–4751. Admission: BF75. Open Tues.–
Sun. 10–5.*

On the opposite side of Meir is the elegant 18th-century
Osterriethhuis, now occupied by a bank. The continuation of Meir,
Leysstraat, crosses the broad Frankrijklei and becomes De
Keyserlei. On your right is the **Diamond District,** a few nondescript
city blocks bordering on the Central Station to the east. Shop signs
in Hebrew and the characteristic Hasidic clothing and ringlets worn
by many men are the only clues that this area is any different from
the rest of Antwerp. Below the elevated railway tracks a long row of
stalls and shops gleams with jewelry and gems, a bit like New York's
West 47th Street.

Diamond cutting began in Brugge but moved to Antwerp in the 16th
century along with most other wealth-creating activities. Given
Antwerp's twin preoccupations with beauty and money, craft and
trade both flourished. Twenty-five million carats are cut and traded
in Antwerp every year, more than anywhere else, and the industry
employs some 18,000 people, divided among 6,000 independent
firms. In addition to cutters, grinders, and polishers, there are
about 3,000 traders, of whom two-thirds are Jewish and one-fifth Indian, with a heavy sprinkling of Lebanese and Armenians. Nearly
all come from old diamond families. Some of Antwerp's Jews managed to flee Belgium during the war, but many more perished in the
camps.

Turning right off Meir into Appelmansstraat you come quickly to
(15) Lange Herentalsestraat and the **Provinciaal Diamantmuseum** (Provincial Diamond Museum). Maps, models, and videos tell the story
of the diamond trade, and exceptional jewelry is displayed in the
treasure room. *Lange Herentalsestraat 31–33, tel. 03/231–8645.
Admission free. Open daily 10–5; demonstrations Sat. PM.*

In this business, security is of the essence, and traditionally visitors
have not been able to see much of the bustling activity. To remedy
(16) this situation, the industry has created **Diamondland.** The spectacular showrooms have three floors of slide shows and films, showcases
of rough and polished diamonds, and several diamond cutters at
work. *Appelmansstraat 33A, tel. 03/243–3612. Open Mon.–Sat.
9–6.*

(17) The Neo-Baroque **Centraalstation** (Central Station) at the end of De
Keyserlei was built between 1895 and 1905 during the reign of Leopold II, a monarch not given to understatement. Architect Louis
Delacenserie's magnificent exterior and splendid, vaulted ticket-of-
fice hall and staircases call out for hissing steam engines, peremplo-
ry conductors, scurrying porters, and languid ladies wrapped in
boas. Alas, most departures and arrivals are humble commuter
trains. The square in front of the station, Koningin Astridplein, is
depressingly seedy, and the blocks north of it are best avoided.

(18) East of the station the **Antwerp Zoo** offers a refreshing change from
most city center zoos. A Moorish villa is home to the rhinoceroses,
an Egyptian temple is the elephant house, and the thriving okapi
family graze around an Indian temple. There's also a dolphinarium,
an aquarium, and a house for nocturnal animals. *Koningin
Astridplein 26, tel. 03/231–1640. Admission: BF390 adults, BF240
children. Open daily 9–4:45 in winter, until 6:30 in summer.*

Excursion from Antwerp

Lier The small town of **Lier** lies 17 kilometers (10½ miles) southeast of Antwerp on N10. It may seem a sleepy riverside town, but it has long attracted poets and painters and has even known its moment of glory. It was here in 1496 that Philip of Burgundy married Joan of Aragon and Castile (known as Philippe le Beau—Philip the Handsome—and Juana la Loca—Joan the Mad). From that union sprang Emperor Charles V.

The **Sint-Gummaruskerk,** where they were wed, is yet another product of the De Waghemakere–Keldermans partnership. It is well endowed with stained-glass windows from the 15th and 16th centuries. Those in the choir were the gift of Maximilian of Austria, who visited in 1516, and he can be seen in one of them with his wife, Mary of Burgundy.

Along the riverside, willows bend over the water, and in summer, boats can be hired for 40-minute sightseeing rides (Netelaan, weekends 2–8). The Kleine Nete flows straight through the heart of the town; the Grote Nete and a canal also encircle the center.

Across the river is the **Zimmertoren,** a 14th-century tower renamed for Louis Zimmer, who designed its astronomical clock with 11 faces in 1930. His studio, where 57 dials show the movements of the moon, the tides, the zodiac, and other cosmic phenomena, is inside the tower. *Zimmerplein 18, tel. 03/489–1111. Admission: BF40. Open daily 9–noon and 1–7; winter, 9–noon and 1–5.*

Time Out If you want sustenance, don't pass up the delicious syrup-filled biscuits, *Lierse Vlaaikens,* that are the local specialty.

Nearby is the **Begijnhof,** which differs from most other beguinages in that its small houses line narrow streets rather than being grouped around a common. A Renaissance portico stands at the entrance, and on it a statue of St. Begge, who gave his name to this congregation and who probably derived his own from the fact that he was *un begue* (a stammerer).

What to See and Do with Children

The **Antwerp Zoo** is perhaps the greatest attraction for the younger generation in Antwerp (*see* Exploring Antwerp, Tour 2, *above*). **Planckendael,** the breeding station for the zoo, is a huge park where more than a thousand animals live in a state of almost total freedom. *Southeast of Mechelen, 25 km (15 mi) from Antwerp: Leuvensesteenweg 582, Muizen, tel. 015/414921. Admission: BF280 adults, BF180 children. Open Apr.–Sept., daily 8:30–6:30; Oct.–Mar. daily 10–5.*

Kids can see the entire city in miniature at **Mini-Antwerpen** in a transformed quayside warehouse. *Hangar 15, Scheldekaai, tel. 03/ 237–0329. Admission: BF130 adults, BF100 children. Open daily noon–6.*

The region's chief amusement park is **Bobbejaanland,** which has 45 rides, plus slides, swings, and shows. *43 km (27 mi) from Antwerp on E313, exit Herentals West, direction Kasterlee; Steenweg op Olen, Lichtaart, tel. 014/557811. Admission: BF510. Open Apr.– June and Sept., daily 10–6; July–Aug. 10–7.*

Off the Beaten Track

Berchem, to the southeast of the city center, is the first train station on the line to Brussels. The 19th-century entrepreneur Baron Edouard Osy and his sister Josephine Cogels, bought an old castle, demolished it, and built some refreshingly eccentric houses reflecting the confident and eclectic tastes of that era. There are houses in Renaissance, Greek classical, and Venetian styles, but most of all, there are beautiful Art Nouveau buildings, especially at the southern end of Cogels Osylei and Waterloostraat.

South of the Old City, in Leopold de Waelplaats, is the **Koninklijk Museum voor Schone Kunsten** (Royal Museum of Fine Arts). The permanent collection is long on monumental Rubens works and short on more intimate paintings; the prosaic explanation is that the latter were more easily taken away from Antwerp. Rubens's friends and followers are also well represented. The collection of Flemish primitives is perhaps even more rewarding; it includes works by van Eyck, Memling, Roger van der Weyden, Joachim Patinier, and Quinten Metsys. On the ground floor there's a representative survey of Belgian art of the past 150 years—Emile Claus, Rik Wouters, Permeke, Magritte, Delvaux, and especially James Ensor. *Leopold de Waelplaats 1–9, tel. 03/238–7809. Admission free. Open Tues.–Sun. 10–5.*

The **Museum voor Hedendaagse Kunst** (Museum of Contemporary Art) occupies a renovated warehouse a few blocks west of the Fine Arts Museum, near the waterfront. Exhibits include contemporary painting, installations, video art, and experimental architecture. *Leuvenstraat 16–30, tel. 03/238–5960. Admission: BF100. Open Tues.–Sun. 10–5.*

South of the beltway—above the tunnel for the expressway to Brussels—is the 30-acre **Middelheim Park** with its **Openluchtmuseum** (Open Air Sculpture Museum). There are close to 500 sculptures in this very attractive setting, providing an excellent survey of three-dimensional art from Rodin to the present. There is also a new pavilion that houses smaller or more fragile sculptures. *Tel. 03/828–1350. Admission free, except during exhibitions. Open Tues.–Sun. 10–dusk, (i.e., 5 PM in midwinter; June–July, 9 PM).*

Shopping

Antwerp takes pride in being young, with-it, and trendy, and this is reflected in the city's shops and boutiques, which are as smart as they come.

Shopping Streets The elegant **Meir,** together with its extension to the east, **De Keyserlei,** and at the opposite end, **Huidevettersstraat,** is where the smart and long-established shops are. Shopping galleries branch off from all three—**Century Center** and **Antwerp Tower** from De Keyserlei, **Patio** from Meir, and **Nieuwe Gaanderij** from Huidevettersstraat.

The boutiques along pedestrian malls often cater to more avant-garde tastes. The best-known area is **De Wilde Zee,** consisting of Groendalstraat, Wiegstraat, and Korte Gasthuisstraat. Another pedestrian area is **Hoogstraat,** between Grote Markt and Sint-Jansvliet, with its appendix **Grote Pieter Potstraat.** Here you find good secondhand bookshops and all kinds of bric-a-brac.

Street Markets Public auction sales of furniture and other secondhand goods are held on **Vrijdagmarkt** (Wed. and Fri. 9–noon). There's an antique market on **Lijnwaadmarkt** (Easter–Oct., Sat. 9–5), just north of the cathedral. Oudevaartplaats (a block south from Rubenshuis on Wapper) is home to the most popular and animated of Antwerp's markets, the **Vogelmarkt** (bird market, Sun. 9–1). It includes flowers and plants, fruit and vegetables, and lots of pets.

The **Rubensmarkt** (Rubens Market, Aug. 15 annually) is held on the Grote Markt, with vendors in 17th-century costumes hawking everything under the sun.

Specialty Stores
Clothing A group of fashion designers collectively known as the Antwerp Six has been making waves internationally. Two of them, Ann Demeulemeester and Dirk Bikkenbergs, are represented at **Louis** (Lombardenstraat 2, tel. 03/232–9872). Other leading fashion boutiques are **Modepaleis** (Nationalestraat 16, tel. 03/233–9437) and **Closing Date** (Korte Gasthuisstraat 15, tel. 03/232–8722).

Gifts **Calico House** (Zand 1, tel. 03/233–6023) specializes in quilts and patchwork. **Extra Large** (Oude Beurs 30, tel. 03/232–9841) is a place for outsize, fun gifts.

Diamonds Diamonds are an excellent investment for individual customers, as well as for the many dealers who come to Antwerp for them; they can be bought tax-free. (Note: tax-free does not mean duty-free when you return home.) If you are not an expert, you can rely on the advice given by the staff at **Diamondland** (Appelmansstraat 33A, tel. 03/243–3612). The quality of the stones is guaranteed by a Diamond High Council certificate.

Sports and Fitness

Golf The **Brasschaat Open Golf Club Center** (Miksebaan 248, Brasschaat, tel. 03/653–1048) is 15 kilometers (9 miles) from the city center.

Skating Two popular skating rinks are **Antarctica** (Moerelei 119, Wilrijk, tel. 03/828–9928) and **Zondal** (Ruggeveldlaan 488B, Deurne, tel. 03/325–0374).

Tennis Courts at **Het Rooi** (Berchemstadionstraat 73, tel. 03/239–6610) rent for BF200–BF300 per hour. Tariffs at **Beerschot** (Stadionstraat, tel. 03/220–8687) are a bit lower, at BF150 an hour. Try to book courts for as early in the day as you can.

Spectator Sports

Most indoor sports events are staged in the **Sportpaleis** (Schijnpoortweg 113, tel. 03/326–1010) just outside the ring road northeast of the city center, including cycling and tennis championships.

Dining

Belgium's second city—its Flemish capital and one of the most active ports in the world—offers an impressive variety of restaurants and even some ethnic options, though not on the level of its once-more-colonially inclined Dutch neighbors. In fact, despite a certain amount of exotic influence, Antwerp remains remarkably conservative in its culinary tastes, focusing with understandable devotion on fish—fish presented with few frills in even the finest restaurants, often poached or steamed, and accessibly priced. From the chilled welks and winkles picked out of their shells with pins, to piles of tender little crevettes grises, to the mammoth turbot heavy with steamy white flesh, the odor of salt air and fresh brine is never far from your table. The ubiquitous *mosselen* (mussels) and eels, show-cased in middle-class restaurants throughout the city center, provide a heavier, heartier version of fish cuisine; they are bought alive from wholesalers, and are thus irreproachably fresh.

$$$$ De Matelote. In a house down a narrow street, this tiny bi-level restaurant has a mezzanine which is reached by a winding staircase. Self-taught Chef Didier Garnich turns out such delicious creations as langoustines in a light curry sauce, sea scallops cooked with a stock of mushrooms and sorrel, and grilled asparagus with fresh morels and a poached egg. The crème brulée is outstanding. Local gourmets consider this the best seafood restaurant in town. *Haarstraat 9, tel. 03/231–3207. Reservations required. Jacket and tie advised. AE, DC, MC, V. Closed Sat., Sun., July.*

$$$$ La Pérouse. When the good ship *La Pérouse*, which carries tourists on pleasure trips in summer, ties up at the Steen for the winter season, it becomes an outstanding gourmet restaurant. Whole turbot is presented in its kitchen steamer before being filleted and served with fennel, carrots, and cream-thickened stock; bass is cooked in salt-crust and served with saffron butter. There's plenty of meat as well: beef in Pomerol with marrow, lamb in orange rind and basil. The ambience is relaxed, almost casual. The dining room is small, so make reservations far in advance. *Ponton Steen, tel. 03/231–3151. Reservations required. Jacket and tie advised. AE, DC, MC, V. Closed Sun.–Mon. and mid-June–Sept.*

$$$ In de Schaduw van de Kathedraal. Cozier and more traditional than the wave of contemporary restaurants dominating the scene, this comfortable little dining room faces the cathedral square and, in warm weather, sets up terrace tables in its namesake's shadow. Try the nutmeg-perfumed gratin of endive and crevettes grises or steamed sole with scampi in fresh basil. *Handschoenmarkt 17, tel. 03/232–4014. Reservations advised. Jacket advised. AE, DC, MC, V. Closed June–Sept., Tues.; Oct.–May, Mon.–Tues.*

$$$ Neuze Neuze. Composed of five small 16th-century houses, the restaurant has plenty of nooks and crannies on different levels. Its chichi name ("nose-nose," referring to what children call an Eskimo kiss) sets the tone: This is a young, fashionable dining spot with a downtown air, an arty mix of intimate, old-beamed rooms with halogen and waitresses in stretch velour. But the cooking is strictly uptown—terrine of goose liver and pear; warm smoked salmon with chicory and a light, white beer sauce; monkfish rolls with caviar. The genial patron, Domien Sels, is ever present, and the wine list is exceptionally deep. *Wijngaardstraat 19, tel. 03/232–5783. Reservations advised. Jacket advised. AE, DC, MC, V. Closed Sun., 2 weeks in July/Aug.*

$$$ Petrus. The owner/chef has named his restaurant for Château Petrus, the prince of Pomerols; he stocks it, too, at prices starting at BF12,000, and serious wine lovers should visit the extensive cellar. The terrine of duck's liver interleaved with filet d'Anvers (lightly smoked beef) is a specialty of the house, and the sliced, sautéed sea scallops on a galette of potatoes with olive oil and white truffles are a dream. The restaurant is opposite the Bourla Theater; the fixed-price theater menu is an excellent buy. *Kelderstraat 1, tel. 03/225–2734. Reservations advised. Jacket and tie advised. AE, DC, MC, V. Closed Sat. lunch, Sun. lunch, Mon., 2 weeks in July.*

$$$ Sir Anthony Van Dijck. Once one of Belgium's top restaurants, this dining spot was dropped by some restaurant guidebooks when owner/chef Marc Paesbrugghe decided to simplify and cut prices in 1992. But while it's true the restaurant is no longer one of the country's very best, it's still quite good. The brasserie-style fare includes a fine salad liègeoise, with haricots, smoked salmon, and caramelized onions; duck à l'orange; and tuna steak. Diners sit under high, massive beams and stone pillars, surrounded by flowers and carved wood, at tables overlooking an interior courtyard. There are two seatings a night. *Vlaykensgang, Oude Koornmarkt 16, tel. 03/231–6170. Reservations advised. Jacket and tie advised. AE, DC, MC, V. Closed Sun., first 3 weeks of Aug.*

$$ De Peerdestal. For chalkboard specials (mixed grill, scallops *maison*), café standards (mussels, fish, steaks), and yes, horse meat, this beam-and-brick stable is an appealing place for a casual meal. It has been renovated in a two-story atrium design, with checkered-cloth tables scattered around the open loft and stools around the pine-topped bar below. *Wijngaardstraat 8, tel. 03/231–9503. Dress: casual. AE, DC, MC, V. Closed Sun.*

$$ Het Nieuwe Palinghuis. This is a good Old Antwerp landmark, with dark wood, pottery, and a comfortable bourgeois air, and its seafood specialties—above all, its *paling* (eel)—are well prepared and reasonably priced. There's eel in green sauce, grilled turbot, grilled scallops, and sole in lobster sauce. *Sint-Jansvliet 14, tel. 03/231–7445. Reservations advised. Jacket advised. AE, DC, MC, V. Closed Mon.–Tues.*

$$ Rooden Hoed. Though it was founded by an Alsatian family in the 1930s, this atmospheric restaurant/tavern is pure Old Antwerp (the building itself dates from 1467), with high, dark wainscoting and plenty of pottery and knickknacks. Classic *cuisine bourgeoise* and Antwerp specialties are combined here—eel, oysters, sole, and mussels dominate. However, some more ambitious (read: pretentious) dishes—Chateaubriand, turbot *Noilly Prat*—try to lift the restaurant into an altogether uncalled-for higher class. *Oude Koornmarkt 25, tel. 03/233–2844. Reservations advised. Dress: casual. AE, V. Closed Wed.–Thurs., Carnival week, mid-June–mid-July.*

$ 't Brantyser. This old café, with dark rafters, brick, and stucco in two open levels, offers more than just drinks and the usual snacks: There are imaginative salads (endive with bacon and Roquefort), fish and meat dishes, and affordable specials. *Hendrik Conscienceplein 7, tel. 03/233–1833. Reservations advised at lunch. Dress: casual. No credit cards. Closed Mon.*

$ Kiekekot. Antwerp students satisfy their craving for spit-roasted chicken and frites at this no-frills "chicken coop," which offers a juicy, golden half chicken for little more than its retail price. *Grote Markt 35, tel. 03/232–1502. No reservations. Dress: casual. No credit cards.*

$ Panaché. This Antwerp institution, north of the Diamond District and close to the Central Station, makes the best sandwiches in town. Good-value meals are served in the back room. *Statiestraat 17, tel. 03/232–6905. No reservations. Dress: casual. AE, DC, MC, V.*

$ Zuiderterass. The striking five-story building, with its black-steel-and-glass facade, was designed by avant-garde architect bOb (his spelling) Van Reeth. Surrounding a central bar, tables in the café/restaurant offer river views on one side, views of the cathedral and Old Town on the other. There's a wide choice of salads, fish and meat dishes, and desserts, and you can have just a snack or a complete meal. The servers are young, as are the customers. *Ernest Van Dijckkaai, tel. 03/234–1275. No reservations. Dress: casual. AE, DC, MC, V.*

Lodging

The tourist office can reserve hotel rooms for you up to a week in advance for reduced prices. You pay a deposit of BF200, which is deducted from the price of the room. Write for a reservation form and return it, specifying your needs. If you land in Antwerp on a weekend, you'll benefit from tremendous reductions on hotel rooms, as most are filled with expense-account businesspeople during the working week. The hotels below are categorized by their weekday price; some fall easily into a lower range on weekends and in July and August.

$$$$ **Alfa DeKeyser.** This is one of the more deluxe versions of a business hotel, with music piped into the muffled anonymity of the corridors. Newly refurbished "executive" doubles sport post-modern pearwood cabinetry and granite-look laminate. Standard doubles, though not as up-to-date, are fresh nonetheless. Ask for a room in the back, overlooking an Astroturfed "court." It's just next door to the train station and zoo. *De Keyserlei 66–70, B-2018, tel. 03/234–0135. 117 rooms. Facilities: restaurant, bar, indoor pool, whirlpool, sauna, solarium, fitness center, no-smoking rooms. AE, DC, MC, V.*

$$$$ **Classic.** Formerly the Villa Mozart, this small, modern hotel is in a pedestrian area, and thus quiet. The decor is a bit fussy, with floral-print Austrian blinds, but the emphasis is on business-class comforts: air-conditioning, electronic security. The rooms are slightly cramped—due, in part, to the generous beds—but many look out toward the cathedral. *Handschoenmarkt 3–7, B-2000, tel. 03/231–3031, fax 03/231–5685. 25 rooms with bath. Facilities: restaurant, bar. AE, DC, MC, V.*

$$$$ **Hilton.** After digging up the entire Groenplaats to construct an underground garage (and then putting the Groenplaats together again), and incorporating the former *fin de siècle* Grand Bazaar department store, Antwerp's newest luxury hotel, a five-story complex, opened in 1993. Rooms have mahogany doors, three telephones, safes, and executive desks. Afternoon tea is served in the marble-floored lobby, and buffet breakfast, lunch, and dinner is offered in the Isabella and Helena restaurant, named for Rubens' two wives. *Groenplaats, tel. 03/204–1212, fax 03/204–1213. 211 rooms. Facilities: 2 restaurants, bar, sauna, fitness center, conference rooms, ballroom, no-smoking floors, shopping arcade, garage. AE, DC, MC, V.*

$$$$ ★ **De Rosier.** Leaving would-be competitors in the deluxe market behind by several laps, this is the only choice in town for luxury on an intimate scale. Literally cloistered behind discreet double doors (it functioned as a cloister from 1932 to 1972), this lovely hotel is nearly invisible from the narrow back street it faces, focusing inward instead on the aristocratic garden court and its sumptuously furnished interiors. Downstairs, guests move freely from Louis Quinze to Empire to Victorian chinoiserie; rooms upstairs vary from skylighted, modernized garrets to the beamed-and-leaded-glass suite in pure Old Antwerp style, which has been favored by the likes of Madonna and Marlene Dietrich. The mansion dates from 1627. *Rosier 21–23, tel. 03/225–0140, fax 03/231–4111. 12 rooms with bath. Facilities: breakfast room, garden terrace, indoor pool. AE, DC, MC, V.*

$$$ ★ **Firean.** This Art Deco gem, built in 1929 and restored in 1986 not only to its architectural style but also to the welcoming grace of its era, offers sweet relief to travelers benumbed by the uniformity of chain hotels. Its location—a residential neighborhood south of the

center but on the way into town from the Brussels expressway—reinforces the tranquillity inside, expressed in fresh flowers, rich fabrics, and a tasteful mix of antiques and reproductions. Breakfast eggs come in floral-print cozies, and jazz piano is discreetly piped into public areas but doesn't leak into the rooms—which are sanctuaries. A tram to the Old Town stops outside the door. *Karel Oomsstraat 6, B-2018, tel. 03/237–0260, fax 03/238–1168. 11 rooms, 6 in annex next door, all with bath. Facilities: breakfast room, bar. AE, DC, MC, V. Closed first half of Aug., Christmas Eve–weekend after Epiphany (Jan. 6).*

$$ **Cammerpoorte.** All modern but comfortably nestled in the Old Town, this simple hotel was opened in 1990 and since then has added seven new rooms. The structure is solid, the rooms are slick, with all-weather carpet and graphite-look laminate. The breakfast buffet is served in a conference-room atmosphere. *Nationalestraat 38–40, B-2000, tel. 03/231–9736, fax 03/226–2968. 46 rooms. Facilities: breakfast only. AE, DC, MC, V.*

$$ **Prinse.** Set well back from an Old Town street, this 400-year-old landmark with an interior courtyard opened as a hotel in 1990 and is a member of the Relais du Silence (Quiet Inns) group. The hotel has a modern look, with black leather chairs, soft blue curtains, and tiled baths. Exposed beams give top-floor rooms more character. The 16th-century poet Anna Bijns lived here. *Keizerstraat 63, tel. 03/226–4050, fax 03/225–1148. 30 rooms with bath. Facilities: breakfast room. AE, DC, MC, V.*

$$ **Waldorf.** In an attractive area south of the Diamond Center, this modern hotel hosts many guests who are in the diamond business. The smallish rooms are attractively decorated in gray and brown, and the restaurant is pleasant. *Belgielei 36, tel. 03/230–9950, fax 03/230–7870. 100 rooms. Facilities: restaurant, bar. AE, DC, MC, V.*

$ **Pension Cammerpoorte.** Owned by the managers of the
★ Cammerpoorte Hotel and just up the street, this small, familial pension has been scrubbed and decorated with the enthusiasm of a home owner by its proud proprietor. Breakfast is served in the tidy brick-and-lace café downstairs, while rooms—on landings up the narrow staircase—are full of bright pastels and sad-clown art. *Steenhouwersvest 55, B-2000, tel. 03/231–2836. 9 rooms with toilet and shower. Facilities: breakfast only. AE, DC, MC, V.*

$ **Scoutel.** Co-ed, although owned by the Boy Scouts, Scoutel occupies a modern building five minutes' walk from the Central Station. The double and triple rooms are simple but adequate; all have toilets and showers. Rates are lower for those under 25, and most of the guests *are* young people. Breakfast and sheets are included; towels can be rented. Guests are provided with front-door keys. *Stoomstraat 3, tel. 03/226–4606, fax 03/232–6392. 24 rooms with shower. Facilities: breakfast room, meeting room. No credit cards.*

The Arts and Nightlife

The Arts Check *The Bulletin* for details on arts events in Antwerp.

Antwerp has acquired a reputation for innovative and exciting ballet, and its school is internationally renowned. The principal company is the **Koninklijk Ballet van Vlaanderen** (Royal Flanders Ballet, Britselei 80, tel. 03/234–3438). The opera is nearby: **Koninklijke Vlaamse Opera** (Royal Flanders Opera, Frankrijklei 3, tel. 03/233–6685).

The **Koninklijk Philharmonisch Orkest van Vlaanderen** (Royal Flanders Philharmonic) can most frequently be heard at **De Singel** (Desguinlei 25, tel. 03/248–3800), where modern and contemporary music is often performed. Another venue for classical music is the **Koningin Elisabethzaal** (Koningin Astridplein 23, tel. 03/233–8444), where there are also rock concerts. Visiting rock musicians can also be heard at the **Sportpaleis** (Schijnpoortweg 113, tel. 03/326–1010).

The flagship of the over two dozen theaters in Antwerp is the **Koninklijke Nederlands Schouwburg** (KNS, Theaterplein 1, tel. 03/231–0750). Two independent theaters of special interest are **Vrije Val** (Namenstraat 7), and **Monty** (Montignystraat 3–5). The **Poppenschouwburg Van Campen** (Van Campen Puppet Theater, Lange Nieuwstraat 3, tel. 03/237–3716), puts on traditional puppet performances in Flemish dialect.

Nightlife There are 2,500 taverns in Antwerp—one per 200 inhabitants. The
Bars most famous is probably the **Bierhuis Kulminator** (Vleminckveld 32–34, tel. 03/232–4538), which stocks, cools, and pours 550 different kinds of beer, including EKU-28, the strongest beer on earth. Other bars in the Old Town include **Pelgrom** (Pelgrimsstraat 15, tel. 03/234–0809), a 16th-century tavern; **De Engel** (Grote Markt 3, tel. 03/233–1252), an ordinary café but the most popular in town; **Blauwe Steen** (Ernest van Dijckkaai 34, tel. 03/231–6710), with buskers performing Antwerp music; and **Beveren** (Vlasmarkt 2, tel. 03/231–2225), an old-fashioned café. **Il Mondo** (Grote Pieter Pot 6, no phone) is small and caters to the fashionable fringe, while next door **Het Spiegelbeeld** (tel. 03/225–3010) is large and unpretentious.

Discos The best-known upscale disco remains **Jimmy's** (Van Ertbornstraat 12, tel. 03/233–3515), but it is challenged in popularity by a new place in the red-light district, **Café d'Anvers** (Verversrui 15, tel. 03/226–3870), where the music is as mixed as the clientele. Other discos of note are **Prestige** (Anneessensstraat 18, tel. 03/225–1717) and **New Casino** (Kloosterstraat 70, tel. 03/237–8846). Check opening hours.

Gay Bars These include **Oscar Wilde** (Van Schoonhovestraat 84, tel. 03/226–1118) and **Marcus Antonius** (Van Schoonhovestraat 82, tel. 03/231–4384) for gay men; for gay women, there are **Shakespeare** (Oude Koornmarkt 24, tel. 03/231–5058) and **Lady's Pub** (Waalsekaai 56, tel. 03/238–5490).

Jazz Clubs There isn't live music every night in these clubs, so check beforehand. Try **Swingcafé** (Suikerrui 13, tel. 03/233–1478), **De Muze** (Melkmarkt 15, tel. 03/226–0126), or **De Hopper** (Leopold De Waelstraat 2, tel. 03/248–4933).

Excursion to Limburg

Limburg is the easternmost Flemish-speaking province, stretching from the sandy moorlands of the Kempen area in the north to the fertile plains of the Hesbaye, which the Flemings call Haspengouw, with its prosperous-looking farms, orchards, and undulating fields. On the east it borders on the narrow Dutch corridor stretching south to Maastricht. Its history and spiritual affinity are closest to Antwerp's.

Two great physical features have shaped much of Limburg's recent economic history. One is the coalfields, now a thing of the past but formerly very extensive. The other is the Albert Canal, which leaves the Meuse just north of Liège to follow a course parallel to the river and then veers off across the country to carry the heavy Liège traffic to Antwerp. Thanks to the canal, Genk is a center for the auto and petrochemical industries.

Important Addresses and Numbers

Tourist Information The Provincial Tourist Office for Limburg is at Universiteitslaan 1, **Hasselt** (tel. 011/237980). City Tourist Offices are at Lombaardstraat 3, **Hasselt** (tel. 011/239540); Grote Markt 68, **Sint-Truiden** (tel. 011/686872); and Stadhuisplein 9, **Tongeren** (tel. 012/232961).

Emergencies **Police:** tel. 101. **Ambulance:** tel. 100. The address of the on-duty **late-night pharmacy** is posted in all pharmacy windows.

Getting There

By Car Hasselt is 77 kilometers (48 miles) from Antwerp on A13/E313, almost as the crow flies.

By Train You can get to Hasselt by train from Antwerp, Brussels, and Liège, but there are quite a few stops en route.

Exploring Limburg

Numbers in the margin correspond to points of interest on the Excursion to Limburg map.

Limburg has the youngest population in Belgium, and it is the province where the rate of development is fastest. This is particularly noticeable in **Hasselt,** a town with busy shopping streets, innovative museums, and lively music life.

Hasselt enjoys the slightly raffish distinction of having had gin distilling as its major industry; one of the country's oldest surviving distilleries, from 1803, has become the delightful **Nationaal Jenevermuseum,** jenever meaning "gin" in Dutch. A tour of the installations, which include changing exhibits such as vintage gin advertisement posters, ends in the paneled tasting room, which offers a menu of gin of various ages, flavors, and proofs from two dozen Belgian distilleries. *Witte Nonnenstraat 19, tel. 011/241144. Admission: BF80. Open Tues.–Sun. 10–5, weekends 2–6.*

Stadsmuseum Stellingwerf-Waerdenhof (Stellingwerf-Waerdenhof Municipal Museum) consists of two impressive mansions whose interiors have been turned into a strikingly modern space with white walls, red balconies, and large mirrors in which the collection of decorative arts has been dramatically arranged. *Maastrichterstraat 85, tel. 011/241070. Admission: BF80. Open Tues.–Sun. 10–5, weekends 2–6.*

The third among Hasselt's unusual museums is the **Modemuseum** (Fashion Museum), installed in a 17th-century hospital, which illustrates the development of fashion trends over the past two centuries. At press time it was being refurbished and was scheduled to reopen in early 1995; check with the tourist office (tel. 011/239540). *Gasthuisstraat 5. Admission: BF80. Open Tues.–Sun. 10–5, weekends 2–6.*

Time Out **La Galette** (Fruitmarkt 26) is an ice cream parlor whose product is 100% homemade, free of all additives, and very good.

In the **Sint-Quintinus Kathedraal** you'll find the **Stedelijk Beiaardmuseum** (Carillon Museum) at the top of several flights of wooden steps. The 47-bell carillon is one of the best in the country. *Vismarkt, tel. 011/241070. Admission: BF80. Open June and Sept.,*

Excursion to Limburg

weekends 2–6; July–Aug., Tues.–Fri. 2–5, weekends 2–6; concerts July–Aug., Sun. at 3.

② **Sint-Truiden** is 19 kilometers (12 miles) southwest of Hasselt on N80. This is the center of the fruit-growing district; in spring thousands upon thousands of trees are in bloom. The town developed around the abbey founded by St. Trudo in the 7th century. The **Begijnhof** (Beguinage), dating from 1258, has a well-restored church, from the end of the 13th century. It is now the **Provinciaal Museum voor Religieuze Kunst** (Provincial Museum of Religious Art) and is known for its 38 frescoes, executed over four centuries. *Begijnhof, off Speelhoflaan; tel. 011/688579. Admission: BF100. Open Apr.–Oct., Tues.–Fri. 10–noon and 1:30–5, weekends 1:30–5.*

At the **Festraets Studio** you can see the astronomical compensation clock, constructed by Camille Festraets out of 20,000 mechanical parts. It is more than 6 feet tall and weighs more than 4 tons. *Begijnhof 24, tel. 011/688752. Admission: BF80. Visits Easter–June and Sept.–Oct., weekends 1:45, 2:45, 3:45, and 4:45; July–Aug., Tues.–Fri. 9:45, 10:45, 1:45, 2:45, and 3:45, and weekends 1:45, 2:45, 3:45, and 4:45.*

Lace making has been revived in Sint-Truiden over the past few decades with a great deal of originality. The results can be seen at the **Museum van Hedendaagse Kantwerken** (Contemporary Lace Museum) in the school of the Ursuline sisters. *Naamse Straat 5, tel. 011/682356. Admission: BF25. Open Sun. and bank holidays 10–noon and 2–6.*

The **Sint-Gangulfskerk** is worth the small detour to Diesterstraat. It is a Romanesque basilica from the 11th century and has been carefully restored.

In **Zoutleeuw,** a couple of miles west of Sint-Truiden, is the **Sint-Leonarduskerk** (St. Leonard's Church), which dates from the 13th century and is quite out of proportion to the town's present population. The great treasure is one of the finest brassware pieces in Belgium, a tall paschal candlestick incorporating a Crucifixion scene, made by Renier van Thienen in 1453. *Open Mon.–Sat. 9:30–noon and 1:30–6, Sun. 1:30–5 (winter, Sun. 1:30–4).*

❸ **Tongeren,** 20 kilometers (12½ miles) east of Sint-Truiden on N79, is one of the two oldest cities in Belgium (the other being Tournai). It started life as a Roman army encampment. Here Ambiorix scored a famous but short-lived victory over the Roman legions in 54 BC. The Roman city was considerably larger than the present one; over the centuries following its foundation, it was repeatedly sacked and burned. By the end of the 13th century, the city had retreated within its present limits and enjoyed the occasionally burdensome protection of the prince bishops of Liège. The Moerenpoort gate and sections of the ramparts remain from that period.

Tongeren's outstanding sight is the 12th-century Romanesque cloister in the **Onze-Lieve-Vrouwebasiliek** (Basilica of Our Lady). The Chapter House contains the Treasury, also known as the **Basilica Museum Tongeren.** This is the richest collection of religious art in the country, including a 6th-century ivory diptych of St. Paul, a Merovingian gold buckle from the same century, and a head of Christ sculpted in wood in the 11th century. *Grote Markt, tel. 012/235719. Admission: BF100. Open May–Sept., daily 9–noon and 2–5; Oct.–Apr., by appointment, tel. 012/231417.*

The basilica is a very handsome Gothic church, dating in part (the central nave up to the pulpit, the choir, and the south transept) from 1240. The candlesticks and lectern from 1372 are the work of Jehan de Dinant, one of the outstanding artists of metal working who flourished in the cities of the Meuse Valley. The basilica has excellent acoustics and is used for symphony concerts on Saturdays during the Festival of Flanders.

❹ Exit 30 from A13/E313 takes you via Genk to **Bokrijk,** the largest (1,360 acres) open-air museum in Europe. The nature reserve shows the unspoiled Kempen country of heather and pine, sand and broom, with marshes and ponds frequented by waterfowl. There's also a big playground with pony rides and other attractions, and a sports center with tennis courts, minigolf, and even a soccer field.

Time Out   **In den Dolphin** is an old Flemish inn where you can enjoy traditional fare such as spicy sausages, smoked ham, rich cheeses, and red Rodenbach beer.

Much of Bokrijk's charm derives from the carefully restored farm buildings, which have been transplanted from Limburg and other Flemish provinces. Each building has its own custodian, many of whom are mines of local folklore. The interiors are filled with old peasant furniture and ancient utensils. *Domein Bokrijk, Genk, tel. 011/224575. Admission: BF200 adults, BF75 children, under 7 free. Open Apr.–Oct., daily 10–6.*

What to See and Do with Children

Bokrijk (*see* Exploring Limburg, *above*) is certainly the leading contender for family fun in the province.

At **Lanaken,** near the Dutch border northeast of Tongeren, you can rent a horse and wagon through the local tourist office and set off for a one-day excursion along a route mapped out for you. *Tel. 089/722467. Open May–Oct.*

Sports and Fitness

For general information on sports facilities and opportunities, contact the **Sportdienst** (Universiteitslaan 1, Hasselt, tel. 011/237111).

The local tourist offices can supply maps and information on attractive **bicycle** trails. Two of the most popular are the **Trudofietsroute,** 54 kilometers (33½ miles) long, based on the travels of St. Trudo, and Tongeren's **Tongria** route, 45 kilometers (28 miles) long.

Golf aficionados will find excellent facilities in Hasselt (Vlaams-Japanese Golf & Business Club, Vissenbroekstraat 15, tel. 011/223793). The 18-hole course is for members only, while the nine-hole training course is open to the public.

Dining and Lodging

With its combination of historic towns and idyllic country, this region offers an attractive mix of bucolic inns and burnished urban cafés.

Hasselt
Dining

De Egge. This charming little one-horse restaurant offers the best efforts of a young couple who believe in their excellent taste: The decor is pretty and discreet, with whitewashed brick and café curtains, and the cooking is imaginative and beautifully executed. Try monkfish on a bed of leeks, or goat cheese brushed with honey and fresh thyme and served hot on a bed of julienned apple, endive, and *mâche* (lamb's lettuce). *Walputstraat 23, tel. 011/224951. Reservations advised. Jacket advised. AE, DC, MC, V. Closed Thurs. $$*

Majestic. This big, leaded-glass, high-ceilinged tavern on the Grote Markt has a grand, historic feel, and it draws locals for drinks, cards, snacks, and light meals: sandwiches, trout, steak, and a cheap daily menu. *Grote Markt, tel. 011/223330. Dress: casual. AE, DC, MC, V. $*

Dining and Lodging

Scholteshof. Owner/chef Roger Souvereyns created a mecca for many a Belgian and foreign gourmet on an 18th-century farm, and he keeps adding new touches, his most recent being a beautiful fountain in the interior courtyard, where you can have a drink. There's also a sculpture-filled English garden and an extensive herb garden. A meal in the candlelighted dining room is a romantic and relaxing experience; the imaginative menu includes such tempting creations as pumpkin soup with langoustines, carpaccio with a ball of caviar on green tomato jelly, sweetbreads roasted with rosemary, and grilled turbot with a rhubarb mousse. Rooms are spacious and furnished with magnificent antiques. *Kermtstraat 130, Stevoort (6½ km/4 mi west of Hasselt), tel. 011/250202, fax 011/254328. 9 rooms, 9 suites, all with bath. Facilities: restaurant (reservations required; jacket and tie required), garden, park, meeting rooms. AE, DC, MC, V. Closed Wed., Jan., second half of July. $$$$*

Lier **'t Suyckeren Schip.** Just across from the church, this restaurant of-
Dining fers *cuisine bourgeoise:* steaks with a variety of sauces, and five different preparations of sole. The setting has an informal,
comfortable, brick-and-beams look. Sunday crowds come after
church. *Rechtestraat 49, tel. 03/489–0140. Reservations advised.
Jacket advised. AE, DC, MC, V. $$*

Sint-Truiden **De Fakkels.** In an extravagantly decorated 19th-century town
Dining house, with tapestries, carved wood, leaded glass, and terrazzo
floors, this ambitious restaurant offers well-executed French cook-
ing: *pot-au-feu de St-Pierre aux raviolis de langoustines* (John Dory
stew with lobster ravioli), sweetbreads on a bed of zucchini and
mushrooms. *Stationstraat 33, tel. 011/687634. Reservations ad-
vised. Jacket and tie advised. AE, DC, MC, V. Closed Sun. dinner,
Mon., last week of Jan., second half of Aug. $$$*
Century. A classic old tavern/restaurant on the Grote Markt, with
oak, green-plush banquettes, and great windows framing the market scene, this simple spot is as comfortable for a drink as for a meal.
Typical "snacks" include half a roasted chicken with frites and salad,
omelettes, steaks, sole, and sandwiches. *Grote Markt 5, tel. 011/
688341. Dress: casual. AE, DC, MC, V. Closed Tues. dinner. $*

Lodging **Regency.** Expanded and renovated from its origins as an early 19th-
century town house, this city hotel offers two styles: graceful old
rooms with high, molded ceilings, or those in the new wing, all modern. It's on a quiet street but close to the city center. *Schepen
Dejongstraat 43, B-3800, tel. 011/684881. 30 rooms with bath. Facili-
ties: restaurant, bar. AE, DC, MC, V. $$*

Tongeren **Clos St. Denis.** This enormous 17th-century farmhouse with at-
Dining tached barns has been completely restored as a fresh, elegant coun-
★ try inn, where chef Christian Denis serves extravagant fare: grilled
turbot in Chablis butter; gratin of oysters in champagne and caviar;
raviolis of *foie d'oie* (goose liver) in truffle cream. There's
choucroute with suckling pig and mustard as well. Four dining
rooms outdo each other for period luxury—burnished parquet, Per-
sian runners, chinoiserie. *Grimmertingenstraat 24, Vliermall-
Kortessem, tel. 012/236096. Reservations required. Jacket and tie
advised. AE, DC, MC, V. Closed Mon.–Tues., week after Easter, 2
weeks in July–Aug., first week of Nov., 2 weeks in Dec.–Jan. $$$$*

The Meuse and the Ardennes

Wallonia is everything that Flanders is not. The northern half of the
country is flat, the *"platte land"* of Jacques Brel's songs. The south
is hilly, even mountainous. You visit Flanders primarily for its his-
toric towns; Wallonia attracts people who enjoy its rapid streams,
deep forests, and hamlets. The northerners are all Dutch speakers;
the southerners speak French, but one in three also understands
Walloon, a dialect descended from demotic Latin; the linguistic fron-
tier corresponds roughly to the northern boundary of the Roman
empire. Flanders has a sense of regional identity going back a thou-
sand years; Wallonia consists of several smaller regions joined to-
gether not much more than 150 years ago.

The Meuse The Meuse River rises in France and reaches the sea in Holland un-
Valley der a different name, the Maas. It is in Belgium that it reveals real
character, at first foaming along narrow ravines. In Dinant it is
joined by the Lesse and flows, serene and beautiful, toward Namur,

overlooked by ancient citadels. At Namur comes the confluence with the Sambre, tainted from its exposure to the industries of Charleroi. The river becomes broad and powerful, and gradually the pleasure craft are replaced by an endless procession of tugboats and barges.

From the name of the river is derived the adjective "Mosan," used to describe an indigenous style of metalworking of extraordinary plasticity. It reached its finest flowering in the 12th and 13th centuries with masters such as Renier de Huy, Nicolas de Verdun, and Hugo d'Oignies. They worked with brass, copper, and silver to achieve artistic levels equal to those of the Flemish painters a couple of centuries later.

Roman legions commanded by Julius Caesar marched up the Meuse valley 2,000 years ago and made it one of the principal routes to Cologne. Later, it served a similar purpose for Charlemagne, linking his Frankish and German lands. The French came through here under Louis XIV and again under Napoleon; a century later it was the turn of the Germans pushing west and south in World Wars I and II. They were seen off here, too.

The Ardennes The Ardennes are an ancient mountain range worn down to wooded hills, largely bypassed by modern development, where villages and isolated farmhouses all have slate walls and slate roofs, and where you can walk alone for hours. German is spoken in cafés and restaurants in the easternmost reaches of the country, and shop and road signs are in that language. German is in fact spoken by less than 1% of the Belgian population but is one of the three official languages. These cantons were part of the Duchy of Limburg for centuries. They were awarded to Prussia after the Napoleonic wars and reverted to Belgium a century later.

Liège Many Belgians feel that visiting Liège, gateway to the Ardennes, is almost like going abroad. The Liègeois, for their part, see little reason for going to Brussels; if they hanker for bright lights, they head for Paris. They are the most Francophile among the Francophones, and it was no accident that Georges Simenon could so easily transplant the cafés and streets of the Liège of his boyhood to Maigret's Paris.

The history of Liège does differ fundamentally from that of the rest of the country. For eight of its 10 centuries it was an independent principality of the Holy Roman Empire, from the time Bishop Notger transformed his bishopric into a temporal domain at the end of the 10th century. His successors had to devote quite as much time to the defense of the realm—much larger than the present province—as to pastoral concerns. The power of the autocratic prince bishops was also hotly contested by the increasingly independent-minded cities. The end was brought about by the French Revolution, which many Liègeois joined with enthusiasm. The ancient cathedral of St. Lambert was razed, and the principality became a French *département*.

The 19th century, after Belgian independence in 1830, saw an upsurge in industrial activity. The first European locomotive was built in Liège, and the Bessemer steel production method developed; it is to the burning furnaces that Liège owes its nickname *la cité ardente* (the Fiery City). Drawing on a centuries-old tradition of weapons manufacturing, the Fabrique Nationale started to build precision firearms, and Val-St-Lambert began to produce glassware that has gained wide renown.

Belgian The Belgian province of Luxembourg is almost twice as large as the
Luxembourg independent Grand Duchy of Luxembourg. Luxembourg made common cause with Belgium against the Dutch in 1830, but while Belgium gained its freedom, the Grand Duchy remained under Dutch domination for another 50-odd years; meanwhile Leopold I of Belgium had claimed the western half. This is the largest and, with just a couple of hundred thousand inhabitants, by far the most sparsely populated province of Belgium. Here you can fill your lungs with fresh mountain air. It's a land of forests and dairy farms, slate gray houses and fortresses perched on high rocks, swift streams, and flowering meadows.

Important Addresses and Numbers

Tourist The tourist office for **Wallonia** as a whole, Office de Promotion du
Information Tourisme, is at rue du Marché-aux-Herbes 61 in Brussels (tel. 02/504–0200). The provincial tourist office for the **Meuse Valley** is at rue Notre-Dame 3, **Namur** (tel. 081/222998). City tourist offices: **Dinant** (rue Grande 37, tel. 082/222870) and **Namur** (Square de l'Europe Unie, tel. 081/246449).

The provincial tourist office for **Liège** is at boulevard de la Sauvenière 77 (tel. 041/224210). The **Liège** city tourist office is at En Féronstrée 92, (tel. 041/219221) and is open weekdays 9–6, Saturday 10–4, and Sunday 10–2. Other city tourist offices in the region are at Marktplatz 7, **Eupen** (tel. 087/553450); Hospice d'Oultremont, 4 quai de Namur, **Huy** (tel. 085/212915); Ancienne Abbaye, pl. du Châtelet 10, **Malmédy** (tel. 080/330250); rue Royale 41, **Spa** (tel. 087/772519); and Ancienne Abbaye, **Stavelot** (tel. 080/862339).

The provincial tourist office for **Belgian Luxembourg** is at 9 quai de l'Ourthe, La Roche-en-Ardennes (tel. 084/411011). City tourist offices are at pl. MacAuliffe 24, **Bastogne** (tel. 061/212711); Bureau du Château-Fort, **Bouillon** (tel. 061/466257), and (during the high season) at Porte de France, also in Bouillon (tel. 061/466289); Hôtel de Ville, place du Marché, **La Roche-en-Ardenne** (tel. 084/411342); and place de l'Abbaye, **St-Hubert** (tel. 061/613010).

Emergencies **Police,** tel. 101; **ambulance,** tel. 100.

Late-Night Addresses of all-night pharmacies are posted in all pharmacy win-
Pharmacies dows.

Arriving and Departing

Meuse There are two to three trains an hour from Brussels to Namur. The
By Train trip takes an hour from Brussels's Gare du Midi; 10 minutes less from Brussels's Gare du Nord. For train information in Namur, call 081/223675.

By Car Namur is 64 kilometers (40 miles) from Brussels on the A4/E411 motorway, which continues to Luxembourg and on to eastern France, Germany, and Switzerland. It is 61 kilometers (38 miles) from Liège on A15/E42, which continues to Charleroi and links up with E19 to Paris.

Liège There are 20 trains a day from Brussels. The trip takes an hour from
By Train Brussels Nord, 10 minutes more from Brussels Midi. All express trains from Oostende to Cologne stop at Liège. So do international trains from Scandinavia and Hamburg to Paris. Liège's station is the Gare des Guillemins (tel. 041/529850).

By Car   Liège is 97 kilometers (60 miles) east of Brussels on A3/E40, which continues 122 kilometers (76 miles) to Aachen and Cologne. The distance from Antwerp is 119 kilometers (74 miles) via A13/E313. Paris is 360 kilometers (224 miles) from Liège on A15/E42, which links up with A7/E19 near Mons.

Belgian   There are half a dozen daily connections from Brussels to Bastogne,
Luxembourg but you have to change at Libramont, and the trip takes 2½ hours.
By Train   Secondary lines run into the region from Liège and Namur, but services are neither frequent nor fast.

By Car   The main artery through the region is the A4/E411 highway from Brussels.

Getting Around Meuse and the Ardennes

The Meuse   There's hourly train service between Namur and Dinant. The trip
Valley   takes about 20 minutes. From April to August, excursion steam
By Train   trains are operated from Dinant to Givet, across the French border, and east–west from Treignes to Momignies. Each takes about two hours round-trip. For reservations, call 060/312440.

By Car   The main route from Brussels is the A4/E411 motorway. Elsewhere in the region, you travel chiefly on two-lane roads.

Liège   Taxis are plentiful and can be picked up at cabstands in the principal
By Taxi   squares. Call a cab at 041/676600.

By Bus   A single trip on a bus in the inner city costs BF36, and eight-trip cards sell for BF200.

The Ardennes   Having your own wheels is almost indispensable in exploring the
By Car   Ardennes. The northeast is traversed by two motorways, A3/E40 from Brussels via Liège to Aachen, Cologne, and points east, and the nearly completed A27, which runs south from E40 via Verviers to St. Vith and stops at the German border.

Belgian   The road network seems to have been designed to get cars through
Luxembourg Luxembourg as fast as possible rather than to serve its towns. Thus
By Car   St-Hubert and Bouillon are on either side and about 25 kilometers (16 miles) from A4/E411, and La Roche-en-Ardennes is about 15 kilometers (9 miles) away on E5 from Liège and on the old N4 from Namur. Some secondary roads are four-lane highways, but most are two-lane.

Guided Tours

The Meuse   Boat tours ranging from short excursions to full-day trips are avail-
Valley   able in both Dinant and Namur; for details, contact **Compagnie des Bateaux** (rue Daoust 64, 5500 Dinant, tel. 082/222315). For trips from Dinant, contact also **Bateau Bayard** (rue Caussin 13, 5500 Dinant, tel. 082/223042).

With some advance planning, you could probably arrange to sail the entire length of the Meuse from France to Holland by sightseeing boats. In Huy, river trips are organized on the *Bateau Val Mosan* (1 quai de Namur, tel. 025/212915).

In Liège, one-day excursions are arranged on board *Le Pays de Liège* (Port des Yachts, tel. 041/874333) from Liège to Maastricht in the Netherlands.

Liège   Your best bet is to hire an English-speaking guide from the city **tourist office** (En Féronstrée 92; BF1,200 for 2 hrs, BF600 per additional hr).

If you understand French, you're welcome to join a guided walking tour starting from the tourist office. *En Féronstrée 92. Cost: about BF100. Apr.–June and Sept.–Oct., weekends 2 PM; July–Aug., daily 2 PM.*

Exploring the Meuse and the Ardennes

This region is crowded with Belgian vacationers and weekend visitors, especially in July and August.

Tour 1: The Meuse Valley

Numbers in the margin correspond to points of interest on the Meuse and the Ardennes map.

1 At **Han-sur-Lesse,** 60 kilometers (37 miles) south of Namur on A4/E411, at Exit 23, are the magnificent **Grottes de Han** (Han Caves), which have been visited by tourists since the 1850s. Before that, they had provided refuge for threatened tribes since Neolithic times. Tickets are sold in the center of the small town, where you board an ancient tram that carries you to the mouth of the cave. Multilingual guides take groups through 3 kilometers (2 miles) of dimly lighted chambers, with occasional glimpses of the underground River Lesse, past giant stalagmites, into the vast cavern called the Dome, 145 meters (475 feet) high. The final part of the journey is by boat. The trip takes about 90 minutes. *Rue J. Lamotte, tel. 084/377213. Admission: BF275 adults, BF195 children. Open Apr.–Nov., daily 10–4, until 5 May–June, until 6 July–Aug.*

Time Out At the **Taverne Ardennaise** (rue des Grottes 2), you can enjoy regional specialties such as *civet de marcassin* (jugged wild boar) washed down by a locally brewed Trappist beer.

The Lesse is one of the liveliest tributaries of the Meuse, and shooting the rapids in a kayak has great appeal to the adventure-minded. **2** The starting point for organized river trips is **Houyet,** near Exit 22 on the motorway. The 21-kilometer (13-mile) ride takes you through two rapids and past the eagle's-nest Walzin castle to Anseremme on the Meuse, just south of Dinant. Train service back to the starting point is available, and reservations are recommended. *Lesse-Kayaks, 2 pl. de l'Eglise, Anseremme, tel. 082/224397. Price: BF250–BF600. Open Apr.–Oct., daily embarkation at Houyet 9:30–11.*

The Meuse is at its most attractive upstream from Dinant, and it's worth crossing the river and driving along it at least as far as **3** **Hastière-Lavaux.** Its charmingly named twin town, **Hastière-par-Delà**—on the other side of the river—has an 11th-century church, well worth seeing, in Romanesque Mosan style. The drive back toward Dinant offers many vistas over the river to the towering rock formations on the opposite shore.

4 **Freÿr,** on the left, is considered the best rock-climbing center in Wallonia. The **Château de Freÿr** is an impressive Renaissance building with beautiful interiors decorated with 17th-century woodwork and furniture. Louis XIV visited here during the siege of Dinant in 1675. The park has been laid out in accordance with the design principles of Le Nôtre, the French landscape architect. *Domaine de Freÿr, Waulsort, tel. 082/222200. Admission: BF200. Guided visits for groups by request.*

Just before Dinant, the needle-shaped **Rocher Bayard** looms on the right bank. Legend has it that Bayard, the steed of the four Aymon

The Meuse and the Ardennes

NETHERLANDS

GERMANY

Heretals

TO
ANTWERP

Geel

Balen

Bree

Maaseik

N13

Diest

E313/A13

A2/E314

Demer

Genk

Leuven

TO
BRUSSELS

Tienen

Hasselt

Bilzen

St.
Truiden

Geet

Maas

Borgloon

E40/A3

TO
BRUSSELS

Hannut

N3

A13

E25/A2

A278

Visé 15

Val-
Dieu

Henri-
Chapelle 11

N627

Dalhem 14

12

N28

TO
CHARLEROI

E411/A4

E42/A15

Blegny 13

Liège 9

Clermont

Eupen 21

N80

Ivoz

Herve 10

E40/A3

N3

Verviers

N68

Meuse

20

Neuville-
en-Condroz 19

N62

A27

N629

HAUTES FAGNES

Botrange

Namur 8

Huy 16

18

St-
Severin

Ourthe

Spa 26

Baraque
Michel 22

23

Robertville

N681

Sambre

Meuse

Andenne

Hoyoux

N641

17

Modave

Francorchamps

Reinhardstein 24

Annevoie-
Rouillon 7

Crupet 6

N97

N63

Manhay

A26

Stavelot

25 Malmédy

Godinne

Spontin

Cliney

N4

Hotton

N89

N68

St-Vith

Hastière-
Lavaux

Dinant 5

3 4

Freÿr 2

Marche-en-
Famenne

La Roche-en-
Ardenne

Vielsalm

E4N/A4

Lesse

27

28

Bovigny

Hastière-
par-delà

Houyet

35

Rochefort

Belvédère
des Six Ourthes

Beauraing

Han-sur-
Lesse 1

Fourneau
St-Michel

N834

Noville

GERMANY

A
R
D
E
N
N
E
S

34

St-Hubert

29 Bastogne

Our

Bièvre

Libramont

E25

Sûre

LUXEMBOURG

F
O
R
Ê
T

Semois

Bertrix

Neufchâteau

Martelange

E25/A4

D
E
S

N884

32

Bouillon
33

Herbeumont

Florenville

N83

Habay-la-
Neuve

Arlon

A
R
D
E
N
N
E
S

Chiers

31

Abbaye
d'Orval

30

N88

N82

N

Meuse

Virton

0   20 miles

0   30 km

FRANCE

Alzette

brothers who were the implacable foes of Charlemagne, split the rock with his hoof. The passage was widened by the troops of Louis XIV as they advanced on the city.

⑤ **Dinant** has a most scenic location; unfortunately, its strategic importance led to its involvement in an interminable series of wars. The French word *dinanderie*, meaning the art of brass- and copperworking, is derived from Dinant, where it was developed in the 12th century and spread downstream to Namur and Huy. The copperware sold today in Dinant's souvenir shops is not, alas, of the same quality.

Dinant was the birthplace of the 17th-century painter Joachim Patenier, who worked in Antwerp; his biblical scenes are set in landscapes recognizably inspired by the Meuse Valley. Another native son was Adolphe Sax, inventor of the saxophone.

The 13th-century collegiate church of **Notre-Dame** huddles under the citadel. The bulbous blue bell tower is a 17th-century addition. Back of the church is the starting point for cable cars to the **Citadel,** which is not as ancient as you might think, for the ancient fortifications were razed in 1818 by the Dutch, who replaced it with a new fort just before they were evicted. The view is splendid, and there is an arms museum. *25 le Prieuré, tel. 082/222119. Admission plus cable car: BF170 adults, BF130 children. Open Apr.–Oct., daily 10–4, until 6 in summer; Nov.–Mar., Sat.–Thurs. 10–4.*

On the left bank about 450 meters (1,500 feet) from the bridge on the road toward Philippeville you'll come to the entrance to the cave called **La Merveilleuse,** whose many stalactites are remarkably white. A visit takes about 50 minutes. *142 rte. de Philippeville, tel. 082/222210. Admission: BF170, children BF130. Open Mar.–Nov., daily 10–6.*

Time Out Dinant has two specialties: *flamiches* (cheese, egg, and butter tarts), to be eaten piping hot; and the hard, spicy *couques*, made with carved molds in many fanciful shapes from pastry and honey. The streets are lined with cafés. The **Patisserie Solbrun** offers the advantage of a great view over the river.

From N96 toward Namur, cross the river just after Anhee for a 23-kilometer (14-mile) detour. From Yvoir, take the steeply rising N937 to **Spontin.** The moated **Château de Spontin** is an excellent example of medieval architecture, with a Renaissance brick superstructure. The drawbridge can still be operated, and there are secret staircases and lookouts. The castle is still inhabited, and the interior presents the same contrast between austerity and elegance as does the exterior. *8 chaussée de Dinant, tel. 083/699055. Admission: BF150, children BF100. Open daily 10–1 and 2–5.*

⑥ In nearby **Crupet** stands a massive, river-encircled square dungeon from the 12th century; it was the stronghold of the powerful French Carondelet family for centuries.

⑦ You return to the Meuse at Godinne, and at the other end of the bridge is **Annevoie-Rouillon.** A greater contrast to medieval keeps cannot be imagined than the **Château et Jardins d'Annevoie** (Chateau and Gardens of Annevoie). The 30-acre park is a happy blend of 18th-century French landscaping and romantic Italian garden design, remarkable for its use of natural waterfalls, fountains, and ponds to animate the gardens with their flower beds, lawns, statues, and grottoes. The château blends perfectly with the gardens; the furniture, paneling, and family portraits all contribute to an ambience of elegant refinement. *Rte. des Jardins, tel. 082/611555. Admission: BF200 adults, BF100 children. Gardens open Apr.–Oct., daily 9–7; château open 9:30–1 and 2–6:30 daily July–Aug., weekends Apr.– June and Sept.*

❽ You enter **Namur** under the shadow of the Citadel, perched on a cliff on the promontory overlooking the confluence of the Meuse and the Sambre. The city is the seat of the body governing the affairs of the semiautonomous French-speaking community, chosen as a compromise acceptable to Charleroi and Liège, both of which are twice as large. Much of the center of Namur is a pedestrian zone, with cafés, art galleries, and boutiques. The appealing streets are lined with pink-brick 17th-century houses, and here and there is a rich Baroque church. Namur is a university town, and the student population helps to liven up what passes for nightlife around the rue St-Loup. Right in the center is the quiet place du Marché-aux-Légumes, with the **Eglise de Saint-Jean Baptiste** (St. John the Baptist's Church).

Time Out   On this square you'll find a new café in an old building, **Le XVIIIe**, so named for its stuccoed 18th-century ceiling. The specialty is pancakes with generous fillings.

The **Institut des Soeurs de Notre-Dame** (Institute of the Sisters of Our Lady) is the home of the **Trésor Hugo d'Oignies**. The crosses, reliquaries, and other religious artifacts, made by Brother Hugo for the priory in nearby Oignies in the beginning of the 13th century, were rescued during the bombardments of 1914. The finesse with which he worked the silver and enamel inlays, often with miniature hunting scenes, was remarkable, and Hugo d'Oignies has been recognized as one of the masters of Art Mosan. *Rue Billiart 17, tel. 081/ 230342. Admission: BF50. Open Wed.–Sat. and Mon. 10–noon and 2–5, Sun. 2–5. Closed bank holidays.*

The **Musée Archéologique** (Archaeological Museum) is installed in the handsome 16th-century Butchers' Hall on the waterfront. It contains Roman and Merovingian antiquities from the Namur area, and the collection of jewelry from the 1st century to the 7th century includes some magnificent specimens. *Rue du Pont, tel. 081/231631. Admission: BF80. Open Mon. and Wed.–Fri. 10–5, weekends 10:30–5.*

A special museum, dedicated to the work of Namur's leading 19th-century artist, is the **Musée Felicien Rops.** Rops was a friend of Baudelaire and illustrated his and many other books. A surrealist before his time, Rops created works by turns satirical and erotic. *Rue Fumal 12, tel. 081/220110. Admission: BF100. Open Nov.–Apr., daily 10–6, May–June and Sept.,–Oct., daily 10–5, July–Aug., Wed.–Mon. 10–5.*

You can reach the **Citadelle** (Citadel) by car up the hairpin curves of a mile-long road called la route Merveilleuse, or you can ride up by cable car. From the plateau at the top you have great views in all directions. The 15th-century bastions were further fortified by the Spanish. The Dutch also constructed fortifications here, called the Fort d'Orange. *Rte. Merveilleuse 8, tel. 081/226829. Admission: BF195 adults, BF100 children. Open Apr.–Oct., daily 11–7. Cable car: BF100.*

There are several museums on the site, including the **Musée Provincial de la Forêt** (Provincial Forestry Museum), contained in an old hunting lodge, which gives an overview of the region's fauna and flora. *Rte. Merveilleuse 9, tel. 081/743894. Admission: BF50 adults, BF 20 children. Open Apr.–mid-June and mid-Sept.–Oct., Sat.–Thurs. 9–noon and 2–5; mid-June–mid-Sept., daily 9–noon and 2–5.*

Tour 2: Liège

9 The bustling city of **Liège**—Luik to the Flemish and Dutch, Lüttich to the Germans—is in many ways quietly romantic. Surrounded by hills, it sits deep in the Meuse Valley at the confluence with the Ourthe. Here the river is slate-gray, and pleasure craft play second fiddle to coal barges and tankers. Liège is a city riddled with secret courtyards, narrow medieval lanes, and steeply stepped streets. Above all, it is a city of joie de vivre, where you easily get into conversation with strangers. The institution that best expresses the Liège spirit is the *café chantant* (singing café), where everyone is welcome to burst into song and frequently does.

The **place de la Cathédrale** is a pleasant square with flower beds in the center, lined with sidewalk cafés on two sides, and flanked by the north wall of the Gothic **Cathédrale St-Paul** (St. Paul's Cathedral). Inside, you'll see some handsome statues, including one of St. Paul by Jean Delcour. Other graceful 18th-century sculptor dot the old city. The cathedral's most highly prized possessions are found in the **Treasury,** especially the *Reliquaire de Charles le Téméraire* with gold and enamel figures of St. George and the bold duke himself on his knees; curiously, their faces are identical. This reliquary was presented to Liège by Charles the Bold in 1471 in expiation for having had the city razed three years earlier. *Admission: BF50. Open daily (except during services) 10–noon and 2–5. Ring bell next to cloister door.*

From the place de la Cathédrale, turn left on pont d'Avroy. Despite the name, there's no bridge in sight. Many street names here reflect a maritime past, when the arc of the boulevard de la Sauvenière, which surrounds the district, was a branch of the river. Pont d'Avroy is crammed with shops and cafés, giving a taste of what the neighborhood is like. Everyone in Liège knows it by its informal name of **Le Carré.**

Time Out   **Le Panier Fleuri** (20 pont d'Avroy) is a period piece from the Belle Epoque. This combination tavern and brasserie serves Belgian beer, 200 brands of spirits, and 80 different permutations of ham and cheese on toast.

Three blocks from the pont d'Avroy is place Xavier Neujean and the **Eglise St-Jean** (St. John's Church), an octagonal church founded by Prince Bishop Notger in the 10th century and heavily restored. Here you can see the *Sedes Sapientiae* (Seat of Wisdom), a magnificent wood carving of the Virgin and Child from 1220—one of the finest sculptural examples of Art Mosan. *Pl. Xavier Neujean, tel. 041/237042. Open Mon.–Sat. 4–5, Sun. 11–1; in summer, daily 10–noon and 2–5.*

Time Out   On the rue St-Adalbert in a single block there are more than half a dozen antiques dealers, as well as a traditional Liègeois café, **Le Seigneur d'Amay,** and two student hangouts, **Le Saloon** and **Les Trois Frères.**

Bearing left, you come to the charming and animated triangular square called **Vinâve-d'Ile,** where a fountain is ornamented by a Virgin and Child by Delcour.

Liège's most prestigious shopping addresses are along the covered Passage Lemonnier, which stretches from here to the rue de l'Université. On the left you come to the place de la République Française. Turn right into the narrow medieval lane called rue de la Wache to the **Eglise St-Denis** (Church of St. Denis), also founded by Bishop Notger, with a handsome reredos portraying the Suffering of Christ. *Pl. St-Denis, tel. 041/235756. Open Mon.–Sat. 9–6, Sun. 9–11:30.*

Turning left from place St-Denis, you shortly arrive at a true eyesore, the place St-Lambert. What should be the city's most prestigious square has in fact been a hole in the ground for more than 200 years. It's as though the destruction of Cathédrale St-Lambert (St. Lambert's Cathedral) during the French Revolution has cast a spell on the site. The word is that a solution has been agreed upon and work is about to start, but the Liègeois aren't holding their breath.

On the other side of the square stands the enormous **Palais des Princes-Evèques** (Palace of the Prince Bishops), rebuilt at different stages since Notger's days. The present facade dates from after the fire of 1734. It's worth picking your way across the square to have a peek inside the colonnaded 16th-century courtyard, which has remained unchanged. Each column is decorated with stone carvings of staggering variety. The palace is now used by local government offices and law courts, which explains the presence of police and metal detectors.

Just to the left as you leave the palace is the **place du Marché** (Market Square), as old as the city itself. For centuries, this was where the city's commercial and political life was concentrated. A number of the old buildings surrounding it were among the 23,000 houses destroyed by German "flying bombs" toward the end of World War II. In the center stands the **Perron,** a large fountain sculpted by Jean Delcour, a symbol of municipal liberty.

Time Out   The **Café à Pilori** (pl. du Marché 5) is another essentially Liègeois tavern, with a large fireplace and beamed ceiling. It sells good pub-style food and its own homemade brew called La Rousse, a mellow brown beer.

Turning down En Neuvice toward the Meuse, you can take the first passage to the left, a 1-meter-wide (3-foot-wide) alley called rue du Carré. The second right is rue de la Goffe, which takes you past several attractive houses on the right and, on the left, the **Halle aux Viandes** (Butchers' Hall), from the 16th century, a handsome building that served its original purpose until rather recently. Thus one arrives at the riverside.

On Sundays from 9 AM to 2 PM, this is the site of the mile-long street market known as **La Batte,** ranging from bric-a-brac and foodstuffs to songbirds and pets to clothing, books, records, and toys. Visitors from neighboring Holland and Germany descend regularly on Liège to join the locals at the Sunday market, but it's not so much the merchandise that makes it attractive as the good-natured ambience.

A couple of blocks downstream you come upon rue St-Georges, which takes you into the **Ilôt St-Georges,** an interesting example of urban archaeology. Twelve dilapidated buildings were taken apart, brick by brick, and put together again to form an attractive architectural whole. Here, too, is the new **Musée de l'Art Wallon,** containing works by Walloon artists from the 17th century to the present day, including Magritte and Delvaux. *En Féronstrée 86, tel. 041/219231. Admission: BF50. Open Mon.–Sat. 1–6, Sun. 11–4:30; closed first week of May.*

Farther down the quay stands the handsome neoclassical **Musée d'Armes** (Armaments Museum). Napoléon slept here, and there's a portrait of him as first consul by Ingres. Liège was famed for its arms manufacturing from the Middle Ages on, and the collection includes many rare and beautifully executed pieces. *Quai de Maastricht 8, tel. 041/219400. Admission: BF50. Open Mon., Thurs., Sat., and Sun. 10–1; Wed. and Fri. 2–5; closed first week of May.*

Next door is the **Musée Curtius.** This patrician mansion was built in the style typical of Mosan Renaissance for the arms manufacturer Jean Curtius in the 16th century. Among its archaeological and decorative art treasures are three outstanding pieces: a 12th-century tympanum, representing the Apollonian Mystery; the Virgin of Dom Rupert, from the same century; and, above all, Bishop Notger's Evangelistery, an exquisite 10th-century manuscript of the gospels. *Quai de Maastricht 13, tel. 041/219404. Admission: BF50. Open Mon., Thurs., and Sat. 2–5; Wed. and Fri. 10–1; 2nd and 4th Sun. of month 10–1, 1st and 3rd Sun. guided visits only at 10 and 11:30. Closed first week of May.*

Time Out **A la Bonne Franquette** (En Féronstrée 152) is a no-frills neighborhood eatery where you can enjoy a meal or snack.

Liège's greatest treasure awaits you in the **Eglise St-Barthélemy** (St. Bartholomew's Church). Follow rue du Mont-de-Piété to an archway (an *arvô* in the local patois), turn left, and then turn right. The entrance to this Romanesque church retains its original aspect of sober austerity. The nave has been touched up in baroque fashion, and the choir is under restoration. In this church stands the brass masterpiece of Art Mosan, the Baptismal Font of Renier de Huy, which dates from the period between 1107 and 1118. The high relief figures of the five Biblical baptismal scenes are of an extraordinary suppleness, and there is also great variety among the 10 oxen on which the font rests. *Pl. St-Barthélemy, tel. 041/234998. Admission: BF80. Open daily 10–noon and 2–5 except during services.*

Leaving the square in front of the church by the rue des Brasseurs and bearing right at the first opportunity, you reach the **Cour St-Antoine,** a hidden square combining postmodern architecture with Mosan Renaissance buildings and a daring use of color. In the old days, prominent citizens in the service of the prince bishops lived along En Hors-Château. Their servants were tucked away in tiny houses up narrow mews, or *impasses*. As late as the 1970s it was believed that the best approach to urban redevelopment was to tear them down. Luckily, common sense prevailed, and many small houses have been restored to mint condition. The **Impasse de l'Ange** and its neighbor **Impasse de la Couronne** are fine examples. Here, as in many other places around Liège, you find a number of *potales* (wall chapels), devoted mostly to the Virgin or Saint Roch, the latter venerated as the protector against epidemic diseases.

As you return toward the center on Hors-Château, the **Montagne de Bueren** ascends as a broad flight of 373 steps toward the Citadel. The stairway is not much more than a hundred years old, but it evokes the memory of Vincent van Bueren, a leader of the resistance against Charles the Bold. In 1468 he climbed the hill with 600 men, intending to fall upon the duke and kill him. Betrayed by their Liègeois accents, they lost their lives instead, and the city was pillaged and burned. Charles was loved in Burgundy, but he never got good press in Liège.

At the foot of the stairs, you can turn left through the cobbled **Impasse des Ursulines,** which mounts to the small and peaceful Beguinage. Next to it stand old buildings rescued from demolition elsewhere in Liège. Continuing uphill, you come to a gate in the wall on the left. Push through it, and you're in a large and verdant hillside park. From rue du Pery, you can return down the Montagne de Bueren.

Back on Hors-Château, you come to the last two museums of note, past another Delcour fountain. The **Musée d'Art Religieux et d'Art Mosan** (MARAM) has inherited the treasures of the old diocesan museum. They include an 11th-century *Seat of Wisdom,* two centuries older than its namesake in St. John's. This is a stiff and stern-faced Virgin, reflecting a more austere age. *Rue Mère Dieu 11, tel. 041/218944. Admission: BF50. Open Tues.–Sat. 1–6, Sun. 11–4.*

Across the courtyard, in the old Franciscan convent, is the **Musée de la Vie Wallonne** (Museum of Walloon Life), where carefully reconstituted interiors give a vivid and varied idea of life in old Wallonie, from coal mines to farm kitchens to the workshops of many different crafts, as well as a court of law complete with a guillotine. One gallery is populated by the irreverent marionettes—Tchantchès and his band—who have always represented the Liège spirit. *Cour des Mineurs, tel. 041/236094. Admission: BF80. Open Tues.–Sat. 10–5, Sun. 10–4.*

You can follow rue des Mineurs back to the place du Marché.

In the Vicinity
Herve Region

The gently rolling **Herve region,** northeast of Liège, is a land of orchards and fields, hedgerows and copses. Herve has given its name to a particularly pungent cheese, which connoisseurs rank among the world's top cheeses.

⑩ You get to the village of **Herve** most easily by taking E40 toward Aachen and following N3 northeast from Exit 37. Nearby is the **Fort de Battice,** which held out against the Germans for 12 days in May 1940 while the German tanks rolled on into France. *Rte. d'Aubel, tel. 087/311350. Admission: BF100. Open last Sat. of Mar.–Nov., at 1:30.*

⑪ Farther along N3 you'll come to the Cimetière de **Henri-Chapelle,** an American military cemetery that is the resting place of 7,989 GIs who fell in the Battle of the Bulge during the last winter of World War II. The crosses and steles (commemorative stones) are arranged in arcs converging on the central monument, which also contains a small museum. From here, there is a great view over the plateau of Herve. *Rte. du Mémorial Américain, Hombourg, tel. 087/687173. Open Apr.–Sept., daily 8–6, Oct.–Mar., daily 8–5.*

In the opposite direction, you pass through attractive villages such ⑫ as **Clermont,** where you can take N650 to **Val-Dieu.** The ancient but much rebuilt abbey here is open for visits and sells local produce. ⑬ N642 will take you on to **Blegny,** where it is possible to visit the old colliery. The wealth of Liège was based on coal, which was mined from the Middle Ages until 1980. An audiovisual presentation illustrates this history, and former miners lead tours of the facility. A complete visit takes 3½ hours. *Complexe Touristique de Blegny, rue Lambert Marlet 23, tel. 041/874333. Admission: BF270 adults, BF175 children. Open May–Sept., daily 10–4; Apr. and Oct., weekends 10–4.*

⓮ To the north is **Dalhem,** formerly a walled town, with castle ruins and an old keep.

At **Mortroux,** the **Musée de la Vie Régionale de Mortroux** (museum of the life of the region) has been installed in an old farm where syrup, cider, butter, and cheese are still produced in the old, artisanal way. There's also a rustic self-service restaurant, where you can try local beers and the celebrated Herve cheese. *Chemin du Trimbleux, tel. 041/766297. Admission: BF50 adults, BF30 children. Open May–Sept., daily 10:30–7; Apr. and Oct., weekends 10:30–7.*

⓯ **Visé** on the Meuse was sacked and burned early in World War I and abandoned when the survivors fled to Holland. It is an old town, proud of its ancient guilds of crossbowmen and harquebusiers, each of which maintains a small museum. The reliquary of Saint Hadelin, in the collegiate church, is decorated with scenes of his life, presumed to have been done by Renier de Huy, the master of the baptismal font in Liège. Water sports are available off the Ile Robinson.

Huy and the The small and charming town of **Huy** (pronounced "we") on the River
Condroz Meuse is 33 kilometers (20 miles) southwest of Liège off A15/E42. It is an ancient place; its city privileges of 1066 are the oldest that have
⓰ been preserved in Europe. The Gothic **Eglise Collégiale de Notre-Dame** (Collegiate Church of Our Lady) has a rose window, the so-called Rondia, with a diameter of 9 meters (30 feet), and its treasury contains several magnificent reliquaries, two of them attributed to Godefroy de Huy, who followed in the footsteps of Renier. *Admission: BF50. Open Mon.–Thurs. and Sat. 9–noon and 2–5, Sun. 2–5 except during services.*

On the Grand'Place is the **Hôtel de Ville** (Town Hall), in Louis-XV style, and in the center stands a remarkable copper fountain, the Bassinia; the bronze cistern decorated with saints dates from 1406, and in the 18th century the Austrians topped it all with their double eagle. From the square you can wander through winding alleys to the old Franciscan monastery, which is now the **Musée Communal,** a mine of local folklore and history, with an exceptional Art Mosan oak carving of Christ. *Rue Vankeerberghen 20, tel. 085/232435. Admission BF60. Open Apr.–Oct., Mon.–Sat. 2–6, Sun. 10–noon and 2–6.*

An easy way to get a great view of town and country is to take a mile-long ride on the cable car from the left bank of the Meuse, across the river and to the cliff-top fort. This **Citadelle** was part of the defenses built by the Dutch in the early 19th century. During World War II it served as a prison for resisters and hostages. *Chaussée Napoléon, tel. 085/215334. Admission: BF120. Open Apr.–June and Sept., weekdays 10–6, weekends 10–7; July and Aug., daily 10–8.*

It's in Huy that the Meuse is joined by the Hoyoux, clearest and coldest of the rivers of the Ardennes. Following its valley south on
⓱ N641, you come to **Modave** with its 17th-century **Château des Comtes de Marchin,** on a cliff overlooking the river. Its elegant rooms feature stuccoed polychrome ceilings. The hydraulic machinery that brought water from the river to the cliff top was copied in France to bring water from the Seine to the Palace of Versailles. *Tel. 085/411369. Admission: BF150 adults, BF90 children. Open Apr.–mid-Nov., daily 9–6.*

You are now in the heart of the **Condroz,** a fertile plateau of the lower Ardennes remarkable for the opulence of its farms and manors.
⓲ Traveling toward Liège on N63, you reach **St-Severin** on the left, with the beautiful and harmonious Romanesque **Eglise de Sts Pierre**

et Paul (Church of Sts. Peter and Paul) from the 12th century, one of the best preserved in Belgium. The architecture is based on that of the Abbey of Cluny in Burgundy, of which this was once a priory. *Tel. 041/714034. Open daily 10–6. In case of temporary closure, ring the bell at No. 17 in the churchyard.*

Where N63 forks, take the road to the left, N677. You arrive in **Neuville-en-Condroz**, the site of the **Cimitière Américain des Ardennes**, final resting place for 5,327 soldiers of the U.S. First Army who fell in the Ardennes, at the Siegfried Line, and around Aachen. The memorial, decorated with an immense American eagle, contains a nondenominational chapel. *Rte. du Condroz 164, tel. 041/714287. Admission free. Open mid-Apr.–Sept., weekdays 8–6; Oct.–mid-Apr., weekdays 9–5.*

At **Ivoz**-Ramet on the Meuse, turn right on N90 and you arrive at the **Cristalleries du Val St-Lambert.** You can see glassblowers and engravers at work, walk through well-restored factory buildings from the 19th century, see an exhibition of museum and contemporary glassware, and visit the shop. *Admission: BF100 adults, BF50 children. Open Apr.–Dec., Tues.–Sun. 10–5; Jan.–Mar., weekends and bank holidays 10–5.*

Tour 3: Eupen to Spa

Eupen, 40 kilometers (25 miles) east of Liège, is a newcomer as Belgian towns go, dating from the 18th century. The church, with its bulbous towers and extravagant altars, is typical of the period. Following N68 in the direction of Malmédy, you are soon in dense woods, which then open up into the **Hautes Fagnes** (High Fens). This is now a national park of almost 10,500 acres. Here the vistas open over vast tracts of moor, with bushes and copses harboring rich and varied vegetation and bird life. The marshland is waterlogged, and wooden walks have been laid out across the area. You're well advised not to stray from them and to be exceedingly careful with matches in dry periods. Paths are clearly marked.

Just past the Baraque Michel (Michael's Shack, named for a former innkeeper), take N676 toward Robertville and you'll reach the Centre Nature à **Botrange**, where you can get a professional introduction to the flora and fauna of the High Fens. Parts of the area can only be visited with a guide, especially the peat bogs and the feeding areas of the *capercaillies* (large and very rare woodland grouse). You can book an individual guide in advance, and you can also rent boots and bikes. *Robertville, tel. 080/445781. Admission: BF70. Open daily 10–6; closed mid-Nov.–mid-Dec.*

Schloss **Reinhardstein,** the loftiest and possibly the best-preserved medieval fortress in the country, is reached by a mile-long walk. It sits on a spur of rock overlooking the River Warche and has been in the hands of such illustrious families as the Metternichs, who spawned the prince who masterminded the Congress of Vienna in 1815. The castle has been well restored; the Hall of Knights and the Chapel are gems. *Robertville, tel. 080/446868. Admission: BF150 adults, BF60 children. Tours mid-June–mid-Sept., Sun. 2:15, 3:15, 4:15; July–Aug., also Tues., Thur., and Sat. 3:30.*

The High Fens act as a huge sponge; dams have been built on some of the rivers that drain them, and water sports are available on the artificial lakes at **Robertville** and neighboring **Bütgenbach.**

Malmédy and its neighbor Stavelot formed a separate, peaceful principality, ruled by abbots, for 11 centuries before the French

Revolution. The center of Malmédy was destroyed in error during an Allied air raid in December 1944. Most years there's at least a short skiing season. The carnival, beginning on the Saturday before Lent, is among the merriest in Belgium. To learn more about it, you might want to visit the **Musée du Carnaval.** Pl. de Rome 11 (3rd floor; no elevator), tel. 080/337058. Admission: BF50 adults, children free. Open July–Aug., daily 3–6; Sept.–June, weekends 2:30–5:30. Closed carnival and Lent.

Time Out **Le Floreal** (pl. Albert I) serves breakfast, lunch, dinner, and snacks such as *jambon d'Ardennes*.

㉕ **Stavelot** is only 15 kilometers (9¼ miles) from Malmédy, but its traditions differ. Here carnival is celebrated on the fourth Sunday in Lent and is animated by a couple of thousand Blancs-Moussis, dressed in white with long capes and bright red long noses, who swoop and rush through the streets. The Blancs-Moussis commemorate the monks of Stavelot, who in 1499 were forbidden to participate in the carnival, but got around it by celebrating Laetare Sunday (3 weeks before Easter), instead. Stavelot, too, was badly damaged in the Battle of the Bulge, but some picturesque old streets survived, particularly rue Haute (off place St-Remacle). Remacle founded the abbey in 647, and his reliquary, now in the **Eglise St-Sébastien** (St. Sebastian's Church), is one of the wonders of Art Mosan. Dating from the 13th century, it is 2 meters (6½ feet) long and is decorated on the sides with statuettes of the apostles and, on the ends, of Christ and the Virgin. *Rue de l'Eglise 7, tel. 080/864437. Admission: BF40. Open Mon.–Sat. 9–noon and 2–5, Sun. 11:30–noon and 2–5 except during services.*

Only a Romanesque tower remains of the **Ancienne Abbaye** (Old Abbey). The present buildings date from the 18th century, and the refectory has become a concert hall. The old stable has been converted into a **Musée d'Art Religieux Régional** (Regional Museum of Religious Art), and the vaulted cellars of the abbey have been put to somewhat anachronistic use in housing the **Musée du Circuit de Spa-Francorchamps** (Museum of the Spa-Francorchamp Racecourse), which displays Formula I racing cars, sports cars, and motorcycles illustrating the history of motor racing since 1907. *Tel. 080/862706. Admission: BF100 adults, BF40 children; valid also for Museum of Religious Art. Open daily 10–12:30 and 2:30–5:30 (winter to 4:30).*

㉖ The road from Stavelot north to **Spa** runs through very attractive landscape. Spa is indeed the original spa. The Romans came here to take the waters, and they were followed over the centuries by crowned heads such as Marguerite de Valois, Christina of Sweden, and Peter the Great. Less welcome was Kaiser Wilhelm II, who established his general headquarters in Spa in 1918. By then Spa was already past its prime. During the 18th and 19th centuries, Spa had been the watering place of international high society, and many gracious houses remain from that period. The pleasures of the cure and the surroundings were supplemented in those days by high-stakes gambling, playing *pharaon* or *biribi* for rubles, ducats, piastres, or francs. Today's casino is more sedate.

The two best-known sources in the center of town—locally known as *pouhons*—are the **Pouhon Pierre-le-Grand** and the **Pouhon Prince-de-Condé**, which can be visited by tourists as well as *curistes* (people taking the cure). The price for a glass straight from the source is a modest BF7. *Tel. 087/772510. Open Easter–Oct., daily 10–noon and 2–5:30; Nov.–Easter, weekdays 2–5, weekends 10–noon and 2–5.*

Tour 4: Belgian Luxembourg

㉗ **La Roche-en-Ardenne** is 77 kilometers (48 miles) from Liège, 127 kilometers (79 miles) from Brussels, and 66 kilometers (41 miles) from Namur. It's a small town, beautifully situated, and is packed with tourists and trippers in the summer season, when it's wise to avoid it on weekends. The **Musée de la Bataille des Ardennes** (Battle of the Ardennes Museum) displays uniforms, vehicles, weapons, and personal belongings found on the battleground in the vicinity. *Rue Châmont 5, tel. 084/411725. Admission: BF150 adults, BF80 children. Open daily 10–6.*

The main attraction is a trip out of town to admire the view, and the principal part is played by the River Ourthe, a torrent that splashes through a landscape of great beauty. Follow N834 south and turn left on N843 to Nisramont, which has an excellent view. Cross the river and go left on N860 to Nadrin, and left again on N869 to the **㉘** **Belvedère des Six Ourthes.** A 120-step climb to the top of the observation tower will reward you with a magnificent view of the quintessence of the Ardennes: wooded hills and meandering river valleys. You can return on the pretty N860, following the banks of the Ourthe toward La Roche.

㉙ You reach **Bastogne** by going southwest on N89 and then southeast on N4. La Roche and a number of other Ardennes towns were also destroyed during the Battle of the Bulge, but Bastogne was the epicenter. The town was surrounded but held by the American 101st Airborne Division. The weather was miserable. On December 22 Brigadier General MacAuliffe was invited to surrender. His four-letter-word reply, "Nuts!" is one of the famous quotes from World War II. On December 26, the skies cleared and supplies could be flown in, but it took another month before the last German salient had been wiped out.

Colline du Mardasson (Mardasson Hill), just east of the town, is the site of a memorial to the Americans lost in the battle. Mosaics by Fernand Léger decorate the crypt with its three chapels, Protestant, Catholic, and Jewish. The **Bastogne Historical Center,** next to the memorial monument and built in the shape of a five-pointed star, illustrates the ebb and flow of the battle with photos, films (including footage shot during the battle), uniforms, and arms. *Tel. 061/ 211413. Admission: BF245 adults, BF185 children. Open Mar.– Apr. and Nov.–Dec., daily 10–4; May–June and Sept.–Oct., daily 9:30–5:30; July–Aug., daily 8:30–7.*

The **Victory Memorial Museum,** 40 kilometers (25 miles) south, near Arlon, expands on the same theme. The museum traces the progress of World War II from Africa to Berlin with the help of realistic reconstructions, using 200 vehicles, arms, uniforms, matériel and a film compiled from contemporary sources. There's also a souvenir shop and a specialized book shop. *Messancy, tel. 063/219988. Admission: BF345 adults, BF195 children. Open daily 10–5; summer, daily 8–7.*

㉚ In **Arlon,** the **Musée Luxembourgeois** contains a number of Roman tombstones from the first three centuries AD, sculpted with reliefs of mythical or allegorical figures as well as scenes from daily life. There is also a section featuring Merovingian tombstones and jewelry. *Rue des Martyrs 13, tel. 063/221236. Admission: BF100. Open mid-June–mid-Sept., Mon.–Sat. 9–noon and 2–5, Sun. 10–noon and 2–7.*

You are now in the southernmost part of Belgian Luxembourg, La Gaume, which is part of Lorraine rather than the Ardennes. N83 leads west to Florenville, where you can turn south on N88 to reach **31** the **Abbaye d'Orval** in the middle of the woods, almost on the French border. This abbey, founded by Italian Benedictines in 1070, gradually became one of Europe's richest and most famous. Destroyed twice by French troops in the 17th and 18th centuries, the monastery was finally re-consecrated as a Trappist abbey in 1948. The medieval and 18th-century ruins are remarkable. The tomb of Wenceslas, first duke of Luxembourg, is in the choir of the abbey church, and outside it is the spring where Mathilde, duchess of Lorraine, once dropped her wedding band, only to have it miraculously returned by a trout. The monks are known not only for their spirituality, but also for the excellence of their bread, cheese, and potent Trappist beer. *Villers-devant-Orval, tel. 061/311060. Admission: BF80. Open daily (except Mon. AM in winter) 10–noon and 1:30–5:30.*

The focus of this region is the Semois River, flowing west to join the Meuse. A few miles west of Florenville you can head north on N884 **32** to **Herbeumont,** a thousand-year-old village with a hilltop castle ruin, which offers a splendid view of the river valley. Just to the north, N865 west follows the river from Mortehan/Cugnon to Dohan (both possible starting points for kayak trips to Bouillon), Noirefontaine, and Bouillon.

33 The small town of **Bouillon** was capital of a duchy almost equally small, which managed to remain independent for 800 years. Its most famous native son, Godefroy de Bouillon, sold it to the bishop of Liège in 1096 to improve his cash flow before departing on the first crusade. Bouillon owed its independence to the **Château Fort,** an impressive example of medieval military architecture. Successive modifications have done little to alter the personality of this feudal stronghold with its towers, drawbridge, guardroom, torture chamber, dungeons, and enormous walls. *Rue du Château, tel. 061/466257. Admission: BF140 adults, BF70 children. Open Mar.–June and Sept.–Nov., daily 10–5; July–Aug., daily 9:30–7; Dec., Wed.–Sun. 10–5; Jan. and Feb., weekends 10–5.*

34 **St-Hubert** is 56 kilometers (35 miles) northeast of Bouillon on N89. Its name recalls the patron saint of hunters. According to legend, Hubert, hunting in these woods on Good Friday in 683, saw his quarry, a stag, turn its head toward him, and its antlers held a crucifix. Hubert lowered his bow, and later went on to become a bishop and a saint. On the first Sunday in September, Mass in the old basilica is played with hunting horns, followed by a historical procession, and on November 3, St. Hubert's feast day, animals are blessed.

North of the town is, appropriately enough, the **Parc à Gibier de St-Hubert,** where one can observe the animal life of the Ardennes—deer, mountain sheep, and wild boars. *Rue St-Michel, tel. 061/611715. Admission: BF60 adults, BF40 children. Open daily 9–6.*

35 To the north past Han-sur-Lesse (*see* Tour 1, *above*) is **Rochefort,** where the caves excavated by the River Lomme are even wilder and colder than those at Han-sur-Lesse. *Drève de Lorette, tel. 084/212080. Admission: BF150 adults, BF105 children. May–Aug., visits every 45 min. 9:45–5:15; April and Sept.–mid-Nov., 10, 11:30, 1:30, 3, and 4:30.*

You are now only 13 kilometers (8 miles) from A4/E411 and the network of motorways.

What to See and Do with Children

The Meuse Valley
The **Réserve d'Animaux Sauvage** (Wildlife Reserve) in Han-sur-Lesse, which covers more than 600 acres, provides an opportunity to see the wildlife, past and present, of the Ardennes, including stags and wild boars, lynx and bears, bisons and wild oxen. *Rue J. Lamotte 2, tel. 084/377213. Admission: BF185 adults, BF130 children. Open May–Aug., daily 9:30–11:30 and 1–5; Mar.–Apr. and Sept.–Nov., guided visits daily 10–4.*

Mont-Fat in Dinant, 122 meters (400 feet) above the city, offers the combination of a guided tour of prehistoric caves and a chair-lift ride to an amusement area. *Rue en Rhée 15, tel. 082/222783. Admission: BF150 adults, BF120 children. Open Easter–Aug., daily 10:30–7, Sept.–Oct., weekends 10:30–5.*

The **Reine Fabiola** center in the Citadel grounds at Namur includes a large playground with miniature golf, go-carts, boat rides, and electric cars. *Rte. Merveilleuse, tel. 081/226829. Admission and hrs as for the Citadel (see Tour 1, above).*

Liège
The **Wegimont Domaine** is just a few minutes south of E42 at Exit 37. An area of 50 acres around the château offers sporting facilities, fishing, rowing, swimming in a heated outdoor pool, minigolf, and signposted walks. *Soumagne, tel. 041/771020. Admission: BF90 adults, BF55 children. Open May–Aug., daily 9–8.*

Eupen to Spa
At **Telecoo,** chair lifts take you up from Coo to a plateau where there's a splendid view of the Ambleve River valley and an extensive amusement park. *Stavelot, tel. 080/684265. Admission: BF520. Open Apr.–Oct., daily 10–7; Nov.–Mar., weekends 10–7.*

You get to the **Monde Sauvage Safari** (Savage World Safari) at Deigné near Aywaille on E25 south from Liège, Exit 46. The safari park, home to a number of different species of African animals, is visited by car or tourist train. This is followed by a visit on foot to a zoo with lions, tigers, polar bears, and others. *Fange de Deigné 3, tel. 041/609070. Admission: BF225 adults, BF150 children. Open Easter–mid-Nov., daily 10–7; in winter, weekends 10–5.*

Belgian Luxembourg
On a very different note, you'll find a **Musée du Jouet** (Toy Museum) in Ferrières (motorway A26, Exit 48). Its collection consists of more than a thousand early 20th-century toys. *Rte. du Lognoûle 6, tel. 086/400452. Admission: BF100 adults, BF40 children. Open weekends 2:30–5:30.*

Off the Beaten Track

Liège
To the northwest of central Liège, the **Fort de Loncin** has remained as it was at 5:15 PM on August 16, 1914, when a German shell scored a direct hit, killing most of the garrison. *Rue des Héros 15bis. Admission: BF50. Open Wed.–Sun. 9–6; winter, Wed.–Sun. 9–5; guided visits Apr.–Sept., Sat. at 2:30.*

The right bank of the river, **Outremeuse** (On the Other Side of the Meuse), is a sort of Alternative Liège. It was the home of two personages, Georges Simenon and Tchantchès. Simenon left Liège as early as he could, and only one of his more than 400 books, *Le pendu de Saint-Pholien,* is set in the city; nevertheless the tourist office arranges occasional Simenon walks for his fans. Tchantchès is strictly a local character, a marionette that impersonates the "true Liègeois"—caustic, irreverent, and funny. His home is the **Musée**

Tchantchès. *Rue Surlet 56, tel. 041/427575. Admission: BF20. Open Tues. and Thur. 2–4.*

The **Aquarium/Musée Zoologique,** on the waterfront, owned by the University of Liège, presents 300 different species in 30 carefully created biotopes. The museum collection of 18,000 pieces illustrates the process of evolution. *Quai Van Beneden 22, tel. 041/665001. Admission: BF100. Open weekdays 10:30–12:30 and 1:30–5:30, weekends 10:30–12:30 and 2–6.*

The **Maison de la Métallurgie** (House of Metallurgy) is south of Outremeuse. Huge 19th-century steel mills have been converted into a museum of industrial archaeology, including a 17th-century Walloon forge. *Blvd. Raymond Poincaré 17, tel. 041/426563. Admission: BF100. Open weekdays 9–5.*

On the attractive University of Liège campus at **Sart Tilman,** a wooded plateau south of the city, is the **Musée en Plein Air** (Open-Air Museum) conceived by architect Claude Strebelle. It contains many contemporary sculptures and some murals, all integrated with the striking modern architecture. *Domaine Universitaire Sart Tilman, tel. 041/562220 for info on guided visits (BF100). Admission free. Open 24 hrs.*

The **Eglise St-Jacques** (St. James's Church) is a few blocks south of Liège's center. The grimy exterior belies a wonderful interior in which marble, stained glass, and polished wood combine to create an outstanding visual harmony. The glory of the church are the Gothic vaults, decorated in intricate patterns of vivid blue and gold and containing myriad sculpted figures. *Pl. St-Jacques, tel. 041/221441. Open Mon.–Sat. 8–noon.*

Shopping

Huy   The artisans of modern Huy produce pewter plates that make attractive souvenirs; one of the best shops is **Les Potstainiers Hutois** (av. des Fosses 34).

Liège   The **Carré** is almost exclusively a pedestrian area, with boutiques and shops. The most important shopping arcades are the **Passage Lemonnier** (between Vinâve d'Ile and rue de l'Univérsité), **Galerie en Ile** (between Vinâve d'Ile and rue du Pot d'Or), **Galerie du Pont d'Avroy** (off the street of the same name), and **Galerie Nagelmackers** (between pl. de la Cathédrale and rue Tournant St-Paul).

Glassware from Val St-Lambert can be found in a number of shops and most advantageously at the glassworks in Seraing (*see* Tour 2, *above*). **Firearms,** an age-old Liège specialty, are still handmade to order by some gun shops, notably Lebeau-Courally (rue St-Gilles 386, tel. 041/524843). (Keep in mind that only a licensed arms importer may carry arms into the United States.)

Sports and the Outdoors

The Meuse   Biking is a popular sport in this region. You can rent mountain bikes
Valley   at **Meuse et Lesse** (rue Caussin 13, Dinant, tel. 082/226186).

Biking   Rowing is also popular, and boats can be hired under the auspices of
Boating   the **Clubs Nautiques** at Namur and Dinant. If you find riding a kayak down the Lesse a bit too tricky, canoeing on the Meuse may be more to your liking. Contact **Meuse et Lesse** (*see* Biking, *above*).

Climbing   The sheer cliffs along the Meuse lend themselves extremely well to rock climbing, and many hopeful mountaineers learn the skills here for more dramatic exploits. Contact **Club Alpin Belge** (Belgian Alpine Club, rue de l'Aurore 19, Brussels, tel. 02/648–8611).

Fishing   Fishing is permitted on several stretches of the Meuse, where it is mostly of the sitting-on-the-bank kind, and on some livelier tributaries. Licenses can be purchased at local post offices (Dinant: rue St-Martin).

Horseback   The Provincial Tourist Office can supply a list of more than 20 sta-
Riding   bles, and the region is great for horseback riding. Horses can be hired for about BF500 per hour, and several stables organize treks of several days with overnight accommodations.

Sailing   Sailing is extremely popular, with yacht harbors at Namur, Profondeville, Dinant, and Waulsort. Contact **Royal Nautique Club de Sambre et Meuse** (chemin des Pruniers 11, Wepion, tel. 081/461130).

Liège   **Boating.** There's a yacht harbor along the boulevard Frère Orban,
Participant   and water sports are popular upstream from the Pont Albert I. An-
Sports   other water-sports center is the Ile Robinson at Visé.

Golf. The **Royal Golf Club du Sart Tilman** (rte. du Condroz 541, Angleur, tel. 041/362021) has 18 holes. Another 18-hole course is at **International Gomzé Golf Club** (rue de Gomzé 30, Gomzé-Andoumont, tel. 041/609207).

Swimming and Skating. The **Palais des Sports de Coronmeuse** (quai de Wallonie 7, tel. 041/271324) provides facilities for swimming in a heated outdoor pool in summer and skating in winter.

Spectator   **Motor racing.** Motor sport fans know **Francorchamps** (near Spa) as
Sports   one of Europe's top racing circuits. The Formula I Grand Prix de Belgique race is run in August, and there are several other motorcycle and automobile races throughout the year. Contact Intercommunale du Circuit de Spa-Francorchamps (rte. du Circuit 55, Francorchamps, tel. 087/275138) for information.

Eupen to Spa   There's a lovely 18-hole golf course at **Balmoral** (tel. 087/771613),
Golf   just outside Spa.

Horseback   The **Worricken Sports Center** (rue Worricken 9, Bütgenbach, tel.
Riding   080/446961) offers horseback riding.

Skiing   Venues for downhill and cross-country skiing are dotted around the region. Equipment is generally available locally. Snow conditions vary wildly, however; check before setting out by calling Belsud (tel. 02/504–0280) in Brussels.

Tennis   The **Worricken Sports Center** (*see* Horseback Riding, *above*) has tennis facilities.

Water Sports   Water sports can be enjoyed at Robertville and Bütgenbach (*see* Horseback Riding, *above*).

Virtually all the rivers of the Ardennes are great for canoeing, and the meandering Amblêve is one of the best. Single or double kayaks can be rented at **Cookayak** (Stavelot, tel. 080/684245) for a 9-kilometer (5½-mile) ride from Coo to Cheneux (about 1½ hrs) or a 23-kilometer (14-mile) ride to Lorcé (about 3½ hrs). Bus service back to the starting point is provided.

Belgian   Biking in these parts is for those with sturdy legs. Mountain bikes
Luxembourg   can be rented from **Ardenne Adventures** (*see* Canoeing, *below*),
Biking   **Ferme de Palogne** (*see* Canoeing, *below*), and **Moulin de la Falize** (Bouillon, tel. 061/466200). The last is a multisport facility with a swimming pool, bowling alleys, a sauna, and a fitness room.

Canoeing The rapid rivers are ideal for canoeing in this part of the Ardennes. Kayaks can be rented by day or by distance, generally with return transportation to the point of departure. For the River Ourthe, contact **Ardenne Adventures** (la Roche-en-Ardennes, tel. 084/411347; kayaks Apr.–Oct., rafting Nov.–Mar.) or **Ferme de Palogne** (Vieuxville, tel. 086/212412). For the Semois River, contact **Récréalle** (Alle-sur-Semois, tel. 061/500381), which also functions as a general sports center, with facilities for tennis, bowling, fishing, and volleyball.

Cross-Country Skiing It is possible to ski cross-country for a few precious winter weeks at the **Centre de Tourisme Equestre** (*see* Horseback Riding, *below*) and at **Moulin de la Falize** (*see* Biking, *above*).

Horseback Riding Contact the **Centre de Tourisme Equestre** (Grand-Halleux, tel. 080/21–64–43), which offers both instruction and treks.

Dining and Lodging

Eating in the Ardennes is one of the most straightforward pleasures Belgium has to offer. The territory is chockablock with atmospheric gray-stone inns. The cuisine is redolent of forest and farm, with ham, sausage, trout, and game in the forefront. The region's *charcuterie* (cured meats and sausages) is some of the best in central Europe. Ardennes sausage, neat and plump, is made with a blend of veal and pork, and smoked over smoldering oak; its flavor is a wholesome compromise between simple American summer sausage and the milder Italian salamis. The real charcuterie star is *jambon d'Ardennes*, ham that is salt-cured raw and delicately smoked so its meat—surely among the most supple among its Parma and Westphalian competitors—slices up thin, moist, and tender, more like a superior roast beef than ham. Restaurateurs offer generous platters of it, garnished with crisp little gherkins and pickled onions or, if you're lucky, a savory onion marmalade.

Though game figures prominently throughout Belgian cuisine, nowhere is it more at home, and rarely do you find it fresher than in these deep, forested hills. Cooks pride themselves on buying their game *à poil*—that is, fresh and furry—from the back of the hunter's station wagon. *Lièvre*, a specialty, is true hare, an enormous rabbit with sail-sized ears and haunches thick with dark flesh. Its most delicate meat lies along the backbone (saddle or *râble*) and can be roasted and served in tenderloin-like slices. The rest of the hare is often, well, gamier (that is, stronger flavored), which prompted the invention of another Ardennes treat: *civet de lièvre*, a rich, aromatic, marinated stew often thickened with blood. A second popular Ardennes stew is *civet de marcassin*, made from the meat of young wild boar, closer to veal than to pork, but considerably more pungently flavored. Ardennes game is usually served with poached fruit and *airelles*, cranberrylike red berries; it also is cooked so often with *genièvre* (juniper berries) that the French call this seasoning *à l'ardennaise*.

Trout offers diners a slightly lighter meal, though once poached in a pool of butter and heaped with toasted almonds it may be as rich as red-meat alternatives. One pleasant relief, though not always available, is *truite au bleu:* Plunged freshly killed into a boiling vinegar stock, the trout turns steely blue and retains its delicate flavor.

Hotel rooms in this region tend to be low-priced, even if there's an outstanding restaurant downstairs. They tend to fill up on weekends and during summer high season (June–Aug.). If you prefer to eat somewhere other than in the hotel you've booked, clear it with the management: You're often expected (and sometimes obligated) to eat in their restaurant. Many hotels offer *demi-pension* (half-board) arrangements, as well as "gastronomic weekends," which include two or three lavish meals with two nights' lodging.

Bastogne
Dining

Wagon-Restaurant Léo. Originally a tiny chrome railroad diner, this local institution has spilled over across the street into the new, chicly refurbished Bistro Léo. In the restaurant, huge platters of plain Belgian standards—mussels, trout in riesling, *filet Américain* (steak tartare), frites—are served up; in the bistro, only cold ham plates, quiche, and homemade lasagna are the fare. *Rue du Vivier 8, tel. 061/216510. Dress: casual. MC, V. $*

Lodging

Du Sud. Airy and solid in its new, postwar form, this straight-forward little hotel kept its local atmosphere—oak details, game trophies, tile floors—and offers simple comforts. Back rooms are quietest. *Rue de Marche 39, B-6600, tel. 061/211114. 13 rooms with shower. Facilities: café, breakfast only. MC, V. $*

Dining and
Lodging
★

La Ferme au Pont. On a country road between Bastogne and La Roche, this idyllic little farmhouse inn has forests surrounding it and the Ourthe rushing just behind. Dating from 1747, with white-washed brick, flower boxes on every sill, and a dining room taking in views of the landscaped greenery behind, the inn offers good, simple cooking—grilled ham, smoked trout—and comfortable rooms decked with ivy-print fabrics. *16 km/10 mi from Bastogne on N834, near Ortho. B-6983, tel. 084/433161. 7 rooms, 4 with bath. AE, DC, MC, V. $*

Bouillon and
Environs
Dining and
Lodging

Auberge du Moulin Hideux. No, the mill isn't hideous, but there used to be two of them ("*il y a deux*"), and the name stuck. Nestled in a valley in leafy woods, this inn has become synonymous with gracious living. The fountain is illuminated at night, swans glide in the small pond, and breakfast is served on the flower-bedecked terrace. The cuisine is traditional but updated with a lighter touch; woodcock mousse, black and white boudins (blood sausage) with truffles, and fabulous game in season are among the menu highlights. The rooms, all with balconies, have been decorated with great taste by the patronne herself. *Rte. de Dohan 1, Noirefontaine (4 km/2½ mi north of Bouillon), tel. 061/467015, fax 061/467281. 10 rooms, 3 suites, all with bath. Facilities: restaurant (closed Wed., Thurs. lunch Mar.–July), bar, guided walks in the woods, bicycles for rent, shop. AE, DC, MC, V. Hotel and restaurant closed Dec.–mid-Mar. $$$$*

★

Au Gastronome. This swank Paliseul auberge, once a roadside café, explores the usual stellar routes of haute gastronomy but specializes in a local delicacy: suckling pig, roasted in its crisp skin, its juices blending with those of its stuffing of green pepper and lime. The setting is a little stuffy, but rooms upstairs are pleasantly old-fashioned, in shades of pink and cream, with floral prints. *Rue Bouillon 2, B-6850 Paliseul (15 km/9 mi north of Bouillon), tel. 061/533064. 9 rooms with bath. Facilities: restaurant (reservations required; jacket and tie advised; closed Sun dinner, Mon.). AE, DC, MC, V. Hotel $$; Restaurant $$$$*

★

Auberge d'Alsace. In the center of Bouillon, with the River Semois across the street and the château towering behind, is this ambitious little hotel/restaurant. Having had the interior rebuilt from the ground up, the proprietress has lavished the rooms with flashy fabrics, brass, lacquer, lace, and the occasional baldachin. Striking a similar tenuous balance between store-bought chic and Old Ardennes, the restaurant downstairs offers good cooking nonetheless: monkfish with kiwi, curried shrimp, but also home-smoked trout and homemade *civet de marcassin* (stew of preserved young boar). *Faubourg de France 3, B-6830, tel. 061/466588, fax 061/468321. 18 rooms with bath or shower. Facilities: restaurant (closed off-season, Mon. dinner, and Tues.), café, terrace café. AE, MC, V. Hotel $; Restaurant $$*

De la Poste. This is the most historic and atmospheric hotel in town, but not consistently the most comfortable. Since Napoleon III, Emile Zola, and Victor Hugo stayed at this 1730 stagecoach stop, its original rooms have been left virtually unchanged, balancing burnished oak and antiques with aged fixtures and small baths. The all-new annex, built in 1990, offers modern comfort. Downstairs, the grandeur remains intact, with a charming mix of Victorian antiques and rustic brocante. The restaurant stretches along the riverfront; the menu features French classics. *Pl. St-Arnould 1, B-6830, tel. 061/466506, fax 061/467202. 77 rooms, 68 with bath or shower. Facilities: restaurant, bar, terrace café. AE, DC, MC, V. Hotel $; Restaurant $$*

Dinant and Environs
Dining

Le Vivier d'Oies. This country inn lies northeast of Dinant, about 3 kilometers (2 miles) east of Yvoir, in a lovely stone farmhouse with a modern stone-and-glass wing. The ambience is strictly urbane, and the cuisine is above reproach: goose liver sautéed with caramelized pears, farm duck with honey and cinnamon, trout with caviar. *Rue Etat 7, Dorinne, tel. 083/699571. Reservations advised. Jacket and tie advised. AE, DC, MC, V. Closed Tues. dinner, Wed., Carnival week, 2 weeks in June–July, 2 weeks in Sept.–Oct. $$$*

Le Jardin de Fiorine. Opened in May 1991 and a great success, this young, ambitious restaurant holds forth in a restored gray-stone mansion with a pretty garden behind. Specialties include a fine lobster and sweetbread salad, satiny lobster flan with Chablis, veal in tarragon and pears, and roast pigeon with corn cakes. *Rue Georges Cousot 3, Dinant, tel. 082/227474. Reservations advised. Jacket advised. AE, DC, MC, V. Closed Wed., 3 weeks from Carnival, last week in Aug. $$-$$$*

Thermidor. All the elements are here for a mediocre meal—stodgy bourgeois decor with game trophies, an excess of wine glasses, the combination of the words "*touristique*" and "*gastronomique*" on the same menu—yet the cooking here is all it should be: old-time French cuisine, sauces made fresh on the spot, a few experiments in new combinations. Try the grilled salmon steak with fresh-whisked mustard sauce, or chicken breast with a drizzle of vanilla butter. *Rue Station 3, Dinant, tel. 082/223135. Reservations advised. Jacket advised. AE, MC, V. Closed Mon. dinner, Tues. $$*

Dining and Lodging
★

Auberge de Bouvignes. This 1830 roadhouse just north of Dinant combines beautifully restored architecture—beams, stonework, whitewashed brick—with a chic decor and superb cooking. Its wine caves are blasted into the solid stone bluff behind, and its rustic bedrooms overlook the Meuse. Lobsters of all kinds are a specialty as in a ragout with asparagus, morels, and fresh pasta; or there may be Bresse pigeon with braised endive and truffles. *Rue Fétis 112, B-5500 Bouvignes-sur-Meuse, tel. 082/611600, fax 082/613093. 6 rooms with bath. Facilities: restaurant (reservations required; jacket and tie advised; closed Sun. dinner, Mon.; Oct.–Mar., lunch only except weekends.) AE, DC, MC, V. Hotel $; Restaurant $$$*

Le Mosan. In Anseremme, just downstream from Dinant, this welcoming old roadside hotel sits right on the riverbank. It's very well kept, with fresh, light decor in pretty pastels—worth the mild inconvenience of bathrooms down the hall. Downstairs, the traditional restaurant offers trout specialties, kidneys, and steaks, either on the glass porch or in the charming dining room. *Rue Dufrenne 2, B-*

5500 Anseremme-Dinant, tel. 082/222450. 8 rooms without bath. Facilities: restaurant (closed off-season, Mon.). AE, DC, MC, V. $

Durbuy
Dining and Lodging

Le Sanglier des Ardennes. Dominating the center of town (with 432 inhabitants, Durbuy is the smallest incorporated city in the world), this inn has a stone fireplace, beams, and public spaces punctuated by glass cases hawking perfume, leather, and French scarves. Rooms are classic pastel-modern, with a businessy look, and the bathrooms are quite large. The restaurant offers grand French cooking with some regional touches. Back windows overlook the Ourthe River. *Rue Comte d'Ursel 99, B-5480, tel. 086/213262. 45 rooms. Facilities: restaurant (closed off-season, Thurs.), bar, garden, terrace café. AE, DC, MC, V. $$$*

Han-sur-Lesse
Dining and Lodging

Des Ardennes. Run casually and not very well maintained, this is a good roadhouse stopover for families visiting the caves. Rooms are musty, with spongy beds and old bath fixtures; those overlooking the garden are more pleasant. Guests are required to eat in the hotel, which is no great punishment: There's good regional cooking with some French fuss, friendly and competent service, and an unusually well-chosen wine list. *Rue des Grottes 2, B-5580, tel. 084/377220, fax 084/378062. 26 rooms with bath. Facilities: restaurant (closed Wed., Jan.), bar, terrace café. AE, DC, MC, V. Hotel $; Restaurant $$*

Henri IV. In a much quieter setting outside town, with forest behind and fields in front, this is more like a country inn than its competitors. It was built in 1948 for the new wave of tourism, and rooms have been kept up to date with a bit of handiwork and fresh decor. The restaurant features *la poule au pot d'autre fois* (old-fashioned stewed chicken, made with ham, turnips, and cabbage) and its own trout. *Rue des Chasseurs Ardennais 59, B-5580, tel. 084/377221. 8 rooms, 6 with bath or shower. Facilities: restaurant (closed off-season, Thurs.), bar, terrace café. AE, MC, V. Hotel $; Restaurant $$*

Huy
Dining and Lodging
★

Du Fort. Tucked under the Citadel, across from the arching bridge over the Meuse, this is the simplest of roadhouses, but its rooms have been carefully decorated and maintained at a solid middle-class level, and its owners pamper you in the unpretentious tavern downstairs. There's a brief, standard menu with trout, sole, or chicken, each with frites and salad, at reasonable prices. *Chaussée Napoléon 6, B-4500, tel. 085/212403, fax 085/231842. 34 rooms, 25 with bath. Facilities: restaurant, bar. AE, DC, MC, V. $*

Liège
Dining

Vieux Liège. The money you spend here on classic, old-school French cuisine—foie gras, lobster, beef in three-pepper sauce—functions less as a cost of fine dining than as a museum entry fee into one of Belgium's extraordinary buildings, a sprawling, appealingly ramshackle cross-timbered beauty dating from the 16th century. Interiors, all creaking parquet and glossy wood beams, have been furnished in Old-Master luxury—Delft tiles, brass, pewter, Oriental runners. *Quai de la Goffe 41, tel. 041/237748. Reservations advised. Jacket and tie advised. AE, DC, MC, V. Closed Sun., Wed. night, Easter week, mid-July–mid-Aug. $$$$*

★ **Chez Max.** There's never a dull moment at this wonderful, elegant brasserie run by the charismatic Alain Struvay. The brasserie cuisine is enlivened by specialties like lobster and langoustines au gratin, turbot in champagne sauce, very tender lightly smoked salmon—and more than 100 brands of whiskey. There is a spectacular *banc d'écailler* (oyster and seafood display). *Pl. de la République Française 12, tel. 041/237748. Reservations advised. Jacket and tie advised. AE, DC, MC, V. $$$*

★ **Ma Maison.** This sleek, intimate little restaurant chose to showcase its timbers and casement windows in cool, modern decor, focusing its energies instead on varied, imaginative cooking, chic presentation, and discreet service. Daily specialties may include skate in a cool aspic of bouillabaisse, tiny beignets (fritters) of ham in mustard sauce, airy potato pancakes with minced smoked salmon, and a smörgåsbord of cunning sweets. *Rue Hors-Château 46, tel. 041 233091. Reservations advised. Jacket advised. AE, DC, MC, V. Closed Sun., Mon., first half of Aug. $$$*

Lodging **Bedford.** Opened in 1994, this new hotel on the banks of the Meuse is just a few blocks from major museums and the old city. The bright, air-conditioned rooms have leather armchairs and marble bathrooms with blow-dryers. The brasserie-style restaurant is in the oldest part of the hotel, which dates from the 17th century. *Quai St-Léonard 36, tel. 041/288111, fax 041/274575. 149 rooms. Facilities: restaurant, bar, conference rooms, parking, garden. AE, DC, MC, V. $$$*

Holiday Inn. Next door to the Palais des Congrès, this is the hotel of choice for congress delegates and businesspeople. The lobby and guest rooms have recently been refurbished, and the riverfront location is very pleasant, but there's no restaurant. *Esplanade de l'Europe 2, tel. 0041/426020, fax 041/434810. 214 rooms. Facilities: bar, conference facilities, no-smoking rooms, fitness center, sauna, indoor pool, garage. AE, DC, MC, V. $$$*

Simenon. Named for Liège's most famous native son and in his old neighborhood east of the river, this splendid Belle Epoque house has been converted into a theme hotel: Each room is named for one of the author's novels, which are also available from a lending library. Excellent homemade ice cream is served in the tearoom (there's no restaurant). *Blvd. de l'Est 16, tel. 041/428690, fax 041/442669. 11 rooms with bath. Facilities: salon, tearoom, library. AE, DC, MC, V. $*

Univers. A cut above most train-station hotels, this landmark has been kept up to date with double windows, sharp room decor (business-class beige and burgundy), and a modernized brasserie/bar downstairs. *Rue des Guillemins 116, B-4000, tel. 041/522804, fax 041/521653. 49 rooms. Facilities: restaurant, bar. AE, DC, MC, V. $*

Malmédy **Hostellerie Trôs Marets.** Up the hill on the road toward Eupen, this
Dining and inn offers a splendid view over the wooded valley. In fall, the fog
Lodging hangs low over the nearby High Fens; in winter, cross-country skiing beckons. The main building contains the restaurant and five rustic, cozy rooms. A modern annex has suites (furnished in contemporary English style, with fireplaces) and a large indoor pool. The restaurant serves up such specialties as duck's liver with caramelized apples, asparagus in truffle vinaigrette, grilled duckling with honey, and Herve cheese soufflé with Liège liqueur. Half-board is a good value. *Rte. des Trôs Marets 2, Bévercé (3 km/2 mi north on N68), tel. 080/337917, fax 080/339710. 5 rooms, 4 suites, all with bath. Facilities: restaurant, pool. AE, DC, MC, V. Closed mid-Nov.–Christmas. $$$$*

★ **Chez Guy.** In the very center of this now-thriving town (well recovered and even friendly to Americans despite being accidentally bombed by the Allies three times in December 1944), this solid, comfortable hotel combines fresh decor (pretty floral prints, fresh linens in the rooms) with regional charm (fireplace and beams downstairs). The restaurant features Ardennes specialties, of course—ham, trout, game—on a number of moderately priced menus. *Pl. de Rome 26, tel. 080/330314, fax 080/339998. 9 rooms, 6 with bath. Facilities: restaurant. (closed Tues. dinner, Wed., Thurs. dinner, 1* *week in Mar., 2 weeks in June–July, 1 week at Christmas). AE, DC, MC, V. $*

Namur **Le Temps des Cerises.** On a narrow old-town street chockablock with
Dining little restaurants, this retro café serves rich, hearty fare—fish soup
★ with *rouille* (garlic and red-pepper sauce), homemade sausages,
kidneys in garlic-juniper sauce—in artful but generous portions.
The setting is charmingly Old Belgium, with lace café curtains, vin-
tage postcards, knickknacks, and furniture and paneling painted a
glossy cherry red. *Rue des Brasseurs 22, tel. 081/225326. Reserva-
tions advised. Dress: casual. V. $$*

Dining and **Saint-Loup.** Making a real break away from posh old city hotels and
Lodging jazzy new chains, this central lodging is urban to the core, convert-
★ ing an 18th-century town house to an avant-garde downtown delight. Rooms have been designed in super-mod angles and candy-
bright colors, some with marble baths; downstairs, lovely old spaces
(including a quiet, green garden court) have been slicked up with
halogen and high-tech furniture. *Rue St-Loup 4, B-5000, tel. 081/
230405, fax 081/230943. 10 rooms with bath. Facilities: restaurant,
bar, garden court. AE, DC, MC, V. Hotel $$; Restaurant $$–$$$*

Château de Namur. At the top of the Citadel's bluff above the city, in
a grand old mansion built in 1930, this is a hotel school first and fore-
most, with much of its former grandeur subjugated to its current
role as a teaching vehicle. Public spaces are spare and underfur-
nished, but rooms are comfortable and fresh and the views above re-
proach. Ask for a corner, with double views. In the dining room,
students practice the art of serving rough-edged but ambitious
French cooking. *Av. Ermitage 1, B-5000 tel. 081/742630, fax 081/
742392. 29 rooms with bath. Facilities: restaurant, bar. AE, DC,
MC, V. $$*

★ **Ferme du Quartier.** Just outside Namur, near the Bouge exit from
the highway, this delightfully restored old stone farmhouse stands
in a silent country oasis. Interiors are modern, in natural materials,
with some brick-vaulted ceilings and beams. The locals dine in its
simple, traditional restaurant on varieties of steak, rabbit in mustard sauce, grilled salmon, or *pintadeau* (guinea fowl) in beer.
Rooms in the converted barn are smaller but even quieter than those
in the main house. *Pl. Ste-Marguerite 4, B-5004 Bouge-Namur, tel.
081/211105, fax 081/215918. 14 rooms with bath or shower. Facilities: restaurant, bar. AE, DC, MC, V. Closed Sun. dinner, July,
last week of Dec. $*

Lodging **Beauregard.** Built into a wing of the Casino, this is a polished, fashionable business hotel, with vivid color schemes (lime, salmon, teal)
and sleek room decor. Rooms with wide views of the river cost
slightly more. A breakfast buffet is served in a vast, windowed hall
with more river views. *Av. Baron de Moreau 1, B-5000, tel. 081/
230028, fax 081/241209. 51 rooms. Facilities: access to Casino Club
(restaurant/bar) and Casino. AE, DC, MC, V. $$*

La Roche-en- **La Huchette.** Though a bit out of place in this hardy forest resort,
Ardenne this middle-class restaurant serves good, classic French cooking—
Dining delicate quenelles of pike in lobster *coulis* (broth), salmon tournedos
in tarragon, pigeon with red cabbage—in a decidedly unrustic set-
ting of pink, brass, and terra-cotta. *Rue de l'Eglise 6, tel. 084/
411333. Reservations advised. Jacket advised. AE, MC, V. Closed
Tues. dinner, Wed. $$*

Dining and **Hostellerie Linchet.** At the best address in an otherwise touristy
Lodging town, this new hotel has large rooms that overlook the Ourthe val-
★ ley. The cuisine is traditional in the best sense of the word, including

such dishes as stuffed crayfish, poached trout in Alsatian white wine, and fillet of venison with truffle sauce; there's alfresco dining in season. In fall, patron André Linchet is apt to invite you to join him when he goes hunting. Half-board gives very good value for money. *Rte. de Houffalize 11, tel. 084/411223, fax 084/412410. 13 rooms, 12 with bath. Facilities: restaurant. AE, DC, MC, V. Closed Tues., Wed., Feb., 3 weeks in June–July, weekdays Jan. and Mar.–May. $$–$$$*

★ **Du Midi.** This tiny old cliff-side hotel is worth a visit for the food, which is the Real Thing: straightforward regional specialties, simply and stylishly served. Game in season is superbly cooked (tenderloin of young boar in old port) and served with *gratin Dauphinois* (scalloped potatoes) and poached pear; air-dried Ardennes ham comes with candied onions. The setting is local—oak, green plush, brass lamps, spinning-wheel chandeliers—though not old. The rooms have been recently renovated, and all now have bath or shower. *Rue Beausaint 6, tel. 084/411138, fax 084/412238. 8 rooms with bath or shower. Facilities: restaurant. AE, DC, MC, V. Closed second half of June, first half of Dec., second half of Jan. $*

★ **Les Genets.** Even the rooms are pretty in this romantic old sprawl of a mountain inn, with its stenciled wallpaper and homey-chic mixes of plaid, paisley, and chintz. Picture windows take in valley views on two sides. The restaurant offers gastronomic menus (grilled and smoked trout salad with hazelnut vinaigrette, pigeon in juniper). They prefer guests to take half-board. *Corniche de Deister 2, B-6980, tel. 084/411877, fax 084/411893. 8 rooms, 7 with bath. Facilities: restaurant (closed off-season, Wed.–Thurs.), bar. AE, DC, MC, V. Closed 3 weeks in June–July, first half of Jan. Hotel $; Restaurant $$*

Rochefort
Dining and Lodging

Les Falizes. On the edge of town, on the way to Han-sur-Lesse, this is yet another comfortable, upmarket country inn. It is cozily furnished with old oak, leaded glass, a working fireplace, and overstuffed furniture; sizable rooms upstairs are furnished with a palatable mix of Victorian plush and florals. The focus is food, however: *chartreuse* (a layered mold) of sole and beets; pigeon roasted in truffle juice; and duck-liver *pot au feu* (hot pot). *Rue de France 90, B-5580, tel. 084/211282, fax 084/221086. 6 rooms with bath. Facilities: restaurant (closed Mon. dinner, Tues., end of Jan.–early Mar.). AE, DC, MC, V. Closed end of Jan.–early Mar. Hotel $$ Restaurant $–$$*

La Malle Poste. Despite its location on the main road through town, this former *relais de poste* (coach stop), dating from the late 18th century, affects a grand, manicured garden. Its architecture merits the fuss, as the stonework, moldings, and burnished oak of the main house evoke a lavish past. The new wing, built into a neighboring building, is more rustic, with exposed timbers and heavy stone. The restaurant specializes in luxuries—foie gras, lobster, and pigeon—though they do a mean truite au bleu as well. *Rue de Behogne 46, B-5580, tel. 084/210986, fax 084/221113. 11 rooms with bath. Facilities: restaurant (closed Wed. except July–Aug., Feb.–Mar.), bar, garden, terrace. AE, DC, MC, V. $*

Saint-Hubert
Dining

Le Clos Saint-Michel. In an area where tourist menus predominate, you'll find an oasis of haute cuisine inside this handsome gray-stone villa with a terrace and garden. Chef Eric Lekeu's game dishes are second to none; other dishes worth a detour include turbot with young onions and carrot juice, lamb with herb-and-truffle salad, and *pain perdu* (French toast) with pineapple. *Rue St-Michel 46, tel. 061/612559. Reservations advised. Jacket and tie advised. AE, DC,*

MC, V. Closed Mon. dinner, Tues., first half of Jan., few days at end of June, 5 days at beginning of Sept. $$$$

Spa **La Brasserie du Grand Maur.** This graceful 200-year-old city man-
Dining sion houses a lovely restaurant. The cuisine served here has become
★ quite a bit more sophisticated, to the delight of a loyal clientele. Tartare of salmon, lamb infused with tomato and thyme, and duck's
breast with raspberries and red currants are current favorites. The
setting, all polished wood, linens, and antiques, enhances the meal.
*Rue Xhrouet 41, tel. 087/773616. Reservations advised. Jacket ad-
vised. AE, DC, MC, V. Closed Mon.–Tues., 3 weeks in Dec.–Jan., 3
weeks in June. $$*

Old Inn. A simple, slightly touristy little lunch stop on the main
street across from the baths, this beamed and wainscoted res-
taurant serves inexpensive regional menus (ham, game) as well as
mussels and crepes. It's one step up from a tavern, with pink linens
covered by paper mats with ads for local businesses. *Rue Royale 17,
tel. 087/773943. Dress: casual. AE, DC, MC, V. Closed off-season,
Wed. $–$$*

Lodging **Cardinal.** Offering a real taste of old Spa, this grand urban resort
★ hotel opened in 1924—but, the host asserts, it was completely renovated in 1948. Its period decor and interior architecture is completely intact and fresh as new. Have tea in the muraled salon, hot
chocolate in the beautiful all-oak café, or dinner in the swanky
chandeliered dining hall. Most rooms are 1948-modern (smooth gold
oak paneling). *Pl. Royale 21–27, B-4880, tel. 087/771064, fax 087/
771964. 29 rooms with bath. Facilities: restaurant, bar, tearoom.
AE, DC, MC, V. $$$*

The Arts and Nightlife

Liège Check times at **Infor-Spectacles** (En Féronstrée 92, tel. 041/221111).
You can also buy tickets there. For all sorts of events in Liège, look
under "Other Towns" in *The Bulletin.*

The Arts Liège has its own opera company, the **Opéra Royal de Wallonie** (Thé-
âtre Royal, rue des Dominicains, tel. 041/235910).

The city also has its own symphony orchestra, **l'Orchestre
Philharmonique de Liège.** The Wallonie Chamber Orchestra and oth-
er ensembles participate in the annual Festival de la Wallonie, with
concerts also in Spa and Stavelot.

The most interesting **theater** performances in French or Walloon are
generally at the **Théâtre de la Place** (pl. de l'Yser, tel. 041/428118).
It's also worth checking out what's on offer at **Les Chiroux** (pl. des
Carmes, tel. 041/231960) or at the **Foyer Culturel du Sart Tilman**
(Domaine Universitaire, tel. 041/563299). You can see **puppet theater**
performances featuring the irrepressible Tchantchès at the grandly
named **Théâtre Royal Ex-Impérial de Roture** (rue Surlet 56, tel. 041/
427575; Wed. 2:30 PM and Sun. 10:30 AM), at the theater of the **Musée
de la Vie Wallonne** (Cour des Mineurs; tel. 041/236094 same hrs), and
at the **Théâtre Al Botroule** (rue Hocheporte 3, tel. 041/230576; Sat. 8
PM for adults, Wed. 3 PM for children).

Nightlife The Liégeois have an amazing ability to stay up until all hours, and
nightlife is booming on both sides of the Meuse. The Carré quarter,
on the left bank, is favored by students and those who go to a show
first and decide to go out afterwards. Two cafés chantant, than
which nothing is more typical of this city, should be tried: **Les
Olivettes** (rue Pied-du-Pont des Arches, tel. 041/220708) and **Les
Caves de Porto** (En Féronstrée 144, tel. 041/232325). Other cafés

with lots of traditional ambience include **Le Seigneur d'Amay** (rue d'Amay, tel. 041/220044) and **La Taverne St-Paul** (rue St-Paul, tel. 041/237217) near the Cathedral. Rue Tête-de-Boeuf contains some fashionable clubs and discos such as **Estoril** (tel. 041/210937).

You go to the Roture quarter in Outremeuse more specifically for a night's entertainment. There's hardly a house without a café, club, or jazz hangout. Here's where the best jazz clubs are, including **Le Lion s'envoile** (En Roture 11, tel. 041/429317) and **Le Cirque Divers** (En Roture 13, tel. 041/410244). Both branch out from time to time into literary and other kinds of happenings. Or you may choose to finish the evening more quietly in an ambience of Liège folklore at the **Café Tchantchès** (rue Grande-Beche, tel. 041/433931).

Stavelot
The Arts The **Stavelot Chamber Music Festival** (tel. 080/862734) is held every August.

5 Luxembourg

By Nancy
Coons

Updated by
Eric Sjogren

Entering the eponymous capital of tiny Luxembourg across the Grande-Duchesse Charlotte Bridge, first-time visitors are greeted by an awe-inspiring view: Up and down the length of the Alzette River stretches a panorama of medieval stonework—jutting fortification walls, slit-windowed towers, ancient church spires, massive gates—as detailed and complete as a 17th-century engraving come to life. Then the visitors turn left—and enter the 20th century. The boulevard Royal, little more than five blocks long, glitters with glass-and-concrete office buildings, each containing a world-class bank and untold, anonymous, well-sheltered fortunes. There's plenty of time to gawk, because traffic, thick with Jaguars, Mercedes, and BMWs, crawls through town, dodging extravagant new roadworks and construction projects. Luxembourg, once sovereign to lands that stretched from the Meuse to the Rhine, reduced over the centuries to a powerless pawn and lobbed from conqueror to conqueror like a tennis ball, until recently little more than a cluster of meager farms and failing mines, flaunts new wealth, new political muscle, and the fourth-highest standard of living in the world.

The Grand Duchy of Luxembourg, one of the smallest countries in the United Nations, measures only 2,597 square kilometers (999 square miles), less than the size of Rhode Island. It is dwarfed by its neighbors—Germany, Belgium, and France—yet from its history of invasion, occupation, and siege, you might think those square miles built over bedrock of solid gold. In fact, it was Luxembourg's very defenses against centuries of attack that rendered it all the more desirable: From AD 963, when Charlemagne's descendant Sigefroid founded a castle on the high promontory of the Bock, the duchy encased itself in layer upon layer of fortifications until by the mid-19th century its very invulnerability was considered a threat to those *not* commanding its thick stone walls. The more impregnable it became, the more desirable it became; the more its enemies tried to grasp it, the greater its holder's efforts to thicken the shell.

It all started when Sigefroid, a beneficiary of the disintegration of central Europe that followed Charlemagne's death, chose a small gooseneck carved by the Alzette to develop as a fortress and the capital of his considerable domains. Thanks to his aggressions and the ambitions of his heirs, Luxembourg grew continuously until, by the 14th century, its count, Henry IV, was powerful and important enough to serve as Henry VII, king of the German nations and Holy Roman emperor. In fact, in that epoch, Luxembourg contributed no fewer than five kings and emperors to the empire, including Henry VII's son, the flamboyant John the Blind (Jean l'Aveugle), who, despite leading his armies to slaughter in the Battle of Crécy (1346), remains a national hero.

After his death, Luxembourg commanded the greatest territory it would ever rule—from the Meuse to Metz and the Moselle—and its rulers Charles IV, Wenceslas I and II, and Sigismund carried the name of the House of Luxembourg to pan-European renown. If Luxembourg had a golden age, this was it, and it was short-lived. Plague, the decay of feudalism, marital and financial intrigues among leaders who rarely, if ever, set toe in Luxembourg—all these factors finally left the duchy vulnerable, and Philip the Good, duke of Burgundy, took it by storm in 1443.

From that point on, Luxembourg lost its significance as a geographical mass and took on importance as a fortress. It was controlled from 1443 to 1506 by Burgundy, from 1506 to 1714 by Spain (with a brief period—1684 to 1697—under Louis XIV of France), and from 1714 to 1795 by Austria; Napoléon took it from the

Habsburgs in 1795. Each, in taking the fortress, had to penetrate miles of outworks whose battlements, pointed like the arms of stars, were thrust into the threatening countryside. And having penetrated the outer defenses, the aggressor faced a citadel perched on sheer stone cliffs with weapons bristling from every pore, its soldiers outnumbering its citizens. To take it by frontal attack was out of the question; the solution, usually, was siege and starvation.

Having been torn and ravaged for 400 years by conquerors' games of tug-of-war, Luxembourg continued to provoke squabbles into the 19th century, when Prussia's leader, Bismarck, Solomon-like, decided that no one should have it at all. Named a grand duchy in 1815 and granted independence in 1839, Luxembourg was declared an independent and neutral state in 1867 by the Treaty of London, and its battlements were dismantled, stone by stone. What remains of its walls, while impressive, is only a reminder of what was one of the strongholds of Europe—the "Gibraltar of the North."

Today Luxembourg is besieged again, this time by bankers and Eurocrats. Its more than 120 banks rival Switzerland's, and just outside the old city a new colony has been seeded, a self-contained ecosystem of *fonctionnaires* for the European Union (EU), the heir to the Common Market. Fiercely protecting its share of the expanding bureaucracy from Strasbourg and Brussels, which, with Luxembourg, form the triumvirate of capitals that head the EU, the duchy digs its heels in once again, this time fighting not only for independence but also for its newfound prosperity and clout. Thus the national motto takes on new meaning: *Mir wölle bleiwe wat mir sin* (We want to stay what we are)—nowadays, a powerful, viable grand duchy in the heart of modern Europe.

And yet, really, all this new wealth and power has very little to do with the average Luxembourger, beyond increasing exponentially the value of his cabbage patch. This was, and remains, an agricultural country, a close-knit, self-contained community of small farmers who, until the 19th century, suffered a plague of natural and political disasters and produced little more than enough to support themselves. In 1878 breakthroughs in both farming and mining technology turned the country around (ironically, it was discovered that a new, efficient technique for purifying iron ore created an indispensable by-product: fertilizer) and started a boom that ended up putting Luxembourg on 20th-century maps.

Luxembourgers have remained proud farmers at heart, trading their Bruno Magli shoes for garden clogs every weekend and digging row upon row of brussels sprouts and cabbage; until the mid-'60s, foreign residents were hard put to find greengrocers, as the natives grew their own fruits and vegetables. Often wealthy enough to mortgage Grandpapa's now astonishingly valuable farmlands and buy each of their children suburban bungalows as wedding gifts, many Luxembourgers nonetheless scrub their sidewalks weekly, keep their manure pile in front of the adjoining barn (in old times this was a measurable status symbol), play in the community band, spend Sunday afternoon at the local *jeu de quilles* (bowling) café, and walk to the cathedral every year to thank the Virgin for sparing their forefathers from the plague.

Threatened and encroached upon for a thousand years, isolated by Luxembourgish, their only recently codified Frankish dialect, and now smothered under a new eruption of foreign laborers and Eurocrats, the Luxembourgers are a far from effervescent lot; the public face is dour, sober, hardened against foreign approach. Nor are they socially promiscuous among themselves, entering one another's homes only on formal invitation. The family is sacred, and though children are expected to go to university in Brussels, Strasbourg, or Cologne (there is no university here), they also are expected to come home, where they will often live and lunch until marriage—and sometimes after. While their education prepares them to deal with the world in French, German, and English, they are only truly at home in their mother tongue—and few in the world besides Mother speak it.

Observing the Luxembourgers out on a Sunday afternoon in their loden-green overcoats as they walk their long-haired dachshunds down their tidy streets, past their shutterless, unsentimental modernizations of ancient buildings; speak their guttural dialect, with its scraps of Alttrier-Moselle German and flinty, scolding tone; and treat themselves to their afternoon coffee and cake, a visitor might conclude that Luxembourg is a Germanic culture at heart. Hitler tried to convince them of it: Suppressing Luxembourgish, converting French names, he launched a campaign to convince Luxembourgers to come *Heim ins Reich*—to come home to the fatherland as ethnic Germans. Yet a visit to any war museum will show that the Luxembourgers weren't having any of it, and that the majority have yet to forget that the German invasions left Luxembourg hideously scarred, that thousands of its men were conscripted during the German occupation and sent as so much cannon fodder to the Russian front. There are Luxembourgers today who refuse to drive German cars and who will welcome American veterans come back to trace the *Route de la Liberation*.

Yet that era is passing, too, and the Germans, like the Spanish, the French, and the Dutch who conquered before, have been for the most part forgiven—and even accepted as frequent tourists. Today Luxembourg welcomes all nationalities as visitors; they swarm through its ruins, churches, museums, forests, and vineyards every summer. And whatever their origin, Luxembourg greets them, quite often, in a common tongue. Centuries of occupation have prepared the inhabitants well for such grudging hospitality. But despite—or perhaps because of—the onslaught, Luxembourg remains intact, autonomous, independent: *Mir wölle bleiwe wat mir sin*.

Before You Go

Government Tourist Offices

In North America **Luxembourg National Tourist Office** (17 Beekman Pl., New York, NY 10022, tel. 212/935–8888).

In the United Kingdom **Luxembourg Tourist Office** (122 Regent St., London W1R 5FE, tel. 0171/434–2800).

Tour Groups

General-Interest Tours Listed below is a sample of the tours and packages that concentrate on Luxembourg. *See* Tour Groups in Chapter 1, Essential Information, for tours that cover more than one country in the region. Most tour operators request that bookings be made through a travel agent—there is no additional charge for doing so. For additional resources, contact your travel agent or the tourist office of Luxembourg.

Luxembourg

From the **Olson Travelworld** (Box 10066, Manhattan Beach, CA 90226, tel. 310/
United States 546–8400 or 800/421–2255) tailors excursions in Luxembourg for individuals or groups.

From the **Time Off Ltd.** (Chester Close, Chester St., London SW1X 7BQ, tel.
United 0171/235–8070) has packages from two to seven nights to Luxembourg.
Kingdom

Package Deals for Independent Travelers

Extra Value Travel (683 S. Collier Blvd., Marco Island, FL 33937, tel. 813/398–4848 or 800/336–4668) offers self-drive tours of Luxembourg that include hotel choices and car rental. **Jet Vacations** (1775 Broadway, New York, NY 10019, tel. 800/538–0999) offers Flexiplan Europe, a choice of hotels, car rentals, airport transfers, and sightseeing options for Luxembourg. **Travel Bound** (599 Broadway, Penthouse, New York, NY 10012, tel. 212/334–1350 or 800/456–8656) offers three- to six-night packages to Luxembourg.

When to Go

Luxembourg is a northern country—parallel in latitude to Newfoundland in Canada—and experiences extreme changes in day- and night-length from season to season. Thus late spring, summer, and early fall allow you long days that stay light up to 10 o'clock; in winter, however, be prepared for dusk closing in before 4 PM. There's rarely a long spell of heavy snow, but winters tend to be dank and rainy. Many attractions, especially outside the city, maintain shortened visiting hours (or close altogether) from late fall to Pentecost (late spring), except for a brief time around Easter. Summer is tourist time, when Luxembourg polishes up its sightseeing train, and restaurants set out terrace tables under the sycamores; gardens are in full bloom and weather can be comfortably hot. Spring is attractive as well, but it is riddled with church holidays and inconvenient closings.

Climate The following are average daily maximum and minimum temperatures for Luxembourg.

Luxembourg	Jan.	38F	3C	May	65F	18C	Sept.	67F	19C
		31	– 1		47	8		50	10
	Feb.	40F	4C	June	70F	21C	Oct.	56	13C
		31	– 1		52	11		43	6
	Mar.	50F	10C	July	74F	23C	Nov.	45F	7C
		34	1		56	13		38	3
	Apr.	58F	14C	Aug.	72F	22C	Dec.	40F	4C
		40	4		54	13		32	0

Festivals and Seasonal Events

Apr. 17: At the **E'maischen** fair on Easter Monday, ceramic bird-flutes (*Peckvillchen*) are sold to usher in spring.

May 21: During **Octave** (beginning the fifth Sunday after Easter) since the 17th century when the Holy Mother spared the devout from a raging plague, grateful villagers have walked from their local church to the cathedral in Luxembourg City, accompanied by chants, incense, and often the community band. During Octave, a fair holds forth in the place Guillaume, offering arcade games, crafts, and food stands selling fried sausages, fried potato patties, fried crepes, fried waffles, and the traditional batter-fried *merlan* (whiting).

June 6 (Whit Tuesday): During Echternach's **Spring Sprang-procession** (Dance-Procession), the most famous spring pageant, the townspeople dance through the streets, hopping from one foot to the other, chanting prayers to St. Willibrord.

June 23: Luxembourg's National Day honors its beloved grand-duke with parades and ceremonies; the night before, there's a spectacular fireworks show launched from the Pont Adolphe.

Aug. 15–31: The **Schobermesse** (trade fair begun in 1340) dominates the Parking Glacis (near the Grande-Duchesse Charlotte bridge), with rides and games as well as the usual abundance of greasy treats.

What to Pack

Clothing Bring a woolen sweater, even in summer; if you hit a rainy spell, a raincoat and umbrella may prove indispensable, as rain often takes hold for weeks at a time. Practical walking shoes are important, whether for rough cobblestones or forest trails. Women here wear skirts more frequently than do women in the United States, especially those over 35: If you would rather fit in with the natives than with fellow tourists, a casual skirt is appropriate for day wear. Men would be wise to include a jacket and tie, especially if you're planning to visit one of the upper-echelon restaurants.

Miscellaneous Americans will need an electrical adapter for hair dryers and small appliances. Voltage is 220, with 50 cycles, so you may want to invest in portable appliances with changeable voltage and cycles. You will need to adapt the plug to fit Luxembourg outlets; Luxembourg plugs have two round prongs, the thicker of two standard options.

Taking Money Abroad

Luxembourg, as an international banking capital, makes it easy for travelers to pay with credit cards or to withdraw cash advances. Make sure the bank (or shop, restaurant, or hotel) has a sticker in the window for the credit card you wish to use. There is no limit to the amount of cash you can bring into Luxembourg.

Luxembourg Currency

The Luxembourg franc (abbreviated Flux), equivalent to the Belgian franc and used interchangeably with it within Luxembourg, comes in notes in denominations of 100 and 1,000 francs; Belgium issues 500- and 5,000-franc notes as well. Coins are issued in denominations of 1, 5, 20, and 50 francs; you will rarely be required to use the 50-centime piece. If you're traveling in France as well, be careful not to mix up French 10-franc pieces with Belgian and Luxembourgian 20-franc coins; the French coin is three times as valuable. At press time, rates of exchange average Flux 32 to the U.S. dollar, Flux 49 to the pound sterling, and Flux 23 to the Canadian dollar. Rates fluctuate daily, so be sure to check at the time you leave.

What It Will Cost

As Luxembourg continues to prosper, the cost of living skyrockets annually, pumping up real estate costs and thus prices everywhere. Yet hotel and restaurant prices tend to be up no more than 5% over last year's. Because of Luxembourg's tax privileges, gasoline, cigarettes, and liquor continue to be notably cheaper here than in neighboring countries; you'll find combination gas station/liquor stores clustered at every border crossing. High-octane, unleaded gas costs about 21 Flux a liter; in Belgium, you'll pay 8 or 9 francs more.

Taxes A visitor's tax of 5% for overnight stays is included in your hotel bill. Value-added taxes (TVA) are in upheaval now as the EU makes gradual adjustments toward equality; they range from 3% to 15%, depending on the type of purchase. Purchases of goods for export only to non-EU countries may qualify for a refund; ask the shop to fill out a refund form. You must then have the form stamped by customs officers on leaving Luxembourg, Belgium, or Holland. A minimum purchase of Flux 3,000 is required before you're eligible for a refund.

Sample Costs Cup of coffee, Flux 50; glass of beer, Flux 40; movie ticket, Flux 170–200; 4¾-kilometer (3-mile) taxi ride, Flux 500 (10% higher nights, 25% higher Sundays).

Customs and Duties

On Arrival **Americans and other non-EU members** are allowed to bring in no more than 200 cigarettes, 50 cigars, 1 liter of spirits or sparkling wine, two liters of wine, 50 grams of perfume, and .25 liters of toilet water. **EU members** may bring in 300 cigarettes (200 if bought in a duty-free shop), 75 cigars, 1.5 liters of spirits or sparkling wine, 5 liters of wine, 75 grams of perfume, and .375 liters of toilet water.

On Departure **U.S. citizens** may take home $400 worth of foreign merchandise as gifts or for personal use without having to pay duty, provided they have been out of the country for more than 48 hours and provided they have not claimed a similar exemption within the previous 30 days. Every member of a family is entitled to the same exemption, regardless of age, and the exemptions can be pooled. For the next $1,000 worth of goods, inspectors will assess a flat 10% duty, based on the price actually paid, so it is a good idea to keep your receipts. Included in the $400 allowance for travelers over the age of 21 are one liter of alcohol, 100 cigars, and 200 cigarettes. Any amount in excess of those limits will be taxed at the port of entry, and it may be additionally taxed in the traveler's home state. You may not take home meats, fruits, plants, soil, or other agricultural items.

Canadian citizens may take home 50 cigars, 200 cigarettes, and 40 ounces of liquor. Be sure to carry receipts for your purchases abroad, as any totaling more than $300 will be taxed.

British citizens may take home the same quantity of goods they were allowed to carry into Luxembourg (listed above). Because of strict rabies control, no pets or animals may be brought into the United Kingdom.

Language

Luxembourg is a linguistic melting pot, with its citizens speaking an essentially oral tongue called Lëtzeburgesch (Luxembourgish) descended from an ancient dialect of the Moselle Franks. Luxembourgers themselves are educated in German while learning French, eventually completing higher studies in French; the current generation also learns English and is, for the most part, easily conversant. The language used for government documents is French, but many are translated into German as well; a simple church service will often include German, French, Luxembourgish and a soupçon of Latin. Within the tourist industry, most Luxembourgers you'll meet will speak some English with you, better French, and even better German; but they'll talk *about* you in Luxembourgish.

Staying Healthy

Whatever their linguistic leanings, Luxembourgers cleave to their Germanic roots when it comes to cleanliness, scouring their sidewalks and airing their linens. Its tap water is as safe to drink as that of any other urban source, though widespread manure fertilization and heavily salted streets in winter may make you think twice; most locals drink bottled water. Otherwise, the greatest health threat to be found here is to your waistline.

Car Rentals

Luxembourg is one of the cheapest sources in Europe for rental cars, with easy pickup at the airport and at the train station in Luxembourg City *(see* Car Rentals in Chapter 1, Essential Information). A valid driver's license from your own country is required, as is proof of insurance.

Traveling with Children

Getting There A car is by far the best way to get around with children in this tiny country, where few rail connections and limited bus excursions make it difficult to sightsee beyond the main attractions.

Rentals The National Tourist Office publishes a free pamphlet listing available holiday flats and houses and all their facilities. There's also a new brochure for "Rural Holidays" listing a number of farms that take in visitors.

Baby-Sitting Services **Action Familiale et Populaire** (tel. 460004) offers names of screened baby-sitters in the Luxembourg City area; **Luxembourg Accueil** (tel. 41717) offers a similar service.

Hints for Travelers with Disabilities

In Luxembourg, the Ministry of Health handles provisions for people with disabilities. Most trains and buses have special seats for riders with disabilities, and spaces reserved for people with disabilities are available in parking lots.

Further Reading

The Grand Duchy of Luxembourg: The Evolution of a Nationhood by James Newcomer (University Press of America, Lanham, MD, 1984) is an extensive, fairly readable history of the Grand Duchy's early woes. *A Time for Trumpets* by Charles B. MacDonald (William Morrow and Company, New York, 1985) gives a blow-by-blow, 600-page account of the Battle of the Bulge.

Arriving and Departing

From North America by Plane

Airports and Airlines **Icelandair** is the only airline to offer direct flights from the United States (New York, Washington, DC, Fort Lauderdale, FL), with a stopover in Reykjavik. However, most of the main international airlines—**British Airways, Northwest, KLM, Sabena, Lufthansa**—offer connections (usually with **Luxair**) allowing you to fly to London, Frankfurt, Amsterdam, or Paris, then connect into Luxembourg as a final destination with little or no additional cost. All flights land at **Findel Airport,** 6 kilometers (4 miles) from the city center. Their numbers, locally and in the United States: British Airways, tel. 348347 or 800/247–9297; Icelandair, tel. 40272727 or 800/223–5500; Luxair, tel. 47982690; Sabena, tel. 221212 or 800/632–8050.

Flying Time Brussels–Luxembourg, 45 minutes; New York–Brussels, eight hours. Reykjavik–Luxembourg, three hours, plus New York–Reykjavik, six hours, or Fort Lauderdale–Reykjavik, 7½ hours.

From the United Kingdom by Plane, Car, and Train

By Plane Airlines **Luxair,** the Luxembourg airline that connects to all major airports in Europe, has regular flights to London (reservations, tel. 436161; information and arrivals/departures, tel. 47982311), as does **British Airways** (information, tel. 348347).

Flying Time London–Luxembourg, one hour and 15 minutes.

By Car and Ferry The entire Benelux region is easily accessible in a day from London and the southeast. Nearly all ferries from Britain to the Continent take cars, as does the long-awaited Channel Tunnel. Several companies operate sailings direct to the Belgian ports of Oostende and Zeebrugge. Sailings are most frequent from the south coast ports; during the summer months there are up to six sailings a day from Ramsgate to Oostende, by **Sally Line** (tel. 01843/595522). The quickest (but most expensive) ferry crossing is from Dover to Calais via the Hovercraft link, operated by **Hoverspeed** (tel. 01304/240241). After a mere 35-minute crossing, you continue south from Calais to Lille and cut across Belgium, via Mons, Charleroi, and Namur, to reach Luxembourg. If weather and short queues permit, you'll make it from the south coast to Luxembourg in five hours. You also can take a standard ferry from Dover to Calais, with P&O alternating departures with **Stena** (tel. 01233/647047).

Fares vary considerably according to season, journey time, number of passengers, and length of vehicle. However, the approximate cost of crossing the Channel by ferry on one of the short sea routes in high summer, with an average vehicle of 4¼ meters (14 feet) and two adult passengers, works out to about £110 one way. By traveling off-peak, early in the morning or late evening, or in June and September, you can reduce costs.

The Channel Tunnel The Channel Tunnel opened officially in May 1994, providing the fastest route across the Channel—35 minutes from Folkestone to Calais, or 60 minutes from motorway to motorway. It consists of two large 50-kilometer (31-mile)-long tunnels for trains, one in each direction, linked by a smaller service tunnel running between them. **Le Shuttle** (tel. 0345/353535 in the U.K., 800/388–3876 in the U.S.), a special car, bus, and truck train, which was scheduled to begin service in June 1994, operates a continuous loop, with trains departing every 15 minutes at peak times and at least once an hour through the night. No reservations are necessary, although tickets may be purchased in advance from travel agents. Most passengers stay in their own car throughout the "crossing"; progress updates are provided on display screens and radio. Motorcyclists park their bikes in a separate section with its own passenger compartment, while foot passengers must book passage by coach (*see* By Train, *below*).

The Tunnel is reached from exit 11a of the M20/A20. Drivers purchase tickets from toll booths, then pass through frontier control before loading onto the next available service. Unloading at Calais takes eight minutes. Ticket prices start at £130 for a low-season five-day round trip in a small car and are based on season, time of day, length of stay, and car size regardless of the number of passengers. Peak season fares are not always competitive with ferry prices.

By Train Air travel may offer the fastest point-to-point service, car travel the greatest freedom, and bus transportation the lowest fares, but there is still an unparalleled air of romance about setting off for Europe by train from one of the historic London stations. The fastest route via conventional rail service is to take an early morning train from Victoria Station to Ramsgate, ferry by **Jetfoil** to Oostende, train to Brussels, then cross the tracks at the Gare du Midi and continue into Luxembourg, arriving early that evening. It's advisable to reserve seats for the whole trip (including Jetfoil) in advance.

The Channel Tunnel **Eurostar** (for information, tel. 0171/922–4486 in the U.K., 800/942–4866 in the U.S.) high-speed train service was scheduled to begin in July 1994, with passenger-only trains whisking riders between new stations in Paris (Gare du Nord) and London (Waterloo) in three hours and between London and Brussels (Midi) in 3¼ hours, where there's conventional train service to Luxembourg City. The service of one train daily each way was scheduled to increase in January 1995 to 15 trains daily in each direction. At press time, ticket prices had not been set. Tickets are available in the United Kingdom through **Intercity Europe,** the international wing of BritRail (London/Victoria Station, tel. 0171/834–2345 or 0171/828–8092 for credit-card bookings), and in the United States through **Rail Europe** (tel.

800/942–4866) and **BritRail Travel** (1500 Broadway, New York, NY 10036, tel. 800/677–8585).

Staying in Luxembourg

Getting Around Luxembourg

By Train Train travel within the Grand Duchy is very limited; a north–south line connects Luxembourg City with Clervaux in the north and Bettembourg in the south; another line carries you to Grevenmacher and Wasserbillig, along the Moselle. For additional information, write or call the **Chemins de Fer Luxemborgeois** (CFL, pl. de la Gare 9, Boite Postale 1803, L-1018 Luxembourg, tel. 492424).

By Bus The Luxembourg bus system carries tourists and citizens to points throughout the Grand Duchy; most buses leave from the train station. You can buy an *horaire* (bus schedule) to plan complex itineraries, or you can ask at the tourist office for suggestions on a logical schedule for getting to, say, Vianden or Echternach from Luxembourg City. The **Oeko-Billjee,** a special day ticket (Flux 140), allows you to travel anywhere in the country by bus (including city buses) or rail from the time you first use it until 8 AM the next day. They're available at the **Centre Aldringen,** the underground bus station in front of the central post office (corner rue Aldringen and av. Monterey; av. Monterey 8A) and at any train station.

By Car The best way to see Luxembourg outside Luxembourg City is by car, as castles and attractive villages are scattered around and connected by pleasant, well-maintained country roads. Observe standard middle-Europe driving laws: *Priorité à droite* (yield to the right) applies here and should be strictly observed; drivers may shoot out from side streets at top speed without glancing to their left. Speed limits are 50 kph (31 mph) in built-up areas, 90 kph (55 mph) on national highways, and 120 kph (75 mph) on expressways.

Telephones

Local Calls Public phones are relatively rare, except at post offices and in cafés, usually near the toilets. A local call costs Flux 5 or 10, depending on the phone booth; pick up the receiver, slip in the coin, listen for the tone, then dial. No area codes are necessary within the Grand Duchy.

International Calls To dial direct internationally, start with the country code (001 for the United States, 0044 for the United Kingdom), then dial the local number. A **Telekaart,** available with 50 or 150 time units, works in specially equipped booths, usually in post offices, where they are sold. The AT&T U.S.A. Direct number out of Luxembourg is 08000111. Phone cabins for timed long-distance calls are provided inside most post offices; you may be required to make a down payment before the call. Luxembourg's country code is 352. To make an international call without direct access, you must dial 0010.

Operators and Information For international information, dial 016; for local information, dial 017.

Mail

Postal Rates Airmail postcards and letters weighing less than 20 grams cost Flux 22 to the United States. Letters and postcards to the United Kingdom cost Flux 14.

Tipping

In Luxembourg, service charges of 15% are included in your restaurant bill; for a modest meal, most people leave the small change. At a grander restaurant, you will be expected to leave a larger tip—up to 10% extra when a large staff is involved. A tip of Flux 50 per bag is adequate for porters. Cab drivers expect a tip of about 10%.

Opening and Closing Times

Most shops open at 9 and close at noon, reopening at 1:30 or 2 and closing for the night at 6. Many banks now stay open through the lunch hour, opening at 8:30 and closing at 4:30. Nearly all shops and businesses stay closed Monday mornings.

Shopping

As Luxembourg has only partially and recently abandoned its rural roots, its citizens are for the most part unsentimental about the traditional blue-and-gray crockery and burnished pewter that once furnished every home; nowadays, they prefer their indigenous Villeroy & Boch vitro-porcelain in jazzy, modern designs. Nonetheless, all three can be found in most home-furnishings and gift shops. For souvenirs, there are lovely photography books on Luxembourg's historic sites, as well as reproduced engravings of the city in all its fortified glory. *Taaken*, miniature cast-iron firebacks with bas-relief scenes of Luxembourg, are made by the Fonderie de Mersch and are available in gift and souvenir shops.

Sports and the Outdoors

Biking The Luxembourg National Tourist Office, as well as those of Luxembourg City, Diekirch, and Mersch, all publish booklets suggesting cycling tours within the grand duchy; good routes include Ettelbruck–Vianden and Luxembourg City–Echternach.

Boating/Water Sports The Wiltz and the Clerve rivers offer challenging waters for small craft or canoes, but the Our, with its wooded gorges, is the wildest; the Sûre is most rewarding, for its length and for the thrills it offers. For further information, write to the **Fédération Luxembourgeoise de Canoë et de Kayak** (rue de Pulvermuhle 6, Luxembourg). People windsurf and sail on Lac de la Haute Sûre.

Camping Visitors from all over Europe, but especially the Netherlands, descend on Luxembourg's campgrounds every summer, making them sociable, populous places, often near forests and riverfronts. Write for the pamphlet "Camping/Grand-Duché de Luxembourg," made available through the national tourist office. The **Fédération Luxembourgeoise de Camping et de Caravaning** (rte. d'Esch 31, L-4450, tel. 591274) also publishes information.

Fishing If you're in search of trout, grayling, perch, and dace—as well as relaxation—apply for a government fishing permit from the **Administration des Eaux et Forêts** (Boite Postale 411, L-2014 Luxembourg, tel. 405310), and a local permit from the owner of the waterfront, which is in many cases your hotel.

Hiking/ Walking Luxembourg is full of well-developed forest trails, often on state lands with parking provided. *171 Circuits Auto-pedestres*, a book with 171 maps of walking itineraries, is available in bookshops for Flux 895. Trails will be full of strollers late Sunday afternoons, the traditional time for such outings.

Hunting The District Commissioners of the Administration des Eaux et
Forêts (*see* Fishing, *above*) also issue one- or five-day hunting per-
mits on request, but the application must be franked by the owner of
the hunting rights for the area.

Dining

"French quality, German quantity"—that's an apt and common description of Luxembourg cuisine. A quick study of local posted
menus might lead visitors to think the locals eat nothing but *cuisine
bourgeoise*—veal with cream and mushrooms, beef entrecôte with
peppercorn sauce, veal *cordon bleu* (breaded veal stuffed with ham
and cheese)—all served in generous portions, with heaps of *frites*
(french fries) on the side. Yet this tiny country has its own earthy
cuisine, fresh off the farm: *judd mat gardebounen* (smoked pork
shoulder with fava beans), *E'slecker* ham or *jambon d'Ardennes*
(pearly-pink raw-smoked ham served cold with pickled onions),
choucroute (sauerkraut), *treipen* (blood pudding), *kuddelfleck
paniert* (plain breaded tripe), *fierkeljelli* (suckling pig in aspic), batter-fried merlan, and spicy *gromperekichelcher* (fried potato patties). A few restaurants still feature them, for sentimental locals as
well as for visitors. More upscale additions to the national specialties are *ecrevisses* (crayfish), cooked with local wine, and all
manner of trout. In Luxembourg City, though, you're as likely nowadays to find Chinese, Thai, Japanese, Indian, Mexican, and—leading the ethnic selections by several laps—Italian, its hold on the
dining scene due in part to the vast immigration of Italian miners
who settled and assimilated at the turn of the century. (Pizza, in
fact, is Luxembourg's de rigueur fast food.) Of course, Belgium's
penchant for *moules* (mussels) has leaked over the border; here,
they're savored with the local white wines. And some of
Luxembourg's French cuisine isn't so bourgeois: There are more
star-studded *gastronomique* restaurants per capita than in any other European country. Many restaurants—including some of these
world-class venues—offer an accessibly priced menu at lunch.

Luxembourg takes pride in its Moselle wines, grown on the hills
that rear up from the riverside and take maximum advantage of the
region's muted sunlight. Their bottles—slim and tapered—and
some of their names suggest Alsatian and German wines, and they
do share a certain straightforward fruitiness with these fellow
white wines. But Luxembourg's versions are sharper and lighter,
and when poured from an iced bottle into a green-stemmed glass,
they're an ideal counterpoint to a cream-sauced veal dish—or a plat-
ter of choucroute. The best names: a crisp Riesling or Auxerrois, a
dry Pinot Gris or a rounder Pinot Blanc, and the rare, rosé-like
Pinot Noir. More commonplace varieties, often served in pitchers or
by the glass, are Rivaner and Elbling.

Luxembourg's Moselle wines lend themselves well to the French
aperitif called *kir*, a glass of white wine tinted pale pink with a touch
of *cassis* (black currant liqueur), a version of which is made in the
castle village of Beaufort. After a meal, be sure to try the local eaux-
de-vie, reducing the fruity essence of *quetsch* (a little blue plum),
mirabelle (halfway between a plum and a yellow cherry), *kirsch*
(cherry), or—for the hard core—grain, the latter best mixed in a
mug of strong coffee.

Though Luxembourg is a hardworking business town, its workers
drop everything at noon and rush home, jamming the streets, to a
leisurely hot meal, then rush back, jamming the streets once more,

at 2 PM. Many restaurants offer a relatively speedy *plat du jour* (daily one-course special) for those who don't commute twice a day. Evening meals at home tend to be an early cold supper of ham, sausage, dark bread, and cheese; the evening meal out is a celebration and is enjoyed at length, à la Française. The Sunday noon meal is the most important of the week, and the best restaurants are booked up with three-generation families, who plan to spend the afternoon eating and drinking before their late-afternoon stroll, after which the menfolk retire to the local pubs.

Price categories in the Dining sections are based on a three-course meal without beverages or additional tip. Italian restaurants are rated $$, but simple pizza or one-course pasta meals would fall well within the $ range. Service is included.

Category	Cost
$$$$	over Flux 3,000
$$$	Flux 1,500–3,000
$$	Flux 750–1,500
$	under Flux 750

Lodging

Hotels in Luxembourg tend to be tidy and straightforward, with prices considerably higher in the city than in the surrounding countryside; outside town, prices vary remarkably little. Hotels outside the city may well close up during low season—late fall to Easter—so check in advance with the tourist office. Breakfast is usually included in the price; that information, along with prices, should be posted at the door, at the front desk, or in the room itself. Rooms with bathtub tend to cost slightly more than rooms with showers; specify your preference. Categories are based on the nightly rate for a standard double room with bathroom. A 5% visitors' tax is automatically included in the price.

Category	Cost
$$$$	over Flux 8,000
$$$	Flux 5,000–8,000
$$	Flux 2,500–5,000
$	under Flux 2,500

Luxembourg City

If you visit one place only in the Grand Duchy of Luxembourg, it will be, of course, Luxembourg-Ville (Luxembourg City), the city of 79,000 people in a nation of 400,000. Here, at leisure, you can explore all the must-sees—the fortifications, the old cobbled streets, the parks, the cathedral, the museum—and, after shopping, relax in a shaded terrace café, listening to street musicians or a brass band. For first-time visitors to Europe with big eyes—those who plan to take in Paris, Florence, Stonehenge, and the Matterhorn in 10 days—it can be "done" in a day; indeed, many train travelers check their bags in a station locker and make a satisfying tour of the town without spending the night. But if you have more time to ration, you may find quiet little Luxembourg a romantic base for excursions and a lovely place at night, with its illuminated monuments and walls and its inviting public squares.

Important Addresses and Numbers

Tourist Information
The **Luxembourg National Tourist Office (ONT)** (tel. 481199) maintains an information desk at the Air Terminus Building (Aerogare) in the place de la Gare; it's open daily (except Sun. from Nov. to March) mid-September–June, 9–noon and 2–6:30; July–mid-September, 9–7:30.

The **Luxembourg City Tourist Office** (pl. d'Armes, tel. 222809) is open mid-September–mid-June, Monday–Saturday 9–1 and 2–6; mid-June–mid-September, weekdays 9–7, Saturday 9–1 and 2–7, Sunday 10–noon and 2–6.

Embassies
United States: Boulevard Emmanuel Servais 22, tel. 460123.

Canada (in Brussels): avenue de Tervuren 2, B-1040 Brussels, tel. 0032/27356040.

United Kingdom: Boulevard Franklin Roosevelt 14, tel. 229864.

Emergencies
Police, Ambulance, Doctors, Dentists: Dial 409401 for the police. Dial the central emergency number, 112, for instructions in English on where to go in case of medical or dental emergencies. Do *not* go to the nearest hospital, as it may not accommodate you—hospitals firmly adhere to a rotation schedule for handling emergencies.

Late-Night Pharmacies
Check in the windows of pharmacies for a sign listing the *pharmacie de garde* (pharmacy on duty), or call 112.

Where to Change Money
Banks throughout Luxembourg display CHANGE signs in their windows and doors; there's also a *bureau de change* at the central rail station, open 9–9.

English-Language Bookstore
The **Magasin Anglais** (Allée Scheffer 19, tel. 224925) carries some English books among its teas, greeting cards, Weet-a-bix, chutneys, and custard mixes.

Travel Agencies
American Express is at avenue de la Porte-Neuve 34 (tel. 228555). **Wagons-Lits Tours** is at rue Aldringen 6 (tel. 460315). **Sotour,** at place du Théâtre 15 (tel. 461514), offers several English-speaking agents.

Arriving and Departing by Plane

Airport and Airlines
Luxembourg's Findel Airport, 6 kilometers (4 miles) from the city center, serves the entire grand duchy, particularly by Icelandair.

Between the Airport and Center
By Bus
Luxembourg city Bus 9 leaves the airport at regular intervals for Luxembourg City's main bus depot (pl. de la Gare), just beside the train station. Buses 2, 4, and 11 go to the city center. Individual tickets cost Flux 30. As city buses make stops along the way, you may be willing to pay more for the **Luxair** buses, which leave hourly 6 AM–10 PM, heading nonstop for the train station. Tickets cost Flux 120.

By Taxi
To the center, a taxi ride will cost about Flux 600.

Arriving and Departing by Car, Train, and Bus

By Car
The proper motorway exits for Luxembourg City are poorly indicated for newcomers; if you're arriving from France, watch for

"Belgique/Brussels–Liège/Luxembourg aeroport" with "centre-ville" in fine italics; from Belgium, exit for Strassen and turn left on the route d'Arlon. From Germany, the motorway empties directly into the center.

By Train Luxembourg is served by frequent direct trains from Brussels (under 3 hrs) and Paris (4 hrs). From Amsterdam, you travel via Brussels (6 hrs). Most connections from Germany channel through Koblenz.

Getting Around Luxembourg City

By Bus Luxembourg City has a highly efficient bus service. The blue-and-yellow buses outside the city train station will take you all around town and also to some of the outlying areas. Get details about services at the information counter in the station arrivals hall. Fares are low, but for an extended stay, the best bet is to buy a 10-ride ticket (Flux 270), available from banks or from the bus station in the Aldringen Center. Other buses, connecting Luxembourg City with towns throughout the country, leave from the train station. For information on bus routes or departures, call the information desk at the train station (tel. 492424) or write to Chemins de Fer Luxemborgeois (Boite Postale 1803, L-1018 Luxembourg).

By Taxi Taxis (tel. 482233 or 405252) are available at stands by the central post office and at the train station.

By Car As traffic is unusually thick for a city this size, and problems are compounded by extravagant roadworks, you will be wise to deposit your car in a central parking area, either Parking Glacis (near the Grande-Duchesse Charlotte bridge), or in Parking Knuedler, under the place Guillaume.

On Foot Luxembourg's diminutive scale allows you the luxury of covering nearly every neighborhood on foot.

Guided Tours

Orientation **Sales-Lentz** (26 rue de Curé 26, L-1368, tel. 461818) offers tours of the city 9:30–11:30 every morning during the peak tourist season (Apr.–Oct.) and several days a week in winter. The tours leave from the bus station, next to the railway station, platform 5, or from place de la Constitution, under the Gëlle Fra, and visit the historic sights of the center, the new European area, and some of the villas on the city outskirts, together with the military cemeteries. Tours cost Flux 290. Another tour of the city and countryside takes visitors to the monuments of Luxembourg City, the cemeteries, and on to the village and restored castle at Bourglinster. Tours run 2:30–5:45 every Saturday and Sunday during April, May, and October; from June through September, they run every Tuesday, Thursday, Saturday, and Sunday. Other more complete tours of the sights in the grand duchy are available for groups of 10 or more.

Special-Interest Tours **Luxembourg Live!** is a guided minitrain tour of the Old Town and Petrusse Valley, with multilingual commentary and dramatic music; tickets are sold at the bus booth on the place de la Constitution, and trains leave every 45 minutes (11:30–5:30, later in midsummer). Tours last 60–90 minutes. Tickets cost Flux 220 for adults, Flux 160 for children 4–15; families with up to two children, Flux 650; additional children, Flux 140.

Walking Tours A self-guided City Tour offers visitors a cassette player and earphones with a choice of commentaries on cassette: either "Discovering Luxembourg" (45 minutes, Flux 170) or "Luxembourg the fortress" (60 minutes, Flux 190). The players and cassettes are available for rental at the bus booth on the place de la Constitution.

Highlights for First-Time Visitors

Bock/Corniche
Casemates
Cathédrale Notre-Dame
Citadelle St-Esprit
Diekirch (excursion)
Echternach (excursion)
Grand Ducal Palace
Maquette
Moselle wine country (excursion)
Musée National
Vianden Castle (excursion)

Exploring Luxembourg City

Numbers in the margin correspond to points of interest on the Luxembourg City map.

This walk takes you through the maze of ancient military fortifications of Luxembourg City, now transformed into peaceful paths. Begin at the train station, in the southern section of the city. As you head right from the station toward the city center, along avenue de la Gare, you will pass through a bustling shopping district.

❶ Take the **Passerelle** (Viaduct), a 19th-century road bridge that links the station with the valley of the Petrusse. The Petrusse is more of a brook than a river and is now contained by concrete, but the valley has become a singularly beautiful park. From here you'll see the rocky ledges—partly natural, partly manmade—on which the city was founded.

At the cathedral end of the Viaduct, immediately on the right, take
❷ the steps and curving sidewalk up to the **Monument de la Solidarité Nationale** (National Monument to Luxembourg Unity), with its perpetual flame. It was erected in 1971 to commemorate Luxembourg's sacrifices and survival during World War II. The stark walls and enclosed chapel are dedicated *"D'Hémecht hiren Doudegen 1940–1945"* ("From the homeland to their dead"). To the right of the monument, continue up the road along some of the typically wedge-shaped remains of the old city fortifications, known here as the
❸ **Citadelle du St-Esprit** (Citadel of the Holy Spirit). This 17th-century citadel was built by Vauban, the great French military engineer, on the site of a former monastery. From the "prow" you'll see wraparound views: the three spires of the cathedral, the curve of the Alzette, and the incongruous white tower of the European Parliament secretariat.

Retrace your steps along the old city fortifications, cross boulevard
❹ F.D. Roosevelt, and continue on to the **place de la Constitution**, marked by the war memorial, a striking gilt *Gëlle Fra* (Golden Woman). She was destroyed by the Nazis in 1940 and rebuilt, with original pieces incorporated, in 1984. Here you'll find the entrance to the ancient **Casemates** (military tunnels) carved into the rocky **Petrusse** fortifications. At the height of her power and influence, Luxembourg was protected by three rings of defenses comprising 53 forts and strongholds. During the many phases of the fortress's construction, the rock itself was hollowed out to form a honeycomb of pas-

Luxembourg City

Bock, **11**
Boulevard Royal, **16**
Cathédrale
Notre-Dame, **5**
Chapelle de
St-Quirin, **15**
Citadelle du
St-Esprit, **3**

Corniche, **14**
Grand Ducal Palace, **9**
Grand'rue, **17**
Maquette, **8**
Monument de la
Solidarité Nationale, **2**
Musée National, **10**
Passerelle, **1**
Place d'Armes, **7**

Place de la
Constitution, **4**
Place Guillaume, **6**
Plateau du Rham, **12**
St-Michel, **13**

sages running for nearly 24 kilometers (15 miles) below the town. Ten gates controlled admittance through the walls, and the town was, in effect, 440 acres of solid fort. The Casemates served not only defensive purposes but were also used for storage and as a place of refuge when the city was under attack. Two sections of the passages are open to the public. These sections contain former barracks, cavernous abattoires, bakeries, and a deep well. *Pl. de la Constitution. Admission: Flux 50 adults, Flux 30 children. Open Easter, July–Sept. daily 10–5.*

Back across boulevard F. D. Roosevelt, take rue de l'ancien Athénée past the former Jesuit college, now the National Library. On rue Notre-Dame, to your right, is the main entrance to the late-Gothic
❺ **Cathédrale Notre-Dame.** There's an attractive Baroque organ gallery and a crypt containing the tomb of John the Blind, the beloved 14th-century king of Bohemia and count of Luxembourg. The valley side of the church was rebuilt in 1935; the roof of the main tower was rebuilt after a fire in 1985. *Open Easter–Oct., weekdays 10–5, Sat. 8–6, Sun. 10–6; Nov.–Easter, weekdays 10–11:30 and 2–5, Sat. 8–11 and 2–5, Sun. 10–5.*

❻ Opposite the cathedral lies the **place Guillaume,** known locally as the Knuedler, a name derived from the girdle worn by Franciscan monks who once had a monastery on the site. On market days (Wed. and Sat. mornings) the square is a mass of retail fruit and vegetable stands, vivid flower vendors, cheese and fish specialists, and a few remaining Luxembourg farmers who bring in their personal crop of potatoes, apples, cabbage, and radishes—as well as homemade jam, sauerkraut, and goat cheese. That's Grand-Duke William II on the bronze horse; he reigned from 1840 to 1849, while Luxembourg was flush with new independence. The Hotel de Ville (Town Hall), its stairs flanked by two bronze lions, was inaugurated in 1844.

Opposite the Town Hall, leave the place Guillaume through the yel-
❼ low sandstone arched passageway, then turn left. The **place d'Armes,** lined with symmetrical plane trees and strung with colored lights, was once the innermost heart of the fortified city; today it is the most welcoming corner of town, and in fine weather its cafés and benches are full of locals and tourists. The bandstand shelters visiting bands, who offer concerts every summer evening. Every second and fourth Saturday, a *brocante* (antiques/flea) market fills the square. The tourist office holds forth on the southwest corner, in the **Cercle Municipal,** with its bas-relief of the Countess Ermesinde granting Luxembourg its charter of freedom in 1244.

Behind the tourist office, look for the doorway marked Forteresse
❽ de Luxembourg: **Maquette.** Inside, there's a relief model of the fortress at various stages of its construction. *Rue du Curé, tel. 47962496. Admission: Flux 40 adults, Flux 20 children. Open Sept.–June, Sat. 10–1 and 2–6; July–Aug., Wed.–Sun. 10–12:30 and 2–5:30.*

Continue two blocks down rue du Curé and turn right; on the left
❾ you'll see the city's finest building, the **Grand Ducal Palace.** The palace has been closed for restoration but is scheduled to reopen by June 1995; restoration of the facade has already been completed, with superb results. Portions of the building were constructed in the late-16th century as part of the town hall commissioned by Peter Ernst, the count of Mansfeld and then governor; the elaborate ornamentation bears the stamp of the Spanish Renaissance. (The cross of Burgundy is on one of the consoles supporting the balcony.) Al-

though the royal families used to reside here, they now use the palace for business and entertaining.

To the right of the palace, turn left and continue up rue de l'Eau into the city's most ancient quarter. Here, rue de l'Eau turns into a tiny cobbled street and leads downhill to the right; some say this portion is the oldest street in town. It empties into a large, open crossroads, called the **place Marché aux Poissons;** this is the site of the old fish market and originally the crossing point of two Roman roads. Look to your right: Just up and behind the Pizzeria Um Bock, you'll see an oriel (bay-window tower) inscribed with the national motto.

⑩ To your left stands the **Musée National** (National Museum), in an attractive row of 16th-century houses. The Gallo-Roman collection, on the ground floor, has a fascinating assortment of small, local treasures—toga buckles, miniature deities—unearthed along the ancient routes that crisscrossed Luxembourg in the first centuries AD. This is the home of the 8th-century altar stone that guarded the tomb of St. Willibrord in Echternach; it's the oldest known of its kind. There's a series of rooms reproducing middle-class home life in 17th- to 19th-century Luxembourg, more models of the city's fortifications, and a collection of art ranging from old masters to local heroes, including the notable works of Luxembourg's own Joseph Kutter (1894–1941) and Sosthène Weiss (1872–1941), and works by Bruegel, Rembrandt, and Canaletto. *Marché-aux-Poissons, tel. 479330. Admission free. Open Tues.–Fri. 10–4:45, Sat. 2–5:45, Sun. 10–11:45 and 2–5:45.*

Time Out   Down rue Wiltheim, which runs alongside the museum, you'll find the tavern **Welle Mann** (rue Wiltheim 12, tel. 471783), the quintessentially Luxembourgish museum café. Sit on the tiny terrace and enjoy the magnificent view along the Alzette Valley, or admire the oak, the tile, and the old-city photos and posters inside. As there's no kitchen, only snacks are available—croques monsieurs, pizza baguettes, hot dogs—but the ambience makes it worth the stop.

At the bottom of rue Wiltheim stands the gate of the **Trois Tours** (Three Towers), the oldest of which was built around 1030. During the French Revolution, a guillotine was set up in these towers. To your right, up boulevard Victor Thorn, you can clearly see **⑪** Luxembourg's raison d'être: the **Bock** (from the Celtic "büück," meaning the promontory supporting a castle). Jutting dramatically out over the valley, this tongue of cliff served as the principal approach to the town from Celtic and Roman times until later bridges were constructed. Over its farthest point looms the ruined tower of the castle of Sigefroid himself. He founded the fortress Lucilinburhuc in 963; it was expanded, over the centuries, from this dominant point. In the surrounding ruins, you can walk over stone foundations, tour yet another set of **casemates,** or hang over the wall and take in vertiginous views of the valley, just as Sigefroid did: **⑫** You'll see the **Plateau du Rham** across the way, on the right, and before it, the massive towers of the Wenceslas fortifications, which in 1390 extended the protected area; the blocklike *casernes* (barracks) were built in the 17th century by the French and function today as a hospice for the elderly. Below them, at the bottom of the valley, is the 17th-century **monastery,** which from 1869 to 1984 served as the prison. Looking down the length of the Grund (meaning "valley"), it's easy to imagine the ground covered with thousands of banner-topped tents and campfires waiting out a siege. *Casemates admission: Flux 50 adults, Flux 30 children. Open Mar.–Oct., daily 10–5.*

⓭ Just uphill from the Bock, the prominent church of **St-Michel** looks over the valley, its bulbous steeple visible from all directions. Its congregation dates back to the 10th century, and there are visible signs of the original Romanesque structure to the left of the entrance. Most of the current structure mixes late Romanesque, Gothic, and Baroque, all heavily restored. From the Bock, you can

⓮ continue right along the **Corniche,** scenic ramparts overlooking the Grund, to the newly cobbled Plateau St-Esprit and take the elevator down to the Grund itself; or double back from the Bock to the place Marché aux Poissons and cut left down a steep cobbled street (rue Large) to reach the same point.

Time Out On the Corniche, stop at the shady outdoor tables of **Restaurant Breedewé** (rue Large 9, tel. 222696; you can cut through from rue Large as well) for a drink or a light, French-accented plat du jour. Or at the bottom of the valley, have a pint of bitter or Anglo-American cuisine at the English gathering point, **Scott's Pub** (Bisserwé 4, tel. 475352), where outdoor tables line the picturesque Alzette.

Once considered dank and squalid, twice buried under the flooding Alzette, the Grund is suddenly recherché, and you'll find chic restaurants, exclusive clubs, and skylighted renovated town houses among the tumbledown laborers' homes. Continue down rue St-Ulric and cut left into the **Vallée de la Petrusse,** a broad canyon-park full of willows, cherry trees, and illuminated bluffs. Before you pass

⓯ under the high Passerelle viaduct, you'll see the **Chapelle de St-Quirin** (St. Quirin's Chapel) built into the rocks on your left. The cave it surrounded is said to have been carved by the Celts; it is known to have housed a chapel since at least the 4th century. The relics of St. Quirin, transferred in 1050 from Avignon to Deutz-on-Rhine, spent a night in the chapel. The current structure was first built in 1355 by Teutonic Knights, though it has been repeatedly restored.

Continue through the park, with the cathedral and the Golden Woman looming above you, and cut right, uphill, under the Pont Adolphe.

⓰ Narrow switchbacks will carry you back up to the **boulevard Royal** and the beginning of banking territory. For shopping, cross the boulevard and turn right on rue Notre-Dame, walk two more blocks, then cut left on rue Philippe II. This busy shopping street empties

⓱ onto the **Grand'rue,** Luxembourg's pedestrian-only shopping street, where pastry shops and high-priced clothing boutiques vie for your tourist dollars. From here, it's half a block down rue des Capucins to the place d'Armes.

What to See and Do with Children

Luxembourg City itself is small and congested and, as such, not entirely user-friendly for children. Older kids may enjoy the loud music, dramatic stories, and novelty ride on the **Petrusse Express** (*see* Luxembourg Live! in Special-Interest Tours, *above*). Children often fill the central square of the place d'Armes during the summer **band concerts;** it's easy to have an ice cream at one of the surrounding café tables and dance when the spirit moves. The best **playground** by far is in Merl Park, off avenue X Septembre in a residential neighborhood west of the center; it offers plenty of high-adventure equipment for all ages.

Off the Beaten Track

Walk up boulevard Royal to Rond-point Robert Schuman, named for one of the fathers of the European Common Market, and cross the Grande-Duchesse Charlotte bridge to **Plateau Kirchberg,** a moonscape of modern architecture housing the European Court of Justice and various branches of the **EU.** Its most prominent structure—at 23 stories, Luxembourg's only skyscraper and, some complain, a bit of an eyesore looming over the old city's graceful stonework—houses the secretariat of the European Parliament. The Plateau is increasingly decorated with modern sculpture. Recent additions include a work by Henry Moore near the Court of Justice, a replica of Carl Fredrik Reutersward's "Non-Violence" in front of the Jean Monnet Building, and a sculpture by Frank Stella in front of the Hypobank in rue Alphonse Weicker. Note also German architect Gottfried Boehm's Deutsche Bank building in boulevard Konrad Adenauer.

Shopping

Luxembourg City has a reputation for being expensive, as it shelters a population of bankers and well-paid Eurocrats as well as Luxembourg's own newly wealthy. Thus the city supports a disproportionate share of luxury and designer shops. Service is usually European-style, meaning the client often isn't allowed to browse alone, but is expected to be shown goods by a clerk. Clerks are often aloof in a manner bordering on rudeness.

Shopping Districts The **Grand'rue** and radiating streets concentrate the best of high-end shopping; shops along the **avenue de la Gare** and **avenue de la Liberté,** both forking north from the train station, offer more affordable goods.

Department Stores **Rosenstiel** (4–6 rue Philippe II) is a glamorous little mini–Trump Tower, with atrium escalators, fountains, marble, brass, and a mix of its own departments with independent boutiques. **Monopol** (branches at Grand'rue 33, av. de la Gare 42, and av. de la Liberté 53) has more middle-brow goods.

Street Markets The main **farmers' market** holds forth in the place Guillaume every Wednesday and Saturday morning. An **antiques fair** takes over the place d'Armes every second and fourth Saturday. The annual **Braderie,** a massive, citywide sidewalk sale, slashes prices on the last weekend in August or the first weekend in September.

Specialty Stores
Chocolates **Oberweis** (Grand'rue 19, tel. 470703) is one of the city's finest patisseries, with a mean sideline in *knippercher,* Luxembourg chocolates.

China **Villeroy and Boch** porcelain has been manufactured in Luxembourg since 1748. If you have a favorite pattern, this is the place to invest in it: The seconds-quality factory outlet, on the edge of town, offers good reductions on virtually flawless goods and rock-bottom bargains on pieces with slightly visible flaws. The factory (rue Rollingergrund 330, tel. 468211) lies on the northwest edge of town. Take Bus 2, direction Rollingergrund, from Aldringen Center, by the post office. The outlet will not ship, so weigh your purchases carefully. The glossy main shop (rue du Fossé 2, between the Grand'rue and the pl. Guillaume, tel. 463343) shows first-quality goods at full price.

Prints **Correspondances** (rue de la Boucherie 16, tel. 252060) carries lovely antique engravings and maps of Luxembourg, along with a serious assortment of antique books. **Galerie Kutter** (rue des Bains 17, tel. 223571) offers good framed prints and stationery taken from the works of Luxembourg watercolorist Sosthène Weiss, who painted Cezanne-like scenes of Luxembourg's old town. **Librairie Bruck** (Grand'rue 22, tel. 499888717) sells maps and engravings in its showroom downstairs.

Sports and Fitness

Biking In Luxembourg City, you can rent bicycles for forays throughout the grand duchy from **Velo en Ville** (rue Bisserné 8, tel. 47962383), in the Grund.

Golf The **Golf Club Grand-Ducal** (tel. 34090) at Senningerberg, about 7 kilometers (4¼ miles) east of the city, has narrow fairways surrounded by dense woods; it is open only to members of other private clubs. The **Kikuoka Country Club Chant Val** (tel. 356135) is at Canach, about 10 kilometers (6 miles) east of Luxembourg City.

Dining

Luxembourg City has a wide variety of restaurants, offering everything from top French cuisine to simple local specialties; you'll also find an assortment of international choices and a plethora of pizzerias. It's easy to find a fixed-price menu or plat du jour by wandering from restaurant to restaurant, but beware: The best places are often booked up at weekday lunchtime; if you know where you want to eat, phone ahead. Dress is casual unless indicated.

$$$$ **Clairefontaine.** Airy, bright, and chic, and on the place de Clairefontaine near the Foreign Ministry, this fine gastronomic restaurant offers foie gras specialties, innovative fish dishes such as *vinaigrette tiède de grenouilles et homard* (warm vinagrette of frogs' legs and lobster), and seasonal game (wild duck with truffles). There's a business lunch, a three-course fixed price menu, and a lavish *dégustation* (tasting menu). The wine cellar met with the approval of both French President Mitterrand and the pope. *Rue de Clairefontaine 9, tel. 462211. Reservations required. Jacket and tie required. AE, DC, MC, V. Closed Sat. dinner, Sun., 3 weeks in Aug., and 1st week of Nov.*

$$$$ **St-Michel.** In a 16th-century building behind the ducal palace,
★ warmly lighted, intimate, and filled with antiques, this is one of the finest restaurants in the region and is rich in historical atmosphere. It was bought in 1993 by German chef Joerg Glauben, who is making new friends with his lobster salad with green asparagus tips, pigeon stuffed with foie gras and accompanied by rhubarb compote, and sumptuous desserts. The staff is young, skilled, and unstuffy, and the ambience is genuinely welcoming. *Rue de l'Eau 32, tel. 223215. Reservations required. Jacket and tie required. AE, DC, MC, V. Closed weekends and 3 weeks in Aug.*

$$$ **La Lorraine.** Strategically set on the place d'Armes, with terrace tables under its awnings, this seafood specialist caters to tourists passing by but also serves serious meals upstairs in its dignified dining room. The retail shop around the corner shows off the quality of the restaurant's wares: heaps of briny oysters, glistening turbot and sole, wriggling crabs. Once prepared, they live up to their promise: Baked skate in hazelnut butter with capers and grilled salmon in white wine sauce are good bets. *Pl. d'Armes 7, tel. 474620. Reservations advised. Jacket advised indoors. AE, DC, MC, V. Closed Sat. lunch, Sun., and 3 weeks in Aug./Sept.*

Dining

Ancre d'Or, **12**
Bacchus, **13**
Casa d'Italia, **18**
Clairefontaine, **15**
Ems, **27**
Kamakura, **17**
La Lorraine, **8**
La Trattoria dei Quattro, **23**
Mousel's Cantine, **16**
Osteria del Teatro, **1**
Speltz, **9**
St-Michel, **14**
Taverne Bit, **2**
Um Dierfchen, **10**

Lodging

Arcotel, **22**
Auberge du Coin, **19**
Bristol, **25**
Carlton, **24**
Dauphin, **21**
Empire, **28**
Cravat, **11**
Hostellerie du Grunewald, **3**
InterContinental, **4**
International, **26**
Italia, **20**
Le Royal, **7**
Parc, **5**
Sofitel, **6**

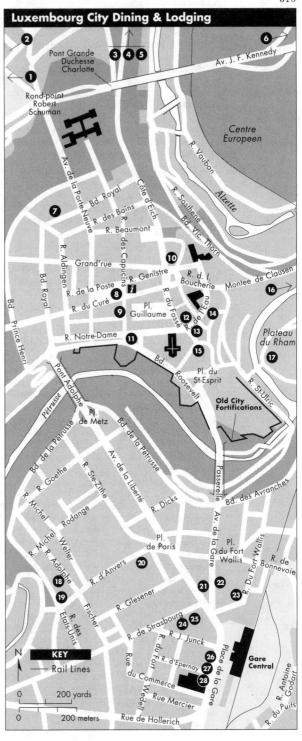

Luxembourg City Dining & Lodging

$$$ Speltz. In a chic, restored 17th-century house in the middle of the pedestrian shopping area, this stylish, relatively new restaurant caters to a young business crowd by serving a reasonable fixed-price lunch menu that may include lobster in local Riesling sauce with fricassee of mushrooms, or veal kidneys roasted in balsamic vinegar and mustard. *Rue Chimay 8, tel. 474950. Reservations advised. Jacket and tie advised. AE, DC, MC, V. Closed weekends, Easter week, and 2 weeks in July/Aug.*

$$ Bacchus. This Italian pizzeria attracts an upscale, downtown set, as much for its location in the historic center and for its slick peach-and-brass decor as for its food, which is straightforward and reasonably priced. Wood-oven pizza and classic pastas are dependable choices. Reserve for a seat in the tranquil courtyard. *Rue Marché-aux-Herbes 32, tel. 471397. Reservations advised. AE, DC, MC, V.*

$$ Um Dierfchen. While you'll find *steak de cheval* (horse meat) a standard in pubs throughout the region, this simple downtown establishment used to raise its own stock on farms near the French border. Still in the same family but without the farm source, it continues to specialize in entrecôte and *tournedos de poulain*—the horsey equivalent of veal. Both colt- and horse meat come sauced, either with a mild paprika or rich mushroom blend. Other specialties include lentil soup with smoked pork, and steaks of the more customary bovine sort. Portions are astounding, so you'd be wise to skip the first course. *Côte d'Eich 6, tel. 226141. Reservations advised at lunch. V.*

$$ Kamakura. If heavy Western cuisine palls, take the elevator down from St-Esprit to the up-and-coming Grund and try this chic Japanese restaurant. A number of fixed-price menus offer a variety of delicate, nouvelle-accented dishes, artfully presented and graciously served. À la carte specialties, considerably more expensive, include impeccably fresh sashimi (raw fish) and light tempura vegetables. *Rue Munster 2–4, tel. 470604. Reservations advised. AE, DC, MC, V. Closed Sun.*

$$ Mousel's Cantine. The great Mousel brewery dominates the valley of
★ Clausen (just across the bridge from the Bock), the waters of the Alzette reflecting its old walls. Directly adjoining its works—there are windows that open into the plant and beer taps that feed from tanks within—this fresh, comfortable café serves up heaping platters of local specialties to be washed down with crockery steins of creamy *Gezwickelte Béier* (unfiltered beer). There's braised and grilled ham, sausage, and smoked suckling pig (order in advance, minimum five diners), as well as the usual smorgasbord of choucroute, *gardebounen* (fava beans), and fried potatoes. *Montée de Clausen 46, tel. 470198. Reservations advised. MC, V. Closed Sun.*

$$ Osteria del Teatro. Across the Parking Glacis from the Municipal Theater, this popular restaurant offers a wide variety of pizzas, gnocchi, and risottos as well as grilled meats and fish in a lavish decor of scarlet brocade and *faux* Renaissance art. *Allée Scheffer 21–25, tel. 228811. Reservations advised. AE, DC, MC, V. Closed Thurs.*

$$ La Trattoria dei Quattro. Despite an undesirable location—on one of
★ the sleazier back streets around the train station—and despite an overabundance of pizzerias in town, this merits a trip off the beaten track. It's in a 150-year-old town house with an impressive carved wood ceiling and fireplace, and the Sardinian-accented cooking is a cut above the usual. Pastas are all homemade and are rarely run of the mill: Try *maccheroni alla Sarda* (sauced with tomato, onion, tuna, and fennel seeds) or *bucatini alla melanzani e funghi* (with eggplant and mushrooms). There are several good risottos, a mixed fish grill, and *filetto al gorgonzola* (steak with blue-cheese sauce).

Rue Fort-Neipperg 64, tel. 490039. Reservations accepted. AE, DC, MC, V. Closed weekends.

$ **Ancre d'Or.** This tidy, friendly brasserie, just off the place Guil-
★ laume, serves a wide variety of old-time Luxembourgish specialties
as well as good bourgeois cuisine. Try their judd mat gardeboenen,
kuddelfleck, or a pair of rich blood sausages served with red cabbage
and applesauce. Other country classics include a fine version of tête
de veau (stewed calf's head and tongue with onion vinaigrette) and
choucroute. Their veal in cream-and-mushroom sauce is prototypi-
cal, and the delicious apple tart (Luxembourgish style, with custard
base) is homemade. Try to book ahead; it's usually full on market
days. *Rue du Fossé 23, tel. 472973. Reservations strongly advised.
MC, V. Closed Sun.*

$ **Casa d'Italia.** Though the cooking isn't anything to write home
about, you can get a substantial two-course hot meal at absurdly low
prices in this comfortable, clublike meeting place crowded with loyal, local Italian immigrants. Order and pay at the cash register when
you enter, choosing between a big slab of lasagna followed by roast
veal, or pasta in Bolognese sauce followed by plain, fresh mozzarel-
la. *Centro di ristoro Italiano, rue Adolphe Fischer 56, tel. 483568.
No reservations. No credit cards.*

$ **Ems.** Directly across the street from the train station, this lively
diner equivalent (vinyl booths, posted specials) draws a loyal clientele for its vast portions of moules in a rich wine-and-garlic broth,
accompanied by frites and (unlike in Belgium, where they drink
beer) a bottle of sharp, cold Moselle wine. There also are local meat
and fish specialties—*tomates aux crevettes* (tomatoes stuffed with
mayonnaise-coated tiny shrimp), herring, Thuringer sausages—
and substantial ice cream specialties. Food is served until 1 AM. *Pl.
de la Gare 30, tel. 487799. No reservations. DC, MC, V.*

$ **Taverne Bit.** With sanded tabletops and dark-wood banquettes, this
is a cozy and very local pub, where you can drink a *clensch* (stein) of
draft Bitburger beer (from just across the German border) and have
a plate of sausage with good potato salad, a plate of cold ham, or
kachkeis, the pungent local cheese spread, served with baked potatoes. *Allée Scheffer 43, tel. 460751. No reservations. No credit
cards. Closed Sat. dinner, Sun.*

Lodging

It's more expensive to stay in Luxembourg than in hotels outside the
city, but worth it for the convenience of having an interesting home
base. Hotels tend to be modern here; more options are clustered
around the train station, which is a trek (or a bus ride) from the old
town.

$$$$ **InterContinental.** Rising above the outskirts of Luxembourg like a
20th-century château-fort, this all-modern 19-story deluxe hotel
opened in 1985 and competes directly with Le Royal downtown, offering a big indoor pool, good fitness facilities, and gracious rooms
with good, broad beds. The restaurant Les Continents attracts locals for its upscale French cooking. *Rue Jean Engling, L-1466, tel.
43781, fax 436095. 344 rooms. Facilities: restaurant, café, bar, terrace, indoor pool, sauna, fitness room. AE, DC, MC, V.*

$$$$ **Le Royal.** In the city center, on the Wall Street of Luxembourg and
★ within steps of parks, shopping, and the old town, this is the best
choice for luxury. It's solid, modern (opened 1984), and sleek, with a
great deal of lacquer, marble, and glass, and all facilities stress business: There are six phone booths in the lobby and a separate counter
for faxes and telexes. Rooms facing boulevard Royal have traffic

noise leaking through the double-glazed windows; opt for a back room toward the park if possible. The gourmet restaurant, Le Relais Royal, serves French cuisine with a Mediterranean accent. The piano bar is popular, as is the Le Jardin brasserie, especially when the fountain terrace is open. *Blvd. Royal 12, L-2449, tel. 41616, fax 225948. 180 rooms. Facilities: 2 restaurants, piano bar, exercise equipment, pool, sauna, tennis, hairdresser. AE, DC, MC, V.*

$$$$ Sofitel. Formerly the Pullman, this hotel is on the moonscape of the Kirchberg Plateau, surrounded by the architectural experiments of various branches of the EU. Nearly a hundred new rooms were added in 1993, making this the largest hotel in Luxembourg. The hotel maintains an all-American look (big beds, generic decor) and a friendly attitude. *Centre Européen, L-2015, tel. 437761. 349 rooms. Facilities: restaurant, bar, café, garden, shopping arcade. AE, DC, MC, V.*

$$$ Cravat. ★ While Luxembourg is quickly bulldozing away its bourgeois past and tacking up the glitziest *nouveau* international styles, this relic—moderately grand, modestly glamorous—continues to hold forth at the best location in town: the edge of the old town, along the Petrusse Valley. Built in several phases since the turn of the century, it features a mix of solid old architectural details—an Art Deco brass elevator, caryatids framing the lounge fireplace—and though corridors have a dated, institutional air, the rooms are fresh and welcoming in a variety of tastefully retro styles. Bathrobes and hair dryers add a bit of luxury. The bar is comfortably swank, though you may want to drink in the adjoining Art Deco coffee shop, another period piece that still draws fur-hatted ladies of a certain age to tea. General Bradley stayed here during World War II. *Blvd. F.D. Roosevelt 29, L-2011, tel. 221975, fax 226711. 60 rooms. Facilities: restaurant, coffee shop, bar. AE, DC, MC, V.*

$$$ Parc. On the edge of the forest, just outside the city and away from its traffic-clogged streets, this modern hotel with extensive conference and sports facilities and a large outdoor swimming pool is a good base for excursions to the Ardennes and Petite Suisse. Rooms are restful, the bar cheerful, and the restaurant quite acceptable. *Route d'Echternach 120, Dommeldange, tel. 435643, fax 436903. 271 rooms. Facilities: restaurant, bar, room safes, rooms for guests with disabilities, non-smoking rooms, conference facilities, pool, sauna, solarium, horseback riding, tennis, bowling, playground, garage. AE, DC, MC, V.*

$$ Arcotel. Opened in 1985 on the busy shopping street between the old town and the train station, this modernized hotel provides a quiet getaway from the city outside. Decorated in warm shades of beige and rose, with polished wood and brass, it offers solid baths and extra comforts—blow-dryers in the bathroom, drinks in the Bukhara-lined lounge—to make up for the typically small rooms. *Av. de la Gare 43, L-1611, tel. 494001, fax 405624. 30 rooms with bath. Facilities: breakfast room. AE, DC, V.*

$$ Auberge du Coin. ★ At the edge of a quiet, dignified residential area but within easy reach of the station and the old town, this pleasant hotel is done in pure "new Luxembourg" style—that is, stone and terra-cotta floors, wood-framed double windows, polished oak, Persian rugs, and tropical plants. Rooms are freshly furnished in bright knotty pine with new tile baths and oil paintings of the old town. There's a lovely French restaurant and a comfortable oak-and-stone bar as well. The nine-room matching annex down the street has no elevator and costs slightly less. *Blvd. de la Pétrusse 2, L-2320, tel. 402101, fax 403666. 23 rooms with bath. Facilities: restaurant, bar. AE, DC, MC, V.*

$$ Empire. Slick, freshly decorated, simple, and aimed at single business travelers (there are only three double rooms), this station hotel offers all comforts and a few bargain no-bath rooms (though all have toilets). A pizzeria and a French restaurant adjoin. *Pl. de la Gare 34, tel. 485252. 27 rooms, 21 with bath or shower. Facilities: restaurant, pizzeria, bar. AE, DC, MC, V.*

$$ Hostellerie du Grunewald. Just outside the city center, near the InterContinental, this former auberge offers the antithesis of anonymous business travel: a quiet, illuminated garden out back; cozy, old-fashioned lounges crammed with mixed wingbacks, knickknacks, and old master prints; and plush rooms full of Persian rugs, rich fabrics, and cream-patina Louis XV furniture. Serene garden-side rooms are worth booking ahead, though street-side windows are triple glazed. The current owner took over in 1963, upgrading rooms to full comfort and creating the detail-rich decor that merits their membership in the Romantik hotel group. The cozy restaurant, more like an upscale country inn than a city hotel dining room, serves classic, luxurious French cuisine, catering to a business crowd with different *menus d'affaires* at lunch and dinner. *Rte. d'Echternach 10–14, L-1453, Dommeldange, tel. 431882, fax 420646. 28 rooms with bath. Facilities: restaurant (tel. 420314; closed Sat. lunch, Sun., 1st 3 weeks of Jan.), garden terrace. AE, DC, MC, V.*

$$ International. In the midst of a gradual upgrade, this large postwar station-area Best Western hotel offers a mixed bag of comforts and decors without making a price distinction. Sixty percent of the rooms have been redone with fresh Eurostyle baths and built-in cabinetry; be sure to request one of these, otherwise you may end up with chipped laminate, chenille, and elderly toilets. Despite double-glazed windows on the street side, back rooms are much more desirable. *Pl. de la Gare 20–22, L-1016, tel. 485911, fax 493227. 60 rooms, 53 with bath. Facilities: restaurant. AE, DC, MC, V.*

$$ Italia. This is a valuable and remarkably inexpensive find in the train-station area: a former private apartment converted into hotel rooms, some with plaster details and cabinetry left behind. Rooms are solid and freshly furbished, all with private tiled bathrooms. The restaurant downstairs is one of the city's best Italian venues, and prices are considerably higher than those in neighboring pizzerias. In summer, try to dine in the quiet back garden. *Rue d'Anvers 15–17, L-1130, tel. 486626, fax 480807. 20 rooms with bath. Facilities: restaurant, bar, garden. AE, DC, MC, V.*

$ Bristol. Though rue de Strasbourg is part of the network of questionable streets that lead off the place de la Gare, and thus is lined with strip joints and flophouses as well as legitimate shops and restaurants, this modest hotel offers comfortable, secure lodging and a fresh decor. The lobby/bar is warm and cozy, and the breakfast room is lined with game trophies won by the owner's family. A few bathless rooms on the first and fourth floors go for bargain rates. *Rue de Strasbourg 11, L-2561, tel. 485830, fax 486480. 30 rooms, 22 with shower/toilet. Facilities: bar for guests only. AE, DC, MC, V.*

$ Carlton. In this vast 1918 hotel, buffered from the rue de Strasbourg scene by a rank of stores and opening onto a quiet inner court, tight-budget travelers will find roomy, quiet quarters. Nothing has been renovated, which means the beveled glass, oak parquet, and terrazzo floors are original, but so are the toilets, all down the hall. The lounge, reception, and breakfast room are vast and lavishly furnished. Upstairs is only a little bleaker: Each room has antique beds, floral-print comforters, and a sink; wood floors, despite creaks, are white-glove clean; and while there's blistered plaster in the shower, the heat works. The maid even leaves an apple when she makes your bed in the morning. *Rue de Strasbourg 9, L-2561, tel. 484802. 50 rooms, 8 with shower. Facilities: breakfast room, bar. No credit cards.*

$ **Dauphin.** Another budget option, this modern hotel offers plain, clean rooms with splashy '60s decor—daisy prints, linoleum—and all-private baths. Back rooms avoid heavy street noise. *Av. de la Gare 42, L-1610, tel. 488282, fax 489661. 36 rooms with bath. Facilities: breakfast room. AE, DC, MC, V.*

The Arts and Nightlife

The Arts Luxembourg has been named **Cultural Capital of Europe** for 1995; for details on the many events, contact Luxembourg 95, rue Aldringen 23, tel. 221995, fax 222000. Even without this title and the wealth of events that go with it, Luxembourg City would still host a disproportionate number of arts events for its size. Although many of them are sold out on a season-ticket basis, there are often seats available at the last minute, and there are also independent concerts with tickets sold immediately before. Watch for posters on kiosks, and check at the tourist office on the place d'Armes, where tickets to many events are sold. Tickets to events at the Municipal Theater (Rond-point Robert Schuman, tel. 470895) may be sold at its box office. The *Luxembourg News*, an English-language weekly translating local news from the city dailies, offers up-to-date events listings; it is sold at bookstores and magazine stands. *Weekend* and *Rendez-vous Lëtzebuerg*, both available at the tourist office, also offer listings.

Theater Good traveling plays in French and German pass through the Municipal Theater; there also are English-language amateur productions from time to time. Watch kiosks or check at the tourist office on the place d'Armes.

Music Luxembourg is home to the **Radio-Télé-Luxembourg** (RTL) **Orchestra,** which performs a series of weekly concert pairs, usually on Thursday nights in the Municipal Theater and Friday nights at the Conservatoire de Musique (rue Charles Martel 33, tel. 47962950). Watch for posters announcing "Concerts du Midi": They may feature the RTL Orchestra, its members as soloists, or other professional chamber groups, and they are free of charge. They take place at the RTL Villa Louvigny, in the central municipal park. Though Luxembourg supports no opera company of its own, several German companies pass through on tour every season.

Film Luxembourg films are usually shown in their original language, with subtitles in a variety of tongues. If you want to see something other than an English-language film, check the posters to see what language subtitles will be in. The best films in any language usually come to **Cine Utopia** (av. de la Faiencerie 16, 47–21–09), where reservations are accepted by phone.

Nightlife **Lentzen Eck** (rue de la Boucherie 2, tel. 222477) offers a very tradi-
Bars and Cafés tional old-Luxembourg setting, plus a good list of local eaux-de-vie. The **Cockpit Inn** (blvd. General Patton 43, tel. 488635) pulls together the Icelandair and American residents for mixed drinks and an aviation theme. **Scott's Pub** (Bisserwé 4, tel. 475352) in the Grund makes Brits feel at home; across the way, **Am Häffchen** (Bisserwé 9, tel. 461617) serves cocktails and cocoa in an intimate, retro setting, complete with bookshelves. **Interview** (rue Aldringen 21, tel. 473665) draws a very young, chic crowd (mostly students from the European School) to a setting of Warholesque urban decay. **Taverne Bit** (allée Scheffer 43, tel. 460751) serves draft Bitburger Pils in a cozy

German-pub setting. The **George and Dragon** (rue Unden 217, tel. 474186) has an open fire, fish and chips, and Guinness stout on tap. The **piano bar** at the hotel Le Royal (blvd. Royal 12, tel. 41616) has live music and cocktails in a swank setting. **Yucatan** (rue Notre-Dame 13, tel. 226871) draws a stand-up local crowd for mixed margaritas and, as an afterthought, a reasonable approximation of Mexican food.

Discos The enormous **Metropolis** (rue du Fort Neipperg 56–58, tel. 482211) has occasional live music. **Le Biblos** (av. Monterey 10, tel. 223229) stays open until 3 AM. **Casa Blanca** (blvd. d'Avranches 36, tel. 496940) is the current weekend hot spot, while **Bugatti** (rue des Bains 19, tel. 227066) draws an upscale, flashy crowd. Upstairs at **Jamaïque** (rue Aldringen 23, 47–08–22), there's a mix of soul and country music.

Jazz Clubs **Melusina** (rue de la Tour Jacob 145, tel. 435922) draws top local musicians and touring guests for jazz, rock, and folk.

Excursion to the Luxembourg Ardennes

Vast, rolling green hills and dense fir forests alternate in Luxembourg's northern highlands, the southeast corner of the rocky, wooded Ardennes plateau. Higher, harsher than the duchy's southern *Bon Pays* (Good Country), with bitter winters and unwilling soil, it has remained isolated and inaccessible; indeed, even in the 1940s, no one expected the Germans to attempt attacking across such rough and uneven terrain. They did, of course—twice. The second led to one of the most vicious conflicts in World War II, the Battle of the Ardennes, or the Bulge (*see* Chapter 2, Portraits). It has been the hunting grounds of kings and emperors, Celts, Romans, and Gauls; shaggy deer and great, bristling wild boar still occasionally charge across a forest road. Castles punctuate its hills and valleys, and rocky rivers and streams pour off its slopes, making this an attractive vacation area for Europeans—especially from the flat Netherlands—to experience wilderness and medieval history. Clervaux, the northernmost point of our tour, lies some 60 kilometers (37 miles) north of Luxembourg City; thus it, and any points below it, lie within reach for a day trip. To follow the complete tour as described below, give yourself at least an overnight stop; though distances are small, roads do tend to wind a bit, so plan on a leisurely drive. If you're interested in tracing the ravages of World War II, allow plenty of browsing time, for there are three museums devoted to the subject in this hardest-hit area. And if you want to hike, you may want to settle in for a wilderness sojourn of two or three days—or more.

Important Addresses and Numbers

Tourist Information **Clervaux:** Syndicat d'Initiative, L-9700, tel. 92072. **Diekirch:** Syndicat d'Initiative, esplanade 1, Boite Postale 29, L-9201, tel. 803023. **Esch-sur-Sûre:** Syndicat d'Initiative, Parking (at entrance to town), L-9650, tel. 89367. **Vianden:** Syndicat d'Initiative, rue de la Gare 37, L-9420, tel. 84257.

Emergencies Police **Clervaux:** tel. 92811; **Diekirch:** tel. 803185; **Esch-sur-Sûre** (Heiderscheid): tel. 89005; **Vianden:** tel. 84841.

Ambulance Throughout Luxembourg, dial 012.

Emergency **Ettelbruck:** Clinique St. Louis (Sq. Dr. Marx, tel. 81661); **Wiltz:**
Rooms Clinique du Nord (rue G. D. Charlotte 10, tel. 95951).

Late-Night Inquire at 112 for the number and address of the local *pharmacie de*
Pharmacies *garde* (emergency pharmacy).

Getting There

By Car Driving is by far the most efficient and satisfying way to explore this
region, and roads are well-kept though slow and winding. From
Luxembourg City, follow signs for Ettelbruck (via route E 420/RN
7). An alternative—and very attractive—route is E27 toward
Echternach, turning left almost immediately on the road to
Larochette, and thence to Diekirch.

By Train Small rail lines out of Luxembourg City can carry you to Ettelbruck,
Bourscheid, Clervaux, and Wiltz, but other sites on this tour remain
out of reach by train.

By Bus Luxembourg buses connect throughout the grand duchy, both from
Luxembourg City and from exterior towns. If you're staying outside
the city, invest in the thick *horaire*, which has complete listings of
connections.

Guided Tours

Sales-Lentz (*see* Guided Tours in Luxembourg City, *above*) offers
coach tours to groups of 10 or more.

Exploring the Luxembourg Ardennes

Numbers in the margin correspond to points of interest on the Ex-
cursion to the Luxembourg Ardennes map.

Leave **Luxembourg's** center via the Côte d'Eich, passing the red
Grande-Duchesse Charlotte bridge, and follow signs toward
Ettelbruck/Diekirch (E 420/RN 7). About 25 kilometers (15 miles)
❶ up the road, past Mersch, you'll reach **Colmar-Berg** and the **Grand**
Ducal Castle, where the royal family has maintained their castle
quarters for centuries; it is visible from the road (to the left), but
well protected from close-up public viewing. Colmar-Berg is also
home to a large branch of America's Goodyear tire company.

Another 2 kilometers (1¼ miles) takes you to the outskirts of
Ettelbruck, an important crossroads; just short of town, take a right
❷ toward **Diekirch.** This small, easygoing city, with a pleasant pedestrian shopping area, offers several points of interest. **Eglise St-**
Laurent (St. Lawrence's Church), a lovely, ancient little Romanesque church, has portions dating from as far back as the 5th century. Its earliest incarnation was constructed on the foundations of a
Roman temple, the older parts functioning as a cemetery; in 1961,
that lower section was uncovered, and with it 30-some Merovingian
sarcophagi, many of them containing intact skeletons. Since 1978,
the cemetery has been restored and open to the public. Some of
the ancient underbelly of the church can be seen through a grate in
the nave; you may enter the crypt by an exterior door on the right of
the building. At the **Musée Municipal** (Municipal Museum), in the
basement of the primary school, there are two more sarcophagi and
remains found under the church, along with well-preserved Roman
mosaics from the 4th century, found a couple of blocks away;
Diekirch is riddled with remains of Roman culture, though most of
its treasures were carried away by invading Franks. *Pl.*

Excursion to the Luxembourg Ardennes

BELGIUM

Asselborn

Wincrange

Eschweiler

❹ Clervaux

Hosingen

Wilwerwiltz

Wiltz ❺

Büderscheid

Gœsdorf

Esch-sur-Sûre ❻

Bigonville

Martelange

Mertzig

Colmar-Berg ❶

Redange

Useldange

Hollenfells

Septfontaines

Marienthal

Ansembourg

Valley of the Eisch

Steinfort

GERMANY

Mt. St.-Nicolas ▲

❸ Vianden

Göbelsmuhle

❼

Bourscheid

❷ Diekirch

Ettelbruck

Beaufort

Larochette

Mersch

PETITE SUISSE LUXEMBOURGEOISE

Junglinster

Echternach

Rosport

Mompach

Wasserbillig

Grevenmacher

Wormedange

Sandweiler

Ehnen

Luxembourg

Hamm

KEY

Rail Lines

0 — 20 miles

0 — 30 km

N

Guillaume. Admission: Flux 20. Open mid-Mar.–Oct., Fri.–Tues. 10–noon and 2–6.

In the **Diekirch Historical Museum** (Museum of the Battle of the Bulge), 10 life-size, authentically equipped dioramas depict personal aspects of the hardships of the battle. Unlike the museum at Bastogne, this thoughtful, neutral effort sidesteps discussions of strategies and fronts; it brings out individual details instead, from yellowed letters and K rations to propaganda flyers—both German and American—scattered to demoralize already homesick soldiers at Christmastime. All paraphernalia are authentic period pieces. The staff often welcomes veterans personally. *Bamertal 10, tel. 808908. Admission: Flux 120 adults, Flux 80 students under 18. Open Easter–Oct., Wed.–Mon. 10–noon and 2–6.*

Diekirch is also the home of the brewery of a beer bearing its name; it is one of the most popular beers in Luxembourg. And you may want to head briefly out of town, following the route to Larochette; as you climb the switchbacks above town, park across from the sign for the **Diewelselter,** an impressive dolmen (stone altar) attributed to the Celts, then walk up the trail marked "D" into the forest (about 15 minutes). No one is sure who piled the great stones that form this ancient arch—or how they did it.

❸ From Diekirch, follow route 17 east and north to **Vianden,** where coming around the last bend, you'll suddenly see a full-length view of its spectacular **castle** rearing up on a hill over the village, replete with conical spires, crenelation, step gables, and massive bulwarks. Its dramatic position enhances the tiny village's medieval air, with its steep, narrow main street and shuttered houses crouched at the feet of the feudal lord. The castle was built on Roman foundations in the 9th century, but its most spectacular portions date from the 11th, 12th, and 15th centuries. It has been completely and, to some eyes, ruthlessly restored. *Tel. 84108. Admission: Flux 110 adults, Flux 30 children. Open Mar. and Oct., daily 10–5; April–Sept., daily 10–6; Nov.–Feb., daily 10–4.*

In the village below, the 13th-century **Gothic church** once functioned as a Trinitarian monastery; its ancient cloisters, too, have been restored to sparkling modernity. Down the hill, by the banks of the River Our, the **Musée Victor Hugo** displays letters and memorabilia from the famous French author's sojourn here in 1871. *Tel. 84257. Admission: Flux 25 adults, Flux 15 children. Open Apr.–Oct., Wed.–Mon. 9:30–noon and 2–6.*

The **Hotel Heintz,** on the main street, billeted American intelligence and reconnaissance (I&R) men in the chilly last days of 1944; one of the bits of intelligence they picked up was the story of Elise Delé, a Luxembourgish farm woman from Bivels, just up the road. On route to her evacuated house to retrieve warm clothing, she had been picked up by German soldiers and carried across the Our, all the way to Bitburg. Along the way she witnessed a beehive of activity—soldiers, trucks, artillery, SS troops, and river-crossing pontoons—heading west. With help from the Luxembourg underground, she escaped and described what she had seen to the I&R Americans at the Hotel Heintz. On December 14 her story had made it as far as the First Army headquarters in Spa, but it hadn't crossed the desks of Eisenhower or Montgomery. At 5:30 AM on December 16, the Germans attacked and continued to attack, with a passion and brutality born of desperation, until well after Christmas—and well into Belgium.

From Vianden, wend your way back toward Diekirch, but cut north (right) on a smaller scenic road over Mont St-Nicholas (with widespread views of the Our Valley from its summit) and on to **Clervaux.** This forest village, surrounded by deep-cleft hills, draws vacationers to hike, hunt, and visit its sprawling **castle,** founded by the de Lannoi family. It was from this castle that Philip de Lannoi, an ancestor of Franklin Delano Roosevelt, left in 1621 to make his fortune in America. The castle was virtually reduced to rubble in the Battle of the Bulge but has been completely restored. Two floors in the right wing of the castle house the restored exhibition of photo portraits of *The Family of Man*—considered by some to be the greatest photographic exhibition of all time—taken by Luxembourg native Edward J. Steichen. *Tel. 5224241. Admission: Flux 150. Open Mar.–Dec., Tues.–Sun. 10–6.*

Clervaux is also home to the striking **Benedictine Abbey of Saints Maurice and Maur,** built in 1910 in the style of the Abbey of Cluny and perched high above town. In the pedestrian center, there is a new memorial to the Americans who fought in Clervaux in 1944.

From Clervaux, double back to route 7 and head south, then (in about 7 kilometers/4¼ miles) cut west (right) on winding route 25 toward **Wiltz.** This unusual town is divided into two separate levels, with its Oberwiltz (upper town) dominated by the fully restored **castle.** Built in the 12th century, it was completely remodeled in 1631; it now houses a small **Musée de la Battaille des Ardennes** (Museum of the Battle of the Bulge), with documents and photographs from the war. *Tel. 957444. Admission: Flux 50 adults, Flux 25 children. Open Whitsun (7th weekend after Easter), June–mid-Sept., daily 10–noon and 1–5.*

Also in town is a **Musée arts et métiers** (Museum of Arts and Handicrafts), which displays tools and objects from old local bakers, tanners, and distilleries. *Tel. 957444. Admission: Flux 50 adults, Flux 25 children. Open Whitsun (7th weekend after Easter)–June, daily 2–5, July–Aug., daily 10–noon and 1:30–5:30, 1st half of Sept., daily 2–5:30.*

The amphitheater behind the museum hosts the Wiltz Festival of classical music in July and August; the rest of the château serves as a retirement home and cannot be visited.

Leaving Wiltz, head south on route 12 to Büderscheid, then continue south briefly on N15. Turn right, cutting through a tunnel in the rock cliff, and in 2 kilometers (1¼ miles) you'll enter pretty little ❻ **Esch-sur-Sûre.** Completely circled by densely forested hills, this miniature gooseneck on the River Sûre was once a stronghold, and its ruined **fortress-castle** still towers over the town. (Unrestored, it is open to the public.) Legend has it that an Esch Crusader brought home a Turk's head and hung it outside the castle gate, and that it reappears to this day to warn of disaster; some claim to have seen it before the German invasion in 1940. Nowadays Esch is the gateway to a water recreation area, on the shores of the **Lac de la Haute Sûre,** created by a dam just upstream from town.

Head south again on route 15, then immediately cut left toward Goebelsmühle, following the green Sûre Valley along a wild and isolated winding road. Continue along the river, following signs for Bourscheid Moulin-Plage, where you'll see the romantic ruins of ❼ **Bourscheid** Castle looming 500 feet above the Sûre, commanding three valleys. Restorations have made this rambling hodgepodge of towers and walls more accessible; the views are magnificent, and there's a snack bar built in. *Tel. 90570. Admission: Flux 80 adults, Flux 50 children. Open Apr.–June and Sept., daily 10–6; July–Aug., daily 10–7; Oct., daily 11–4.*

From Bourscheid, follow signs to Lipperscheid, from where N7 leads back to Luxembourg City.

What to See and Do with Children

Kids who finally tire of pouring imaginary boiling oil and shooting flaming arrows from Ardennes castles, and who balk at another uphill forest hike, will enjoy a trip to swim or windsurf on the waterfront of the **Lac de la Haute Sûre,** accessible on the south shore at Insenborn and on the north shore below Liefrange. There's also a **Musée de la poupée et du jouet** (Museum of Dolls and Toys) in Vianden, with antiques dating back to the 16th century. *Grand'rue 96, tel. 84591. Admission: Flux 80 adults, Flux 60 children. Open Easter–Oct., Tues.–Sun. 10–noon and 2–6.*

Off the Beaten Track

For more castles, make an extra circle tour west of **Mersch** (with its own three towers) and visit the **Valley of the Seven Châteaux,** cutting west to Reckange, south to **Hollenfels, Marienthal,** and **Ansembourg** (which has an old castle in the heights and a new one in the valley below), then working west to **Septfontaines** and south to **Koerich.** The castles, in various stages of repair and representing a broad historical spectrum, have not been developed for visitors, but they loom above forests and over valleys much as they did in Luxembourg's grander days. Follow the road signs marked "Vallée des Sept Châteaux": This rather obscure and never-direct itinerary takes you through pretty farmlands, woods, and—just outside Koerich, at **Goeblange**—to the foundations of two 4th-century **Roman villas,** their underground heating and plumbing systems exposed; the rough cobbles leading into the woods are original, too.

Shopping

There's good, moderate shopping for clothes and kitchen wares in the downtown sections of **Diekirch** and **Ettelbruck.** A few souvenir shops in **Clervaux** and **Vianden** offer rustic goods and (grimly enough) World War II–model war toys for children inspired by the horrors of Battle of the Bulge museums.

Sports and the Outdoors

Biking Bicycles can be rented in Diekirch at **Camping de la Sûre** (tel. 809425) and at **Outdoor Centre** (tel. 809792).

Golf There's an 18-hole course at **Eselborn** (tel. 929395), 3 kilometers (1.8 miles) northeast of Clervaux, with the inexpensive, 10-room Hôtel du Golf (tel. 929395) right by the course.

Dining and Lodging

Clervaux
Dining and
Lodging

Koener/International. These two hotels, owned by brothers and adjoining a shared indoor pool, offer sleek new mall-look decors and modern details; rooms on the International side are somewhat more attractive (and more expensive), with dark-green and brass decors. Neither half, aside from some rooms with forest views, has much Ardennes atmosphere, but both offer full comfort. *Koener: Grandrue 14, tel. 91002, fax 92826. International: Grand-rue 10, tel. 929391, fax 92492. 48/42 rooms. Facilities: restaurant ($$), café, terrace, piano bar, indoor pool, sauna, solarium. AE, DC, MC, V. Closed mid-Jan.–mid-Mar. Koener: $. International: $$*

Le Commerce. Directly below the castle and slightly apart from the hotel-packed center, this spacious hotel has been in the family for two generations, and shows their pride: It combines slick, spare modernity—tile, stucco, polished oak—with homey old details (fringed lamps, heavy upholstery), and there's an open fireplace in the restaurant. Some rooms have balconies over the river and hills. *Rue de Marnach 2, L-9709, tel. 91032, fax 929108. 54 rooms. Facilities: restaurant, bar, garden, terrace café. MC, V. Restaurant and hotel closed mid-Nov.–mid-Mar. $*

Diekirch
Dining and
Lodging
★

Hiertz. This small hotel/restaurant looks stark and unwelcoming from the outside, but inside, its tiny dining rooms are homey little parlors, with heavy carpet, flocked wallpaper, and ornate silver appointments. Sit in the pretty terraced garden on the hill behind for summer aperitifs and after-dinner coffee; for the meal in between, try *rouget* (red mullet) in rosemary cream sauce or roast Vosges quail with juniper berries. The hotel plays second fiddle to the food, but rooms are comfortable, their decor in the same stuffy-lavish vein (green satin, mixed floral stencils) as downstairs; ask for one of the three back rooms facing the garden. *Rue Clairefontaine 1, L-9220, tel. 803562, fax 808869. 8 rooms with bath. Facilities: restaurant (closed Mon. dinner, Tues.), garden bar. AE, DC, MC, V. Closed 2nd half of Aug. and mid-Dec.–mid.-Jan. Hotel $$; Restaurant $$$*

Esch-sur-Sûre **Beau-Site.** At the edge of a village and overlooking the river, this
Dining and comfortable landmark hotel/restaurant has been updated with new
Lodging woodwork and fresh tile. The rooms are modern, some with flower
boxes and river views. The restaurant offers grilled meats and
cream-sauced standards at prices slightly higher than average—but
the portions are staggering, and the kitchen cuts no corners. *Rue de
Kaundorf 2, L-9650, tel. 89134, fax 899024. 21 rooms with bath. Facilities: restaurant (closed Wed.), terrace café. No credit cards.
Closed Jan.–mid-Feb. $$*

Lipperscheid **Leweck.** Just off the main north–south route between Diekirch and
Dining and Clervaux, this big, comfortable hotel/restaurant has evolved over
Lodging the years into a fairly luxurious lodging, with an indoor pool, green
grounds, and an upscale restaurant. The rooms are modern; the
back rooms (higher priced) take in valley views toward Bourscheid.
The restaurant walks a delicate line between deluxe and bourgeois,
with rustic pine, copper decor, and highbrow service hovering over
the steaks and lamb chops. You can have simpler fare—local ham
with frites and salad—in the adjoining casual café. *Rte. de Diekirch,
L-9378, tel. 90022, fax 90677. 25 rooms with bath or shower. Facili-
ties: restaurant (closed Tues.), café, garden terrace, indoor pool,
tennis court, whirlpool, sauna, solarium, game room. DC, MC, V.
Closed mid-Feb.–mid-Mar. $$*

Vianden **Oranienburg.** In the same family since 1880, this once-traditional
Dining and lodging has gone deluxe, decorating its rooms and restaurant in
Lodging lush, new fabrics and modern, built-in fixtures. Only the café and
stairwell retain the old-Vianden atmosphere, with game trophies
and burnished oak. The restaurant, Le Châtelain, now contemporary and posh as well, attracts nonguests for its ambitious French
cooking and its views toward the village and castle. *Grand'rue 126,
L-9411, tel. 84153, fax 84333. 36 rooms with bath. Facilities: restaurant (closed mid-Dec.–Mar.), café, terrace, private garden terrace.
AE, DC, MC, V. Closed 1 week in Nov. and mid-Jan.–Feb. Hotel $$;
Restaurant $$$*

Aal Veinen. Dark, cozy, and casual, this 1683 auberge serves a menu
of simple standards—*bouchée à la reine* (chicken à la king) with
frites, omelettes, cold sausage plates—and a wide selection of
grilled meats, cooked in full view of the dining area over a sizzling
wood fire. (If you've given up on pork chops, this is the place to get
reacquainted.) Rooms upstairs are tidy and sparely furnished, with
some beams, stucco, and oak armoires. *Grand'rue 114, L-9411, tel.
84368, fax 84084. 8 rooms with bath. Facilities: restaurant (closed
Tues. except in Aug.), bar. MC, V. $*

★ **Heintz.** Expanded from its origins as a Trinitarian monastery, this
atmospheric hotel has been in the family for four generations. During the war, owner Grandma Hansen worked with the Resistance,
hiding hams, cash, and Luxembourgers with equal aplomb. The
public spaces are rich with history, from the cross-vaulted oak café
to the hallways filled with local antiques; rooms are simple and up-
to-date. The oldest rooms, on the first floor, have antique oak furniture and original doors, but baths are down the hall; the best rooms
are upstairs, with balconies over the garden and fountain. The restaurant offers French classics—grilled beef with béarnaise sauce,
salmon in chives, and pure-German apple strudel with vanilla sauce.
*Grand'rue 55, L-9410, tel. 84155, fax 84559. 30 rooms, 26 with bath.
Facilities: restaurant (closed Wed. except July–Aug.), café, garden
terrace. AE, DC, MC, V. Closed mid-Nov.–March. Hotel $; Restau-
rant $$*

The Arts and Nightlife

The Arts   **Wiltz** sponsors a popular classical music festival, with concerts in the church and outdoor amphitheater (for ticket and schedule information, call 95–74–41 or write to the Syndicat d'Initiative, L-9516 Wiltz).

Nightlife   Wiltz's **Cocotier** (rue de la Fontaine 68, tel. 95501), a disco, attracts a young, local crowd. Otherwise, head back to Luxembourg City for dancing and late-night action.

Excursion to Petite Suisse and the Moselle

Important Addresses and Numbers

Tourist   **Echternach:** Syndicat d'Initiative, Boite Postale 30, L-6401, tel.
Information   72230. **Remich:** Syndicat d'Initiative, Gare Routière, L-5553, tel. 698488.

Emergencies   **Echternach:** Police, tel. 729995. Doctor/Dentist/Hospital/ Ambulance, tel. 012. **Remich:** Police, tel. 698687. Doctor/Dentist/ Hospital/Ambulance, tel. 012.

Getting There

By Car   Everything on this excursion can easily be reached by car within 40 minutes of Luxembourg City; there is no rail service connecting these sights.

By Bus   *See* Getting Around Luxembourg, *above.*

Guided Tours

Sales-Lentz (*see* Guided Tours in Luxembourg City, *above*) offers tours into the Moselle area to groups of 10 or more. To view the Moselle by cruise boat, contact **Navigation Touristique** and its M.S. *Princess Marie-Astrid* (rte. du Vin 10, L-6794 Grevenmacher, tel. 758275); this graceful little ship stops at Wasserbillig, Grevenmacher, Wormeldange, Stadtbredimus, Remich, Bech-Kleinmacher, and Schengen. It runs, on average, twice a day between 11 AM and 6 PM; a comfortable itinerary for sightseers would be to leave Remich at 2:30, arrive at Schengen at 3:10, then double back to Remich by 4. Another company offers entertainment on board: **Navitours** (rue de Luxembourg 1, L-6750 Grevenmacher, tel. 758489).

Most of the wine houses along the Moselle offer guided tours and tastings. Contact **Bernard-Massard** (rue du Pont 8, L-6773 Grevenmacher, tel. 75545), **St-Martin** (L-5570 Remich, tel. 699091), and **St-Remy** (L-5501 Remich, tel. 69084).

Exploring Echternach and the Moselle

Leave Luxembourg City via the Côte d'Eich, following signs for **Echternach.** You'll pass through some lovely forests—and some devastated wastelands, where the windstorms of 1990 cut tornadolike swaths through ancient beech timber; the damage is still evident throughout the grand duchy. The next town of consequence is the now bedroom community of Junglinster, where you'll see three transmitter towers and buildings of **RTL** (Radio-Télé-Luxembourg), made famous during World War II and still one of the most powerful radio stations in Europe. Just past town, turn left toward those towers, following signs to **Larochette.** This forest resort, on the western edge of the region known as **Müllerthal** (or, because of its high bluffs, woodlands, and rushing streams, as La Petite Suisse), hosts a striking step-gabled castle that looks down on the town. The castle is privately owned and occupied, but adjoining ruins from an earlier incarnation (with evocative views over the small houses below) may be visited. *Admission: Flux 50.*

From the center of Larochette, cut east, following signs to **Beaufort.** Here yet another splendid ruin, only partially restored to its 15th-century form, rises over green grounds full of sheep and forests full of walking trails. This one is well worth crawling around in: You can step into guard towers with archers' slits, look down wells, visit the kitchen fireplace, cross a drawbridge, and ogle very serious-looking torture equipment in a dungeon, including a rack. At the ticket counter, you can buy (or drink) samples of the local kirsch and cassis. *Tel. 86002. Admission: Flux 60 adults, Flux 20 children. Open Apr.–Oct., daily 9–6.*

From Beaufort, head northeast for N10, and follow the River Sûre south to **Echternach,** a flourishing tourist center all but adopted by the Germans across the Sûre, who fill its hotels, restaurants, and monuments every weekend. Their influence is strongly felt, in the all-German-language labels on artifacts and attractions, and in the spic-and-span, better-than-ever restorations—as well as in the shrapnel scars that pock the stonework still, 45 years after the Battle of the Bulge. This ancient town was founded in 698 by Saint Willibrord, who came from Northumberland in England to establish a Benedictine abbey, which thrived until 1795. In the Middle Ages, the Echternach Abbey was known throughout the Western world for its fine school of illuminations (miniature paintings that illustrated holy, hand-copied texts). The magnificent quadrant of abbey buildings dates from the 18th century (though damaged and restored after the war); nowhere else in Luxembourg can you wander among buildings of such noble line and classical scale. Examples of the artwork produced in the abbey can be viewed in the **Musée de l'Abbaye** (Abbey Museum) in the abbey basement. The books displayed here are painstakingly executed reproductions of the originals, down to their gem-studded covers. The originals are now in various museums abroad. Even so, the exhibition provides an interesting introduction to the art of illumination in the Middle Ages. *Admission: Flux 40. Open Apr.–Oct., daily 10–noon and 2–6; Nov.–Mar., weekends 2–5.*

The once-early-Romanesque **basilica,** built originally in the 11th to 13th centuries but destroyed in World War II and reconstructed in 1952, combines a very spare, squeaky-clean modernism with the few Romanesque details that remain; note the alternating square and round pillars. It was first built to house the remains of St. Willibrord; they were rediscovered after World War I behind an 8th-century altar (on display in the National Museum in Luxembourg City) and are enshrined in the **crypt** in a neoclassical marble sarcophagus. Behind the elaborate carvings, you can just get a glimpse of the simple tooled-stone sarcophagus cut in the 7th century. A few token traces of the original 7th-century chapel, founded by the saint himself, have been left exposed under heavy, modern cosmetic repairs. On a hill just behind the basilica, the **Eglise SS. Pierre et Paul**

(Saints Peter and Paul's Church) stands on remains of a Roman castellum and shows, in its spare architecture, signs of Merovingian, Romanesque, and Gothic influence. Every spring, the two churches host one of Luxembourg's most important arts events: the Echternach Festival of Classical Music.

Time Out Just below Saints Peter and Paul's, have coffee and a sizable fresh pastry at the **Café-Tea Room Zimmer,** and pick up something for later in the adjoining bakeshop/confiserie, perhaps its specialty, *Macarrons Moux.*

Echternach's cobbled **place du Marché,** in the old town center, offers a charming mix of Gothic arcades and restored medieval town houses, festooned with wrought-iron signs and sculpted drain spouts; the arched and turreted 13th-century **Hôtel de Ville** (Town Hall) is its centerpiece.

Take rue André Duchscher 2 kilometers (1¼ miles) from the place du Marché to the **Troosknepchen** belvedere. On foot, follow path B through the beechwood to the **Gorge du Loup** (wolf's gorge). The rock face rises 50 meters (160 feet) on either side of the crevice; at the entrance stands the pointed rock known as Cleopatra's Needle. From the **Bildscheslay** belvedere on the other side of the gorge, there is a magnificent view over the Sûre River valley.

On Whit Tuesday (the eighth Tuesday after Easter), Echternach is transported to the Middle Ages: Well over 10,000 pilgrims (most of them young people) from throughout the region come to town to join in—and tourists come to watch—the famous **Springprozession,** a dancing parade down the streets of the town, the marchers bouncing from one foot to the other, all the way to the basilica. Their chanted prayer: "Holy Willibrord, founder of churches, light of the blind, destroyer of idols, pray for us." One of the few Christian forms of worship today that include dancing, this unique pilgrimage has been repeated every year since the 15th century.

Leaving Echternach, follow signs for Wasserbillig/Trier and head south on N10 along the Sûre and the German border, passing **Rosport,** the source of the ubiquitous green-bottled mineral water you will be served wherever you go. You'll also pass several small artisanal schnapps or eaux-de-vie distilleries, making the most of nearby orchards. At Wasserbillig cut through town toward Grevenmacher; at the other end, you will greet the **Moselle,** whose waters nourish Luxembourg's famous vineyards, cultivated since Roman times. The vines cover every exposed slope in sight, and the farther south you drive, the more romantic the scenery becomes. About 6 kilometers (4 miles) down, you'll find **Grevenmacher,** a principal wine center and home of Bernard-Massard (who make a widely exported champagne substitute). Ten kilometers (6 miles) south lies graceful little **Wormeldange,** another key wine center; cut inland and follow signs up into Wormeldange-Haute (Upper Wormeldange) for sweeping views over the Moselle.

Time Out Stop at Wormeldange's enormous pink-stuccoed **Caves Cooperatives** to sample the local product, as its tidy adjoining pub offers a dégustation of five wines served on a wrought-iron, vine-shaped rack. There's local grape juice, too, for the designated driver.

Return to the main Moselle highway. **Ehnen,** just down the road from Wormeldange, is worth a stop and a stroll as well, as its narrow old streets, carved-wood doors, and circular church (a 15th-century design reconstructed in 1826) seem frozen in time. It's home to a **musée du vin** (wine museum), set in a typical group of Luxembourgish farm buildings, with pink stucco and cobbled courts. Its rooms are full of tools, equipment, and photographs of the wine-making industry, and there's a demonstration vineyard planted with samples of each of the local varietals. There are labels in English. *Tel. 76026. Admission: Flux 70. Open Apr.–Oct., Tues.–Sun. 9:30–11:30 and 2–5.*

Twelve kilometers (7 miles) farther down the highway, **Remich** is a popular waterfront town, where cruise boats roll past a pleasant riverside promenade, and sizable wineries can be visited. You can take a leisurely round-trip boat ride from here to **Schengen,** which, at the southeast tip of Luxembourg, intersects with both Germany and France (*see* Guided Tours, *above*).

Just south of Remich, in a small wine village named **Bech-Kleinmacher,** stop at **A Possen,** a 17th-century stone wine maker's house restored and furnished. Its extraordinarily atmospheric displays include a "black kitchen," with a ham-smoking chimney, and a cozy bedroom with a four-poster and homespun linens; there are museum displays on the wine industry, and a toy collection as well. *Rue Sandt 16, tel. 698233. Admission: Flux 120. Open May–Oct., Tues.–Sun. 2–7; Nov.–Apr., Fri. and weekends 2–7.*

Time Out   After viewing the displays, you can stop in the **Waistuff** (wine *stube* or café) to taste the local wine and sample dark bread smeared with kachkeis, Luxembourg's favorite cheese spread.

Double back to Remich, then take E27/N2 toward Luxembourg. Just before reaching the city, stop between Sandweiler and Hamm to visit the **American Military Cemetery,** where General George Patton chose to be buried with his men. More than 5,000 soldiers of the Third Army were buried here, having died on Luxembourg soil; there are also 117 graves of unknown soldiers. Each grave is marked with either a Star of David or a simple cross, but they are not separated by race, rank, religion, or origin—except for the 22 pairs of brothers, who lie side by side. Only Patton's cross, identical to the others, stands by itself.

From the parking lot, a small road leads a kilometer toward Sandweiler, and across an intersection to the **German Military Cemetery,** which shelters more than twice as many war dead. During the Ardennes conflict, the U.S. Army Burial Service recovered the bodies from both sides and buried them in two temporary cemeteries, the Americans near Hamm, the Germans near Sandweiler. For the Germans, 300 graves served 5,000 soldiers. Yet another 5,000 had been buried on battle sites throughout the country, with little or no identification, mostly in mass graves. In 1952, those bodies were transferred here. Blunt stone crosses identify multiple burial sites, some marked with names and serial numbers, other marked simply "Ein Deutscher Soldat" (a German soldier). At the top of the lot, a tall stone cross heads the mass grave, where the other 5,000 are, for the most part, identified by a bronze plaque.

What to See and Do with Children

The **Jardin des Papillons** (Butterfly Garden) in Grevenmacher seethes with fluttering wildlife, from butterflies to birds to tropical insects, all enclosed in an attractive greenhouse. *Rte. du Vin, tel.*

758539. Admission: Flux 160 adults, Flux 80 children. Open Apr.–mid-Oct., daily 9:30–5:30.

Off the Beaten Track

If you've seen enough castles and want to wander through dense fir and beech forests, with high limestone bluffs and twisting brooks, drive through the **Müllerthal,** also known as La Petite Suisse. The forests are rich, and there are auberges (inns) sprinkled along the roadside, with terrace tables and welcoming cafés. Starting at Junglinster, follow signs for Larochette, then toward Consdorf and Berdorf, where hotels and restaurants are concentrated.

Shopping

The best souvenirs of this region are meant to be drunk: Moselle wines, both sparkling and regular, can be tasted and purchased in gift packs from most of the caves cooperatives. Artisanale distilleries sell their eaux-de-vie along the Moselle highway, too. And at Beaufort, you can pick up a bottle of their house-label kirsch or cassis.

Sports and the Outdoors

Bicycling   In Echternach, contact **Cycles Schmitt** (rue Ermesinde 27, tel. 72148).

Dining and Lodging

Echternach   **La Bergerie.** One of the best restaurants in the country, this 19th-
Dining   century farmhouse nestles in an idyllic setting of forest and fields,
★   with windows and a garden-terrace making the most of the expanse of greenery. The graceful, unfussy dining room features the cooking of owner/chef Claude Phal, whose specialties include classics (simple foie gras; turbot in champagne sauce) and sophisticated experiments (smoked sole; young pigeon in pastry, its own juice caramelized). The strawberry gratin in orange butter uses fruit from their own garden; all baked goods are made in their full-scale pastry kitchen. It's a family effort, with wife, son, and daughter-in-law running the restaurant and their offshoot hotel in Echternach, 7 kilometers (4¼ miles) away (there's a free shuttle between). *Geyershaff, tel. 79464. Reservations required. Jacket and tie advised. AE, DC, MC, V. Closed Sun. dinner, Mon., Jan.–mid-Feb. $$$$*

Dining and   **Du Commerce.** Tucked back from the place du Marché, with quiet
Lodging   bordering streets and an idyllic garden behind, this simple hotel has been kept in top running order, with efforts at upgrades in every corner. Rooms have fixtures of varying vintage but all-fresh decors, and there's an enormous fitness center free to guests. The restaurant and café are atmospheric, with oak wainscoting, beams, and pink linens; standards (trout, bouchée à la reine) are moderately priced and well prepared. *Pl. du Marché 16, L-6460, tel. 72301, fax 728790. 48 rooms. Facilities: restaurant, café, terrace café, garden, fitness room, sauna, solarium. AE, MC, V. Closed mid-Nov.–mid-Feb. Hotel $; Restaurant $$*

Lodging   **La Bergerie.** Managed by the owners of the partner restaurant out-
★   side town (*see* Dining, *above*), this 1988 addition to the downtown hotel scene is one of a kind: a small mansion, enclosed in a shady garden, completely converted to creamy, modern luxury, with glis-

tening tile baths, opulent fabrics and cabinetry, and all comforts—
except a restaurant, which requires a pleasant shuttle ride into the
countryside. Breakfast is served in the big bay window overlooking
the garden and fountain, or on the terrace in good weather; crois-
sants come from the restaurant's pastry kitchen. *Rue de Luxembourg 47, L-6450, tel. 7285041, fax 728508. 15 rooms with bath.
Facilities: breakfast only, sauna, solarium, fitness equipment. AE,
DC, MC, V. Closed Jan.–mid Feb. $$*

Ehnen
Dining and
Lodging

Bamberg's. Looking for all the world as if a world war had never
passed through, this comfortable, friendly old hotel/restaurant,
across from the Moselle and flanked by vineyards, maintains a reas-
suring retro formality: oak wainscoting, leaded glass, ceramics,
pewter coasters under cut-glass crystal goblets. The cuisine is
equally old school, and just as appealing: plump vineyard snails
swimming in butter; boned quail stuffed with grapes and wrapped
in pastry; sweetbreads and morels in rich cream sauce. Wines, of
course, are local and modestly priced. The breakfast room is a cozy
parlor, complete with antiques and a porcelain collection, and some
of the stuffy/comfy (chenille, sculptured carpet) rooms upstairs of-
fer balconies toward the Moselle. *Route du Vin 131, L-5416, tel.
76022, fax 76056. 14 rooms with bath. Facilities: restaurant, (closed
Tues.). AE, MC, V. Closed Dec.–mid-Jan. Hotel $; Restaurant $$*

★ **Simmer.** This Moselle institution, built in 1863 and maintained in a
welcoming Victorian-rustic style, is the preferred riverfront retreat of the royal family and political luminaries, though its ambience remains comfortable and homey. Incorporating portions of a
1610 house and the founder's butcher shop, it was taken over by the
current family in 1955 and built into an elegant hotel/restaurant.
The details they added—a 17th-century fireplace in the dining
room, carved oak grotesques paneling the salon—complete the effect of elegant warmth. Rooms are roomy and solid, decked with
dated glamour (brocade, gilt, crystal) and some antiques; in front,
there are balconies, in back, small suites. Restaurant specialties include braised *brochet* (pike) in cream and *sandre* (pike perch) in local
Auxerrois; in summer, you can dine on the full-length, open front
porch. It's next door to the wine museum. *Rte. du Vin 117, L-5416,
tel. 76030, fax 76306. 17 rooms, 12 with bath. Facilities: restaurant
(closed Tues.), terrace, bar. AE, MC, V. Closed early Jan.–early
Mar. Hotel $; Restaurant $$$*

Frisange
Dining
★

Lea Linster. As the first woman to win France's culinary Oscar, the
Paul Bocuse d'Or, Ms. Linster has earned international attention
and keeps her modest farmhouse—once her mother's rustic café,
with *jeu de quilles* (bowling)—full of prominent guests. Have a glass
of champagne in the shady garden out back (cows may wander near-
by), then relax in the elegant dining room over her prize-winning
dishes: lobster with truffled fettuccine, lamb in crisp potato crust,
and hot chocolate soufflé. The wine list is weighted toward the high
end, as are prices. It's on the southern border, 4 kilometers (2½
miles) east of the Bettembourg exit off the motorway (E25). *Rte. de
Luxembourg 17, tel. 68411. Reservations required. Jacket and tie
advised. AE, DC, MC, V. Closed Mon.–Tues. $$$$*

★ **Lëtzebuerger Kaschthaus.** Secure in her success in haute
gastronomie, Lea Linster hasn't forgotten her roots; in 1992 she
opened a simple farmhouse restaurant to cook nothing but Lux-
embourg specialties, superbly prepared and served without frills in
a comfortably retro setting. Pretty print linens, stenciled wallpa-
per, and original ceramic flooring make everyone feel at home, from
hip young nationalists to fur-hatted ladies of a certain age. Try the
green-bean soup, rich bouchée à la reine with sweetbreads, savory

lentils with sausage, and mouth-watering fruit tarts. Immediately off the motorway (E25) between Bettembourg and Frisange, it's an easy drive from Luxembourg City. *Rte. de Bettembourg 4, Hellange, tel. 516573. Reservations advised. Dress: casual. AE, DC, MC, V. Closed Tues., Wed. lunch, 3 weeks in Aug./Sept., and Christmas week. $–$$*

Remich **Caves St-Martin.** This long, open oak-and-tile sprawl of a restaurant/
Dining café offers comfortable old-style dining—fried fish, veal in cream sauce—to be washed down with a bottle of the house specialty, which you can sample on a tour of the winery. *Rte. du Vin 21, tel. 69102. Reservations advised. Dress: casual. MC, V. $$*

Lodging **Saint-Nicolas.** Named for the patron saint of fishermen, whose small shrine adjoins the building, this hotel got its start in 1885 as a *relais* (relay station) for changing teams of horses that hauled barges up the Moselle. Now, under the same family management and fully rebuilt after the war, it offers guests modern facilities but the same roomy scale and grace of its earlier days. There's a long, glassed-in front porch with a restaurant, and an open terrace just above, both taking in full-length views of the Moselle, as well as an enclosed garden court for summer breakfasts. Rooms have bright fabrics, and some have double casement windows over the river (and highway). *Esplanade 31, L-5533, tel. 698333, fax 699069. 43 rooms. Facilities: restaurant (closed mid-Nov.–mid-Dec.), bar, terrace, sauna, solarium, fitness equipment. AE, DC, MC, V. $$*
Esplanade. This big, postwar waterfront hotel offers much of the same comfort as the Saint-Nicolas but none of the historic tradition. There's a big porch and a terrace café, and plenty of rooms overlooking the waterfront, some with sheltered balconies. *Esplanade 5, L-5533, tel. 69171, fax 698924. 20 rooms with bath. Facilities: restaurant (closed Wed. mid-Sept.–Nov. and Feb.–mid-June, and Dec.–Jan.), bar, terrace café. MC, V. $*

Wormeldange- **Schmit-Hengel.** Perched high over the Moselle valley, with some
Haut windows taking in the view, this is a family restaurant specializing
Dining in cuisine bourgeoise standards: asparagus in fresh-whisked *sauce*
★ *mousseline* (a blend of hollandaise sauce and cream), *escalope de veau crème champignons* (veal in mushroom cream sauce), rump steak, and *friture de la Moselle* (fried freshwater fish). It's packed with three-generation groups for Sunday dinner. *Berreggaass 9, tel. 76046. Reservations advised. Dress: casual. AE, MC, V. Closed Tues. $$*

The Arts and Nightlife

The Arts The **Echternach Festival** of classical music is one of the most important arts events in Luxembourg, bringing in world-class artists and ensembles and showcasing them in the basilica and the smaller Saints Peter and Paul's Church. It takes place on weekends for a month during May/June, and tickets sell out quickly; if you're interested, write ahead to Lux-Festival (Boite Postale 30, L-6401 Echternach). Tickets, if available, can be bought in person at the Echternach Syndicat d'Initiative and at the Luxembourg Syndicat on the place d'Armes.

Nightlife For all its touristic charms, if you're interested in late nights and bright lights, this is not the region to linger in—head back for Luxembourg City. The one exception: the small treatment spa Mondorf-les-Bains, on the French border southeast of Luxembourg City, offers **Casino 2000** (rue Flamang, tel. 661–0101), with full gaming facilities. Jacket and tie are required.

Vocabulary

Dutch Vocabulary

	English	Dutch	Pronunciation
Basics	Yes/no	Ja,nee	yah,nay
	Please	Alstublieft	**ahls**-too-bleeft
	Thank you	Dank u	**dahnk** oo
	You're welcome	Niets te danken	neets teh **dahn**-ken
	Excuse me, sorry	Pardon	pahr-**don**
	Good morning	Goede morgen	**hoh**-deh **mor**-ghen
	Good evening	Goede avond	**hoh**-deh **ahv**-unt
	Goodbye	Dag!	dah
Numbers	one	een	ehn
	two	twee	tveh
	three	drie	dree
	four	vier	veer
	five	vijf	vehf
	six	zes	zehss
	seven	zeven	**zeh**-vehn
	eight	acht	ahkht
	nine	negen	**neh**-ghen
	ten	tien	teen
Days of the Week	Sunday	zondag	**zohn**-dagh
	Monday	maandag	**mahn**-dagh
	Tuesday	dinsdag	**dinns**-dagh
	Wednesday	woensdag	**voons**-dagh
	Thursday	donderdag	**don**-der-dagh
	Friday	vrijdag	**vreh**-dagh
	Saturday	zaterdag	**zah**-ter-dagh
Useful Phrases	Do you speak English?	Spreekt U Engels?	sprehkt oo **ehn**-gls
	I don't speak Dutch	Ik spreek geen Nederlands	ihk sprehk **ghen** **Ned**-er-lahnds
	I don't understand	Ik begrijp het niet	ihk be-**ghrehp** het neet
	I don't know	Ik weet niet	ihk **veht** ut neet
	I'm American/English	Ik ben Amerikaans/Engels	ihk ben Am-er-ee-**kahns**/Ehn-gls
	Where is . . .	Waar is _____?	vahr iss
	the train station?	het station	heht stah-**syohn**
	the post office?	het postkantoor	het **pohst**-kahn-tohr
	the hospital?	het ziekenhuis	het **zeek**-uhn-haus
	Where are the restrooms?	waar is de WC	**vahr** iss de **veh**-seh

Left/right	links/rechts	leenks/rehts
How much is this?	Hoeveel kost dit?	hoo-**vehl** kohst deet
It's expensive/ cheap	Het is te duur/ goedkoop	het ees teh **dour**/ **hood**-kohp
I am ill/sick	Ik ben ziek	ihk behn zeek
I want to call a doctor	Ik wil een docter bellen	ihk veel ehn **dohk**-ter **behl**-len
Help!	Help!	help
Stop!	Stoppen	**stop**-pen

Dining Out	Bill/check	de rekening	de **rehk**-en-eeng
	Bread	brood	brohd
	Butter	boter	**boh**-ter
	Fork	vork	fork
	I'd like to order	Ik wil graag bestellen	Ihk veel khrah behs-**tell**-en
	Knife	een mes	ehn mehs
	Menu	menu/kaart	men-**oo**/kahrt
	Napkin	en servet	ehn ser-**veht**
	Pepper	peper	**peh**-per
	Please give me . . .	mag ik [een] . . .	mahkh ihk [ehn] . . .
	Salt	zout	zoot
	Spoon	een lepel	ehn **leh**-pehl
	Sugar	suiker	**sigh**-kur

French Vocabulary

	English	*French*	*Pronunciation*
Basics	Yes/no	Oui/non	wee/no
	Please	S'il vous plaît	seel voo play
	Thank you	Merci	mare-**see**
	You're welcome	De rien	deh ree-**en**
	Excuse me, sorry	Pardon	pahr-**doan**
	Good morning/ afternoon	Bonjour	bone-**joor**
	Good evening	Bonsoir	bone-**swar**
	Goodbye	Au revoir	o ruh-**vwar**
Numbers	one	un	un
	two	deux	dew
	three	trois	twa
	four	quatre	**cat**-ruh
	five	cinq	sank
	six	six	seess
	seven	sept	set
	eight	huit	wheat
	nine	neuf	nuf
	ten	dix	deess

Days of the Week	Sunday	dimanche	dee-**mahnsh**
	Monday	lundi	lewn-**dee**
	Tuesday	mardi	mar-**dee**
	Wednesday	mercredi	mare-kruh-**dee**
	Thursday	jeudi	juh-**dee**
	Friday	vendredi	van-dra-**dee**
	Saturday	samedi	sam-**dee**
Useful Phrases	Do you speak English?	Parlez-vous anglais?	par-lay vooz ahng-**glay**
	I don't speak French	Je ne parle pas français	jeh nuh parl pah fraun-**say**
	I don't understand	Je ne comprends pas	jeh nuh kohm-prahn **pah**
	I don't know	Je ne sais pas	jeh nuh say **pah**
	I'm American/ British	Je suis américain/ anglais	jeh sweez a-may-ree-**can**/ahng-**glay**
	Where is . . .	Où est . . .	oo ay
	the train station?	la gare?	la gar
	the post office?	la poste?	la post
	the hospital	l'hôpital?	low-pee-**tahl**
	Where are the restrooms?	Où sont les toilettes?	oo son lay twah-**let**
	Left/right	A gauche/à droite	a goash/a drwat
	How much is it?	C'est combien?	say comb-bee-**en**
	It's expensive/ cheap	C'est cher/pas cher	say sher/pa sher
	I am ill/sick	Je suis malade	jeh swee ma-**lahd**
	Call a doctor	Appelez un docteur	a-pe-lay un dohk-**tore**
	Help!	Au secours!	o say-**koor**
	Stop!	Arrêtez!	a-ruh-**tay**
Dining Out	Bill/check	l'addition	la-dee-see-**own**
	Bread	du pain	due pan
	Butter	du beurre	due bur
	Fork	une fourchette	ewn four-**shet**
	I'd like . . .	Je voudrais . . .	jeh voo-**dray**
	Knife	un couteau	un koo-**toe**
	Menu	la carte	la cart
	Napkin	une serviette	ewn sair-vee-**et**
	Pepper	du poivre	due **pwah**-vruh
	Salt	du sel	dew sell
	Spoon	une cuillère	ewn kwee-**air**
	Sugar	du sucre	due **sook**-ruh

Index

Personal Itinerary

Departure *Date*

Time

Transportation

Arrival *Date*   *Time*

Departure *Date*   *Time*

Transportation

Accommodations

Arrival *Date*   *Time*

Departure *Date*   *Time*

Transportation

Accommodations

Arrival *Date*   *Time*

Departure *Date*   *Time*

Transportation

Accommodations

Personal Itinerary

Arrival	*Date*	*Time*
Departure	*Date*	*Time*
Transportation		
Accommodations		

Arrival	*Date*	*Time*
Departure	*Date*	*Time*
Transportation		
Accommodations		

Arrival	*Date*	*Time*
Departure	*Date*	*Time*
Transportation		
Accommodations		

Arrival	*Date*	*Time*
Departure	*Date*	*Time*
Transportation		
Accommodations		

Personal Itinerary

Arrival *Date*   *Time*

Departure *Date*   *Time*

Transportation

Accommodations

Arrival *Date*   *Time*

Departure *Date*   *Time*

Transportation

Accommodations

Arrival *Date*   *Time*

Departure *Date*   *Time*

Transportation

Accommodations

Arrival *Date*   *Time*

Departure *Date*   *Time*

Transportation

Accommodations

Personal Itinerary

Arrival	*Date*	*Time*
Departure	*Date*	*Time*
Transportation		
Accommodations		

Arrival	*Date*	*Time*
Departure	*Date*	*Time*
Transportation		
Accommodations		

Arrival	*Date*	*Time*
Departure	*Date*	*Time*
Transportation		
Accommodations		

Arrival	*Date*	*Time*
Departure	*Date*	*Time*
Transportation		
Accommodations		

Personal Itinerary

Arrival *Date*   *Time*

Departure *Date*   *Time*

Transportation

Accommodations

Arrival *Date*   *Time*

Departure *Date*   *Time*

Transportation

Accommodations

Arrival *Date*   *Time*

Departure *Date*   *Time*

Transportation

Accommodations

Arrival *Date*   *Time*

Departure *Date*   *Time*

Transportation

Accommodations

Personal Itinerary

Arrival   *Date*   *Time*

Departure   *Date*   *Time*

Transportation

Accommodations

Arrival   *Date*   *Time*

Departure   *Date*   *Time*

Transportation

Accommodations

Arrival   *Date*   *Time*

Departure   *Date*   *Time*

Transportation

Accommodations

Arrival   *Date*   *Time*

Departure   *Date*   *Time*

Transportation

Accommodations

Addresses

Name	*Name*
Address	*Address*
Telephone	*Telephone*
Name	*Name*
Address	*Address*
Telephone	*Telephone*
Name	*Name*
Address	*Address*
Telephone	*Telephone*
Name	*Name*
Address	*Address*
Telephone	*Telephone*
Name	*Name*
Address	*Address*
Telephone	*Telephone*
Name	*Name*
Address	*Address*
Telephone	*Telephone*
Name	*Name*
Address	*Address*
Telephone	*Telephone*
Name	*Name*
Address	*Address*
Telephone	*Telephone*

Addresses

Name	*Name*
Address	*Address*
Telephone	*Telephone*
Name	*Name*
Address	*Address*
Telephone	*Telephone*
Name	*Name*
Address	*Address*
Telephone	*Telephone*
Name	*Name*
Address	*Address*
Telephone	*Telephone*
Name	*Name*
Address	*Address*
Telephone	*Telephone*
Name	*Name*
Address	*Address*
Telephone	*Telephone*
Name	*Name*
Address	*Address*
Telephone	*Telephone*
Name	*Name*
Address	*Address*
Telephone	*Telephone*

Addresses

Name	*Name*
Address	*Address*
Telephone	*Telephone*
Name	*Name*
Address	*Address*
Telephone	*Telephone*
Name	*Name*
Address	*Address*
Telephone	*Telephone*
Name	*Name*
Address	*Address*
Telephone	*Telephone*
Name	*Name*
Address	*Address*
Telephone	*Telephone*
Name	*Name*
Address	*Address*
Telephone	*Telephone*
Name	*Name*
Address	*Address*
Telephone	*Telephone*

Notes

Notes

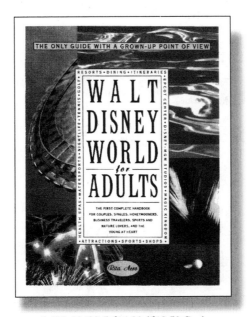

Fodor's Travel Guides

Available at bookstores everywhere, or call 1–800–533–6478, 24 hours a day.

U.S. Guides

Alaska

Arizona

Boston

California

Cape Cod, Martha's Vineyard, Nantucket

The Carolinas & the Georgia Coast

Chicago

Colorado

Florida

Hawaii

Las Vegas, Reno, Tahoe

Los Angeles

Maine, Vermont, New Hampshire

Maui

Miami & the Keys

New England

New Orleans

New York City

Pacific North Coast

Philadelphia & the Pennsylvania Dutch Country

The Rockies

San Diego

San Francisco

Santa Fe, Taos, Albuquerque

Seattle & Vancouver

The South

The U.S. & British Virgin Islands

USA

The Upper Great Lakes Region

Virginia & Maryland

Waikiki

Walt Disney World and the Orlando Area

Washington, D.C.

Foreign Guides

Acapulco, Ixtapa, Zihuatanejo

Australia & New Zealand

Austria

The Bahamas

Baja & Mexico's Pacific Coast Resorts

Barbados

Berlin

Bermuda

Brittany & Normandy

Budapest

Canada

Cancún, Cozumel, Yucatán Peninsula

Caribbean

China

Costa Rica, Belize, Guatemala

The Czech Republic & Slovakia

Eastern Europe

Egypt

Euro Disney

Europe

Florence, Tuscany & Umbria

France

Germany

Great Britain

Greece

Hong Kong

India

Ireland

Israel

Italy

Japan

Kenya & Tanzania

Korea

London

Madrid & Barcelona

Mexico

Montréal & Québec City

Morocco

Moscow & St. Petersburg

The Netherlands, Belgium & Luxembourg

New Zealand

Norway

Nova Scotia, Prince Edward Island & New Brunswick

Paris

Portugal

Provence & the Riviera

Rome

Russia & the Baltic Countries

Scandinavia

Scotland

Singapore

South America

Southeast Asia

Spain

Sweden

Switzerland

Thailand

Tokyo

Toronto

Turkey

Vienna & the Danube Valley

Special Series

Fodor's Affordables

Caribbean

Europe

Florida

France

Germany

Great Britain

Italy

London

Paris

**Fodor's Bed &
Breakfast and
Country Inns Guides**

America's Best B&Bs

California

Canada's Great
Country Inns

Cottages, B&Bs and
Country Inns of
England and Wales

Mid-Atlantic Region

New England

The Pacific
Northwest

The South

The Southwest

The Upper Great
Lakes Region

The Berkeley Guides

California

Central America

Eastern Europe

Europe

France

Germany & Austria

Great Britain &
Ireland

Italy

London

Mexico

Pacific Northwest &
Alaska

Paris

San Francisco

**Fodor's Exploring
Guides**

Australia

Boston &
New England

Britain

California

The Caribbean

Florence & Tuscany

Florida

France

Germany

Ireland

Italy

London

Mexico

New York City

Paris

Prague

Rome

Scotland

Singapore & Malaysia

Spain

Thailand

Turkey

Fodor's Flashmaps

Boston

New York

Washington, D.C.

Fodor's Pocket Guides

Acapulco

Bahamas

Barbados

Jamaica

London

New York City

Paris

Puerto Rico

San Francisco

Washington, D.C.

Fodor's Sports

Cycling

Golf Digest's Best
Places to Play

Hiking

The Insider's Guide
to the Best Canadian
Skiing

Running

Sailing

Skiing in the USA &
Canada

USA Today's Complete
Four Sports Stadium
Guide

**Fodor's Three-In-Ones
(guidebook, language
cassette, and phrase
book)**

France

Germany

Italy

Mexico

Spain

**Fodor's
Special-Interest
Guides**

Complete Guide to
America's National
Parks

Condé Nast Traveler
Caribbean Resort and
Cruise Ship Finder

Cruises and Ports
of Call

Euro Disney

France by Train

Halliday's New
England Food
Explorer

Healthy Escapes

Italy by Train

London Companion

Shadow Traffic's New
York Shortcuts and
Traffic Tips

Sunday in New York

Sunday in San
Francisco

Touring Europe

Touring USA:
Eastern Edition

Walt Disney World and
the Orlando Area

Walt Disney World
for Adults

**Fodor's Vacation
Planners**

Great American
Learning Vacations

Great American
Sports & Adventure
Vacations

Great American
Vacations

Great American
Vacations for Travelers
with Disabilities

National Parks and
Seashores of the East

National Parks
of the West

**The Wall Street
Journal Guides to
Business Travel**

At last — a guide for Americans with disabilities that makes traveling a delight

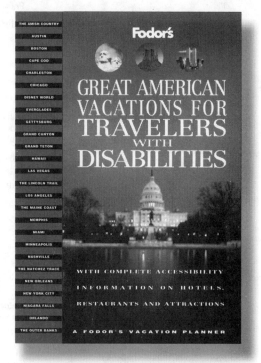

0-679-02591-X $18.00 ($24.00 Can)

This is the first and only complete guide to great American vacations for the 35 million North Americans with disabilities, as well as for those who care for them or for aging parents and relatives. Provides:

- Essential trip-planning information for travelers with mobility, vision, and hearing impairments

- Specific details on a huge array of facilities, along with solid descriptions of attractions, hotels, restaurants, and other destinations

- Up-to-date information on ISA-designated parking, level entranceways, and accessibility to pools, lounges, and bathrooms

 At bookstores everywhere,
or call **1-800-533-6478**